The Collecte

ELIZABETH JENNINGS was born in B lived most of her life in Oxford, where she moved in 1932. She was educated at Rye St Antony and Oxford High School before reading English at St Anne's College, Oxford, where she began a B.Litt., but left to pursue a career in copy-editing in London. Returning to Oxford to take up a full-time post as a librarian at the city library, Jennings worked briefly at Chatto and Windus before becoming a full-time poet. Her second volume of poetry, *A Way of Looking* (1955), won the Somerset Maugham Award, which allowed her to travel to Rome, a city which had an immense impact on her poetry and Roman Catholic faith. While she suffered from physical and mental ill health from her early thirties, Jennings was a popular and widely read poet. She received the W.H. Smith award in 1987 for *Collected Poems 1953–1985*, and in 1992 was awarded a CBE. She died in Rosebank Care Home, Bampton, in 2001 and is buried in Wolvercote Cemetery, Oxford.

EMMA MASON is a Reader in the Department of English and Comparative Literary Studies, University of Warwick. She was previously a British Academy Postdoctoral Fellow at Corpus Christi, Oxford and has also been a Fellow at the University of Wisconsin-Madison and the Huntington Library, California. She is the author of *The Cambridge Introduction to Wordsworth* (2010), *Women Poets of the Nineteenth Century* (2006) and *Nineteenth-Century Religion and Literature* (2006; with Mark Knight); and a co-editor of *The Blackwell Companion to the Bible in English Literature* (2009) and *The Oxford Handbook of the Reception History of the Bible* (2010). With Mark Knight, she co-edits the monograph series New Directions in Religion and Literature for Continuum.

Also by Elizabeth Jennings from Carcanet Press

Celebrations and Elegies
Consequently I Rejoice
Every Changing Shape
Extending the Territory
Familiar Spirits
In the Meantime
Moments of Grace
Praises
Selected Poems
Timely Issues
Times and Seasons
Tributes

Translation
The Sonnets of Michelangelo

Criticism
Every Changing Shape: Mystical Experience and the Making of Poems

Edited
A Poet's Choice

Elizabeth Jennings

The Collected Poems

Edited by Emma Mason

CARCANET

New Collected Poems first published in Great Britain in 2002 by
Carcanet Press Limited

This newly edited, revised and enlarged edition first published
in Great Britain in 2012

Carcanet Press Limited
Alliance House
Cross Street
Manchester M2 7AQ

A CIP catalogue record for this book is available from the British Library

ISBN 978 1 84777 068 4

Research for this book was partly funded by an AHRC award.

Arts & Humanities
Research Council

The publisher acknowledges financial assistance from Arts Council England

Supported by
ARTS COUNCIL
ENGLAND

Typeset by XL Publishing Services, Tiverton
Printed and bound in England by SRP Ltd, Exeter

♪ ♫
with love

Elizabeth Jennings, c. 1950

CONTENTS

EARLY WORKS

COLLECTIONS 1953–2001

POEMS (1953)

A WAY OF LOOKING (1955)

SONG FOR A BIRTH OR A DEATH (1961)

RECOVERIES (1964)

THE MIND HAS MOUNTAINS (1966)

New poems from COLLECTED POEMS (1967)

THE ANIMALS ARRIVAL (1969)

LUCIDITIES (1970)

CONSEQUENTLY I REJOICE (1977)

AFTER THE ARK (1978)

MOMENTS OF GRACE (1979)

EXTENDING THE TERRITORY (1985)

TRIBUTES (1989)

TIMES AND SEASONS (1992)

FAMILIAR SPIRITS (1994)

IN THE MEANTIME (1996)

PRAISES (1998)

TIMELY ISSUES (2001)

UNPUBLISHED POETRY

JUVENILIA

UNDATED POEMS

ILLUSTRATIONS

PREFACE

Elizabeth Jennings gave me a small ceramic sheep once, although one of its legs had fallen off and most of its spaghetti-like wool had disintegrated. I was in the first year of my English degree at Cardiff University, and had gone to visit my school friend Debbie, who was studying at Oxford Brookes. Debbie worked in a café called Beau Champs next to Gloucester Green coach station, and I arrived early and sat down to wait until she had finished her shift. As I did so, an elderly woman, who I later learned from the owners of the café was a published poet called Elizabeth Jennings, struck up conversation. According to the café owners, Jennings sat there for most of the day every day, reading the newspaper and discussing the latest films (she was a frequent cinema-goer) or Thatcher (whose politics she despised) with anyone with time to talk. After I had made a few visits to Oxford, and enjoyed several brief conversations with Jennings, she showed me a shoe-box of objects that she carried around with her in the last years of her life, filled with broken china, doll's house furniture, lockless keys, elastic bands and old pencils, and presented to me, without explanation, a ceramic sheep.

With the onset of exams, I stopped visiting the café and it wasn't until I started to study Jennings' poetry that I thought again about our meetings. The incident had, on the surface, confirmed her widely commented-on title as Britain's 'bag lady of the sonnets', and, as her older sister Aileen Albrow told me, she often played up to this eccentric role, notoriously receiving her OBE in an over-sized duffle coat and woolly hat. And yet, like many readers of Jennings' poetry, I soon discovered that this bag-lady image was something of a smokescreen for a profoundly devotional, thoughtful and emotionally observant poet, one engaged in exploring love, joy, friendship, loneliness, depression, faith and poetics. Her published and unpublished poems alike often speak in raw and stark terms of what it means to undergo sadness, despair and breakdown, experiences from which she often claimed to have been rescued by her intense and moving commitment to Roman Catholicism. This faith served as a kind of elastic seal around her poetry, quieting and holding in its content while allowing the narrator to push a little at its boundaries, allowing for what she called the 'silence of a tripped tongue' ('Towards a Religious Poem') to confide a humane and consoling devotion to God.

The sense of words falling through a reflective silence defines much of Jennings' poetry, and meaning breathes through the page rather than being stated or declared. The reader can almost feel this breath through the countless 'O's that appear throughout her volumes of published work. While her handwritten manuscripts variously use the spelling 'Oh' or 'O', Jennings tended to correct her typescripts to the single 'O', a letter that punctures her poems with holes through which their sound whistles. 'O love is kind, O love is kind' Jennings sings in 'Love Poem', a characteristically Romantic verse that evokes Christian and human affection while also separating her work stylistically and affectively from that of her literary contemporaries. This new edition of her poetry seeks to reinstate Jennings as one of the most discerning and lyrical Christian poets of the twentieth century, and does so by reproducing both her published work (including several neglected volumes never before anthologised) and a sample of her unpublished poetry, now spread across several archives in both Britain and North America.

Jennings wrote an astonishing number of poems and prose essays, enough to fill a volume of this size many times over. This edition collects nearly all of her published work (with the exception of two weak volumes, *An Oxford Cycle* and *In Shakespeare's Company*); and a representative group of her unpublished poems (although her attempts at limericks are excluded, a form I think Jennings used for writing practice rather than publication). A small number of obvious typographic errors in her published poems have been corrected, otherwise the texts are reproduced as they appeared in the first editions of the original collections. Jennings often did not sign her manuscript poems, and so many of them are undated. I have listed her unpublished dated poems chronologically, and, where several poems appear under the same date, in the order by which they are catalogued in the archive (Jennings' work is housed in four main archives: University of Delaware Library Special Collections; John Rylands, Manchester, Special Collections; Georgetown University, Special Collections and Washington University in St Louis, Special Collections). Undated poems are included under a separate heading, and printed in the order in which they are catalogued. My transcriptions of these manuscript poems are faithful to Jennings' unrevised drafts, although her handwriting very occasionally forced an element of interpretation. Usefully, Jennings tends to divide stanzas with a dash and signifies the end of a poem with a ÷ sign, although repeated crossings-out and scribbles render some poems more uncertain than others. I have included only poems that Jennings legibly completed; and added some minor formatting that accords with those methods she uses in her published work (for example, her preference for placing punctuation inside, not outside, quotation marks).

I owe thanks to many people for assistance and encouragement during the development of this edition, in particular Grover J.

Askins, Catherine Bates, Jane Dowson, Stella Halkyard, Cathia Jenainati, Mark Knight, Erin Lafford, Peter Larkin, Rebecca Lemon, Jon Roberts, Sophie Rudland, Jason Rudy, Nicholas Scheetz, Jeremy Treglown, Rhian Williams, Judith Willson, and my students and colleagues at the University of Warwick. I am grateful to the Arts and Humanities Research Council, and the K. Blundell Trust at the Society of Authors, for financial support; and to the archivists at the British Library, London; University of Delaware Special Collections; Georgetown University Special Collections; John Rylands, Manchester; and the University of Washington, St. Louis for guidance with Jennings' manuscripts. I would like to especially thank Amjad Shad, neurosurgeon at the University Hospital, Coventry, physiotherapist David Howells and my parents for their continued support during and following my work on this edition; Rachel Buxton and Michael Schmidt for generously and amiably sharing their knowledge of and research on Jennings; and Helen Tookey for her editorial assistance with the volume. Finally, many thanks to Jennings' sister, the late Aileen Albrow, and Jennings' friends, Gina Pollinger and Priscilla Tolkien, who each offered invaluable help with contextual details about Jennings' life and works.

EARLY WORKS

The Elements

The elements surround us,
Earth, water, air and fire,
And O my love I bring you
Those thoughts that long since found us
And quickened our desire;
So this desire I sing you.

Earth with its rich enfolding
I lay before your feet:
I lay it for your waking
And for your body's moulding,
This earth, a golden sheet,
Smoothed sweetly for your taking.

Water I bring for lovers
To wash their golden hands,
Water that gently hovers
And falls on arid lands;
Take it, my love, this river
It will not flow for ever.

Air I bring with caresses
Fluttering on your breath,
And silver-thin my kisses
Laid on your lips beneath,
Laid between life and death.

The last gift that I give you,
My love, is quickening fire,
It curls in blood-red fingers
And in its flame I leave you:
O guard it while it lingers,
It keeps my whole desire.

Estrangement

Neither map nor compass tells the heart's decay,
No chisel cuts across the lines of love:
Night still is night and day remains but day,
Only our thoughts and not our bodies move.

No dial reasons why we fall apart,
The clock goes ticking on, we cannot see
The palest indication that the heart
Will not strike out the night's futurity.

The Lucky

Sailors and gamblers and all such,
These least expect and most deserve my praise
Who, not didactic, yet most ably teach
The tranquil taking of the splendid days.

For whom a spot of breeze, a turned-up penny
Bring golden lights into their lucky eyes –
These face the world and have no fear of any,
And strut the daily storms without disguise.

Modern Poet

This is no moment now for the fine phrases,
The inflated sentence, words cunningly spun,
For the floreate image or the relaxing pun
Or the sentimental answer that most pleases.

We must write down an age of reckless hunger,
Of iron girders, hearts like plumb-lines hung
And the poet's art is to speak and not to be sung
And sympathy must turn away to anger.

Time

Why should we think of ends, beginnings,
Who for a moment draw our pace
Through moons and sunsets, risings, wanings,
Who brush the moment, seek a place
More than a minute's hopes and winnings?

Why cannot we accept the hour,
The present, be observers and
Hold a full knowledge in our power,
Arrest the falling of the sand?
And keep the watchful moment, pour
Its meaning in the hurried hand?

The Clock

The old clock
With its tick reluctant, slow,
Makes me wish there were some clock within
More regular than heart, steady as rock,
That we might know
The time to end, begin,
The time for stopping love or war
Or hate,
And see the stiff hand turning O before
Before it is too late.

Deception

Children who find their strength in loneliness,
Discouraging the bright sun on the roofs
(The sun that nullifies their secret caves)
Are desperate before the lovers' kiss
Acknowledging defeat and laugh at love's

Cowardly despair in loneliness.
They swear that they will never love like this,
And boys in gangs harry the girls and run
In many lonelinesses, quick to shun
The female wrath, the pity of the sun.

They keep their separateness like a disease
Until the darkness can no longer hide
Their ebbing strength, their impotent despair,
And out they come at last and wear their need
Like conquerors. Their coming they declare
Is but to end the women's loneliness.

Warning

Child do not tell your images, we kill them
With argument and I would wish you deaf
Rather than hear the mad cries of our logic
Aiming at beauty, wounding it with grief.
Be silent now and do not tell your magic.

And when your children dream O never tell them
Those dreams were yours, for if they should believe
Such dreams belong to others it would fill them
With knowledge that displaces dreams and if
You argue truth for images you kill them.

John the Baptist

Growing from old age he was close to death,
When he was born carried the look of death.
The mouth sharp as a sword forbade the touch
Of softness. In the desert he found sand
And friendly thistles for his hardened hand.

He was a god a short time, camped within
A wilderness and found his childhood there,
Built sand castles, was tempted first to sin
But pleasure was repellent. With long hair
He frightened and baptised throughout Judea.

Ironic for him that was precursor
Of one who turned the water into wine
And multiplied the loaves, one who was wiser
In knowing peace. The tawny lion John
Hated the path that he had trodden on.

He had been careless of the power of women
But a voluptuous feast was his own death –
The head upon a plate, the sword-sharp mouth
Condemning dancing with a sad inhuman
Face that shook above Salome's hips.

Tuscany

His stopping here grows close to living as
He marks a landscape for his thoughts. Before
His mind inhabited itself and not
Outside itself could pass,
But here
Built ready for him, to be recognised
His thoughts confront him in the light, the trees.

And contemplation active as the sea,
Purposeful yet half drawing back will come
At last in single meeting up the shore.
So all his questions answered outside him
Enrich his prayer,
Expose this different landscape as his home,
All to restore him perfect inwardly.

Cave Dwellers

Outside the cave the animals roar and whine,
Inside they move upon the walls and stride
Only within the pattern that the men
Who worked in careful patience have allowed.
So rich they are it seems they're painted in
The creatures' blood, the blood that burns outside.

Caves are our minds. How to relaxing peace
Our animals withdrawn there! They are tamed
To tapestries and dance on musicless
Obedient only to what we have named
Their laws, yet pacify our own distress.

But still outside the ravenous creatures rove
And set us burning, willing to be consumed
And to consume even the painted cave.
Their claws become our hands which seized and stormed
The peaceful animals who speak of love
And which possessed by power we say we dreamed.

COLLECTIONS 1953–2001

POEMS
(1953)

Delay

The radiance of the star that leans on me
Was shining years ago. The light that now
Glitters up there my eyes may never see,
And so the time lag teases me with how

Love that loves now may not reach me until
Its first desire is spent. The star's impulse
Must wait for eyes to claim it beautiful
And love arrived may find us somewhere else.

Winter Love

Let us have Winter loving that the heart
May be in peace and ready to partake
Of the slow pleasure Spring would wish to hurry
Or that in Summer harshly would awake,
And let us fall apart, O gladly weary,
The white skin shaken like a white snowflake.

Woman in Love

All familiar thoughts grow strange to her,
One thought insists on opening each door,
Each window on to love, the others stir
And creep as strangers, skulking on the edge
To find an entry by some subterfuge.

But she dismisses them and grows one thought
Whatever hands obey, whatever voice
Speaks of indifference. She is tamed, self-taught.
Peace in a high room now defines the noise
As meaningless and she, beyond the range
Of conversation, finds no dreaming strange.

Yet when he comes will then unlearn it all,
Find thought within her mind and fact in him
At variance, almost inimical,
And as peacemaker will exile the dream,
Escape her own mind and acknowledging
This love as strange enact a truer pledging.

Weathercock

A hard tin bird was my lover
Fluttering with every breeze
To north and west would hover
In fierce extremities
But I would never find
Him quietly in the south
Or in the warmest east
And never near my mouth
And never on my breast.

A hard bird swinging high
Glinting with gold and sun
Aloft swung in the sky
Ready to run
O would I were that sun
He swings to with desire
Could see my love's gold eye
And feel his fire.

The Substitute

He rehearsed then with an understudy
(Love he had cast not ready to play the part
Nor knowing yet disturbance in the heart).
Nearly indifferent he explored the body
Of one untutored, ready to be hurt,
Absolute, being unpractised in the role.

She took the lesson wholly in the school
Of his rehearsal, learnt it thoroughly,
Played it entire while his mind still was full
Of the other with whom he could not be,
Who played a passion quite away from him.

If she his waking love and she his dream
Used cruelly should meet, his love would stir
A sympathy and union in them,
The loved and loving have a common theme,
And he the instigator be in neither
But as the cause they recognised each other.

The Meeting

This meeting now blurs all we have become
Though not quite back to then,
And asks that here we build ourselves not dream
Each other out as when love had begun,
For now each one must fashion himself of
No other but himself and not of love.

So only can we greet and meet in calm
And watch the once mixed love divide and go
To where the other cannot know
And not to you or me as home.
So we construct
Pure meeting of pure self we think and yet
Envy those others moving into love
Strange and oblique where we are now direct.

The Infatuation

She looks in mood of dream to take his meaning
And loves what she is thinking that she sees
And gathers it so close about her ways
She cannot see he has a true beginning
Within her only, imaged there to dress
All her own passion in a deep distress.

But knows him still away and what she holds
No flesh held deep to love, so wills her passion
Close in a child to argue in a child's
Absolute power, as object of compassion
To prove her love not inward. But she folds,
As their child moves away, the true negation
Of love; it is a lover that she builds
And this real child no child of such relation.

The Three

Between them came
Not pleasure from their love
But always, past their senses, her own dream
Of what she made him for herself would move
And each grew helpless wondering at that life.

And making love was not between these two
But her own making this, this image of
What he was not, would never grow,
So in their gestures each grew less to know
Where their minds met and what each had to love.

Two Voices

'You are more than your thoughts' he said
Watching her wandering away from him
In a landscape her own where she denied
Entry to any, kept a private dream
Where all love met rebuff, remained outside,

'You are more than your love' she replied
Watching him searching, how his eyes
And hands demanded to include
Her landscape where his loving was
Yet when he entered it it died.

And she beyond her thoughts he thought to hold
Made absolute in love. And he withdrawing
Behind his hope of love, she wished to build –
The seeker and the sought each one pursuing
Where each was, not in love, not in thought, held.

The Exchange

'I will unlearn myself for you' he says
Gazing away from him into her eyes
And drowning some old notion of himself
Within that gaze,
Relinquishing his meaning to her will.

And she discards the self she once would call
Her only self, seems gone entire and all
Given in patience, given in peace to love.
Yet both will fail
To see their old self copied in the full
Glance of the other, an exchange of life.

Sequence from Childhood

I

Children ponder our possessions with
Minds that are free, they play with curious fears
Adept at suffering second-hand, their legends
Are dire with cruelty. As overseers
They watch with fascination from the path.

Their truth being other than the facts, their brigands,
Pirates and thieves can be shut up at night,
But move like mice within their dreams beneath
The floor of sleep and with the morning light
Appear, unlike ours, fabulous as death.

II

A looking-glass is not where they indulge
Self-scrutiny, it is a country that
Opens before them in a lucky journey
Where animals are waiting to divulge
Important secrets, where the children meet
And threadbare rulers begging for a penny.

The sudden likeness seen is not their will,
They look beyond it curious to spy out
New topsy-turvy landscapes without any
Images of themselves. They would wipe out
Their own reflections clearly to reveal
The tempting country ever in retreat.

III

Children ask that stories be repeated
And if we change a word they catch us out;
Wanting no ends they trace the well-known route

As if it is new land they have created.
Their history is of animals who live
Lives within lives, are always on the move,
Of kings who fall but to be reinstated.

Their detailed countries live by being told
Over and over, they unwrap new meaning
From stories, learnt by heart, when we repeat them,
A dream made verbal is for them no dream
And boring narratives are where they build
A power of love, a world without beginning.

Adopted Child

'This' they say 'Is what we could not have.
How strange for other lovers to impart
A meeting thus. And separate from the love
Barren between us, this child grows to move
Almost against the turning of our heart.'

'Our failure thus shall walk about our son,
Learn to speak dutifully to his parents
Who know him their escape, whose love moves on
To gesture at so tender a pretence
And make a home in others' innocence.'

But love is inward still, however they
Walk in the child and make him weather all
The tenderness that neither could fulfil,
And never 'This is you' will either say
Passing a passion to the child to seal
Their lack, but watch a stranger ignorantly.

The Alteration

He argued with his thoughts, they would not stir
To go out ceremoniously, wear

The other side of passion. In strict hate
They would not be sent strutting proudly out

But dressed up quietly for no inspection
And tiptoed round and called themselves affection.

And all the tenderness he willed before
Came then unwanted and with much to spare.

Love could be held a little dressed as hate
But turned to fondness must be quite cast out.

Reminiscence

When I was happy alone, too young for love
Or to be loved in any but a way
Cloudless and gentle, I would find the day
Long as I wished its length or web to weave.

I did not know or could not know enough
To fret at thought or even try to whittle
A pattern from the shapeless stony stuff
That now confuses since I've grown too subtle.

I used the senses, did not seek to find
Something they could not touch, made numb with fear;
I felt the glittering landscape in the mind
And O was happy not to have it clear.

Fantasy

Tree without a leaf I stand
Bird unfeathered cannot fly
I a beggar weep and cry
Not for coins but for a hand

To beg with. All my leaves are down
Feathers flown and hand wrenched off
Bird and tree and beggar grown
Nothing on account of love.

Jealousy

She spoke the word at last and gave him cause
To fatten on the treachery and grow jealous,
To see the underside of his own love

And find a new power, to be worshipped with
As much care as the love which bound them both,
To tame to tricks or burn incense before.

But when the fever by her malice stirred
Be changed to health before a gentle word,
He will be helpless in his love and wish

The absolute jealousy to touch him further
That he may hold his failure as a mother
Cherishes most the misbegotten one.

Italian Light

It is not quite a house without the sun
And sun is what we notice, wonder at
As if stone left its hard and quarried state
To be reciprocal to light and let
The falling beams bound and rebound upon
Shutter and wall, each with assurance thrown.

So on descending from the snow we meet
Not warmth of south but houses which contrive
To be designed of sun. The builders have
Instructed hands to know where shadows fall
And made of buildings an obedient stone
Linked to the sun as waters to the moon.

A View of Positano

He builds the town, puts houses random down
Though they have stood there long. But this is new,
He brings the angles narrow on the view,
Cracked plaster peels, breaks under sun, its rind
Composing then and white within his mind.

The maps, sunglasses and binoculars
Are to detach the place from what he makes it,
To hold it off there in a clear perspective
And out of reach, placed apt in all particulars.
This needful to the town for staring fakes it

And leaves too personal a spirit there.
Afterwards, from the sea, it will grow dim
But rich in promises and seem to air
Its meaning publicly. Be as before
White houses fallen down the cliff
But rooted there as in no traveller's dream.

A Tuscan Village

Anchored to its appearance this town yet
Grants you a guess at what goes on in it.
And moving past and never to walk there,
You shape it to perfection, build the walls
With no paint peeling off in sun, you bear

It meaning that it may not have,
A kind of love,
Held on a hill fragile as eyes that stare
Yet firm for ever as your mind fulfils.

The Place Between

Not here to be exalted
Though the church cries out vividly as there
Up in the mountains where the snow invites
To stations out of ordinary paths.
Many have climbed and wilted
Many whose deaths
Make stories here
Were urged within their own excitement to
A sudden way of being something new.

Here there is peace
To move in circles of a private will,
To chime as bells, in order, to release,
To move as winds move trees upon their roots.
The sailor lets
His ship exceed his pride,
Beyond himself his hand can feel
But he is out there, you inside.

This is the place to fall
To reason, here to learn no mile
Beyond which you may step.
You lie between the hills and sea
To grow what you can be,
Your only aspiration looking up.

Afternoon in Florence

This afternoon disturbs within the mind
No other afternoon, is out of time
Yet lies within a definite sun to end
In night that is in time. Yet hold it here
Our eyes, our minds, to make the city clear.

Light detains no prisoner here at all
In brick or stone but sends a freedom out
Extends a shadow like a deeper thought,
Makes churches move, once still,
Rocking in light as music rocks the bell.

So eyes make room for light and minds make room
For image of the city tangible.
We look down on the city and a dream
Opens to wakefulness, and waking on
This peace perpetuates this afternoon.

Deepsea Diver

Strange above water he is exiled in
The freedom of the air, the kinder sea
Was guardian of his thought, explained his will
In terms of fish and tides. Islands begin
Insisting upon choice and he is full
Of loss, uneasy wondering what to love.

Uses the knowledge found in deepsea waters
To ward off every gesture of his will,
Turns into language where the water fell,
What fish intruded. But the watching faces
Inquire in other terms and all he utters

Loses its interest. A quick escape,
One will accuse, you must come up and choose
In your own element of land the shape
Of what you love. Water, he thinks but knows
Waves were indifferent and the mainland asks
A chosen attitude, a dive more deep.

The Planners

Some who fell in love with lack of order
And liked the random weather, were made angry,
Accused the planners thus 'It is not brick
Only you set upright and scaffolding
And the roof bending at a perfect angle,
But all our love you end in measurements,
Construct a mood for any moment, teach
Passion to move in inches not by chance'.

And swarming from the forests to new houses
They chipped the walls a little, left footmarks
Across the thresholds, would not scan each other
By clock or compass, terrified the silence
With rough words that had never been thought out.

And builders, poets fell upon them, saw
A just disorder for their alteration,
Would turn the conversation into music,
Tidy the house and from the lovers' quarrel
Shape a whole scene with middle, end, beginning,
Never be wearied of the straightening out
Though would not recognise they fell in love
Most deeply at the centre of disaster.

The Harbour

No ship is stationed here for greatness, white
Sails urge forward only momentary
Prowess and funnels strike brief attitudes.
Each cargo lifted out is commentary
On all small voyages, all seaward loss,
No sunburn on a sailor what it was.

Mere idleness is proud, is a lifted thought.
(Here leaning upon a bollard or tapping a pipe
On a boat's steep side means 'I am entirely myself')
All ships but shuffle through the harbour, bells
Suggest that tides are seeking something else,
And only cargo at a looked-for end
Is rich for promise or giving hand.

So this is not the place to ask a tragic
Meaning, a gesture that decides a pause
In ordinariness. Movement is loss,
Yet sailors draw up anchors from their peace
And all pass forward to a wave's rough logic.
Even the watchful one upon the wharf
Is less himself because the ships must hurry
Relative always, hindrances to love.

The Arrival

See how travel conveys him as love can
Out of himself. This is not I I feel,
He thinks, but sets himself in will
Newmade to stare, to take a virtue out,
And wonders how to meet all those who fill
The jetty there and wonders how they wait

For him who does not know himself at all;
And though his movement states 'I am'
He argues with his own identity,
Sees, somewhere back, himself at sea,
Him starting out, him, further still, at home,
And wonders which to gather up to greet
Those waiting who are nothing but their thought
Of strangeness and another way to meet.

The Stranger

This stranger looks for no encouragement,
Concerns himself with silence, ceases movement
To learn a landscape, yes to grow in it,
And trade all old familiar settings for
The slightest cypress, or one shuttered villa,
A sharp incline, so long as not familiar.

And finds this loss of past a gain to him,
Confronts another's eyes and finds a candour
A warmer look as if he took it from
A recent love-making, and this is love –
To find new roots strike in this country deep
And feel a friendship like wind through the landscape.

Identity

When I decide I shall assemble you
Or, more precisely, when I decide which thoughts
Of mine about you fit most easily together,
Then I can learn what I have loved, what lets
Light through the mind. The residue
Of what you may be goes. I gather

Only as lovers or friends gather at all
For making friends means this –
Image and passion combined into a whole
Pattern within the loving mind, not her or his
Concurring there. You can project the full
Picture of lover or friend that is not either.

So then assemble me,
Your exact picture firm and credible,
Though as I think myself I may be free
And accurate enough.
That you love what is truthful to your will
Is all that ever can be answered for
And, what is more,
Is all we make each other when we love.

The Geologist

Knows shells wait here holding no life now
Nor overcome by waves to be flung on shore
And gathered by children. Here escape, his thought
Continues, timelessness for him
Where shells are monuments to mock his time
And all the land afraid of sea no more.

Not the rare fossil crowns his search but looking
(Strata hard of access easy to him
Since time is backward to catch up on them).
Soil upon soil is still, and an earth shaking
Under old years grows quiet to be discovered.

In time again, abandoning the quarry
His life seems mocked as children gather round
Glass cases of his finds, not knowing that
It was himself and not the stones he found,
And dug for peace. And they collect with eyes
Shells as they might on seashores. But he is
Released and confident at their inquiry.

The Settlers

A land once questioned only by the sea
Which carried pebbles off as property,
And spoken to by bird or animal
Or a weight of wind trespassing a little,
But now the water throws explorers up
Whose eyes possess and hearts begin to settle.

Climate becomes a privilege for them
Offered to later visitors like love,
And all the corn cut down and packed away
Loses the sun a little and casts off
The lash of wind. The complete natural kingdom
Is tamed and ruled, even the sea discouraged.

And the rebellion of an earthquake shaking
The crops awry, throwing the houses down,
Killing a few, finds only the next morning
Bruised dreamers planning and the workmen taking
The broken bricks to build another town.

And men who come to meditate a mountain
Are tamed too by the dwellers here and offered
Weather for happiness, children to show
The white church in the market-place, the fountain
That mocks the uncouth sea. They go away
Ignorant that they alone are undiscovered.

The Seer and the Blind

Sea falling wide and a fresh wind from the forests
Show us homecoming to ourselves, we are so apt
In outward peace. The rain across the face,
A longer shadow startling us, each casts
A new man in us. Only one man wrapt,

(Some say in dream, but others looking closer
Know how his mind avoids the landscape) is
Unmoved by what the sea decides or land conveys,
Relinquishes the senses and the looser
Dreams in which we who guess ourselves are trapped.

So we try out our hands at casting off
The sea before us and the trees behind,
The wind and rain constructing a new face,
Would grow, as this man does in prayer, clear mind
And a heart in a deeper kind of love,
Yet have within no meaning to replace

The landscape that we move in. We have not
Perturbed as he has a remoter silence
Where prayer and aspiration cast out thought.
Only we can learn deeper the wind's violence,
Let seas continue where our hearts fall short.

The Idler

An idler holds that rose as always rose,
Will not, before the bud discloses it
Within a later season, in his thought
Unwrap the flower and force the petals open
And wish in mind a different rose to happen.

So will not colour it with his own shadow
As we contrive, living beyond the present,
To move all things away from their own moment
And state another time for us. O who
Watches may yet make time refuse to grow.

So has his subtle power wiser than ours
And need elaborate no peace at all.
Watch how a landscape kindest is to idlers
Helping their shiftlessness grow to new powers,
Composing stillness round their careless will.

Bell-Ringer

The bells renew the town, discover it
And give it back itself again, the man
Pulling the rope collects the houses as
Thoughts gather in the mind unscanned, he is
Crowding the town together from the night

And making bells the morning, in remote
Control of every life (for bells shout 'Wake'
And shake out dreams, though it is he who pulls
The sleep aside). But not into his thought
Do men continue as in lives of power;

For when each bell is pulled sufficiently
He never sees himself as any cause
Or need; the sounds had left his hands to sing
A meaning for each listening separately,
A separate meaning for the single choice.

Yet bells retire to silence, need him when
Time must be shown a lucid interval
And men look up as if the air were full
Of birds descending, bells exclaiming in
His hands but shouting wider than his will.

The Climbers

To the cold peak without their careful women
(Who watching children climbing into dreams
Go dispossessed at home). The mountain moves
Away at every climb and steps are hard
Frozen along the glacier. Every man
Tied to the rope constructs himself alone.

And not the summit reached nor any pole
Touched is the wished embrace, but still to move
And as the mountain climbs to see it whole
And each mind's landscape growing more complete
As sinews strain and all the muscles knot.

One at the peak is small. His disappointment
The coloured flag flown at the lonely top,
And all the valley's motive grown obscure.
He envies the large toilers halfway there
Who still possess the mountain by desire
And, not arriving, dream in no resentment.

Fishermen

This to be peace, they think beside the river
Being adapted well to expectation
And their wives' mutiny at no achievement,
And yet can sit watching the promises
Escape through weeds and make a trial of biting,
Can lose them, thankful that it is not yet
Time to draw in the line and drain the net.

Learning themselves in this uncertainty
Each hardly cares whether a fish is caught,
For here is privacy, each warns himself,
The fish, inquiries in the river, not
When drawn out promises at all
Being so solid on the bank and still.

Only the boys who live in certainty,
With expectation other than the stream,
Jeer at the patience and draw up their net
Of future frogs, the river vague to them
Until it's emptied. But the old men fill
Their eyes with water, leave the river full.

From the Cliff

He watches but would be out there
Falling and divided as the waves
And many things knocked by the winds that tear
The separate patterns into other patterns.
He gazes from himself and knows he loves
Seeming division and the chance of final wreck.

But for the sailors whose sun-burned arms are will
The necessary journey is simple, is straight,
To lean out carefully to the wind, to let
Storm go otherwhere and not to look back
Or forward, but be inward and direct
Merging all patterns in a way to act.

The Island

All travellers escape the mainland here.
The same geology torn from the stretch
Of hostile homelands is a head of calm,
And the same sea that pounds a foreign beach
Turns strangers here familiar, looses them
Kindly as pebbles shuffled up the shore.

Each brings an island in his heart to square
With what he finds, and all is something strange
But most expected. In this innocent air
Thoughts can assume a meaning, island strength
Is outward, inward, each man measures it,
Unrolls his happiness a shining length.

And this awareness grows upon itself,
Fastens on minds, is forward, backward, here.
The island focuses escape and free
Men on the shore are also islands, steer
Self to knowledge of self in the calm sea,
Seekers who are their own discovery.

A Way of Looking

It is the association after all
We seek, we would retrace our thoughts to find
The thought of which this landscape is the image,
Then pay the thought and not the landscape homage.
It is as if the tree and waterfall
Had their first roots and source within the mind.

But something plays a trick upon the scene:
A different kind of light, a stranger colour
Flows down on the appropriated view.
Nothing within the mind fits. This is new.
Thought and reflection must begin again
To fit the image and to make it true.

Reflections on Southern Light

Sun dazzles thoughts until ideas seem
To stand before us visible and solid
Hard as the marble, cool as the mountain stream.

And light assures us that these things are valid,
Transfers our thoughts to what our eyes can bear
And shows idea and image really married.

For instance, then, that statue in the square –
The truculent hero calmed into the stone
Confident and with confidence to spare

For us – sun helps us fashion him again,
Making him fit our own idea of hope
Taut to our thought and showing what we mean.

For light falls deeper than our minds can grope,
O better then to let the mind alone
And sun find symbols even for our sleep.

Florence: Design for a City

Take one bowl, one valley
Assisted by hills to peace
And let the hills hold back the wind a little
Only turning the trees
Only dividing the shadows
With a simple movement of sun
Across the valley's face.

And then set cypresses up,
So dark they seem to contain their repeated shadows
In a straight and upward leap,
So dark that the sun seems to avoid them to show
How austere they are, stiff admonishing gestures
Towards the city, yet also protective
To the deep houses that the sun makes more deep.

Here I say the mind is open, is freed.
Anchored only to frailest thoughts we are
Triumphantly subdued to the light's full glare.
It is simple then to be a stranger,
To have a mind that is wide
To permit the city to settle between our thoughts,
As between those hills, and flower and glow inside.

Fiesole: The Search

We did not know that we had come to search.
The journey, in easy stages, kept us remote
From the further joy or despair. We told ourselves
How little we altered, how stable we really were
As if all space and time were emanations
Of our own thoughts, as if we were the centre
Of any country that we strayed into.

And so no marvel was a miracle.
The hills suggested only aspirations
We might, in time, fulfil. The sea announced
(Being flat and pale, the colour of the sky)
Many journeys that we might embark on
And never be transfigured at the end.
And so we came like merchants to this valley

But merchants without wares. It was the valley,
Easy and warm like our most simple thoughts,
That sent us up to gaze upon the city.
The hill we climbed sent glory down below
Investing the whole city with desire
Yet moving us a distance from desire.
And still yoked only to ourselves we came
Most unprepared for any revelation.

What we did not know we searched for, here
We found – something between the single bell
Enforcing prayer, something between the words
Of one who offered hospitality.
It was as if the people and the hill
Were active only to give shape to silence
And in the centre of the silence let
Peace be discovered like a memory.

And through the bell and through the voice and through
The mesh of woven baskets we distilled it –
Peace without name or question in this village
That has a name though rests as though it were
Waiting for any name a man might give
Looking out words to echo exaltation.

A Sense of Place

Now we cannot hold a sense of place
Entirely by ourselves, we need to share,
Look round for hands to touch, for eyes to bear
Upon the same horizon that we love,
Until we cannot part the hands, the eyes
From the loved view and the close love we prize.

And when the eyes, the hands are gone we accuse
The place, say the horizon is at fault,
Thinking it has withdrawn a glory we felt,
Finding in it not in ourselves the loss.
Yet when the sharer is again with us
And the whole landscape seems renewed, rebuilt,
Not mountains or the sun are what we praise
But his mood shared with us, his sense of place.

The Image and the View

I seek now to compose
This country of my mind
Which I built long ago
In an extended dream
With what it is to them –
The men who love and tend
The vineyards of the place,
Who watch through every season
In mood that is half passion,
Half deepest contemplation.

And I would test the scene
That stood before I came
(Hills softly rising to
A round completed view)
With what I built long since –
A country which a child
Could animate and build
With images enough
To reckon up his love –
And make them both convince.
For as we can impose
Our image upon those
We fashion into love
And in the fusion make
Two separatenesses break
So with a place felt for
In dreams or visions or
Conjectures of the mind –
What we have shaped can be
With what we see combined
In one identity.

So now this Italy
Approached by mind and heart
Can never separate
From the old dream. For look
The men are walking through
The vineyards now and take
Their place within the view,
And grope within our vision
(Half love, half contemplation)
For us to make them true.

Not in the Guide-Books

Nobody stays here long;
    Deliberate visitors know
There is nothing here the guide-books show,
    No ruin or statue to sustain
Some great emotion in their stone.
    So visitors soon go.

Some travellers stay a little
    To collect wine or corn
And here breathe in the over-subtle
    Smell of places worn
Not by a marvellous death or battle
    But by their insignificance brought down.

Yet good, a place like this,
    For one grown tired of histories
To shape a human myth,
    A story but for his
Delight, where he might make the place
    His own success
Building what no one else had bothered with –
    A simple life or death.

Fisherman in the Arno

Yesterday he was fishing
Motionlessly, as if rooted in the river,
His hat sloping backwards on his head,
And I wondered what he was thinking,
Whether his thoughts were as still as the river-bed
Or if he was mere concentration on the act
Of fishing, and wanting the fish dead.

Today he is still there.
The light is the same
And the river
Would seem to have flowed forward then backward
To remain the similar stream I watched yesterday.
He is standing stooped in the same way
And no fish in his bag.

Only I have changed while he
With neither epilogue nor prologue
Has time in his net caught
As the mind holds a thought.

Children in the Square

I play now with the thought of being a child
As children in the square below me play
Soldiers or emperors, play at being me.
Almost we reach each other and convey
Ourselves almost into the other's world.

Theirs is the large and the complete success
Since wholly built by them. But I because
I have been in the square indeed like them
Must build from facts, must take my present theme
Not from imagination but from time.
They make a future from suggestions, hints,
While I must reconstruct my innocence.

Children are still in the square and I am here:
It is not I but they who have the power
To offer back a childhood to share.
Passive I let them play at being me.
And slip into their country by that way.

Poem in Winter

Today the children begin to hope for snow
And look in the sky for auguries of it.
It is not for such omens that we wait,
Our world may not be settled by the slow
Falling of flakes to lie across our thought.

And even if the snow comes down indeed
We still shall stand behind a pane of glass
Untouched by it, and watch the children press
Their image on the drifts the snow has laid
Upon a Winter they think they have made.

This is a wise illusion. Better to
Believe the near world is created by
A wish, a shaping hand, a certain eye,
Than hide in the mind's corner as we do
As though there were no world, no fall of snow.

Song at the Beginning of Autumn

Now watch this Autumn that arrives
In smells. All looks like Summer still;
Colours are quite unchanged, the air
On green and white serenely thrives.
Heavy the trees with growth and full
The fields. Flowers flourish everywhere.

Proust who collected time within
A child's cake would understand
The ambiguity of this –
Summer still raging while a thin
Column of smoke stirs from the land
Proving that Autumn gropes for us.

But every season is a kind
Of rich nostalgia. We give names –
Autumn and Summer, Winter, Spring –
As though to unfasten from the mind
Our moods and give them outward forms.
We want the certain, solid thing.

But I am carried back against
My will into a childhood where
Autumn is bonfires, marbles, smoke;
I lean against my window fenced
From evocations in the air.
When I said Autumn, Autumn broke.

Music and Words

No human singing can
  Express itself without
Words that usurp the sounds
  That pour forth from the throat.
But when the music ends
  There lie within our minds
Thoughts that refuse to fit,
  That will not sing or scan
Or alter what they mean.

Yet we believe in song
  Some meaning that no word
Can catch is finely caught,
  That music is a state
Where truth is overheard.
  But we are wrong, are wrong:
Thoughts still are shaped of hard
  Unalterable stuff
We think we can forget
  If we sing loud enough.

Astronomer: A Song

Astronomer bring your telescope to bear
Upon this planet. Do not think that since
  Everything stands and moves about you near
    You have its meaning clear.
Find out some glass that probes beyond the stance
Of men perceived by their own measurements.

Useless to hunt the stars in outer space
Merely to have a superficial look
  At a mere size. Your glass will but disclose
    The limits of a glass.
O find a clearer, closer one to take
Deep looks into this planet or to break.

Different Visions

Sighing so often for a separate vision,
    For something shown to no one else but us
(A splendid moment entering the mind
    And losing all the attributes of time)
We certainly ignore the fact that much
    We hardly notice is quite near a vision.

A rapture cast off as without importance
    Might, watched more carefully, grow to the form
We hanker after, something we could lose
    Ourselves in and become the sense of glory.
We have accepted that a vision's static
    And if it will not stay then has not come.

Better discard the hope for the great moment,
    The pure illumination and make do
With partial ecstasies not cast them out.
    The whole thing is a question of degree:
The great inhabit their appropriate grandeur
    And the full vision. We, aware of this,

Should also be aware of how our glimpses
    Fit us as perfectly. It is the ardour
That visionaries bring to what they see
    That we most lack and should be most arraigned for.
It is our flawed conception of the flawless
    That makes us miss true visions of our own.

Kings

You send an image hurrying out of doors
When you depose a king and seize his throne:
You exile symbols when you take by force.

And even if you say the power's your own,
That you are your own hero, your own king
You will not wear the meaning of the crown.

The power a ruler has is how men bring
Their thoughts to bear upon him, how their minds
Construct the grandeur from the simple thing.

And kings prevented from their proper ends
Make a deep lack in men's imagining;
Heroes are nothing without worshipping,

Will not diminish into lovers, friends.

Map-Makers

After the journey we can fill the map
We shall not need; that map can only show
The journey that we need no longer go

Because we know its contours. And we love
Only what has not yet a certain shape;
The love we feel is the dimension to

Any great work, it is completed powers
Only diminishing when we survive
Beyond the journey and the mapping. Ours

Is will to steer upon a wider course,
Not charted afterwards, not formed by love,
But yet to be the finish and the cause.

The Enemies

Last night they came across the river and
Entered the city. Women were awake
With lights and food. They entertained the band,
Not asking what the men had come to take
Or what strange tongue they spoke
Or why they came so suddenly through the land.

Now in the morning all the town is filled
With stories of the swift and dark invasion;
The women say that not one stranger told
A reason for his coming. The intrusion
Was not for devastation:
Peace is apparent still on hearth and field.

Yet all the city is a haunted place.
Man meeting man speaks cautiously. Old friends
Close up the candid looks upon their face.
There is no warmth in hands accepting hands;

Each ponders, 'Better hide myself in case
Those strangers have set up their homes in minds
I used to walk in. Better draw the blinds
Even if the strangers haunt in my own house.'

Napoleon

Many who spoke with him a little found
Him most indulgent to the common voice
And sensitive to quirks of character.
I wonder, then, was this sent underground,
This gift for understanding, when he chose
All the impersonal power of emperor?

So much the legend haunts us. His last days
Slide easily into the sentiment
We like to hide our great men in. But was
The truth elsewhere, his talk with valet and
Children a screen while his real thinking went
Still to the thought of Europe in his hand?

There is no answer. Emperors elude
Our logic and survive within the small
Moment when they seemed ordinary. All
Our thoughts of greatness disappear when we
Can catch the emperor quite off his guard
And think he lived such hours continually.

In This Time

If the myth's outworn, the legend broken,
    Useless even within the child's story
Since he sees well they now bring lights no longer
    Into our eyes: and if our past retreats
And blows away like dust along the desert,
    Not leading to our moment now at all,
Settling us in this place and saying 'Here
    In you I shall continue' – then what kind
Of lives have we? Can we make myths revive
    By breathing on them? Is there any taper
That will return the glitter to our eyes?

We have retreated inwards to our minds
    Too much, have made rooms there with all doors closed,
All windows shuttered. There we sit and mope
    The myth away, set by the lovely legends;
Hardly we hear the children shout outside.
    We only know a way to love ourselves,
Have lost the power that made us lose ourselves.
    O let the wind outside blow in again
And the dust come and all the children's voices.
    Let anything that is not us return.
Myths are the memories we have rejected
    And legends need the freedom of our minds.

New Worlds

    Atlantis now will be ignored forever.
    No more the eyes of sailors in a calm
    Seem to descry a promontory, discover
    A twig or tree between two waves. The dream
        That all the swelling waters cover
    Is drawn back to the mind and called a dream.
    Atlantis soon will even lose its name.

    And other hoped-for continents that have
    More substance in their myth will also go.
    We shall not even wish we could believe
    That they exist. We shall not want to know
        How some have seen a shadow move
    Out of the mythical past. For now we know
    Countries in space that may be travelled to.

        Yet quite untrue to say the need is still
        The same, that all we want's a kind of hope.
        Atlantis certainly existed while
        It stood up in our minds as on a map:
        It was our past and quite accessible.
        But the far stars are nothing we can feel
        Save at a distance. Should we travel up
            To them they would not fill the gap
        Atlantis leaves with our minds but steal
        Even the hope that made Atlantis real.

The Lost Symbols

Missing the symbol they restore the fact:
How seven years back this city was burned down
And minds were gutted too. Men learnt to act
As though there were no meaning in the town,
And chose at last to make as derelict
All dreams they fostered. Dreams are also one
With walls and roofs and they like ashes lie
When a fired city cries for elegy.

Soon stone was piled on stone, another city
Replaced the ruin with its shadow and
Men walked in it but new it had a beauty
Not like the one that burnt beneath their hand.
The dreams would not return. Men's minds were weighty
With all the sense of searching for a land
Revealing symbols that a man might hold
Within the heart and from those symbols build.

It is a fine tradition they have lost
That spoke in architectural styles, that rang
Out with the bells when all the bells were tossed
And voices spoke up in the sounds and sang,
And men put feet down firmly in the dust
That flowered a legend and the legend was
Their way of life and a man's peaceful cause.

Now they assemble all the facts to learn
New symbols. For their minds are so constructed
That every fact that must to image turn
And dream new dreams when towns are resurrected.
The meaning is not clear – the burning down
And the charred minds. They would have all collected
In visions to be lived. The only style,
The only symbol is in each one's will.

The Nature of Tragedy

We will the tragedy upon
Ourselves. There is more suffering
In watching jealousy or grief
Move to completion in a life
Not ours, than in the offering
To have the entire burden on
Our hearts and feel the pain within.

How can the senses play their part
In Hamlet's hesitation or
Othello at the bedroom door
Consumed entirely by the heart?
Feelings are forced that are not used
Upon their own occasion and,
Close to a tragedy, at most
We only move it through the mind.

O we should stride upon the stage,
Not stand to watch and cogitate
And change the hero and his rage
Into a merely mental state.
We must set free the mind, enlarge
Our thoughts until we cannot tell
What we most nearly, deeply feel
From what we carefully contemplate.

Perhaps the deeper tragedy
Is then the inability
To change a thought into emotion
And still to be an onlooker
When all else passes by in passion.
O could we smooth that conflict out
We might know tragedy entire
And reach into the heart of it,
Where there is neither anger nor
Grief nor jealousy nor hate –
These being but an attribute
While the real tragedy is here,
An almost missed and simple state.

The Rescuer

Once trapped upon a ledge without a rope,
Stranded between the cliff-top and the sea,
Or caught mid-way between a hope and hope
Did we not feel some pleasure in despair,
Seem stripped down to our bare identity
And feel resentment towards the rescuer

Who threw a coil of rope and drew us up
And set us down among familiar things,
Or pushed us into one or other hope?
Did we look kindly on our safety or
Wish for our loneliness again, the pangs
Prevented by the adept rescuer?

We owe a gratitude to him yet rather
We yearn towards that slippery edge, despair,
Because we felt ourselves complete there, neither
Fashioned of what men think or we prefer,
But concentrated into pure fear;
Now we are fragments we must put together,
Sundered by the apparent rescuer.

The Conqueror

Revolution gives men only the possibility of dignity;
it is for every one of them to turn that dignity into a possession.

                                                            Malraux

Then was all that for this? To stand at ease
With your own blood and with your adversary's
Clogged indistinguishably on your coat?
To feel your courage growing stronger now
You do not need to prove it, and to see
The natural world again collected round you,
Animals on the move, birds flying over?

All this you had before the war began –
No need to test your strength, no enemy,
Man, beast and bird upon their usual exploits.
Only this dignity is new, is strange,
Something you have not yet learnt how to use
And will not learn until you bring it out,
word from its sheath, bright for another battle.

The Humanists

These had no wish to make
A gesture out of death
As if an audience,
Intent with bated breath,
Were building from mischance
A dream to conjure with:
No, these made death an act,
A final sense of choice,
A secret separate voice,
Used by a man alone
With nothing else to own
But loneliness at last.

For this great buildings were
Disturbed upon the air,
Bronze horses, statues cast
Not for man's glory or
Something to replace fear,
But merely as a kind
Of comment. Death was plain,
Not decorated on,
And grandeur was designed
As mere contrast. No man
Believed he could assemble
Death and be wholly noble.

And yet how much we all
Conjure from what they built.
It is our minds that bring
Their death to everything.
It is our way of seeing
That draws their stature up
To stone, to buildings. Whole
Tragedies that they felt
As private, as their own,
We now possess and feel
The act they willed alone
As part of us. We dress
Death in our loneliness.

Missing the Point

No one was brave there, many turned away
With every thought a backward step for them
And all excitement echoes. Others who
Would turn the future into an escape
And so assembled it before it came
Found nothing but themselves to emulate,
Would not let any other world take shape.

The closest to a courage halted where
His past seeped almost out of him and he
Reacted to himself as wholly present,
But too much braced himself as if a wind
Of speculation would knock life from him
And he diminish into his own madness;

Patience he never quite attained, but had
He consummated calm and watched as children
Succumb to wonder yet remain themselves,
He might have felt the city building round
(As visionaries gather in their prayer
And are transformed by it) and felt the peace
Of when a man puts out his hand to touch
The moment not himself but all his freedom.

Beyond Possession

Our images withdraw, the rose returns
To what it was before we looked at it.
We lift our look from where the water runs
And it's pure river once again, we write
No emblems on the trees. A way begins
Of living where we have no need to beat
The petals down to get the scent of rose
Or sign our features where the water goes.

All is itself. Each man himself entire,
Not even plucking out his thought, not even
Bringing a tutored wilfulness to bear
Upon the rose, the water. Each has given
Essence of water back to itself, essence of flower,
Till he is yoked to his own heart and driven
Inward to find a private kind of peace
And not a mind reflecting his own face.

Yet must go deeper still, must move to love
Where thought is free to let the water ride,
Is liberal to the rose giving it life
And setting even its own shadow aside;
Till flower and water blend with freedom of
Passion that does not close them in and hide
Their deepest natures; but the heart is strong
To beat with rose and river in one song.

On Making

All you who build, whether the marvellous columns
  Or the splendid stanza echoing itself,
Is there a place for you to stand and watch
  And truthfully swear 'My part in this is finished'
With a mind quite empty of its images
  That fit best in another kind of freedom?

There is no place at all. Your satisfaction
  Fails with the last brick laid, with the final word.
There is no place for minds to stand at ease
  Nor any mood where passion may partake
Of stillness and be still. Move on, move out
  Riding your mind with reckless animation.

Look there are men living within your houses,
  Look there are minds moving through your poems,
Proving how much you left unmade, unsaid.
  Your work is done yet there is no completion.
Only when inspiration is lived along
  Dare you exclaim 'I'm near the perfect thing
That is not mine nor what I made at all.'

Tribute

Sometimes the tall poem leans across the page
And the whole world seems near, a simple thing.
Then all the arts of mind and hand engage
To make the shadow tangible. O white
As silence is the page where words shall sing
And all the shadows be drawn into light.

And no one else is necessary then.
The poem is enough that joins me to
The world that seems too far to grasp at when
Images fail and words are gabbled speech:
At those times clarity appears in you,
Your mind holds meanings that my mind can reach.

Are you remote, then, when words play their part
With a fine arrogance within the poem?
Will the words keep all else outside my heart,
Even you, my test of life and gauge?
No, for you are that place where poems find room,
The tall abundant shadow on my page.

Looking Forward

Those waiting for a child or looking out
For landscapes to grow up within the mind
Release as much as men dare lose of self,
Instruct themselves in doubt
Letting the child grow, the landscape be defined.

But children argue down the avenues
Of all men's wonder and take something of
The marvel from them, and a landscape is
So patterned that no man need move
As if the trees to grow required his love.

To watch is hardest kind of work for us,
Forgetting how we feel ourselves alone;
The child achieved is soon unknown,
And landscapes send men hunting deep within
Homesick for waiting, learning about loss.

For a Child Born Dead

What ceremony can we fit
You into now? If you had come
Out of a warm and noisy room
To this, there'd be an opposite
For us to know you by. We could
Imagine you in lively mood

And then look at the other side,
The mood drawn out of you, the breath
Defeated by the power of death.
But we have never seen you stride
Ambitiously the world we know.
You could not come and yet you go.

But there is nothing now to mar
Your clear refusal of our world.
Not in our memories can we mould
You or distort your character.
Then all our consolation is
That grief can be as pure as this.

Communication

No use to speak, no good to tell you that
A love is worn away not by the one
Who leaves but by the one who stays and hopes,
Since you would rather have the hoping still
Than be yourself again. What can I say
Who know, better than you, the one who has
Moved on, away, not loving him at all?

And certainly to you I would relinquish
This knowledge held in other ways of feeling
Though dressed up in the properties of passion
Looked at by you. Something is deeply held
By me who never deeply searched at all
And we are not yet wise enough or subtle
To offer anyone a state of mind.

This the particular problem, and I search
A power over our general condition,
Where love is like a landscape we can change
And where desire may be transformed to friendship
If friendship gives the really wanted knowledge,
Where we can see the end and have the power
To take the journey there a different way,
And we can move our minds as we move houses:
Where love is more than lucky in the land.

Mirrors

Was it a mirror then across a room,
A crowded room of parties where the smoke
Rose to the ceiling with the talk? The glass
Stared back at me a half-familiar face
Yet something hoped for. When at last you came
It was as if the distant mirror spoke.

That loving ended as all self-love ends
And teaches us that only fair-grounds have
The right to show us halls of mirrors where
In every place we look we see our stare
Taunting our own identities. But love
Perceives without a mirror in the hands.

The Recognition

'But I was here before,'
You said, 'Before you came
I filled this narrow room,
Nor did I need your stare
To prove that I was here:
Yet coming in you show
A self I did not know.'

And certainly I feel
New vigour moving through
My blood and it is you.
Will moving into will
Makes separate beings whole,
Though each of us is sure
He was himself before.

All the room widens to
Your waiting and my coming
As mind with mind in dreaming
Compiles one thought from two.
Each says 'It's you, it's you'
And never ravels out
His own self-willed self-doubt.

The Return

One might return with April in his face,
Looking as if a glory had escaped,
A vision missed, yet he had brought some remnants,
Shreds of old dream for you to conjure with,
A Winter unwrapped from him and he giving
Himself, explorer, to you from the snow.

Yet he would never grow to truth from this
As if the travelled pole were nothing to him,
Nothing the all-day, all-night glare of sun
And men resuming something in the waste,
Something made rife and to be grasped in treeless,
Flowerless country. All your south evades

Some issue he explores; the light's not bold
In sky stretched out as far as it will go
(And seeming to enlarge horizons too)
As in the north, but southern sun drifts round
The flowers and separates, dividing life
From life, nothing in common men with plants.

The altered man returning brings a vestige
Of snow, a hint of how the Arctic looked
However he transfigures his own face
To speak of love for you. Receive him then
Not to that narrow place within your thoughts
But make your mind a country to include
Even withdrawal, even the two poles.

Escape and Return

Now from the darkness of myself
I turn to let the lightness in.
Is it the raging of the sun
Or my own thoughts made free again?
I between hills of light and light
Stand and, composed of my own doubt,
Wonder where they, where I begin.

For I would travel from the mind
And move beyond the intellect
And search and search until I find
Identity clear in total act;
Then learn how landscape is combined
With images we mint and make
From the mind's fret and the bones' ache.

And I would feel the invading vision
Without a self to stand and watch,
Without these hands to trap and touch;
Bodiless I would prove my passion
By learning the character of each
Landscape or person that I love,
Clothing them only with contemplation.

Out of this will to be beyond
Myself I come, return again
Into the struggling thoughts within
The boundaries of my own mind.
Yet something of those loves, that land
Batters and batters on my thought,
And, once more separate in the heart,
I feel the images that strained
Within me join the landscape drained
Of everything but its own light.

In the Night

Out of my window late at night I gape
And see the stars but do not watch them really,
And hear the trains but do not listen clearly;
Inside my mind I turn about to keep
Myself awake, yet am not there entirely.
Something of me is out in the dark landscape.

How much am I then what I think, how much what I feel?
How much the eye that seems to keep stars straight?
Do I control what I can contemplate
Or is it my vision that's amenable?
I turn in my mind, my mind is a room whose wall
I can see the top of but never completely scale.

All that I love is, like the night, outside,
Good to be gazed at, looking as if it could
With a simple gesture be brought inside my head
Or in my heart. But my thoughts about it divide
Me from my object. Now deep in my bed
I turn and the world turns on the other side.

The Acknowledgement

Since every touch or glance before seemed but
The mirror-image that myself had made,
Seemed but yourself constructed from my thought,
What images may now be singled out
To show me you indeed?
What symbols now will answer to this need?

Even the word of greeting intervenes
And puts you at a distance when you are
Most close to me yet your own self entire.
All the old images were but the means
Towards this moment. Images occur
When we desire
Still to impose ourselves on what we sense
Is not ourselves. No image now can wear
The simple recognition of your glance
Except the image of acknowledger.

Recapitulation

Being a child it was enough to stand
    The centre of a world and let success
Come crowding in, be taken by the hand.
    This was one way to lose a loneliness.

Until success itself became a part
    I played. It was the shell and centre too.
My mind was somewhere else, also my heart.
    I could not tell the false self from the true.

Now I abandon all my attributes –
    Failure, success, despair – until I have
Nothing at all but hard invincible doubts
    Shaping the one self that I can believe.

Answers

I kept my answers small and kept them near;
Big questions bruised my mind but still I let
Small answers be a bulwark to my fear.

The huge abstractions I kept from the light;
Small things I handled and caressed and loved.
I let the stars assume the whole of night.

But the big answers clamoured to be moved
Into my life. Their great audacity
Shouted to be acknowledged and believed.

Even when all small answers build up to
Protection of my spirit, still I hear
Big answers striving for their overthrow

And all the great conclusions coming near.

A SENSE OF THE WORLD
(1958)

The Child and the Shadow

Your shadow I have seen you play with often.
O and it seems a shadow light before you,
Glittering behind you. You can see what lies
Beneath its marking dappled on the water
   Or on the earth a footprint merely;
No total darkness is cast by your body.

Say that it is a game of identities this —
You chasing yourself not caring whatever you find.
You have not sought a use for mirrors yet,
It is not your own shadow that you watch,
   Only our world which you learn slowly:
Our shadows strive to mingle with your own,

Chase them, then, as you chase the leaves or a bird,
Disturb us, disturb us, still let the light lie gently
Under the place that you carve for yourself in air;
Look, the fish are darting beneath your reflection
   But you see deep beyond your glance:
It is our shadow that slides in between.

Old Woman

So much she caused she cannot now account for
As she stands watching day return, the cool
Walls of the house moving towards the sun.
She puts some flowers in a vase and thinks
   'There is not much I can arrange
In here and now, but flowers are suppliant

As children never were. And love is now
A flicker of memory, my body is
My own entirely. When I lie at night
I gather nothing now into my arms,
   No child or man, and where I live
Is what remains when men and children go.'

Yet she owns more than residue of lives
That she has marked and altered. See how she
Warns time from too much touching her possessions
By keeping flowers fed, by polishing
    Her fine old silver. Gratefully
She sees her own glance printed on grandchildren.

Drawing the curtains back and opening windows
Every morning now, she feels her years
Grow less and less. Time puts no burden on
Her now she does not need to measure it.
    It is acceptance she arranges
And her own life she places in the vase.

Old Man

His age drawn out behind him to be watched:
It is his shadow you may say. That dark
He paints upon the wall is his past self,
A mark he only leaves when he is still
    And he is still now always,
At ease and watching all his life assemble.

And he intends nothing but watching. What
His life has made of him his shadow shows –
Fine graces gone but dignity remaining,
While all he shuffled after is composed
    Into a curve of dark, of silences:
An old man tranquil in his silences.

And we move round him, are his own world turning,
Spinning it seems to him, leaving no shadow
To blaze our trail. We are our actions only:
He is himself, abundant and assured,
    All action thrown away,
And time is slowing where his shadow stands.

The Child and the Seashell

Never the certainty of it now but only
Far-off forebodings, tides tending to silence,
The lip of the sea usurping the shell not shore
And this is the lip he puts to his ear and listens,

Listens and waits for the far-off hum, the drowning,
   The sliding and suck of shingle
As if an echo were lifted off the surface

Of water, as if the sea, withdrawn for long,
Left only the sound of itself and this he hears
Dim in the corridors of the twisted shell;
For him now, more than the real sea, this is
Promise and expectation of worlds where he
   Might possibly sail. The shell,
Sleeping in its own silence, admits all seas.

And the child, still in the mood for every promise
Rewarding him, listens to great commotions,
To storms abating, to men dragging on driftwood,
And does not know that never will sea so sound,
That shores which wait for his footprints now will never
   So slip like a shadow beneath
His mind, as this shell now in perfect silence
Steeps his whole being in seas now forever nameless.

The Dandy

The elegance you wore was more than grace,
I watched the way you lifted up your hand,
No casual gesture, each limb knew its place,
And every pause in speech was carefully planned.
Also the shifting surface of your face

Changed with no diffidence. And where you stepped
On path or ballroom, there your shadow ran
Suave without vagueness, much as if you clipped
The darkness like a solid thing and then
Carved through the chaos where your life began.

A surface thing, some say, for underneath
Your brilliant colours and your flaunting air
They sense the human and immoderate breath;
Yet what bright bird puts off its plumage where
Colour may flash upon the dark of death?

Young Boy

It was too much of gazing into mirrors
Your sickness then, you said. You could not love
In any way but as reflections do –
Drinking their own denials and dark glances.
  Passing from glass to glass
Your feverish fingers only grasped yourself.

And passionate for passions known elsewhere
You turned away from those cold corridors,
Those long-receding glimpses of yourself.
Flinching from self-regarding you walked where
  Shadows were thrust aside
And all reflections faded from your sight.

And girl or boy who met you in this mood,
Who did not know how mirrors can deceive,
Gave all audacity into your hands,
Offered a love you had not learnt to use,
  Made innocence a skill.
How could they know it was pain more than passion

And suffering more than sensuality
That gave you up into their lives? Too soon
In each surrender you would come upon
That cold bright mirror glance; yourself stared back
  Even from deepest looks
And when they turned you had escaped again.

Taken by Surprise

Before, the anticipation, the walk merely
Under the oaks, (the afternoon crushed down
To his pressed footprints), noon surrendered, forgotten –
And the man moving, singular under the sun
With the hazel held in his hand lightly, lightly:
On the edge of his ear the lisp of the wind among
Untrembling leaves. Sun at the tips of the trees
Looked down, looked cold, and the man felt easy there.
His shadow seemed fitting as never before it was,
And the almost silence a space a man may enter

And be forgotten by all but his secret thoughts.
Then, something taking his fingers: 'Is it the wind?'
He thought and looked to see if the branches moved.
But nothing unusual stirred the trees, again
His fingers trembled, the hazel shook, he felt
Suddenly life in the twig as a woman feels
Abrupt and close the stir of the unborn child.
O and the afternoon was altered then;
Power from all quarters flung at him, silence broke
And deft but uneasy far in the back of his mind
A word like water shuddered, streams gushed and fountains
Rose as the hazel leapt from his mastered hand.

The Storm

Right in the middle of the storm it was.
So many winds were blowing none could tell
Which was the fiercest or if trees that bent
So smoothly to each impulse had been waiting
All of their growing-time for just that impulse
To prove how pliable they were. Beneath,
Beasts fled away through fern, and stiffest grasses,
Which bent like fluid things, made tidal motion.

These who had never met before but in
Calmest surroundings, found all shadows mingling;
No stance could be struck here, no peace attained,
And words blew round in broken syllables,
Half-meanings sounded out like trumpet blasts,
Decisive words were driven into hiding.
Yet some hilarity united them
And faces, carved and cleared by rain and lightning,
Stared out as if they never had been seen.

And children now, lost in the wood together,
Becoming the behaviour of the wind,
The way the light fell, learnt each other newly
And sudden gentleness was apprehended
Till the abating winds, the whole storm swerving
Into another quarter, left them standing
Unwild and watching in bewilderment
Their own delusive shadows slow and part.

Her Garden

Not at the full noon will she pick those flowers
For sudden shade indoors would make them wilt.
The petals would drop down on polished wood
Adding another element to decay
Which all her old rooms are infected with.

Only outside she can put off the course
Of her disease. She has the garden built
Within high walls so no one can intrude.
When people pass she only hears the way
Their footsteps sound, never their closer breath.

But in her borders she observes the powers
Of bud and branch, forgetting how she felt
When, blood within her veins like sap, she stood,
Her arms like branches bare above the day
And all the petals strewn along her path.

No matter now for she has bridged the pause
Between fruition and decay. She'll halt
A little in her garden while a mood
Of peace so fills her that she cannot say
Whether it is the flowers' life or her death.

The Bird Catchers

Is it the song they wish to catch, to hold
The thrilling voices in a purer way
By keeping the birds captive all the day?
And will the resonance seem more possessed
By being concentrated in a world
Where birds sing only that they be released?

Such calm yet suffering men these catchers seem;
Stalking those fields, in patience they prolong
The final echoes of the birds' free song
As if they knew no singing in a prison
However desperate could have the passion
Of a bird shouting in its natural home.

In any tree we can hear singing too
But want it brought indoors as men for years
Strain to bring inward all their outward powers,
And every bird tamed down at last onto
Finger or window-ledge withholds the clear
Notes that it lavished on the stormiest air.

The men perform their task and sell what they
Caught on an ordinary working day.
Look, colours vie with voices in the cage.
Such violence of sense we buy when we
Take home the birds: their songs make us unfree
And even if we let them fly away
We own a torment that we can't assuage.

Five Poems from 'Sequence in Venice'
For J.

You were also there: I can't
Detach the place from what you meant.
Beneath my hands the earth is felt,
Within my mind the landscape built.
Something is missing. Add it. You
Were something essential there, a true
Gauge of my feeling, an event.

I Introduction to a Landscape

Difficult not to see significance
In any landscape we are charged to watch,
Impossible not to set all seasons there
Fading like movements in a music one
To other, slow Spring into the fast rage
Of Summer that takes possession of a place
Leaving the residue of time to Autumn
Rather than just a used and ravished landscape.

And never long able to see the place
As it must be somewhere itself beyond
Any regard of the ecstatic gazer
Or any human attitude of mind,
We blame all human happiness or grief

Upon a place, make figures of our feeling
And move them, as a story-teller might
Move modern heroes into ancient legends,
Into the solid and receptive land.

For who can keep a grief as pure grief
Or hold a happiness against the heart?
Noble indeed to impute our worthiest thoughts
To a serene and splendid countryside,
And therefore logical to let our loathing
See a storm looming in the Summer light,
The hills about to learn of landslides and
The entire landscape be quite swallowed up
In a surrender – a type of our death.

II First Reflections

No one would need to find a logic for
Living within this city; no man need
Have cause to ponder out his livelihood.
In other places far from sun or sea
Even the certain man has had to brood
Upon the nature of his certainty
And think of other ways to live instead.

Legends and allegories grow from such
Strong doubt. It is those cities where men look
Within themselves to wonder where they are
That shadows of great stories stir and stretch.
Myths are built up not where men love but where
They feel most ill at ease. Our fables reach
Back to the places where our hearts could break.

III The Islands: Torcello

Here you may find the purest style, a way
To be direct. This little island floating
On the same sea where Venice preens herself
Is island only, smells of sea and soil:
The style is in the toil,
Seamen with boat or farmer with his hay.
All is an action, nothing merely waiting.

Words would come easily and aptly here.
There is no grandeur to disturb
The mind, no squares where our selves disappear
Into a sense of wonder. Here we may
Partake of the particular
And put all generalities away.

Soil, salt and peasants with one tower to ride
The sky – and this is all.
Calmly our statements step away,
Substance and form elide.
Nothing of symbol's here, no rhetoric,
Yet we who are obsessed with what we make
Everything mean, yes even here compile
Torcello an archetype, a new and simpler style.

IV Piazza San Marco, The Mystics and Makers

Now they return to the one world we know
And do you recognise this man who comes
Rubbing the marble flakes between his fingers,
Pulling a splinter from his thumb? Are you
Prepared to welcome him to this one place
Which we, for lack of closer truth, declare
Is common ground for every one of us?

Mystics and sculptors come together here:
One feels a vision fading from his mind
And needs renewal from this downward world;
The other, so collected round his carving,
Is still withdrawn. Then bring him back to life –
Wine and the dusty sandal and our talk.

We, questioning ourselves, never believe
Entirely in a world that we can share.
Our characters, our faiths are where we move
Alone; yet we must act as if there were
A common ground if only fashioned of
Sun and a square deserted by the noon.
O put your hand on what the world is made of –
Water and dust. Let the creators take
Their time off here among this kindly chaos:
Let there at least be some way to return.

V Last Reflections

Now in this different perspective see
Another side of Italy.
Can you believe that history occurred
Within those squares, upon that sea
With you no witness there delightedly?
Turn to the books upon the shelf, the word
Of conquerors and kings who have not stirred

Merely to beckon your imagination.
See them in cold print now and watch their wars
Solemnly marching through the pages' progress.
Nothing can meet these things except the mind
Since you have left the five senses behind,
Put Italy into its proper past
Where nothing is diminished or revised.

Now Venice is surrendered to the maps,
The Adriatic falling sheer away
Downward to Greece and Africa;
And pity that you cannot put your own
Character down so easily on known
Papers or histories. No calm full-stops
Mark us on maps, we are dependent on
Our own ideas or those of friends perhaps.
There is no sign of us where we have been.

Summer and Time

Now when the days descend
We do not let them lie
But ponder on the end,
How morning air drained dry
Of mist will but contend
Later with evening sky.

And so we mix up time.
Children, we say, ignore
Before and after, chime
Only the present hour.
But we are wrong, they climb
What time is aiming for

But beg no lastingness.
And it is we who try
In every hour to press
Befores and afters, sigh
All the great hour's success
And set the spoiling by.

Heavy the heat today,
Even the clocks seem slow.
But children make no play
With Summers years ago.
It is we who betray
Who tease the sun-dial so.

At Noon

Lying upon my bed I see
Full noon at ease. Each way I look
A world established without me
Proclaims itself. I take a book
And flutter through the pages where
Sun leaps through shadows. And I stare

Straight through the words and find again
A world that has no need of me.
The poems stride against the strain
Of complex rhythms. Separately
I lie and struggle to become
More than a centre to this room.

I want the ease of noon outside
Also the strength of words which move
Against their music. All the wide
And casual day I need to stuff
With my own meaning and the book
Of poems reflect me where I look.

Still Life

Light on the table and the roses standing
Between the moment of their petals bending
And falling on the wood. Here there is no
Suppression of mere surface things; the glow
Of light and opaque petals are unwinding

Into each other. Soon you cannot tell
Whether the petals opened or light fell
Into the bud, an opening core of light;
Only you judge a lifting of some weight,
Fanning of petals, folding out yet still.

And watching all day long you would not touch
In time the moment when the petals each
Turned into cups of light. You'd merely see
The table strewn with shadows suddenly
And only broken roses within reach.

The Dancers

See how they move with strange smooth faces now.
Their feet find sympathy they never found
In words, their joy is bouncing on the ground.
The faster that they move the more they show
Soft and impassive features. It's as though

Thought were abandoned and the mind grown small,
And we sense peace however fast they move.
Some centre they have found, silent and still
Round which they dance. It looks like love until
The music stops, they separate and send
Shudders of some betrayal through us all.

Ghosts

Those houses haunt in which we leave
Something undone. It is not those
Great words or silences of love

That spread their echoes through a place
And fill the locked-up unbreathed gloom.
Ghosts do not haunt with any face

That we have known; they only come
With arrogance to thrust at us
Our own omissions in a room.

The words we would not speak they use,
The deeds we dared not act they flaunt,
Our nervous silences they bruise;

It is our helplessness they choose
And our refusals that they haunt.

During the Hungarian Uprising

In crisis now I walk
The tidy troubled street
And every face I meet
Seems deeper than before
And when we stop and talk
Our sentences mean more.

Strangers as well as friends
Set subterfuge aside
And now refuse to hide.
What they hugged hard and near,
I mean their private ends,
On this day disappear.

Yet even so I see
Not general looks of pain,
Not eyes whose surface strain
Is like all other eyes:
The differences remain,
For all identities

Clutch at compassion which
Joins but can never make
Faces the same. We break
Towards each other. Here
In helpless grief we reach
And bear each other's fear.

Absence

I visited the place where we last met.
Nothing was changed, the gardens were well-tended,
The fountains sprayed their usual steady jet;
There was no sign that anything had ended
And nothing to instruct me to forget.

The thoughtless birds that shook out of the trees,
Singing an ecstasy I could not share,
Played cunning in my thoughts. Surely in these
Pleasures there could not be a pain to bear
Or any discord shake the level breeze.

It was because the place was just the same
That made your absence seem a savage force,
For under all the gentleness there came
An earthquake tremor: fountain, birds and grass
Were shaken by my thinking of your name.

Disguises

Always we have believed
We can change overnight,
Put a different look on the face,
Old passions out of sight:
And find new days relieved
Of all that we regretted
But something always stays
And will not be outwitted.

Say we put on dark glasses,
Wear different clothes and walk
With a new unpractised stride –
Always somebody passes
Undeceived by disguises
Or the different way we talk.
And we who could have defied
Anything if it was strange
Have nowhere we can hide
From those who refuse to change.

The Parting

Though there was nothing final then,
No word or look or sign,
I felt some ending in the air
As when a sensed design
Draws back from the completing touch
And dies along a line.

For through the words that seemed to show
That we were learning each
Trick of the other's thought and sense,
A shyness seemed to reach
As if such talk continuing
Would make the hour too rich.

Maybe this strangeness only was
The safe place all men make
To hide themselves from happiness;
I only know I lack
The strangeness our last meeting had
And try to force it back.

Resemblances

Always I look for some reminding feature,
Compel a likeness where there is not one,
As in a gallery I trace the stature
Of that one's boldness or of this one's grace.
Yet likenesses so searched for will yield none;
One feature, yes, but never the whole face.

So every face falls back into its parts
And once-known glances leave the candid look
Of total strangeness. Where the likeness starts
We fix attention, set aside the rest,
As those who scan for notes a thick-packed book,
Recalling only what has pleased them best.

And doing this, so often I have missed
Some recognition never known before,
Some knowledge which I never could have guessed.
And how if all the others whom I pass
Should like myself be always searching for
The special features only one face has?

Always the dear enchanted moment stays.
We cannot unlearn all whom we have loved;
Who can tear off like calendars the days
Or wipe out features fixed within the mind?
Only there should be some way to be moved
Beyond the likeness to the look behind.

A Death

'His face shone' she said,
'Three days I had him in my house,
Three days before they took him from his bed,
And never have I felt so close.'

'Always alive he was
A little drawn away from me.
Looks are opaque when living and his face
Seemed hiding something, carefully.'

'But those three days before
They took his body out, I used to go
And talk to him. That shining from him bore
No secrets. Living, he never looked or answered so.'

Sceptic I listened, then
Noted what peace she seemed to have,
How tenderly she put flowers on his grave
But not as if he might return again
Or shine or seem quite close:
Rather to please us were the flowers she gave.

The Misunderstanding

See how the window groups the landscape there
(You sit back half-reluctant in your chair)

And how the sky looks brighter closed into
One square of light, one sharp constricted view.

It is the depths we do not wholly see
But most imagine which are really free,

As memories far back within the mind
Are unperturbed by what we later find.

(Still you are sitting there, your head bent down.)
Your shadow, like your mood, is dark and thrown

Over the floor but fades before the glass
Which filters darkness but lets sunlight pass

Much brighter than it ever was outside.
(With hands across your face you seem to hide.)

Dare you pluck one bright thought from what you feel,
Measure the memories your hands conceal?

Or can you find a darkness we can share,
Slip off our shadows, meet each other there?

The Shot

The bullet shot me and I lay
So calm beneath the sun, the trees
Shook out their shadows in the breeze
Which carried half the sky away.

I did not know if I was dead,
A feeling close to sleep lay near
Yet through it I could see the clear
River and grass as if in bed

I lay and watched the morning come
Gentle behind the blowing stuff
Of curtains. But the pain was rough,
Not fitting to a sunlit room.

And I am dying, then, I thought.
I felt them lift me up and take
What seemed my body. Should I wake
And stop the darkness in my throat

And break the mist before my eyes?
I felt the bullet's leaps and swerves.
And none is loved as he deserves
And death is a disguise.

Song for a Departure

Could you indeed come lightly
Leaving no mark at all
Even of footsteps, briefly
Visit not change the air
Of this or the other room,
Have quick words with us yet be
Calm and unhurried here?

So that we should not need –
When you departed lightly
Even as swift as coming
Letting no shadow fall –
Changes, surrenders, fear,
Speeches grave to the last,
But feel no loss at all?

Lightest things in the mind
Go deep at last and can never
Be planned or weighed or lightly
Considered or set apart.
Then come like a great procession,
Touch hours with drums and flutes:
Fill all the rooms of our houses
And haunt them when you depart.

Choices

Inside the room I see the table laid,
Four chairs, a patch of light the lamp has made

And people there so deep in tenderness
They could not speak a word of happiness.

Outside I stand and see my shadow drawn
Lengthening the clipped grass of the cared-for lawn.

Above, their roof holds half the sky behind.
A dog barks bringing distances to mind.

Comfort, I think, or safety then, or both?
I warm the cold air with my steady breath.

They have designed a way to live and I,
Clothed in confusion, set their choices by:

Though sometimes one looks up and sees me there,
Alerts his shadow, pushes back his chair

And, opening windows wide, looks out at me
And close past words we stare. It seems that he

Urges my darkness, dares it to be freed
Into that room. We need each other's need.

Telling Stories
For M.

Telling you stories I forget that you
Already know the end
And I forget that I am building up
A world in which no piece must be put back
In the wrong place or time
Else you will make me go back to the start.

My scope for improvising will not ever
Deceive you into taking
A change of plan. You are so grounded in
Your absolutes, even the worlds we build
Of thin thoughts, lean ideas
You will not let us alter but expect

The thing repeated whole. Is this then what
We call your innocence –
This fine decision not to have things changed?
Is this your way of stopping clocks, of damming
The thrusting stream of time?
Has a repeated story so much power?

Such is the trust you have not in large things
But in the placing of
A verb, an adjective, a happy end.
The stories that we tell, we tell against
Ourselves then at the last
Since all the worlds we make we stand outside

Leaning on time and swayed about by it
While you stand firm within the fragile plot.

A Fear

Always to keep it in and never spare
Even a hint of pain, go guessing on,
Feigning a sacrifice, forging a tear
For someone else's grief, but still to bear
Inward the agony of self alone –

And all the masks I carry on my face,
The smile for you, the grave considered air
For you and for another some calm grace
When still within I carry an old fear
A child could never speak about, disgrace
That no confession could assuage or clear.

But once within a long and broken night
I woke and threw the shutters back for air
(The sudden moths were climbing to the light)
And from another window I saw stare
A face like mine still dream-bereft and white
And, like mine, shaken by a child's nightmare.

In a Foreign City

You cannot speak for no one knows
Your language. You must try to catch
By glances or by steadfast gaze
The attitude of those you watch.
No conversations can amaze:
Noises may find you but not speech.

Now you have circled silence, stare
With all the subtlety of sight.
Noise may trap ears but eye discerns
How someone on his elbow turns
And in the moon's long exile here
Touches another in the night.

The Roman Forum

Look at the Forum
Commanded now by Roman pines:
Walk down the ancient paths
Rubbed smooth by footprints in the past and now
Broken among the baths
And battered columns where the lizards go
In zig-zag movements like the lines
Of this decorum.

Not what the man
Who carved the column, reared the arch
Or shaped the buildings meant
Is what we marvel at. Perfection here
Is quite within our reach,
These ruins now are more than monument.
See how the houses disappear
Into a plan

Connived at by
Shadows of trees or light approved
By sun and not designed
By architects. Three columns eased away
From all support are moved
By how the shadows shake them from behind.
The pine trees droop their dark and sway
Swifter than eye

Can catch them all,
O and the heart is drawn to sense,
Eye and the mind are one.
The fragments here of former markets make
(Preserved by the intense
Glare of the Roman unremitting sun),
Such cities that the heart would break
And shadows fall

To see them pass.
Removed from Rome you, half-asleep,
Observe the shadows stray.
Above, the pines are playing with the light.
Dream now so dark and deep
That when you wake those columns, lucid, free,
Will burst like flowers into white
Springing from grass.

A Conversation in the Gardens of the Villa Celimontana, Rome

For A.

Deeper the shadows underneath the pines
Than their own trunks and roots. Under the hard
Blue of the sky (a Roman blue, they say)
I watched the afternoon weave its designs
Lucid as crystal on this first June day.

The fountains softly displayed themselves. The grass,
Unpressed by footprints yet, looked cool and young;
Over the paths we saw our shadows pass
And in the air the glittering moments strung
Together like a brilliance under glass.

Suddenly to this fullness our words went
Talking of visionaries, of those men
Who make a stillness deeper than an act,
Who probe beyond a place where passion's spent
And apprehend by purest intellect.

You talked of this and in between your words
I sensed (still shadowed by my own warm flesh)
That you had known such apprehension and
Back in this garden where the pine-trees stand
Held to that moment where all hungers hush.

Yes but the garden held a stillness too.
My mind could seize upon the pleasures there,
Yet in between the fountains and the grass,
The leaning pines, the overriding air,
I glimpsed a radiance where no shadows pass.

Companions

Strictly across the urgent street
The eager voices probe and pale.
'It is the noon, it is the heat
That make the flesh and world prevail'
We say who know the calm defeat
Of those who vanish when they fail.

But still there is another way
Of entering these different lives.
Under the fragile, piercing day
An understanding now arrives.
Our shadows substitute our stay.
See how this town connects, contrives.

And far away from what I know
Deeper than I can now relate,
I watch the people come and go,
Their faces like the sudden, slow
Enchantments of those friends who wait.
For us – too early or too late.

A Roman Window

After the griefs of night,
Over the doors of day,
Here by this window-sill
I watch the climbing light
As early footsteps steal
Enormous shadows away.

Tenderly from this height
I feel compassion come –
People pestered by hours,
The morning swung to sight
As all the city stirs
And trembles in my room.

So from a stance of calm,
A stepping out of sleep,
My shadow once again
Disperses in the warm
Day with its lives more deep
Than any pleasure or pain.

Strangers

Each face repeats its former attitude.
How with our glances we beset the street!
Each man and woman in their separate mood
Pass through the dust of wind and do not know
It is their own reflections that they meet,
So shared are feelings which we undergo.

Yet straining towards a meeting we depart
(Still fixed upon stark shadows we have grown)
The simple, present and intrinsic heart,
And feel that others move in worlds which we
Could pass as foreigners but never own:
There are more meeting-places than we see.

Stripped to the cries of children or the words
A blind man speaks who begs an alms to come,
We move in doubt and stealthily towards
Wide squares where shadows draw back from a place
Sun is set free in, and it feels like some
Room where we recognise each human face.

Fountain

Let it disturb no more at first
Than the hint of a pool predicted far in a forest,
Or a sea so far away that you have to open
Your window to hear it.
Think of it then as elemental, as being
Necessity,
Not for a cup to be taken to it and not
For lips to linger or eye to receive itself
Back in reflection, simply
As water the patient moon persuades and stirs.

And then step closer,
Imagine rivers you might indeed embark on,
Waterfalls where you could
Silence an afternoon by staring but never
See the same tumult twice.
Yes come out of the narrow street and enter
The full piazza. Come where the noise compels.
Statues are bowing down to the breaking air.

Observe it there – the fountain, too fast for shadows,
Too wild for the lights which illuminate it to hold,
Even a moment, an ounce of water back;
Stare at such prodigality and consider
It is the elegance here, it is the taming,
The keeping fast in a thousand flowering sprays,
That builds this energy up but lets the watchers
See in that stress an image of utter calm,
A stillness there. It is how we must have felt
Once at the edge of some perpetual stream,
Fearful of touching, bringing no thirst at all,
Panicked by no perception of ourselves
But drawing the water down to the deepest wonder.

Santa Maria Maggiore, Rome

According to the legend, snow fell on the Esquiline Hill in August 358 AD
as a sign that a great Basilica was to be built there

Say the snow drifted down
On the Esquiline Hill in August and the light
Easily changed to Winter. Say the hill
Heaved for a moment over the town
And suddenly in the dear defeated night
The snow was still.

So I could well believe
Watching it now, the church completed there,
Altered and added to but still the same;
Senses and not the heart deceive –
Snow grown solid and grey in the Easter air.
I think there came

Once to the Pope and king
Who set the great basilica upright
A snowstorm in their hot and Summer sleep
That when they woke they swore to bring
Such solid coolness to that sultry light
As snowdrifts deep.

San Paolo Fuori Le Mura, Rome

It is the stone makes stillness here. I think
There could not be so much of silence if
The columns were not set there rank on rank,
For silence needs a shape in which to sink
And stillness needs these shadows for its life.

My darkness throws so little space before
My body where it stands, and yet my mind
Needs the large echoing churches and the roar
Of streets outside its own calm place to find
Where the soft doves of peace withdraw, withdraw.

The alabaster windows here permit
Only suggestions of the sun to slide
Into the church and make a glow in it;
The battering daylight leaps at large outside
Though what slips here through jewels seems most fit.

And here one might in his discovered calm
Feel the great building draw away from him,
His head bent closely down upon his arm,
With all the sun subsiding to a dim
Past-dreamt-of peace, a kind of coming home.

For me the senses still have their full sway
Even where prayer comes quicker than an act.
I cannot quite forget the blazing day,
The alabaster windows or the way
The light refuses to be called abstract.

Letter from Assisi

Here you will find peace, they said,
Here where silence is so wide you hear it,
Where every church you enter is a kind
Continuing of thought,
Here there is ease.
Now on this road, looking up to the hill
Where the town looks severe and seems to say
There is no softness here, no sensual joy,

Close by the flowers that fling me back to England –
The bleeding poppy and the dusty vetch
And all blue flowers reflecting back the sky –
It is not peace I feel but some nostalgia,
So that a hand which draws a shutter back,
An eye which warms as it observes a child,
Hurt me with homesickness. Peace pales and withers.

The doves demur, an English voice divides
The distances. It is the afternoon,
But here siesta has no place because
All of the day is strung with silences.
Bells wound the air and I remember one
Who long ago confided how such ringing
Brought salt into their mouth, tears to their eyes.
I think I understand a mood like that:
Doves, bells, the silent hills, O all the trappings
We dress our plans of peace in, fail me now.
I search some shadow wider than my own,
Some apprehension which requires no mood
Of local silence or a sense of prayer –
An open glance that looks from some high window
And illustrates a need I wish to share.

The Annunciation

Nothing will ease the pain to come
Though now she sits in ecstasy
And lets it have its way with her.
The angel's shadow in the room
Is lightly lifted as if he
Had never terrified her there.

The furniture again returns
To its old simple state. She can
Take comfort from the things she knows
Though in her heart new loving burns,
Something she never gave to man
Or god before, and this god grows

Most like a man. She wonders how
To pray at all, what thanks to give
And whom to give them to. 'Alone

To all men's eyes I now must go'
She thinks, 'And by myself must live
With a strange child that is my own.'

So from her ecstasy she moves
And turns to human things at last
(Announcing angels set aside).
It is a human child she loves
Though a god stirs beneath her breast
And great salvations grip her side.

The Visitation

She had not held her secret long enough
To covet it but wished it shared as though
Telling would tame the terrifying moment
When she, most calm in her own afternoon,
    Felt the intrepid angel, heard
His beating wings, his voice across her prayer.

This was the thing she needed to impart,
The uncalm moment, the strange interruption,
The angel bringing pain disguised as joy,
But mixed with this was something she could share
    And not abandon, simply how
A child sprang in her like the first of seeds.

And in the stillness of that other day
The afternoon exposed its emptiness,
Shadows adrift from light, the long road turning
In a dry sequence of the sun. And she
    No apprehensive figure seemed,
Only a moving silence through the land.

And all her journeying was a caressing
Within her mind of secrets to be spoken.
The simple fact of birth soon overshadowed
The shadow of the angel. When she came
    Close to her cousin's house she kept
Only the message of her happiness.

And those two women in their quick embrace
Gazed at each other with looks undisturbed
By men or miracles. It was the child

Who laid his shadow on their afternoon
  By stirring suddenly, by bringing
Back the broad echoes of those beating wings.

Agony in any Garden

And anybody's agony might be
This garden and this time. A different prayer,
A hand put out with no one else to touch
And faltering stammered words that cannot bear
The breadth of passion – anyone might reach
His pitch of hopelessness. We judge despair

By who cries out, by greatness underneath.
The dark night and the friends who would not wake
Are where we choose to place them. Now and here
Dumbness between thumped ribs may tear and break
And some small whimper shelter a great fear.

Gift of Tongues

Now the simple table laid,
  The bottles full of wine, the loaves of bread,
And the one woman coming and twelve men
Not as to that last supper when great doubt
Was washed away and finally cast out:
Visions were past now and their lives began

Again, had to be lived in usual ways
In new simplicity with all the blaze
Of glory passed into a chafing dish.
Their lord had risen and they waited for
The promised word, the message to restore
Aspiring souls back to the naked flesh.

At first they spoke of ordinary things,
Not the great days now gone but gatherings
Of men who sought an order to their lives.
Then suddenly their speech became confused,
They spoke of things they did not know, they praised
As a man praises his new-found beliefs.

Yet they grew strange to one another, stared
At faces unfamiliar now. The word
That each man found was made for him alone.
The broken bread lay by each plate uneaten,
The flasks of wine stood by, untouched, forgotten,
The easy friendship of the meal was gone.

Each man rode on the skill of his own tongue
As children do who take a foreign song
And shape their lives within its rise and fall.
Each was enlarged by language and went out
To test his eloquence beyond, to shout
And make great silence subject to his call.

So each went on his way and spread his speech
And marvelled at the sound of words, the rich
Music that held the people. Yet there was
Such distance between words and what they spoke
About, the marvels would not stand but broke
Away. This language seemed no fitting place

To hold a glory known, for words stay still
While myths burst out of languages they fill.
'This is no way to share the peace we knew'
They said, 'We must find silence once again.
Only a faithful silence can contain
The mystery we watched.' They went back to

The place where all the leaping tongues had come
Where now was shadowed silence in the room.
The story that they preached was sheltered here,
Not in the echoes of their garrulous speech
But in the sudden moment held when each
Could not distinguish ecstasy from fear.

Statue and Candlelight

The candle burns upright, the statue's face
Averted, in half-shadow, seems to turn
Some tenderness away. Beneath she bends
Her head and fingers, sees the candle burn
Then shuts her eyes as if to shut this place

Away, close doors and keep the senses out.
But still the dark is sensual, she feels
The candle burning like a sweet suave touch,
Then the huge shadow of her constant doubt,
Prayer thwarted by the flesh in which she kneels.

Open again, her eyes resume the world
And the prayer grows as hands and lips unite.
'I am a being turned away like this
Statue I kneel before' she thinks 'But press
My eyes, my hands against the candle's light.'

The Virgin at Noon
By Paul Claudel

It is noon. I see that the church is open. I must go in.
Mother of Jesus Christ, I have not come to pray.

I have not come to offer anything or to ask for anything.
I come simply, Mother, to look at you.

To look at you, to weep with happiness, to know
That I am your son and that you are there.

Nothing happens for a moment: everything pauses.
Mid-day!
Be with us, Mary, in this place where you are.

There is nothing to say, I only want to look at your face
And let my heart sing in its own language.

There is nothing to speak about but only a need to sing
                                    because the heart is too full,
Like the blackbird who delights himself with sudden snatches of song.

Because you are beautiful, because you are spotless,
The girl in whom Grace is finally given back to us.

The creature in her first dignity and in her last flowering
Such a one comes forth from God in the morning of her
                                    original splendour.

Ineffably pure because you are the Mother of Jesus Christ

Who is the truth you carry in your arms and the only
                                    hope and the only fruit.

Because you are the woman, the Eden of all ancient
                                    forgotten tenderness,
The very contemplation of which suddenly pierces the heart and
                                    makes all suppressed tears spring forth.

Because you have saved me, because you have saved France,
Because she also, like myself, was the thing which you cared for,
Because at the hour when everything failed, it was then
                                    that you intervened,
Because you have saved France yet again,
Because it is noon, because we are in this day of days,
Because you are there always, simply because you are Mary,
                                    simply because you exist,
Mother of Jesus Christ, accept my gratitude!

Augustine

And Augustine, gazing toward the invisible.

Ezra Pound, *Canto* XVI

Not in Ostia, not where the slant moon slid
Down to the afternoon and the evening came
Lightly, lightly where you and your mother were
Waiting it seemed save that your stance was so
Peaceful as if you expected nothing to come –
No not there indeed where the hushed world shook
To stillness and dark drew back like a curtain. No,
Rather it is in Milan that I place you, set
You simply there among your doubts and dreaming,
Those aspirations which great Ambrose had
Too little time for. There I see you stand
No lights flung clearly to you and no days
Caught like a fragile vision in your gaze.

You learnt yourself there more than on the coast
Where ecstasy came quite unasked. I think,
Torn by the wanton image of your life
You framed the finger-tip and footstep way
How flesh may be discarded. Love became,
Entered as anguish, calmed into a mode
Of thought and claiming. Yes, like water falling

Dear to the dried heart, images bypassed
Your body and you welcomed prayer that comes,
Like prodigal's return, childlike at last.

Teresa of Avila

Spain. The wild dust, the whipped corn, earth easy for foot-steps,
shallow to starving seeds. High sky at night like walls. Silences
surrounding Avila.

She, teased by questions, aching for reassurance. Calm in confession
before incredulous priests. Then back – to the pure illumination, the
profound personal prayer, the four waters.

Water from the well first, drawn up painfully. Clinking of pails. Dry lips
at the well-head. Parched grass bending. And the dry heart too –
waiting for prayer.

Then the water-wheel, turning smoothly. Somebody helping unseen. A
keen hand put out, gently sliding the wheel. Then water and the aghast
spirit refreshed and quenched.

Not this only. Other waters also, clear from a spring or a pool. Pouring
from a fountain like child's play – but the child is elsewhere. And she,
kneeling, cooling her spirit at the water, comes nearer, nearer.

Then the entire cleansing, utterly from nowhere. No wind ruffled it, no
shadows slid across it. Her mind met it, her will approved. And all
beyonds, backwaters, dry words of old prayers were lost in it. The
water was only itself.

And she knelt there, waited for shadows to cross the light which the
water made, waited for familiar childhood illuminations (the lamp by
the bed, the candle in church, sun beckoned by horizons) – but this
light was none of these, was only how the water looked, how the will
turned and was still. Even the image of light itself withdrew, and the
dry dust on the winds of Spain outside her halted. Moments spread not
into hours but stood still. No dove brought the tokens of peace. She
was the peace that her prayer had promised. And the silences suffered
no shadows.

SONG FOR A BIRTH OR A DEATH
(1961)

Song for a Birth or a Death

Last night I saw the savage world
And heard the blood beat up the stair;
The fox's bark, the owl's shrewd pounce,
The crying creatures – all were there,
And men in bed with love and fear.

The slit moon only emphasised
How blood must flow and teeth must grip.
What does the calm light understand,
The light which draws the tide and ship
And drags the owl upon its prey
And human creatures lip to lip?

Last night I watched how pleasure must
Leap from disaster with its will:
The fox's fear, the watch-dog's lust
Know that all matings mean a kill:
And human creatures kissed in trust
Feel the blood throb to death until

The seed is struck, the pleasure's done,
The birds are thronging in the air;
The moon gives way to widespread sun.
Yes but the pain still crouches where
The young fox and the child are trapped
And cries of love are cries of fear.

Family Affairs

No longer here the blaze that we'd engender
Out of pure wrath. We pick at quarrels now
As fussy women stitch at cotton, slow
Now to forget and too far to surrender.
The anger stops, apologies also.

And in this end of Summer, weighted calm
(Climate of mind, I mean), we are apart
Further than ever when we wished most harm.
Indifference lays a cold hand on the heart;
We need the violence to keep us warm.

Have we then learnt at last how to untie
The bond of birth, umbilical long cord,
So that we live quite unconnected by
The blood we share? What monstrous kind of sword
Can sever veins and still we do not die?

A Game of Chess

The quiet moves, the gently shaded room:
It is like childhood once again when I
Sat with a tray of toys and you would come
To take my temperature and make me lie
Under the clothes and sleep. Now peacefully

We sit above the intellectual game.
Pure mathematics seems to rule the board
Emotionless. And yet I feel the same
As when I sat and played without a word
Inventing kingdoms where great feelings stirred.

Is it that knight and king and small squat castle
Store up emotion, bring it under rule,
So that the problems now with which we wrestle
Seem simply of the mind? Do feelings cool
Beneath the order of an abstract school?

Never entirely, since the whole thing brings
Me back to childhood when I was distressed:
You seem the same who put away my things
At night, my toys and tools of childish lust.
My king is caught now in a world of trust.

My Grandmother

She kept an antique shop – or it kept her.
Among Apostle spoons and Bristol glass,
The faded silks, the heavy furniture,
She watched her own reflection in the brass
Salvers and silver bowls, as if to prove
Polish was all, there was no need of love.

And I remember how I once refused
To go out with her, since I was afraid.
It was perhaps a wish not to be used
Like antique objects. Though she never said
That she was hurt, I still could feel the guilt
Of that refusal, guessing how she felt.

Later, too frail to keep a shop, she put
All her best things in one long narrow room.
The place smelt old, of things too long kept shut,
The smell of absences where shadows come
That can't be polished. There was nothing then
To give her own reflection back again.

And when she died I felt no grief at all,
Only the guilt of what I once refused.
I walked into her room among the tall
Sideboards and cupboards – things she never used
But needed: and no finger-marks were there,
Only the new dust falling through the air.

Passage from Childhood

Where hell was open and the threshold crossed,
With seven deadly torments in my head
I walked and lived. At dark, wide-eyed I tossed
Feeling my body feverish on the bed
Certain I was among the chosen lost.

Each impulse paused before me, not my own
But rather like a rag flung in my face,
And wishes to apologise, atone,
Feel eight years' wickedness wrapped up in grace –
The terror, yet the need to be alone.

Looked back at now, the fires of hell retreat
Yet the responsibilities still feel
Like breath blown at me from that furious heat.
I move beyond the gestures of my will,
Careful of each handshake, of each heartbeat.

But now I know that all the agony
Built a compassion that I need to share.
The torment of that childhood teaches me
That when I listen now or simply stare
Fears are exchanged and exorcised – and free.

In Praise of Creation

That one bird, one star,
The one flash of the tiger's eye
Purely assert what they are,
Without ceremony testify.

Testify to order, to rule –
How the birds mate at one time only,
How the sky is, for a certain time, full
Of birds, the moon sometimes cut thinly.

And the tiger trapped in the cage of his skin,
Watchful over creation, rests
For the blood to pound, the drums to begin,
Till the tigress' shadow casts

A darkness over him, a passion, a scent,
The world goes turning, turning, the season
Sieves earth to its one sure element
And the blood beats beyond reason.

Then quiet, and birds folding their wings,
The new moon waiting for years to be stared at here,
The season sinks to satisfied things –
Man with his mind ajar.

World I have Not Made

I have sometimes thought how it would have been
if I had had to create the whole thing myself –
my life certainly but also something else;
I mean a world which I could inhabit freely,
ideas, objects, everything prepared;
not ideas simply as Plato knew them,
shadows of shadows, but more like furniture,
something to move around and live in,
something *I* had made. But still there would be
all that I hadn't made – animals, stars,
tides tugging against me, moon uncaring,
and the trying to love without reciprocity.
All this is here still. It is hard, hard,
even with free faith outlooking boundaries,
to come to terms with obvious suffering.
I live in a world I have not created
inward or outward. There is a sweetness
in willing surrender: I trail my ideas
behind great truths. My ideas are like shadows
and sometimes I consider how it would have been
to create a credo, objects, ideas
and then to live with them. I can understand
when tides most tug and the moon is remote
and the trapped wild beast is one with its shadow,
how even great faith leaves room for abysses
and the taut mind turns to its own requirings.

Harvest and Consecration

After the heaped piles and the cornsheaves waiting
To be collected, gathered into barns,
After all fruits have burst their skins, the sating
    Season cools and turns,
And then I think of something that you said
Of when you held the chalice and the bread.

I spoke of Mass and thought of it as close
To how a season feels which stirs and brings
Fire to the hearth, food to the hungry house
    And strange, uncovered things –
God in a garden then in sheaves of corn
And the white bread a way to be reborn.

I thought of priest as midwife and as mother
Feeling the pain, feeling the pleasure too,
   All opposites together,
Until you said no one could feel such passion
And still preserve the power of consecration.

And it is true. How cool the gold sheaves lie,
Rich without need to ask for any more
Richness. The seed, the simple thing must die
   If only to restore
Our faith in fruitful, hidden things. I see
The wine and bread protect our ecstasy.

A World of Light

Yes when the dark withdrew I suffered light
And saw the candles heave beneath their wax,
I watched the shadow of my old self dwindle
As softly on my recollection stole
A mood the senses could not touch or damage,
A sense of peace beyond the breathing word.

Day dawdled at my elbow. It was night
Within. I saw my hands, their soft dark backs
Keeping me from the noise outside. The candle
Seemed snuffed into a deep and silent pool:
It drew no shadow round my constant image
For in a dazzling dark my spirit stirred.

But still I questioned it. My inward sight
Still knew the senses and the senses' tracks,
I felt my flesh and clothes, a rubbing sandal,
And distant voices wishing to console.
My mind was keen to understand and rummage
To find assurance in the sounds I heard.

Then senses ceased and thoughts were driven quite
Away (no act of mine). I could relax
And feel a fire no earnest prayer can kindle;
Old parts of peace dissolved into a whole
And like a bright thing proud in its new plumage
My mind was keen as an attentive bird.

Yes, fire, light, air, birds, wax, the sun's own height
I draw from now, but every image breaks.
Only a child's simplicity can handle
Such moments when the hottest fire feels cool,
And every breath is like a sudden homage
To peace that penetrates and is not feared.

Notes for a Book of Hours

I

Kneeling to pray and resting on the words
I feel a stillness that I have not made.
Shadows take root, the falling light is laid
Smoothly on stone and skin. I lean towards
Some meaning that's delayed.

It is as if the mind had nervous fingers,
Could touch and apprehend yet not possess.
The light is buried where the darkness lingers
And something grateful in me wants to bless
Simply from happiness.

The world dreams through me in this sudden Spring.
My senses itch although the stillness stays.
God is too large a word for me to sing,
Some touch upon my spirit strums and plays:
What images will bring

This moment down to words that I can use
When not so rapt? The hours, the hours increase.
All is a movement, shadows now confuse,
Darkening the soft wings of the doves of peace,
And can I tame or choose?

II

I have to start the whole thing from the source,
Go back behind the noisy tower of tongues,
Press on my words new meanings, make my songs
Like breath from uncontaminated lungs
Or water from a new-found water-course.

Not to convince you, that is not my aim,
Simply to speak and to be gladly heard.
I have the oils, the waters, but the name
Eludes me still. Within a single word
I want the christening, the flowering flame.

Men had it once who carved far out of sight
Demons and angels, all anonymous;
Skill was another name for pure delight.
My angels must convince, be obvious.
I must create the substance and the light.

The cosmic vision fades. Within my mind
The images are laid, books on a shelf
Dusty and old. I only need to find
Some way to show the struggle in myself –
The demons watchful but the angels blind.

III

In the cool cloisters and the choirs I hear
The open-handed words, the pleading psalms.
The chant is sober and it soothes and calms
Though what the words depict is full of fear;
I gather all the shadows in my arms.

I cannot sing but only hear and trace
The meaning underneath the echoes, wait
For the resumption of a scattered state.
Such concentration screwed into my face –
Can it reflect an inner mood of grace?

What do they think who kneel within those stalls,
Young, old, white, black? The world outside still gropes
Not for a paradise but for its hopes
Come true in time. The chanting sinks and falls –
The great bell silent, none to pull the ropes.

IV

The sound is ordered, cool.
I heard somebody say
Once that the liturgy is diffused
Theology. I think they meant the way
The music and the words are used,
Austere yet beautiful.

A world of dogma can
Within these hours be pressed.
Both day and night are counted by
The times of exhortation and of rest.
The psalms can both rejoice and sigh,
Serve every need of man.

I need to make my own
Great book of hours, record
Matins and lauds, prime, terce and vespers,
With no authority but my own word.
The psalms are loud with truth; in whispers
I mark my hours alone.

A Confession

It seemed the most unlikely place to bring
One's childhood back. Outside, the grown world clung
To light, or did the light engender it?
Within the church, all that was old revived –
Gold on the roof, and in the shining apse
Mosaics stood within a lively stillness.
All was perpetual and precious here.

And here a foreigner, though recognised
By gentleness that leaps ahead of language,
I could discourse of every shameful topic,
Reveal the secret passions of a childhood,
Speak, fumblingly, the fears of adolescence.
And still the gold mosaics went on shining
And still, outside, the city played with light.

Exiles, perhaps, are people without shadows,
Movers beyond the sequences of time.
Simply to speak here is to be accepted.
Or does the light play tricks with one's own past,
Show it unshameful? Does one here mark time
Not with the stamping foot's impatient beat
But with surrender, attribute of love?

A Requiem

It is the ritual not the fact
That brings a held emotion to
Its breaking-point. This man I knew
Only a little, by his death
Shows me a love I thought I lacked
And all the stirrings underneath.

It is the calm, the solemn thing,
Not the distracted mourner's cry
Or the cold place where dead things lie,
That teaches me I cannot claim
To stand aside. These tears which sting –
Are they from sorrow or from shame?

At a Mass

Waiting restlessly the coming event,
Hearing the three bells ringing the loud warning,
I look for the lifted moment, the lifted cup,
Feeling upon my skin the Roman morning.
I watch with a critical eye the bread raised up
And confuse aesthetics now with a sacrament.

It is the veils drawn over, the decent hiding
That recall the decorum the test of art demands.
Around me the people pray, forgetful of
Even their painful eyes, their well-worn hands.
I struggle now with my own ideas of love
And wonder if art and religion mean dividing.

Each has his way and mine perhaps is to
Suffer the critical sense that cannot rest.
If the air is cool, the colours right, the spoken
Words dramatic enough, then I am pleased.
But why must I ask a sense of style in the broken
Bread and bring God down to my limited view?

Pride enfolds me, pride in the gift of tongues;
Envy too, since I long to be like these
Who approach with empty hands, an open heart –
The simple men lost in simplicities.
I have to endure the ecstatic pain of art
And shape from the silence all my encroaching songs.

John of the Cross

Emptiness, space. Darkness you could put walls round, set stars in, light from far off but never unthinkingly enter. To approach was to become the darkness, not even assisted by shadows.

And the senses, too, disarmed, discouraged, withdrawn by choice from pleasure. Finger not touching, crushing cool leaves. Lips closed against mouth or assuagement. Ears unentered by voices. Hands held out but empty. Even the darkness could not be possessed.

All indescribable then, but still the urge to depict, descry, point out, picture, prepare. The deep darkness had to be spoken of, touched beyond reach of stars, entered without indications.

Flame, then, firm – not the inward flame of passion, urgent, wanting appeasement, close to the senses and sighing through them: but a pure light pouring through windows, flooding the glass but leaving the glass unaltered.

More than this too. Not light limited by tapers, drawn to its strength by the darkness around it, not puffed out by wind or increased by careful breath.

It is held in being by patience, by watching, suffering beyond signs or words. Not your light either. You are receiver, requirer. And when the flame falters nothing of yours can revive it: you are resigned to the darkness. And you open your eyes to the world.

Catherine of Siena

Bridges. Ways over and ways to wait. Place for a stance or a stillness. Places, too, for violence. Bridges are blown and a war starts.

And in the water you can see the fish – if you watch carefully, if you side-step your own shadow, if you gaze deeper than self-love or arrogance.

Many have paused here. Have noted the faint sky reflected, the full moon falling, it seems, in the water. Have fallen in love with the dark.

For her, they were ways merely. Bridges meant building, meant the creak of planks, the delicate balance where wood is articulate, where men move as one, where the water is conquered.

Where prayer is most painful, she sought for an image. Others learnt light, air, steps, birds (the dove as a pretext or omen). All insubstantial for her. She needed the passion, the building, something to cleave – and connect.

Not standing there, letting the night drown in the water, watching the dear shadows that hold off the mountain. For her, the poise before the moment's abandon, all the reprisals of pain.

Pope, people, kings, confessors came to her. Proud professions passed over her bridges. Only Siena – round hill-city, seething with feud and friendship – was the safe place, solid ground, sweet summit where winds meet. Only here were bridges redundant.

Can light heal? Can the fountain surrender? Dare the fisher-man pause? Her bridges were built for a journey. The unconcerned waters flowed on.

The Resurrection

I was the one who waited in the garden
Doubting the morning and the early light.
I watched the mist lift off its own soft burden,
Permitting not believing my own sight.

If there were sudden noises I dismissed
Them as a trick of sound, a sleight of hand.
Not by a natural joy could I be blessed
Or trust a thing I could not understand.

Maybe I was a shadow thrown by one
Who, weeping, came to lift away the stone,
Or was I but the path on which the sun,
Too heavy for itself, was loosed and thrown?

I heard the voices and the recognition
And love like kisses heard behind thin walls.
Were they my tears which fell, a real contrition
Or simply April with its waterfalls?

It was by negatives I learnt my place.
The garden went on growing and I sensed
A sudden breeze that blew across my face.
Despair returned but now it danced, it danced.

The Counterpart

Since clarity suggests simplicity
And since the simple thing is here inapt,
   I choose obscurities of tongue and touch,
The shadow side of language and the dark
   Hinted in conversations close to quarrel,
Conceived within the mind in aftermaths.
   The intellect no crystal is but swarming
Darkness on darkness, gently ruffled by
   The senses as they draw an image home.

If art must be abstract that needs to speak
In honesty, in painful honesty,
   Then every scene must be composed likewise,
Familiar objects turn to careful shapes,
   Gestures be stiff, emotions emblematic.
So art makes peace with honesty and we
   Detect a blazing, a Byzantine world,
A formal image shining from the dark
   But no less enigmatic than the dark.

   Only in such decorum can our pain
Survive without dilution or pretence.
   The agony of loss, the potent thrust
Of seed that never will become a child
   Need the severity of metaphor,
The symbol on the shield, the dove, the lion
   Fixed in a stillness where the darkness folds
In pleated curtains, nothing disarranged:
   And only then the eye begins to see.

Mantegna's Agony in the Garden

The agony is formal; three
Bodies are stretched in pure repose,
One's halo leans against a tree,
Over a book his fingers close:
One's arms are folded carefully.

The third man lies with sandalled feet
Thrust in the path. They almost touch
Three playful rabbits. Down the street

Judas and his procession march
Making the distance seem discreet.

Even the praying figure has
A cared-for attitude. This art
Puts down the city and the mass
Of mountains like a counterpart
Of pain disguised as gentleness.

And yet such careful placing here
Of mountain, men and agony,
Being so solid makes more clear
The pain. Pain is particular.
The foreground shows a barren tree:
Is it a vulture crouching there,
No symbol but a prophecy?

The Retreat

Here in this room, the very top of the tower,
I live a little. On these checkered walls
Some past is written and some ancient power
Is whispered in those finger-marks and scrawls –
Childhood or family history or war?
Or were the things inventions, always false?

One window, steep enough to hold the sky,
Holds the sea too; today the water's calm,
The cumbered breakers have smoothed out and lie
As if no ripple cut across their firm
And balanced movement. Meanwhile, slowly I
Sit meditating, head upon my arm.

Silence is spread for me and no one knows
That I am here; no one can point and say
'Escaper both from failure and applause.'
The tongues of fire have not come down today
Nor the descending doves of peace. I close
My door and make my peace in my own way.

And shall be better when I climb the stairs
Downward to darkness and the still-calm sea.
Voices will snatch me and the old despairs
Return. One moment, recollectedly
I understand old silences and prayers
Yet know that something else is meant for me.

Visit to an Artist

For David Jones

Window upon the wall, a balcony
With a light chair, the air and water so
Mingled you could not say which was the sun
And which the adamant yet tranquil spray.
But nothing was confused and nothing slow:
Each way you looked always the sea, the sea.

And every shyness that we brought with us
Was drawn into the pictures on the walls.
It was so good to sit quite still and lose
Necessity of discourse, words to choose
And wonder which were honest and which false.

Then I remembered words that you had said
Of art as gesture and as sacrament,
A mountain under the calm form of paint
Much like the Presence under wine and bread –
Art with its largesse and its own restraint.

The Clown

I

Balloon on finger he watches us, the clown;
White cheeks conceal what eyes are witness of
And nimble body hides in pantaloon.
If you love this it is yourself you love,
Your own absurdity, your pride brought down.

But is this what he means, or does he mean
A dancing childish world where play is fact?
The rubber ball returns unburst and clean –
Your world so shapely, blown up but intact?
Are *you* the dancer in a pasteboard scene.

I am afraid of things which can be hurt.
The clown as much as cringing animals
Invites my wounding. Yet my pain will start
Because I wound. The clown prevails in art;
Gently as his balloon, my pity falls.

II

Aloof, reserved, yet strangely vulnerable,
Making of art a nonchalance, mere skill

As though a skill were something not to care
Too much about. You throw balls in the air,

You make yourself ridiculous, your face
Fitting nowhere but in a taut white space.

Yet sometimes carelessly you have been drawn
By painters in their note-book moments when

A special grace appears but fits nowhere –
A harlequin who leans upon a chair,

A youth who idly strums an old guitar,
Each lazy gesture meaning 'I don't care.'

III

Others are noble and admired –
The ones who walk the tightrope without nets,
The one who goes inside the lion's cage,
And all the grave, audacious acrobats.
Away from fear and rage
He simply is the interval for tired

People who cannot bear
Too much excitement. They can see in him
Their own lost innocence or else their fear
(For him no metal bars or broken limb).
Have they forgotten that it takes as much
Boldness to tumble, entertain and jest
When loneliness walks tightropes in your breast
And every joke is like a wild beast's touch?

IV

If I painted you
It would not be as juggler or as one who
Played the fool and entertained the crowds.
I would have you entirely alone,
Thoughtful and leaning
Against a dark window that needed cleaning.

I would want to show you
Not as victim or scapegoat,
Not like one who is hurried away, loaded
With other people's fears, goaded
Into the distance, but rather
As one who uses distance as a tether,
Tied but detached,
Sympathetic yet remote.

Strangely you remind
Of Christ on the cross.
Is it the seeming surrender or the white face,
The acceptance of loss?
Or simply that you seem like one not fallen from grace,
Innocent through knowledge,
Assenting yet resigned?

V

The eager one unconscious of himself,
Drawing the bow across the strings, absorbed
In music or the version that he makes,

The smiling one who never seems afraid,
Something to offer always yet not hoarding
His own or others' thoughts of what he is –

Simply the one who does not analyse
But still can gauge the feelings that surround him,
Loosen the taut voice, spread the narrow smile.

My childhood stands abruptly at my elbow
Forbidding demonstration, looking in,
Seeing the wishes and the dancers there.

VI

Something he has to say
Concerning pain. You have to watch the dance
With utmost concentration, in the way
A child will watch until the view enchants
And he is lost in it. The clown is gay
    And terrible at once.

His face will never show
You any hint of what you ought to feel:
White greasepaint spreads across his cheeks like snow.
His jokes seem feeble and his tricks are slow,
    He seems a game, unreal.

    And yet his helplessness,
His lack of tragic gesture, tragic mood,
Remind me of the abject beast we press
Our own despairs on, Christ nailed to the wood.
There are more ways to make a wilderness
    Than we have understood.

Lazarus

    It was the amazing white, it was the way he simply
Refused to answer our questions, it was the cold pale glance
Of death upon him, the smell of death that truly
Declared his rising to us. It was no chance
Happening, as a man may fill a silence
Between two heart-beats, seem to be dead and then
Astonish us with the closeness of his presence;
This man was dead, I say it again and again.
All of our sweating bodies moved towards him
And our minds moved too, hungry for finished faith.
He would not enter our world at once with words
That we might be tempted to twist or argue with:
Cold like a white root pressed in the bowels of earth
He looked, but also vulnerable – like birth.

The Diamond Cutter

    Not what the light will do but how he shapes it
    And what particular colours it will bear,

    And something of the climber's concentration
    Seeing the white peak, setting the right foot there.

    Not how the sun was plausible at morning
    Nor how it was distributed at noon,

    And not how much the single stone could show
    But rather how much brilliance it would shun;

Simply a paring down, a cleaving to
One object, as the star-gazer who sees

One single comet polished by its fall
Rather than countless, untouched galaxies.

Stargazers and Others

One, staring out stars,
Lost himself in looking and almost
Forgot glass, eye, air, space;
Simply, he thought, the world is improved
By my staring, how the still glass leaps
When the sky thuds in like tides.

Another, making love, once
Stared so far over his pleasure
That woman, world, the spiral
Of taut bodies, the clinging hands, broke apart
And he saw, as the stargazer sees,
Landscapes made to be looked at,
Fruit to fall, not be plucked.

In you also something
Of such vision occurs.
How else would I have learnt
The tapered stars, the pause
On the nervous spiral? Names I need
Stronger than love, desire,
Passion, pleasure. O discover
Some star and christen it, but let me be
The space that your eye moves over.

To a Friend with a Religious Vocation
For C.

Thinking of your vocation, I am filled
With thoughts of my own lack of one. I see
Within myself no wish to breed or build
Or take the three vows ringed by poverty.
    And yet I have a sense,
Vague and inchoate, with no symmetry,
Of purpose. Is it merely a pretence,

A kind of scaffolding which I erect
Half out of fear, half out of laziness?
The fitful poems come but can't protect
The empty areas of loneliness.
    You know what you must do,
So that mere breathing is a way to bless.
Dark nights, perhaps, but no grey days for you.

Your vows enfold you. I must make my own;
Now this, now that, each one empirical.
My poems move from feelings not yet known,
And when the poem is written I can feel
    A flash, a moment's peace.
The curtain will be drawn across your grille.
My silences are always enemies.

Yet with the same convictions that you have
(It is but your vocation that I lack),
I must, like you, believe in perfect love.
It is the dark, the dark that draws me back
    Into a chaos where
Vocations, visions fail, the will grows slack
And I am stunned by silence everywhere.

Children and Death

Not to be spoken of, they will not let
    Us enter rooms where anyone has died,
And they put candles by our beds, a light
    That keeps us watchful and more terrified

Than any dear familiar darkness where
    Our shadows slip away. We dream of death
Sweet and apparent in the freedom there
    And ape a dying by a withheld breath.

Nor do they know our games have room enough
    For death and sickness. We have stretched them out
Further than childhood or parents' love
    And further even than the breath of doubt.

A Kind of Understanding

You could say anything; she'd listen
Sitting in the corner (a bundle of fur
With cobwebs for string, somebody called her),
Deep in her sewing. Her eyes seemed to glisten
With help and encouragement. Yes, you could stir

And never be punished, always could say
Just what you thought. She seemed beyond shock
Or fear. There was something about the way
She held her sewing, like a child to rock:
She would not drop stitches or let edges fray.

A complete world – yet with a door
For anyone's entrance. An old midwife
Ready for birth or death, to restore
Things to their places. If it was life
She could cut cords: if death, she'd prepare
Fresh flowers and sympathy. Each knew the knife.

Sometimes you'd find her holding her beads,
Begging for silence, gesturing you
To sit down and wait. Always she knew
Time for the harvest and place for the seeds,
Having no words for the things that she grew
Yet, like an instinct, fulfilling all needs.

Visit to a Friend in Hospital

Always I was afraid of hospitals,
The green, inhuman, quiet corridors,
The dark impersonal numbers on the doors;
No echo could exist along those walls.
Death would be easy there and quite expected –
A sigh, a silence, and a room rejected.

Thus nursing-homes and hospitals appeared
To me, a child. Now when I visit you
I have to live the older horror through –
The smells, the dry heat, and the voices heard
Low and discreet. I fight away the fear
That death may stand behind each quiet door.

You are the one to whom I bring distress,
The troubles, dreams and all the broken things.
The roles reverse and I'm the one who brings
Solicitude and help and tenderness.
And yet it is a mask I wear, an act
Where terror hides behind the look of tact.

I walk upright and strong, yet I am weak,
While you who lie in pain have all the power.
I come to call at the appointed hour
Like one who long ago had learnt to seek,
Through sickness, darkness, death, a hem to touch.
The cure was granted. Do I ask too much?

Greek Statues

These I have never touched but only looked at.
If you could say that stillness meant surrender
These are surrendered.
Yet their large audacious gestures signify surely
Remonstrance, reprisal? What have they left to lose
But the crumbling away by rain or time? Defiance
For them is a dignity, a declaration.

Odd how one wants to touch not simply stare,
To run one's fingers over the flanks and arms,
Not to possess, rather to be possessed.
Bronze is bright to the eye but under the hands
Is cool and calming. Gods into silent metal:

To stone also, not to the palpable flesh.
Incarnations are elsewhere and more human,
Something concerning us; but these are other.
It is as if something infinite, remote
Permitted intrusion. It is as if these blind eyes
Exposed a landscape precious with grapes and olives:
And our probing hands move not to grasp but praise.

The Pride of Life: A Roman Setting

Old men discourse upon wise topics here:
Children and women pass the shadows by,
  Only the young are desperate. Their clear
And unambiguous gazes strike
  Against each brushing hand or eye,
    Their faces like

O something far away, maybe a cave
Where looks and actions always moved to hunt,
  Where every gesture knew how to behave
And there was never space between
  The easy having and the want.
    I think the keen

Primitive stares that pierce this decorous street
Look to some far back mood and time to claim
  A life beyond the urbane and effete
Where youth from coolest childhood came,
  And look to look was like the hunter's throw –
    Perpetually new and long ago.

Men Fishing in the Arno

I do not know what they are catching,
I only know that they stand there, leaning
A little like lovers, eager but not demanding,
Waiting and hoping for a catch, money,
A meal tomorrow but today, still there, steady.

And the river also moves as calmly
From the waterfall slipping to a place
A mind could match its thought with.
And above, the cypresses with cool gestures
Command the city, give it formality.

It is like this every day but more especially
On Sundays; every few yards you see a fisherman,
Each independent, none
Working with others and yet accepting
Others. From this one might, I think,

Build a whole way of living – men in their mazes
Of secret desires yet keeping a sense
Of order outwardly, hoping
Not too flamboyantly, satisfied with little
Yet not surprised should the river suddenly
Yield a hundredfold, every hunger appeased.

An English Summer

An English Summer – and a sense of form
Rides the five senses that dispute their claims.
Lawns levelled against nature, airs which warm
Each plant, perpetuate the hours and names.
We cannot see beyond the blue; no storm
Vies with the children ardent at their games.

Childhood returns with Summer. It is strange
That such a season brings one's memories back.
Springs have their homesickness, Autumns arrange
The sweet nostalgias that we long to lack.
But Summer is itself; it's we who change
And lay our childhoods on the golden stack.

My fingers rest and eyes concern their sight
Simply with what would live were I not here.
It is the concentration of the light
That shows the other side of pain and fear.
I watch, incredulous of such delight,
Wanting the meaning not the landscape clear.

Was it for this the breath once breathed upon
The waters that we rose from? I can see
Only a Summer with its shadows gone,
Skies that refuse an alien dignity.
But gardens, gardens echo. What sun shone
To make this truce with pain and ecstasy?

The Room

This room I know so well becomes
A way to keep proportion near.
In other houses, other rooms
Only anomalies appear.

I chose these books, the pictures too,
Thinking that I would often look
Upon a canvas like a view
Or find a world within a book.

They lie or hang, each laden now
With my own past, yet there's no sign
For anyone who does not know
Me, that these attributes are mine.

Strange paradox – that I collect
Objects to liberate myself.
This room so heavy now, so decked
Has put my past upon a shelf.

And this is freedom – not to need
To choose those things again. I thus
Preside upon the present, cede
The ornaments to usefulness.

And yet I know that while I clear
The ground and win back liberty,
Tomorrow's debris settles here
To make my art, to alter me.

Two Deaths

It was only a film,
Perhaps I shall say later
Forgetting the story, left only
With bright images – the blazing dawn
Over the European ravaged pain,
And a white unsaddled horse, the only calm
Living creature. Will only such pictures remain?

Or shall I see
The shot boy running, running
Clutching the white sheet on the washing-line,
Looking at his own blood like a child
Who never saw blood before and feels defiled,
A boy dying without dignity
Yet brave still, trying to stop himself from falling
And screaming – his white girl waiting just out of calling?

I am ashamed
Not to have seen anyone dead,
Anyone I know I mean;
Odd that yesterday also
I saw a broken cat stretched on a path,
Not quite finished. Its gentle head
Showed one eye staring, mutely beseeching
Death, it seemed. All day
I have thought of death, of violence and death,
Of the blazing Polish light, of the cat's eye:
I am ashamed I have never seen anyone die.

About These Things

About these things I always shall be dumb.
Some wear their silences as more than dress,
As more than skin-deep. I bear mine like some

Scar that is hidden out of shamefulness.
I speak from depths I do not understand
Yet cannot find the words for this distress.

So much of power is put into my hand
When words come easily. I sense the way
People are charmed and pause; I seem to mend

Some hurt. Some healing seems to make them stay.
And yet within the power that I use
My wordless fears remain. Perhaps I say

In lucid verse the terrors that confuse
In conversation. Maybe I am dumb
Because if fears were spoken I would lose

The lovely languages I do not choose
More than the darknesses from which they come.

No Reply

Between acceptance and the sense of loss
I pause, reluctant to admit the blame.
Leaves lie along the streets as if to gloss
A grief they never knew, could never name.
I watch them, knowing I am still the same.

Love has its battles and its counterparts
But friendship has to make rules of its own
Both for betrayals and for broken hearts,
Also for feelings that were never shown;
Emotion's not explained by thought alone.

Love could be stressed in touches and in looks.
We only have the easy words we say
When close together. Words seem out of books
When there is any absence or delay;
Distances not our selves, perhaps, betray.

My letters go, hectic with crossings-out,
Having no substitute for pause in speech.
I wait for answers, building out of doubt
More feeling than mere friendships ever reach,
Learning a lesson I would fear to teach.

The Unfulfilled

It was love only that we knew
At first. We did not dispossess
Each other of the total view
That is quite blurred when passions pass.
I felt myself, acknowledged you.

When did desire enter and
Confuse the sweetness, heat the blood?
On meeting we could understand,
Wordless, each other's every mood.
Where does love start and friendship end?

Impediments have set apart
The impulse from fruition. We,
Who have no compass but the heart,
Must learn an immaturity,
Though all the later passions hurt.

By acts of will we now must find
Each other as we were at first,
Unthwarted then and unconfined.
Yes, but I have an aching thirst
That can't be quenched by a cool mind.

We must stand side by side and live
As if the past were still to come.
It is our needs we need to give
And fashion from their anguish some
Love that has no wish to deceive
But rests contented, being dumb.

No Child

We touch and when our hands
Meet, a world rises up,
A hemisphere extends,
Rivers we cannot stop.
Yet something is withheld –
No marriage and no child.

Our fields that seem so thick
With corn, that make an edge
Of gold, play us a trick;
It is a barren hedge,
A stony, sterile field:
No marriage and no child.

Yet barrenness also
Is tender. Others give
To children what we show
Each other. We can live
Sufficiently fulfilled,
No marriage and no child.

And what a child might take
In flesh and blood and mind
To the edge of heartbreak,
We hand over and find
That each of us can build
Out of this love, a child.

The Instrument

Only in our imaginations
The act is done, for you have spoken
Vows that can never now be broken.
I keep them too – with reservations;
Yet acts not done can still be taken
Away, like all completed passions.

But what can not be taken is
Satiety. Cool space lies near
Our bodies – a parenthesis
Between a pleasure and a fear.
Our loving is composed of this
Touching of strings to make sounds clear.

A touching, then a glancing off.
It is your vows that stretch between
Us like an instrument of love
Where only echoes intervene.
Yet these exchanges are enough
Since strings touched only are most keen.

Remembering Fireworks

Always as if for the first time we watch
The fireworks as if no one had ever
Done this before, made shapes, signs,
Cut diamonds on air, sent up stars
Nameless, imperious. And in the falling
Of fire, the spent rocket, there is a kind
Of nostalgia as normally only attaches
To things long known and lost. Such an absence,
Such emptiness of sky the fireworks leave
After their festival. We, fumbling
For words of love, remember the rockets,
The spinning wheels, the sudden diamonds,
And say with delight 'Yes, like that, like that.'
Oh and the air is full of falling
Stars surrendered. We search for a sign.

THE SONNETS OF MICHELANGELO
(1961)

I   On Dante Alighieri

From heaven he came, in mortal clothing, when
All that was worst and best had been observed.
Living, he came to view the God he served
To give us the entire, true light again.

For that bright star which with its vivid rays
Picked out the humble place where I was born –
For this, the world would be a prize to scorn;
None but its Maker can return its praise.

I speak of Dante, he whose work was spurned
By the ungrateful crowd, those who can give
Praise only to the worthless. I would live

Happy were I but he, by such men scorned,
If, with his torments, I could also share
His greatness, both his joy and exile bear.

II   On Dante Alighieri

It is not possible to say how much
We owe to him, because his splendour blinds
Our eyes. Simpler it is to blame those minds
Too small to honour him, to sense his touch.

He did not fear to plumb to places where
Failure alone survives. But this was done
For our example. Always he was near
To God. Only his country dared to shun

His greatness. Her ingratitude at last
Turned on herself. As proof of this, observe
How always to the perfect sorrows fall

Most painfully. To those who are the best
Most ill occurs. Dante did not deserve
Exile; his equal never lived at all.

III   To Pope Julius II

My Lord, of all the ancient proverbs, this
Is surely true – 'Who *can* doth never will.'
You have believed in saws and promises
And blest those men whom falsehoods, not truths, fill.

Always I have been faithful and would give
Honour to you as rays do to the sun.
Yet all my pain has never made you grieve,
The less I please, the more work I have done.

Once I had hoped to climb by means of your
Great height, but now I find we rather need
Justice and power, not echoes faint indeed.

Heaven, it appears, itself is made impure
When worldliness has power. I live to take
Fruit from a tree too dry to bear or break.

IV   On Rome in the Pontificate of Julius II

Here they make helms and swords from chalices:
The blood of Christ is sold now by the quart.
Lances and shields are shaped from thorns and crosses,
Yet still Christ pours out pity from his heart.

But let him come no more into these streets
Since it would make his blood spurt to the stars:
In Rome they sell his flesh, and virtue waits
Helpless, while evil every entrance bars.

If ever I desired reward, oh now
All chance is gone. My work has come to naught.
Medusa hides beneath that mantle there.

Heaven rewards poverty, but here below
What chance have we to find the good we sought
When men are false to the great signs they bear?

V To Giovanni da Pistoja on the Painting of the Sistine Chapel

Like cats from Lombardy and other places
Stagnant and stale, I've grown a goitre here;
Under my chin my belly will appear,
Each the other's rightful stance displaces.

My beard turns heavenward, my mind seems shut
Into a casket. With my breast I make
A shield. My brush moves quickly, colours break
Everywhere, like a street mosaic-cut.

My loins are thrust into my belly and
I use my bottom now to bear the weight
Of back and side. My feet move dumb and blind.
In front my skin is loose and yet behind
It stretches taut and smooth, is tight and straight.

I am a Syrian bow strained for the pull –
A hard position whence my art may grow.
Little, it seems, that's strong and beautiful
Can come from all the pains I undergo.
Giovanni, let my dying art defend
Your honour, in this place where I am left
Helpless, unhappy, even of art bereft.

VI Invective against the People of Pistoja

I have received your word now twenty times,
Read it as many. May it do you good.
As little, I hope, as teeth can do for food
When stomach aches and indigestion climbs.

Now I know certainly that evil Cain
Was your own ancestor. You do again
What he and all his followers did. What good
They had has gone with your ingratitude.

Proud you are, envious, enemies of heaven,
Friends to your own harm and, to your own neighbour,
The simplest charity you find a labour.

See, to Pistoja Dante's curse was given.
Remember that and if good words you say
Of Florence, you but wish to wheedle me.

A jewel far beyond all price is she.
This is a thing you cannot comprehend:
It takes real virtue thus to understand.

VII To Luigi del Riccio

It happens sometimes even in the great
Sweetness of courtesy, of life and honour,
That an offence can hide. Thus, in this manner
Some good is spoilt and mars my healthy state.

He who can give to others wings of hope
Yet stretch a hidden net along their way,
Is false to the great fire of charity
And brings true friendship to a sudden stop.

Therefore, keep clear, Luigi, that first grace
To which I owe my life, let no storm mar
Its calm, let no wind stir its steady peace.

Contempt can make all gratitude obscure,
But, with true friendship, nothing can displace
Its strength. For this, pain is a way to please.

VIII To Liugi del Riccio After the Death of Cecchino Bracci

I scarcely knew him when his eyes were shut
For ever, he who was your life and light.
His eyes closed fast at death's last parting, but
Opened on God and found a love more bright.

I know and weep; yet it was not my fault
That I should meet him too late to admire
His grace. Your memory becomes his vault,
Lost not to you, only to my desire.

Then if, Luigi, I must carve the form
Of him, Cecchino, whom I speak about,
And change him from this dust to living stone,

You, his friend, must keep his image warm,
And if you fail, my art is called in doubt.
I'll find his likeness now in you alone.

IX

Your gifts – the sugar, candles and the mule,
Also the cask of Malmsey wine – so far
Exceed necessity, I must defer
Thanks to St Michael, let him tip the scale.

Like weather in a calm, prosperity
Can make sails drop. Thus my frail barque seems lost
Amid a raging, wild and cruel sea;
Like a soft feather, it is tempest-tossed.

As for your kindness and your gifts, for all
The food and drink, the journeys to and fro,
Which for my need and pleasure have been set –

Dear Lord, I cannot pay you what I owe;
To give you all I have would be to fail
Because it is no gift to pay a debt.

X   *To Gandolfo Porrino on his Mistress Faustina Mancina*

Unique in heaven as on this wicked earth
(Though cheaply by the vulgar crowd is she
Named – that crowd, too blind to see her worth),
This new high beauty was designed to be

For you alone. Neither with tools nor pen
Would I know how to fashion her or trace
The radiant beauty of her living face.
For that, you must return to life again.

And if she overwhelms imagination
As the great sun outshines the other stars,
Still you may rate her at her real price.

To calm your pining and your desolation
God moulds her beauty which can far surpass
All I can make. My art will not suffice.

XI To Giorgio Vasari on The Lives of the Painters

With pen and colours you have shown how art
Can equal nature. Also in a sense
You have from nature snatched her eminence,
Making the painted beauty touch the heart.

Now a more worthy work your skilful hand,
Writing on paper, labours and contrives –
To give to those who're dead new worth, new lives;
Where nature simply made, you understand.

When men have tried in other centuries
To vie with nature in the power to make,
Always they had to yield to her at last.

But you, illuminating memories,
Bring back to life these lives for their own sake,
And conquer nature with the vivid past.

XII To Vittoria Colonna

Oh happy spirit, who with so much zeal
Remembers me though I am soon to die.
Among so many other joys you feel
The wish to greet me. What great loyalty!

You, who delighted me when I could see
Your face, now comfort me within my mind.
You bring new hope to all my misery
That old desires will always leave behind.

Finding in you a willingness to plead
My cause, although you have so many cares,
He who now writes returns you thanks for this.

It would be shame and usury to press
These ugly pictures on you when I need
To bring to life again your loveliness.

XIII *To the Same*

To be more worthy of you, Lady, is
My sole desire. For all your kindnesses
I try to show, with all I have of art
And courtesy, the gladness of my heart.

But well I know that simply by my own
Efforts I cannot match your goodness. Then
I ask your pardon for what's left undone,
And failing thus, I grow more wise again.

Indeed, I know it would be wrong to hope
That favours, raining from you as from heaven,
Could be repaid by human work so frail.

Art, talent, memory, with all their scope
Can never pay you back what you have given.
At this, a thousand tries would always fail.

XIV (i) *To the Same*

Whenever perfect works of art are planned,
The craftsman always makes a model to
Be the first simple part from which shall grow
The finished object underneath his hand.

Later, in living stone, more perfect still,
A lovelier thing is shaped; beneath the blows
Of the fierce hammer, he can feel the thrill
Of art emerging from its own birth throes.

So was I born as my own model first,
The model of myself; later would I
Be made more perfect, born of one so high.

If all my roughness, then, should be so blest
By your comparison, then what penance ought
My feverish ardour by your rules be taught?

XIV (ii)

If noble concepts have a birth divine
In human looks and acts, the value is
Doubled – that from such petty images
A face, not art's, should in the dull stone shine.

Likewise on roughest paper, artists will
Make sketches, long before they use the brush.
Among a hundred efforts, crude and rash,
The right one springs at last from so much skill.

And so with me, among all models least:
For I was born to a great destiny –
To find new birth in you, Lady most high.

If all my roughness, then, should be so blest
By your compassion, then what penance ought
My feverish ardour by your rules taught?

XV

The marble not yet carved can hold the form
Of every thought the greatest artist has,
And no conception ever comes to pass
Unless the hand obeys the intellect.

The evil that I fly from, all the harm,
The good as well, are buried and intact
In you, proud Lady. To my life's sad loss
My art's opposed to the desired effect.

Thus love, and your own beauty and the weight
Of things, are not to blame for my own plight.
Fate, scorn or chance can never be accused

Because both death and pity are enclosed
Within your heart, and I have only breath
And power to draw from you not life but death.

XVI

Just as in pen and ink, the high and low
And mediocre styles can find expression,
And as in marble, the imagination,
Noble or base, will its own worth bestow;

So, my dear Lord, whatever finds its place
Within your heart – pride or humility –
I draw from it only what moves in me,
As you can tell from what shows on my face.

For he who sows both sighs and tears will find
(Since heaven, whose dew is always pure and clear,
To different seeds will variously appear),

That what he reaps is sorrow. Heart and mind,
When grievously afflicted, still will see
In greatest beauty only misery.

XVII

Lady, how can it be that what is shown
Through long experience and imagination
Endures so long in hard and mountain stone,
While years enact the maker's consummation?

The cause to the effect yields and gives place,
Nature by art is overcome at last.
I know too well who work with sculptor's grace
That time and death resign me to the past.

Thus, in one way, I give to you and me
Long life, either in stone or else in paint
Which seems to show each other's faces true.

Thus, in a thousand years all men shall see
How beautiful you were, how I was faint
And yet how wise I was in loving you.

XVIII

With heart of sulphur and with flesh of tow,
With bone designed of dry and rotting wood,
With spirit lacking any guide to show
Which impulses are evil and which good,

With reason which displays itself so weak
Confronted with a world so full of snares,
It is no wonder that my flesh should break
When it first stumbles on such furious fires.

With glorious art – that gift received from heaven –
That conquers nature and in every way
Clings to all human longing and desire;

If such a gift I truly have been given
And yet, divided, torn, still burn and stray,
He is to blame who fashioned me for fire.

XIX

More precious am I to myself than ever
I used to be, since you possessed my heart,
Just as the stone that's chiselled by the carver
Has far more value than in its rough state.

Or as a card or paper is more scanned
When sketched upon than when left blank and plain.
Such is my state since I became the end
Of your attention, nor do I complain.

Always I am secure with such a seal,
Like one who carries arms or charms with him
And finds that every peril has grown less.

Against both fire and water I prevail,
And with your sign light everything that's dim.
My spit makes pure all that's most poisonous.

XX

How much a garland pleases when it lies,
Woven with flowers, upon some golden hair;
It seems as if each blossom thrusts and tries
To be the first to kiss that forehead fair.

Contented all day long that garment is
Which spreads itself but first clings to her breast.
The golden thread asks nothing but to rest,
Touching her cheeks and throat with tenderness.

More honoured still that ribbon which can lie,
Gilded and shaped in the most cunning fashion,
Touching the breast which it so carefully laces.

And that small belt that knots so easily
Seems to declare, 'Unceasing my caresses.'
Would that my arms might join in such a passion!

XXI

To others merciful and only to
Itself unkind, this lowly creature who
Sloughs off its skin in pain that it may give
Pleasure to others, dies that they may live.

So do I long for such a destiny –
That from my death, my Lord, you might alone
Take life; then by my death I too might be
Changed like the worm which casts its skin on stone.

For if that skin were mine I could at least
Be woven in a gown to clasp that breast,
And so embrace the beauty which I crave.

Then would I gladly die. Or could I save
My Lord's feet from the rain by being shoes
Upon his feet – this also would I choose.

XXII

If in the face, if in the gazing eyes,
The human heart indeed can be observed –
I have no other sign, this must suffice
To show, Lord, what my deep faith has deserved.

Your strength will give me more fidelity,
I trust, for you can see the honest fire
Which does consume me now and begs your pity.
Abundant grace will answer my desire.

Happy the day if this indeed is true!
May time and hours a moment then stand still,
May day and sun pause in their ancient track:

That, not through anything that I may do,
My dear, desired Lord my arms may fill –
His greatness making up for all I lack.

XXIII

Both near and far my eyes can see your face
Wherever it appears. When you are near,
Let your demeanour shy and quiet appear,
And walk with hands held both together close.

The intellect, being untrammelled, pure,
Can through the eyes attain true liberty;
All your great beauty it can clearly see;
Not so the flesh, so vulnerable and poor.

So hard it is to trace an angel's flight
Since we are wingless. We can only praise
And glory in the momentary sight.

If you are both in heaven and with us here,
Make of my flesh a single eye to gaze,
And let no part of me uncouth appear.

XXIV

Well-born spirit, in whom we see reflected
All that is noble in man's character.
How much by heaven and nature is effected
When nothing mars what they have both made clear.

Spirit of grace, in which we put our trust
With inward faith, since on your face appear
Love, pity, kindness, qualities so rare
That seldom with such beauty are they blest.

Love casts a spell and beauty has a hold
Unbreakable upon my eager heart.
Pity and kindness rule me with their glances.

What government or custom in the world,
What cruelty in time or random chances,
Would not from death set such a face apart?

XXV

'Tell me, I beg, Love, if my eyes indeed
See all the truth of beauty which I claim,
Or if I have within me now the same
Power to see all the beauty that I need?

You ought to know the answer since you came
With her to break my peace, disturb my rest.
I would not let the smallest sigh be lost
For such a love, nor ask a lesser flame.'

'The beauty that you see is truly hers,
But as it grows it rises higher still
If through the eyes it reaches to the soul.

Here it becomes divine and beautiful,
And on a mortal thing it now confers
An immortality your eyes to fill.'

XXVI

Grace, Lady, equally with sorrow may
Cause death. A man condemned to mortal pain
May find a sudden pardon sets him free
When long past hope and cold in every vein.

Likewise, your kindness which so far exceeds
My worth, so far surpasses all my needs,
Can cheer my misery with such compassion
That life itself reaches its consummation.

Death can be found in news bitter and sweet,
For joy and sorrow both possess the power
To fill the heart or tighten it too much.

Your beauty has a power just as great;
Then curb it lest my life should fail before
A gift that overwhelms my feeble clutch.

XXVII

I cannot shape an image or acquire,
Either from shadow or from earthly skin,
A counterpart to lessen my desire:
Such armour is your beauty shut within.

Obsessed and moved by you, I seem to get
Weaker. My passion takes my strength away.
By trying to diminish grief I but
Double it. Like death, it comes to stay.

And it is useless now for me to try
To win the race against such loveliness,
Which far outstrips the fastest runner here.

Love with its hands so tenderly will dry
My tears and make all labour seem most dear.
He is no coward who discovers this!

XXVIII

The living portion of my love is not
My heart; the love with which I love has no
Heart, for in human hearts things mean and low
Always exist, in impulse or in thought.

Love which came, like the soul, from God's own hands
Made me without eyes, made you full of light;
That light cannot be seen in what death ends –
The mortal part which hurts me with delight.

Just as from fire the heat cannot be parted,
Neither can I be separated from
That Beauty in whose likeness she is made.

Ardent, I run to joys which cannot fade,
That paradise where your own beauty started,
Eternal loveliness from which you come.

XXIX

The first day I beheld so much unique
Beauty, I trusted that I might be one
Who, like the eagle soaring to the sun,
Finds such a radiance makes its own eyes weak.

The fault was mine; I knew that I had failed,
Since he who follows angels and lacks wings
Is sowing seed on stone, his words are whirled
Away by wind; God takes his questionings.

My heart will not support me when I know
So great a beauty's near; my eyes grow blind
Though, from a distance, it persuades me still.

What will become of me? What guide will show
Some value in myself I still may find?
When near, you burn me, when far off, you kill.

XXX   To Tommaso de' Cavalieri

This glorious light I see with your own eyes
Since mine are blind and will not let me see.
Your feet lend me their own security
To carry burdens far beyond my size.

Supported by your wings I now am sped,
And by your spirit to heaven I am borne.
According to your will, I'm pale or red –
Hot in the harshest Winter, cold in sun.

All my own longings wait upon your will,
Within your heart my thoughts find formulation,
Upon your breath alone my words find speech.

Just as the moon owes its illumination
To the sun's light, so I am blind until
To every part of heaven your rays will reach.

XXXI   To Tommaso de' Cavalieri

Why, more than ever, do I give such vent
To my desire, when neither tears nor words
Can change the destiny I move towards?
Nothing I do can my own fate prevent.

Why does the weary heart make death appear
Desirable, since every man must die?
There is no consolation for me here
Where joy is far outweighed by misery.

Yet if the blows must come decreed by fate
And I am powerless, there's comfort in
The thought that nothing now can intervene.

If to be blest I must accept defeat
It is no wonder if, alone and nude,
I am by one in arms chained and subdued.

XXXII

If love is chaste, if pity comes from heaven,
If fortune, good or ill, is shared between
Two equal loves, and if one wish can govern
Two hearts, and nothing evil intervene:

If one soul joins two bodies fast for ever,
And if, on the same wings, these two can fly,
And if one dart of love can pierce and sever
The vital organs of both equally:

If both love one another with the same
Passion, and if each other's good is sought
By both, if taste and pleasure and desire

Bind such a faithful love-knot, who can claim,
Either with envy, scorn, contempt or ire,
The power to untie so fast a knot?

XXXIII (i)

So that your beauty may not lose its power,
I pray that nature now herself may gather
All that she gave you once, and bring together
Those lovely things that leave you hour by hour.

May nature then restore to you the grace
That you owned formerly, but may it be
Celestial beauty now which lights your face
And shows your tenderness and charity.

May nature also treasure all my sighs
And hoard my scattered tears, that she may give
Such things to those who love the one I loved.

Thus in another age the man who tries
To win her, may by my own tears be moved
And find in all I lost the power to live.

XXXIII (ii)

In order that your beauties may endure
And triumph over time which takes away,
I hope that nature may again restore
All that slips slowly from you day by day.

And may these things be handed over to
A happier life and fate. Thus in the place
Of attributes that brought such pain to you,
May there shine forth a peaceful, heavenly grace.

Willing I am that heaven should keep my sighs
And hoard my scattered tears to hand them over
To him who loves the one that I have loved.

Thus in another age the man who tries
To win her may by my sharp grief be moved
And in my loss a greater strength discover.

XXXIV

Eternal fire is kindly to cold stone
And draws strength from it. And though stone may fall
To ashes, it has never really gone
But lives in fire and is not lost at all.

And if, in furnaces, through every season
It lasts, it has achieved a higher place,
Just as a purged soul moves from its own prison
And flies to heaven adorned with every grace.

It is the same with me when fierce desires
Reduce me to pale ashes, dry and cold:
I am not lost but find new life indeed.

If I can rise from ashes which seem dead
And come unscathed from these consuming fires,
I am not forged from iron but from gold.

XXXV

This fire, which burns me fiercely and consumes,
Illuminates her face with lights that freeze;
I find a strength in two frail, graceful arms
Which move great weights though they stay motionless.

Matchless spirit! I only understand
That you, so full of life, can yet cause death,
That you, unfettered, yet can bind me with
Chains; you, my only hope, can still offend.

How can it be, my Lord, that beauty has
Such opposite effects, that harm can spring
From one who has no wish to wound or hurt?

Where is my happy life and everything
That had the power to satisfy? She is
Like sun which heats though it is cold at heart.

XXXVI

If the immortal longing which inspires
The thoughts of others can coax my desires,
Perhaps this longing may, in the same fashion,
Give to the tyrant lord of love compassion.

But since the heavenly ordinance disposes
A short life for the flesh, long for the soul,
Sense in itself never quite discloses
Those qualities which are invisible.

Oh then, alas, how can a love that's chaste
(Such as burns now so strongly within me),
Be seen by him whose love is otherwise?

My happy days are ruined and disgraced
Because my lord pays heed to falsity;
If he believes this, then he also lies.

XXXVII

If someone has been favoured with a great
Kindness – they have, perhaps, been saved from death –
What quality can honour such a debt
Which he who owes may find his freedom with?

Yet if such payment could indeed be made,
He who accomplished it would feel some lack,
For when a debt we owe is fully paid
It seems as if we give the favours back.

Therefore, in order to maintain your grace,
Lady, I will myself deliberately
Covet not kindness but ingratitude.

And for this reason I have chosen thus:
Between two equal loves no rule can be.
I want not partnership but servitude.

XXXVIII

Give to my eyes a natural stream or spring,
Not that great wave which raises you so high
Above a level that is customary.
Such weary labour's an unnatural thing.

And you, thick air, that temper to my sight
Celestial radiance, give back to me
My sighs and tears and all my misery;
Strangely your dark face makes my vision bright.

May earth yield up my footsteps that once more
The grass may sprout where it was torn away;
Let echoes which were deaf return my cries.

Beloved, may your glances now restore –
That I may love elsewhere – light to my eyes,
For I know well you are displeased with me.

XXXIX

Reason is sympathetic when I claim
To find in love a lasting happiness.
With strong examples and true words, my shame
Reminds me of the weakness I possess.

She says, 'The living sun can only give
Death, not a phoenix, now to one like you.'
He who himself has no desire to live,
No hands can save, however willing to.

I understand the truth and know my fate:
I have another heart which cruelly
Kills me the more I yield to its demands.

It is between two deaths that my lord stands.
One baffles me, the other one I hate.
In such suspense body and soul will die.

XL (i)

I know not if it is the longed-for night
Of its first maker that the spirit feels,
Or if some old and honoured memory steals
The heart and makes its beauty shine so bright;

Or maybe fame or dreams themselves can bring
A lovely object to the eyes and heart.
From such a vision many tears can spring
And many memories remain to hurt.

I know not what I feel or seek, or who
Guides me, or where I should true guidance seek,
And yet I feel that someone points the way.

This is my state, my Lord, since I saw you;
Both bitterness and sweetness now can sway
My heart. You are the reason I am weak.

XL (ii)

I know not if it is imagination
Which makes the light that every man can feel,
Or if from mind or memory will steal
Some other glorious illumination.

Or maybe in the soul the scorching fire
Of heaven still burns, and has the power to draw
Our thoughts into an ardent, fierce desire
For truth itself, the one compelling law.

Oh may I always search for what is true,
Although, without a guide, this fire I seek.
Yet still I feel that someone points the way.

Lady, this is my state since I saw you;
Both bitterness and sweetness now can sway
My heart. You are the reason I am weak.

XLI

He who from nothing made all things ordained
That time in two parts should be severed; one
He handed over to the mighty sun,
The other with the nearer moon remained.

From this event, fortune and fate sprang forth,
Mischance or happiness to each man fell.
To me was sent the dark time, I know well,
For it has always been with me since birth.

And like all things which make a counterfeit
Of their own nature, so I make my fate
More black by feeling full of pain and grief.

Oh then it is a comfort to find one,
Like you, whose fate is always in the sun,
And shares some part of what is your whole life.

XLII

Each shuttered room and every covered place,
Whatever they are made of, hold the night.
The day exists where the sun leaps and plays,
Distributing its full and generous light.

But if night can indeed be overcome
By fire or flame, even a glow-worm may
Conquer her as effectively as day;
One little light can break her powerful gloom.

The open land, where seeds and plants allow
The sun to give them light and life, can be
Broken and hurt by the encroaching plough.

Only in darkness can men fully be
Themselves, and therefore night is holier than
Day; no plant has half the worth of man.

XLIII

Since Phoebus does not stretch his shining hands
Around this cold, soft globe, men tend to say
That night holds all that no one understands,
The great enigma following the day.

She is so weak that one small, simple glare
Cast by a torch can take her life away;
She is so foolish that a musket may
Smash her whole being with its shot and flare.

If one must find a name for such as she,
Then call her daughter of the sun and earth –
The one holds shade, the other fashions it.

The truth remains – for no praise is she fit
Who is so dull and lacking in all mirth,
And, for the firefly, can feel jealousy.

XLIV

Oh night, oh sweetest time although obscure,
All things you consummate with your own peace.
He who understands and has a clear
Vision of you, honours you, knowing this.

You carry every weary thought away,
You make it possible for peace to grow;
From lowest things to highest, you convey
Me in my dreams to where I want to go.

Shadow of death, for whom all sufferings pause,
At whose arrival every sorrow goes,
Comfort of the afflicted at the last:

You strengthen our weak flesh and make it whole,
You dry our tears and rest the weary soul,
And from the just man snatch the painful past.

XLV

When a lord thrusts his servant into prison
And binds him in cruel chains, that man will be,
After some time, reluctant to be free,
So used will he become to the oppression.

Custom still keeps the tiger, lion and snake
Under restraint; some limits must be set.
The inexperienced artist too must make
Redoubled efforts with much toil and sweat.

But fire does not behave in such a way,
Since if it is extinguished by green wood
It still can warm and nourish an old man.

Then love, like youth's green sap, urges him on,
And all the world seems glorious and good
And he is full of boyish energy.

That man who scoffs and says there should be shame
When old men love – that man profanes and lies.
It is no sin when human creatures dream
Of natural loveliness; no sins arise
As long as prudence keeps its sovereign claim.

XLVI

If a small, steady flame can quickly dry
The sap within a young green heart, what power
Will raging bonfires have when they but try
An old man's heart which moves to its last hour?

If time in general gives a meagre span
To life with all its values and its claims,
How much less will it grant a dying man
Who, in old age, still plays at lovers' games?

The answer lies in my experience:
The wind which blows my ashes far away
Deprives the worms of their own rightful prey.

If in green youth I wept at milder pains,
In flames more fierce I've little hope that I
May overwhelm them now my wood is dry.

XLVII

If any fire could equal that great light
Of your own eyes from which I part with sorrow,
The world itself contains no part that might
Not be consumed as by a flaming arrow.

But heaven, tender to our weakness, takes
The power of sight from us and with it all
The beauty which you share; and thus she makes
This bitter, mortal life more bearable.

Beauty and passion are not equal then,
For only that deep centre of the heart
That falls in love, with heaven has any part.

So in my age, this happens, Lord, again:
Because for you I do not burn or die,
Blame not my love but human frailty.

XLVIII

Though long delay breeds greater tenderness
Than our desires in youth can ever know,
Still I regret my love's belatedness –
That passion has so short a time to go.

Heaven is perverse indeed if in its care
For us it still can set old hearts on fire.
This is the fate I must accept and bear –
To love a woman with a sad desire.

Yet maybe when the sun sinks in the west
And end of day is reached, I can at least
Be in the greater dark a single shade.

If love has come to me when life must fade,
If I desire, though death must touch me soon,
Oh, of my sunset, Lady, make my noon!

XLIX

From gloomy laughter and delicious tears,
From everlasting to a short-lived peace,
I've lapsed indeed. When truth breeds silences
Then sense is sovereign over truth's affairs.

I cannot say whence these misfortunes come,
Whether from me or from your face. I know
The pains are easier the more they grow.
What heaven are your piercing eyes snatched from?

Your loveliness was never meant to die,
But wrought in heaven to be released among
Men on the earth. Thus I exhausted lie,

Yet find more comfort than when close to you.
If God indeed has planned my death, then who,
When I must die, dare say that you were wrong?

L

Too late I realised that from your soul
I might, much like the phoenix in the sun,
Have warmed myself and been made strong and whole;
So often, in old age, this can be done.

What's swifter than the leopard, lynx or stag
After their prey or flying from a snare?
I could have run once, now I only lag
After the good things I've discovered here.

And yet there is no reason now to grieve
Since in this matchless angel I perceive
My health, my rest and true serenity.

When I was young I should less easily
Have found this joy. Now, when it flies away,
I follow after with much less delay.

LI (i)

Now give me back that time when love was held
On a loose rein, making my passion free.
Return that calm, angelic face to me,
That countenance which every virtue filled.

Bring back those frequent journeys, swift before,
But now so slow to one who's full of years.
Give to my breast the waters and the fires
If you require my service any more.

If you can only live upon the tide
Of bitter-sweet and mortal tears, dear heart,
What pleasure can an old man's tears return?

My soul has almost reached the other side
And makes a shield against your kindly dart.
Charred wood will never make a new fire burn.

LI (ii)

Now give me back that time which held my passion,
Fervent and sweet, upon a gentle rein.
Give back the water and the fire again
If you desire my tears, my consummation.

Return those easy journeys which are now
So difficult to one of many years;
Give back that peaceful and angelic brow
Which snatched from nature all her secret powers.

Love, I am slow now to pursue your wings.
The nest is changed; it is, if I am right,
A blessed place where good intentions live.

Bring to the bow your arrows strong and bright,
And if death is no longer deaf to grief,
I'll find my peace among more blessed things.

LII

I do not need to look on outward forms
Of beauty which must die. I gaze within
Using your sight, finding a peace which calms.
Bringing such love, you banish every sin.

Even if she whom God created is
Not perfect outwardly, I ask no more,
For even if her loveliness has flaws,
She far transcends what I have seen before.

That man who is consumed by what must die
Can never quench his passion. Though it seems
To last for ever, it is transitory.

From sense not love, unruly passions come
And kill the soul. Our feelings sanctified
Even on earth, but more when we have died.

LIII

An ardent love of a great beauty is
Not always wrong, for such a love can melt
The heart and let divine desire be felt;
The heavenly dart may penetrate with ease.

Love wakes prepared and soon adjusts its wings;
Such flight as it will make cannot compare
With those first stumbling steps, but these will bear
The soul up to the maker of all things.

To this, the love of which I speak aspires.
Woman is different and seldom worth
The fiery love which only strong hearts know.

One pulls me to the heavens, the other to earth.
One in the soul dwells, one in sensual fires
And to attain base things will draw the bow.

LIV

I see in your fair face, my dearest Lord,
That which in life I cannot fitly tell.
Your soul already, though flesh holds it still,
Has many times ascended to its God.

And if the vulgar and malignant crowd
Misunderstand the love with which we're blest,
Its worth is not affected in the least:
Our faith and honest love can still feel proud.

Earth is the meagre source of all that we
Can know while still fleshbound. To those who see
In the right way, it gives most copiously.

All that we have of wisdom and of faith
Derives from earth, and if I love you with
Fervour, I shall reach God and find sweet death.

LV

My Lord, you know that I know that you know
That I have come to be more close, more near.
You know that I know what is known to you,
Why then do we delay in greeting here?

If all that you have said is really true,
And if, which you admit, my trust is real,
Then break the wall dividing us, and know
A double strength can greater woes conceal.

If in you, I love only, my dear Lord,
What you love more yourself, do not be hurt
That with one soul another should accord.

That in your noble face which I love most
Is scarcely known by human mind and heart.
He who would see it must become a ghost.

LVI (i)

When you came back into this earthly prison,
It was as if an angel had sprung forth;
You were so full of that divine compassion
Which heals the mind and dignifies the earth.

This only draws me and with this alone
I fall in love, not with the outward grace
Of gentle features. Love will not grow less
When such a lasting good it fixes on.

In this way value always is detected
In proud and natural things. Heaven will not fail
To give what's needful when their birth takes place.

God in no other way has shown His grace
Than in a lovely and a mortal veil
In which I find He is Himself reflected.

LVI (ii)

I know not whence it came and yet it surely
Sprang from that deathless soul which in your breast
Remains, yet seeks the universe entirely,
Healing the mind, making the whole earth blest.

This alone draws me, and with this alone
I fall in love, not with the outward grace
Of gentle features. Love will not grow less
When such a lasting good it fixes on.

If such a form should find new beauties growing
Upon itself as part of its own life,
Then from the sheath I can detect the knife.

Only in this way is God truly showing
His love, for heaven indeed can rival nature,
Letting a chaste love frame a lovelier creature.

LVII (i)

It passes from the eyes into the heart
In a split second. Thus all beauties may
Find by this means an open and broad way,
And thus, for thousands, their desires start.

I am afraid of love like this, being so
Burdened with sin, committing so much wrong.
Nor, though I seek a thousand souls among,
Can I find one whose loving is not low.

Yet love still lives however much it errs;
The world is full of it and man still flies
To things which often are a trap and curse.

If graces do not climb to heaven, then
Noble desires may, for otherwise,
What grief and torment to be born a man!

LVII (ii)

It passes from the eyes into the heart
In a split second. Thus all beauties may
Find by this means a wide and generous way;
And so, for countless men, desires start.

Burdened by grief and gripped by jealousy,
I am afraid of such a powerful passion.
Nor, among countless faces, can I see
One which in life can give me more consolation.

If mortal beauty satisfies desire
Completely, then it did not come from heaven;
Such strong emotion comes from human fire.

But if I pass beyond this and have striven
For heavenly things, I need not be afraid
That I by base desires shall be waylaid.

LVIII

When to my inward eyes, both weak and strong,
The idol of my heart appears, I know
That always in between us death will go;
It frightens me while driving me along.

Yet, strangely, such an outrage gives me hope
And I take courage from so rare a fate.
Indomitable love moves in great state
And thus he puts his strong defences up:

Dying, he says, can never happen twice,
Nor is one born again. If a man dies
By fire when he already is aflame

With burning love, then death can do no harm.
Such love's the magnet of all burning hearts
Which, purged, returns to God from whom it starts.

LIX

Only through fire can the smith pull and stretch
Metal into the shape of his design.
Only through fire can the artist reach
Pure gold which only furnaces refine.

Nor can the phoenix rare itself remake
Unless it first be burnt. For my part, I
Hope to ascend triumphantly on high
Where death fulfils, where time itself must break.

The fire of which I speak has brought salvation,
I find in it new powers and restoration
Although I seemed already with the dead.

Since fire by nature reaches up to heaven
I may, through it, be reconciled, forgiven,
For it must surely bear me overhead.

LX (i)

Sometimes hope rises strongly with desire,
And surely such a hope may not be held
As false; if heaven is angry with such fire,
Then to what end did God create the world?

What better reason can there be to love,
Than to give glory to the God on high?
He who is pleased with you dwells up above,
And every good heart he will purify.

Only false hopes can claim a love that dies.
Such love depends on beauty which grows less,
And the swift change of mortal loveliness.

Sweet is that hope which in the modest heart
Is steadfast though all surface things depart!
Such faithful love's a pledge of paradise.

LX (ii)

At times, pure love may justly be equated
With fervent hope; nor need it be deceived.
If by all human loves the heavens are grieved,
Then to what end was the whole world created?

If I indeed honour and love you, Lord,
And if I burn, it is a heavenly calm
That emanates from you and makes me warm;
Such peace is far removed from all discord.

True love is not a passion which can die,
Or which depends on beauty that must fade;
Nor is it subject to a changing face.

That love is true and holy which finds place
Within a modest heart, and which is made,
Far above earth, a pledge of love on high.

LXI   On the Death of Vittoria Colonna

If my rough hammer makes a human form
And carves it in the hard, unyielding stone,
My hand is guided, does not move alone,
But follows where that other worker came.

Yet the first worker, God, remains above,
Whose very motion makes all loveliness.
To make a tool I need a tool, but his
Power is the first cause and makes all things move.

That stroke which in the forge is raised most high
Has the most strength. Now she who lifted me,
Has, by her death, been raised much higher still.

So I am left unfinished now until
She gives her help to God himself that I
May be completed, not abandoned lie.

LXII   On the Death of the Same

When she who was the cause of all my sighs
Withdrew both from the world and from my eyes,
Nature itself was full of shame to see
Men weeping at the loss of such as she.

But nature may not boast as once it did.
Not it but death has quenched this sun of suns.
But death by love is conquered; love has laid
This glorious creature with the blessed ones.

Thus death, so pitiless, is now deceived;
It has no power to harm such pure perfection,
Or dim her triumph, as it once believed.

History is shining with her soul's reflection
Since she, though dead, lives more abundantly,
She, who would never leave us willingly.

LXIII   On the Death of the Same

Ah yes, when I was fortunate and when
Phoebus blazed down on every hill for me,
I should have risen from the crude earth then,
Using his wings to seek death willingly.

Those promises were in vain; it is too late,
For now my soul, ungrateful, full of guilt,
Lacking both wisdom and what once it felt,
Is now exiled, for Heaven has shut the gate.

I climbed the hills; feathers were wings to me,
Phoebus himself lifted my feet, and I
Thought death itself was wonderful indeed.

I die now without wings and cannot be
Borne up to Heaven. Even my memories die.
Afflicted thus, what comfort can I plead?

LXIV   On the Death of the Same

What wonder is it if, when near the fire,
I burned and melted, now that it is cold
I still am eaten with a fierce desire
And turn to ashes, sad and unfulfilled.

I saw the place, so burning and so bright,
Where my great torment hung. It only could
Turn death into a gay fiesta mood,
And make me happy at the simple sight.

But since the splendour of that fire, which would
So nourish me, is snatched into the dark
By Heaven, I am a lighted coal concealed:

And if by words of love I can't be healed,
Then I am nothing now, not even a spark,
But turn to ashes what the fire once held.

LXV   To Giorgio Vasari

Already now my life has run its course,
And, like a fragile boat on a rough sea,
I reach the place where everyone must cross
And give account of life's activity.

Now I know well it was a fantasy
That made me think art could be made into
An idol or a king. Though all men do
This, they do it half-unwillingly.

The loving thoughts, so happy and so vain,
Are finished now. A double death comes near –
The one is sure, the other is a threat.

Painting and sculpture cannot any more
Quieten the soul that turns to God again,
To God who, on the cross, for us was set.

LXVI

By the world's vanities I've been distracted,
And thus have squandered hours which should have been
Reserved for God. His mercy I've rejected,
And my misuse of it has made me sin.

The knowledge which makes others wise has made
Me blind. I recognise my faults too late.
Hope lessens, yet, before desires fade,
Oh friend, dissolve my self-love and self-hate.

And God, divide, I beg, the road that leads
To Heaven; I cannot climb its length alone,
I need your help through all the snares and strife.

Help me to loathe the world and all its deeds;
I'll cast its beauties out but to atone,
And find the promise of eternal life.

LXVII

There is no lower thing on earth than I
Conceive myself to be when I lack you.
My weak and tired spirit makes me sigh
For pardon for all things I've failed to do.

Stretch down to me, Oh God, that powerful chain
That knots all heavenly gifts. Such faith and trust
Are what I long forever to attain;
It is my fault I am not fully blest.

The more I think of faith, more rare and good
It seems, and even greater may it be
Since all the world depends on it for peace.

You never were a miser of your blood:
If Heaven is locked to every other key,
What kind of gifts of mercy, then, are these?

LXVIII *To Monsignor Lodovico Beccadelli*

By cross and grace and every kind of pain,
I am convinced, sir, we shall meet in Heaven.
Yet, long before such joys, we can attain,
It seems to me, the good things earth has given.

If sharp and bitter ways through hills and sea
Part me from you, my zeal has set at naught
Such icy obstacles. And, inwardly,
Nothing can slow or stop the wings of thought.

In my own thoughts I am with you for ever.
I weep and talk and nothing now can sever
Me from my dead Urbino who, were he

Alive, might now indeed converse with me.
But he is dead, so by another way
I hope to lodge with him without delay.

LXIX

My death is certain but the hour unsure,
Life is so brief and little now have I;
So sweet it is to sense, yet cannot lure
The soul. My spirit prays that I may die.

The world is bad, and evil customs still
Defeat good habits, cast good actions out.
The light's extinguished, pride and daring will
Make false things triumph, call the truth in doubt.

Oh God, when will that time arrive which he,
Who trusts in you, expects? Hope falls away,
And fatal to the soul is great delay.

What good is it that light and clarity
Should shine for others if, before it dies,
The soul is lost in such uncertainties?

LXX

Loaded with years and full of all my sins,
Rooted in habits evil and yet strong,
I feel two deaths approach me. Now begins
The heart's division, poisoned for so long.

Nor have I all the forces which I need
To change my life and love, custom and fate.
Only your grace and power can intercede
And guide our steps before it is too late.

It is not now enough, Oh Lord, that I
Wish to be made anew. I cannot be
The same as when, from nothing, you made me.

I beg you – halve that way so steep and high
Before you take my body from my soul:
And may I come back purified and whole.

LXXI

Now that I need men's pity and compassion,
And can no longer scoff and laugh at all
The faults of others, now my soul must fall
Unguided, lacking its own domination.

Only one flag can I now serve beneath,
And with it conquer life. I speak of faith.
Only with this can I face the attack
Of all my foes, when other help I lack.

Oh flesh, Oh blood, Oh wood, Oh pain extreme!
Let all my sins be purified through you
From whom I came, as did my father too.

So good you are, your pity is supreme;
Only your help can save my evil fate:
So close to death, so far from God my state.

LXXII

Then let me see you everywhere I go.
If merely mortal beauty makes me burn,
How much more strongly shall I shine and glow
When to your fiery love at last I turn.

Dear God, I call and plead with you alone,
For only you can help my blinding pain;
You only have the power to sustain
My courage. I am helpless on my own.

This everlasting spirit, which you gave
To me on earth, is locked within a frail
Body and doomed to an unhappy fate.

What can I do? Myself I cannot save;
Without your strength I certainly shall fail.
Only divine power can improve my state.

LXXIII

Unburdened by the body's fierce demands,
And now at last released from my frail boat,
Dear God, I put myself into your hands;
Smooth the rough waves on which my ship must float.

The thorns, the nails, the wounds in both your palms,
The gentleness, the pity on your face –
For great repentance, these have promised grace.
My soul will find salvation in your arms.

And let not justice only fill your eyes,
But mercy too. Oh temper your severe
Judgment with tenderness, relieve my burden.

Let your own blood remove my faults and clear
My guilt, and let your grace so strongly rise
That I am granted an entire pardon.

LXXIV (i)

Simply the longing for more years to live
Seems to hold out a promise. Yet I know
That death's approach is never made more slow,
That only sorrows have the power to give

A sense of halting. Yet how foolish is
A longing for more life and pleasure when
God is found best in human miseries.
The happier life, the more it hurts again.

And if, dear God, your grace assails my heart
And sets it burning with a fiery zeal,
Which deep within my spirit I can feel,

Then I from my own gifts would gladly part
And rise to Heaven at once, since I am sure
My good desires on earth will not endure.

LXXIV (ii)

Often, I think, a great desire may
Hold out the promise of more time to me.
Yet death has power to whittle me away
The more I live and breathe delightedly.

What better time for my sure transformation
Than when I pray, in grief, to God above?
Then lead me, Lord, to my true destination,
And all my earthly cares and joys remove.

For in this way your grace assails my heart
With faith and all its strong and fervent zeal.
From such a comfort I would never part.

Alone, I shall for certain always fail:
Then plant in me that faith such as you give
To angels who, without you, cannot live.

LXXV

I wish, God, for some end I do not will.
Between the fire and heart a veil of ice
Puts out the fire. My pen will not move well,
So that the sheet on which I'm working lies.

I pay you mere lip-service, then I grieve;
Love does not reach my heart, I do not know
How to admit that grace which would relieve
My state and crush the arrogance I show.

Oh tear away that veil, God, break that wall
Which with its strength refuses to let in
The sun whose light has vanished from the world.

Send down the promised light to bless and hold
Your lovely bride. So may I seek for all
I need in you, both end there and begin.

LXXVI

Those souls for whom you died were sad as well
As happy that you chose death for their sake.
The blood you shed had locked the doors of Hell,
And opened Heaven for all mankind to take.

Happy they were because you had redeemed
Man from his first mistake and final loss.
But they were sad such suffering had claimed
Your flesh which died for all men on the cross.

Heaven gave a sign that she had seen it all;
Her eyes grew dim, the earth beneath her showed
A gulf, the waters rushed, the mountains shook.

Christ snatched the Fathers from their dark abode
But sent the devils to a greater fall;
All baptised men for his own joy he took.

LXXVII

Although it saddens me and causes pain,
The past, which is not with me any more,
Brings me relief, since all that I abhor –
My sin and guilt – will not come back again.

Precious it is to me because I learn,
Before death comes, how brief is happiness:
But sad also, since when at last I turn
For pardon, grace may yet refuse to bless.

Although, Oh God, your promise I attend,
It is too much to ask you to forgive
Those who for pardon have so long delayed.

But in the blood you shed, I understand
What recompense and mercy you've displayed,
Showering your precious gifts that we may live.

LXXVIII

Dear to me is sleep: still more, being made of stone.
While pain and guilt still linger here below,
Blindness and numbness – these please me alone;
Then do not wake me, keep your voices low.

RECOVERIES
(1964)

Sequence in Hospital

I Pain

At my wits' end
And all resources gone, I lie here,
All of my body tense to the touch of fear,
And my mind,

Muffled now as if the nerves
Refused any longer to let thoughts form,
Is no longer a safe retreat, a tidy home,
No longer serves

My body's demands or shields
With fine words, as it once would daily,
My storehouse of dread. Now, slowly,
My heart, hand, whole body yield

To fear. Bed, ward, window begin
To lose their solidity. Faces no longer
Look kind or needed; yet I still fight the stronger
Terror – oblivion – the needle thrusts in.

II The Ward

One with the photographs of grandchildren,
Another with discussion of disease,

Another with the memory of her garden,
Another with her marriage – all of these

Keep death at bay by building round their illness
A past they never honoured at the time.

The sun streams through the window, the earth heaves
Gently for this new season. Blossoms climb

Out in the healthy world where no one thinks
Of pain. Nor would these patients wish them to;

The great preservers here are little things –
The dream last night, a photograph, a view.

III After an Operation

What to say first? I learnt I was afraid,
Not frightened in the way that I had been
When wide awake and well. I simply mean
Fear became absolute and I became
Subject to it; it beckoned, I obeyed.

Fear which before had been particular,
Attached to this or that scene, word, event,
Here became general. Past, future meant
Nothing. Only the present moment bore
This huge, vague fear, this wish for nothing more.

Yet life still stirred and nerves themselves became
Like shoots which hurt while growing, sensitive
To find not death but further ways to live.
And now I'm convalescent, fear can claim
No general power. Yet I am not the same.

IV Patients in a Public Ward

Like children now, bed close to bed,
With flowers set up where toys would be
In real childhoods, secretly
We cherish each our own disease,
And when we talk we talk to please
Ourselves that still we are not dead.

All is kept safe – the healthy world
Held at a distance, on a rope,
Where human things like hate and hope
Persist. The world we know is full
Of things we need, unbeautiful
And yet desired – a glass to hold

And sip, a cube of ice, a pill
To help us sleep. Yet in this warm
And sealed-off nest, the least alarm

Speaks clear of death. Our fears grow wide;
There are no places left to hide
And no more peace in lying still.

V The Visitors

They visit me and I attempt to keep
A social smile upon my face. Even here
Some ceremony is required, no deep
Relationship, simply a way to clear
    Emotion to one side; the fear
I felt last night is buried in drugged sleep.

They come and all their kindness makes me want
To cry (they say the sick weep easily).
When they have gone I shall be limp and faint,
My heart will thump and stumble crazily;
    Yet through my illness I can see
One wish stand clear no pain, no fear can taint.

Your absence has been stronger than all pain
And I am glad to find that when most weak
Always my mind returned to you again.
Through all the noisy nights when, harsh awake,
    I longed for day and light to break –
In that sick desert, you were life, were rain.

VI Hospital

Observe the hours which seem to stand
Between these beds and pause until
A shriek breaks through the time to show
That humankind is suffering still.

Observe the tall and shrivelled flowers,
So brave a moment to the glance.
The fevered eyes stare through the hours
And petals fall with soft foot-prints.

A world where silence has no hold
Except a tentative small grip.
Limp hands upon the blankets fold,
Minds from their bodies slowly slip.

Though death is never talked of here,
It is more palpable and felt –
Touching the cheek or in a tear –
By being present by default.

The muffled cries, the curtains drawn,
The flowers pale before they fall –
The world itself is here brought down
To what is suffering and small.

The huge philosophies depart,
Large words slink off, like faith, like love.
The thumping of the human heart
Is reassurance here enough.

Only one dreamer going back
To how he felt when he was well,
Weeps under pillows at his lack
But cannot tell, but cannot tell.

VII   For a Woman with a Fatal Illness

The verdict has been given and you lie quietly
Beyond hope, hate, revenge, even self-pity.

You accept gratefully the gifts – flowers, fruit –
Clumsily offered now that your visitors too

Know you must certainly die in a matter of months,
They are dumb now, reduced only to gestures,

Helpless before your news, perhaps hating
You because you are the cause of their unease.

I, too, watching from my temporary corner,
Feel impotent and wish for something violent –

Whether as sympathy only, I am not sure –
But something at least to break the terrible tension.

Death has no right to come so quietly.

VIII   Patients

Violence does not terrify.
Storms here would be a relief,
Lightning be a companion to grief.
It is the helplessness, the way they lie

Beyond hope, fear, love,
That makes me afraid. I would like to shout,
Crash my voice into the silence, flout
The passive suffering here. They move

Only in pain, their bodies no longer seem
Dependent on blood, muscle, bone.
It is as if air alone
Kept them alive, or else a mere whim

On the part of instrument, surgeon, nurse
I too am one of them, but well enough
To long for some simple sign of life,
Or to imagine myself getting worse.

Nerves

The wind is playing round the curtains,
The bowl of flowers throws shadows on the sill.
There is nothing to do now, nothing at all
But to lie still.

The mind has never been like this room, clear,
Containing only what I really need.
It has been full of antique objects, rubbish,
And dust indeed.

The objects seemed to swell, their shadows spread
More darkness than I knew how I could handle.
There was no sudden shock, simply a slow
Feeling that strength would dwindle,

That I would one day find myself like this –
Lying in bed, watching the curtains blow,
Seeing the flowers fall, petal by petal,
Longing for something to grow.

Old Man Asleep

He takes the snuff-box from his pocket and,
As many times before, taps on the lid.
The day's newspaper slips on to the floor;
He does not notice now, so near to sleep.
    His chin falls on his chest.
He sleeps more in the daytime than at night.

He has antagonised so many people,
Argued with them and scoffed and cursed their views,
Few men or women come with pleasure now;
All are afraid, except his wife who must
    Have kept the image of
Him being gentle, does not see he's changed.

All meanings lie in fragments; explanations
Of motive – disappointment, love, revenge –
Are too far scattered to reveal a pattern.
Only his anger holds this man together
    And keeps him safe within
The little circle no one dares to cross.

He has loved once with hands and eyes but now
Both are like useless tools. His hands are cunning
Only with his small pleasures, will not stretch
In love or trust. He hates, yet wants, our pity,
    Having so little time
To find compassion for his own near death.

Works of Art

So often it appears like an escape,
That cool, wide world where even shadows are
Ordered and relegated to a shape
Not too intrusive and yet not too spare.
How easy it has seemed to wander deep
Into this world and find a shelter there.

Yet always it surprises. Nervous hands
Which make the first rough sketch in any art,
Leave their own tension, and the statue stands,
The poem lies with trouble at its heart.
And every fashioned object makes demands
Though we feel uncommitted at the start.

Yeats said that gaiety explained it all,
That Hamlet, Lear were gay, and so are we.
He did not look back to a happy Fall
Where man stood lost, ashamed beneath a tree.
There was no art within that garden wall.
Until we chose our dangerous liberty.

And now all making has the bitter-sweet
Taste of frustration yet of something done.
We want more order than we ever meet
And art keeps driving us most hopefully on.
Yet coolness is derived from all that heat,
And shadows draw attention to the sun.

Man in a Park

One lost in thought of what his life might mean
Sat in a park and watched the children play,
Did nothing, spoke to no one, but all day
Composed his life around the happy scene.

And when the sun went down and keepers came
To lock the gates, and all the voices were
Swept to a distance where no sounds could stir,
This man continued playing his odd game.

Thus, without protest, he went to the gate,
Heard the key turn and shut his eyes until
He felt that he had made the whole place still,
Being content simply to watch and wait.

So one can live, like patterns under glass,
And, like those patterns, not committing harm.
This man continued faithful to his calm,
Watching the children playing on the grass.

But what if someone else should also sit
Beside him on the bench and play the same
Watching and counting, self-preserving game,
Building a world with him no part of it?

If he is truthful to his vision he
Will let the dark intruder push him from
His place, and in the softly gathering gloom
Add one more note to his philosophy.

Still Life and Observer

The jar
Holds the shadows.
The shining apple
Exults in its own being,
Exacts
Not appetite but observation.
The light folds, joins,
Separates.
Here energy is in abeyance,
Silence is tamed and tethered.
The one observer
(Himself almost a still life)
Watches eagerly but quietly,
Content to let the light be the only movement,
The shadows the only interruption.
Not the objects here but their setting
Is what is important.
So with the observer,
Whose slightest movement will shift the shadows,
Whose gaze balances the objects.

Father to Son

I do not understand this child
Though we have lived together now
In the same house for years. I know
Nothing of him, so try to build
Up a relationship from how
He was when small. Yet have I killed

The seed I spent or sown it where
The land is his and none of mine?
We speak like strangers, there's no sign
Of understanding in the air.
This child is built to my design
Yet what he loves I cannot share.

Silence surrounds us. I would have
Him prodigal, returning to
His father's house, the home he knew,

Rather than see him make and move
His world. I would forgive him too,
Shaping from sorrow a new love.

Father and son, we both must live
On the same globe and the same land.
He speaks: I cannot understand
Myself, why anger grows from grief.
We each put out an empty hand,
Longing for something to forgive.

For a Visionary Poet

You will expect the light to come to hand
As birds to other men; you will demand
(So gently that it seems a mere suggestion)
An image to impose itself: for instance,
This middle-light that in September glows
Half-way between the earth and trees, a point
Where things fall down or rise, say fruit, or smoke.

You gather and possess, since your detachment
Looks out for words, asks you to annotate.
Light least infringes on the fragile view
And keeps the meaning. Fractured glass also
Serves for a symbol. You will find a use
For any light that falls, especially
The calming glow that does not burn to ash.

It is an aristocracy of style
You seek, the perfect object, artifice
That shows no touch of human hands but bears
Only the weight of history, tradition.
You are the history behind your vision,
The shadow that you will not let intrude
Except that it makes all light impossible.

Domestic Dramas

Children could stamp their feet or slam a door
And parents pick the tools of punishment.
Rancour remained perhaps but something more:
Each knew precisely what the other meant –
The terms of truce, the weapons in the war.

But growing up the children made their whole
Existence a rebellion, did not try
To treat for peace or make a truce at all.
The roots were up, the older bonds set by.
Many were wounded, someone had to fall.

Later we hide the weapons and pretend
There was no war, and yet we cannot meet
In any honest way. Our voices send
Out messages that really mean defeat.
Beginnings vanish: we can see no end.

We have discovered ways to love apart
From family loyalty and family pride.
The child stamping on the floor could start
A war, a peace. We only want to hide,
Fearful of showing a divided heart.

Perhaps if we could meet as strangers do,
Behaving well and not expecting much,
We would find understanding and break through
Passions, resentments that we dare not touch,
Because, like fire, coldness can burn us too.

Exodus

I

Down from the cliffs we came. Hand in hand. Children with all
afternoons before us. The tide was out and the rocks were shining. We
had nets for shrimping and bare feet.

The war was a sea away. Time was someone else's story. Only the
afternoon for us, the air wide and breathless, the sea standing at ease.

I can remember the catches we made – and the clear pools we gazed in.
Not for our own reflections were we staring. Our young unfinished
faces were attentive. Look, the fish darting, the water clouding.

Everything was silent. A circle of silence. Sometimes the sea broke the
circle. You could hear its crisp murmur, its hint of disasters. Not for us
the hour of calamity.

Above was the cottage. The hammocks slung in trees for sleeping, the
sure smoke from the chimney. The determined hour.

Love was far off – and passion. The milked cow, the fed chicken, the
tired unhunting dogs – they were our setting.

I can remember sleep so deep that the sea seemed to enter it. Water
washed on my window. I was curled in the shape of a seed, dreaming
of being unborn.

But the morning was always there, over the window. Time was the sea
slowing, the sand spreading, rocks drying and the cool wind breathing.

My world was the sea's edge, the warm breakers, the grey rocks.
Distance was the Atlantic with huge convoys. I could not believe in the
distance, though my gaze was as wide as the sky.

II

The wide emptiness of it: not snow in Winter stretching the sky, not a
dream breaking through a sleep and a sleep, but a calm safe place, a
quiet place, a landscape.

(Children touch but never own. Children pick but never truly mutilate.
Old men are made for madness and corruption. Yet only children can
be truly cruel.)

Not whiteness here either, not harvest or snow or sunk sky or sea
grown wilful. Simply the fields – and the child watching.

You could take air into your hands then, you could breathe and a word
was assured. You could understand all taming yet never wish to
capture. You could feel the world turning.

(Only the old are arrogant: what have they left but wishes? The old
man at the corner grasps your money. The woman puts her hand
against her breast. These beg for pity out of hopelessness.)

The child is anonymous, casual: his name surprises him. He is the air he breathes and earth he touches. Later the christening with the salt, the oils.

The harvest grows. He only sees the corn. The old man dies, his seed along with him. The child cannot penetrate the future: therefore he does not need or fear the past.

III

It was a night that nobody else knew: it was a wide breaking night. And the dreams came, deep and dark, places of blood and slaughter. Strange beasts slain but there was no executioner.

It was as if whiteness was taken away, as if when you looked for it, there was no place for whiteness, no room for it. Even the dead lacked their lilies.

My own shadow was strange to me – strange yet aware. Every sense had become painful. Everyone's gaze was inimical.

Yet I could recall, still, the cool corridors of childhood, the open delighted gardens, the body bare to the sun. Where was the sun-dial's shadow now? Would the sun never return?

Everything then was a looking, a gaze of candour. Eyes met fully, meaning a friendship. Body met body untouched by desire. Fear was over the wall, a ball flung by an unseen child, a shadow that crept up the stair.

I could remember it all, like somebody else's story, like somebody else's innocence. I was wholly aware now – trapped beast ready to flinch, fearful of touching or tasting.

And all this strangeness – the pain in the body, the child's flesh paling, the shadow grown wider – all this was a country I feared to discover. I would not believe it was mine.

Love was something else, nothing to do with this, no part in the stretching body, the blood leaping. Over the wall I could hear the whisper of lovers, a child crying across their voices. And hearing them – I was afraid.

IV

There are no white rooms now, no places where you can be seen and not recognised, no fields untrampled on. What will defend you now is all your own.

Can you relinquish the mood of childhood? Wholly resign the care, the urgent need? Dare you contract responsibilities? Who lives in white rooms now?

(So many are explorers. Children with sleds and dogs and fur-lined boots. Who needs to see the Pole or any star? What is there now to prove?)

On the edge of childhood, tilted towards maturity, on a grey world turning and a moon changing, I can be stable yet susceptible. I crave for causes now and lasting things.

I am English – and on the surface made of gentle moods. Yet long for south and sun, seek for the white cities, vines on walls, sea left where the sands mould it, flesh sun-burnt and surrendered.

(Can childhood be cast off on a coast? What seas will bear such flotsam? Can suffering surrender and survive?)

High now in Europe, with a window that shapes me a world – I am the child that gathered broken grasses, that dreamt and screamed across the night. Yet every gentle thing has stalwart roots. The sensitive survive and tell their story.

(Order is found, not imposed. Explorers find but do not legislate. Kings crumble with the ruins that they build. The young throw shadows which they have not earned. Our darkness is a promise of survival.)

The world is older than our steps across it. Yet who can bear the pressure of the past? Or move into the future unconcerned? We are no longer children, are full-grown.

Clumsy the climbers now, and bold explorers. We have more seasons than we care to name.

V

It is discovery without ownership, it is trading a word for a vision, it is touching without possession.

(Who understands his own ambition, dare anchor in a sense of his survival, pocket a life and let the profits pass? None is quite arrogant or sure enough.)

So we collect, pack drawers, put books on shelves, plant gardens with perennial flowers. Our seed becomes a son.

All for a reassurance. We dare not be quite feckless or quite wild. We fear the weather and the wind which scatters. Mostly our wishes are concerned with building.

(Where is the child now, the adolescent. We eat and change but still the flesh remains. I am the self I always was. Who fails to recognise himself in mirrors?)

We have grown apt at ballasting and softening. We know the power of palliatives. Have come to terms, it seems, with pain. Yet still we envy every child's delight. Our sleep is shallow and we fear to wake.

Books, bric-a-brac and *objets d'art*. Photographs of the past. The lovely Summer when we fell in love. The church we prayed in and forgot ourselves. The open window and the unclaimed view – we cling to such and bring the wild birds down, yet cannot even guard the things we love.

Retort to the Anti-Abstractionists

The world had grown too complicated, so
He went back to the cause of things and laid
The fiery day within an early shade.
It was impossible to see things grow.

And this he knew and meant. Do not believe
This picture was achieved without much care.
The man drew dangerously toward despair,
Trying to show what inward eyes perceive.

The pattern now demands our firm attention,
But still spectators say, 'What does it mean?
This is not anything that I have seen.'
There is so much the painter could not mention.

His picture shows the meaning, not the things –
The look without the face, flight without wings.

The Confidence

After that moment when at last you let
The whole thing out, the grievances, the fear,
Did you then find it all could disappear,
Clothed in the kindly words 'Forgive, forget'?

It was not so. You only felt the shame
Of being caught out in a hopeless hour,
Of being once again within men's power,
A pawn, a puppet in a grown-up game.

Yet if you loved them and if they loved you
Beyond the carefully chosen words, the wide
Disarming land where terror seemed to hide
But could not, would the older wish come true?

Would someone still be able to confess
That he was more than his unhappiness?

Warning to Parents

Save them from terror; do not let them see
The ghost behind the stairs, the hidden crime.
They will, no doubt, grow out of this in time
And be impervious as you and me.

Be sure there is a night-light close at hand;
The plot of that old film may well come back,
The ceiling, with its long, uneven crack,
May hint at things no child can understand.

You do all this and are surprised one day
When you discover how the child can gloat
On Belsen and on tortures – things remote
To him. You find it hard to watch him play

With thoughts like these, and find it harder still
To think back to the time when you also
Caught from the cruel past a childish glow
And felt along your veins the wish to kill.

Fears are more personal than we had guessed –
We only need ourselves; time does the rest.

Happy Families

The Strangers came and offered to stand in
For one of us still missing. So we dealt
The cards, and hoped that someone would begin.
Each hid what he imagined he had felt.

Oh, look how Mrs Beef, how Master Bun
Step out and stare; someone has got the set.
We sit about, cards clutched, each one alone,
Wishing our blood, our minds had never met.

Someone upstairs is weeping on his bed
(Families can hurt much more than strangers do).
No one consoles; we take our cards instead,
Watching Miss Grit and Mr Satin go.

But when the game is put away at last
And each goes quietly to his own room,
How many then will weep for some lost past
Or see a private shadow in the gloom?

Darkness

The water is troubled and the dark
Wind moves over it.
How do I know the wind is dark?
I only guess how the crowded world discovers my window,
How wild creatures, even in this city, stir
About their dark purposes.
And I too, unable now to be dark,
Unable now to be heavy
Under the sleep the pills will bring me,
Lie awake thinking –
'I can balance the world on my thought.'
Like the lips of a bowl where a flower is brooding,
I hold my fingers.
Wait, wait. Soon, softly
And darkly
A flower will come,
A creature will move
Out of the moss, the grass, the hole; the earth
Will discard it. Soon,

With flickering eyes (and the flowers with trembling petals),
It will wait for the world to discover it.

I am lying here and I wait
For the dark to open, for something whole to welcome
My staring eyes. A moth is beating about
The lamp. So many twitchings and stirrings.
I wish for some support of my sleeplessness,
For fingers around a bowl,
Someone, perhaps, just waiting.
I have pushed the earth aside, I am waiting, alert.

Mah Jong

Intricate pieces: children,
We could not understand them,
Played with them like bricks, built
On the card-table's soft felt,
A world, a city, then
You suddenly broke the dream.

We knew you as presence, a far
Mood, something close to war.
That evening, the cups on the dresser
Shook; my sister and I
Watched fear fall from the sky.

You carried away the game,
Offered it to our nurse.
We had lost, you said, the rules –
Both of us too young for schools
Or for parents' stratagem.
In bed we had nightmares.

Not at Home

This room is dead; the occupant has gone.
Why are we frightened? Is it simply that
So much taut stillness, so much neatness stun
The rough intruder? Under that glass dome
A bird peers out. The furniture is flat
With knowledge of so many who've gone home.

Why do we come so eagerly who once
Shrank from her invitations? What is there
In this old, moth-balled room, dead at a glance,
That holds us? Here there are no hauntings; we
Perhaps are held by the cold atmosphere,
The sudden stress on all we would not be.

We turn away and the whole room falls back
To junk-shop value; there is nothing more.
The things of worth would fit into a sack,
The rubbish keep a rag-and-bone man for
Longer than he'd believe. Yet, stripped and bare,
The room will hint of something still trapped there.

The Storm House

The wind is shaking this house,
This new house, nine storeys high and no one guessing
Such newness could ever be broached. The storm has done it,
The only natural sound in the whole city.

Along the river the boats are hooting farewell
And lights are coming on in the dingy streets.
Somebody, far-off, kicks a can and then
Returns to his separateness, his only gesture
Echoing down the street against the storm.

This moderate skyscraper is full of sickness,
A hospital houses a hundred different ailments.
The wind grows strong, winding a noisy bandage
Around the building; human sounds are unheard.

And if you cried, you would have to cry so loudly
That the wind was stilled a moment as if a hand,
In godlike supplication, laid peace upon it,
But the gods we invoke are quiet here as our prayers.

Problems of Viewing

I The Open Capital

Smoke rises and houses emerge
In geometric squares.
It is a question of how much the eye can hold
As it stares, impossibly filling
Its small space with a crowd, a street,
A distant hill;
And then the sky (that is another problem).
One thing is clear:
Only a little can be taken away,
The view will break but will not give itself wholly.

I am speaking of looking.
There is no emotion,
No choice clouded by desire
As, say, when one sees a glass of water.
Here is a city smudged with smoke,
Stirring towards noon.
To look is to make a simple decision.

No one persuades you.
It is, perhaps, peculiarly human
To gaze upon this and, uncontemplative,
Hoarding the view for a further occasion, turn
To something that needs your touch, your arbitration.

II The Unfolding

It was the way
The eye opened on to it,
And then how all
The other four astonished senses came
To its assistance.

Say that the Spring is late,
Say that we needed some attentive pause:
All these but add to a devoted Spring.
That flower is pushing through the earth, I see,
And in an air that scarcely moves the skin,
Something is growing. Watch it how you will
(And use a whole night's vigil for the act),
Still you can never say the second when
The petals pushed to independent life.

III To Paint the Dawn

You will need more than a northern light for this:
You will need hard thick paint,
To give this strange light emphasis,
To suggest life and half-life.

Nothing human will help you
But your own breathing, your own calm.
All the power that holding a brush has ever
Brought you will surely be needed now; the view
Is moving away but still warm.

Before it goes, before it finally goes,
At least fill out the darkness with some brief
Positive clarity – the hint of a rose
Towering a moment, say, above its leaf.

IV Provisional Attempt

Daily the cars race past.
Seasons seem irrelevant where the traffic
Coasts so constantly. Flowers are dusty before
Their blossoming, and air
Is filled with petrol and smoke before it reaches
The nose. The hand is gritty, the eye unsure.

Somebody swiftly pulls a curtain back
And then you can see the street either as they
See it, expectantly, or else
Can force your eyes into that darkened room
Swarming with shadows, and train your tired vision
To choose and affirm the solid objects there.

Admonition

Watch carefully. These offer
Surprising statements, are not
Open to your proper doubt,
Will watch you while you suffer.

Sign nothing but let the vague
Slogans stand without your name.
Your indifference they claim
Though the issues seem so big.

Signing a paper puts off
Your responsibilities.
Trust rather your own distress
As in, say, matters of love.

Always behind you, judges
Will have something trite to say.
Let them know you want delay;
No star's smooth at its edges.

The Nightmare

The dream was that old falling one;
Sometimes it comes when, half-awake,
You drop down deep into the bed
And rouse yourself. The first sleeps break.

But this was further in the night.
I was upon a high trapeze,
Not in a circus but a street,
Myself the audience I must please.

And past and present met there in
The dangerous clarity dreams have.
I hated every detail yet
Saw all the world I swayed above.

I moved into a shallow doze
And not for hours could I convince
Myself that all this was a dream:
Nightmares can leave such finger-prints.

And, later still, I lived again,
As in an adolescent trance,
The terror of the acrobat.
And could all this be due to chance?

No doubt if I was laid upon
A doctor's couch, he soon would learn,
And teach to me, the meaning there,
And yet I'm sure I still would turn

Dizzy above a dizzy world.
I feel it sometimes now by day:
The streets I walk seem built of air
And all the solid houses sway.

Parts of a Zodiac

I Scales

Under this star they will expect always
A sense of balance, a calm which spreads
Out from your life to the world. You will
Find many coming to you for advice.
Heed emotion, offer few words,
Whatever you say will be repeated.
To yourself, perhaps, the balance will seem

Always precarious; nervous fingers
Will seem to thrust from every quarter
Swaying your sense of perfect justice.
Nor does this inborn balance denote
A lukewarm heart. Rather, you hide
All that might breach your detachment. You hold
The weights in your hand; only you can decide.

II Pisces

From a sliding smooth element
These came and to this they return,
Fish-like bobbing to a word, a hint,
Then back, back, quick under the stern

Of somebody else's thought (borrowers these, ever)
And nothing but a smooth surface left. You would guess
Under this star is born The Deceiver;
Not so, simply a kind of shyness.

In this month, skies are not clear yet, stars
Uncertain, not easily seen; they swim
On their own mysterious adventures.
Those born under them know the same whim.

The Young Ones

They slip on to the bus, hair piled up high.
New styles each month, it seems to me. I look,
Not wanting to be seen, casting my eye
Above the unread pages of a book.

They are fifteen or so. When I was thus,
I huddled in school coats, my satchel hung
Lop-sided on my shoulder. Without fuss
These enter adolescence; being young

Seems good to them, a state we cannot reach,
No talk of 'awkward ages' now. I see
How childish gazes staring out of each
Unfinished face prove me incredibly

Old-fashioned. Yet at least I have the chance
To size up several stages – young yet old,
Doing the twist, mocking an 'old-time' dance:
So many ways to be unsure or bold.

Bewilderment

Not to enter the haunted house,
Not to let the talkers go too deep,
Not to travel without maps, and not
To analyse one's restless sleep –
Is this then cowardice and shamed refusal?

To say we need to go away,
To shout we cannot listen any more,
To travel only well-known streets;
When strangers come, to lock the door –
What judgment will be passed on this?

To be open always to experience,
To welcome change and newness, eager talk,
To give oneself away in conversation,
Never to use the map but always walk
Calm into darkness. Is this wisdom?

I do not know the answers, yet I ask
Myself these questions over and over again.
Is this willingness to ask itself perhaps
A way to live? Is the house haunted then
Only with dust and dark and silences?

Planck's Theory of Chance

So, at the base of all we know
And think most ordered, there presides
Chance, the prime mover who provides
The thrust and pull, the ebb and flow,
The seed which scatters and divides.

Yet at the surface we but see
Smooth order, flowing waves, control
That makes us think of clarity,
That gives us some sense of a whole;
Yet chance provides the destiny.

The theory works and has been proved,
But still it is the surface thing
That is admired by us and loved.
To the smooth clarities we cling
Although we are at random moved.

Is love like this also and do
Our fluctuating feelings fall
By chance from me, by chance to you?
If so, the wonder is how all
The depths we plumb ring clear and true.

The Sumach Tree

The sumach gathers light into its folds,
Consumes the Summer. You can see the blaze
Of months of heat in every branch. It holds
Light like a dying ember. Candles raise
No brighter tokens in the realms of praise.

It looks as if a touch would burn the hand –
Both the beginning and the end of fire.
Red fingers lift themselves. The tree extends
Itself; O we would burn if we drew near
This blazing bush, this emblem of desire.

'Wedding Rites at Tipasa'
By Albert Camus

In the Spring, Tipasa is inhabited by gods, and the gods talk in the sun and the scent of absinthe; the sea is severed with shafts of silver, the sky is a raw blue, ruins are smothered with flowers, and light makes great bubbles of air among the heaps of stones. At certain hours, the country is black with sun. The eyes try vainly to seize every drop of light and colour which trembles on the edge of the eye-lashes. The pervasive smell of fragrant plants catches at the throat and stifles one in the enormous heat. At the edge of the landscape, I can hardly see the black bulk of Chenoua which strikes its roots into the hills that surround the village, and moves with a slow and sure rhythm in order to settle in the sea.

We reach the village which already opens on to the bay. We enter a yellow and blue world where the strong, sharp breath of the Summer earth of Algeria gathers about us. On all sides, the rosy bougainvilleas cover the walls of the houses; in the gardens, the red hibiscus turns pale again, a profusion of tea-roses looks as thick as cream, and on the delicate borders of flower-beds the long, blue iris flourishes. All the pebbles are warm. When we descend to the bus, which is as gold as a button, the butchers in red vans make their morning round and the sounds of their horns summon the inhabitants.

To the left of the port, a staircase of dry stones leads to the ruins, among the mastic-trees and broom. The road passes in front of a small lighthouse and then plunges at once into wild country. Already, at the foot of the lighthouse, great plants with mauve, yellow and red flowers climb across the first rocks which the sea laps with the sound of kisses. Upright in the gentle wind, under the sun which warms one side of the face only, we watch the light descending from the sky, the sea without a ripple and the smile of its glittering teeth. Before entering the kingdom of ruins, we are, for the last time, spectators.

After a few steps, the scent of absinthe trees seizes us by the throat. Their grey foliage covers the ruins and quite conceals them. Their essence ferments under the heat, and from earth to sun there climbs upon the outstretched world an intoxicating spirit which makes the very sky totter. We move to a meeting of love and desire. We do not find any instructions, nor the bitter philosophy which one demands of greatness. Apart from the sun, the kisses and the savage perfumes, all else seems futile to us. As for myself, I do not want to be alone here. I have often come with those whom I have loved and I have read on their features the clear smile which love stamps upon the human face. Here, I leave order and reason to others. The great opulence of nature and of the sea engrosses me entirely. In the marriage of ruins and of Spring, the ruins have become stones again and, losing the polish imposed by man, have returned to nature. For the return of these prodigal children, nature has provided flowers abundantly. Between the flagstones of the forum, heliotrope thrusts its round, white head, and red geraniums shed their blood on what were once houses, temples and public squares. Just as much knowledge leads these men back to God, in the same way many years have returned these ruins to their mother's house. Today, then, their past leaves them, and nothing distracts them from the profound power which leads to the centre of all things which must fall.

What hours pass in absorbing the scent of absinthe, in caressing the ruins, in trying to harmonise my breathing with the tumultuous heartbeat of the world! Aroused by the savage scents and the sounds of drowsy insects, I open my eyes and my heart to the unbearable grandeur of the sky swollen with heat. It is not easy to become what one really is, to discover again a deep sense of proportion. But observing the solid back-bone of Chenoua, my heart is soothed with a strange certainty. I have learnt to breathe, I have made myself whole and complete. I have climbed one after another the hillsides which each give me some reward, such as the temple whose columns measure the course of the sun and from which one can see the entire village, the white and red walls and the green verandas. Such, also, as this basilica on the hill to the east: she is protected by walls, and in a great circle around her are set excavated tombs, most of which are scarcely raised out of the earth into which they sink again. They have contained the dead; at present they are penetrated by sage and wallflowers. The basilica of Sainte-Salsa is Christian, but every time we search for an entrance, it is the rhythm of the world which enfolds us: slopes planted with pines and cypresses, or the good sea which sends in its white horses for the length of twenty metres. The hill which supports Sainte-Salsa is bare to its summit and the wind blows more freely across its porticos. Under the morning sun, a great happiness pauses in the open space.

Poor indeed are those who have need of myths. Here the gods serve as beds or as marks on benches during the course of the day. I discredit them and I say: 'Here, things are red, blue, green. That is the sea, the mountain, the flowers.' And what need is there for me to speak of Dionysus in order to say that I love to crush the bulbs of the mastic-trees under my nostrils? That old hymn of which, so much later, I shall dream without constraint, is addressed to Demeter herself: 'Happy are those living on this earth who have seen these things.' To see, and to see on this earth – how can one forget the lesson? To discover the Eleusinian mysteries, it is sufficient simply to contemplate. I myself know that I shall never have moved close enough to them in this world. I need to be naked and then plunge into the sea, still scented with the essences of the earth, then rinse these essences in the sea, and feel on my flesh the embrace for which lips have sighed to lips since the beginning of the world. When one has plunged into the water, there is the sudden shock, the rising of a cold, opaque glue, then the dive with ears buzzing, the nose streaming and the mouth salty – swimming, arms polished by the escaping waters of the sea, in order to become golden in the sun and beaten by a clenching of all the muscles; the rushing of water on my body, this tumultuous possession of the waves by my arms - and the absence of any horizon. On the shore, there is the slipping into sand, abandoned to the world, admitted into the heaviness of my own flesh and bones, stupefied by sun, with at long intervals, attention to my arms where the flakes of dry skin begin to show, under the evaporating water, the blond down and the salty dust.

Here I can understand what it is that we call glory: the right to love without limits. It is the only love in the world. To clasp the body of a woman is also to hold close to oneself this strange joy which descends from the sky towards the sea. At the same time, when I fling myself into the absinthe trees in order to let their scent enter my body, I become aware, against all prejudice, of accomplishing a truth which is that of the sun and will also be that of my death. In a sense, it is my whole life that I play out here, a life of touching the warm stone, full of the murmurs of the sea and of the cicadas which now begin to sing. The breeze is fresh and the sky is blue. I love this life with abandon and I want to speak with complete freedom: she gives me pride in the condition of man. Yet people have often said to me: 'There is nothing to be proud of.' Yes, there is this: this sun, this sea, my heart leaping with youth, my body tasting of salt, and the immense background where tenderness and glory mingle in the yellows and blues. It is to gain this that I ought to exert all my strength and all my resources. Everything here leaves me intact, I lose nothing of myself. I clothe myself in every mask: it is enough for me to learn patiently the difficult science of living which is worth all the good breeding in the world.

A little before noon, we return by way of the ruins to a small café at the edge of the port. For the head still ringing with the clash of light and colour, what a fresh welcome the shade of the open room provides, and the great glass of iced green mint! Outside is the sea and the burning path of dust. Seated at the table, I try to catch between my trembling eyelashes the many-coloured dazzling of white sky and heat. Our faces damp with sweat, but our bodies cool in the light cloth which covers them, we spread ourselves out in the joyful lassitude of a day of union with the world.

The food is not good in this café, but there is plenty of fruit – above all, peaches of the kind which one eats as one cuts them, the kind whose juice trickles down on to one's chin. With my teeth closed upon the peaches, I listen to the great throbs of my blood mounting right up to my ears, I watch with complete concentration. Upon the sea, the enormous silence of noon has fallen. Every lovely thing that exists takes a natural pride in its beauty and today the world lets its pride spread everywhere. Confronted by this, do I deny the joy of life because I know that not everything is contained in the joy of living? There is no shame in being happy. But today, the fool is a king and I call foolish whatever is afraid of frolicking. We have certainly been told of pride: 'You know, it is the sin of Satan,' 'Take care,' they cry. 'You will be lost, together with all your living forces.' However, I have learnt that a certain pride … But at other times, I can make it my business to claim the pride of life which the whole world conspires to give me. At Tipasa, I see as much as I believe, and I refuse to deny what my hands can touch and my lips caress. I have no need to fashion a work of art but need only give an account of something different. Tipasa appears to me like those personages we select to signify indirectly some point of view about the world. Like them, she bears witness, and most potently. Today she is my personage and it seems to me that in caressing this view and describing it, my intoxication will have no end. There is a time for living and a time for bearing witness to life. There is also a time for creating, which is less natural. It is enough for me to live with my whole body and to bear witness with my whole heart. I exist through Tipasa and testify to her, and the work of art will come afterwards. That is the meaning of freedom.

* * *

I have never stayed longer than a day at Tipasa. There always comes a moment when one has seen a landscape already, just as it must be a long time before one has seen enough. The mountains, the sky, the sea are like faces on which one discovers aridity or splendour, according to the place from which one sees them. But the whole face, to be eloquent, ought to undergo a renewal. And we complain of being too quickly tired when we ought to marvel that the world appears new to us when it had only been forgotten.

Towards evening, I reach a section of the park, arranged like a garden, on the edge of the main street. Moving out from the tumult of scents and of sun into the air now freshened by the evening, the spirit becomes calm, the relaxed body tastes the interior silence which springs from satisfied love. I have sat on a bench. I have seen the country enlarged by the day. I have been satiated. Above me, a pomegranate tree has let the buds of its flowers hang down, sealed and wrinkled like the little closed fists which contain all the hope of Spring. There has been the rosemary behind me and I have sensed in it only the perfume of alcohol. Hills have been framed by trees and, further off still, an edge of sea above the sky, like a stretched sail, has rested with extreme tenderness. In my heart I have had a strange joy, like that which arises from a conscience at peace. There is a feeling which actors know when they have a sense of having accomplished their part well, that is to say, more precisely, of having made their gesture fuse with those of the ideal personage whom they are bringing to life, of having entered in some way into a preconceived pattern and which they have, with one stroke, made to live and breathe with their own heart. It was precisely that which I experienced: I had played my part. I had vindicated my position as man and to have known this joy for a whole day did not seem to me an exceptional success but rather the ecstatic achievement of a condition which, in certain circumstances, insists on the duty of being happy. It is then that we rediscover solitude, but this time with satisfaction.

* * *

Now, the trees were filled with birds. The earth sighed gently before entering the darkness. Suddenly, with the first star, night will fall on the stage of the world. The brilliant gods of day will return to their daily death. But other gods will come. And in order to be darker, their ravaged faces will be born meanwhile in the heart of the earth.

For the time being at least, the incessant falling of waves on the sand has reached me across a space where golden pollen has danced. Sea, country, silence, perfumes of this earth, I have filled myself with a fragrant life and I have bitten the already golden fruit of the world, transported by feeling its strong sweet juice flowing along the length of my lips. No, it was not I who counted, nor the world, but only the peace and silence which between them have given birth to love. Love which has not the weakness to claim me alone but, wise and proud, is shared with the whole race, is born of the sun and the sea, vital and relished: love which draws its splendour from simplicity and, above the beaches, directs her secret smile to the brilliant smile of the heavens.

For Albert Camus

Under the burning, dry Algerian sun
You read philosophies and fashioned one
To fit the climate and the intellect,
To fall between the impulse and the act
And show a reasoned choice for what was done.

The world, you thought, was complex and absurd,
Brutal to sentiment, but to the word
Pliant and supple. Every thought you wrote
Bore back as tribute from abstract, remote
Ideas, the senses and the things they stirred.

Easy to think our thoughts upon you now,
To wish on you our wisdom and allow
The stubborn world you faced to grow obscure.
Easy to let your sentiments endure –
A false inheritance – and to endow

Our thought with what you never really meant.
You made the universe your argument
And drew from man all things that can console,
Leaving him with a longing for some whole,
Honest idea to which he could consent.

A thinking rebel in the universe,
Supplied with feeling – thus you saw man's curse
But saw it also as a link which bound
Man to his fellows and to his own ground –
A creature lovable, also perverse.

Not what you thought but what you were still stands –
A man who built a world with his own hands
And lived in it. Self-love and suicide
Were abstract notions always set beside
The ache for certainty that never ends.

It was a city riddled with disease,
Bereft of rats, that gave you thoughts like these,
And deep in suffering that Calvary knew
You learnt the sacrifice and torment too –
Man, empty-handed, groping on his knees.

A Picture

That dark one in the corner strokes his knife,
Knowing that he can use it if too much
Is asked of him, or if a sudden touch
Shocks him to new awarenesses of life.

The light surrounds the stronger one who fills
The middle distance. Is he thief or saint?
The artist here has shown a bold restraint,
Guessing the hint and not the climax kills.

There is a shadow that he could not find
The colour for. It haunts the picture and
Seems a deliberate gesture of the hand.
But no one saw inside the painter's mind.

The Shells

I have the shells now in a leather box –
Limpets and cowries, ones like hands spread out.
Lifeless they are yet bear the weight of doubt
And of desire with all its hidden shocks.

Once, as a child, I might have pressed the shell
Close to my ear and thought I heard the sea.
Now I hear absence sighing quietly.
I am the one who makes and pulls the bell.

You gathered these and so they bear your print.
I cannot see it, yet the simply knowing
That you have marked these shells keeps my love growing.
Passion can hide in any lifeless hint.

A sentiment perhaps, yet every gift
Carries the weight of all we did not do.
The shells are fragments and the fragments few,
But you still sound in what the shells have left.

Eighty-one Years Old

She wants to die and all of us
Agree although we do not say;
Instead, we tend her every day,
Bring flowers and food without much fuss.
She stares at us and we stare back,
Each knowing what the others lack.

She cannot die. At times, her heart
Moves slowly, almost stops and then
The lingering life begins again,
New days of sickness have to start.
Someone must always be near by;
She must not be alone to die.

And that is what she longs for most –
To be alone, when no one stands
With filled but with unhelping hands.
Even the priest who brings the Host
Cannot provide the peace but stays
To join in mumbled words of praise.

An empty space, a dusted room –
These will be left when she at last
Becomes her own self-willed outcast.
And guilty thoughts, no doubt, will come
To nurses who had wished her dead
And now have nothingness instead.

A Thought from Aquinas

I

Narcissus need not gaze into a stream,
A Wonderland exists within the glass,
Not your reflection. No man is his dream
But lives within the gazers he must pass.

II

Self-knowledge, then, is not what we expected;
A thousand starers search the world about
Begging to see identity collected
In others' eyes, and daring them to doubt.

III

If knowledge thus begins, how does it end,
With all the feverish seekers looking for
Some proof of their existence to extend
And fill the vacuum which they all abhor?

IV

You live, therefore I am. Is this enough?
If so, what is the difference between
Two people searching through the gaze of love
And one man staring at a crowded scene?

The Destroyers

There was a little damage done that day.
A few bricks crumbled and a few men said
Words at the worst to kill, at best betray.

There was no violence, no sudden dead
Strewn in the streets. Things simply wore away.
Where once were houses, there were stones instead.

There was discomfort everywhere, no one
Felt quite at ease. Even the madmen stirred
In their cold beds. Some evil had been done.

And yet the journals scarcely hold a word
Of crucial pain, disaster or decay.
No one has spoken though they all have heard.

We gaze at one another now afraid
Of what we think, of what we long to love.
Handshakes, like kisses, also have betrayed.

Later there will be sacrifice enough.
Can nothing now be done to cause delay?
Within myself the slow destroyers move.

How do they work? What is it that they say?

Pigeons

How we are used by these creatures who seem
To make obeisance to us, allow us for
A moment to be monuments, a dream
Of being statues in a public square.

And always we're exploited. Our arms ache
Being made perches for the birds to settle
As long as they will, to rest their wings or peck
Into our hands for food. We are a little

World for them, all power gone, returned
To objects, something static to be used
As feeding-ground or nesting-places, spurned
When air's their element again. Upraised

Our eyes stride clouds to see the birds descend
Once more. The pigeons make us feel at home,
Safe, with admiring smiles and out-thrust hand,
The brief security to which they come.

A Game of Cards

Determined to be peaceful, we played cards,
Dealt out the hands and hid from one another
Our power. Our only words were weightless words
Like 'Your turn', 'Thank you' – words to soothe and smother;
Our pulses, slowed to softness, moved together.

So we became opponents and could stare
Like strangers, guessing what the other held.
There was no look of love or passion there.
The pasteboard figures sheltered us, compelled
Each one to win. Love was another world.

And yet within the concentration which
Held us so fast, some tenderness slipped in,
Some subtle feeling which could deftly breach
The kings and queens and prove the pasteboard thin:
Another battle thundered to begin.

A New Pain

When you have gone, I sit and wait, diminished
More than I ever was when quite alone.
Where nothing started, nothing need be finished;
Something of love I learn when you have gone,

Something I never knew before; I mean
The ache, the rending and the dispossession.
When I was quite alone I felt no keen
Edge of the blade, the other side of passion.

Absence becomes almost a presence since
It casts so deep a shadow on my mind:
No trivial lights will comfort or convince,
I lack your way of looking and am blind.

But when you come expectedly, it is
As if more absences than one were cast
Into oblivion. Present ecstasies
Thrive on the very anguish of the past.

THE MIND HAS MOUNTAINS
(1966)

In a Mental Hospital Sitting-room

Utrillo on the wall. A nun is climbing
Steps in Montmartre. We patients sit below.
It does not seem a time for lucid rhyming;
Too much disturbs. It does not seem a time
When anything could fertilise or grow.

It is as if a scream were opened wide,
A mouth demanding everyone to listen.
Too many people cry, too many hide
And stare into themselves. I am afraid.
There are no life-belts here on which to fasten.

The nun is climbing up those steps. The room
Shifts till the dust flies in between our eyes.
The only hope is visitors will come
And talk of other things than our disease …
So much is stagnant and yet nothing dies.

Diagnosis and Protest

To be surprised because someone is kind,
To fear to walk into a room and find

Stares of hostility, to try to please
By giving presents, saying 'My fault', – these

Have been my lifelong habits, and I'm told
Now that they are a sign I have not grown

In many ways, that part of me – emotion –
Is infantile. And yet I have known passion,

Wanted requited love, desired a child.
Perhaps if I were wholly undefiled

(Too strong a word and yet not wholly false)
I would not feel these conflicts now. Such ills

(And that is what they're called) can yet produce
A vivid work of art. But who would choose –

If this must be the price – such childlike pain?
I think the answer is we cannot learn

Completely to be bitter; if we did,
Whatever art we practise would be dead.

Maybe for me it's necessary to
Feel guilt always. I love the scapegoat so,

Also the clown – by Chaplin or Rouault.

Madness

Then this is being mad; there is no more
Imagining, Ophelias of the mind.
This girl who shouts and slobbers on the floor,
Sending us frightened to the corner, is
To all the world we know now deaf and blind
And we are merely loathsome enemies.

It is the lack of reason makes us fear,
The feeling that ourselves might be like this.
We are afraid to help her or draw near
As if she were infectious and could give
Some taint, some touch of her own fantasies,
Destroying all the things for which we live.

And, worse than this, we hate the madness too
And hate the mad one. Measured off a space
There is a world where things run calm and true –
But not for us. We have to be with her
Because our minds are also out of place
And we have carried more than we can bear.

Reflections on a Mental Hospital

'A pretty flower,' one says. No answers come;
A nurse turns out the helpless visitors.
Silence at last seeps slowly through the room.
One in a corner, deeply drugged, just stirs
And screens are brought; no one

Must see the tossing, though they are allowed
To hear the sounds and build from them a whole
Body of pain and hopelessness. Aloud,
One getting well, says 'I can't bear it all,'
But does and grows less proud;

Because she knows how near an edge it is
To cast out reason, lie beneath the sheets
Abandoning oneself to kindnesses
One has, perhaps, no right to. A nerve beats
Harsh in these heads. What is

The quick of sicknesses that run like this?
I never thought I would be cast among
The textbook symptoms and the illnesses
That cannot be defined. I feel too young
To be locked up with these.

Little is known about the human brain.
This is the truth. All is empirical:
Oh is the horoscope come back again,
Or are we reaching back but to the Fall,
The fruit, the grasp, the pain?

The Interrogator

He is always right.
However you prevaricate or question his motives,
Whatever you say to excuse yourself
He is always right.

He always has an answer;
It may be a question that hurts to hear.
It may be a sentence that makes you flinch.
He always has an answer.

He always knows best.
He can tell you why you disliked your father,
He can make your purest motive seem aggressive.
He always knows best.

He can always find words.
While you fumble to feel for your own position
Or stammer out words that are not quite accurate,
He can always find words.

And if you accuse him
He is glad you have lost your temper with him.
He can find the motive, give you a reason
If you accuse him.

And if you covered his mouth with your hand,
Pinned him down to his smooth desk chair,
You would be doing just what he wishes.
His silence would prove that he was right.

Van Gogh

All your best paintings, I have heard, were made
When you were mad. I know you sliced your ear
Off, went insane. Yet only that church in
The Louvre might possibly suggest you had
Something that most men call a mental flaw;
Yet even there's a woman with a thin

Bonnet and skirts raised from the dusty ground.
Detail you saw, and foolish men suggest
Such probing gazes are a sign of being
A little crazy, not quite balanced, found,
When tested, passionate, too much depressed,
Quickly in tears. This was your way of seeing.

There is a theory that the very heart
Of making means a flaw, neurosis, some
Sickness; yet others say it is release.
I only know that your wild, surging art
Took you to agony, but makes us come
Strangely to gentleness, a sense of peace.

The Jump

They say there was no plan. Why are they sure?
Apparently the police have evidence.
One clue they think is that she had with her
New clothes, just bought. Now, who would lay their plans

For death, and then go in a shop and buy
An anorak and shoes? Yes, they insist
That human beings who elect to die
Do not behave with such a curious twist.

Oh certainly she jumped, but everyone –
Doctors and police – says that the impulse came
In one split second. Down below, the town
Must have looked ordinary, just the same

As any Friday afternoon. I think
That no one knows how long she had thought over
Committing suicide; she saw the brink,
The dark ... That day I'd helped her with the Hoover.

Attempted Suicides

We have come back.
Do not be surprised if we blink our eyes
If we stare oddly
If we hide in corners.
It is we, not you, who should show surprise.

For everything looks strange.
Roofs are made of paper
Hands are muslin
Babies look eatable.
There has been too much change.

And where do we come from?
Where did the pills take us,
The gas,
The water left pouring?
Limbo? Hell? Mere forgetfulness?

It was a lost moment,
There were no dreams,
There was simply the beyond-endurance
And then the coming-to
To you and you and you and you.

Do not ask us,
As if we were Lazarus,
What it was like.
We never got far enough.
Now we touch ourselves and feel strange.
We have a whole world to arrange.

Lisa

'You don't like being touched,' she said, that kid
Of only fifteen. She was very quick,
Very mature in some things that she said;
At others, certainly unstable, sick.

Like most of us, she was disturbed, distressed,
And yet she had a natural touch with things
Like toys and children. She was not depressed,
Only quite lost among her sufferings.

I liked her very much and she liked me,
She taught me much, I know. But I taught her
Only how little age and family
Matter when one has loved in terms of fear.

Questions

You have said
Over and over again
You are only there to help,
I must grow the grain,
Break down, break down,
Then build up again.

But what are these talks doing?
And these silences?
Something in me holds on to personalities;
Are you really destroying
What I need and love?
I speak through a veil of incoherences.
You never move.

I have done
The ultimate thing,
Tried death and was brought back,
Played at Judas but not known
That someone would turn off the gas –
The one who has grown
Close into lovelessness.
We are tied together now on a rack.

But only I have to learn
Childhood, sex, love
All over again.
He is too old, has moved off.
Yet I, his seed
Have come closer to death,
And further, perhaps, than his need.

Night Sister

How is it possible not to grow hard,
To build a shell around yourself when you
Have to watch so much pain, and hear it too?
Many you see are puzzled, wounded; few
Are cheerful long. How can you not be scarred?

To view a birth or death seems natural,
But these locked doors, these sudden shouts and tears
Graze all the peaceful skies. A world of fears
Like the ghost-haunting of the owl appears.
And yet you love that stillness and that call.

You have a memory for everyone;
None is anonymous and so you cure
What few with such compassion could endure.
I never met a calling quite so pure.
My fears are silenced by the things you've done.

We have grown cynical and often miss
The perfect thing. Embarrassment also
Convinces us we cannot dare to show
Our sickness. But you listen and we know
That you can meet us in our own distress.

The Illusion

The sun, a child at play, and one or two
Young people lying on the lawn, a place
That seems so peaceful that they can't be true,
Those horrors, and so much unhappiness.

Much is the same as what we know outside –
People hold hands here, others sit apart.
A casual glance could never quite divide
The normal from the sick and frightened heart.

Oddly, it's *here* I learn, with fear and pain
Rooted within myself, new words, new tongues,
New honesties and courage that sustain
The power to bear what man has made of things.

Only one horror haunts and lives with me
And won't be shed. I have learnt here also,
In one long look of naked cruelty,
How man can dream of Belsen, make it grow.

Hysteria

It was at breakfast only yesterday
(Patients, like children, gobbling porridge up),
That suddenly this loud inhuman voice
Broke through the semi-peace, the childish noise.
A few of us crashed down a spoon or cup,
But all, I think, willed her to go away.

Not only what is just irrational
Infected us. It was the staring eyes,
The knowledge, too, how close all people are
To what is meaningless. Hysteria
Is like a zoo where each wild creature lies
Ready to pounce, not wanting man's control.

Yet at the end of all this shrieking came
The whimper, 'I regret the things I do.'
Most of us were too shaken then to try
And treat her like a baby who must cry,
Although we do not guess the cause.
I envy those who've learnt what they must do
Though honest nurses say they too feel shame.

Words From Traherne

You cannot love too much, only in the wrong way.

It seemed like love; there were so many ways
Of feeling, thinking, each quite separate.
Tempers would rise up in a sudden blaze,
Or someone coming twitch and shake the heart.

Simply, there was no calm. Fear often came
And intervened between the quick expression
Of honest movements or a kind of game.
I ran away at any chance of passion.

But not for long. Few can avoid emotion
So powerful, although it terrifies.
I trembled, yet I wanted that commotion
Learnt through the hand, the lips, the ears, the eyes.

Fear always stopped my every wish to give.
I opted out, broke hearts, but most of all
I broke my own. I would not let it live
Lest it should make me lose control and fall.

Now generosity, integrity,
Compassion too, are what make me exist,
Yet still I cannot come to terms or try,
Or even know, the knot I must untwist.

A Nurse Gone Sick

You cared for us and now I hear that you
Are sick. I sometimes guessed at it perhaps.
There were those days when you seemed near to tears
As if you could not bear the trials and traps
Of nursing those whose minds have gone askew.
They seemed too much for you – our pains and fears.

And once I said in secret to a friend
'She understands since she has suffered too.'
Odd that I should so nearly comprehend
Yet learn your pain the wrong way round. For you
Had come not to a starting but an end.
Now I regret that far too late I knew.

Final Considerations

The bottle or the needle or the gas;
More choose the pill. They leave themselves a chance
Of getting back. Others grip hopelessness.
But why was no one there with some defence
That might have shown despair as something less

Than their thin world – within, without? I too
Know what it means to want to reach the end,
Have made attempts. There seemed no need of friend
Or hope of future. Terror simply drew
Me on to dark I did not understand;
I did not know then what I wished to do.

Oh, Judas hanging on a tree was close
To Christ in time; in pain perhaps also.
He had the chance to make his peace, God knows,
But only God knows why he had to go
Swinging upon the rope. Men suffer so;
I am with them now who revived but chose.

Samuel Palmer and Chagall

You would have understood each other well
And proved to us how periods of art
Are less important than the personal
Worlds that each painter makes from mind and heart,

The greatest – Blake, Picasso – move about
In many worlds. You only have one small
Yet perfect place. In it, there is no doubt,
And no deception can exist at all.

Great qualities make such art possible,
A sense of TRUTH, integrity, a view
Of man that fits into a world that's whole,
Those moons, those marriages, that dark, that blue.

I feel a quiet in it all although
The subject and the scenes are always strange.
I think it is that order pushes through
Your images, and so you can arrange

And make the wildest, darkest dream serene;
Landscapes are like still-lives which somehow move,
The moon and sun shine out of the same scene –
Fantastic worlds but all are built from love.

On a Friend's Relapse and Return to a Mental Clinic

I had a feeling that you might come back,
And dreaded it.
You are a friend, your absence is a lack;
I mean now that

We do not meet outside the hospital:
You are too ill
And I, though free by day, cannot yet call
Myself quite well.

Because of all of this, it was a shock
To find that you
Were really bad, depressed, withdrawn from me
More than I knew.

You ask for me and sometimes I'm allowed
To go and sit
And gently talk to you – no noise too loud;
I'm glad of it.

You take my hand, say odd things, sometimes weep,
And I return
With rational talk until you fall asleep.
So much to learn

Here; there's no end either at second-hand
Or else within
Oneself, or both. I want to understand
But just begin

When something startling, wounding comes again.
Oh heal my friend.
There should be peace for gentle ones, not pain.
Bring her an end

Of suffering, or let us all protest
And realise
It is the good who often know joy least.
I fight against the size

And weight of such a realisation, would
Prefer no answers trite
As this; but feeling that I've understood,
I can accept, not fight.

Old Age

You were quite silent till the doctor came
Kindly to question, breaking through your thoughts.
And were you glad that he recalled your name,
    Asked you about your pets,
Or would you rather doze there, much the same

As some old cat or dog, some lump of fur
Beside the fire, unmoving and unmoved,
Grateful that no one made you speak or stir,
    Yet wanting to be loved
And finding it in warm sheets and soft chair?

You know who gives real kindness, none the less,
Not to child's shouting like some old ones do.
You feel for certain hands as though to bless,
    And beg a blessing too;
And then you weep, simply from happiness.

Night Garden of the Asylum

An owl's call scrapes the stillness.
Curtains are barriers and behind them
The beds settle into neat rows
Soon they'll be ruffled.

The garden knows nothing of illness.
Only it knows of the slow gleam
Of stars, the moon's distilling; it knows
Why the beds and lawns are levelled.

The all is broken from its fullness.
A human cry cuts across a dream.
A wild hand squeezes an open rose.
We are in witchcraft, bedevilled.

A Baby Born in Hospital

For M.

One normal voice – a child's across the night.
Its sleep is broken by some natural need.
The corridor is blazing with a light
But he screams in the darkness, wants to feed.

Out of the mother's anguished pain he came,
Fragile to touch, and strangely beautiful.
He smiles and thrusts his finger out to claim
Each being here – the sick, the getting well.

From parents wishing perfect love, he grew
And lives with us in innocent compassion.
Will some rare pity linger in him too
When out of childhood? A dream, a vision?

But yet to mother and to child I wish
Oblivion of all they have known here.
Love wrought this wonder from the simple flesh
Where no pain need be and no grief to bear.

Personal Easter

Let them bring gifts, let them bring pious eggs.
There are no kings at Easter, only men.
Two nights ago, we drained cups to the dregs
And did not know if we should live again.
The stars move on, we battle with our plagues.
What god will rise now from the frozen stone?

A few flowers sprinkle over ravaged earth.
Birds hover, dive. Why do they fill my mind?
The Holy Ghost has more august a birth
Than this, the tongues of fire could singe and blind.
Oh God, last year I chose my own poor death
Yet you arose me, left Limbo behind.

A Depression

She left the room undusted, did not care
To hang a picture, even lay a book
On the small table. All her pain was there –
In absences. The furious window shook
With violent storms she had no power to share.

Her face was lined, her bones stood thinly out.
She spoke, it's true, but not as if it mattered;
She helped with washing-up and things like that.
Her face looked anguished when the china clattered.
Mostly she merely stared at us and sat.

And then one day quite suddenly she came
Back to the world where flowers and pictures grow
(We sensed that world though we were much the same
As her). She seemed to have the power to know
And care and treat the whole thing as a game.

But will it last? Those prints upon her walls,
Those stacks of books – will they soon disappear?
I do not know how a depression falls
Or why so many of us live in fear.
The cure, as much as the disease, appals.

Grove House, Iffley

For Vivien

Your house is full of objects that I prize –
A marble hand, paperweights that uncurl,
Unfolding endlessly to red or blue.
Each way I look, some loved thing meets my eyes,
And you have used the light outside also;
The Autumn gilds collections old and new.

And yet there is no sense of *objets d'art*,
Of rarities just valued for their worth.
The handsome objects here invite one's touch,
As well as sight. Without the human heart,
They'd have no value, would not say so much.
Something of death belongs to them – and birth.

Nor are they an escape for anyone.
Simply you've fashioned somewhere that can give
Not titillation, pleasure, but a sense
Of order and of being loved; you've done
What few can do who bear the scars and prints
Of wounds from which they've learnt a way to live.

Suicides

For a psychiatrist

I wish that I could help you when this happens,
When patients you have tended seek their end.
It does not matter what the way, the weapons.
What does it feel like? How can you pretend

All is the same, that something merely failed?
How do you know that a chance word of yours
May have affected them until they willed
To die, and made you the unwilling cause?

Stupid and childish now, I want to cry
To think of threats that I have made to you.
I've said, 'You would not worry if I die.'
It is not true: I know it is not true.

You take on more than many other men –
The quick and sick of life. I wish I knew
How I could help. But I have also been,
And am, your burden and your thread of pain.

Caravaggio's Narcissus *in Rome*

Look at yourself, the shine, the sheer
Embodiment thrown back in some
Medium like wood or glass. You stare,
And many to this gallery come
Simply to see this picture. Clear
As glass it is. It holds the eye
By subject and by symmetry.

Yes, something of yourself is said
In this great shining figure. You
Must have come to self-knowledge, read
Yourself within that image who
Draws every visitor. You made
From gleaming paint that tempting thing –
Man staring at his suffering.

And at his joy. But you stopped where
We cannot pause, merely make sure
The picture took you from the stare,
Fatal within: Chagall or Blake
Have exorcised your gazing for
A meaning that you could not find
In the cold searchings of your mind.

Chinese Art

You said you did not care for Chinese art
Because you could not tell what dynasty
A scroll or bowl came from. 'There is no heart'
You said, 'Where time's avoided consciously.'

I saw your point because I loved you then.
The willows and the horses and the birds
Seemed cold to me; each skilfully laid-on, thin
Phrase spoke like nothing but unpassionate words.

I understand now what those artists meant;
They did not care for style at all, or fashion.
It was eternity they tried to paint,
And timelessness, they thought, must lack all passion.

Odd that just when my feeling need for you
Has gone all wrong, I should discover this.
Yes, but I lack the sense of what is true
Within these wise old artists' skilfulness.

It would be easy now to close again
My heart against such hurt. Those willows show,
In one quick stroke, a lover feeling pain,
And birds escape fast as the brush-strokes go.

Late Child
For L.L.

If many children had been born to them,
They would have seen, after the first delight,
Another note being added to the theme –
A pleasure and a joy – sometimes a fright.

But you have made yourselves more vulnerable,
Put at the mercy of such ecstasy;
Everything that this baby does you feel
As a new wonder, nothing is casually

Observed or, let alone, taken for granted.
The sperm, the seed, the blood, the milk – all these
Are something that you passionately wanted;
All are embodied in the child you praise.

Few are as innocent or glad as this.
This child come to a childless pair has made
Me think of times before the serpent's hiss.
Yet I am frightened too, since this delayed

Daughter means everything. What if she died?
Or if some sickness ruined all she seems
To be (so perfect now)? You have defied
Disaster, living only in your dreams.

I *think* I know a little what you feel,
Being myself childless a different way.
When I see babies, they are not quite real.
I know, like you, the wonder – and dismay.

Love Poem

There is a shyness that we have
Only with those whom we most love.
Something it has to do also
With how we cannot bring to mind
A face whose every line we know.
O love is kind, O love is kind.

That there should still remain the first
Sweetness, also the later thirst –
This is why pain must play some part
In all true feelings that we find
And every shaking of the heart.
O love is kind, O love is kind.

And it is right that we should want
Discretion, secrecy, no hint
Of what we share. Love which cries out,
And wants the world to understand,
Is love that holds itself in doubt.
For love is quiet, and love is kind.

One Flesh

Lying apart now, each in a separate bed,
He with a book, keeping the light on late,
She like a girl dreaming of childhood,
All men elsewhere – it is as if they wait
Some new event: the book he holds unread,
Her eyes fixed on the shadows overhead.

Tossed up like flotsam from a former passion,
How cool they lie. They hardly ever touch,
Or if they do it is like a confession
Of having little feeling – or too much.
Chastity faces them, a destination
For which their whole lives were a preparation.

Strangely apart, yet strangely close together,
Silence between them like a thread to hold
And not wind in. And time itself's a feather
Touching them gently. Do they know they're old,
These two who are my father and my mother
Whose fire from which I came, has now grown cold?

Thinking of Love

That desire is quite over
Or seems so as I lie
Using the sky as cover
And thinking of deep
Dreams unknown to a lover.

Being alone is now
Far from loneliness.
I can stretch and allow
Legs, arms, hands
Their complete freedom:
There is no one to please.

But soon it comes –
Not simply the ache
Of a particular need,
But also the general hunger,
As if the flesh were a house
With too many empty rooms.

Van Gogh Again

This place is too mild,
Nothing dangerous could
Happen here, I think:
Nothing great, either.
If somebody screams or throws
A tea-cup through a window,
They are removed elsewhere.

It is chastening to reflect
That had Van Gogh been brought
(By accident, of course)
Into this mild ward,
And gone berserk one night
In the middle of painting,
Oh, say, the moonlight,

He would soon have gone
To a more hectic place,
And there, no doubt, have entered
A remote, fearful calm
Where everything was clear,
And, searching for something to do,
Would then have struck off his ear.

A Birthday in Hospital
Written on the day

Soon I shall be in tears this birthday morning:
Cards are propped up beside me, people come
And wish me happy days. In ceremony
(Even of childish sorts), I can behave,
Look interested, grateful, courteous,
Be to each one who comes a kind of warmth
And so give back not gratitude, but gifts.

Yet I shall cry, no doubt from loneliness,
From being far away from those I love,
Or any reason I can conjure later.
But are the tears themselves, I wonder, still
A sort of ceremony I must follow,
A childish ritual, necessity,
Something expected by the wishers-well?
I've heard of 'gift of tears' but did not know,
Until this moment, what the words could mean.

New Poem Simply

Orwell invented the idea of a machine which makes novels
ten years ago my friends and I met
for group writing
it was a bit like Consequences
we took a subject
wrote a line
turned down the paper
passed it on
sometimes we got a real poem
but it was a hazard
(who said the so-called conventional poem isn't a hazard
anyway? and what is 'inspiration'?)
Our group worked better though at prose
it must be admitted
and when we had had a certain amount of rough wine

I am aware of the conventionality of all this
and of writing about it
What I really want
is a new kind of art altogether
trade all tradition
make music stand still
buildings be mobile
and everyone say (and mean it)
    'How beautiful!'

Blue Candles

    and burn
    you are a kind of flower
    I worship you flowers
    you are white in churches
    and I have lighted you for prayers
    in Barcelona they make wax legs wax babies
    as thank-offerings
      blue candles
        you are not poetic
          not like the sea or the moon
            (i have not lighted you yet –
            i am holding my breath against the draught)

children, light your sparklers
blue will come at the end
and the smell of burning
Rembrandt you knew about light
i'm putting the candles back in the box
maybe i'll light them at Christmas
blue, blue, blue

My Room

it is full of things from my childhood
oh anyone could analyse it
but to paint it
that would be harder
it is mine yet not mine
Bonnard might have had a shot at it
dear Van Gogh – he would have had a go
and made it just like his own!
Vermeer? he'd have been concerned with mirrors:
and Picasso? it depends what period he was in
and what mood.

    I have two rooms
    the other is not so important
    but it's full of my things
    only the other day I dreamt that someone had come in
    and smashed my treasures –
    china, pots, wood, *papier maché*, books
    the nightmare seemed to go on and on for hours

sometimes I want to clear everything out
except a table, a chair, a typewriter
but I know what would happen
first I'd try to make a mural
then books would appear
then papers
toys
bits and pieces from friends and holidays
and one enormous mirror, in which to stare.

    this is my nursery and I like it.

    it is my growing-up room also.

Trees

trees
    and the blowing through them
wind storm rain gale
oak ash sycamore beech
we cannot stand back and admire you long
not like the Roman pines
part of history
erect in the Forum
silent under the sun
layer on layer –
emperor, Pope, fascist, communist
and the trees still standing
in the churches you can munch God's bread
at any moment of the morning:
outside the Vespas race through Constantine's arch.

want a drink?
in the Via Veneto?
very good, *molto caro?* the Cafe Greco
or a Bloody Mary in the Via Condotti?
(oh stop showing off and talking like guide-books
everyone's been abroad now anyway)
why on earth should we feel proud that we've been to Ravenna
                                    or Florence?
it only needs money and perhaps a certain judgement.

Let's go to Brighton or Blackpool instead
Let's sleep in cold rooms with a single bed
bed and breakfast – what's wrong with that?
only it's likely to make you grow fat.

pink rock, fruit machines, 'what the butler saw'
we won't go to Paris or Rome any more
we'll pick up the shells as the rain falls down
or carry our boredom all round the town.

and what's the point of this?
it's only another affectation.

      Romanesque
      Gothic
      Baroque –

why pretend they haven't got something
anyway, if you don't like history, you always get the sun abroad;
Casinos are more fun than bingo

but we were talking of trees ...

Just Another Poem

Words
stop it
you talk too much
words words words
Hamlet –
where do they get you
this sort of thing is old hat
anyway
(why 'hat'? Stop asking questions.)
don't censor it, just let the words flow she said
(this girl lies on a couch)
what about Joyce
and *Finnegans Wake*
and the end of *Ulysses?*
The funny *thing* is that Virginia Woolf
('Who's afraid of ... ' Don't *do* that)
got the feeling of stream of consciousness
by the most delicate writing in the world
poor thing, look what happened to her
it was all too much –
words and tears and war.
she was afraid even of reviews in *Granta*
all right, I know I'm involved in this
who says I shouldn't care anyway?

they say 'don't think about it'
I tell you I can't stop – at times that is

Hart Crane jumped into the sea
they covered up the reason
too many people are dying and unhappy
(when you mean what you say why does it sound like a cliché?)
what's God doing?
don't be blasphemous
the great big fathers are throwing rocks at you
but the Holy Ghost is settling down to sleep

Unkind Poem about People who are Mildly Deranged

I'm ill   I want psychoanalysis
i want oblivion
i want pills
'what's the matter with that woman?' ('don't speak so loudly')
'i don't care if she does hear'
'i slit my wrists you know: life was too much to bear
it gave my husband a shock all right'

they take away your money mirror and nail file
the lavatory doors won't lock
'would you like to go to the toilet dear' a nurse said
well '*toilet*': I mean to say

if anyone cries the others don't take the slightest notice
one keeps on about her operations
gall bladder
ulcers
tonsillitis
and *of course*
hysterectomy

some keep on about sex
'i can't bear my husband to touch me; it's "the change" you know'
give me the beatniks
with their jeans long hair drugs and dirt.

there are a few gentle ones who never talk about themselves
at times there are tears on their cheeks
they would give anything to hide them
other people's grief upsets them too;
odd what a touch on the wrist can do –
nurse's or patient's.

at times, I confess, I've thought there was nothing wrong with most
                                            of us

then why do we do what we do?

A Limerick and So On

at Chartres the masons made
a church within the shade
they didn't claim
to sign their name –
the place was where you prayed.

God bless everyone
(are you being coy by any chance?)
i'm serious
you can't try to be simple
you either are or you're not
those men at Chartres were
so is Picasso
grinning as he finishes a plate

Poem about the Breakdown of a Breakdown

even the psycho admits it
they don't know much about the human brain
poets know it is very delicate –
hit it and the brains and blood will pour out like egg yolk.

what is the couch for then?
to protect this poor head
to hide the psycho's perplexity from you?
or make you feel like a baby again?

Ring-a, ring-a-roses
Freud is picking posies
Guess what he will use them for?
To make a sexual metaphor.

this poem is giving itself away too much

Hi Jung
How are you getting along?

Pity you didn't like trinities or triangles
that makes you a square
but still, Freud is top of the Hit Parade
heard his latest?
no but I can guess it's the old boy-meets-girl stuff

Adam sat under the magic tree
    Eve came up and kissed him
Oh Adam my darling one said she
    Get that bright apple down for me
    God isn't looking now, you see,
And anyway he was teasing us
When about *this* tree he made such a fuss

Adam looked up at the bough above
    And said, 'All right, let's do it.
God keeps talking to us of love
    This garden itself was made to prove
    Our life is simple, a shady grove,
Our lovely bodies.' Then why did they steal
    Apart when they'd eaten the fruit and feel
Something had disappeared – a game?
Or God himself? and feel such shame?

ever since we have been trying to get
    back to that garden
    Christ had to go, alone, to another one

this poem has slipped away in the usual manner –
Oh the bright apple-trees and skyscrapers.

Sea

i'll have a go at it
some things are felt more if not mentioned
but that blue bloody sea
is too powerful
    I'm not going to mention the moon
or tides or anything like that
    i think of sex
      and the great urges
      and then of a child
(the only true picture Dali painted)
'a child lifting the edge of the sea'
    he called it
      he's a smooth operator
        he even had to be clever about the crucifixion
          but something about the sea got him
            it's got me too
            always always:
            classical yet moving –

      there just aren't any words

THE SECRET BROTHER
AND OTHER POEMS FOR CHILDREN
(1966)

The Secret Brother

Jack lived in the green-house
When I was six
With glass and with tomato plants,
Not with slates and bricks.

I didn't have a brother
Jack became mine.
Nobody could see him,
He never gave a sign.

Just beyond the rockery,
By the apple-tree,
Jack and his old mother lived,
Only for me.

With a tin telephone
Held beneath the sheet,
I would talk to Jack each night.
We would never meet.

Once my sister caught me,
Said 'He isn't there.
Down among the flower-pots
Cramm the gardener

Is the only person.'
I said nothing, but
Let her go on talking.
Yet I moved Jack out.

He and his old mother
Did a midnight flit.
No one knew his number:
I had altered it.

Only I could see
The sagging washing line
And my brother making
Our own secret sign.

Thomas the Ginger Cat

A marmalade cat,
Who sat on my mat,
Was well fed and fat.
But that is *not* that.

This creature of fur
With his resonant purr
Would always prefer
To let others stir.

At times, it is true,
He went out to view
His kingdom; but few
Other cats came there too.

Though weather was bad,
And statesmen went mad,
This cat was not sad.
In fur he was clad.

No moral can grow
From this story, I know.
But at least it may show
The world is not so

Strait-laced, strict, and trim,
As it sometimes might seem.
If you doubt of this theme,
Take Tom, look at him.

In spite of my care,
I have, I declare,
Taught men to beware
Of not daring to dare.

Holidays at Home

There was a family who, every year,
Would go abroad, sometimes to Italy,
Sometimes to France. The youngest did not dare
To say, 'I much prefer to stay right here.'

You see, abroad there were no slot-machines
No bright pink rock with one name going through it,
No rain, no boarding-houses, no baked beans,
No landladies, and no familiar scenes.

And George, the youngest boy, so longed to say,
'I don't *like* Greece, I don't like all these views,
I don't like having fierce sun every day,
And most of all, I just detest the way

The food is cooked – that garlic and that soup,
Those strings of pasta, and no cakes at all.'
The family wondered why George seemed to droop
And looked just like a thin hen in a coop.

They never guessed why when they said, 'Next year
We can't afford abroad, we'll stay right here,'
George looked so pleased and soon began to dream
Of piers, pink rock, deep sand, and Devonshire cream.

Kites

My kite's blue.
What colour's yours?
Bright green and shining
With silver stars.

I've got a box-kite.
No need to boast,
Mine's like a sausage
Ready to roast.

The sea is mine
And the sky is too.
The wind blows the kites
In a net that is blue.

But, thinking again
And tugging my kite,
I'd rather have *that*
Than the whole day and night.

A Sort of Chinese Poem

The Chinese write poems
That don't look like poems.
They are more like paintings.

A cherry-tree, a snow-storm,
An old man in a boat –
These might be their subjects.

It all looks so easy –
But it isn't.
You have to be very simple,
Very straightforward,
To see so clearly.
Also, you have to have thousands of years of skill.

When I was a child, I once wrote a Chinese poem.
Now I'm too complicated.

The Ginger Cat

I once had a marmalade Tom,
Who invented an unusual bomb.
He filled it with mice
And placed the device
So that no one knew where they came from.

The Hamster

A hamster by name of Big Cheek
Stored up nuts that would last him a week.
Alas, he ignored
That their being so stored
Made him look the most terrible freak.

My Animals

My animals are made of wool and glass,
Also of wood. Table and mantelpiece
Are thickly covered with them. It's because
You cannot keep real cats or dogs in these

High-up new flats. I really want to have
A huge, soft marmalade or, if not that,
Some animal that *seems* at least to love.
Hamsters? A dog? No, what I need's a cat.

I hate a word like 'pets': it sounds so much
Like something with no living of its own.
And yet each time that I caress and touch
My wool or glass ones, I feel quite alone.

No kittens in our flat, no dog to bark
Each time the bell rings. Everything is still;
Often I want a zoo, a whole Noah's ark.
Nothing is born here, nothing tries to kill.

The Ugly Child

I heard them say I'm ugly.
I hoped it wasn't true.
I looked into the mirror
To get a better view,
And certainly my face seemed
Uninteresting and sad.
I *wish* that either it was good
Or else just very bad.

My eyes are green, my hair is straight,
My ears stick out, my nose
Has freckles on it all the year,
I'm skinny as a hose.
If only I could look as I
Imagine I might be.
Oh, all the crowds would turn and bow.
They don't – because I'm me.

Chop-Suey

There was a man who in the East
Made sweet-sour soups, a Chinese feast
Of birds' nests, sharks' fins, pancake rolls
And piles of rice with shrimps in bowls.

In many cities in the West
This man built cafés. Every guest
Was given plastic chopsticks and
A finger-bowl to wash each hand.

The menu written out was good
And many people liked the food.
The dishes offered pleased the young,
And *no one* jested, 'Who flung dung?'

Now every town and every street
Serves pancake rolls, pork sour and sweet,
And yet amongst the bamboo-shoots
We taste old hot-pots, chips, and sprouts.

The Radio Men

When I was little more than six
I thought that men must be
Alive inside the radio
To act in plays, or simply blow
Trumpets, or sing to me.

I never got a glimpse of them,
They were so very small.
But I imagined them in there,
Their voices bursting on the air
Through that thin, wooden wall.

The Ark

Nobody knows just how they went.
They certainly went in two by two,
But who preceded the kangaroo
And who dared follow the elephant?

'I've had enough,' said Mrs Noah.
'The food just won't go round,' she said.
A delicate deer raised up his head
As if to say, '*I* want no more.'

In they marched and some were sick.
All very well for those who could be
On the rough or the calm or the middle sea.
But I must say that ark felt very thick

Of food and breath. How wonderful
When the dove appeared and rested upon
The hand of Noah. All fear was gone,
The sea withdrew, the air was cool.

Tiffany: a Burmese Kitten

(who is real)

For Mrs Graham Greene

My friends keep mice – white ones and patched.
I wish I could pretend
I really like the creatures, but
I cannot and I spend

Just hours and hours admiring them.
I think my friends soon guess
They're not my kind of animal.
My secret wish, oh, yes,

Is for a Burmese kitten, one
Of those pure chocolate brown
Cats that I know are seldom seen
In any usual town.

I once met one called Tiffany:
She used to come and see
Me when I was in hospital.
She'd jump all over me,

Knock flowers down, explore the place
From door to door, and leap
Up all the tawdry furniture.
I know she helped me sleep:

I know she helped me get quite well,
Although I did not see
That at the time she came she was
Doctor and nurse to me.

London

When I first went to London
My parents were amazed
That nothing seemed to please me,
That everything they praised
Just left me looking sullen
And feeling slightly dazed.

Oh, Piccadilly Circus
Was just a roundabout,
No monkeys there, no horses,
No tigers leaping out.
You see, I thought a circus
Was always just the same.
I never guessed that it could be
A lying, cheating NAME.

Friends

I fear it's very wrong of me,
And yet I must admit,
When someone offers friendship
I want the *whole* of it.
I don't want everybody else
To share my friends with me.
At least, I want *one* special one,
Who, indisputably,

Likes me much more than all the rest,
Who's always on my side,
Who never cares what others say,
Who lets me come and hide
Within his shadow, in his house –
It doesn't matter where –
Who lets me simply be myself,
Who's always, *always* there.

At Night

I'm frightened at night
When they put out the light
And the new moon is white.

It isn't so much
That I'm scared stiff to touch
The shadows, and clutch

My blankets: it's – oh –
Things long, long ago
That frighten me so.

If I don't move at all,
The moon will not fall,
There'll be no need to call.

But, strangely, next day
The moon slips away,
The shadows just play.

Rhyme for Children

I am the seed that slept last night;
This morning I have grown upright.

Within my dream there was a king.
Now he is gone in the wide morning.

He had a queen, also a throne.
Waking, I find myself alone.

If I could have that dream again,
The seed should grow into a queen

And she should find at her right hand
A king to rule her heart and land:

And I would be the spring which burst
Beside their love and quenched their thirst.

Mirrors

Mirrors have haunted me
Since I was four –
Mirrors to be stared into, mirrors on the door,
Mirrors in the fairground, mirrors in the sea:
Each and every one of them
Has haunted me.

Windows in the buses,
Puddles in the street –
Each can be a mirror. You can splash your feet,
See your face exploding, watch the world go 'Puff.'
Yet it's not enough.

Old People

Why are people impatient when they are old?
Is it because they are tired of trying to make
Fast things move slowly?
I have seen their eyes flinch as they watch the lorries
Lurching and hurrying past.
I have also seen them twitch and move away
When a grandbaby cries.

They can go to the cinema cheaply,
They can do what they like all day.
Yet they shrink and shiver, looking like old, used dolls.
I do not think that I should like to be old.

Chocolate Adam and Eve

Adam and Eve were edible,
One brown, the other white.
The only difference you may feel
If you will take a bite

Of chocolate white and chocolate brown,
And firmly close your eyes.
You will not *taste* the difference,
There won't be a surprise.

Each tastes of chocolate, you see,
Forget the colours – EAT.
Adam and Eve sat under the tree –
Oh, melting in the heat.

The moral of this poem is –
Don't go by looks alone;
You'll miss such strange experiences
Like chocolate white and brown.

Love Poem

You needn't be a princess
To tell your love aloud.
You don't need films or photographs
Or a football crowd:
Just say, 'I love you, love you
More than the world can say.'
Bells will ring around for you, bands begin to play.

Love your love with trumpets,
Love your love with voice.
Love is just the same today
As it always was.
But when you love most truly,
It will seem to you
A thing discovered newly,
A vague wish come true.

Oh, love your love on radio,
Love him to the sky.
Swear that you will love him
Till you both must die.
You needn't be a princess
To sing your love song. Tin
Trumpets will turn gold for you
And royal bells begin.

Clothes

My mother keeps on telling me
When she was in her teens
She wore quite different clothes from mine
And hadn't heard of jeans,

T-shirts, no hats, and dresses that
Reach far above our knees.
I laughed at first and then I thought
One day my kids will tease

And scoff at what *I'm* wearing now.
What will *their* fashions be?
I'd give an awful lot to know,
To look ahead and see.

Girls dressed like girls perhaps once more
And boys no longer half
Resembling us. Oh, what's in store
To make *our* children laugh?

Mary

I am afraid of people who move quickly,
Who jerk about and don't let you see their eyes.
Sometimes I think there are tigers lurking there.

At other times, I think these people move
Because they are not brave enough to be still.
If they stayed still,
If they stayed very still,
The tigers would be quiet.
Then one could feel their rough tongues licking,
And stroke their skins asleep.

The Dead Bird
a poem I wrote when I was a child

I held it in my hand
With its little hanging head.
It was soft and warm and whole,
But it was dead.

Christmas

For weeks before it comes I feel excited, yet when it
At last arrives, things all go wrong:
My thoughts don't seem to fit.

I've planned what I'll give everyone and what they'll give to me,
And then on Christmas morning all
The presents seem to be

Useless and tarnished. I had dreamt that everything would come
To life – presents and people too.
Instead of that, I'm dumb.

And people say, 'How horrid! What a sulky little boy!'
And they are right. I *can't* seem pleased.
The lovely shining toy

I wanted so much when I saw it in a magazine
Seems pointless now. And Christmas too
No longer seems to mean

The hush, the star, the baby, people being kind again.
The bells are rung, sledges are drawn,
And peace on earth for men.

Lullaby

Sleep, my baby, the night is coming soon.
Sleep, my baby, the day has broken down.

Sleep now: let silence come, let the shadows form
A castle of strength for you, a fortress of calm.

You are so small, sleep will come with ease.
Hush now, be still now, join the silences.

New poems from COLLECTED POEMS
(1967)

For Love

I did not know the names of love
And now they have grown few.
When I this way or that behave,
I want the meaning too.
I want the definition when
The feelings starts to go.

'Yes now,' 'Yes now,' or 'It has come' –
Lovers have used these names;
But each one thinks he has found some-
thing separate and strange.
In all the lonely darknesses
We think a new truth gleams.

I am worn out with thinking of
The feelings I have had.
Some strange hand seems to grasp my love
And pull it from the bed.
I wait for clear, undreaming nights
And letters now instead.

The Circle

The circle closes
And we are locked in it.
It is complete, it impinges
Only on what it knows, it
Stays always the same size, only
We (cowering in the centre)
Swell and shrink,
Love or are afraid.

All our known worlds
We make circular. They

Complete us. Round
Or flat does not matter.
They are our idea of safety
And of eternity.
It seems then that,
Of all our aphorisms,
This one is true –
The endless is our home.

The Shaking World

Under all this
There is violence.
The chairs, tables, pictures, paper-weights
Are all moving, moving,
You can't see it but they are being carried
Along with currents and continents.
We too are carried (our peace two quarrelling doves)
And nothing, nothing is still.

A Buddhist monk at his most uplifted
High in the Himalayas
Is moved too.
Great wheels of the world bear him round and round.
We have tried to tie the universe to horoscopes
While we whirl between star and star.

A Dream of Birth

It was a coming out to newness,
It was a hatching, a breaking,
I stretched my limbs finally and they came, came
Newmade, I could feel my own pulse.
And the shell around me dissolved, I let it go,
And then I began to feel green things and grow.

A pulse was under my fingers, a baby's, a child's pleasure,
Also a marriage rite was being performed.
I took part in it gently, gently.
In the spine of pleasure, a power was rising, rising,
I watched and the world was warmed.

The Boy

The pulse
Of the city
Beats loudly.
He waits
Leans against shop-doors, on gates,
Watches people boldly, puts
His hand in his belt, feels proud
Of his face and genitals.

The crowd
Moves past
Like low thunder.
Girls too move past.
He is like a young bull under
Some self-chosen yoke.
He will move soon.
An invisible matador will brandish his cloak,
And a girl will throw down a red flower
In the middle of the wide afternoon.

The Operation

The operation is over now:
He lies in clean linen, hands stretched out.
He is asleep still, mercifully.
When he arouses, the pain will be harsh.

Where is he now, in what limbo?
What kind of creatures hover over him?
What dark beasts terrify him?
The ward is hushed to a kind of death.
There is the smell of ether and medicines.

A few huge flowers bow beside him;
They breathe scent, they mean life,
Someone thrust them in a high vase.
They speak, mutely, of life and creation
And go on speaking as their petals fall.

The Novice

She turns her head demurely. In a year
Or two she will
Be able to smile openly at all.
She once enjoyed so much. Now there's a wall,
Also a grille.
Only the narrow, indoor things are clear.

She is not certain yet if she will stay.
She watches those
Who have been living here for many years.
No doubt upon each timeless face appears.
These stayed and chose
And in their suffering learn how to pray.

Upon her window-sill two turtle doves
Gently demur.
All of the noisy world is here brought low
To these quiet birds who come and go
And seem to her
So far removed from all she hates and loves.

Shock

Seeing you cry
Is, for me
Like seeing others die.

You have been changeless, permanent
As the Equator,
Equal to all tides and suns.
Now it is as if you were a volcano
With a shattered crater.

It is elemental – this.
It is like plants budding, animals mating.
There would be fires and stars in a swift kiss,
Your tears are a storm starting.

The Bonfire

It is burning the Winter away.
The smoke is coming like clouds over sea,
It has its own tides,
Its own laws.
There are only small flowers to see:
Nothing like fireworks or stars.

But it is a herald,
An augury.
These tight buds of flame
Will burst later on borders and flower-beds
Most decorously.

All passion is like this —
Like the spent rose
Veering and turning in a bevy of winds
Till the seed overflows.

Volcano and Iceberg

There will be an explosion one day,
This calm exterior will crack,
Seas will come up,
New islands,
New devastations.
This is me, this is me.

Sail round me, yachts, smacks, steamers,
Explorers come nearer,
Seven-eighths of me is below the surface.
One day, soon, that seven-eighths is coming to the top.

So beautiful I am
With my calm face
But I am cold to the touch,
I can also burn you,
I am saying something about stars and climates.
Soon the explosion is coming.
I don't want to be there then.

Gale

There is an inland gale
And I dream of sea-winds and lobsters.
My mind is open to the full
Places, the islands and the harbours:

Also to the lonely ones
The far-off wave
Topped by a bird long-since
Seeming to speak of love.

And of Noah's Ark I dream –
The gentle animals
Two by two they come –
I hear their footfalls.

And last of all the salt
Taste of the sea and Spring
So far inland is felt
Stranger than anything.

THE ANIMALS' ARRIVAL
(1969)

The Animals' Arrival

So they came
Grubbing, rooting, barking, sniffing,
Feeling for cold stars, for stone, for some hiding-place,
Loosed at last from heredity, able to eat
From any tree or from ground, merely mildly themselves,
And every movement was quick, was purposeful, was proposed.
The galaxies gazed on, drawing in their distances.
The beasts breathed out warm on the air.

No one had come to make anything of this,
To move it, name it, shape it a symbol;
The huge creatures were their own depth, the hills
Lived lofty there, wanting no climber.
Murmur of birds came, rumble of underground beasts
And the otter swam deftly over the broad river.

There was silence too.
Plants grew in it, it wove itself, it spread, it enveloped
The evening as day-calls died and the universe hushed, hushed.
A last bird flew, a first beast swam
And prey on prey
Released each other
(Nobody hunted at all):
They slept for the waiting day.

The Day

I get up shaken by all my nightmares,
the day is grey and pushes itself against
my windows. 'Greyness', I say, 'come in,
you have after all merged with magnificent night
and know its contours and stars.' Here there is nothing
but a few awkward objects. I have to salute them
and learn them again and even perhaps love them.

The lunar mysteries seem so far away
and the sun is also hidden. Someone below
is shaking a carpet, someone is clipping the lawn,
Good labours these, and behind the many windows
men are sporting with what their minds contain,
making them almost computers. Noises are what
this world is really mapped with, the scrape on a scythe,
a man whistling, a bird pecking for food,
a carpet-sweeper next door. Down the lane are coming
taxis and lorries. Next door a very old woman
opens the door and smiles at remaining flowers.
Something is plucking her too, beyond the daybreak.
I am my senses letting the day come in.

Sculptor

Not his hands but his face, watch,
It opens suddenly, suddenly,
He knows that something will happen
And with the most gentle touch
And a fierce inward cry
He waits for the clay to open.

Then he is most eloquent,
Hands move, depart, return,
Slowly a statue appears.
Against his clay he is a faint
Force, yet he can make it burn
Like a hundred blazing fires.

He is different with bronze,
Must build up, build up.
The final cast will show
How much he had to arrange.
His hands will fall back, drop,
Only now he begins to know.

A Pattern

A pattern will emerge, is emerging,
Not simply the embroidered sky showing

What we could never do, but in ourselves,
In our thoughts even, there evolves

A strange mystery and the clue to it,
Pick up the images, let them fit.

And let the astounding earth reveal its creatures,
Each with its own peculiar features.

I am, standing here watching, watching
And if I move, everything is touching me, is touching.

First Man

There must be language found for this –
The first man prodding without emphasis,

For soft ground, a warm home,
A kind of living, a rhythm.

Behind him is all
The past painted on a wall –

Intrepid deer, unusual birds
And everything, everything without need of words.

There is a sudden halting. The man has found
Need for a god in the forefront of his mind.

He appears, O the daring and beauty,
This suddenly needed deity.

And man kneels
Knowing that this god heals.

The spreading tree holds the harsh fruit
That will call man and sear him to the root.

A Simple Sickness

Sickness so simple that a child could bear it
And bear it better. There would be so much –
The soldiers flung among the pillows: dolls
Brought to abrupt confusion down the bed,
And violent Chanticleer, *his* voice gone hoarse,
Crowing quite soundlessly at all the farm –
A child would have all this and know it too.

I only have my grown-up troubles now
And grown-up, half-dead words to speak them in.
Illness for me has no true absolute
Since so much of my daily action is
Dressed up in pain. Why am I lying here,
Voice gone, lips dry, chest fiery, mind quite wild
Begging the past back, longing to be a child?

The Plough

Plough there and put your seed in deeply.
The sky wants it and our eyes too.
Look how gently moon shows you to us,
But there is heaving, deep working there.

I watch you from a telescope,
I hold you for an instant
Then I must run to the world of images.
Speculation is gone. It is we who are human
Who named that happy arrangement of stars
The plough and suggested the planting of seeds?

Fire

It is a wild animal,
It is curling round objects,
It is greasy with candles,
And they run trickling down the walls
Making tributaries.
It is as if bad weather were perpetual.

And we found it
Only just in time.
We threw wet rags on the flames
Flung the books out,
Stamped on the sparks.
At last it was over
And we looked at the dead objects.

Not still-lives any more but still-deaths.
Ruin comes so easily and reminds us
We too might have been destroyed;
I picked up a loved book but was dumb to tears.

And today I am numb still
Shocked to silence and lost
From such little tragedy.
Big ones build in the mind;
We are so near to paper
To nothingness
So, in the power of nature
I shall not light candles again for a long time.

Of Languages

That time is approaching just
When the old imperious request
Can be forgotten in an hour of lust:

When the climates of terror retire
And leave only an aching fear
And the huge longing not to be here.

If I were painting I would put
A head down and hands – the paint still wet –
And eyes pleading something to forget.

As it is, with only a dry word I seek yeast for my own bread
Yet find that it has, unnoticed, stirred.

That hour is approaching now
When the language must be sudden and new
And the images sharp, still, slow.

The Soldiers

Sometime they will come.
Maybe upon an easy August day.
They will come swaggering into a room,
Loosen their belts and say,
'We are not what we seem.'

The way that they behave is quite at odds
With all their easy speeches.
Something in this invasion is like the god
Or like a man who preaches,
Catching up all the congregation's moods.

I woke this morning early, could not hear
The noise of soldiers moving round the house.
Silence was simple: it was everywhere
Enclosing us.
And yet within the distance the taut drums
Were trembling for the fingers' throb and stir.

The Unknown Child

That child will never lie in me, and you
Will never be its father. Mirrors must
Replace the real image, make it true –
So that the gentle love-making we do
Has powerful passions and a parents' trust.

That child will never lie in me and make
Our loving careful. We must kiss and touch
Quietly, watch our own reflexions break
As in a pool that is disturbed. Oh take
My watchful love; there must not be too much.

A child lies within my mind. I see
The eyes, the hands. I see you also there,
I see you waiting with an honest care,
Within my mind, within me bodily,
And birth and death close to us constantly.

Never to See

Never to see another evening now
With that quick openness, that sense of peace
That, any moment, childhood could allow.

Never to see the Spring and smell the trees
Alone, with nothing asking to come in
And shake the mind, and break the hour of ease –

All this has gone since childhood began
To go and took with it those tears, that rage.
We can forget them now that we are men.

But what will comfort us in our old age?
The feeling little, or the thinking back
To when our hearts were their own privilege?

It will be nothing quiet, but the wreck
Of all we did not do will fill our lack
As the clocks hurry and we turn a page.

Resolve

So many times I wrote (before I knew
The truth of them) of horror and of fear;
The words came easily, each phrase seemed true,
And yet there was a polar atmosphere,
A coldness at the heart. I knew it too.

Now that I have lived in the midst of pain
And madness, and myself have gone half mad,
I shall not make the same mistake again
Or write so glibly of the sick, the sad.
I want Equators in my writing, rain
Warm from the Tropics, pungent, quick and sane.

Birth

That was a satisfaction of the sense –
That country where no reason reigned at all.
We heard the cries, we saw the apple fall.
This was how every animal begins.

I could put out my hand and touch the source
Of life; intensest pleasure filled my blood.
And then the waking-up: what conscience could
Restrain, it stopped. The throbbing water-course

Was dammed, the sense of drowning played a drum
Deep in my ears, then silence and I came
Like children to a country I could name
Because one trusted voice had whispered 'Come'.

Hospital Garden

This is the first time I have been alone
For one whole month. Summer is really here
And silence too. Yes, you could drop a stone
Into the hazy, humming atmosphere.

They will return – the nurse, the patients too
And I must write down this before they come.
My inward needs and fears still stir and grow
Into a hideous and a nightmare form.

I am not drugged as all the others are.
My naked senses, totally awake,
Respond at once to pleasure and endure
Immediate pain. I know that I must make

My life again. Yes, make myself as well.
(I hear a ringing in the distance stop)
Now for a second I am out of hell
And Limbo too. The screams, the voices drop.

But only for an instant is there peace.
Someone is walking swiftly down the lawn.
Was it a dream that I felt quite at ease?
In the stark day all answers are withdrawn.

Interviews

For S.S.

'You hate him', 'No, you love him', so they say,
Simply because I meet him every week
And talk. We are a doctor, patient and
Know well the various terms on which we speak.

I thought I hated him, but I was wrong;
I found that out one day when he, in pain,
Bore two hours' suffering while I talked on.
I shall not make the same mistake again.

What then is generated by these speeches?
Compassion, pity, envy? None of these.
It is because we know no rock-bare beaches
That we can anchor, fitfully at ease.

The Source

It was as if I went back to the source
Of life. I smelt the things, the strings of birth –
Milk, grass, a stable and a water-course,
And always the rank stench of fertile earth.

Primeval slime found stirring on a rock –
That is how life and history were viewed
By our great-grandfathers. I say a shock,
A flash of nerves, a glimpse of something nude –

All these are nearer to the truth, but still
Something is unexplained. Why should we fear
To love as deeply as we dread to kill?
I do not know. Too many dreams crowd near.

The Broken Minds

These broken minds of which I too am one
Have no power now to shake my faith at all,
I do not ask: What has this person done
That they should have such punishment? The Fall
Explains it all.

But many question how the Fall took place
Or wonder if it is a fancy built
By man to save his reason and his face
And exorcise the sharp, fierce sense of guilt
Of which we are built.

The madness here increases every day;
The screams invade each room, each corridor.
Dreams overlap my waking in a way
That troubles and confuses me much more
Than when the corridor

Is paved with vomit and with broken glass.
Terror has many forms: it can appear
Gently like shadows which discreetly pass
Or as an all embracing atmosphere,
The very absolute of fear.

Cold Winter

I wait and watch. The distances disperse,
Snow is stored up within the lowering sky.
Only still life would seem to spill and lie
Waiting for someone to observe it there,
Stand for a moment, warm behind thin glass.

Chatter of birds, cars in the distance hum
Yet everything seems moving in my head.
This is the silent season when the dead
Slip from their bodies in a cold dark room,
What once was life is memory instead.

And yet one shift of snow, one shaft of light
And all I know of Spring comes back to me.
It is as if my arms could be a tree,
Bearing and blossoming within the night
And then at daylight struggling to be free.

Loving

Loving, I return
Years back into a time
Where only the young burn
While the old ones rhyme.

I have thought too much
Of this thing and of that.
I become out of touch
And everything seems flat:

Is it? Or do I
Change what I half-perceive,
Half-look, so falsify
And keep up my sleeve

Mask, tricks and children's games.
(I know the tricks of some)
Yet with my passions, dreams,
I am silent, struck dumb.

Hunting

All night long they are hunting in the dark,
The doctors, patients, nurses, children, and birds.
Some are flying in actual forests and some
Are merely moving in conversation or dreams.

But all are searching, all have weapons or traps,
Most have become quite expert at their sport.
For some it is not a sport but life itself –
For the birds, I mean, and perhaps the children too.

What will they do when they finally run it down,
Stare in the steady, gleeful eyes of the foe?
Will the ropes, the stones, the shot, the bullets, the words,
The dangerous dreams, be enough for its overthrow?

Ago

Old.
Few years more attend me, I am redundant
A useless tool, a broken body, seedless.
Look at me and you see a season regretting.

I foresaw this once
But it was not like this. I saw
An age of goodness, of gifts spent out and needed.
Age is a going back.

Is a kind of return,
To the breast, the womb, the mother.
I do without all and face the Winter regretting.
The child in me who can play no longer.

Waking

I have woken out of this cunning sleep;
Beasts – heraldic – formed my memories.
My nightmares were masters. No servant tended them
But they demanded my coherence and clear acceptance.
I am awake, awake among crumpled sheets.

The beasts in my mind, the acts will not leave me,
A moment ago I was running
Down green lawns to a sheer cliff,
I stopped with my feet on the edge of the grass
And behind, behind

One nameless pursued me, went over the cliff,
And wingless flew to a certain death.
Meanwhile my fingers turned on the sheets.
I was coming alive, I was coming to.
The nightmares were ending.

So we make globes and so they are visited.
In the shape of the skull, the lobes of the brain;
Worlds are forming on numerous pillows,
And what if we met each other within them –
What cliffs there would be, what deaths, what encounters!

Bonnard

Colour of rooms. Pastel shades. Crowds. Torsos at ease in
brilliant baths. And always, everywhere the light.

This is a way of creating the world again, of seeing differences,
of piling shadow on shadow, of showing up distances, of bringing
close, bringing close.

A way of furnishing too, of making yourself feel at home – and
others. Pink, flame, coral, yellow, magenta – extreme colours
for ordinary situations. This is a way to make a new world.

Then watch it. Let the colours dry, let the carpets collect a
little dust. Let the walls peel gently, and people come, innocent,
nude, eager for bed or bath.

They look newmade too, these bodies, newborn and innocent.
Their flesh-tints fit the bright walls and floors and they take
a bath as if entering the first stream, the first fountain.

Matador

He will come out with grace and music.
Watch his clothes fit him,
How he struts before you,
Now he is proud, proud.

No matter what happens,
Whatever blood is shed,
There will always be elegance;
This is what we have come for,
This is his *raison d'être*.

Oh I am thrilled by the excited air,
By the trumpets, the voices.
We are near to death here yet strangely, strangely,
It is life we celebrate.
We vaunt and taunt the rainbow spectacle,
Olé, olé, olé.

Sand

It is falling through my hand,
It is stretching along beaches,
The tide draws and drags it
But look, look,
I have caught it in my fingers.
I am holding the tides.

But wait, wait,
There is order here also.
The glass holds the sand,
The sand holds the sea.
At night the moon intervenes
But it cannot break my glass.

Only I can do that
But I am holding the sea at a distance.

This Summer

It is endless – this Summer.
Roses topple over and their petals
Strew the lawn, scar the turf.
Wasps are beginning to swarm.

And at night we feel
All the heats subdued under the stars.
Flies batter against lampshades,
Moths make huge shadows.

And in our sleeps (O enter them, enter them)
There are strange losses and searches,
A feverish hunting, an unquiet pulse,
Then the warm morning suddenly waiting.

The Sea

It is over there, far out.
It comes at us in hints, in salt and sounds
Or a few birds playing carry it
As the dove carried the olive-branch.
It is calm, calm from here.
We are safe inland.

But if we move toward the beach
A thousand shells will ring out the music of distance,
Shingle will slide, sand be fingered.
It is all, all there.

You can watch it for ever.
It is the symbol of variety,
Never, never the same,
And if you enter it and let the waves cover you
A spectrum of colour appears.
This is a science of seeing.

Anything can be likened to it, birth, death, love,
Most of all love.
Those breakers carry pure sound and pleasure,
Then they recede to gentleness.
But the sea is never subdued.

Demands

Perhaps I ask
That life shall always
Excite, enchant.
I do not want
Drab, calm days,
The facile task.

Yet what I have
Now, this hour
Is still, is smooth,
Days pass with
Ease I deplore.
And so with love –

It has become
A matter of
Patience, waiting
And I am getting
A kind of love
I did not dream

Quite possible.
Absence has made
This mood, and you,
Withdrawn into
A different need,
Have made me feel

And learn also
That love in dead,
Dark times can grow.

Lodgings

It isn't my house; only part of it
Contains a few of my own possessions –
A shadow flitting across the window,
An owl at night tending my ears,
And the books and papers I brought in with me.
I have no roots here. I do not fit.

And when I am lonely, loneliness is
Worse than at home, it brings all dreads,
Everything suddenly seems unfamiliar,
Even a letter I may be writing,
Even the doorbell ringing for me,
And the light on that opposite unfolding tree.

The Nightmares

They are coming slowly, slowly.
No act of faith is needed to credit them.
They inhabit your skull.

They inhabit your skull and people it,
People it not with shadows but with sharp light:
Your best moments are perverted.
You wake – sweating.

And turning, turning, you cry in a way children never do
Nor wild men.
There is a sad sophistication in it.
There is too much knowledge.
You stretch and reach to corruption.

Outside

Out there the darkness,
Here warmth, stillness,
Out there, frozen to still life
The world halts.
Inside the fire imitates the sun.
All South is there.
Outside no barometer,
No measurement for ship or bird,
No compass.

We move and fall in love
But our love is careful.
It has to be shielded
As you shield the flame of a lamp,
But it is entrance,
And central also
The great silence
The long nights.
Touching is always a caress, a warming.
Some lonely planet must be like this also.
I could not contend with it.

Silence of Winter

It grips hands, feet, whole body,
It reaches the heart by a quick route,
It makes portraits of faces, rearranging features
And always, always is quiet.

Soft, let the footsteps sink in the snow,
Let the voices disappear into whispers;
Think of the animals huddling in hibernation.
Of birds making small spurts for a crumb,
Of children hidden in mufflers.

It seems forever – this;
It seems as if fires will burn for ever,
As if logs will tumble to ashes.
Far off ships look for shelter and signals
And men are alive on their decks.

Transfigurations

The words will have to come without much ease –
Difficulty of tongue, an aching hand.
Sometimes they will not come at all, I know,
Merely belong to birds and far-off seas.
I shall be silent standing on the cliff.

And gulls will come and seem like symbols then.
I must know they are no such things, I must
Thrust them to their rock ledge once again
And hear the sea uninterrupted, coming
White, without words but meaning messages.

And I must learn a kind of morse, a signal,
Think of long strings being plucked, of the wheel turning
Bringing the pot to life. I shall need my fingers
But still not heed my older languages.
Hush for the silence in between the trees.

One word, perhaps, will come after this silence,
After this stillness; I must cherish it
And think how all the swooping of the gulls,
The sea, the cliff-top moved towards this end
And learn also how stars possess a pulse.

A Letter to Peter Levi

Reading your poems I am aware
Of translucencies, of birds hovering
Over estuaries, of glass being spun for huge domes.
I remember a walk when you showed me
A tablet to Burton who took his own life.
You seem close to fragility yet have
A steel-like strength. You help junkies,
You understand their language,
You show them the stars and soothe them.
You take near-suicides and talk to them,
You are on the strong side of life, yet also the brittle,
I think of blown glass sometimes but reject the simile.
Yet about your demeanour there is something frail,
The strength is within, won from simple things

Like swimming and walking.
Your pale face is like an icon, yet
Any moment, any hour, you break to exuberance,
And then it is our world which is fragile:
You toss it like a juggler.

These Silences

And they are there always, these silences:
Between drum and flute they utter their echoes,
Between voice and voice intervene with a laugh,
I have considered sometimes how one might catch them
As a note in music, a pause in feeling.
We are passionate men but need these intervals,
Our children break them with their first cry.

In each other's arms, lovers achieve them,
A haunting, a hunting, they are sure.
Beasts lurk in the long wait, or pursue their resting place.
Moments of peace are allowed like this.
I have felt them at night under many stars,
Under many truces, after all passion.

Once in the desert a man dragged himself
Far to oasis, his clothes gone to ribbons,
At first he wept with dry lips calling,
Then parched, as forever, gripped the sand in his fingers.
Water was scraped. Oh, water is silence
Or at least its likeness. He quenched his thirst.

Congo Nun Raped

This man tore open what I fiercely closed
Ten years ago. I do not hate him though
I lie here bleeding, cruelly exposed.

I chose cold weather just ten years ago
And he brought heat and sweat and nightmares too.
Why was I quick to him? I had been slow.

His seed is in me and a child may grow
Within nine months. I weep my vows away.
Fear fills me, all the statues seem to sway.

O God of love, what is it that I know?

Motor-Racer

It contains your intelligence,
The wheels spin, the gears hold,
Nothing is by chance.

From a distance one might
Suppose oneself on another planet
Or at the centre of the night.

Love, desire, all our human wants
Are in the movement, the sliding over oil.
Also in every distance.

Think yourself there, the perfect control
With the road spinning out for you
And with the whole

Globe, it seems, waiting for you to take over.
You watch, watch, then suddenly pounce
Either as enemy or as lover.

Mediterranean

Yes it is hard to believe
There are no tides, and yet
Its many moods convey
Sometimes a sense
Of a lithe suppleness
That always falls back to
Exactly the same place.

To this sea edge the sun
Is moon and draws along
Our helpless flesh and minds.

Our minds grow small, and bodies
Stretch to complete themselves.
They need this kind of sun,
Bold eyes and genitals
Ready to fling themselves
At once into embraces.
Yet everyone's apart
However much they cling.
The storm the sun demands
Is in the single heart.

Any Poet's Epitaph

It does this, I suppose – protects
From the rough message, coarseness, grief,
From the sigh we would rather not hear too much,
And from our own brief gentleness too.

Poetry – builder, engraver, destroyer,
We invoke you because like us
You are the user of words; the beasts
But build, mate, destroy, and at last
Lie down to old age or simply sleep.

Coins, counters, Towers of Babel,
Mad words spoken in sickness too –
All are considered, refined, transformed,
On a crumpled page or a wakeful mind,
And stored and given back – and true.

LUCIDITIES
(1970)

Light

To touch was an accord
Between life and life;
Later we said the word
And felt arrival of love
And enemies moving off.

A little apart we are,
(Still aware, still aware)
Light changes and shifts.
O slowly the light lifts
To show one star
And the darkness we were.

For My Dead Father

I reached you a moment and gently spoke.
You turned and from your half-world came back.
It seemed that you had learnt the knack
Of being near death: no tears broke.
I kissed you and it was strange,
I had all my emotions to rearrange.

Hate and fear quickly receded.
We were at one as never before.
I wanted more of this for you, more.
It appeared though that I really needed
The sudden joy and affection,
A child again with a fresh attraction.

Now you have finally gone away.
I cannot apologise for all that went wrong
Between us. Nor can I wring
A false tear from false dismay.
There was love now I see of a strange kind.
We could move about in each other's mind.

Considerations

Some say they find it in the mind,
A reason why they should go on.
Others declare that they can find
The same in travel, art well done.

Still others seek in sex or love
A reciprocity, relief.
And few, far fewer daily, give
Themselves to God, a holy life.

But poetry must change and make
The world seem new in each design.
It asks much labour, much heartbreak,
Yet it can conquer in a line.

Literary Fashions

A youth of prizes, smiles, and generous praise –
Now it has gone and others must take over
The stance of prowess and the famous days.

Oneself, feeling like a discarded lover
But still in love it needs the strongest will
To live this role and learn that one must suffer

Neglect, dispraise. I know all this and feel
Some starlike patience must be found at last
And reached and held and lived through. I could fill

So many pages in the happy past.

Port Meadow, Oxford
Summer evening

End of day and still the people passed
With open shirts and rosy faces open
To sun that had a few short hours to last.

So much was green and so much seemed to happen
Gently, as in a southern country where
The sunburn comes so easily, to deepen

Everyone with a light out of the air.
We are not used to this but we delight
In grateful warmth; we are so happy here.

There is a glow, a vision for our sight.

For George Seferis, Greek Poet

I learnt his ancient language when at school
And in long dreams could see the Parthenon
And the Acropolis. His poems fill
Me with the sense of sea, of sky, of sun.

Great men are often tardy with their truths
But he comes out before us, speaks his mind
About his country's many troubles with
A wisdom that can never be defined.

Poets in their middle years encounter much
That hurts and bruises them. But older men
Like this find a tranquillity to touch
And write of it and give it back again.

Moving In

They come in, box by box —
China, glass, furniture,
A carpet, a lot of books,
And then, in the dusty air
There suddenly appears
A debris of knick-knacks.

These are things which could never
Wholly be parted from.
To lose them would be to sever
All that really means home.
My thoughts suddenly are
'I am unhappy here.'

Letters of welcome stand
Over the fire-place,

Books, now composed in rows,
Lie ready to my hand.
I feel as if some sudden grace
Should show how a life grows.

Revival

I think it has returned
Though I scarcely dare say it.
I am speaking of the gift of verse.

Words are once again arriving,
Like leaves, like flowers, like dearest friends.
Such a return, so sudden, is almost unbearable.

But I rejoice, I am happy, I am so grateful.
Now, perhaps, I can give back again
A little of what I owe to so many.

Forebodings

I am tired but I cannot sleep.
Within me, there is some strange deep

Love, tenderness – call it what you will –
Under its influence, I cannot lie still,

Nor rest at all when the dreams of the whole
Universe appear, perhaps falsely, to enter my soul.

And yet, what does this all amount to in the end?
Perhaps merely a child with a shaking castle to defend.

Weeping

You burst into tears and my first reaction was shock.
One does not often see a man cry but when
It happens, one's whole universe falls, rocks.

At first I was completely helpless, and then
Though you had spoken harsh words to me, I knew
I must somehow comfort you and learn your pain.

You were weeping, you said, because you had certain true
But wounding words to speak. I could scarcely bear
The revelation; but I always trusted you.

I have learnt so much from seeing one man's tear.

Harsh Words

To suffer without understanding why,
To feel the wound and yet be helpless still,
To hear harsh words and not know the reply –

Such are perhaps what make an artist will
His self-destruction. Yet he does not hate,
Nor does he wish to waste his gracious skill.

Sensitive, yes, but be content to wait
Till tears stop falling, sobs themselves at last
Die down to stillness, finally abate –

This is the needful thing but some are pressed
Beyond endurance; then they take their lives.
Their work becomes but something in the past.

The lesson is that suffering survives.

In Retrospect and Hope

When I look back at my past work
I find that the poem I like best
Is one about fountains in Rome.
It seems to me to contain a life-time's reflection,
A true adjustment of art to self.

For years I had been exercised
About the meaning of power, its secret depths;
Then, one day, Maundy Thursday,

The fountains leapt in my mind,
The waters came to life.

I wish all my verse could be like this;
Too often it is hurried, shaken,
Too often it speaks of things
That it would be better for me to forget,
Art for me is that strength, that summoning fountain.

And when love comes into my work
I want passion sufficiently tamed
So that the form, the music are never lost,
When I was a child I wrote verse easily,
Now, every day, new problems enter in.

One day, perhaps, I shall be serene.
My old images – aged women, flowing waters, flowers,
Will find a world in which they can all meet.
But compassion must crown all this
And a great power enter, enter.

A Decision

This is my love and now it must be spoken.
I love you, I have loved you many years.
Now all my love is lapped around with tears.
There are so many things that have been broken.

Love is possession or it partly is.
This I know well and this I understand.
I can't forget our former ecstasies
Or see in what way they can ever end.

My morning fantasies are always full
Of what we did together. I suppose
I must forget all this, give it repose,
Yet keep our love, our passion, constant still.

Is this a dream or is it possible?
I see your face within my heart so clear,
I think we must be chaste yet loving still,
And only thus shall you and I endure.

Revelation

The love, the sun, the beauty and it all
Seems to mean nothing. I am in
A country – Spain – where one could say the Fall

Had never happened. I perceive this, then,
Watch how clear lust shines in a man's hot eyes
Which gaze towards a woman with her thin

Dress and petticoat, her simple breasts
Showing what grown-up women cannot hide –
The place on which a man or baby rests.

The mind is there but thought is set aside.

An Experience

It seems strangely like a flower
Yet I cannot at once
Identify it at all.

I feel like an astronomer
Who knows there is a star in the sky
But cannot remember its name,

But it comes back. It *has* come back;
This is the delicate scent of honeysuckle –
The first flower I ever saw.

How potent it suddenly seems,
Bearing my early memories,
Bearing a child's happiness.

Evening Prayer, by Rimbaud

Like an angel at the barber's shop, I am sitting here;
My neck and stomach are curved and between my teeth
Is a pipe. And I have, of course, a great mug of beer.
Smoke is floating high up, low down and beneath.

Like the dung of doves, strange dreams burn within
My mind. And at times, indeed, my heart overflows,
Like the sap of a tree which seeps out again and again.
My tears are thus, but I do not know why they arose.

After thirty or forty tankards, I rise to relieve
My great need. I have drunk too much, it is true.
Slowly, carefully, I pull myself to life.

Like a great god, I piss towards the new
Stars. The sky is higher than one can perceive.
Enormous flowers approve the act I do.

The Sly One, by Rimbaud

In the dark dining-room with its scent
Of polish and fruit, I was very heartily
Enjoying some Belgian food, and, to me, it meant
Pleasure, life given and accepted free.

As I ate, I listened to the gentle but imperious clock.
The door opened and a girl entered with the gust
Of wind. She certainly had not come in to mock
Or, indeed, to do her best to excite my lust.

Shaking, she passed her finger over her cheek –
Which was pink and white and quietly sleek;
Her mouth pouted, so much like that of a child.

She stood close to me, tidying away the dishes.
She wished for my comfort but also to feel our flesh
Touching. All she said was 'My cheek is chilled.'

Sensation, from Rimbaud

I will go down the paths in Summer and get
Pricked by the corn, feel the crushed grass.
Some kind of reverie will make me wet
My feet. And the wind will bless, will bless.

I shall not think or speak, but a great
Love will fill me; I shall travel far
Like a gipsy and feel grateful for what simple women are.

First Evening, by Rimbaud

She was half-undressed;
A few indiscreet trees
Threw out their shadows and displayed
Their leaves, cunningly and close.

She sat, half-naked in my chair,
She clasped her hands,
And her small feet shook
Where the floor bends.

I watched, on her lips
And also on her breast
A stray light flutter
And come to rest.

First, it was her ankles I kissed;
She laughed gently, and then
Like a bird she sang
Again and again.

Her feet withdrew and,
In an odd contradiction
She said 'Stop, do.'
Love knows such affliction.

I kissed her eyes.
My lips trembled, so weak.
Then she opened her lips again and said,
'There are words I must speak.'

This was too much, too much.
I kissed her breast and, at once,
She was tender to my touch.
She did not withdraw or wince.

Her clothes had fallen aside,
But the great trees threw out their leaves.
I am still a stranger to love,
Yet this was one of my loves.

My Bohemian Life, after Rimbaud
A fantasy

The pockets of my coat were torn; I thrust my hands
Into them, and then travelled far under the sky.
I was indeed a servant to verse and certainly I
Had dreams of love such as no one understands.

One pair of trousers I had, I went on my way rhyming.
The Great Bear was my inn; I could do all the climbing.
My stars in the sky rustled, made the world whole.
In September, at roadsides, I would listen to stars,
Happy on the roadsides I would pass.
Sweat on my forehead seemed like wine with powers

Mysterious. Among the shadows I went
Still rhyming. My boot-strings seemed a lyre which was meant
To help. Near my heart one foot was and it felt like flowers.

The Rooks, by Rimbaud

When the meadow is cold, Lord, and when
The Angelus is no longer heard,
I beg you to let it come,
This delightful kind of bird –
The rook – and here make its home.
One, many, sweep down from the skies.

Such an odd army – you birds.
You have very strange voices.
Cold winds attack your nests,
Yet come, I implore, as if words
Were your medium. Where the river rests,
Dry and yellow, by Crosses

And ditches, come forward, come
In your thousands, over dear France
Where many are still asleep.
This is truly your home.
Wheel over so that a chance
Traveller may see the deep

Meaning within you all.
Be those who show men their duty,
And also reveal the world's beauty.
You, all of you
(And I know this is true)
Are the dark attendants of a funeral.

You, saints of the sky,
Of the oak tree, of the lost mast,
Forget about those of the Spring,
Bring back hope to the lost
Places, to those who feel nothing
But that defeat is life's cost.

Bedsitters

How many people nearly reach the rope,
Lonely in lodgings? How many almost try
To reach the stage that is beyond all hope?

Not many, but enough of them will die –
Students perhaps and others who demand
That we should look into their tragedy.

Imagine bed and breakfast, gas-stoves and
Long hours when no one comes at all to speak.
Death must at such times seem most close at hand.

Some try to make a gaiety to break
The ugly wall-papers, the furniture;
But still they lie long hours in bed awake,

Thinking of love perhaps, some overture
To prove that their existence is no fake.

Mrs Porter

A woman over eighty with a mind
Clear as a child's, and with a sympathy
Gentle, courageous, always quick and kind.

You are that one, my Mrs Porter, the
Old lady with the trembling hands but with
No fear of anything. Your charity

Moves out from where you speak with shaking breath,
And touches us, two friends who listen to
Your conversation, talk of life and death,

But most of all of love and friendship. True
Discernment showed in every word you spoke,
And you made ancient things seem very new.

When you had gone, the gladness, sweetness broke.

To One Who Read My Rejected Autobiography

For Veronica Wedgwood

The publishers returned it; they were right.
So much was egotistical, naive.
Yet you, with all the artist's pure insight,
Saw that I never meant to hurt, deceive.

You read my words and saw that I was trying
To strive towards some aspect of the truth.
You saw that there was no pretence, no lying,
Simply a poet's childhood and youth.

I see the faults, I see the repetitions,
I know I could not say all that I wanted
About my father. There would need additions.
I could not write them, I was too much haunted.

But you observed that there was value here,
Here in this childish tale of love and grief.
I wish that I could thank you for your care
And tell you the great gift you gave – relief.

Vocations

For H.

Of human love – you know it all
Although you may have never known
The pleasure reaching to the bone.
You have a call, you have a call.

Transcending and yet feeling still –
This is the hardest thing, I think.
Your days are busy, you can fill
Each minute up and leave no chink.

Love is for me a constant strain
I have the urge to reach, to touch
And feel the ecstasy again
Come riding back, almost too much,

Almost unbearable. But I
Know that my fantasies engage
My thoughts too constantly. I try
To give my heart a pilgrimage,
To walk along distances and find
Rough stone, rich blossom. Cleansing comes
And enters deftly in the mind.
Christ said that there were many rooms

In his great house. And it is true
And each of them is always new.

Analysis of a Situation

There was a point where everything went wrong –
A word, an act, some insufficiency.
And ever since that time the gift of song
Has come with more and more anxiety.
I wish that I could put a finger on
The trouble, but I can't, some deed has done

Me damage – possibly an act of love
Not fully felt, leaving frustration and
Imagination. We are made up of
Such acts as these. So what has gone awry?
Imprudence or impatience, or perhaps
Simply the ordinary, human traps?

It does not matter; not, at least, if one
Can feel and then accept and further yet,
Learn from the hurt experience has done.
And most of all, maybe, one should forget
And let poems come like flowers which need the sun.

This World

We need to know, we need to feel.
There are great purposes about
And much confusion, much to doubt.
Somebody has to help, to heal.

And personal love is tainted with
A strange despair. I do not know
What forces bring this kind of death.
Animals, flowers, content to grow

In simple ignorance seem all
This planet bears of innocence.
Compassion is the only way
Back to new knowledge and contents.

The stars are out and clear tonight,
The moon is halved. It seems a time
When revelations swiftly come.
Yet it deceives, this light, this light.

We who are lucky calmly live,
Or fairly calmly. Round the world
Men starve and shoot. There seems a hold
Of violence that cannot give.

Lovers and friends meet and depart
And students talk the night away.
It is within our minds, some day
Must flare and blossom with the heart.

Rouault

Rouault, you are a painter of darkness and suffering. Yet you have not the darkness of Rembrandt. There is hope always.

Christ beside the waters, a Madonna and child, a king crowned – these are some of your subjects. And in them all, in them all, there is a sure, strange black outline.

You have a precedence, a princely power over colour and light. In your etchings of the *Miserere* there is, too, so much knowledge of suffering, so much understanding of Christ made Man.

Out of shadows, your colours come, and they illumine, they illumine. I feel very close to you; I feel you understood our present predicaments. I know also that you knew much about God.

The Future

That the gift should go,
That words should cease to arrive,
Poems fail to be alive,
All thought be slow –

I am afraid
Sometimes that this might happen,
That the flower will cease to open,
The world no longer be glad.

Some old men
Have written their best work in their late years;
Like children, they seem close then to laughter and to tears.
I hope this may happen

If I live to be old.
I hope the time may return
When, as in childhood, poems would burn, burn,
And I could still mould

A shapely verse and scan
And sometimes not scan, but still
Make a poem that might fill, fill
Both woman and man.

This Darkness

This darkness
Falls upon me suddenly.

When it will come, I do not know.
I only know that the dark, the dark comes

And suggests doubts and even death.
I have seen it in others but never before

Such a night in myself. No dark night of the soul
But something spread from the world around me.

How do I deal with it? How can I stop these continual tears?
God seems far away and friends are no substitute.

I must wait, wait, try to be patient
And gentle even with my own unhappiness.

But there are no stars in this sky
And no moon, either a slit or a circle.

Doubts

A child, I suffered them. They seemed to me
To show a sudden absence of my God.
I did not dare to look too carefully.
Only I longed to think, be understood.

One afternoon I lay upon my bed
And thought of what the Holy Ghost could mean.
A spirit? No, a monstrous bird. Instead
Of peace, the shades began to intervene.

From that day onwards, I could not take one
Doctrine on trust; I questioned each and all.
Perhaps my adolescence had begun.
And I was now admitted to the Fall.

I took the Host and in a frantic prayer
Said, 'Yes I do believe, I do believe.'
There was no sign of Christ or angel there,
Nor anything that spoke to me of love.

In Rome much later, I confessed my sins
And heard compassionate words. My faith came back.
Is this how each return to God begins?
Perhaps to know no desert is a lack.

Rain

Beautiful rain
Falling so softly
Such a delicate thing

The harvests need you
And some of the flowers
But we too

Because you remind
Of coolness and quiet
Of tenderest words

Come down rain, fall
Not too harshly but give
Your strange sense of peace to us.

Stillness

Only man can make stillness
The trees, the beasts obey him
Only man can order and command.

The first men and the last
Need stillness for their prayers
God exists in it.

Yet wait wait look look
How that petal fell without a noise
How that cat entered without a sound.

Passions

They walk into the meadows two by two
To see the sunset. Also they admire
The quiet air, the gently shaded view.

And then they think of love and of desire,
Of love that they will make a little later.
The sun has turned into a ball of fire.
Love has its violence much like the crater
Of a volcano, but always, later, it
Moves into something gentle, some sweet thing.

We understand so little of the great
Passions that grip us. Love is born with hate.

I Am Myself

I am myself, no other man or woman.
I gaze into the past and see a wall
With animals and men and view them all
As signs of being symbolist and human.
That is the way. That is the garden tall.
Each flower and tree seems now to me an omen.

I love and tell my love. The other comes
Responding to the languages I speak.
There are a hundred thousand different rooms
Where men sit waiting for the final stake.
I speak, I love. I know so many dooms,
So many ways of learning one's heartbreak.

Longings

I am left over
I am a second child
I am singing to a vague tune
I am afraid of men

This August discourses
Of rain and wind
I long for the Summer
The South, the sea
They are too far away
I am lonely, lonely

Child that I was come back
Be at my side
But be more than a shadow
Be a constant guide
I am afraid, afraid
I want my ghosts laid.

The Children

I watched them playing, each with gloves well tied
And hanging down. Each boxed a little, then
Showed how a child's face has peace of mind.
Their toys were scanty yet they could begin

A complex game, a place of stars and spheres,
Also of guns, I watched each separate face,
Noted how little violence there was
And how each sense could fit its proper place.

Always I watch them – children on the run
Or slowed to sleep. I like to see the look
Of peace they have beneath the moon or sun.
They force aside my poetry, my book.

Misfits

What of those ones who in the world
Can find no niche, no place at all?
They have no vow on which to hold

Like the religious. O the Fall
Has so confused us, and we know
So little of each kind of call.

We watch, we live, and poets grow
A kind of strength that holds and heals.
I question why we suffer so
But who'd surrender *that* he feels?

Journey through Warwickshire to Oxford

Beautiful trees, abundant still and green
In this October. As the train flashed by
I watched the rich and almost Summer scene.

There was so much here which absorbed the eye –
Late corn, some sheep, a lake, and all of it
Brought on a mood of happiness. We try

So hard in Winter to keep warm, stay fit
But now the only need is joy and thanks.
To give our gratitude is to permit
The attitude to fit the circumstance.

RELATIONSHIPS
(1972)

Relationships

Understanding must be on both sides,
Confidence with confidence, and every talk
Be like a long and needed walk
When flowers are picked, and almost – asides
Exchanged. Love is always like this
Even when there's no touch or kiss.

There are many kinds of relationships
But this is the best, as Plato said –
Even when it begins in a bed,
The gentle touching of hands and lips –
It is from such kindness friendship is made
Often, a thing not to be repaid

Since there is no price, no counting up
This and that, gift. Humility
Is the essential ability
Before the loved object. Oh, we can sip
Something that tastes almost divine
In such pure sharing – yours and mine.

Friendship

Such love I cannot analyse;
It does not rest in lips or eyes,
Neither in kisses nor caress.
Partly, I know, it's gentleness

And understanding in one word
Or in brief letters. It's preserved
By trust and by respect and awe.
These are the words I'm feeling for.

Two people, yes, two lasting friends.
The giving comes, the taking ends.
There is no measure for such things.
For this all Nature slows and sings.

Upon a Thread

His life hangs on a slender thread;
A jerk upon a step and he
(It is a chance) might soon be dead.
This is his health and destiny.

He is a man of God and so
Has trust, can meditate, say Mass.
For him there is no dread although
He has a natural cautiousness.

But what about the ones who care
And love him, do not want to lose
His inner strength? It's they who fear
And keep on praying, yet refuse,

At times, acceptance of the fact –
The jerk, the trip upon the stair.
A silken thread, a simple act
And then he is no longer there.

A Sonnet

Run home all clichés, let the deep words come
However much they hurt and shock and bruise.
There is a suffering we can presume,
There is an anger, also, we can use;
There are no categories for what I know
Hunted by every touch on memory.
A postcard can produce a heartbreak blow
And sentiment comes seething when I see
A photograph, a Christmas card or some
Association with this loss, this death.
I must live through all this and with no home
But what he was, keep holding on to breath.
Once the stars shone within a sky I knew.
Now only darkness is my sky, my view.

Let Things Alone

You have to learn it all over again,
The words, the sounds, almost the whole language
Because this is a time when words must be strict and new
Not concerning you,
Or only indirectly,
Concerning a pain
Learnt as most people some time or other learn it
With shock, then dark.

The flowers will refer to themselves always
But should not be loaded too much
With meaning from happier days.
They must remain themselves,
Dear to the touch.
The stars also
Must go on shining without what I now know.
And the sunset must simply glow.

Narcissus

Narcissus,
You gazed in a pool once and saw
Your own reflection magnified.
But you saw more than this only;
There was also
The crystalline presence, the glorious loving
Of self and self.
All this Caravaggio also saw
And painted.

Much of our lives is lived
In such vivid gazes,
But it is not enough,
Not enough.
We need to go beyond that translucence
And beyond the delightful waters
See others, see others.

For children, the self is sufficient,
But now, later,
There must be a turning away,
A turning towards another.
Throw a pebble in the stream and then
Look behind you. The world is there.

For Emily Dickinson

She managed it, be
Her world within,
That of a solitary,
Never yearn,

Or not appear to,
For someone by.
She did not fear to
Be alone, lie

Apart. What dreams
By night or day
May, in what seems
The perfect way

To work, to write,
Have come. There were
A few loves, bright
As a star to stir

Her lonely choice,
She wrote, she wrote,
Keeping a voice
Unique, unsought

From any school
Or anyone;
The world a stool
She sat upon.

And turned it to
A royal throne.
Suffering she knew,
Being alone.

The Sea

The sea – so it comes in, the moon trailing it
Or, rather, controlling it.
It goes in and out
Leaving rock-pools
Where we plunge for prawns.

But the Mediterranean
Is not like this.
It is not tidal
Except in a very small way.

Nevertheless, it can have 'White Horses',
Huge breakers against which
Even the rocks and jetties are defenceless.

As for the ships, there are on occasion
Great disasters,
Huge shipwrecks.

It reminds us of so many things – the ocean.
Perhaps love most of all.
The pull and thrust and then the gentle
Subsidence of waves
To a clear, cool wash
Of foam on the sand,
A sudden stillness.

But not for long;
All night through and all day through
The waters can seethe.

It is as if there were a reciprocity,
A continual battling –
Spiral, foam, and then a climax
Lasting a second,

Lasting a lifetime
Perhaps in memory.
Such a union of all the elements,
Such a peace, however short-lived.

And then, in northern waters,
When the tide has gone far out,
People wade, especially children,
Searching for shells and prawns.

Seaweed smells strange. Some of it
Pops at a touch. You can sit
For quite a long time on such beaches.
But the moon is really the power
And the star-satellites support it.

Yet, above everything else,
The sea satisfies every sense,
Specially the salt on the lips,
The swell of the waves on the body.
No wonder the Greeks called 'Thalassa',
Viewing the sea at last.

And though that is all in the past,
The sea has such hints, such symbols,

But alone it moves on without need
Of human words or surrender.
It swirls about our planet
Moving us, moved by the moon.

A Wonder

How much God leans on us;
I do not mean alone
The coming to atone,
But placing so much trust

In changing into bread,
In turning into wine.
Within these fingers, mine,
I hold the whole Godhead.

And when I take the cup
I see what God will risk
Within a tiny disc,
How much is yielded up.

I feel there is no speech
For this, and yet I do
Use words for what is true
Though almost out of reach.

In Memory of Anyone Unknown to Me

At this particular time I have no one
Particular person to grieve for, though there must
Be many, many unknown ones going to dust
Slowly, not remembered for what they have done
Or left undone. For these, then, I will grieve
Being impartial, unable to deceive.

How they lived or died is quite unknown,
And, by that fact gives my grief purity –
An important person quite apart from me
Or one obscure who drifted down alone.
Both or all I remember, have a place.
For these I never encountered face to face.

Sentiment will creep in. I cast it out
Wishing to give these classical repose,
No epitaph, no poppy and no rose
From me, and certainly no wish to learn about
The way they lived or died. In earth or fire
They are gone. Simply because they were human, I admire.

Water

How many forms you assume.
So simple, so harmless you can be,
Yet you are the sea, you are fountains,
You are what quenches fire,
You are what satisfies thirst.

And from many things you come –
A tap, a stream, a water-diviner's magic
Which draws you deep from the earth;
How you cool the face and fingers.
How you delight a child.

But you can be rough also,
In fierce rainstorms, in the sea's White Horses.
Your forms are so many, it sometimes seems
You are the source and end of all things.

All Quarrels

Children throw toys
Adults throw words
We are all girls and boys;
We have no magic birds

To send in peace. In fact
We can only smile and touch
Before the dreadful act.
A dove could mean so much.

Making a Silence

Making a silence
So many different kinds
One that a child may sleep
Another to help someone sick.

So many silences
When everyone else is sleeping
And you can feel the stars
And mercy over the world.

But the greatest one of them all
Is a gift entirely unasked for,
When God is felt deeply within you
With his infinite gracious peace.

This happened to me tonight
And now, now, I am so grateful.

Sympathy

How many people cry themselves to sleep
For broken love-affairs or loneliness?
How many of us sink into the deep

Depression when we long for a caress
Or else a word encouraging us to
Go on, in spite of words of heartlessness?

Not only artists know that this is true,
But almost everyone. To suffer is
A knowledge that is only kept from few;

The rest just struggle, looking for some new
Way out of all their darkness and distress,
Maybe we learn something from all of this

As long as we can keep our thoughts apart
From all self-pity, death to the human heart.

A Very Young Mother

Girl who had a child so young
There is something very wrong
In the look upon your face.
There is beauty, but no grace.

All the shock and all the hurt
Made a wound within your heart.
Wounds like this can never heal.
You stare but do not seem to feel.

Fifteen is too young to have
A child to bear when there's no love.
What, I ask, will come and make
A happiness from such heartbreak?

Hurt

They do not mean to hurt, I think,
People who wound and still go on
As if they had not seen the brink

Of tears they forced or even known
The wounding thing. I'm thinking of
An incident. I brought to one,

My host, a present, small enough
But pretty and picked out with care.
I put it in her hands with love,

Saying it came from Russia; there
Lay my mistake. The politics
Each of us had, we did not share.

But I am not immune to lack
Like this in others; she just thrust
The present over, gave it back

Saying, 'I do not want it.' Must
We hurt each other in such ways?
This kind of thing is worse than Lust

And other Deadly Sins because
It's lack of charity. For this,
Christ sweated blood, and on the Cross

When every nail was in its place,
Though God himself, he called as man
At the rejection. On his face

Among the sweat, there must have been
Within the greater pain, the one
A hurt child shows, the look we can

Detect and feel, swift but not gone,
Only moved deeper where the heart
Stores up all things that have been done

And, though forgiven, don't depart.

Rembrandt

The darkness is not like night. It has
a different purpose, a different meaning.
Within it portraits flare their faces at
you; that is what the dark is for.
    What are the faces like, these figures
with their strange shining? Sometimes,
a youth looks at you boldly – the artist
himself when young. Later, sadness is
scored over the older self-portraits. The
darkness allows the massive light to reveal
it. Its use is never neglected.

Or an old woman with folded fingers
bends, bends; then a group of impudent burghers
appears. Yourself too, at all ages, but
never with self-pity.

Christ enters also, in a delicate
discreet nativity. The painter knows when
to conceal himself.

He was a Dutchman, Rembrandt, one of a
solid people. But beneath their sturdiness
they hide great compassion, great sensitivity.
How else could they have produced this man,
one of the greatest suffering geniuses in
the world?

The Seven Deadly Sins
A sequence

Introduction

They all go together
But you can part them carefully,
Sparely,
Like a surgeon making the incision
With decision
And with dexterity.
So the Seven Deadly Sins are committed,
Deliberately and wilfully.

Sloth

He dies long in bed,
The warmth round body and head.
He will not work because he knows
National Assistance or Sickness Benefit can close
All doors to work.
Watch him shirk
Full of food and with a wide smirk.

Envy

This is hard.It can exist in a word or a thought. The mind
(That delicate thing)
Controls it
As it controls everything.

Envy is subtle.
Unlike jealousy, it will not settle
Just for what others have,
Whether a meal or an expression of love.
It wants deprivation,
It wants what someone else has
And leave them to starvation
Of any kind,
The body or the mind.

Greed

There is not much to be said about greed
Except that it is disgusting and, indeed,
Can consist of too much or too little eating
It is the fleeting
Yet sure intentions that matter.
Food on great platters,
Or a delicacy cooked to a turn,
Can burn, burn
And produce greed.
It is desire dressed up as a need.

Lust

This is the kindliest of the seven
Because it can produce happiness.
It only goes wrong when personal desire
Presses on, with no tiny thought even
Of the other's feeling.
It misses out all that love means –
Giving, taking, accepting, perhaps abstaining,
Always being gentle and full of thought.
It breaks what a life-time has carefully wrought.
All these, Lust demeans,
All it knows is desire,
The bonfire-burning of a fire.

Anger

A child can show its beginnings
By kicking a door.
A murderer knows the end
And with a hand,
A gun, a rope, any weapon
Can open
The door to real ire.
It comes close to desire
Because it is self-seeking.
Of that I am speaking.

Despair

Wishing not to be here –
That is Despair.
But it is, in its stark form
Much more than that.
It is wanting not to exist at all,
Considered, in cold blood;
It is not just a melancholy mood,
But a wish to fall down, down, down
To nothingness,
With no desire to bless.
It is a wish to make everything nothing,
Not just hanging on and still breathing,
But annihilating everything.

Pride

The worst of the seven we call
This one.
And so it is, because it encompasses all
We know of love, beauty, nature,
Every animal and human creature,
Because it wishes to possess,
To own, to caress
Not with love but in order to own
The desired object, whether a human body
Or a distant star.
And we are all prone to this, we are,
And if we give in we are left silently, coldly, justly, alone.

A Dream Undreamt

I never dreamt this, but I wish I had:
I mean a land where queens and kings can ride
And there are forests with no fear at all
Of darkness. And great feasts where everyone
Eats and drinks happily and never shouts.
I wish I'd had a dream resembling this.

I wish I'd dreamt of sky so full of stars
That some just had to fall into your hand
And you could hold them while they kept their light
And then release them back into the sky,
Steadfast, serene and back where they belong.
I wish, just once, I'd had a dream like that.

Sea Love

Strange how the stars make one think of love,
The sea also and the moon enters in,
All of them joining our bodies together,
All of them making us part of a world
Which casts upon us a magic, a marvel.
The world is huge and we are little
So we clutch each other as if to make
A tiny universe which we can fill.
We can smell the gracious flowers of the south
And hear the gentle waves of the sea.
We feel some share in their beauty and movement
So join our hands and exchange a salt kiss.

Fear

Did anyone ever find cure
In fear a terror or fright
An ugly word to stir
By day or worse by night,
Harsh words, brutality?
I don't think any of these
Could assuage or appease.

Kindness always, of course,
Can help. I do not mean
That all firmness must pause,
But a gentle scene
Puppet-show, opera or play,
Can be keen, keen,
We are made that way.

Of Love

It is not in the heart alone.
I cannot find it in the mind;
I know it reaches to the bone,
I know also that you can find

In sign, in touch, all this in look
We give vague words to. Is it best
To find it written in a book
Explaining what is only blessed?

My love is simple but is deep;
I cannot find the fitting words.
Sometimes they come to me in sleep
And when they do they're strong as swords.

Skies

Never the same for a second;
In the South, ecstatic blue
Until a brief dark cloud
Sends down huge hail-stones,
Then the blue returns.

In the North, skies are more subtle,
Clouds more curiously shaped
And always changeable –
Like sheep, like balloons, like puffs of smoke.
Except for the sea,

Skies are the most eye-drawing things,
Especially at night when
Moon can be severally-shaped,
Stars glitter and we have named them,
We should find names for our skies.

Meteorologists have listed the clouds
But, as far as I know, no one
Has found worthy names for the whites,
The daring blue, the darkness.
Soon, perhaps, somebody will

But it will have to be a poet.

From the Heights

From the heights they come,
Prophets, visionaries,
But with such diverse messages –
Moses burning with the tablets of the law,
Our adamant Commandments still,
John of the Cross locked in his tower on a hill
Writing at last words of warning and hope.
Each has his scope.

One does not need to name them
But one must, one must
If only to keep trust
With the power
That comes from a mountain or a tower:
So, here are a few,
Augustine hushed at Ostia Antica,
Teresa of Avila,
Hopkins in Wales finding God in a poem
He'd been asked to write.
But there, as always, was the real darkness and light.

Enough
Of names.
What is left is love,
What was meant was love.
And many who have no names in history
Of any kind
Know this high-up, deep-down mystery,
This terrible, wonderful touch on the human mind.

Missing a Mirage

For V. and J.

They went up the mountains
In snow and with the sun,
With snow I too have seen
From a plane over the Alps.
They'd hired the car
But a tyre went flat.

What to do about that
With no spare but a crowd
Of children with loud
Voices? No help
When they wanted a tyre.
By good luck they were

Helped in the end,
Perhaps helped for the best
For the one who hoped missed
What she had so hoped for –
The whole Sahara.
That missing was surely blessed.

Italian Memories

Lizards slide over my path
Or they used to.
The smell of the orange-grove in Sorrento
Intoxicated me
As I wandered down to the sea
And saw the bay of Naples,
Vesuvius
And all that they mean to us
Who come from the North.

Our poets have died there,
In Rome or elsewhere,
Shelley and Keats,
Even the dusty, haggling streets
Play on every sense.
A glance at a slide and we feel we are there

Drawn by a magnet, or to change the metaphor
By some dream of childhood or before,
The longing to see;

The longing also to taste and touch
The shells, the ruins, the sand.
See how the last trickles through the hand
Seems so much
Like a thought going through the mind,
But it is not so.
To these rainbow-coloured, tideless things we clutch
Because we know
That in them we may find
What reaches the thought and the sense
And can endure.
And we have the pure
Feel of discovery like all four elements
Held in patience and not in suspense.

Happiness in Rome

There were the sparkling lights of that great city.
It could have been another but was Rome;
There out of gentleness, compassion, pity,
I had come home at last, I had come home.

Home to my Faith at last through kind words spoken
In a confessional, open to all.
So much was mended that had long been broken.
What does it matter? Time is small, is small

To measureless events such as this was.
Oh yes, I loved the buildings, all the beauty
But this was different, different because
A simple act, part childlike, done from duty

Ranged through my heart. Of sin I had been shriven
In quiet words, but so much more was there,
The solid city and the stars, all given.
All I could do was watch and thank and stare

And think of all the mysteries of my Faith,
Of the baptismal waters, questions 'Why?'
It did not, does not matter. I stood with
Joy upon the steps and watched the world go by.

Quiet Wars

It does not need barbed wire, bombs or gas,
Barrage-balloons or Air Raid shelters,
Dug-outs, First Aid stations, nothing alters,
I suppose never has
In the human heart
And *there* the armies can start to fight,

There, the fighters begin to fly,
And the bomber too
With its frightened crew.
Oh no:
It need not be so.
There are wars as fierce

As hard, or which can as deftly pierce
As the ancient sword
Or the lance.
There is no elegance,
No tourney, only a word
Perhaps misunderstood but gone so deep
That a battering army comes in the following sleep,
If sleep does come.
There is no home,
No hand or arm
To heal the wound.

The still stars are around
But the individual is more important than them,
Though they look like a precious gem.
Is there an end to such wars?

It is idle to seek for the cause
Will there be a truce?
If there is, what is the use
Since the trouble started where truces do not occur,
They only abuse,
And two people face each other to kiss or to curse.
And I do not know which is worse.

Kinds of Tears

It feels like spoiling something precious,
Like flaunting a gem
Because of the money it cost.
The real value is in the flash
Like that of a star,
Not in a diadem.
Stars,
We are born to them –

But my theme
Is different though of course related.
It must be stated.
To-night, we, after misunderstandings,
Quarrels over words,
Sheathed our swords.
Or rather you did
Simply because you said
'I have been thinking and realise I am insensitive.
Help me.' Just to admit
This was a denial but my tears nearly came
Out of joy that we can live

And believe
In such clarities,
Such apparent inconsistencies.
So to relieve
You, I told you of the many kinds of tears –
Tears of temper when a child appears
Quite out of hand,
Tears of despair
(I knew then that you would understand)
Tears of fear
And of dread
Of the nearly dead.

But lastly I said,
There are tears of gratitude
Expressing human amazement at something good
As you evoked to-night
And another has done before
By their silent sympathy and kindness and
A way to understand;
These are tears without flaw.

Blame Yourself

Never blame
Anyone but yourself.
The rest is a kind of serious game
But full of shame,

Shame to bring on
Anyone else
What you have done or undone
Or where you have gone wrong.

And above all
Do not crawl
Like a scapegoat into some ugly wilderness.
Bear your own distress.

Dignity here
Not pride
Will let you ride
Like a surfer over the passionate waves.
Thus, at its best, blame behaves.

Tears

Held tears are worse than shed ones, much,
Because they never reach the cheek;
They can be bitter, mean heartbreak
But nobody can wipe or touch.

They are stored up in the mind
Or in the brain; we do not know
Precisely how they come and go,
Only that they can stun and blind.

Not Counting Time

No, children never
Spoil the present by thinking
Of the future. Unblinking
They will not sever

The present but enter
Completely into
The happiness though
Sometimes the centre

Is tears, tossed toys.
All ends come home
Whether dear or doom,
Terror or joys.

The child's got it right,
Not the two, then the past,
But lives deep to the last
Whether darkness or light.

The Drunk

The cautiousness of the drunkard –
How he puts the key in the door
Thinking how clever he is,

And then he walks very carefully,
Almost kneels on the floor
But rises up and thinks,

'I must be sure I don't
Lose what I'm searching for
Or wake other people up.'

He reaches the light at last,
Then switches it off before
The bulb may snap and fuse.

Still dressed, at last he falls
On to his bed to steer
Into mere darkness or

A never-remembered dream.
In the morning he'll war
With headache, sickness, wish

He had never *smelt* drink before
And, ice-cold, add up the score.

Craftsmanship with Fish

Ever seen a man boning a fish,
Anything you like from herring to plaice?
Ever seen a waiter making an art

Out of top-and-tailing 'gambas', not scampi,
Not lobster, not, I think, 'langoustine'?
Whatever fish it was, it was certainly an art
Demanding deft hands, great concentration.

I have seen all this with professionals and amateurs
And have marvelled at the skill. Fish of the sea

And of the rivers, you have shown
Through human hands a revelation to me.

Almost Falling Asleep

Slipping, sliding, gliding
Gently, I hope, to sleep.
Everything now is quiet
Except the hiss of my fire
And the busy thoughts in my brain;
They will keep me awake.

A soothing drink, quiet music –
These have come and gone.
And this house, so often noisy,
Is, at present, a nest of peace.
Busy thoughts, be off,
Let the slipping start again

And then, perhaps much later,
The real sleep, dreamless,
No nightmares when I wake sobbing
With self-pitying desire for someone
To soothe the shadows away
And tell me it's really day.

The Climb

The lower slopes are easy, strewn with flowers
And sun comes down almost of heat-wave strength.
But we keep looking upwards at the snow,
Loving the uncorrupted whiteness there,
And wonder for a moment if we ought
Even to try to make our boot-marks on

Such unspoilt loveliness. And then we thought,
'Is the true vision gazing from below
And giving silent wonder, or is it
Enduring all the ardour of the climb?'
The first thought seemed too easy, so we started,
The ropes around us. It was a harsh climb.

Many times we almost slipped right down
And we were bruised and cut. In fact we never
Got to the summit, put our feet on snow.
So we came down, half-disappointed yet
Feeling that something strange had been attained:
The partial vision and the striving limbs.

The Wood

Into the wood we hurried for an hour
Or so it seemed. There was no thread to follow,
No labyrinth or maze, simply we went
To seek out animals, to hear the birds
And undergrowth that crunched beneath our feet.
We had no path, no map; no treasure-hunt

Was in our minds except the kind of treasure
The eager senses bring. We heard the scramble
Of nameless timid creatures darting off;
We were intruders on their solitude
Though did not mean to be. Stealthy we were
But human footsteps never can be silent,

However gentle. What, then, did we find?
Cobwebs and undergrowth, early Spring flowers,
Dexterous nests beginning to be built
And somewhere, far off, smells of damp and smoke.
Our purpose simply was our walking there,
No quest, no hunt, simply the wood itself.

The Caves

Why did we go into those caves at all?
Partly, it's true, because we'd heard of grottoes.
And we saw two, one crowded, the other quiet
And on the most fabulous bay I've ever seen:
Not Naples, no, but the gulf of Salerno.
But still I am not sure quite why we went.

It was not certainly in search of views
(We had no cameras), something more deep –
The Northern mind seeking the Southern heart,
And other things also, intangible.
Motives are meaningless at times like this
And yet we cannot help but seek them out.

There are treasuries we do not know,
Journeys we never really understand.
We go because some impulse urges us
Like those first men who painted in dark caves
(They still exist). Our power is not to paint,
Only to make an unexplained journey.

Sheer Rage

You were right again, oh yes you were,
Whether in bets or silly small rows which
Occur with those who care. But how I rage
So that I tremble when I write a page
And take it out of you (the usual thing)
Because I'm mad you have the flur and fling,
Some unknown instinct – and I'm in the wrong.
Yet I belong to you, yes I belong
Clinging for help upon that rope which winds
And swings between us. But one always finds
The rope is fast, as if to catch and bring
A weighty salmon in. It's no chance thing
That you are dexterous at fishing too.
I hang behind but still I love-hate you.

The Roses

Yes, the rose is heavy
With too much rain.
Nonetheless it can
Bring back to all of us,
As all flowers cruelly can,
Resentments, happiness.
The roses are heavy.

We need them but do they
Need our demanding,
Not just our plucking,
All that we weigh on them
In memory or hope?
We cannot judge at all,
We cannot even guess.
It's beyond our scope.

A Paradox

I feel because I do not feel.
My mind's aloof in one small part
Yet all the rest is bountiful

With images, ideas. My heart –
Yes part of that has gone quite cold.
Still there are children and great art,

Great friends. These never lose their hold
Though something strange has come, a shock;
I have read of or else been told

Indifference can come, a block
Of ice. Mine's small, dropped in a glass
But big enough. Can my heart knock

And beat as others' do with this
Discovery that I can know
Such lack of feeling? Worse, despise

Someone I thought I needed so?
And will the pain, the paradox,
Yes even that, at some time go,

A pattern form, confusion pass?

GROWING POINTS
(1975)

Beech

They will not go. These leaves insist on staying.
Coinage like theirs looked frail six weeks ago.
What hintings at, excitement of delaying,
Almost as if some richer fruits could grow

If leaves hung on against each swipe of storm,
If branches bent but still did not give way.
Today is brushed with sun. The leaves are warm.
I picked one from the pavement and it lay

With borrowed shining on my Winter hand.
Persistence of this nature sends the pulse
Beating more rapidly. When will it end,

That pride of leaves? When will the branches be
Utterly bare, and seem like something else,
Now half-forgotten, no part of a tree?

Growing

Not to be passive simply, never that.
Watchful, yes, but wondering. It seems
Strange, your world, and must do always, yet
Haven't you often been caught out in dreams

And changed your terms of reference, escaped
From the long rummaging with words, with things,
Then found the very purpose that you mapped
Has moved? The poem leaves you and it sings.

And you have changed. Your whispered world is not
Yours any longer. It's not there you grow.
I tell you that your flowers will find no plot

Except when you have left them free and slow,
While you attend to other things. Do not
Tamper with touching. Others pick, you know.

Transformation

Always I trip myself up when I try
To plan exactly what I'll say to you.
I should allow for how my feelings lie
Ready to leap up, showing what is true,

But in a way I never had designed.
How is it you are always ready when
Those linked ideas like beads within my mind
Break from their thread and scatter tears again?

I am amazed, and distances depart,
Words touch me back to quiet. I am free
Who could not guess such misery would start

And stop so quickly, change the afternoon
And, far much more than that, transfigure me.
Trusting myself, I enter night, stars, moon.

To the Core

You have tried so hard to reach the core
Of what you tell us that you think you are.
Friends find you out, mirrors now explore,
Or you yourself, both eyes gripped to a star

Or two defensive eyes you can't stare out,
Feel down your flesh, with careful fingers, thin
As worn-out thoughts, and find the scars of doubt.
You test appearances upon your skin.

Truth tastes strange to you and lips learn warnings.
Are you afraid when you reach out and kiss
The air, your breath accepting every morning's

Terrible trust? We learn all fear in ways
No books describe to us. We must dismiss
All but the ghosts which give back our own gaze.

A Quartet

Four people in a street where houses were
Devoted to their silence. Voices went
Into an argument. The other pair
Looked at each other with a quiet assent.

So speech, so echoes. What were we explaining?
Pitting ourselves against the stars perhaps?
Two did not move, or need a breath-regaining.
Pause meant a stir of love, for us a lapse

In thought. There was no feeling in our speech
Except the easing out to victory.
Tempers were kept. Better if we had each

Been silent, let the other two go off.
There was one lamp disputing with a tree.
Ideas of ours broke through those looks of love.

Rhetoric

He told us that it mattered how a bird
(Not naming it) should have its wings so taut
That it was watchful always, could be stirred
By all events except the being caught

And caged by us. Bright symbols bubbled then
Out of his mouth, poets handed lines
To prove his feelings. Quiet once again,
He gave me territory, gave me signs.

The need to prove had gone now for a time,
Yet I was not at ease, was shouldered out,
First by the echoes of a verse or rhyme,

Then by these people's quiet dexterity.
I had no need of birds to show my doubt
But searched the night for some simplicity.

Trance

Naked as possible in cities, these
Young look enchanted. Each attentive face
Could shine a god or goddess in the trees
Of a great forest where the roots found place

Long before man. Yes, in this daze of heat,
Stripped bodies could have stepped from anywhere
To anywhere. The street's no more a street
Of houses where the people have to share

The sense of time. Look, naked children run
Into the water, splashing fountains too
Constant for usual days. They have begun

To change before the watchers' eyes and show
How light is palpable, how day is new,
And, strangely, more so in the sunset glow.

In a Garden

When the gardener has gone this garden
Looks wistful and seems waiting an event.
It is so spruce, a metaphor of Eden
And even more so since the gardener went,

Quietly godlike, but, of course, he had
Not made me promise anything, and I
Had no one tempting me to make the bad
Choice. Yet I still felt lost and wonder why.

Even the beech tree from next door which shares
Its shadow with me, seemed a kind of threat.
Everything was too neat and someone cares

In the wrong way. I need not have stood long
Mocked by the smell of a mown lawn, and yet
I did. Sickness for Eden was so strong.

Grapes

Those grapes, ready for picking, are the sign
Of harvest and of Sacrament. Do not
Touch them; wait for the ones who tread the wine,
See Southern air surround that bunch, that knot

Of juice held in. In Winter vines appear
Pitiful as a scarecrow. No one would
Guess from their crippled and reluctant air
That such refreshment, such fermenting could

Come from what seem dry bones left after death.
But, look now, how those pregnant bunches hang,
Swinging upon a pendulum of breath,

Intense small globes of purple till the hour
Of expert clipping comes. There is a pang
In seeing so much fullness change its power.

Among Strangers

Changed by the darkness their indifference shed
Can you be undiminished yet and share
The harmony you find in picture, bed,
In that defiant moth that meets the air

And passes through it and flies on? Can you
Find in the punishings of this no-love
Yourself; the bell your mind which still rings true
As you face what must be well-known enough?

Back to your childhood, are you now before
Any demands? You were not powerless though,
You cried your need out, joining others. Why

Do you divide and count the distance so?
Look, they are harmless and you need not try
To prise their difference open any more.

The Quality of Goodness

Brought up perhaps on some quiet wave of sea
When the boat vanishes and surf reclines
And seen from close at hand as suddenly
A figure folded on the sand's designs

And rising, moving inland – so you stare
With a compassionate serenity
And gaze into my moment of despair.
Total decorum and simplicity.

So I survive and step upon the shore
Which you have yielded. No demands are made.
My laughter is not false, there is no more

Deception. I look back at you, return
Your gaze, am calm upon those tide-out sands,
Sea heard and smelt, too distant to discern.

No Rest

Even while I sit and think and see
Patterns around me which my eyes arrange,
Even while battling out of poetry,
I know some rising in me, summon change

And am existing out of literature,
Not among words or papers any more
But moving among freedoms that are pure.
O no I am not artist but restore

All that was there already, only needing
A touch here; I correct but not improve.
Or change the metaphor – say I am weeding

A garden planted on a stair-cased hill.
I climb and pluck and everywhere I move
I feel unsettled but am learning skill.

For the Mind Explorers

What have you done to some of us privately, to perhaps all publicly
since you have
Taken away our fables, a child's toys, taken and hidden, sometimes
destroyed them,
Or so it seems, 'for our good'. What is this 'good' that comes with
no nurses
That a language, a tongue or one imagination require? You have lived,
acted, written, some of you even
Have prophesied, have thus taken over our old role while we stand,
gagged, hands tied, in a small cell.
But not for long. We see to that, we confound you by admitting you,
by letting you

Trespass upon preserves poets once thought theirs alone. We do more,
We grant you a dispensation to take away our symbols, but in our
wakeful nights, since you have now
Taken away at least some of our dreams, we are gentle with you,
own you and like the
Raiders, but not spoilers, we have always been, we have plundered,
your found, held coins and
With extreme delicacy, been Midas with what you have done, said or
thought. So our magnanimity must
Admit its debt to you – no war, no rage, no guilt, only now gratitude
and a gentleness.

Thunder and a Boy

For T.

That great bubble of silence, almost tangible quiet was shattered.
There was no prelude, the huge chords
Broke and sounded timpani over the town, and then lightning, first
darting, then strong bars
Taking hold of the sky, taking hold of us as we sank into primitive
people,
Wondering at and frightened of the elements, forgetting so swiftly how
naming had once seemed
To give them into our hands. Not any longer. We were powerless
now completely.

But today we have risen with the rain and, though it is torrential, we
believe at moments that we

Still have power over that. We are wrong. Those birds escaping
                                through showers show us
They are more imperial than we are. We shift, talk, doze, look at papers,
Though one child is remembering how last night he stood with defiance

    And joy at his window and shouted, 'Do it again, God, do it again!'
Can we say he was less wise than us? We cannot. He acknowledged Zeus,
    Thor, God the Father, and was prepared to cheer or dispute with
                                any of them.
This afternoon he watches the sky, praying the night will show God's
                                strength again
    And he, without fear, feel those drums beating and bursting through
                        his defended, invisible mind.

Freshness

    Good, yes, good, gracious and giving a feeling of
Redemption, is redemption – I mean this open strewn-before-you
                                liberty of
    Knowing small kindnesses deeply. It is like going into those libraries
                                where chained
Books are and, forgetting there is a custodian, librarian, it does not matter.
    You see an illustration, a story from the Bible or an old fable twined
                                round
One letter. It is like that – this awareness of warmth and also returning
                                it.

    The Alphabet is being learnt again, it is new and amazing when you
                                see such
Strange Arabic shapes forming words, telling feelings, assisting,
                                triumphing.
    You read and you understand as deeply as you do these faces,
More deeply. You respond and are illuminated and radiant yourself,
    Finding friendship so unexpectedly, yet so, when acknowledged,
Fitting, in or out of a time sequence, by a need, a renewal, a victory.

A Quiet Enemy

Never doubting, he goes on with a routine of perpetual
Small destructions. It would be childlike were there not, behind the
                                                    thick grin, a
Masterly malice, acquired quickly and willingly so that all others who
Move where he is must either learn an even swifter immunity or else
    Put on a thin mask, say polite words fast, then run, themselves now
Committed to childhood, to that fear which was generated in grates
    Of nurseries or back-rooms. 'You should not be sensitive'

Others mock, others who do not align themselves with this youth
                                                    but can bear,
Even laugh away afterwards, the assurance that his smile will end, if not
                                                    begin
    With a malice you cannot compete with, nor wish to, ever, for
There is power to hurt here and you crave protection. Is there anyone
                                                    strong enough,
    Flexible enough to uphold your cause? It seems doubtful for he will
                                                    at once
Have their prowess recognised, know they are prepared and so hand a
                                                    quick draft
    Of a treaty of courtesy. You, meanwhile, wait for what is, after all,
                    his war to break out again, at any time, any.

I Feel

I feel I could be turned to ice
If this goes on, if this goes on.
I feel I could be buried twice
And still the death not yet be done.

I feel I could be turned to fire
If there can be no end to this.
I know within me such desire
No kiss could satisfy, no kiss.

I feel I could be turned to stone,
A solid block not carved at all,
Because I feel so much alone.
I could be grave-stone or a wall.

But better to be turned to earth
Where other things at least can grow.
I could be then a part of birth,
Passive, not knowing how to know.

Bird Study

A worm writhes and you have some power
Of knowing when and where to strike.
Then suddenly bread in a shower.
Being a bird is like

This and a feathered overcoat,
A throb of sound, a balanced wing,
A quiver of the beak and throat,
A gossip-mongering.

But higher up a hawk will take
Stature of stars, a comet-fall,
Or else a swan that oars a lake,
Or one note could be all.

I am obsessed with energy
I never touch. I am alive
To what I only hear and see,
The sweep, the sharp, the drive.

Towards a Religious Poem

Decrees of a dead tongue gone,
The flicker of Greek in the vernacular,
An age for the East and Yoga,
For lotus and resting. One word
Cannot be spoken or carved.
If music suggests it, it erred.
Christ in this age you are nameless,
Your praises and slanders have sunk
To oaths. Love has somehow slipped by
What once throbbed in an occupied sky.

In my stanzas I'll only allow
The silence of a tripped tongue,
The concerns and cries of creation
To hold you, as always, but more now.
The Prophets and all their books prosper,
But here as a Christmas comes closer,
Awe will be speechless, and magic
Be dropped like an acrobat's pitfall.
The absence, the emptiness echo,
A girl with a cradle to borrow.

After a Time

For a friend dead two years

I have not stood at this grave nor have I
Been where men come at last to silence when
Death sends them to instinctive ceremony,
Whether in torturing sun or fitting rain,
Whether they stare or cry.

What do I say who never put a wreath
Down for a father or this friend? Someone
Will make the speech for me. O this dear death,
Two years of missing all have been undone,
Yet I am growing with

Spontaneous strengths, blessings I did not claim –
Laughter, a child, knowledge of justice and
Faith like a cross which oddly bears my name,
Falls round my neck. In early hours I stand
Reflecting how I came

To this. What takes me through the corridors
Of grief? Was it the touch of love, that leading thread
Which drew me to glad grief from wrong remorse
Wiped off the dust and let me see the dead
With new care now, new laws?

The Lord's Prayer

'Give us this day.' Give us this day and night.
Give us the bread, the sky. Give us the power
To bend and not be broken by your light.

And let us soothe and sway like the new flower
Which closes, opens to the night, the day,
Which stretches up and rides upon a power

More than its own, whose freedom is the play
Of light, for whom the earth and air are bread.
Give us the shorter night, the longer day.

In thirty years so many words were spread,
And miracles. An undefeated death
Has passed as Easter passed, but those words said

Finger our doubt and run along our breath.

Meditation on the Nativity

All gods and goddesses, all looked up to
And argued with and threatened. All that fear
Which man shows to the very old and new
All this, all these have gone. They disappear
In fables coming true,

In acts so simple that we are amazed –
A woman and a child. He trusts, she soothes.
Men see serenity and they are pleased.
Placating prophets talked but here are truths
All men have only praised

Before in dreams. Lost legends here are pressed
Not on to paper but in flesh and blood,
A promise kept. Her modesties divest
Our guilt of shame as she hands him her food
And he smiles on her breast.

Painters' perceptions, visionaries' long
Torments and silence, blossom here and speak.
Listen, our murmurs are a cradle-song,
Look, we are found who seldom dared to seek
A maid, a child, God young.

Christ on the Cross

Forgive them, Father, forgive them Father who
Is in my heart. How frightened she who stands,
My mother with my friend. The soldiers too,
Help me forgive them who have nailed my hands.
It seems so long ago

I talked in Temples. O the streams where John,
Another, poured the fountain on my head.
Father, I tell my mother that a son,
My friend, shall care for her when I am dead.
I am so dizzy on

This wood. The waters flow but now from me.
I have been chosen. Father, I am you
Who breathed, then sapped the great man-offered tree.
Spirit within me, there are risings too.
Father, forgive now, me.

Lent Beginning 1974

This is the beginning of it. Towards
The torn hill, through the ash of earth
We stumble, gathering our words
From staring death, blind birth.

And what round many necks hangs now
As charm, still casts its shadow of
Shame like the noose upon that bough,
The burdenings of love.

Believe or not – we are all kin
When violence sweats out as blood,
When dared compassions smile at sin,
One cruel thought stuns to good.

Easter Duties

They are called duties. People must confess,
Through garlic-smelling grilles or in quiet rooms,
All the year's mis-events – unhelped distress,
Griefs lingered over, *accidie* in dreams,
And hear the words which bless

And unbind, eat the bread and feel the cross
Hurting only a little, hinting more.
Why do I feel, in all these acts, a loss,
As if a marvel I had waited for
Were a cheap toy to toss

Away, the giver gone? Why do I care
In this uncaring? I need gods on earth,
The wonder felt, sleep which I somehow share
Because it is a going back to birth.
And, yes, I want to bear

Anticipated laughter, jokes which once
Meant calibre and bite but did not make
Anyone sad. Prayer yet could be a dance
But still a cross. I offer small heartbreak,
Catch grace almost by chance.

Whitsun Sacrament

Others anoint you but you choose your own name.
This comes with childhood just about to leave.
It comes with new self-consciousness, old shame,
Arrives when we are not sure we believe.
We read about a flame

And answers when we question every word,
Mumble our motives. Spirit, Spirit, where
Are you to be caught now and where be heard
We only feel the pitched-low, taunting air.
There was talk of a bird,

A dove. Where is peace now in our unrest –
The childish questions in the throbbing mind,
The new name, itching loins, the shaping breast?
When we most need a tongue we only find
Christ at his silentest.

Out of the Heights

Out of the preening and impetuous heights
Where we look down and do not fear and risk
The snow escaping, the ice-melting flights,

And where we spin the sun a golden disc
And do not care and watch the clouds attend
The tall sky's dazzling and arched arabesque,

Out of those places where we think we end
Unhappiness, catch love within a final hand,
God, from such places keep us and defend

The innocence we do not understand,
The darknesses to which we must descend.

The Nature of Prayer

a debt to *Van Gogh's* Crooked Church

Maybe a mad fit made you set it there
Askew, bent to the wind, the blue-print gone
Awry, or did it? Isn't every prayer
We say oblique, unsure, seldom a simple one,
Shaken as your stone tightening in the air?

Decorum smiles a little. Columns, domes
Are sights, are aspirations. We can't dwell
For long among such loftiness. Our homes
Of prayer are shaky and, yes, parts of Hell
Fragment the depths from which the great cry comes.

Thomas Aquinas

Thinking incessantly, making cogitations always but as keenly,
                                    freshly as the child
He had been who asked repeatedly 'What is God?' and was pursued by
                                    this inquiry till grown-up,
And family factions argued, as they thought logically, that he
Must be an Abbot, they had long doomed this – he, Thomas of
                                    Aquinas, then revolted, but typically

Mildly and unviolently. No aristocracy for him but in ideas and he
                                    had settled his destiny to be
A Dominican friar. The one act of outrage we know of is when
   Relations sent in women to tempt his body and he drove them out
                                    with a

Burning brand. After that, Albert to instruct him, Plato read and
                                    discarded, then
Aristotle transformed with clarity into a great system coinciding with every
   Christian dogma, dancing metaphysical thought, and he put down
                                    calmly the ending in
The Summa for students, for others more and deeper, if possible, matters.
   And he, who patterned and explained the world, dined with Louis
                                    of France, still
Stayed the child of great questions, saint but like an angel, and rightly, now
   Known among us as the Angelic Doctor, a Church's title for one
               whose sole wish was for the pure gold of continual inquiry.

Open to the Public

They fall in easy poses as if they
   Knew the sun's moods by heart,
Expected it, as in hot lands. Each day
   They soon become a part

Of the stretched grass unmown where shining flowers
   Stare straight into the light.
Grown-ups and children all accept its powers
   As if it were a right.

They are adaptable to changes, so
   Here where the sun can bruise
With brightness where they bask, they all still know
   This climate is for use.

Yet they are not complacent: Watch them run
   Fast when the sun comes out
And for a moment shrug fore-knowledge. Sun
   Is strong before all doubt.

In a Picture Gallery

Show me a gallery of air
And walls shored up with paintings through
Which we can climb. A step, a stair
Takes us to sunsets or a view
Of light sufficient to a square
Of harlequinning people who

Set minds to music. Do you hear
A murmur of continued flight?
Paint, sound and word are everywhere,
A quick kaleidoscope of light.
Are paintings far or are we near
This texture of, this sound of sight?

Mondrian

Attempt a parody of this:
Prepare the paints, make measurements,
Keep an eye cocked on memory,
Call up geometry, stand back,
Extend the rainbow's ready scope.

But Mondrian will not appear.
He starves still with an easel too
Heavy to hang on, fever high,
Caught too late with canvases
For barter in the auction rooms.

Can abstractions tell the tale?
Are portraits put in angles, squares?
Still life, still death and one thing more –
The dignity of distances,
The lofty white a man's last breath.

Rembrandt's Late Self-Portraits

You are confronted with yourself. Each year
The pouches fill, the skin is uglier.
You give it all unflinchingly. You stare
Into yourself, beyond. Your brush's care
Runs with self-knowledge. Here

Is a humility at one with craft.
There is no arrogance. Pride is apart
From this self-scrutiny. You make light drift
The way you want. Your face is bruised and hurt
But there is still love left.

Love of the art and others. To the last
Experiment went on. You stared beyond
Your age, the times. You also plucked the past
And tempered it. Self-portraits understand,
And old age can divest,

With truthful changes, us of fear of death.
Look, a new anguish. There, the bloated nose,
The sadness and the joy. To paint's to breathe,
And all the darknesses are dared. You chose
What each must reckon with.

Mozart's Horn Concertos

Not for war or hunting cry
Is this; it gentles down the heart
So there's no question asking 'Why

Does man exist?' God gave him art,
And God is proved in every note
And every sound takes its own part

In what a young composer wrote
Who ended in a pauper's grave.
The disc is on, the patterns float

And I feel back at some strange start
And marvel at what Mozart gave.

A Scholar Emperor of the Tang Dynasty

Dazzling it was indeed, a golden age,
The lakes ran round the palaces, the park
Was, yes, a turned, illuminated page.
    You did not think of dark

Or only as a time when candles curled
Over a manuscript and filled the air
With pens, with eyes to circumscribe the world,
    And you were moving there,

No autocrat but patron till a strong
And swarming dynasty took off your power,
Put you in exile. Poetry, the long
    Finger of time, its hour,

Gave you the diffidence and dared you look
At moon-extending shadows, short-lived sun.
You also added letters to a book
    But now a home-sick one.

Wasn't it worth it? Didn't all those days
Of letting others write and paint allow
This gift of loss, lament which felt like praise
    And proves it is so now?

Wonder

Homage to Wallace Stevens

Wonder exerts itself now as the sky
Holds back a crescent moon, contains the stars.
So we are painters of a yesterday
Cold and decisive. We are feverish
With meditations of a Winter Law
Though Spring was brandished at us for a day.

Citizens of climate we depend
Not on the comfortable clock, the warm
Cry of a morning song, but on the shape
Of hope, the heralding imagination,
The sanguine making and the lonely rites
We exercise in space we leave alone.

Prophets may preside and they will choose
Clouds for a throne. The background to their speech
Will be those fiery peaks a painter gives
As a composer shares an interval,
As poet pauses, holding sound away
From wood, as worshippers draw back from gods.

A Chinese Sage

A Chinese sage once took every word distilled, altered and perfected
In private till for him it seemed a poem, yes he took this to a peasant
woman,
Read it to her softly and slowly and waited for her rough-voiced
assurance that
Certain words she could understand, others were meaningless to her.
Very discreetly
But decisively, and with no arguments, this sage crossed out every
word that was foreign to
A woman of simplicity who knew labours of the soil and the house,
who had no
Dealings other than this with poetry, art of any kind, yet by his

Magnanimity, more, his humility, became his mentor, guided him
Out of all obscurity, not with wearying argument or even quiet coaxing,
but by the fact
That she was a world he could only enter through her. Hay, beds,
crude meals, lust
Subdued his wit, bodied out his verse, cancelled cleverness. And, I ask,
was he
Most poet or most philosopher in this uncrowned wisdom, writing
In the reign of Charlemagne, paring simplicities to a peace no Emperor
was ever enticed by or even dreamed of?

Elegy for W.H. Auden

Stones endure as your first and last things.
The carpet slippers, the leather skin,
The incorrigible laughter inaccurately aped,

Those late epigrams which obviously were
The acute desperation of that laughter
These are forgotten almost already.

But the stone your student hand held gently,
Schoolboy hair flopped over years later,
The limestone which reminded you of love

And caught the last strains of your lyrical perceptions,
The walks out of Italy into Austria,
All that grey North which you set glowing

Yes, it is geology, quarries and tools,
The precise tap on the finished fossil,
And last the shuffle on Christ Church cobbles,

The cobbles you must have stared at rather
Than look up as Wren's Tom trembled your hours –
All these are a life you refused to surrender.

No glass-cases and no museums.
All your grand operas opened into caves
Where your Orators shout and your Mirror is shining.

The Sea stands still but your landscape moves.

Prospero

All back into their places, steps
Printed on sand, and air to air
Confides, great fruit from spent trees drops.
O Prospero, how you prepare

And ravish in the giving back,
Lamb to the ewe, isle to the sea
And Ariel self-swung and quick
In that good hour of setting free.

Hopkins in Wales

We know now how long that language,
Your language, had been dancing in you but
    Suppressed, held back by hard work, the debt
You owed to discipline. But no one, not one
    Stopped you looking, dissecting at a glance
A leaf, a tree's stump, while in your mind
    The long thought-over, now fermented
Ideas of Duns Scotus were waiting, the vintage
    Years about to be bottled at one sign, a word
From a Superior about the wreck you had read of.
    Worked-out ideas, your 'instress' and 'inscape',
Problems of prosody, 'Sprung Rhythm', came out dancing,
    Linked with that subject, and you wrote at last

Guiltless, no squabble now between your vocation,
Endurance chosen as a priest, with art, two arts
    Now stretching within: you with all the force of
Deliberations held back. And the discipline itself
    Appeared in selected stanzas, half-rhymes, senses once subdued
Unleashed into another order. A nun, a shipwreck
    Were set down, had happened but now would happen
Over and over in the committed, inexorable, also defenceless
    Way in which poems are always vulnerable. And every long look
At a leaf's individuality or the mark, his own, on a man's face
    Was dynamic. And the heroism heard of
Found place with all your admirations, while God's Presence
    Was granted a new kind of immanence in your lines. Doubtless

The no-understanding of others hurt but, far deeper
    And like the sea you wrote of, the fitness,
Inexorably of this exercise and joy, flowered in you, jetsam
    To others in time, acknowledged by you and by us
Years later. Let us hope you had some inkling of this
    As you rode through so many other poems until Dublin
Felled you like an axe or a wave into
    A desirable death, your work around you
Careful as carved stones simply waiting to be picked up,
    Wondered at, not static but dynamically precious,
Named by you, found by us, never diminishing.

Performer

Tight-roper, care, do not look down,
Think of the thread beneath your foot,
Forget the pony and the clown,
Discard the circus, see before
Your gaze a safety held, complete
And, after that, the tidal roar

Of watchers, some of whom no doubt
Wanted a death. You have an hour
When you can cast your terror out,
Depend no more on balance but
On earth whose ground gives you the power,
You think, to snatch that rope and cut.

A Play at Avignon

Emptiness after midnight since the voices
Had stopped at last, no echo left behind
    Within that courtyard. Stars had crowded out
Sound, and because there had been voices once
    There was a vacancy that almost, now,
Seemed to be measurable. The actors had
    Spoken their classic lines and simply bowed
And moved from sight. Day would redeem the view,
    The famous broken bridge turn thoughts to rivers
Or else to painting. Southern atmosphere,
    Pervasive and imprisoning, would return

And pick each small square out, each watered field,
Light point the way to Orange or to Nîmes,
    And all Provence be like a text of which
You know the language, linger on the page
    And hear the voices speaking in your mind
Different from those within the palace of
    Disputed Popes. So Avignon arranges
Itself and seen from any point you choose,
    Softens and ripens as the day proceeds
Never preparing you but letting happen
    Those voices, the whole city slipped from sight.

Opera

These lovers must rely
On the adjustment of the wood and strings
Which, in their turn, are guided by
   The baton beating down the air.
Italian, French or German rings
Towards the fatal hour. The theatre

   Is words subjected to
The stretch and fling of sound. Poets withdraw
Or let their rhythms here subdue
   Themselves. Meanings also demur
Without poetic justice, law.
Yet it is this subjection that can stir

   Us by a story which
Climbs out of farce into high tragedy,
Love thrives upon the rich
   Deceptions winnowing the ear,
While instruments and voices free
Us to rejoicing pain and apt despair.

After a Play

The wind in spasms swept the street
As we walked very quietly
Till cold and silence seemed to meet
And make one point – one star set free
Between two stormy clouds. We leant
Upon both wind and words we meant.

A tense and joyful audience had
Thronged in the theatre we left.
Lovers had laughed at being sad
And justice, mercy were bereft
Of all abstractions. So were we,
Talking so low yet passionately.

Creators in Vienna

That dance we have heard of, so far back now that
We do not know who first pushed it gently into
    A child's mind. But Vienna, Vienna, no mere tapping
In rooms or pavements. Ideas were dancing also, especially in
    Four men's minds, ideas to change us, linking and breaking
Like dancers. The other two, a painter, a philosopher.
    Four kings crowned now by decades of acceptance,

Two trying to heal – Freud, Adler leaping down our
Apparently never-before-discovered minds, entering our dreams,
    Telling us of love and power, changing love and power,
And Kokoschka painting and enriching, purifying, disclosing,
    Wittgenstein quietly challenging centuries of speculation.
                               They are moving, moving still
These men, they pursue us. Time out of mind we
    Check them, deny. As we do so they smile at us because

Our queries continually prove them right, their power
Is no Prospero-wand. They have discarded nothing at all
    For our minds are brimmed with their voices, our hearts
Dance differently now. We are spellbound. We are islands.
    Madness has been given order, painting pours out on posterity.
The thinker, as always, is pressed dry between two pages somewhere
    Of a book containing the world, a book which can never be written.

Orpheus

    Not looking back, not looking back
    For him that was the test. We have,
    All of us, camped out, somewhere, some time
    In a place, underground or in full sunlight,
    Where we must choose. So our myths later
    Instruct us, and our beliefs, whether in Eden
    Or oblivion, take for granted free-will,
    Act on that assumption, even in unbelieving.

    Thus Orpheus running through Hades with
    A lyre so enchantable once, was himself
    Now enchained. That girl, she must, could be his.
    But he must not look back. He saw light,

A little like Lazarus, with the same trust,
The same astonishment, but for him life was behind
In that place there. Misjudging the threshold
Or perhaps forgetting the promise, he turned, stunned,
Seeing only darkness, no lyre could call her back, the girl
Had gone, the gods dealt out their punishment.

Persephone

For Spring and Summer she appeared and was
Blinded at first by light. To us she meant
Autumn and Winter were away because
For those two seasons she retreated, went

Back to the dark world, darker than our own.
When she arrived the petals opened to
Welcome her with their wreaths, twine round her throne.
Birds hatched their eggs and all things richly grew.

She went away quite silently one night.
The air was cold next day. From every tree
Leaves fell in dusty disarray to light
And burn the shadow of Persephone.

Snake Charmer

The body writhes and rounds. The fingers feel
A circle, find a note. Up from the ground
Rears the caught serpent. It unwinds its coil
And dances to the sound

The player blows. His eyes address those eyes.
He is the choreographer who's made
The pattern of the dance, its length and size.
Danger is what is played.

In jeopardy, in thrall, the watchers can't
Help moving to the creature which they fear.
But they are safe as long as music's sent
Though that's not what they hear.

This is a rite but this is power also.
It happens now, yet enterprises such
As this take timid men to long ago
When the first reed's first touch

Haunted a jungle, hypnotised a snake.
This is no charming, this is courage when
At any moment faulty notes can break
Out anarchy again.

The Minotaur

Daedalus designed this. Famous for buildings he did Minos' will.
                         Minos, full of revenge, yet could not
Kill this creature begotten by his wife and a bull coupling. Poseidon
                                punished him in this way,
Making for us a pattern as perfect and intricate as that labyrinth. We
                         want the danger, the escape, above all
We want a happy love story to cancel a passion which was prodigal
                                     only of
A half-bull. Ariadne waited on this, patient as Penelope. She had
                     seen the handsome Athenians one by one
Go into Daedalus' design and die there. But she possessed joyfully the
                       power of a thread and a secret.

At first sight, as even classical writers will show and allow us, she fell
                     in love with Theseus who arrived
Apparently just a victim. But she, and we want this too, always this
                       necessity and ceremony,
Gave him the thread, the clue, the condition to be his wife. Theseus,
                     quick with courage and passion,
Took the twine from her, smiled and walked into the darkness
                     watchfully but fearlessly and found
The Minotaur sleeping. Beautiful indeed but now to be beaten to
                     death by young fists, exalted
In no bull-ring with panoply but providing us with the desired peril
                     before love succeeds,
Leading us gently into labyrinths within us where half-bulls
                   sometimes wake in our own darkness
And where we must always all be both Theseus and Ariadne.

Not Abstract

Where the river bends, where the bridges break,
Where the willow does not quite
Fall to the current – here is the place to stake
Your life in, your delight
Once easily lost. Here again you could make
A day out of half a night.

The moon is assured. The sun has put its back
Against the wood, the trees
Carry their rotten fruit like a swollen sack.
Stand among all of these
And learn from desertion and luxurious lack
Why some fall on their knees.

Gods have given. Gods have taken away
But left us with the need,
In angry arguments, logics which pray
Even for ghosts of a creed.
The bridge is broken and the willows sway.
Where does the river lead?

Little Peace

Through intricacy of sharp air
The urgent messages are sent.
Voices become a thoroughfare,
Crunched leaves are now irrelevant.

For seasons have resigned to let
Emergencies take on the sway
Where rules and governments once met
And legal systems drew each day

A quiet map, imposed a scheme
For living through. Now to exist
Through hours that shake men from a dream
Makes them take care not to be missed.

For not appearing will put them
In cells unwardered and unbarred.
Strange that a child still shouts its game
And has not heard the times are hard.

Trees shake, leaves drop. But who will win
Such trembling apprehensions warred
Where blood runs cold, blood-sheds begin,
That child ignoring and ignored?

Because huge violence is a threat,
A few are frenzied to be kind,
Warm one another yet, and yet
Hope is still hunted. Who will find?

Spy

The cleaving currents of dispute
Hold back. The vengeances now lie
With a few batteries of loot,
While a consenting, unhelped spy

Is wary, wondering what to do.
There may be armistice. He does
Not know the false reports from true
But waits in hiding. Is his cause

Or what he thought a war proclaimed
Ended? How long can he last out,
Starving now simply to be named,
Despair itself a thread of doubt?

Prisoner

Feel up the walls, waters ooze. The cold
Cranes down the spine. The wayward sky won't fit
A window, a square, but a square equates itself
With the eye in the brain, in the nervous system. All
Which flesh becomes without food and a little water.

I am tired. The planet curves, I cannot sleep.
How many moons have shone in how many shapes?
I am wistful in wisdom, honest in rich endearments,
Hollow perhaps, a channel for any whisper.
The long night takes my loneliness into its hands.

Behind All Iron Curtains

Ambassadors were dignified and curt
And even whispered in brocaded halls.
The slightest emphasis made someone start.
Meanwhile, pent anger hid behind the walls.

Answers were easy. It was questions which
Sent the eyes darting and the eyelids down.
One secretary slipped out of this reach,
Preferring all the tumult of the town.

Two wanted to make love but could not find
A room, a park, even a pool of shadow.
There was a haunting in the loving mind
And every mother seemed to be a widow.

One boy went out alone. There was a hush
Of people disappearing, then, far-off
A better tone, the beating, tidal rush.

He stood as though a statue in a hot
Strewn-with-siesta square. He heard a cough.
Smiling, he turned and, with a smile, was shot.

Happenings

Some say contentious Summers drove them to
A mountain range where they could touch the ice.
Then feel the finger-tip of thawing twice
When the hot cities cried 'Our need is you.'

Others were stunned awake, their mouths were sand
Choking, their spread of skin felt like a shore
Whose sweat was tides which only can withdraw.
They woke from this to lineaments of land.

And a forsaken few, who found forsaking
A suffering that pleased them with its skill,
Worked out proud plots their dreams could not fulfil
Though the beginnings had been so breath-taking.

Some kindly quiet ones were swept away
Until their own compassion cried 'Be mild.'
Madness caught up and set a mask that smiled
On such domestic, dutiful dismay.

Twelve great imaginations disappeared
Till someone's memory went deeply down
And grasped a goodness which they gave a crown.
Part of the world for two hours was not feared.

Visions and revolutions such as these
Are trusted to no treasure-hunts but lie
Beneath an unportending birdless sky
Waiting for, O, what men, what histories?

Not for Use

A little of Summer spilled over, ran
In splashes of gold on geometry slates.
The grass unstiffened to pressure of sun.
I looked at the melting gates

Where icicles dropped a twinkling rain,
Clusters of shining in early December,
Each window a flaring, effulgent stain.
And easy now to remember

The world's for delight and each of us
Is a joy whether in or out of love.
'No one must ever be used for use,'
Was what I was thinking of.

Wishes

I hired a boat and told the sailors to
Take me to a hot island where the palms
Give you warm breath, and on the sands a few
Shells wait to be wrapped up in the sea's arms.

I begged a lonely man to show me where
A desert and a mirage might be found
And some oasis would give quenching air
As water blossomed from the ancient ground.

I asked some lovers if they knew the way
To some old friends of mine. They did not know;
They had not even heard the time of day.
The sunlight seemed to make their bodies glow.

I asked a priest where he had found his God.
He handed me a musty-smelling book.
I stared into his eyes and thought it odd
That he should have such an untrustful look.

I asked a child if he could cross the road
Safely. He did not speak but took my hand.
The shaking traffic seemed to shift my load
But there were thoughts I longed to understand.

Ends

A city afraid of its darknesses,
Stone and wood and creeper wore
Their fitful mourning. An odd or even
Light appealed with a tiny gesture.
People ashamed of the cold they hide.

It could be the end of the world. It could
Be the almost last moment. Yes, there might
Have been a warning, men given a chance
To collect together their better feelings,
Create a contrition just in time.

We did not think it would be like this.
We imagined thunder-bolts or a blaze
Of all the stars colliding and clinging,
The moon head on to the sun. And so
It well may be. This is not the end.

In spite of the shame, in face of the fear
Half a cleaned Classical column withstood
The thriving moon which must increase.
Marching clouds were packing the sky
And one or two or three stepped clear.

Particular

Milk is on rocks, sea is only
Faintly tidal. The same sail draws
Its red sheet on a washing blue.
A telescope picks out rocks.
Limpets cling to their fastness.

Somebody's photograph? It wasn't.
Geologist's playground? No.
A scene unglossed by sentiment.
No one has ever been there.

A slice of an island this is.
The hem of a dream held fast.
Immaculate invitation.
A move towards innocence.

A place revered so richly
Is untampered as the moon.
But idylls are earmarked always
And we have set our seal

On the power which pulls a particular
Sea. This fragment of shore
Was sand-castled once by a child
But isn't now any more.

Childhood in Lincolnshire

Six years of a flat land.
Grasses cut your fingers on that shore.
People kept calling it Holland and a child
Thought this on some map somewhere
Linked it with that place
A Dutch doll came from.
So the sea trafficked with imagination
Which was more luminous even
Than the blazing tulips in formidable ranks
Or honeysuckle,
The first flower to be seen and smelt,
Tied to its own event and potent for that, therefore, always.

Losing and Finding

You had been searching quietly through the house
That late afternoon, Easter Saturday,
And a good day to be out of doors. But no,
I was reading in a north room. You knocked
On my door once only, despite the dark green notice,
'Do not disturb'. I went at once and found you,

Paler than usual, not smiling. You just said
'I've lost them'. That went a long way back
To running, screaming through a shop and knocking
Against giants. 'I haven't had lunch', you said.
I hadn't much food and the shop was closed for Easter
But I found two apples and washed them both for you.

Then we went across the road, not hand in hand.
I was wary of that. You might have hated it
And anyway you were talking and I told you
About the river not far off, how some people
Swam there on a day like this. And how good the grass
Smelt as we walked to the Recreation Ground.

You were lively now as I spun you lying flat,
Talking fast when I pushed you on the swing,
Bold on the chute but obedient when, to your question
About walking up without hands, I said 'Don't. You'll fall.'
I kept thinking of your being lost, not crying,
But the sense of loss ran through me all the time

You were chatting away. I wanted to keep you safe,
Not know fear, be curious, love people
As you showed me when you jumped on my lap one evening,
Hugged me and kissed me hard. I could not keep you
Like that, contained in your joy, showing your need
As I wished *I* could. There was something elegiac

Simply because this whole thing was direct,
Chance, too, that you had found me when your parents
So strangely disappeared. There was enchantment
In the emptiness of that playground so you could
Be free for two hours only, noted by me, not you.
An Easter Saturday almost gone astray

Because you were lost and only six years old.
And it was you who rescued me, you know.
Among the swings, the meadow and the river,
You took me out of time, rubbed off on me
What it feels like to care without restriction,
To trust and never think of a betrayal.

An Event

Legs in knee-socks,
Standing on the rough playground,
Suddenly thinking, 'Why am I here?'

No one else seemed near you,
Though they had been, still were
Except for this awareness.

Long before adolescence
This happened, happened more than once.
Is this the onset

Of that long-travelling,
Never answered
Question, 'Who am I?'

It could be.
The state does not last
But the memory does.

And soon the shouts surround you again.
You have a blue and a red marble in your hand.
It is your turn to roll one.

Usage

Creature-comforts other people call them
And what do they mean, just what precisely?
One would gladly starve for weeks to have
That picture pinned up always, while another
Would buy a toy rather than think of bread rolls.
And what exactly are these creatures, are they
Listed in books of mammals? Are they insects?

Birds possibly, the ones who loot a nest
Of one more bright than they. I am amazed
     When I discern the different ways we live,
Tastes we provide for, that we can have in common
     The same five senses and yet still allow,
In these at least, no singularity,
     While creature-comforts thrive upon their vagueness.

A Third

It was not that I intercepted
A look of love, as though trapped between two portraits.
I could have shared that, been included
Simply by recognising what I have seen directed
At me, a look so humanly open that a human being
Cannot bear it long and casts down his eyes.

No, this was altogether different, important
Only because it embarrassed, because it showed the
Gulfs and gaps between three people, also the tributaries
Linking them and separating them. What I saw
Was desire, something which cannot be shared,
Which twists you away not in wonder but horror.

Horror because one human being is appearing
Too appropriately like an animal, the other attempting
To change the look with a smile of longing acknowledged
Publicly. Better surely, to pair off under dark trees than
Confiscate, however briefly, the equal friendship of a third person.

Need

     Only you would notice what lay under
     The practised smile, the just not jumping nerve.
     You would have known this was a hint of thunder
     To break out later. Yes, you would observe

     The manners learnt yet meaning nothing now
     But 'Let's pretend.' You've seen my nursery,
     Sifted the pleasure from the grief, shown how

I need not act. The irony, you know,
Is when I'm with you I enjoy the part
Of playing someone else, put selves on show

Simply because I need not. I don't fit
Either the worn-out or the tempted heart.
Tell me the words to feel the truth of it.

Accepted

You are no longer young,
Nor are you very old.
There are homes where those belong.
You know you do not fit
When you observe the cold
Stares of the old who sit

In bath-chairs or the park
(A stick, then, at their side),
Or find yourself in the dark
And see the lovers who,
In love and in their stride,
Don't even notice you.

This is a time to begin
Your life. It could be new.
The sheer not fitting in
With the old who envy you
And the young who want to win,
Not knowing false from true,

Means you have liberty
Denied to their extremes.
At last now you can be
What the old cannot recall
And the young long for in dreams,
Yet still include them all.

An Abandoned Palace

A palace where the courtiers have vanished fleetly because
The work was too hard, and where they squabbled continually about
                                                       their rights
And the Queen's debt to them – this has foundered as if the close
                                                       sea had
Rolled over and entered the doors. People ran out screaming.
   Two stayed – an old woman bound to rheumatic fingers and the
                                                       now hard
Embroidery she insisted on finishing. The other was the undeposed
                                                       but rejected and
   Uncomplaining Queen, who did not mind that the crown was covered
With mildew, the jewels were sold. She was subdued into a soft, slow,
   Ever-expanding melancholy, though her eyes smiled,
Bidding farewell to the servants gone, asking only that
   The steward should remain, add up the valuables and
Sell them. Then, in the high bedroom, she sat thinking

   Of utter simplicities, the heir who had gone to travel the world and
                                                       had not
Written. In her note-book she wrote two words only, two words
   Of disfigured defiance meaning almost total loss. The words were
'Find me.' Quickly she took a moulting carrier pigeon to trust this
                                                       message to
   And, with careful hands, glided the bird out of the tarnished
                                                       windows and then
Sat, waiting, occasionally visiting the trembling old woman, admiring
   The progress of the stitching, herself hiding tears, still, somehow,
                                                       hoping for
Rescue, reprieve, an escape from a palace now a prison where hope itself
   Taunted her continually with its expert disappointments,
Its refusal to gaze back at her long, caught in its own desperate incapacity.

Rather like a Peacock

You say you saw a bird much like a peacock,
Not proud of its own plumage, powerless with it
And being like a beacon to all corners,
Bedraggled birds, small but with the sharp
Anger and strength that comes when brightness is

Discerned, observed as dangerous, a threat
Simply by being passively attractive.
Yes, but among that gathering of birds,
Helpless, you said it was, and vulnerable.
Beaks bit into the colours and you thought

Of other creatures, human beings who
Have gifts not so flamboyant yet observed,
Envied. Tormentors, tireless as those birds,
Sense there's a threat, that here is something which
Might change their lives if given freedom, so,

They, who are quick at this thing only, find
The weak spot and with hostile words and looks
Darken that dazzle, rid themselves of fear
By forcing it upon the one they won't
Dare let it bring its brilliance to their minds.

What happened to that bird within your garden,
Target upon your turf? Could you scare off
Those small attackers, or were you too late?
Can you suggest a safe place for the being
Harassed just here, alive, alert, laid open?

Given Notice

For Clare

It was the going back which gathered
A pack of thoughts, feelings also.
They spilt from my hands as I looked about.
A window which held contentment once
Framed a sky unfit for viewing,
But the grey of it fell with glare enough

On squat chessmen, a kaleidoscope,
A Russian bear, an Italian mug.
The full and flare of the place were rich,
But I in the middle of it was mute
Begging within myself for one,

Yes just one day and a different sky.
How hot I became with remembrances,
Then a feather of fear with strength enough
To connect the subtle silences,
Unheard discourses valued now.

The room was an animal money-box
Smashed in pieces, the coins thrown down.
It was that returning which did it all,
Unlodged the losses I'd thought well-hidden
People who came or did not come,

The bird outside which seemed to stick
On a single branch through a keepsake June
Of pell-mell skies and unscathed stars,
Broken yet holding petals and leaves,
All too much outside and within.

You who had never been before
Watched my wistfulness, saw the shrug,
Contained the sigh in a silence shared.
Toys are terrible, rooms are let
As blood is sometimes, for transfusion.

Leaving a Room

Somebody said 'Like an amputation,'
Another, 'Part of your character.'
Both were right: growing and breaking,
The nine, nineteen, nine hundred lives
Have been breathed in minutes, hours and weeks here,
Eighteen months by the calendar.
I have put both anchor and roots down.

My seasons were torn off a Summer layered
With raiding sunsets; bonfires blew
Away before me. Pictures faded
Slightly. I bronzed, slightly also.
What a litter of life I have crowded here,
What a residue of authentic gold!
I cannot keep it now.

The gallery, toyshop, study stand.
Clocks are striking round me, pendula
Pursue their energy. I have collected
Stars from that sky, laid them on ledges,
Rubbed shoulders with storms, the glass protecting.
Possessive, feverish, populous, I
Have plaited birds with their sounds. Today

Is not in time, is another order.
Nostalgia echoes, the early hours
Which were not hours are holding me.
I am tied up fast by trails of cards,
The threads of unfinished conversation.
I am a shape, a cube perhaps,
Now being sucked. But apparitions

Install themselves. I did not know
How acutely reliant I could be
On the lean of a card, the look of a toy.
Someone is taking over already.
Bruised by a fleck of dust, I pick
Some papers up and close my eyes

To the stars once fixed for me outside,
Stuff my ears against the insistent
Lovable echoes. I need a conversion,
Change into one who does not own,
Believe my belongings supply no need,
Then am heretic to the bone.

Deaf

Her mind is pushing slowly through the doors
Which others do not think about since they
Toss up their senses like a conjurer's
Five cards or streamers. She must find a way
To catch a tone or pause.

But it is nonsense that the eyes make up
For lack of hearing. Hers, obliquely bright,
Have no exchange with touch or tongue or lip.
Their brown is but a tension, not a sight
But when the eyelids droop

She hunts and stalks her family. Their names
Come out in questions. Silver deaf-aid is
A mockery, a shaken box of themes
Whose high notes are distorted, dissonance,
As though she spoke her dreams

And asked us for the meaning. Hidden mind,
Muffled behind a face which never has
Tautened to adult enterprise, been lined
With cross-hatched disapprovals, your distress
Is terribly unblind.

Night Worker by Nature

Almost the last thing I shall see,
My morning is near waking time
For others. Factory night-workers
Are yawning at conveyor-belts,
    Newspapers fell off trains

Four hours ago. My lean-to hours,
Shaped small by others, not by me,
Are shuffled books, precluding lamp,
A curtain keeping out the stars.
    No stars, though, when I switch

The light off. One long strip of grey,
Where curtains can't be dragged to meet,
I watch, then hump my back against
Sky coming in to spark my feet,
    Sun-rise, two hours away.

Birds call across my almost-sleep,
Draw drowsy waking into my
Drowsing-asleep. Night-worker, I
Have felt reluctant power keep
    Clocks back but not that sky.

The only chanticleer I know
Runs with the wind, washed by the moon.
Its plumage folds. This cock has no
Voice to attend the day. The sun
    May gild it upon show.

I shall not see. My room takes form –
A Cubist's gathering of things
In muted colours, my last sight,
My dream-connected lingerings,
    My last touch on the night.

An Attempt to Charm Sleep

A certain blue
A very dark one
Navy-blue
Going to school
Get back to colour
A pale blue
Somebody's eyes
Or were they grey
Who was the person
Did they like me
Go back to colour
An intolerant blue
A very deep
Inviting water
Is it a river
Where is it going
Shall I swim
What is its name
Go back to colour
Go back to waking
The spell doesn't work
As I stare at the night
It seems like blue.

The Poem at Times

Summons on the mind,
Seizing and questing, an
Attack, a coming to,
Excitement eased at once,
The found word, and the shine

As if, from water plucked
But never losing light,
Wash of the river still
Yet now on land at last
The writing's on a spool.

Box-Room

It is empty. Anyone entering hears
The creak of themselves. Boxes once
Held moth-eaten clothes and Teddy Bears.
That was before the going,
The gathering-up for the dance.

It is almost impossible to feel
Untouched by haphazard memory's glance.
Either your own or another's will steal
Into the gala of going,
The drawing-away to dance.

Cancer

Were the others warned of this also
Who saw the fingers flimsy as that disc
Of palatable bread, the over-flow
Of soda-water swallowed with no risk?
They must have seen the slow

Faltering, the body drooping dress
And cardigan. But they had their own ways –
Deafness, the tilted mind, or loneliness.
At first it was an ectoplasmic haze
I saw her through, distress,

Fear of my own, all that I had been told.
Motives don't mean much when uncoffined death
Walks in a woman not aware of cold,
Knowing, however, that each push of breath
Has not the power to hold.

She talked no stoic talk, nor thrived on past
Promise. She did not know I knew she had
The medical prediction and forecast
A year or maybe two. Below my bed
She lies, but does she rest,

Does the Faith I was told of falter where
She is alone? She only let a hint
Of any creed out with a casual air,
Yes, almost an aside. Acceptance sent
Shivers through me, not her.

Observing

That tree across the way
Has been a magnet to me all this year.
What happens to it is what interests me.
    I've watched a blackbird stay
Glued for a moment, unglue, disappear.
Violence came in April to that tree,
    Made its whole being sway

    Till I was sure it could
Not stand, would snap and in torn fragments lie,
Leaving another entrance for the sky.
    But that frail-seeming wood,
A conifer with intricate small leaves,
Stands under stars now while a new moon conceives
    Itself before the eye.

Celebration of Winter

Any voice is soprano in this air,
Every star is seeding, every tree
Is a sign of belonging or being free,
Of being strong in the Winter atmosphere.
Nobody hesitates here.

There are sounds and there are spaces.
Human creatures could have left long ago,
Birds are migrants except
For an owl which woos and lullabies the night.
We are only waiting for snow.
The wind has swept away the brooding Summer,
Or has it taken flight?
Nostalgias are null. Eyes are a taper alight.

And Winter reaches ahead, it stretches, it goes
Further than dark. A fountain is somewhere still.
What voice will come and fill
The emptiness of its no-longer overflows?
Any birth in Winter is hallowed by more
Than Advents or Bethlehems. The seas compose
Themselves perhaps for an Age of Ice, a shore

Where a child lifts a wave, where one gull chose
Not an inland cluster but broken wing and claw.
Any voice is sharpened upon this air
And if the sky sagged there would be more than one star to spare.

To Go with a Present

I will risk threats of gazing at the most appetising
Mirrors and turning away with bleakness. I will gather more
    As a geologist than a gardener, stones where fossils may be engraved
And give you the completest. This will last and though lacking
    The bounty and exuberance of full Summer flowers
Be quiet as I wish, as I want these words to be. For gratitude

    Is an honour conferred and requires always that subtle
Blend of the spontaneous with the studied. With all thanks
    A present should go. You handed over more
Than a dedication. You gave me a portrait and a mood and I
    Am amazed still at the authority of your perception, your gentleness.

A Little More

        Each minute of a further light
        Draws me towards perspective Spring.
        I fold the minutes back each night,
            I hear the gossiping

        Of birds whose instinct carries time,
        A watch tucked in the flourished breast.
        It ticks the second they must climb
            Into a narrow nest.

        So birds. But I am not thus powered.
        Impulse has gone. My measured cells
        Of brain with knowledge are too stored,
            And trust to birds and bells.

        Yet longer light is fetching me
        To hopes I have no reason for.
        A further lease of light each day
            Suggests irrational more.

Comfort

Hand closed upon another, warm.
The other, cold, turned round and met
And found a weather made of calm.
So sadness goes, and so regret.

A touch, a magic in the hand.
Not what the fortune-teller sees
Or thinks that she can understand.
This warm hand binds but also frees.

This is

This is to be unpossessive,
This is a way to earn
A portion of the clasp
Of sun. An eye can glean
The stars. They ride there still,
Are never gathered in.

And by nocturnal sea
A man may rest his dark
Which one wave laps upon.
This is a blessing, this
Awe which is silent, breath
Borne on a flight of wind.

Never Going

We were always going
Further up the beach
Or further down,
However you regard it.
This was always planned
For after siesta
One afternoon,
But we never went.
Why didn't we?

Stopped by the heat?
More than once certainly.
Or was it the familiar walk
Where, even abroad,
We had made landmarks,
Wanted to stick to them,
Streets become personal
With our private names?

How easily then
We dismissed that journey
Thinking, I suppose,
'There will be another time.
Today is all wrong.'
I shall not go there,
Not even to that town
Where you could have died.
No, that was elsewhere,
And that intended journey
Is prepared and plotted
For other people's footsteps.
There are no spoors of ours
And I won't go there alone.

A Gentle Command

May we retain
Such scope in which we play and love
    That we do not exclude
All those who have no heart to move,
    Fearing to spoil or strain,
Towards what is for us both joy and food.

Abandon, then
Secret looks, I charge you, and
    This self I need to school
From subtle ways which guard a land
    And keep off other men.
This paradox will make us spare and full.

In Itself

The rarity, the root, the flower,
The things themselves, not the abouts,
The magic wand of naming, power
That dreads away the darks, the doubts —

All this and see, a child appears
White as unfootstepped snow and strong
As dissipaters of spread fears.
He stands and sings. It is a song

He's thought, a purpose of pure sound.
This child is conjurer, can make
The roots thrill in the frozen ground,
Petals fold up for buds to break.

Gained

The day is not impoverished any more.
The sun came very late but never mind,
The sky has opened like an unwedged door
And for a moment we are all struck blind,
But blind with happiness. Birds' feathers toss
The air aside, regaining all the loss.

The loss of morning which was quietly grey,
Expectant, but what of? We did not know.
Our disappointment had discarded day
Until this early evening with its show
Of caught-up hours, sun's rising, sunset's glow.

CONSEQUENTLY I REJOICE
(1977)

Lighting a Candle

I have placed candles. I have held the wick
Upright, have shielded match-flames, scalded my
Hands, smelt the burning, tried again, again to keep my eye,
My night-eye on the moon, have laid the quick
Spurt to the candle, watched the flame grow tall
And a soft glow climb quietly up the wall.

The blinds are pulled to, all that gold explores
The room. It touches back across my hands.
I fold them, feeling, seeing lines like scars,
Then look away and up. The candle sends
Curious distributions. When I close
My eyes, the glow moves inward, takes my breath
At all the hauntings which I start to lose
The black hours as I shut a *Book of Hours* for death.

Restlessness

Houses whose dirt and hurt we've kicked off gladly
Soon become perfect in the memory.
Guitars in next-door rooms, a record badly
Scratched or put on too high
Dwindle away and somewhere else we see
And miss that view, that always sunset sky.

This moving which had seemed not only vital
But also something to look forward to
Is retrogressive and we cannot settle
In elsewhere very long.
Houses are only moods which we move through.
Too late we learn that most first moves were wrong.

Almost Drowning

First there was coming,
A coming-to, a sense of giddy
Limbs, another's or wings gleaming
Across the light. I was the body.
Was air or earth unsteady?

Second were voices,
Syllables, vowels were turning, running
Together. I was having races
With these, to overtake their meaning.
Then one word about drowning.

Third was the sea,
The tear of it about me still,
The time in it never to be
Within my compass or my will,
A birth or death writ small.

Invocation and Incantation

I caught a night-bird on a shaft of wind.
I thought and found it sleeping in my mind.

I took a leaf and held it in my palm.
It sent no shiver through me but pure calm.

I went out late at night to taste the air.
A star shone back at me like my own prayer.

Each second someone's born, another dies
But early hours do not contain their cries.

Sleepers are all about. O let them see,
When they wake up, peace garnered now for me

And may they lay their sleep upon my mind –
A bird with folded wings no nightmares find.

Inevitable

I am the haunted house whose doors are locked,
I am the echo of a sickening cry,
I am the ghost by which a child was shocked,
    I am the way you die.

I am the wound which never ceases bleeding,
I am the sun who blinds you with its eye,
I am the garden no one thought of weeding,
    I am the way you die.

Try to escape – I'll find you anywhere,
Attempt to tame me – do not even try,
Use your breath for a final whispered prayer
    For when I come you die.

Fragment for the Dark

Let it not come near me, let it not
Fold round or over me. One weak hand
Clutches a foot of air, asks the brisk buds
To suffer grey winds, spear through
Fog I feel in me. Give me the magic
To see grounded starlings, their polish
As this threat of all-day night. Mind, mind
In me, make thoughts candles to light me
Out of the furthest reach of possible nights.
Lantern me, stars, if I look up through wet hands,
Show assurance in blurred shining. I have
Put every light in the house on.
May their filaments last till true morning.

Tempered

Charted as dangerous that night is now
Because my rage seeped out and sweated through
The books, the toys, pictures hanging how
Some peaceful morning told me. Maps don't view,

They only guide and in the morning I
Marked in my mind that place, hot springs with no
Healing or warming powers. I pass them by
But are they tamed? Turning away won't do

Enough assuaging, I am worn with fight
Yet in me is the pressure to renew.
I feel dimension, growth, accept the right

Not of a passive being but of one
Who knows their rage and all that it can do
And, peacefully powerful, wills it all undone.

Morning Decision

All night lying tossing and loathing and dare I
Tell you how fast love seethed to hatred? Will I
Wound you further by what could be selfish confession,
This need to unload a guilt?
I ask this suitably grey and raining morning
Which is more important – to let you hear
The truth of me or deceive you and keep you happy?

Quickly a little wisdom comes as the sun does,
As the birds sing their own late dawn.
If I do not speak you will, as always, guess,
And if without further probing of self I show
My truth in speech, love will increase since you know
Me as the sun is concerned with the earth and as birds
Are learned in light. So yes, I will speak my words.

Better than a Protest

Tear off the rags of all my loves; you'll find
The scarecrow which you see
Was fashioned long ago in your own mind,
It was not made by me.
Blow tempests on my treasures. When you pick
Sharp pebbles up, treat them with care. You see
You're dazzled by my jewels, the pile is thick.

Remember that the berries and the flowers
You took indoors to die
Have their own strange recuperative powers.
I took them up. They lie
Sprouting already in my hands. I'm quick
To push them in the ground until a tree
Drops healing herbs for you, new buds for me.

Drama

Orchestra floats a quiet theme
To take the argument. Two seem
Once to have quarrelled and can't find
The words for mending. To the mind,
The music stretches. We are sure
That quickly there will be some clear
Words of requital. Shame will go,
Its coward self walk out tip-toe.

We shall see all that we have known
In early hours, sometimes alone,
But here a public act is done
Though private lovers will have won
With music, music always near
When words dare not speak of men's fear
And where the whispered happiness
Is sacramental and will bless.

My Seasons

I am a kind of Persephone perhaps
Would gladly be underground or asleep in the dark
Winters, would certainly hibernate if I could.

I count so many Springs since a hint of one
Excites. I have never learnt the way of seasons
Or not of English ones which I ought to know.

If I were Persephone I would be coming and going
Back to the dark, lacking an instinct for
The precise moment when Spring has arrived for sure.

I smell the nights, I cast a net of hope
Round a morning sun, I rub my shoulders with shoots,
I challenge the sky to be gentle with the lambs,

Gentle with me also. When the cuckoo gives
Its wooing double call I put out my hands
For feathers to drop from nests. I obey the winds

And let them carry me where they will. I give
All astrology up for a spread of stars
And a sickle moon meaning so many kinds of gold.

Winter Night Wish

We are all waiting, waiting,
Waiting for silence perhaps
Darkness ought to be still.
Day-sounds, you trespass upon
Time let loose by the sun.
Stars are not ready to fill
The upward dark with eclipse
Of little lights. Our will,

Our prayers feel for the night,
Knuckle and nudge, demand
A wordless, soundless time.
I have put out an icy hand
To stop a steeple's chime.
The noises are starting to end.
The sounds were strung on my mind

Meditation in Winter

Sealed against cold, I make the world I saw
Is it two months ago?
I shut my eyes and see an opening door
And just beyond the slow
Waves taking all the time there is, a shore
Fragrant with pasts which are not mine and yet
Reach out to me as if
Those waves were hands I recognise. I let
Them slip their warm, salt life
Over my own. How wide the sun has set

Plucking horizons off. Along my arms
The Winter wakens me.
My eyes are opened to a world's alarms
Yet that refashioned sea
Meditates through all seizures, calms, it calms.

Bird Sunrise in Winter

Close eyes. Stay still and you can hear
Rising of sun, ferocious cries
Speaking of birth about your ear,
An eloquence of skies.

Winter perhaps but this is Spring
Wrung from cold earth. Harsh life asserts
Its pressure on the air, will sing
Until the singing hurts.

Open your eyes. The light is birds.
They bear the sun and clip it round.
Almost they break out into words
In this impulse of sound.

Let There Be

Let there be dark for us to contemplate.
Light draws the senses. O that seize of stars
Or even ember-comfort in a grate –

These blind us. Christ, teach us the *Book of Hours*
Which says 'Be silent' as we turn the page
And let the vigil come. Light overpowers.

Give us the night, the lonely privilege
Of offering our praise, a plea within
Enormous spaces lasting to the edge

Of almost dawn, and let the birds begin
To chip at sounds, set fire to tree and hedge.

Song for the Swifts

The swifts have now returned.
They volley, parry, play with the new light,
Dance under pieces of cloud then, out of sight,
Tease us with the pleasure of their flight,
Become our luxury too. The wind's weight
   Is once again to be learned,

   To be taught to us by each swift.
Melancholies are carried away in the stride
Of the tamed clouds and Spring has opened wide
Its windows, these birds assisting. They have defied
Drowning waves, peaks few men have tried
   And they have come to lift

   Our minds and natures too.
Envy cowers with so much to be shared,
Love revives as we count up the paired,
Unthinkingly mating birds. Cold winds are repaired
By South the swifts have brought and we are snared
   By joy, know what to do.

   However dark our lands,
Wisdom is in our bloodstream not in brain
Alone and we take instinct on again
Watching these birds and the soon-to-bear-fruit grain,
And what we never thought we could attain
   Falls, the uneaten apple, in our hands.

Song

   As the sky
Unfolds every morning in Spring, slipping the sun
Over the needing earth, the asking trees, the high
Birds singing in discords sweeter than unison,
So I know with each day love has begun
   Afresh, who knows why

   We know what we mean
When we say 'I love'? Perhaps we are natural then,
Instinctual yet also intuitive, quick and keen
Not only to those we love but to all men,
Women and children when
   We trust we are being seen

As sun sees all
It lights upon, as birds tower to the sky
With the confident largesse of their call,
As animals burrow towards the greenery
Of grass and flowers, and as petals lie
So is love and so am I.

For Their Own Sake

Come down to the woods where the buds burst
Into fragrances, where the leaves make havoc
Of cloudy skies. Listen to birds
Obeying their instincts but also singing
For singing's sake. By the same token
Let us be silent for silence's sake,
Watching the buds, hearing the break
Free of fledgelings, the branches swinging
The sun, and never a word need be spoken.

Hatching

His night has come to an end and now he must break
The little sky which shielded him. He taps
Once and nothing happens. He tries again
And makes a mark like lightning. He must thunder,
Storm and shake and break a universe
Too small and safe. His daring beak does this.

And now he is out in a world of smells and spaces.
He shivers. Any air is wind to him.
He huddles under wings but does not know
He is already shaping feathers for
A lunge into the sky. His solo flight
Will bring the sun upon his back. He'll bear it,
Carry it, learn the real winds, by instinct
Return for food and, larger than his mother,
Avid for air, harry her with his hunger.

Much to be Said

There is much to be said
For undramatic landscapes, for pale skies,
For hills which do not overtire the eyes,
For rivers which yield quickly the treasure at their bed,

And where no sea
Haunts or hunts save when gulls bear
Witness to cold. Within such places you hear
Nature moving calmly with grace and integrity.

Here there is rest
But not so much the dwellers lull and steep
Themselves too long. No, missing here the deep
And high movements of land and bird makes people guest

Rather than those
Who settle, take for granted. I have found
My voice, my language here. It is a ground
Which starts my song, which also tells the proper close.

Instinct for Seasons

As some have divining instincts
For water, gold or diamond,
Can tell by a twitch or a scent,
So others, I among them,
Have a similar gift to tell
Of a season changing. It's not
In the power of one sense only
Or a habit of memory.
If I could tell the causes
I'd lose the knack or gift.

But causes jump to mind
And here are a few: – a concern
For how a bird's song hollows
A distance at early dawn
And climbs to a clarity
Which has something to do with the sun;
And again, the way the petals

Lift the face of a flower
Till it balances on the light
As a gull imposes its stillness
On a crest of impulsive wave.

All these explain but little.
Perhaps, though city-bred
(The house wasn't far from a town),
I have a farmer's feeling
Of when to plough or reap.
In the place where blood and the mind
Meet and are reconciled,
A recognition of seasons,
Days before they have come
Leaps with a throb and a drive
And today exults with the sun
And did so before it arrived.

The Sleep of Birds

We cannot hear the birds sleeping
Under the trees, under the flowers, under the eyes of our watching
And the rustling over of sheets of our unsleeping
Or our final whispers of loving.
How enviable this solemn silence of theirs
Like the quiet of monks tired with their singing hours
And dreaming about the next.
Birds are remote as stars by being silent
And will flash out like stars at their punctual dawn
As the stars are snuffed by the sun.

Does this quiet sleep of birds hide dreams, hide nightmares?
Does the lash of wind and the failing wing and the falling
Out of the air enter their sleep? Let us listen,
Open the window and listen
For a cry of a nightmare to underline the night.
There is no cry, there is only
The one feathered life who's not awake and does not sing
But hoots and holds his own, his own now being
A lordly and humorous comment upon the darkness,
A quiet joke at the changing demands of the moon.

Star Midnight

Isn't the sky wider, isn't the air
Steeper, the stars more preening,
Isn't the mind climbing stair by stair
And gradually winning
Advantage over earth, earning the clear
Precisest meaning?

Summer suggests this or its evenings do
When stars break through the warm
Darkness. The bare hand stretches out to strew
A bracelet from its arm
And the mind is sure that it has caught the true
Ultimate calm.

A moth flits by. A cat calls out. The intent
Moment is held. An hour
Pours out not in bell-notes but by the consent
Of purest thought. Say prayer
Or say this is a settled argument,
Say we are near

Knowing beyond discoveries with names
Or theories, but worldly-wise
In ways astonishing beyond our dreams
Yet here before our eyes.
I take a star down and the air still gleams
More in those skies.

Decision on a July Night

The stars come into their inheritance
In this night of almost
No sound. My very lowest breathing pants,
My body is a ghost.
No one about but my intelligence

Quickening. I animate a whole
Universe. I am
Guardian of the light which does not fall,
Lord of the stars which cram
The opulence of sky. If I should call

The sound would shake the trees. Suppose, suppose
That this were really so,
I could not live it long, I would depose
Myself, would overthrow
My power and risk whatever else I'd lose.

July Island

Frolicking over streets, parading Summer,
Leaves are like little boats.
The wind tides them along, the sunsets shimmer
Upon them, painted coats
As they stand to, but not for long.
Listen a sailor's song

Is on the breeze which comes in warm soft waves.
We swim upon such air.
That wind which was a launcher of those leaves
Combs also through our hair.
A mood of mariners prevails,
Birds' wings are bending sails.

All this until the sun withdraws its slow
Gilding, its mingling with
The drying wind, until horizons glow
And we draw in our breath,
Patter our strolling feet upon
Dark pools left by the sun.

Sonnet for Late Summer

With all this growing I must run a race,
Catch at a leaf the moment just before
It looses to a breeze, unmask a face
And show the future with the present stare.

Or take a jug surrounded by its own
Stillness, then raise it. Words must show the run
Of water. Look, it's pouring on a stone,
A little fountain soaked in jets of sun.

All these and more – a harvestful of time
In between Summer and the total fall
Of seed and leaf, caught in a cadenced rhyme,

Muscular words which stretch and race the course
To the last migrants' *grand finale* call,
The corn swept but each field a field of force.

Towards Migration

Listen, there is a leaving sound,
A slightly urgent note,
Partly from air, partly aground.
It issues from the throat

Of hiders in the trees along-
Side never-going birds.
It fits into a farewell song
And almost hints at words.

To the Ground

Leaf after brown leaf fell
And now is mould.
Bare every branch and tall,
Deeper each field.
Fallow land touched by sun
Is harvest gold.

Patient this pregnancy.
Birds skim across;
Earth hard for us to see
Will be no less
Vigoured to potency
By this darkness.

November Sun

Today is made of light and Winter goes
Away with one cloud darker than the rest.
The others are suggesting later snows.
Put out your hand and feel how it is blessed.

A pagan sacrament, a world of fire,
But sky is also open wings of blue.
Old stones are hoisting up their pale attire
And gently break as early flowers do.

New for a run of hours we cannot guess
As spirit lifts because the flesh has caught
Light. We stare the sun out as we bless
Beyond the very credence of our thought.

Ways of Dying

Shall we go bird-like down out of the air
Falling, falling, vertigo feeling only
Shaking our minds as they slowly blur, blur
And flesh is soon to be finally dust and lonely?

Or shall we scream and roar and make a scene
Like a nursery one, yelling 'It is unjust.
So much I meant to do, so much not seen'
And long for hunger and anger again and lust?

Or shall we lie quietly hoping to keep
The stranger's grip from stopping our hearts' slow beating
Or disappear in the corridors of sleep
But for what darkness there or for what meeting?

Winter Testimony

The last month of the year. I turn
The pages one by one.
They fade the more I look at them
But not with days'-past sun.
Words and events which shaped them ask
'How will you go on?'

The cold air climbs the clouds and breaks
Into a harmony
That would move in my absence
Or so it seems to me.
But this is not what I believe
In all honesty.

Right reason and wrong action
Have filled three seasons. Here,
Biting the wind which took the leaves
I see a child appear
Playing in an empty street,
Beckoning me near.

And further back a graveyard
Shows stones attacked by moon.
Somebody died three years ago
Leaving me alone
But the child I saw wants words from me
To prove it has been born.

All the year's music gathers,
Three parts of a quartet.
The harmony and meaning of
The fourth ask to be set.
That child could be Christ demanding love
From me who am needier yet.

Associations

Streets bore your name. Whole countries must
Be shied away from. Friends who knew
Closed mouths but just in time, but just
To hold me back from you.

And I, alone, shoved out of sight
What only could be memory
Of memory, but back at night
The facts confronted me.

Now I have seen a station with
Its name unblurred. How did yours fade?
I swallow tears and catch my breath
Because I have betrayed.

A death is intricate and grief
Itself is mourned for. Surely such
A loyal passion keeps your life
In closer, deeper touch?

And I may also be caught out
By sudden sights of streets or names.
Yet it's myself I call in doubt.
You never laid such claims.

Dust and a prayer, hope and dread –
Our hearts and minds are clocks which chime
Haphazard requiems for the dead
Contained in numbered time.

Old People's Nursing Home

The men have ceased to be men, the women, women.
Or so it appears at first.
Here are children dressed for a meal, napkins in collars,
Here are meals from the nursery, here is the nurse.
So it appears to one who is half
Within this house and half outside.
'It will be calm', someone suggested.

And so it seemed at first – tidy and calm
With the weather outside tidy and calm,
The carpets, pressed to the walls, forbidding noise,
No smell of a hospital, no smell at all,
And that was what I longed for first, the scent
Of a hyacinth bypassing sickness and pungent with growth,
Perfume thrust on the wrist and rising in clouds
In circles of foreign Summers.

But there was no smell, not even the deathly sick
Odour of death. And then I realised:
Death is shut from this house, the language of death,
The accoutrements of dying.
A ghost would be lively. Ghosts are not allowed here
And neither is talk of birth.

The faces differentiate themselves,
The men half-women, the women half-men
And each entirely children

Except in anger, except in ignorance.
These wrinkled faces knew too much, these gnarled
Hands have touched the pulse of love, have known
The family increase and birth's harvesting.

But that was the past and this house has shut out the past
And it dare not face the future:
So it lives in a perilous present that could be cracked
By a broken cup or a laugh.
Cups are unbreakable here,

Jokes are in print too small
And the noisy future, the passionate past are dammed
Partly by deafness, partly
By doctors' decisions and nurses'
Hiding the stuff of life and death away –
Tear-heavy handkerchiefs, the whiff of pain.

And I who carry compassion find it useless,
I who am very young here feel part-guilty,
Part-helpless. Most, out of place.
For my past and future spread throughout my present,
Time is a scheme of light and dark,
'What is the time' an old woman whispers.
Nobody answers and I,
With a load of compassion to scatter, refuse to tell her
For to do so would set the rainbow over this house,
Of movements and mornings which lead to death, and death
Is an outcast here for a night, for an hour, for how long?

To My Mother At 73

Will you always catch me unaware,
Find me fumbling, holding back? You claim
Little, ask ordinary things, don't dare
Utter endearments much but speak my name
As if you hoped to find a child there,
There on the phone, the same

You tried to quiet. You seem to want the years
Wrapped up and tossed away. You need me to
Prove you are needed. Can you sense the tears
So pent up, so afraid of hurting you?
Must we both fumble not to show our fears
Of holding back our pain, our kindness too?

Elegy for My Father

The bad years slip away and I see you
A generous, passionate man who had his share
Of merriment, who told good stories too.
At death's remove I can unyoke my fear
Of angry things you'd do

And see no 'good side', no, since sentiment
You were too salty for, then see you, rather
As one who never found his element,
His fit vocation. You, my caring father,
Followed me where I went

With claiming hope. Anatomy you would
Have chosen. Medicine took a different way.
You knew my love of words and sometimes could
Quote English verse. More often you would say,
Caught in an envious mood,

That 'There's no money in it', nag me. Yes,
My father, I am truthful here.
I listened to advice more than you'd guess
But could not show it. I am guilty there,
Yet now I want to bless,

To bless your gentle kindness and the great
Care you had for my mother, the quick mind,
The pride in me – all this I want to state,
And most of all the fierce love I can find
When now it is too late.

Death of an Old Lady

The wind came up this afternoon and I,
Blown like a feather, shivering into
The small warmth in me, thought 'Today you die,
Blown out also, clean gone, the whole of you.'
Last night I saw you lie

Sleeping, a little human bag of bone
With pallid skin stretched over it. You were
Alive, heart beating, one flame flickering on.
Then all the usual, human questions, 'Where?'
And 'Why?' pressed down upon

My three months' love of you. The stormy night
In retrospect seemed part of all of this,
The quiet morning suitable with bright
Still air, a calm much like the fantasies
To which you gave me right

Of entry. There were no farewells for us.
The wind lifts branches now, is snapping small
Twigs and there's a wind both boisterous
And grave, like death which needs no dirge or bells
But happens with no fuss.

Her Hands

They have attended to growing things, they have
Whispered along the grass.

They know when to leave alone. Their kind of love
Is often letting pass

Over or under. Learned they are and yet
Have never been possessed.

Lively they are with a dumb and devoted wit.
They punctuate its rest.

For an Old Lady of 96

Because you will not read
These words I write,
They come more carefully made.
You, out of sight,

Give me an honesty
For most poets rare.
Your trade was wool. Your fee
Less in a year

Than most make now in a week.
Your words were full
Of gratitude. You spoke
Of how the wool

Came in at midnight, said
It does not matter
What work one does; it's good
And can be better

If one respects it and
Keeps trying for
More swiftness with the hand.
Yes, you sat there,

Almost a century old
And I, half that,
Listened with awe. You told
Out of a heart

Warm without sentiment,
Memory long.
You said the words you meant,
Lightened your tongue

With country tones, a yeast
To raise the head
And heart. May you outlast
Your century ahead.

A Disabled Countryman

You acknowledge change but not without grief.
You are long-sighted, point the chalk horse out
Reined in on the horizon,
And you approve the cows in the middle-distance,
A jar, close by,
Of wall-flowers is a blur, but you with pleasure
Smell it, smile, and go silent.

Only a moment, though, only a moment.
You are off on the crops, niceties of description,
Forecasts of meteorologists and, most,
The book of biology swiftly turned in your mind,
Page after page lit with your intuitions.

You are a man who is stranger to regret
As the sun down-going does not grieve though it sheds
Its blood on the ritual sky.
It does not grieve but welcomes the moon taking over
With its court of attendant stars.
So you, a countryman who is now disabled
Must watch what once you used to do. You never
Envy the active ones.
The present is your province since it's wide
Enough to let the future enter it.

And the past is part of that open book whose pages
Have room for notes. Nothing is static for you.
You say a snowdrop has always been your favourite
Flower. That fits. You have its gentleness
Concealing toughness, and a suffering
Which goes with the land, the seasons and the weather.
You take on pain as birds take buffets from
The wind, then gather strength and fly and fly.

Military Service

He will not hurt because he is afraid.
He tries to force a hate he does not feel.
He practises all night but is dismayed
When morning comes to shine upon his steel
To find he handles it as if he played

With caps and pistols, noise which never hurt.
He has a bayonet and feels the knife
With fingering pride. He has become alert
As if to kill would give him double life
But plunging steel in sawdust dulls his heart.

He has not proved his manhood, thinks of waste,
Of sweating hours when he's too bored to read.
Then anger starts that he has been so placed,
Playing the guard of others' fear and greed.
His fight is like loveless kisses, a sour taste.

The Hoarder

Strangers might have diagnosed at a glance.
Neighbours took a little longer to
Remark upon the parcels he brought in
And how he tried to hide them, not be seen
Himself. He put his oddments out on show,
A private view but also a defence

Against the public, that is, workmen who
Might come to mend a pipe or check a door
Which would not shut. He never guessed why he
Hurried them out with too much courtesy,
Then, left alone, laid oddments on the floor
And played with them, but not as children do.

Ballad

The sun was firework bright that day
And Spring had broken through
The trees and put the lambs to play,
The flowers knew what to do.

Yet no one walked a street or square
And only birds proclaimed
There could be laughter everywhere,
Though laughter was not named.

The doors were shut, curtains were drawn.
Meanwhile in fields and farms
All life was fresh and newly born,
When suddenly alarms

Rang out, first shrieks, then sirens, then
A darkening in the sky.
Terror was all about but when
One fearless child called 'Why

Won't someone pluck a shaft of sun
Or pick a bunch of stars?'
The noises stopped and everyone
Watched the boy peacefully pass

Through fields and streets and as he went
Softly he sang a song,
And, oddly, all knew what he meant –
That omens had been wrong,

That horrors which they thought they saw
Were phantoms shaped by fear,
That one bold child had halted war
But they must bring peace near.

War

We thought with animals we were at ease.
Our power has overcome us since we named
Them first and then cajoled them to be tamed.
Did we forget they would stay enemies,

Their fury building up with no outlet
As in the plains and jungles? Now we pay
For our false sovereignty as every day
We war with one another, are beset

By fears more cleverly concealed than when
We took the animals and locked them fast
By coward iron bars. Now we are faced
With one another. Daily wars begin,

Bombs fall, guns rattle and we want to hide.
Fear is the fuelling passion with which we
Have built a prison for an enemy
And find too late we've locked ourselves inside.

Childbirth

It is going, leaving me – but the pain
Is making me hate this burden of
What I've been bearing proudly. Again
I am taken over by rough
Hands. They hold me, O but not
Now in the grip of love.

I never reckoned on this before
Or if I did it seemed a thing
To rejoice in, proof of a loving more
Than I had guessed could bring
Such ecstasy. Was passion worth
This life which insists on suffering?

A Child in the Night

The child stares at the stars. He does not know
Their names. He does not care. Time halts for him
And he is standing on the earth's far rim
As all the sky surrenders its bright show.

He will not feel like this again until
He falls in love. He will not be possessed
By dispossession till he has caressed
A face and in its eyes seen stars stand still.

Cradle Catholic

The hope and charity may go
A moment but the faith that's you,
You I can't feel and never see,
Yet feed on my identity.
O Christ, can it be ever just
To make a burden out of trust?

Love does. I mean our human love
And you are man but spoken of
As God. To make life simplified
You were a little child who died.
O take my unlove and despair
And what they lack let faith repair.

A Reflection from Pascal

'God made himself man in order to unite himself with us.'

All before stars, all before sun and seed,
All before planets severed, all before
Word or a breath of birth, there was this need

And not from skyward-peopled gods who war
And look like us and scoff. This God could plead
And cry and feel for friends. Kings might adore

But this one parched and panicked while the greed
Of other kings and men not kings could pour
Wine out and feast. He took the wine to feed

Us as with bread, became like us indeed
And made us like him as we wish to grow
Like those we love. Before the sun and seed

There was the Spirit, Christ who wanted to
Enter the moment when we saw his need.

Meditation on the Fall

Pleasure and passion – yes, we have them still
But somewhere in between a link was broken.
Whatever version we have of the Fall
We prove this in each love-word which is spoken,
A fragment of farewell

Sounds and is shared, sometimes is frantic too.
Man, woman bound in passion, don't you hear
Two clocks, your hearts, make mockery of you
And long at least that every heart-beat were
One clear note ringing true

However fitfully? Is that why we
Demand, contend and try to outstretch hours,
Force growth? Whatever Eve plucked from what tree
Mocks at our passions and outwits our powers.
We cannot be carefree.

O gardens of imagination where
We put an apple back, undo the fault,
The happy fault that sets us fumbling here,
Why do we panic to prolong each halt
And force what we cannot share?

A Magnificat

I make him greater. Yes I magnify
This child, this God, yet hardly understand
How this can come about. He is so high,

So broad, so everywhere. Yet in my hand
His lay, the touch of God. So many days
He was about and needed me to send

Him on his tasks. My task is now to praise
And teach the echo of it to all men
Who make God greater every time they raise

Their voice in need or wonder. My son, when
Will you be satisfied, come back again?

Mary the Huntress

Mother of God, the huntress who
Takes on Diana's part, we are
The creatures you seek out, pursue

So quietly. However far
We stray, you hunt us down not with
Anger, extravagance or fear.

You catch us with a snare of breath
And give us sorrowing words to say
And fill our better moments with

Grief on an ordinary day
As if all Nows were hours of death.

Mary Speaks

I did not sin but, Son of God and mine
I felt temptation, stood one step before
Decisions made in thought or word or sign.
You as all man, I as all woman saw
How far off the divine,

Great arbitrations run, from cell to star,
All the huge spaces. Yes, but you gave me
A way to enter them without men's fear
Since you diminished to maternity
And brought creation near.

My little son who made the universe,
My God who shed your tears upon my breast.
Virgin and mother, daughter, child and nurse,
I heard the whispers of your near-despair
And now, from all men, worse.

Mary's Magnificat

My little child but barely child,
Only a flutter, like the clutch
Upon the air when my words willed
That God should come for man to touch.

My spirit magnifies and flesh
Is growing every hour until
The nine months' nearness has grown full
And in one way I lose my wish.

For little child you are not mine
Again alone nor is God so
Sheltered. Now I must let him go
Who sought me out for his design.

Christmas Request

Cast aside all trappings, let
Tinsel tree and bauble be
Put away, and no more light
For this child's nativity

Than the brightest star you find
As you pace through almost ice.
Bring it down into your mind
Like a wordless prayer for peace.

Shepherds shall draw back. Alone
Shall the young girl with a smile
Clasp a God which is her own
Flesh to feed a little while.

Ours much later, ours as bread
Now let wonder be our gift.
See, that star shines overhead;
All we thought we took is left.

Words for the Magi

'Shall I bring you wisdom, shall I bring you power?'
The first great stranger said to the child.
Then he noticed something he'd never felt before –
A wish in himself to be innocent and mild.

'Shall I bring you glory, shall I bring you peace?'
The second great stranger said when he saw
The star shine down on entire helplessness.
The gift that he offered was his sense of awe.

'Shall I show you riches' the third one began
Then stopped in terror because he had seen
A God grown-up and a tired tempted man.
'Suffering's my gift' he said
'That is what I mean.'

Our Lady's Lullaby

My needy, dwindled creature lie
And weep laments of later men.
Are you also divinity?
I ponder this again, again.

I am all wonder as when you
Sent messages to ask my care.
Child of my free-will, how are you
The God of prophets clinging here?

O power subdued to flesh of mine,
How tangible is our exchange.
From me the milk, then you in wine.
Simplicity, O you are strange.

Christ Recalls 'The Massacre of the Innocents'

I name them now, I think of them always.
Features stand out whenever children lurk
Among the crowds. I catch a hostile gaze.
O children not yet frightened of the dark,
I fall upon my knees,

I sweat, am scourged, am crowned with thorns for you,
Yes, I escaped but Herod took each son.
I'm punished by the screaming mothers too.
Father, where had our endless mercy gone
If there was this to do?

Mystery of man and God, the interplay
Trapped in a prayer but not in argument.
Those children died and yes I went away
To an impassioned, to my own lament
That I too must betray.

Christ on His Loneliness

Alone entirely, I am not like men
Who run to one another's arms or fight
For justice. I am perfect God and man
And feel those two perfections like a weight
I bear about alone.

Where are you, Father, when this sadness comes
And there's no quittance? Love is what I preach
But not that love I found in one girl's arms
When Time and childhood gave their kindly touch.
I need a love which warms.

And yes, long to escape from my vocation,
From my two natures. Being God is too
Vast, while my manhood asks an isolation
At times unbearable. I did not know
This sense of separation,

This chill of air around and mind within
Would hurt. My Father, are you also here,
Looking upon a world of smiling sin?
I weep to see my destiny so clear,
God-Man yet not like men.

The Holy Fool

Who was the holy fool among you chosen?
Perhaps impetuous Peter wanting to
Set altars to applaud a mountain vision,
Who swore his loyalty and when cocks crew
Wept an entire contrition.

Impulsive men have sought you out since then
And been mocked at. Didn't you warn of this
Yet never emphasised what laughs could mean
In terms of martyrdoms – the near-madness
Of those who think they've seen

A god and only babble? These are fools
Of holiness and in our better hours
We study them rather than learned schools
Where wise men exercise and flex their powers
With such cold-hearted tools.

We call men mad when we are most afraid
And in the very words confer a grace
We wonder at, it is so simply made
And when we catch it in another's face
Feel innocence betrayed.

One Who Was Healed

Perhaps the worst temptation. Bitterness.
The pain was unprepared. I was all man,
All child delivered into loneliness.

Tortures to come and promised. Yes, but when
I healed they went away. I needed their
Requital, pleasure. All my Godhead gone

A moment as I begged a childlike prayer
For their return, a sign of gratitude.
I watched the road and blinked at gritty air

Then far off dust took shape. Could, yes it could
Be one had come to thank. The man in me
Felt what I preached and saw how men are good,

At least one was, in perfect liberty,
And all the desert flowered a neighbourhood.

Christ's Final Temptation

Father, in desert, in that wilderness
I took the final, loneliest temptation,
Lassitude, yes, and also helplessness,
The numbness of not having a vocation.
I begged for the distress

Of anger, lust for now I entered man
Entire, the man at any age who finds
Within himself no order and no plan.
Father, I reached the splitting edge of minds
Which care because they can

See nothing but a purposeless lost state.
O how compassion flowed when I learnt this,
I understood how men could torture, hate
Us for allowing them such uselessness.
How could we let them wait

For me to enter into this unbeing?
I was in time and for a moment could
Hate you for this, thus hate myself. The freeing
Made me fall on my knees that man is good.
Yes, I to him was praying.

Christ's Agony in the Garden

Father, the Supper's over. Judas is
Betraying me. My Father, I kneel down
In this dark garden. Now I am helpless.
It's hard to pray. My God, Myself, my own
Being, this loneliness?

Is too unbearable. Did we ask men
To live through such? Why, I demand now, why
Must they be stricken so, why suffer when
Without free-will, they did not have to die?
Father, free-will I know

In its full terror. I am sweating here
Because of liberty. Take time away,
Show me our Now. My Father help me bear
All sufferings of all men every day
And night. Father, the worst pain now's the fear
That I too shall betray.

In Christ's Place

You will be crucified for me,
You will be hunted in the place
You thought most safe. And you will see

The darkness on a threatener's face,
Then hear the shouts of Calvary,
And learn the opposite of peace.

My Temple is not safe from this.
Remember I was angry there
And can be now in silences.

This is the sword I told you of
Which strikes most deeply where there's love.

Prayer to Christ Suffering

Christ, you look afraid. What is your need?
It was a painting that I saw and yet
I thought of blood not pigment, blood you shed,
And then of tears, a child's, a face still wet,
And all that history said.

O be as little as you can so I
May be sufficient comfort. Be as small
As the spent breath which dying creatures sigh.
Or be an impulse or a single call
Or else the question 'Why?'

Christ I can pray to need more than to pain,
Can beg from either too. That wine, that bread
Are too correct for fever or blood-stain.
O be the anxious longing in my head,
The whole of doubt again.

Christ Surprised

Back I came so deftly, felt my body
Healed but light, washed by the sun of morning
And every sense was woken up to newness.
I looked, surprised to see my shadow marking
The earth which slightly hurt my feet – new-grounded.

No one must touch me, no one yet must finger
The hands which had been wounded or the body.
Light-headed was I, yes intoxicated
By air, by light, my godhead brimming over,
My manhood daunted. I was lost a little.

She came so fast along the garden to me.
O Father I was fearful, I was being
Born once again but in a new aloneness.
The sun was heavy and the hours were pressing.
I must grow used to my own Resurrection.

Christ Seen by Flemish Painters

Never the loaves and fishes multiplied,
Never the senses loosed, never the full
Attentive crowd, bloat faces set beside
A landscape opulent with sun and whole
Terraces hung with wide

Sweet fruit. Austerity, the grey face drawn,
The body almost spirit on the wood,
The wood like ash. Perhaps two lookers torn
By watching night through with no sleep or food.
Yes, here God is alone.

And man has seen the solitude of spaces,
The no-star air, the soil which hurts the feet,
The puckered pain on hands, the worried faces,
Triumphant anguish just before defeat,
The cool air of hard graces.

Christmas Poem 1974

Once more you climb down from the cross
Back through the thirty years and lie
Within a young girl's large embrace
And warmed by wonder. Stars are high,

The air is quiet. War has drawn back
An hour or two. The soldiers sleep.
This birth lights up the centuries' dark.
Not yet the message or the cup.

She knows that you must suffer, yet
Perhaps she too fills out this hour
When love and innocence have met
And God himself puts off his power.

One Creed and Many

Those who sing a creed, share a belief,
Are yet not one entirely. Each re-makes
The article he needs, fashions a prayer,
Fingers the same prayer-book leaf.
One will find hope, another suffering there.

Christ turns to each of us
A different face, the one we beg and need.
Open and wise to children, he can show
A doubtful countenance indeed
To those in doubt, who bleed
Arguing thoughts. Doubt too can be a creed.

All we believers share
Is the knowledge of pain which comes to each one in
A different guise. Some know it all their lives,
To others it will begin
As age takes over, they see everywhere
The scar of their own and also of Adam's sin.

This Church we call a Rock
Knows the wearing, washing sea, the insulting wave,
The storms that almost overwhelm, the shock
Of thunder and lightning. We are children of such
But see in that flashing light Christ's sudden love,
Feel through the thunder God the Father's touch.

Michelangelo's First Pietà

Carve a compassion. Older than you are
He lies upon your lap. What can you do
But hold him with a trust you also fear?
    Thus Michelangelo

Saw what a girl may do for gods. O we
Have mercy on this man a woman holds,
God in the grip of our humanity.
    All this the sculptor moulds.

But more. It is a prayer that he is saying
Wordless, except that written on her breast
He writes his name. This girl he is displaying
    Has also brought him rest.

Sufism

This God is a veil over the world but is also shining at us
Through all growth, hides in the detailed veins of a leaf, in the dance
    Of petals in wind, in the four quartered wind also and in
Each different turn of a wave, each diverse groove in the sand, and in
    All eyes, whether of fish or lion or a bold child outstaring
The sun. Let the veil be stripped off, the Sufis say, let God
    Step out of his own inventions. Let us prepare our poems and
                                                        music and
Dervishing dances for his delectation. What we seek is to grow to a full
    Maturity. The way is freedom, the means and the only means is love.

So they gathered in groups and chanted, others wrote poems, some
Tapped or plucked instruments, and all were preparing a home, a
    Paradise for their creator, one who could span the sky and also
Be caught in the cup of a mountain flower, in the wings of a dragon-fly
    Hovering over the water. Let us dance, these seekers, these
                                                    mystics said,
Let us chant for not only in silence is our God at hand, he will
                                                    bound to life
    And sport with and glory in his creation if we
Will play with his games, be serious also with his ways with us as he spins
    The world we are on. Let us take it to us like lovers, embrace the
                                                    God we have summoned.

A Meditation on D.H. Lawrence

One more step from darkness, one more step
From that acceptable darkness.
Breaking you did not fear, the painful breaking
Which brings to birth, which bears above the waters
The soaked wings of a bird, a bird which rises,
Its feathers finding air, each sense awakened.
But one more step, the one the mind must dare take
You could not see or only see your mind as

A stirring, flickering brightness on the waters,
The sun assuming tides. O but your mind was

Brave to all breaking, bearing an unknown God.
Could you not see your mind was searching Christlike,
Bruised and wounded like him,
Clear, bright-thoughted like him?
He walked the waters with such senses as you
Commended to a flower, the grass, a forest,
But mind was sensitive to every feeling,
To every step across the land or water.
The darkness and the bruises which he knew of
Were in the mind immaculate, new-minted.

O one more step and you would have joined hands with
No unknown God but one who praised as you did.

Tolstoy

The terrible nightmare was a cross to bear,
Shadow over your page and no more peace
For others or yourself. Your wife must share
Your huge distrust, angry unhappiness,
The marriage-bed despair.

Stories were written, novels piled up. You
Could not write out the dream. Suspicious of
Your body, hating how your children grew
In number, you at last made war on love.
It takes a passion to

Hurt with such vehemence, hate with such shame.
The woman could not bear the cross you tried
To load her with and would not take the blame.
At last it was your lust you crucified,
Called by a different name.

Elegy for Aldous Huxley

Words had been relegated long ago.
A young man's cleverness was put aside.
You thought you could not feel but feared to show
In speech the pities which you thought collide
And introvert us so.

How well you knew yourself. You put away
The novels, verses, stories where the 'I'
Dominates, makes us masochists. Today
You are the peaks you would not dare to try,
Words you refused to say.

Change of Plan

Instead of painted avenues
Of light, I let that painter play
With all the air about the trees,
And, by good luck, this Winter day
    For six hours was at ease

With sun. Gold trickled slowly first,
Then bled along the roofs and took
Charge of the branches. Blossom burst
Across the sky and on my book.
    So Turner might have thrust

His later hand along this air,
This altered day when plans were changed,
When any moment tears were near.
Yet as I walked the light arranged
    His brush-strokes everywhere.

And his intense search for the pure,
For the acute, the almost, yes
Beyond what any eye can bear
Put fingers on my face to press
    A part of his quest there.

Circles and squares and lines which paused
At pink and turned away to red

Or, for a moment, gold, proposed
An outdoor exhibition spread
As disappointment was dispersed,
    Turner, all ways, ahead.

In a Violent Time

For Andrew

We know of violence but need not add
Our portion to it. There's protection too
Not for ourselves but, say, for keeping bad

Stories from children, pictures with a view
Of bombs and blood. It takes an art to be
A calmness anywhere. To me and you,

To all our friends and to most strangers we
Owe every tact that's learnt by discipline,
The craft which grows from self-severity.

Cheerfulness can look stupid. How to win
A smile without deceiving anyone?
The answers come by practice. We begin

To fight most violence by having won
The long destructions fighting in us from
Our birth. For some those battles aren't begun.

Compassion easily can seem a calm
Evasion. No, it's bound with courage and
The way unhappy people give a warm

Hand to the more afflicted. So, to you
Whose years are fewer but have suffered much
And want to write and make your words sound true,

I offer what you gave me first with such
Flamboyance, openness. To risk a loss
Is more than half of friendship. May I touch

Your griefs sometimes by silence, never lose
The power to bare the painful depths in us.

For Edward Thomas

I have looked about for you many times,
Mostly in woods or down quiet roads,
Often in birds whose question-times
Sound like the echo of your moods

When sombre. I've not found you yet
In day sounds or dream-threaded night
You watched through, tired-eyed. I set
Such places by, finding no sight

Of you in this strange hunt. I turn
Back to your words. You do not haunt
Them either. Suddenly I learn
Your art of being reticent,

Of leaving birds, trees, hills alone.
You left no spirit in any place
Or spoors of yours where you had gone.
Yet, though there is no print or trace

Of you, I *see* a different way,
As if your writing were a shine
Upon cool suns, your words the play
Of stars with water, your dark – mine.

Questions to Other Artists

Tell me, composer, tell me,
When silence comes to you,
The dance of the notes has vanished,
The wave has ceased to flow,
Each instrument is dumb,
What do you do?

Tell me, painter, if there
Is a confusion of
Colours on your palette
Which your brush can't move
Often? Does a canvas
Stare like a flouting love?

When a movement falters,
When the brushes start
Shaking to a pause,
Do you wonder what
Keeps us hunted, hunting
In the luck of art?

Aren't you grateful also
For the truthful song,
Or the colours fitting
Space you left for long
As I when words are offered
Like a Host upon the tongue?

Reflections on a Still Life

Why is looking sufficient? Why do taste
And touch not enter? Isn't there growing here?
Isn't there ripening which was never guessed
Entirely by the painter set before

Our eyes? It must be so or we would not
Return, keep meditating, yet stand back
At the insistence there, the absolute
No doubt of power, its stillness. Who would pluck

Except by staring? Apple, pear and peach
Hold us off as kings will do who know
Instinctively their subjects dare not touch.

And yet we feel a gentleness as though
Protection is required by all this rich
Quiet, this hush of how things have to grow.

Klee's Last Years

You cancel out your face. You score a cross
Over the features. Then you turn away
Into another's mood, unnerving place,
A martyr's final hope, a child at play.
You're in a hurry, chase

Down any background. Jute or sacking is
Planted with points. Nothing haphazard here.
Sometimes you take apart our fantasies,
As others blaze a bonfire from thin air.
And, yes, at times you tease

Yourself and us. That cancelled face yet has
A cared-for colouring. Twelve years of such
Hectic appraisal. Names you thought possess
Each picture. Words are always within touch
But paint does not grow less

Important. The reverse. How you combine
Hurry with purpose! That horizon goes
In steps of pastelling, in runs of line.
You break an arrow on your fruitfulness
Much like a name to sign.

Portrait Painting

To glimpse, catch the appearance, halt the fleeting, the fitful but
Essential glance, to find, net and hold, while keeping alive and
    Somehow suggesting movement – this the portrait-painter is
Attempting always. He fights time, is continually dissatisfied and so
    Discarding. Under his eyes his sitter ages, by the minute
Is altering, by the hour light is hinting at years ahead for we
    Age when so steadfastly gazed at, tire under the tireless

    Scrutiny. Cézanne said his blood was mingled with
The blood of his sitter and both were mixed with each tone
    And colour he selected. Leonardo talked incessantly of
Light and dark, of shifting shadows, told and illustrated how
    Light dwindles dark in ways a painter can measure, how
Dark drenches all pools of light, darkens the sun even while it

    Reaches its headstrong risings. All portraits, then, it
Is agreed, are on the move, and there is a constant tension between
    Painter and subject so that when a portrait is said to be
Completed, the painter possesses his subject even while its imperial
    Gaze holds him in thrall, under its power
With all the painful persuasion he has exercised daily, which is
    Now taken from him so entirely and absolutely.

Cézanne

What others would see as a foreshadowing of, or
Beginning of Cubism was for you a mathematical problem
   Worked out in sketches and later in paint. Then, where
Does the joy, the always-escaping ecstasy enter, that
   Shiver along the skin, that unique excitement never to be
Sought or even hoped for? Maybe the problems presented by
   Stone and light never seemed like such to you. Maybe

The solution was found and appeared like that fitful achieving
All artists recognise but will not try to explain for they
   Are always moving off, always discarding. So you –
The lesson learnt and accepted as an intuition – approached
   Other scenes, faces, objects with a new advantage now, though,
Analyst as you were, you probably, being ahead of what you had
   Attained, were only after more surfaces to break, more
Appearances to probe, the rainbow to you being
   What a syllogism is to a philosopher, only more so, more so since
It leads on, is not sealed off, solves according to the artist nothing at all
            finally, at least for him, above all not for him.

For Virginia Woolf

'Rhythm' you said 'is the deepest instinct' and
Turned conversation inside-out to find
The word that balances. Your huge eyes scanned
The sea. You heard its gossip in your mind.

How daringly the waves came as you passed
Page over peerless page. You looked too long.
You should have paused one page before the last.
Yet who dares say which instinct proved more strong?

A Painter's Wife

Even when I sit for him he's far
Away. I must stay still, I must sit still.
Sometimes he looks with an impersonal stare.
I feel the grinding of his will.
And then he turns as if I were not there.

I smell the paint. I hear the brushes move
And think of when he took me to his bed.
He touched with fingers skilled in ways of love.
It is a stranger's hand which paints my head.
I am a thought he's thinking of
And he is not the man who last night said

'Dearest, I want you. Please, again' and such.
I slept a girl and woke to be a wife,
Made coffee, toasted bread, was quick to fetch
Another spoon and knife.
Now I am shapes he does not even touch
And yet his portrait will tell my whole life.

Spring

Tribute to Botticelli's Primavera

It is a girl. No it is many. They are
Running on flowers, not tampering, are lifting
Hands to thread. Their bodies are all astir
With a dance to escape from love. Their bodies are drifting

With clothes like petals. They will not be running for long.
Their refusing faces will soon be caressed but now
They are safe, a moment are safe from the dangerous, strong
Impulse which cannot entice though Cupid has bow

Ready to snap, to open. Breastlings like fruit
Untouched, unripe are swayed by an impudent breeze,
A breeze for how long remaining a mere salute?
Is seduction waiting for night? What a hoist of trees,

What an easy burden is flaunted, how flesh is revealed!
A youth is pointing but not at the girls. He too
Is fragile and unaware, but how much is concealed
In two arms to the right, in a garment of sky-Summer blue.

Chinese Poem

It would be an error to suppose
This is impersonal.
True the sky is drained of all but palest
Blue, and true that one cool willow here
Repeats itself in water never rough.

But look more closely, watch the handiwork,
The painter gives himself away in his
Careful calligraphy.
He signs himself in letters which themselves
Are further pictures, miniatures and all
Are upright, at attention.

Here we may gaze at coolness which is worked for.
Monet would have understood how closely
This painter's eye studied the way all water
Is on the move, is never still because
Sun whether dazzling or, as here, concealed,
Coaxes it constantly in serious play.
This eastern painter sent his brushes chasing
To marry elements and keep them linked,
Water and airy light, in unison,
But drawn together by a human touch.

Night Concert at Taormina
The Greco-Roman Theatre

The spectacle is changing into sound,
The columns, plucked by song, turn into light,
Two key-boards rise in triumph from the ground
And fill the spaces of a warm good-night.

The century does not matter or the name,
The careful fingers put the stars in place.
Listen, the movements make a kindly claim
And lift the troubled glances from each face.

O hush the huge half-circle and recall
The ruined Greeks, the flaunting Romans. Here
Their echoes are drawn back and lightly fall

From keys which open more than heart or mind
As four hands in a moon-warmed theatre
Release our violence and make us kind.

Ariel's Song

Air is my element. Now he has thrown
His wand away, I can fly anywhere.
Liberty oddly makes me feel alone,
I cannot take the air

As birds do with a gusto of sheer height.
I want an order. Who will give it me?
I need his gaze as I sport with the light.
I'm lost now I am free.

The Aegean

The gods departed and the columns fell,
Heroes had to die and empty thrones
Have little left to tell
Of kings and queens. Only the blatant tones
Of seas are still untarnished. The clean bones,

The debris of a war, are rubbed by wave
Which adumbrates another. None is like
The last. They all behave
With separate precision. Each can break
The rainbow and another rainbow make.

Credence in gods returns, credence in strength
Of heroes living now. The music of
The sea spreads its own sympathy, a length
Of coloured sounds which tell of death and love,
Of what remains when there is most to move.

Poems for a New Greek Anthology

I Death of a Poet

Under the dark cypress, under the long
Shadow, my shadow lies. Come not here
In hope of hearing one last joyful song.
Even its echoes learnt to disappear.

II

He raced, hurled javelins and won much fame.
Now there are no races and no breath.
But he has still to fight a final game,
Close to the Styx, his argument with death.

III

The fountain flows from rock. He cannot move
Who once charmed all Olympia. His feet
And hands lie still and cold. He raced with love.
Now love outstrips him in his one defeat.

IV

He argued that the gods did not exist,
He told men that the love of woman was
Enough. What did he feel when he was kissed
By death and when no woman showed her face?

V

Carve him now who never was so still
Before. But hurry, hurry, soon he must
Be laid within the ground where soil will fill
The air he breathed and he too turn to dust.

VI

Under the cypress and the olive tree
He lies at last who fought and loved too much.
Death is his only perfect liberty,
The only kiss for him the soil's dark touch.

VII

Her love was not returned yet bitterness
Could never darken her. She lies at last
Mourned by a nightingale whose happiness
Echoes a sweet, imaginary past.

VIII

He was admired by most when he was young.
He was in love with youth and did not live
To understand how often he'd been wrong.
Death is his mourner, also his reprieve.

IX

He was so quiet that few of us could see
The peace he brought to us. But now we miss
The generous power of his serenity
And in ourselves discover loneliness.

X

Not till it touches one we love do we
Believe in death. My dearest, you are dead.
This life is a deception. May I be
Without it now and share your dark instead.

AFTER THE ARK
(1978)

The Animals' Chorus

Once there was nothing but water and air. The air
Broke into constellations, waters withdrew.
The sun was born and itself hatched out first light.
Rocks appeared and sand, and on the rocks
There was movement. Under the sea
Something tender survived, not yet a fish,
A nameless object floating. This was how we

Began and how you later followed us,
Much, much later, long before clocks or sun-dials,
Long before time was discovered.
The sun stared hard and the moon looked back and mountains
Pierced the air. Snow was formed, this earth
Was gently beginning to live.

We were your fore-runners, we with fins and tails,
With wings and legs. Under the sun we crawled
To life. How good the air was, how sweet the green
Leaves, the rock-pools, the sturdy trees. And flowers

Flaunted such fragrance we wandered among them, clung
To their petals or, out of the blue and widespread air,
Descended, drew in our wings and settled where
You now stand or sit or walk. We know
So much about you. We are your family tree
But you have power over us for you can name,
And naming is like possession. It's up to you
To give us our liberty or to make us tame.

The Fish's Warning

Stay by the water, stand on your shadow, stare
At my quick gliding, my darting body. You're made of air
And I of water. I do not know if you mean to throw
Your line, I move very fast, swim with fins much quicker
Than your thin arms. Rushes will hide me and will
Darken me. I'm a pulse of silver, something the moon tossed down.
I am frail for your finding but one whom only the night can drown.

The Ladybird's Story

It was a roadway to me.
So many meeting-places and directions.
It was smooth, polished, sometimes it shook a little
But I did not tumble off.
I heard you say, and it was like a siren,
'A ladybird. Good luck. Perhaps some money.'
I did not understand.
Suddenly I was frightened, fearful of falling
Because you lifted your hand.

And then I saw your eyes,
Glassy moons always changing shape,
Sometimes suns in eclipse.
I watched the beak, the peak of your huge nose
And the island of your lips.
I was afraid but you were not. I have
No sting. I do not wound.
I carry a brittle coat. It does not protect.
I thought you would blow me away but superstition
Saved me. You held your hand now in one position,
Gentled me over the veins and arteries.
But it was not I you cared about but money.
You see I have watched you with flies.

The Cabbage White Butterfly

I look like a flower you could pick. My delicate wings
Flutter over the cabbages. I don't make
Any noise ever. I'm among silent things.
    Also I easily break.

I have seen the nets in your hands. At first I thought
A cloud had come down but then I noticed you
With your large pink hand and arm. I was nearly caught
    But fortunately I flew

Away in time, hid while you searched, then took
To the sky, was out of your reach. Like a nameless flower
I tried to appear. Can't you be happy to look?
    Must you possess with your power?

The Moth's Plea

I am a disappointment
And much worse.
You hear a flutter, you expect a brilliance of wings,
Colours dancing, a bright
Flutter, but then you see
A brown, bedraggled creature
With a shamefaced, unclean look
Darting upon your curtains and clothes,
Fighting against the light.
I hate myself. It's no wonder you hate me.

I meddle among your things,
I make a meal out of almost any cloth,
I hide in cupboards and scare
Any who catch me unaware.
I am your enemy – the moth.

You try to keep me away
But I'm wily and when I do
Manage to hide, you chase me, beat me, put
Horrible-smelling balls to poison me.
Have you ever thought what it's like to be
A parasite,
Someone who gives you a fright,

Who envies the rainbow colours of the bright
Butterflies who hover round flowers all day?

O please believe that I do understand how it feels
To be awake in and be afraid of the night.

The Spider's Confession

You with your looms and wheels and every kind of machine,
Don't you marvel at the intricate lace I spin?
Many of you are skilful but have you seen
Working under your hands such delicacy, such thin,
Easily breakable patterns? You think it strange

That one with a squashy, dark and ugly body,
Can make such a wonder. I wish that I could convince
All of you that it hurts to carry around
A creature so greatly at odds with the work it spins.
Some of you are revolted at sight of me
And quickly wash me down drains. All that I ask is that you
At least allow me to do
My work. That is all I honestly want you to see.

Wasp in a Room

Chase me, follow me round the room, knock over
Chairs and tables, bruise knees, spill books. High
I am then. If you climb up to me I go
Down. I have ways of detecting your least
Movements. I have radar you did not
Invent. You are afraid of me. I can
Sting hard. Ah but watch me bask in
The, to you, unbearable sun. I sport with it, am
Its jester and also its herald. Fetch a
Fly whisk. I scorn such. You must invent stings
For yourselves or else leave me alone, small, flying,
Buzzing tiger who have made a jungle out of the room you thought safe,
Secure from all hurts and prying.

The Snake's Warning

A coil of power,
A twist of speed,
Hider in grass,
Content in jungles,
Footless, wingless,
I have powers beasts lack,
Strength birds seek
In clean skies which
Are not my home.
If footsteps approach
Or I hear a twig
Break I alert
At once. My tongue
Means painful death.
Keep your hands off me.

There are men, a few,
With a special gift
To whom I surrender.
I sway to the sound
Of their flutes but I keep
My glance upon them.
They hypnotise me,
Don't ask me how
Or when or why,
If *you* want to be safe,
Keep away, don't try
To tame me with flutes.
If you do, you will die.

The Earthworm's Monologue

Birds prey on me, fish are fond of my flesh.
My body is like a sausage, it lacks the snake's
Sinuous splendour and colour. Yes, I'm absurd.
Yet I also till and soften the soil, I prepare
The way for flowers, Spring depends upon me
At least a little. Mock me if you will,
Cut me in half, I'll come together again.
But haven't you felt a fool, hated your shape,
Wanted to hide? If so I am your friend;

I would sympathise with you were I not so busy
But bend down over me, you who are not yet tall
And be proud of all you contain in a body so small.

The Frogs' History

You caught and carried us, pleased with yourselves.
We were only blobs of black in jars.

You knew what we'd become, were glad to wait.
How hectically we swam in that glass cage!

And there was never hope of an escape.
You put us on a shelf with more care than

You generally move. We were a hope,
A something-to-look-forward to, a change,

Almost a conjuring trick. Some sleight of nature
Would, given time, change us to your possessions.

We would be green and glossy, wet to touch.
'Take them away,' squeamish grown-ups would

Call out. Not you. You longed to hold us in
Your dry palms with surprising gentleness

And with a sense of unexpected justice
Would let us go, wanted to see us leap

And watch our eyes which never seem to sleep,
Hear our hideous but lively croak.

We know as well as you we are a joke.

The Bats' Plea

Ignore the stories which say
We shall fly to and tangle your hair,
That you are wise if you dread
Our mouse-like bodies, the way
Our wings fan out and spread
In gloom, in dusty air.

Eagles are lucky to be
Thought of in terms of light
And glory. Half-bird, half-beast,
We're an anomaly.
But, clinging to darkness we rest
And, like stars, belong to the night.

The Swallows' Speech

We are the bearers of sun, we take
Its rays with us, it rides our wings
And trusts its gold to us. The sky
Enlarges southward, opens for
Our passage. Watch our nestlings fly
After. We carry all warm things.

You in the Winter only know
Our arrow ways in dreams. We keep
A little glow within your minds,
We stoke your loving and your sleep.
Listen, our wings are coming back.
Summer is on. We tell you so.

Gull Thought

Shall I descend? Shall I allow
A buffet of wind to take me? Shall
I hover to stillness over the tides,
Smelling the salt, waiting to pounce
And bruise the waves? The sun's gold slides
Over my wings. I am wide awake
And the earth is mine to take.

I descend to a place of waves and hands,
To water-filled air, to spume and to
five fingers holding me food. I am
August and insolent. Hands, wait there!
I will skim the horizon before I turn,
A tide of my own, and grasp the bread,
Following instinct, possessing the air.

The Rooks' Chorus

Our homes are high,
We sway in the sun and wind
And are not afraid
Of a stormy sky.
At night we sleep
Close to the moon and stars.
Think of us as the deep
Note of the songs which fill your mind
As a lullaby.

Early risers are we.
We want to veer
About as the sun rises
Magnificently.
We open our wings
To protect more fragile things.
Look up at us when you wake
And the turns and curves we make
And fashion your day with the songs
We sing to ease you awake.

The Robin's Song

I am cheerful. You can
Depend on me. I'm around
All the year. In the rain,
When frost is on the ground
Or the sun is dancing, I'm here,
Bright in colour and sound.

Other birds are less stout,
Sing flawless songs in Spring,
Look more beautiful, there's no doubt.
I am always pleased when you fling
Crumbs to me. Yes, I am happy.
Isn't that everything?

The Sparrows' Chorus

How often you forget about us! We are
About all through the year.
Our feathers are drab, beside other birds we appear
Nonentities, no fashion parades for us.
Nobody makes a fuss
Of us and really we don't care,
At least, not too much.
But we are faithful, whatever the weather we stay
Among you. And don't think we're ungrateful for the food
Some of you like to toss.
We need it badly. We can lose half our weight
On an icy night. We depend a lot on you.

Often, we have to admit, we wish we wore
Flamboyant colours. A yellow, a red, a blue.
The robin is lucky and all the tits are too.
But perhaps our smallness is noticeable. Beside
A starling or blackbird we are almost invisible
But don't forget we are here,
Domestic creatures, never flying far.
Just to exist through an English climate is
Remarkable.
It's almost a miracle simply that we are.

The Thrush Confides

The truth about me is I am
One who enjoys life, who feels
Happy most of the time.
Whatever weather may come –
Wind, rain, enormous falls
Of snow – I feel at home –
And would like you to feel much the same.

And please don't imagine that I
Am stupid or priggish. I'm not.
I know I'm not handsome, not one
Who people point at and cry
'What a very remarkable sight.'
I like being left alone
To find worms, look about, feel the sun.

The Owl's Request

Do not be frightened of me.
I am a night-time creature. When the earth is still,
When trees are shadows of shadows,
When only the moon and its attendant stars
Enlarge the night, when the smallest sound is shrill
And may wake you up and frighten you,
I am about with my friendly 'Tu-whit, tu whoo'.

My face is kindly but also mysterious.
People call me wise.
Perhaps they do so because I sometimes close my eyes
And seem to be thinking.
The way I think is not like yours. I need
No thick philosopher's book;
I can tell the truth of the world with a look
But I do not speak about
What I see there. Think of me then
As the certainty in your wandering nights.
I can soothe men
And will snatch you out of your doubt,
Bear you away to the stars and moon
And to sleep and dawn. So lie
And listen to my lullaby.

The Cuckoo's Speech

What a very bad example I set
But never mind.
I have the best of all worlds. I get
Applause and kind
Words from all when they hear the sound
Of me. Winter's behind

And I prove Spring's arrived. Forget the way
I use the homes
Of others, set up house there, always lay
My eggs in the warm
Hard-worked-for nests. O yes, you can certainly say
To me all good luck comes.

The Cockerel Proclaims

I am proud of my pride.
I open the doors of morning.
I shout the trees awake,
Circle your towns with a high,
Magnificent, self-controlled cry.

One by one I snuff out the stars
And I am the first colours,
A reminder of the rainbow,
A singer shaming your small
Complaining voices. I'm tall

And proud of my flaring height.
I am the sun's true herald.
I wind up the small birds' voices,
And tell you it's worth getting up
As I lock the doors of the night.

The Fieldmouse's Monologue

Didn't you know how frightened I was when I came
For shelter in your room? I am not tame.
You looked enormous when I saw you first.
I rushed to the hole I had made, took refuge there,
Crouched behind paper you thrust at me, shivered with fear.
I had smelt some chocolate. The kitchen was warm below
And outside there was frost and, one whole night, great snow.

I only guessed you were frightened too when you
Called out loudly, deafeningly to me.
My ears are small but my hearing strong, you see.
You pushed old papers against my hole and so
I had to climb into a drawer. You did not know
That I could run so high. I felt your hand,
Like my world in shadow, shudder across me and
I scuttled away but felt a kind of bond
With you in your huge fear.
Was I the only friend near?

The Hedgehog's Explanation

I move very slowly,
I would like to be friendly,
Yet my prickly back has a look of danger. You might
Suppose I were ready for war or at least a fight
With a cat on the wall, a gather of birds, but no,
My prickles damage nobody, so you

Must be gentle with me, you with your huge shadow,
Your footsteps like claps of thunder,
The terrible touch of your hands.
Listen to me: I am a ball of fear,
Terror is what I know best,
What I live with and dream about.
Put out a saucer of milk for me,
Keep me from roads and cars.
If you want to look after someone,
Take care of me
And give me at least the pretence I am safe and free.

The Rabbit's Advice

I have been away too long.
Some of you think I am only a nursery tale,
One which you've grown out of.
Or perhaps you saw a movie and laughed at my ears
But rather envied my carrot.
I must tell you that I exist.

I'm a puff of wool leaping across a field,
Quick to all noises,
Smelling my burrow of safety.
I am easily frightened. A bird
Is tame compared to me.
Perhaps you have seen my fat white cousin who sits,
Constantly twitching his nose,
Behind bars in a hutch at the end of a garden.
If not, imagine those nights when you lie awake
Afraid to turn over, afraid
Of night and dawn and sleep.
Terror is what I am made
Of partly, partly of speed.

But I am a figure of fun.
I have no dignity
Which means I am never free.
So, when you are frightened or being teased, think of
My twitching whiskers, my absurd white puff of a tail,
Of all that I mean by 'me'
And my ludicrous craving for love.

The Sheep's Confession

I look stupid, much like a dirty heap of snow
The Winter left.
I have nothing to draw your attention, nothing for show,
Except the craft

Which shears me and leaves me looking even more
Unintelligent.
I do not wonder you laugh when you see my bare
Flesh like a tent

Whose guy-ropes broke. But listen, I have one thing
To charm and delight –
The lamb I drop when Winter is turning to Spring.
His coat is white,

Purer than mine and he wears socks of black wool.
He can move
And prance. I am proud of a son so beautiful
And so worthy of love.

The Deers' Request

We are the disappearers.
You may never see us, never,
But if you make your way through a forest
Stepping lightly and gently,
Not plucking or touching or hurting,
You may one day see a shadow
And after the shadow a patch
Of speckled fawn, a glint
Of a horn.
        Those signs mean us.

O chase us never. Don't hurt us.
We who are male carry antlers
Horny, tough, like trees,
But we are terrified creatures,
Are quick to move, are nervous
Of the flutter of birds, of the quietest
Footfall, are frightened of every noise.

If you would learn to be gentle,
To be quiet and happy alone,
Think of our lives in deep forests,
Of those who hunt us and haunt us
And drive us into the ocean.
If you love to play by yourself
Content in that liberty,
Think of us being hunted,
Tell those men to let us be.

The Riding School

We are at grass now and the emerald meadow
Highlights our polished coats. All afternoon
You trotted, cantered us. How mild we were,
Our bodies were at one
With yours. Now we are cropping at the shadow
We throw. We scarcely stir.

You never saw us wild or being broken
In. We tossed our saddles off and ran
With streaming manes. Like Pegasus almost
We scorned the air. A man
Took long to tame us. Let your words be spoken
Gently. You own the freedom we have lost.

The Black Cat's Conversation

Do not suppose
Because I keep to the fire,
Am out half the night,
Sleep where I fall,
Eye you with stares
Like your finest marbles,
That I am not conscious
Of your slightest changes
In mood. I never
Miss your temper
Although you attempt
To disguise it. I know

How envious you are
Of my lithe body,
My lack of self-consciousness,
My glossy coat,
My imperious air.
All this is instinct,
Something you've lost
Except when you cower
From the rats I bring in,
Proud of my haul.
I am proud of my pride
And I always win.

The Lion Cub

My fur is soft. I am not a lion yet.
You can tease me a little, treat me like a pet.

The keeper is feeding my parents. Trust me to
Be playful. I can warm and comfort you.

Forget the forests and jungle, the great sun-face
Of my father. He has violence and grace

And I have neither yet. For a little time
I am a prince locked safe in a nursery rhyme.

Finale for the Animals

Some with cruelty came, sharp-fanged and clawed,
Tore at the air searching for food which, found,
They ate in an instant – new leaves, the tall and small
Flowers. Carnivores were
Worse, hunters of blood, smellers of victims
More miles away than our instruments measure or we
Imagine. Meanwhile the jungle listened and looked.
The parrot kept its beak shut, the slithering snake
Stilled to a coil. The stars were listening, the sun's
Burning paused at the tear and rampage of
A striped or spotted creature. This was the time
Before we were.

Now we have caged and enclosed but not enchanted
Most of these. Now full of power we are not
Gentle with flowers, pull too hard, break the admired
Rose with abandonment. We should know better.

You have heard of the ark and Noah. Most likely it
Was a local event or a myth but remember men
Bow down to the myths they create.
Perhaps we were kindest, most gentle,
Most at our best
When we coupled all creatures and launched them forth in an ark.
Imagination was gracious then indeed,
Gracious too when we thought up the speeding dove,
Feathery emblem of peace whiter than clouds, its wings
Combing and calming the breakers. The waters stilled.

You have heard now of some of these, learnt of their habits.
Do not haunt zoos too often, do not demand
Affection too often from rabbits or cats or dogs,
Do not tame if taming hurts.
Be grateful for such variety of manners,
For the diverse universe.
Above all respect the smallest of all these creatures
As you are awed by the stars.

MOMENTS OF GRACE
(1979)

Into the Hour

I have come into the hour of a white healing.
Grief's surgery is over and I wear
The scar of my remorse and of my feeling.

I have come into a sudden sunlit hour
When ghosts are scared to corners. I have come
Into the time when grief begins to flower

Into a new love. It had filled my room
Long before I recognised it. Now
I speak its name. Grief finds its good way home.

The apple-blossom's handsome on the bough
And Paradise spreads round. I touch its grass.
I want to celebrate but don't know how.

I need not speak though everyone I pass
Stares at me kindly. I would put my hand
Into their hands. Now I have lost my loss

In some way I may later understand.
I hear the singing of the Summer grass
And love, I find, has no considered end,

Nor is it subject to the wilderness
Which follows death. I am not traitor to
A person or a memory. I trace

Behind that love another which is running
Around, ahead. I need not ask its meaning.

An Answer to Odd Advice

You who would have me often cynical
And even bitter, have you never thought
I have my moments of pure anger bought
Always highly? In my lyrical
Verse you doubtless find what you have sought,

A childishness. You should know it is hard
To keep the clear eye and the trust in men.
I have met cruelty but then, again,
I've found the good more often. I am scarred,
Like others, after unjust charges. When

You tell me to be disillusioned, I
Answer, 'I've tried and never yet succeeded
And I am glad I have not.' Hope is needed
If in a dark world some, like me, will try
To last through mankind's new Gethsemane

And be near any Christ again who's pleaded
For friends, for comfort, and not yet to die.

A Meditation in March 1979

No bravery, no trumpets' festival,
Death is a little circumstance. Our wars
Are scattered, cold, a shadow of us all
And of our lack of awe and tact. We go
Under the neon-lights, under the show
Of signals, barricades, Iron Curtains too.
And we diminish what we mean and are
And crave a comfort out of fashion now.
We eye the spaces which once lit a star
To light the world. Children run wild and how
Are we to tame them who have built Misrule?
Love was a master, now it is a fool.

And grace is caught in seconds unexpected –
Beads of light hung on a chain of stars,
The child's goodnight look. All the recollected
Dead who fill our shelves. They wrote their lives.

They lived by law, but we are otherwise.
Rhodesia, China, Persia are at odds
And so are we. What is important is
That, lacking faith, we do not place false gods
Upon our shaky thrones. Believers claim
They know a God and dare to speak his name.
We need belief and so we put it in
Our children. We invest too much in them.
They turn with scornful eyes and they are right.
The stars hang in old patterns, death so near
Seems just accomplished on the edge of night.
We can reach out and almost touch its hem.
And what is happening in Jerusalem?

The Sermon of Appearances

We are motes dancing,
We are flecks of the rainbow settling down
For a definite twelve hours.
We are appearances,
We are decorators.
We take the elements for frivolous reasons.
We are the bonus seasons.

Chips from a huge bonfire, we are. We are
Today what stars are to the night but better,
Believe that. It is true.
We are the tan on you
And the healthy feel caught in a Summer sea
Or under southern tree after tree.

Glittering on a coming tide, we run
According to our own
Rules. We have them.
What is it we teach?
The value of appearances, the prize
Of a moment. We can give you Midas hands
But remember, always, the price.
We give you different eyes
And remorseless beginnings and ends.

Among Farm Workers

My hands hang loose like gloves a child has.
They're tied through sleeves and won't be lost. Mine are.
I would have work to roughen them, would press
On spade or hoe. Instead, these hands hang here

As I stroll through the country of a season
Not Spring, not Winter. Yet what work I pass –
Digging that ditch, for instance, felling trees.
Instead my hands are hand-cuffs in a prison,

The prison being me. I smell, I taste
The curdling country air but there is no
Work for me. I can't join with the rest

Who smell of labour. Envious, I watch grow
Catkins hanging in the wind. What waste
Walks with me. Yet I reap who never sow.

To be a Sunflower

To be a sunflower, to
Smile on the sad gardeners, to be
  Admired and grow
As cipher of that face which finally
  Will be the death of me.

To look up aslant
At the feasting sun, sun worn as a dress
  By me. I can't, no, can't
Believe my skin will shrivel, that winds will toss
  Even the tallest of us.

I exercise my flesh-
Bound spirit with this freedom of a flower
  Large but never lush.
It bends with dignity, will never cower
  But quietly heel over.

Cypresses

Those definite proportions, those strong shapes,
Are yet among the randomness of things.
The oxen plough on as the tourist sleeps
And in that sleep dreams the cypress is
A shadow-thrower, and the dark it keeps
Is the pure essence of all cypresses.

So in that stalwart upward-turning tree,
That looking-cool black candle with no flame,
We can behold the whole of Tuscany.
Turn to your window as the small hours sound
A spell of time, and under pale stars claim
A score of cypresses shading the ground.

Cyphers of a language we don't need
To learn. It is no lost Etruscan now
Decoded. It's by signs that these trees plead.
They are steadfast, true until you stare.
Then many shadows throng and form and bow
In cypress-surfeited and Tuscan air.

In Renaissance paintings only these
Cypresses stay stark, definite and climb
One by one, a company of trees
Giving bonus landscapes whose fore-view
Is the attraction. In and out of time
Cypress and shadow step away from you.

Outside Greece

Out of the city quickly. There it is –
Pastoral Greece a thousand years ago.
    The air is clear, the sea keeps changing, changing,
Spendthrift alteration of all blues.
    And greens also. Be still and listen here.

    The light embraces you and there are voices
Far away at first and then all round
    Like an invisible pantheon, all gods
Subdued a little. Dryads might walk out
    Of pines surrounding Epidaurus. What

Do clockless voices say that bears upon
Our world? They speak of death and love and fate.
How bleak that wisdom was in this warm air,
Or did the Greeks turn Puritan among
Such natural riches? It could be, it could.

Poor land for farmers. Every tithe of land
Is planted. See, a goat herd blocks the way.
The sun puts out its arms and presses us
To odd conclusions. Air seems much like earth.
Greece mixes up the elements and we
Know ancient people back to our own birth.

The Whole Bestiary

Here they come, wandering, slipping, striding, looming,
The whole Bestiary into a world beginning,
A life to jaunt about on this one globe
Known to be peopled among the galaxies, nebulae,
Southern Cross, all the wide lap of space.

And the beasts are waiting for us, a whole rôle,
Parrot gossips, birds try maiden wings,
All separate, each is another world,
A pulse of life, the one gift shared in common –
Determination to last. Here we breathed in life,

And breathed on life and approved
The animals, birds, contained in their own substance,
Gripped by their own element,
These are savage for life, while we examine
The look and feel of a world of a thousand textures,
Of seething appeals to the five expert senses.

Here we are, and we are on the threshold
Of the reason why life needs death, of the reason why love
Needs suffering over and over.
The world is maimed and the *Bestiary* is shadowed
But it is, some believe, the shadow of a Creator
Brooding over his business with us, attentive
To the first choice we make.

Flies

All through the Winter these tunnel
Torpid air, desert of central heating,
Doubling men's thirst. These live God
Knows where, and they are his creatures.
Buzz, buzz, they insist,
Flies fallen from Summer,
Jig-zagging from cupboards, appearing
At the first left toffee,
And the smoking Christmas cake.

They carry dirt, we know,
They are ugly. They cannot help it.
Aesop would have a message. Creatures are good
For our metaphorical questions
And our necessary teaching.
I will try to admire this toss of a cigarette burning,
Bringing destruction and pain
But being so dogged with it.
'Let the flies come still,' I say
And let no one else complain.

Goldfinch

These claws too contain
A bad crop. The goldfinch preys on the blossom
Of apple, that froth and tide of a white
Spring wedding. The neatness, the tailor-made
Touch of his suit bespeaks a harmlessness,
A wish to please that he is stranger to.

Why must we pet the world's destroyers?
I am not speaking of the soft-handed cream-buyers
Or the vendors of fresh liver
To fill the guts of a cat, no, I speak
A contradiction. I praise the pluck of the goldfinch
But I abhor this lamentable *gourmet*
Who plucks from the Eden branch the Eden flower,
Such a bright appearance, such a dandy to the inch.

Friesian Cows

Muddy-booted and with an acrobatic way
With churns and electric milker,
He calls the litany of these docile Friesians
Who wait with a world's patience to have their milk
Sucked from their bloated udders.

I can, at this distance,
With the memory of the cowman's 'Honey, Snowdrop',
Understand entirely the vegetarian.
More, I can see the point
Of the 'Protection of Animals' people,

'But let them be milked,' I say, 'But not misused,
Let the cow keep her calf for longer than
A day ...' You interrupt and you are right.
'My child needs that milk.' I stammer
'I'm sorry,' and go away with a dream of milkers
Grazing in Paradise. I have shut the gate.

Rook

Lover of natural sky-scrapers, builder in
Face of East winds, and any winds indeed,
Acrobat whose tight-rope is a branch,
And a thin one at that, you survey
The stripes of fields, clutch of cottages here,
And there the factories with their blinds and humming,
There, a motor-way.

No one has called you king of anything,
You rook, you wary traveller, you who don't
Know what vertigo is. Why haven't we admired you
Before? Being a rook is a daring thing
But height and distance are your media,
You evening-dressed, almost haphazard bird.
A little nearer to the sun you are
Than us. You could be photographed by a star.

Cat in Winter

Evader mostly, a glancing cold, a watcher
Of snow from a warm distance, a clever seeker
Of the heated corner, the generous lap, the fingers
Handing tit-bits or filling a shallow saucer –

So the cat in Winter and his movements.
He slinks into hiding places like a dandy
Recovering from a party or preparing
For another appearance in the evening. This one,
Striped, ginger and handsome,

Is a teller of weather, has a machine in his head
Which is a barometer to him. He is inventive,
Enterprising always, always lucky.
We sink into February and its inertia.
The cat's ears are cocked for a Spring of happy hunting.

The Shoot

They are bringing the bright birds down.
The Winter trees are shaken, the sky looks on
    And, far away, a town
Writes its houses on a sky with no sun.
    They are bringing the bright birds down.

    And from my room I can see
Patches of snow which the thaw hasn't reached yet,
    And now I seem to be
Alone. The wind goes off. What birds wait,
    Birds I cannot see?

    And then anger comes on fast.
I storm inwardly at these cold men
    Who will be glad to have passed
An afternoon giving the bright birds pain
    And a violent death at last.

    They are bringing the bright birds down.
Yesterday's pheasant will plummet through the air.
    And I am not guiltless, I own,
For I have eaten pheasants who shelter here.
    I too have brought them down.

A Beseeching

Lord, they suffer, still they suffer,
Lord of the long hills and low fields and the flat
Meadows, Lord of little places, weather
Seldom extreme. Lord, Christ, your heart
Beats in this country. You have gathered together
   Us and what we would offer.

   Lord, we are bold in sin,
Rich in hoardings, fencing your Presence out.
Move in our hearts, we can be kindly, be
The moon to our tide of passion, take our doubt
Down to the rock and the everlasting sea
   Where another world will begin.

Watcher

He is the watcher underneath the stars.
He dresses the dome of night with strings of long
   Meditations. He seldom moves. If he does,
It is to become acquainted with nightly creatures
   And now with hibernators who are creeping
Out of their snowy sleep, their habitations
   Which, perilously, just kept them warm enough.
The watcher is handy and burly but even he

   Rejoices in his own silence at the change
Apparent everywhere as the glacier Winter
   Slides away, as the woken grass speaks
And a chorus of thrushes and blackbirds sings the hours.
   This watcher joins them in his meditations:
But he thinks of a shadow only just beginning
   To creep over grass dressed by the sun.
It is the encroachment of a gallows-tree.
   And the watcher waits for the torment in a garden,
Eden swept out, and a dark figure weeping.

A Christmas Carol for 1978

Again it comes as if
   It never was before –
This trumpet-sound of life,
   This weakness to adore.

God is not hidden when
   This birth takes place again,
O we are unkind men
   But in this – God-made-Man

Who needs us – we use all
   We still have of our best,
To this child's hungry call
   We offer him our trust.

Holly is bleeding, wise
   Men have started out
Upon their enterprise,
   And we have no more doubt,

For Mary sings again,
   Again to the locked heart,
We open it with pain,
   We play our Christmas part.

Forgiveness

Anger, pity, always, most, forgive.
It is the word which we surrender by,
It is the language where we have to live,

For all torn tempers, sulks and brawls at last
Lie down in huge relief as if the world
Paused on its axis. Sorrow does sound best

When whispered near a window which can hold
The full moon or its quarter. Love, I say,
In spite of many hours when I was cold

And obdurate I never meant to stay
Like that or, if I meant to, I can't keep
The anger up. Our storms must draw away,

Their durance is not long. Almost asleep,
I listen now to winds' parley with trees
And feel a kind of comforting so deep

I want to share it. This unpaid-for peace
Possesses me. How much I wish to give
Some back to you, but living's made of these

Moments when every anger comes to grief
And we are rich in right apologies.

Never Such Peace

Never such peace before, never such rest
As when, a gaze away from Summer sky
We watched the bleeding and the burning west.
We did not move, we did not even sigh.
Your hand lay on my breast.

And in that centre, as it were, of calm,
It was as if the acts which we had done
Were flared out in the west. The night was warm
And in this personal peace we saw a sun
That burns but does not harm.

Not what you did or what I said's the drift
Now. I remember silence as the light
Seeped down the sky and you and I were left.
It was not day still and it was not night
When we, though sleep-bereft,

Watched an epic sunset, did not move
But stared out at the final act but one.
The elements were copying our love
And dramatising our small union,
And nobody moved off.

A curtain fell, the night's, so slow to come
We did not notice it until the air,
The outer star-packed air flowed through the room.
And when you pointed at one bigger star
Both of us were dumb.

The Way of it

When it is over or before it starts,
    We know the strength of love.
It is so cool, this literature of hearts.
It lies in books. Only the pages move.

When blood is beating and the pulse unsteady
    And eyes are gladly blurred,
When nouns we use are quite inept but ready,
We lose the wish for any nerveless word.

And yet, and yet, our whispered passion tells
    Us that we should claim
A speech, a part. But we are somewhere else
And where we are is mapless with no name.

When fire is ashes and the hearth shows no
    Burning we start to tell
Our history but cannot make it glow
Even though what we know we know so well.

Love, I stammer monosyllables.
    The heart's dictionary
Falls from my fingers. Tender vocables
Are crying out. We are the lock and key.

Channel Port Night

    Boats signal nothing but night.
This English Channel port town is only eyes
Of green and red and yellow. Tide is in.
Waves keep calm. Only the gulls' cries
Insist on being heeded. Now we begin
    A dream-voyage under the light

    Of little ships and houses. Being near
The rugged clangour of the anchored ships
Tells us swimmers that our dreams will be
Constant with voyages. Love, I touch your lips
And taste their salt. Do the same now to me
    Before the night's *détour*.

A Weather Spell

Seven times seven and seven again,
Come the wind and come the rain,
Come the snow and come the heat
And come where darts of lightning meet.

Come all weather, come all ways
To join and part or walk a maze.
Come, my love, be light to start.
Let no thunder break your heart.

I will take the elements
And move their dangerous charges. Chance
Is tossed away. I give you choice
And a purpose and a voice.

I will take the dark aside,
Make the furious seas divide,
But most I'll breach the wall of you
Come the heat and come the snow.

Thought and Feeling

I have grown wary of the ways of love
And when I find a moment crammed with thought
I cherish that sweet coolness and I move

As only spirits can, as dryads caught
In a Greek grove, then loosed among the trees.
Worship does not mean passion, I was taught.

But I have been brought down upon my knees
Was it by prayer or by the ancient church
In which I found both art and artifice?

I do not know but I know I must touch
And that it is by flesh the spirit lives.
The strides of mind are prisoned in the reach

Of sense so intricate that it receives
All impressions, sieves them as a beach
Takes worn-down, random stones and offers them

To any wanderer there on his way home.

I Count the Moments

I count the moments of my mercies up,
I make a list of love and find it full.
I do all this before I fall asleep.

Others examine consciences. I tell
My beads of gracious moments shining still.
I count my good hours and they guide me well

Into a sleepless night. It's when I fill
Pages with what I think I am made for,
A life of writing poems. Then may they heal

The pain of silence for all those who stare
At stars as I do but are helpless to
Make the bright necklace. May I set ajar

The doors of closed minds. Words come and words go
And poetry is pain as well as passion.
But in the large flights of imagination

I see for one crammed second, order so
Explicit that I need no more persuasion.

Love Needs an Elegy

Move over into your own secrecy.
The planet cools. Our bodies lie apart.
I am not part of you, nor you of me,

We have a separate and a wounded heart,
We hear the world, we see the kings go by
And men and children happy from the start.

Why are they so or is it all a lie?
Listen, a wind is rising. I think Spring
Is skirmishing today. It feels nearby

Yet we are not affected. I hear wings
And flights. The birds need never heed the clock
Or hear a lonely summons. Such light sings

But we fit nowhere. What is it can break
Hearts while there's good faith still? I do not know;
We keep our promises but stay awake.

If love could be a matter of the will
O this would never be most sadly so.

On its Own

Never the same and all again.
Well, no same loss will tear me through
Or the same pain grip me if you
Go on your way. I yet shall gain
Knowledge and never wish unknown
The arguments that reach the bone,

The feelings which lay waste the heart.
No tidy place, no, I will have
All the destructiveness of love
If I can know, beyond the hurt,
Happiness waits or partly so
But not like once and long ago.

My world shall be dramatic then,
No repetitions, many acts,
A few hard treaties, broken tracts,
And peace made stronger yet by pain
Accepted but not chosen when
Love is its own and not again.

Death

They did not speak of death
But went round and round the subject deviously.
They were out of breath
With keeping it at bay. When would they see
That they were burdened with

Dying like other men?
Immediate mourners know the whole of grief
    When they've seen the dying in pain
And the gradual move toward the end of life.
    O death comes again and again

And starts with the crying child and the doctor's knife.

An Elusive One

You slipped away but left your ghost.
Did you expect me, then, to trust
Hauntings like that? I sent them off.
I want no counterfeits of love.

You play me false. Why would you be
That cold, elusive one? I see
No point in indirectness. Say
What your game is. Why do you play

So deviously? Come full, come clear
As out will come a shouldering star
With only one way to be seen.
Are you so unsure who you are?

Haunted House

The house was haunted yet the dwellers there
    Could never run away.
They were accustomed to its chilly air
    And felt calm during day.

It was the night which was their warder and
    Kept them locked within
Half-fear, half-curiosity. A wind,
A draught, then quiet and now ghosts would begin

Their little tappings, moans and then a cry.
    The dwellers lay still then.
Why do we waste time thinking, 'Who next dies?'
Or feel with ghosts half pleasure and half pain?

Spirits

If there are spirits, then they breathe in birds
Tossed by the winds, agile in the frost.
Though the world falls down like a house of cards,
Spirits will soar and in birds put their trust
Who rely on us to feed them as we must

In lengthy Winters like the last; it is
Our happy task to keep these fliers going,
To give them nuts and crumbs. When it is snowing
They huddle in the evergreens and press
Their lean, bright breasts upon that lastingness.

But if there are, say, angels, or the Greek
Nymphs, and though it is a fancy to
Speculate, it's thus we like to speak.
Who could believe a nearly dead thing flew
As cold blackbirds so frequently will do?

These are approximations but they touch
As near as men can through the boundaries
Rounding our senses' exploration. Much
Is still mysterious, but man probes and tries
To halt a hope, a fragment where it lies,

A vestige of his dreams. If he lets go
Of it he cannot live. Our dreams express
Acts we daren't do. But let mankind be slow
To lose the impulse of their images.
Releasing them, they'll let so much more go.

The Dangerous Ones

We are the silences you dread so much,
We are the agonising pauses when
You need to speak. We are the final touch,
   We are acutest pain.

But we are more. We do not come and go
And there is nothing which alleviates
The ache, the bleeding. We are tears which flow
   Through your own eyes' gates.

We look with care for victims, never fail
To find the one who'll catch our sickness worst.
If any tell you this is an old tale,
    Look out, they are the first

Of our whole army. They will weaken you,
Paint you pallid, slowly make you move
Until you limp. We are the acts you do
    That never looked at love.

Spell of the Elements

Fire and water, air and earth
Contend, unite. A magic birth
Is taking place somewhere not far
Celebrated by a star.

Take the music of the wind,
Take the fingers of a mind
Making, breaking, letting go.
Take the blanket of the snow

And a necklace of the stars,
Take the footsteps of the hours.
All can spell-bind, all can build,
All will come if you have called.

We are subject to a spell.
It is married to free-will.
Come the Spring, the earth will lie
Lucky under lucky sky.

No determinism has
Power to hold us long. We pass
Into every element,
Come and gone but never spent.

A Chorus of Creation

With hands and with fingers, with trailing of these in the high
Seas, on the first rock rising and on the first
Bird escaping, taking air on its back,
Carrying a branch and riding up, up,
Up to the still molten sky, across the arteries
Of air and the winds' currents —

Event after event,
Establishment of rules,
Then time suggested, only suggested by
The fall of a drop of quintessential life
On a looming rock. Then, then at last
Breath bringing life, drawing a bud up,
Putting it into the light, light which was air,
All that metal dissolved.

The breath is a force, is also a tremor of music,
Notes taken later up by birds who fall
Into different flights according to their size.
And hands, the rudimentary hands are searching,
Under the water, over the life now going
Up with green breath into a morning sky,
The first dawn dancing, the first clouds passing by.

A Chorus

Over the surging tides and the mountain kingdoms,
Over the pastoral valleys and the meadows,
Over the cities with their factory darkness,
Over the lands where peace is still a power,
Over all these and all this planet carries
A power broods, invisible monarch, a stranger
To some, but by many trusted. Man's a believer
Until corrupted. This huge trusted power
Is spirit. He moves in the muscle of the world,
In continual creation. He burns the tides, he shines
From the matchless skies. He is the day's surrender.
Recognise him in the eye of the angry tiger,
In the sigh of a child stepping at last into sleep,
In whatever touches, graces and confesses,
In hopes fulfilled or forgotten, in promises

Kept, in the resignation of old men –
This spirit, this power, this holder together of space
Is about, is aware, is working in your breathing.
But most he is the need that shows in hunger
And in the tears shed in the lonely fastness.
And in sorrow after anger.

An Education

How rooted this was in
Concrete matters, purposes of time
And nightly circumstance.
If this was visionary, then it was
Not won and not expected.
I'd rather see it as a part of learning
And none of it prepared.

At ten years old, I walked out to the night
In an Oxford suburb not yet spoilt
By hurried building. Fields grew at my back,
And in the evergreens of a front garden
I moved without the fear of shadows or
Any interruption. Then I stared
Up at a sky surely spawning stars
Or was the moon releasing one by one
Her young? Or was the firmament so crammed
With precious stones it gave a few away?

I do not know but what I still store in
The corner of a memory of clutter
Of intellectual bric-à-brac, is this –
The memory of elation, changing too,
Being elevated into wonder
Unknown before. The atmosphere was charged
And so was I. My ten years fell away
As I was caught up in an education
Sublime and starry. Maybe all of this
Lasted no more than seconds, but it stayed
With me, a keepsake for the harder years.
A child I was of moods like many children,
And like them in this strange illumination.
But number does not count nor vanity.
I am a wanderer still among those stars.

A New Patience

He warms his hands at artificial heat
    And puts a blanket round
His legs. He does not want to drink or eat,
He is content with this new sleeping sound

Close by. She fell asleep before he had
    Finished last kisses but he,
With knowledge he hadn't learnt, left her in bed,
And now he is a full discovery
To his own self. The terrible prison years

He can shrug off. Love was an hour ago
    But he is patient and
As purposeful as a sun-dial which can show
The garden darkening on its rigid hand.

Euthanasia

The law's been passed and I am lying low
Hoping to hide from those who think they are
Kindly, compassionate. My step is slow.
I hurry. Will the executioner
Be watching how I go?

Others about me clearly feel the same.
The deafest one pretends that she can hear.
The blindest hides her white stick while the lame
Attempt to stride. Life has become so dear.
Last time the doctor came,

All who could speak said they felt very well.
Did we imagine he was watching with
A new deep scrutiny? We could not tell.
Each minute now we think the stranger Death
Will take us from each cell

For that is what our little rooms now seem
To be. We are prepared to bear much pain,
Terror attacks us wakeful, every dream
Is now a nightmare. Doctor's due again.
We hold on to the gleam

Of sight, a word to hear. We act, we act,
And doing so we wear our weak selves out.
We said 'We want to die' once when we lacked
The chance of it. We wait in fear and doubt.
O life, you are so packed

With possibility. Old age seems good.
The ache, the anguish – we could bear them we
Declare. The ones who pray plead with their God
To turn the murdering ministers away,
But they come softly shod.

The Wrong Subject

So many interests you had. You needed all
To quench your curiosity. I too
Would have a hand in more than the quickening feel
Of prosody. I grew up much like you,
But your wish was to heal,

Or rather study man. Anatomy
Would have made your whole life much happier
But you, wanting to marry, chose to be
A guardian of public health. You were
Good at it, but I see,

Years later, that your craving for a kind
Of study which you loved had made of you
A nervous man, swift to be angry, lined
Too young. I had the luck to find the true
End to ambition, combined

The abstract and the concrete, caught from you
The love of taking things apart and learning
New possibilities. I wish I knew,
Or had known earlier, frustrations turning
Your life slantwise. Words go

As doctor's eyes should to the quick of life.
Words heal the user. It needs gentle hands
To dare to touch sick bodies. Surely if
You'd had man's bones to love, there'd been less grief.
Doctors like poets move to the same ends.
It's largely luck which mends and understands.

Some Never Forgotten Words of My Mother's

'You'll end a murderer' –
The words shiver and thrill me through today.
I was six years old and kicking a door,
    Trying to get my way.

    You, so gentle, were
Yet adamant in this and rightly so.
You've left me with a fear
    Of losing my rash rage, not letting go

    All laws. Yet temper still
Rages in me occasionally and,
    When it does, I feel
A door rise up and kept locked by your hand.
    Then my still untamed will

    Pushes for some small
Favour I have no right to or, perhaps
    Half-want, yes, to kill
A petty stranger. Mother, you've laid traps
    And you protect me still.

The Gardens Stretch

The gardens stretch, happy under a sun
Cantering through the day. It puts its hands
On me and guides me. All the dark has gone
And snow has melted. That stark Winter ends

And so does our imprisonment. Why did
I pause today, as if I'd come upon
A life I did not understand? What led
Me through the woken stems, the spacious sun,

The long debate of seasons we do not
Become accustomed to? It's good we don't.
Freshness rides us. We are gladly caught

In trances of the light and dark. We can't
Choose, as we can choose an abstract thought.
We're beggars always, yet glad of our want.

Summer Scene

Air through a window only, but
    It carried with it scents
Of grass and trees and also caught
    The South with that intense,

Authentic charge, so hot, so strong.
    Time is defeated by
Potent reminders which belong
    Also to that starred sky

Fixed but dazzling. Night comes on
    Slowly, but sitters here
Surrender to the pacific moon
    And that air still, that air.

Sea Song

Listen, the palm trees shake
    In a quick concern of wave.
Hear the breakers make
    New music and now have

An invisible orchestra of
    Sounds to purify
Our lives and make us love
    A little before we die.

Shall we speak or shall
    We let the silence be
As obedient as a shell
    Which stores the voice of the sea?

Well, let the children say
    Their wishes while we are
Only the night and day
    Only the sun or a star.

Sea-Drunk

Acquaint me with some grief
For I am walking half between the air
   And land. There is relief
In feeling thus and having now no share
   Of gravity. This life

   Suits me best when I
Can't see or hear a clock. My roots have come
   Up, I am like the gulls which dignify
The tired shore. My home
   Is half with sea, the other half with sky.

When sleep appears I'll drown yet stay alive,
   The diver and the dive.

Spring Twilight

   This is that good hour when
The dying twitterings of several birds
Speak, but in a lower strain
Of Spring wrought of suggestions moving towards
A world of etched trees, all in silhouette
As the pale, drained sky shows the sun has set.

   One window in my room
Is open to the warmth that channels through
   Shafts of coldness. I have come
Into a season and all acts I do
Are steeped in gold, royal authority.
I am the shadow locked into that tree

   A dozen yards away.
I am the new moon pencilled on the sky
   And I am my whole yesterday,
But most I am this moment, am held by
Its crystal dome around me. When it's night
I shall be all the scattered stars in sight.

   And as I stare around
My room, it interests me with shadows of
   Ruled, careful lines, a geometry

But also an old exercise of love,
Shaped partly of a spirit quick to take
Colour from climate. When it is daybreak

The moment's clarity will sunder and
I'll take the sun's white wafer on my hand.

Night Moment

One cedar tree, one oak, one sycamore
   Turn in a little sigh
Of wind. This is the day's evasive hour,
   For now the quick-change sky

Is restive, paling, sinking, letting go,
   Her anchor pulls away.
Moment by moment all the trees will show
   A branch of stars to stay

Until the morning. Under those stars sleep
   Or at least lie peacefully.
All bird-calls have just stopped. Our world dreams deep
   And for ten hours is free.

Night Power

Am I alone now as the wind comes up
Sweeping huge stretches of the darkened sky,
Threading the stars, enfolding others' sleep?

I am yet am not. In this room that's high
Above a formal garden far away
From crowds and noise, I am the lonely cry

Of owls who tell the hours. I rule the day
As my mind reaches for before-dawn peace
And there is reason in the words I say

Or write. How warm it is. The bluff winds sing
The rise in temperature. I think the end
Of Winter's come, but now is neither Spring

Nor any other season while I stand,
As if the globe were trembling in my hand
And I could still the world's fraught whispering.

The Apt Phrase

To have the apt phrase now and then
But O so much more then than now.
There is rain tapping on a pane
    Of glass. I would teach how
    To be punctilious with words
As clouds are when they forecast rain.
I'd have instinctive flights from birds,
    I would feel any pain

If cadences were at my beck
If images conveyed my drift.
    Where is the one poem I can make?
    How many words are left?

A Proustian Moment

It wasn't a moment. It
Was not possessed by time. Just now a shaft
    Of broad sun shone and set
All Rome before me caught in memory's net.
    I wish I knew the craft

Of Proustian moments when
Five senses link and smell is what we see,
    Light is heard. Again
Touch could strike lightnings in that April rain
    And Rome was palpably

About me, all the great
Churches and ruins rose in the bread-sweet air.
    How do we open the gate
To this? We cannot, we can only wait
    Until again we hear

Nostalgic powers making us surrender
All but attention and an ancient wonder.

A Chinese Poem

It may be hot. This picture does not show
Though in the centre water's coursing down
Rapids from a river we can't see.
Not far from the horizon is a bridge,
An old man leans on it. Whether he is
Wise we do not know.

Nor do we know if those two close together
And yet not touching, under a willow tree
Have reached the end or start of love. It is,
The painter seems to say, not our affair.

The old man's wisdom and the couple's passion
Are left in doubt but what we learn from these
Cautiously offered, careful objects is
That things remain themselves. The rapids flow
Whether a wise man notices or not.
That willow droops but does not weep for these

Lovers. We need reminders now and then,
We, ardents for pathetic fallacies.
What matters is that water will stay cool
If lovers suffer or that man's a fool.

Braque's Dream

You are in a wood and you can hear
    Music playing far off.
Violins are singing, you are sure
    And there are sounds enough

For your exploring. You will take apart
    These violins, these trees,
And from some strength which struggles in your heart
    You will refashion these

Shapes and sounds and, with a quiet shade
    Of brown will tell us more
Of two great arts. A masterpiece is made
    And the world was different before.

Christmas Suite in Five Movements

1 The Fear

So simple, very few
Can be so bare, be open to the wide
Dark, the starless night, the day's persistent
Wearing away of time. See, men cast off
Their finery and lay it on the floor,

Here, of a stable. What do they wait for?
Answers to learned questions? No, they have
Been steeped in books and wear the dust of them.

Philosophy breaks all its definitions,
Logic is lost, and here
The Word is silent. This God fears the night,
A child so terrified he asks for us.
God is the cry we thought came from our own
Perpetual sense of loss.
Can God be frightened to be so alone?
Does that child dream the Cross?

2 The Child

Blood on a berry,
   Night of frost.
Some make merry.
   Some are lost.

Footsteps crack
   On a pool of ice.
Hope is back.
   This baby lies

Wrapped in rags,
   Is fed by a girl.
O if God begs,
   Then we all hold

Him in our power.
   We catch our breath.
This is the hour
   For the terrible truth,

Terrible, yes,
But sweet also.
God needs us.
Now, through snow,

Tomorrow through heat
We carry him
And hear his heart
And bring him home.

3 A Litany

Mary of solace, take our hope,
Girl untouched, take our hands,
Lady of Heaven, come to our homes,
You bring Heaven down.

Mary of mercy, learn our laws,
Lady of care, take impulse to
Your heart, give us grace,
More than enough
And a relish for
The renewal of love.

Queen of formal gardens, reach our forests,
Girl of the fountains, come into our desert.
Mary of broken hearts, help us to keep
Promises. Lady of wakefulness, take our sleep.
You hold God in your arms and he may weep.

4 The Despair

All night you fought the dream and when you woke
Lay exhausted, blinded by the sun.
How could you face the day which had begun?
As we do, Christ, but worse for you. You broke
Into our history. History drives you on.

Love before this was dust, but it was dust
You took upon yourself. Your empty hands
Have scars upon them. You have made amends
For all wrong acts, for love brought down to lust.
God, the world is crying and man stands

Upon the brink of worse than tragedy.
That was noble. Now there's something more
Than careful scenes and acts. Some men make war
On you and we feel helpless, are not free
To struggle for you. God, we've seen you poor

And cold. Are stars dispensing light that you
Should find the universe turned ... can it be
Away from you? No, no, we cannot see
Far or fully. Christ, just born, you go
Back to the blighted, on to the thriving Tree.

5 The Victory

Down to that littleness, down to all that
Crying and hunger, all that tiny flesh
And flickering spirit – down the great stars fall,
Here the huge kings bow.
Here the farmer sees his fragile lambs,
Here the wise man throws his books away.

This manger is the universe's cradle,
This singing mother has the words of truth.
Here the ox and ass and sparrow stop,
Here the hopeless man breaks into trust.
God, you have made a victory for the lost.
Give us this daily Bread, this little Host.

WINTER WIND
(1979)

Near the End

The time may come I'm so old I'll need
To count up animals and birds I can
Depend upon – birds not too shy to feed
Out of my hands, a sentimental cat
Who makes bread on my knees, and things like that.

For all the world of men will draw away,
But peacefully. Perhaps a child or two
Will come to call because they want to stay
An hour, admire my animals and be
Hiders of death and its anxiety.

But may I not invest too much in things,
Be miserly with objects, but rely
More on what walks away, what flies and sings,
In short, what warms my hands, sharpens my eye,
Hoodwinking me with hopes that I shan't die.

A Happy End

Perhaps I'll go to the jungle when I am old,
Go down where the snakes hide and the parrots scream.
I shall not mind the heat or the sudden cold.
Close to death, I shall be at one with extreme

Weathers. Back and back I'll go to when man
First named these creatures. Perhaps, also like him,
I'll paint the ways of beasts when they began,
Use a child's colours before my eyes grow dim,

My body weakens and I start to see
What is not there though I shall not know of this.
With the frantic snake and the poised tiger I'll be
Prepared to take whatever destinies

Await us there, there in the dark and the heat,
In the stiffening nights I'll murmur my last prayers
And one hot morning lie dead at the feet
Of the wild beasts still pursuing their wild affairs.

I shall be lucky if I die this way
With my epitaph what the parrots choose to say.

The Deepest Love

Let us not draw back when you dare
To speak a truth which seems unkind.
Give me the strength to say 'My dear,
I sense through anger crystal care
And mark the keen edge of your mind.'

Love must be hard to last. Also,
All sentiment will break around
This crystal strength, this tower of gold.
A loving touch may taste of cold
But any power needs such to show
It will not yield, it's so well-found.

Winter Wind

Wind rocking and chasing,
Wind with no trees to turn
Over and over, you're lacing
Together the clouds till the moon

Is sly or shivering. Wind,
Whatever the quarter you come from,
Blow through the wakeful mind
And whisper at dawn your way home.

A Widow

He would not want the mourning,
He would reproach the tears
And yet I wish to show him
Some tribute of the years
I spent with his discerning
And bearing of my cares.

Would he if I had been
The first of us to die
Have shown a mask of courage?
I think he would and I,
In shame, would wish him seen
In tears such as I cry.

Van Gogh

Whirling and dizzying as a beginning world,
The planets parting and fixing an order – there
You pushed your vision down. Now it takes hold
Of us. We steady in stilled atmosphere.

Cypress or chair, a landscape, your own face
Reach a conclusion for our pleasure, while
Still leaving finger-marks of skill and grace,
You fumble at your ear with one bleak smile.

The Only Child

How did I come and why alone
When all the other children have,
At least when I look round at play,
A brother or a sister who
Fights for them, is defender of
Their weakness? This is true all day.

They must be luckier still at night
When darkness shakes my curtains and
I am afraid to turn and see
What hovers near; I cannot call
To anyone. Defenceless in
Myself, I want another me.

The Rake

It is their little safeties that I want.
I know they never guess this. I can show
A proud and carefree face.
They love the easy laughs in me, I know,
But do they know I haunt
Their homes and wish that I were in their place?

They do not. That is why they come to me.
I represent no ties, no promises,
I stand for all who say
That they have lost their sovereign liberty.
I am their night, not day.
They do not know I have my enemies.

A dark within, a loneliness I try
To throw away by seeming to them one
Who's always on the move.
Why can't they see that I am on the run
Because I fear their love
Yet long for it until the hour I die?

Eurydice

He with his fluting is always remembered,
He is the model for players and lovers,
I am the one by darkness encumbered.
He is the one that each century discovers,

Discovers, remodels, reshapes for new uses.
What if he had not looked back? O what then?
Would I too be lost? We both are excuses
For every hurt love that is lived through by men.

I listen. No answer. But wait, I can hear
The murmurs of fluting. Excitement returns.
Yes, someone is playing. Sound's growing more clear.

We are more than a myth. We're a truth each one learns
When the joy and the wonder of first love appear,
But also the warning that each victim spurns.

A DREAM OF SPRING
(1980)

Winter Argument

It was a rife and perfect Winter cold,
The scarecrow oaks stood out against the sky.
The sun gave half-an-hour of melting gold
While rooks were grounded. Who lives in this island
For long will never for its mildness cry.
You pull your own place up, hand by rough hand.

You take the weather and tear pages up,
Those chapters full of faulty forecasts and
The massive edges of a rotten crop.
Better expect too little than too much.
What was a feverish is now a spent land,
And yet it yields to a pacific touch.

Squares divided once are now at ease
Fitfully. England looks up in Winter
Suggesting nowhere an enduring place.
We do not ask that, we but ask to wander,
With tacit lack of absolutes. A chanter
In the cold wood sets the mind to ponder

On its own value and the worth of those
Collected trees which kneel into the light,
The falling light which has ways to disclose
The secrets hoarded for a frosty night.
We drift into the dark where each dream goes
With unexpected order. What insight
Will shift in sleep towards us? No one knows.

The Snow

Has it let up at last?
Snow slips its sleeves over the branches of oak,
    Grey clouds have passed
And now off-white is letting the sun soak
    Through it. Will land be possessed

    By Summers again ever?
We are a mute chorus and have had enough
    Of the night-long shiver,
Of the way thick clouds of snow so proudly move
    And alter and take over

    The meadow of horses and
The wilting forest, making one great white
    Expanse, as if weather's hand
Had a sure right to possession of the land.
    It was a pluck-the-heart sight,

    That snow, every fall
Looked designed, and when the sun at last appeared
    Boldly, our minds were full
Of a singular beauty offered, one which we once feared,
    And all the birds stood still.

A Dream of Spring

    I woke to another dream.
The sun was leaping up the sky and I heard
    A chorus which seemed to come
From a nearby wood, from the sky, as if every bird
    Had started to build a home.

    What industry there was,
What a twitter and dash of making. Winter had gone
    And the trees' nakedness.
A gather of leaves pressed and reached into the sun,
    And in the silken, loose

Clouds there was shine enough
For meeting and mating. Daffodils blew in the wind
        And it was as if love
Were insisting on being vocal. Surely the mind
        Of a maker turned the leaf

        Of his book of life and set
Free creation again and love again.
        This was a dream and yet
When I woke and saw the snow turning to rain
        And the trees dripping wet,

I smelt the smack of Spring in the changing air,
Heard the blackbird's triumphant call, and Persephone near.

Instead of an Elegy

What is this calm in which I walk? Does it
Issue from me or is it part of this
So welcome Spring that gathers round my feet?

There is a hesitancy in the trees
As if they needed several weeks to grow
Accustomed to the warmth. I am with these

And with the just-appearing snowdrop who
Looks round for space and throws timidity
Away. What is this peace in which I know

Nothing but tenderness to a dead friend,
No elegiac mood, no painful tears?
I am at a beginning, not an end,

And in this start, I dance with ardent Spring
And join the blackbirds. I learn how to sing,
And think of death and start to understand.

More Than Spring

Spring is a secular sacrament. Today
It healed us as we walked the golden streets.
The leafless trees threw handfuls of birds to
The shafts of sun. Winter, for sure, retreats

But goes off with a laggard look resenting
Sequences of light. In spite of cold
We toss our mufflers off, we are acquainting
Ourselves with Spring and all its spendthrift gold.

The snowdrop pushes slowly up. Why do
Tears hurt? It is for more than Spring they come.
We're back with Eden-longings, want to go

Into Paradise, that fabled home.
A hawk streaks down to kill a mouse and show
What dark we move to, what dark we come from.

A Moment of Childhood

Lizards ran over my palm. I had no fear.
Four or five I was and I knew the bounds
Of my world – the high, white nursery with its air
A mixture of honey and soap. Beneath were grounds

Full of red currant bushes and apple trees
And loganberries and rockeries with plants
Seething over white pebbles. I could please
Myself for hours then. What is it that enchants

Me now, as I fondle a memory of those
Days of rocking-horses and kittens and trust
Taken for granted? Now, sometimes, I close
My eyes and will myself back to that time, but just

As I settle down the present is on me again,
Though the child persists for little. Audacity
Pulses in my blood and I sustain,
A moment only, that identity.

I'm uncircumscribed now but have less liberty.

From Light to Dark

Love was easy then. It did not tear
Through daily circumstances, did not divide
The mind. It had all childhood on its side.
It was a new frock or new suit to wear,
It was a clever toy. We set aside

All this reluctantly. Love changes us
Or do we change it? Darkened years advance
And we must move with them. There's little chance
Of love without the passions which abuse,
Or gratitude without the thrust of sense.

And it is now that a strange homesickness
Haunts us, not for some place where we have been
Happy. It is for one place we've not seen
But where we feel we fit. An Eden is
Our long desire. Among its many trees

One stands and mocks us, one whose fruit has gone.
This is our lost home. Cannot we put back
The fruit forbidden? We can't, since we lack
The proper love, the selfless one. We're sick
With an old pain so prompt in its attack.

Lent and Spring

It has come fast, another Lent,
Hard on the thaw. The Winter went
Suddenly. Few were prepared
For the spilt sun, or singing bird.

The elms are killed. None can be saved,
And every meadow looks bereaved,
Ash on the brow, sin in the mind.
Our spirits burn low, eyes are blind.

But Lent is in the Spring, maybe,
That grace should burst out naturally,
That we may learn from birds and flowers
That we depend on one God's powers,

A God, however, who needs us.
What better motive can we use
To make ourselves at one with these
Blossom-waiting apple trees?

What better way to tell again
The Eden story and its pain?
But there's a death that felled the world.
A God died once. Spring air was cold

But strong belief affirms that this
God-man rose up, kept promises,
O Christ upon a flowering tree,
Be your own Spring, blossom with me.

A Difficulty

Why do words stick in my throat, the ones I want
Poised on the edge of my mind? The drift is love,
And I, so glib at other times, lack proof,
In words I mean, of my gratitude. I can't
Be gracious except in silence. Poems move

And link in ranks and rhythms. They are fleet
Compared with affectionate conversations. I stand,
Angry, frustrated, sometimes put out a hand,
Miming love. Meanwhile you must sit
Till I touch your hand most shyly. Thus I wait

On the mood and minute. You must do the same
And you won't seem to mind. At least, we both know
That nothing is overstated. My words are slow
In coming, but when I at last murmur your name
It is as if ice cracked at the sun's first blow.

Turn

Turn on your side and bear the day to me.
The dawn is on its way. The night has gone.
Gone the full moon and all the Milky Way.

You stand on tiptoe waiting for the sun.
You always were the optimist while I
See through your eyes now, now the dark is done.

Listen, a cock is crowing far away.
The sky blushes to pink. The birds confide
Their secrets to the dawn, the start of day.

Give me your world and turn upon your side.
We have a link more sure than rings of gold.
Our ways together are both deep and wide.

I am the nervous one and you the bold,
So different, though we never can divide.
You have on me what sea has to the cold

Moon. I feel chains. O turn back to my side.

Horse

At first a fume of mist in the morning is
The horse, haltered to dawn, smoke round his feet,
    That herald of the heat.
He canters in a sun-disclosing place
Before day-sounds, before the hounds will meet.

He walks away from psalms and rituals,
Is but the remnant of a Pegasus
    At night riding to us.
He is himself and here and nowhere else,
Hint of a new event or a first cause.

The dawn is clearing but the horse is there
Tossing his mane. The sun is pouring through
    Fragments of mist to go
Upon this beast and be his bridle. Clear
The meadow and we see his shadows throw

Horse after horse. The groom is standing by
With saddle. He himself is spurred. The horse
    Comes from some early source,
A myth now melting underneath the eye
Reminding of some far ... no, some new force.

Spring's Annunciation

This is now to be
In on creation again, the start of all
    The ingenuity
And variousness of a world before the Fall.
    We open our eyes to the

    Rinsed out sky, its blue
Beckoning birds who rise and skirmish and play:
    In a day or two
The snowdrop will tell of so much strength in the way
    It lets the wind run through

    Its petals. What do I say
Who come into Spring unfallen? I cannot find
    Words that would convey
More than gratitude. I open my mind

    And its shadows run off at once.
The blackbird sings there and enjoys its flight.
    My heart is all a-dance
With wonder and love at this overplus of light.
    The world which seemed immense

    In Winter is small again,
Slight as a sparrow, is a gentle of breezes
    And a falling of small rain.
In short, Spring is on. O how it tempts and teases,
    What joy it gives to pain.

Into Spring

I put my hands out and the breezes come
Into my palm. I gather up the light.
Thrushes are building, migrants flying home.

It is as if I'd stepped from prisons of night,
A long sentence, and now had won reprieve.
I ask myself if Spring was ever so bright

Before, so fertile too. There is relief
In simply standing, saying nothing, feeling …
No, being feeling. Leaf after probing leaf

Will soon be riding on dark boughs. What healing
Has come now Winter's gone? I cannot speak,
But feel creation rise again and stealing

My Winter wounds. I watch a blackbird break
Out of a hedgerow into song. I watch
The cruising clouds unveil the sun, and make

A prayer of gratitude. I almost reach
A star at night. I find but never seek.

Sermon of the Clouds

So many shapes are we,
Count us over and over,
Let the sun pitch its camp in our tents,
We, the elusive emperors.
We enter all weathers, we represent
All elements. It is we who waterfall the showers,
We who withdraw and let the sun distribute
Largesse of life or death.

We are chameleon, mercury,
Nothing escapes our attention and nothing is
Too small or large to accommodate our presence.
What is our message to you?
Perhaps we teach that pride need not be too vain,
That elusiveness is not the same as evasion,
That power can attain a singular purity.
We are the high-riders and the drifters,
But drifters with a purpose.
We are the evanescence of the sky.
Set your sights by us, high.

One Man, One Voice

Pascal said it was
Sufficient to justify the world if one
Man could plead his cause,
Demand justice, cry from being alone
To a God with his hand on

This planet and all of space.
We feel near to this now, so divided up,
         Afraid to show our face.
We have almost lost the last garrison, hope,
         And the regiments of grace.

         But there are quite enough
Who want peace. They had better say
         That now they, indeed, have
So much care locked up. This is a day
         To surrender part of love,

And spread it about. The more
We do, the less we lose. There's a habit in
         The most passionate love. To feel sure
We need only offer it. There is torment in men.
         We must make ourselves care.

         The world where we exist
Still has moments of grace, still offers us
         Meadows where the best
Frolic before the fight. The world's for our use
         At our first breath and our last.

English Wild Flowers

Forget the Latin names; the English ones
Are gracious and specific. Hedge-rows are
Quickening fast with vetch and cow-parsley.
And fast along the lawn the daisies rise
For chains or for the murdering lawn-mower.

Look everywhere, there is all botany
Laid between rising corn,
Infesting hay-fields. Look, the buttercup
Stares at the sun and seems to take a share
Of wealthy light. It glows beneath our chins.

Slim shepherd's purse is lost in dandelions,
Scabious will show a little later. See,
The dog-rose in the hedge. It dies at once
When you pluck it. Forget-me-nots disclose
Points of pure blue, the sovereign blue of sky.
And then there are the herbs.

Counting this floral beauty I grow warm
With patriotism. These are my own flowers,
Springing to pleasant life in my own nation.
The times are dark but never too dark for
An Eden Summer, this flower-rich creation.

A Way to a Creed

Mine is a hard creed and often is at odds
With my mercury nature. It informs my mind,
Tells of truths apparent to the blind
But not to me. I am afraid of Gods,
And yet when a line sings through me and I find

A poem telling me what I did not know
Before about myself or my character
I need to thank, for it's then I find myself near
A presence in the universe. I go
About with a new hope and without fear.

So I come into a childhood creed again,
Come to it like the prodigal son and am
Welcomed with understanding, as if there were some
God who, yes, needs me in a daily pain.
He, like me, is also coming home.

Always that dark cross throws its shadow on me
And I am often in the garden where
Christ came so often to the brink of despair.
It is, I think, in my own poetry
I meet my God. He's a familiar there.

CELEBRATIONS AND ELEGIES
(1982)

Goings

A packet of hurried letters, nervous gestures
To do with fingers, voices high and low
But out of key, eyes afraid to meet eyes –
　　All this meaning 'Go'.

A child might hug or rush into its silence
This is the fear of life not fear of death,
And the promises that distances mean nothing
　　Already out of breath.

O our walls are painted with partings we don't notice,
Our minds are galleries of looks averted.
Perhaps the cord was never cut completely
　　And those birth pangs were started

In a universe that's vast with a unique
Structure of inter-connections – star and steeple,
Storm and brain cell. We are born to break.
　　We are departing people.

Autumn

Fragile, notice that
As Autumn starts, a light
Frost crisps up at night
And next day, for a while,
White covers path and lawn.
'Autumn is here, it is,'
Sings the stoical blackbird
But by noon pure gold is tossed
On everything. Leaves fall
As if they meant to rise.
Nothing of nature's lost,
The birth, the blight of things,
The bud, the stretching wings.

Sermon of the Hills
In Tuscany

We are voices but never the voices of mountains,
We have dignity but never condescend,
The good trees burst in flower and fruit upon us,
And the olive prepares its oil and the vineyard loves us;
They speak of us quietly, mostly in the Spring.

There are quarries hacked from our many sides,
Oxen who plough out ledges. But the sun,
Ah the sun nests against us in every season's *siesta*.
All are reticent here, almost silent.
But across our valley a little village speaks

And the old and young live their lives in public air.
We are a distance of sky, a channel of water
Entering the silence of men.
So we teach you calm and diffidence but also
Love which sighs from a midnight street for a few,

Love that surrenders day by day at a Mass,
Love that takes the stranger into its calm.
We lean against the sky and all the stars
Are silver flares struck from our many stones.

The Heart of Night

Time is a dancer now in the dead of night,
    Spirits dance minuets,
Angels present pavanes under starlight
    And each unsleeper meets

His counter-part, attendant, one who knows
    The steps by heart. How much
The sleepers miss in ignorant repose
    Of small hours' magic touch.

But they have their own time. It is the dawn.
    Flights are the movements then.
Stars have thinned out and all the dancers gone
    Back to the mood of angels, or of men.

Arrival in Bibbiena, Tuscany

A huddle of shadows and
Small lights down all the slopes. Dark had come down
And we were racing now through the sweet warmth
Of Tuscany with its slit moon
And its imperial crown.

How fitting it is always to arrive
By night in foreign places. They give hints
Of royalty tomorrow, sovereign sun
At its full height, but now it was the moon,
A goddess, a madonna with full hands

Offering simple, therefore holy things.
Her child had gone to sleep as we drew near
Our destination. No need now to speak.
No words were needed, simply being there,
And feeling night's soft arms, was strong and dear.

Remembering Bibbiena in Tuscany

Green hills assemble in this Northern dawn.
The first birds whisper and there is a haze
Suggesting heat. O Tuscan hills draw near,
Counsel my memory. You walk to me
In a strange landscape, English in a Summer
Not seen till June. You churches,

Little Romanesque ones, lend me prayer
When I pass here or enter ugly ones.
What coolness haunted me. It haunts me still
As those brisk swallows did in Tuscany.
And then, you friendly people, with loud voices,
Milena and Marino, Sergio,

Enter this English morning. No, you would
Be ill at ease and not at all yourselves.
Stay where you are but draw me back to you
When grapes are trodden and the new wine comes
And you stand there and smile a 'Welcome home'.

A Kind of Catalogue

Item, a cloud, and how it changes shape,
Now a pink balloon, then a white shift
From a Victorian doll. The forms won't keep
One pattern long. Item, a flow of wind
Carrying dust and paper, gathering up

Rose petals. Item, a command of sun
Subtly presented on a lifted face,
A shaft of light on leaves, darkness undone
And packed away. Item, limbs moved with grace,
Turning the air aside. Item, my own

Observations, now *Lot This, Lot That*
Ready for an unseen auctioneer.
The bidders are half-conscious choices met
To haggle. Signs are made, sometimes I hear
My whisper bidding for *Lot This, Lot That.*

Sparrow

The hallowed, the special flyer, I mean the sparrow,
A flash of feathers and tiny body, a quick
Nerve, a spirit of speed and certainly one
To copy when you are tempted to turn from the sun.
Sparrow of 'special providence' teach to us
Your joy, your gladness, your success, for you
Live in accord with that power which moves
You fast and far. Your flights and pauses bring
Delight to us. We are not surprised you were chosen
Specially, for even birds who sing
With a rapture of angels lack your flare and fling.

Field-Mouse

Pause for a moment. Look
At the poised power of the universe which holds
All things in place. No book
Telling of earth or sky describes those fields
Which are ready now to break

Corn, make the harvest start.
Observe the purpose everywhere – that man
    Who is about to set
The combine harvester to its business.
    It can work quickly, is a threat

To the field-mouse hearing sound
Come nearer and nearer. He is stiff with fear,
    He has so little ground
To stand on. He will go under the harvester
    And never be found, or mourned.

Blackbird Singing

Out of that throat arise
    Such notes of poignant sound
That circle round the skies
    And never come to ground.

The bird has gone elsewhere
    But its melody echoes on
Through the transported air
    And it even gilds the sun.

Can any of us be
    So utterly outside our
Personal city
    Or the treading of the hour?

Never. O let it go
    On, this blackbird's song.
It has so much to show
    Our weakness. It is strong

But at least we recognise,
    Innocence, purity,
There is eloquence in the sky's
    Space and sweet energy.

Not Mine

Take my hands, full moon, take my
Aspirations. Take my hope,
You stars that spread the sky
And I can feel my scope
For joy increasing but it is not 'I'

Any longer. I am lost in leaves
Falling and staying. In the harvest I
Gathered the corn with power
Of memory and imaginings. I beg,
I cannot stop it, that the last full hour

Of Summer stay with me till Spring next year.

Over and Over

Over and over they suffer, the gentle creatures,
The frightened deer, the mice in the corn to be gathered,
Over and over we cry, alone or together.
And we weep for a lot we scarcely understand,
Wondering why we are here and what we mean
And why there are huge stars and volcanic eruptions,
Earthquakes, desperate disasters of many kinds.
What is the answer? Is there

One? There are many. Most of us forget
The times when the going sun was a blaze of gold
And the blue hung behind it and we were the whole of awe,
We forget the moments of love and cast out time
And the children who come to us trusting the answers we give
To their difficult and important questions. And there

Are shooting stars and rainbows and broad blue seas.
Surely when we gather the good about us
The dark is cancelled out. Mysteries must
Be our way of life. Without them we might
Stop trying to learn and hoping to succeed
In the work we half-choose and giving the love we need.

Rescued

These are the many but they must be praised.
They have known dark valleys but have raised
Their eyes to rings of stars. They have climbed up
Hill-sides and cliffs and felt the vertigo
Of height but have gone on, not looked below
But watched the sky and rested at the top.

Do not imagine these have never been
In *cul de sacs* of near-despair and seen
Death as desirable. They have and they
Have turned away from it. It is good luck
Simply to be and these have turned their back
On the dark stranger who stands in the way

Of life, the breath of it, its primal power
Settled in us, with each one given our
Specific strength. That stranger's had his toll
Of many lost. Some were nearly so
But brought back by great mercy. This I know
For I gave up but felt a great power pull

Me back and now I see why and am glad,
Also ashamed. Call that power God,
As I do, call it fortune. I have found
Some use in all those shadows. They have told
Me of the terror that makes dying bold
But now I hear its soft retreating sound.

An Elegy before Death

For two old ladies aged 94 and 101

They cannot die and they would like to go
On the quiet ferry, slipping out of this world.
They've led rich lives, each differently so.
Onto this life each keeps a careful hold.
    What can my words do?

I'll give an elegy to see them through
The last few stretches. I shall have to say
'We love you still. We cannot bear that you
Should want to leave us every opening day.'
    These words are partly true

But, secretly, I want what these two want
For themselves – a happy drifting off
Into other worlds they trust. We can't
Say that we want what they want now. Our love
    Has to lie. These haunt

Our imaginations. We say we
Need them. We mean it but we realise
We must sound selfish, never let them see
That we can see their own world with their eyes
    But cannot set them free.

Children at Play

'And I shall be a tree,'
The child said to a playmate. He went on,
'You are the river I am growing near,'
And to a third he said, 'You are the boat
Which rows across my clear, fresh water.' So
The ring-leader decided and the game
Went on for days, for weeks. Sometimes a word

Was heard by parents who looked baffled. They
Had quite forgotten how imagination
Had worked with them once. Certainly some have
More intense ones but there can be few
Children who lack some small creative power
Which is how an imagination shows
Itself. But it grows dim. That boy who played

At trees and rivers grew up with no gift
For any art but he became adept
At science and computers. Now he has
Children who, in a year or two, will play
The kind of game he knew. Will he forget
Just how it felt or be quite otherwise,
Feel the cold shudder of a large regret?

Landscapes and Figures

Have you seen a landscape where the people
Do not fit? We always tend to think
Of paintings where, perhaps, a loving couple
Gives the foreground a small, careful link
    With the clouds that topple

Over the mountains in the whole landscape.
Painters are clever. They compose the scene.
It's true that real landscapes sometimes keep
People suited to the place but then,
    Too often they will step

Out of the picture, play no part in what
The trees discourse about, the winds supply.
We jostle for our place and few will not
Try to keep the background from the eye.
    We ought to be taught

The selflessness of figures in a Claude.
They take us to the hazy sky beyond.
They are to hills and sky what a prelude
Is to dramatic music. A background
    Teaches a moral you'd

Hardly expect. But surely a concern
With people, with the land they live in are
The way we lose ourselves. From art we learn
To step back and be self-effacing where
    Dawn enters, sunsets burn.

Heyday

All was a blossom and a bounty then,
A world of learning pulsing with the young
Keen minds at work, quick eyes to speed to eyes,
Libraries of the great to move among
And all those dazzling, wondering young men.

Enough to turn your head. It never did.
I had my flowering too but it came late.
I was surprised into the magic of
Party or ball, the passionate and sweet
Moment of young men moving into love

And moving me, young too. This one would shine
With love of art and read his poetry,
That one was shy and when he first kissed me
It was a child's touch. Vulnerability
Belonged to all of us. I hid in mine.

Only as it went slowly (an eclipse
Would have been kinder) did I realise
How much admired I was, what careful grace
And disguised awkwardness there were. Such eyes
Followed me far, and then the meeting lips.

Leaves in the Wind

Wind muddles energy
But yet brings us the shape and power of peace.
There are tides in each tree.
These could be waves turned by the wind, and this
Could well be an unpeopled world. Such free

Abandonments there are
But there is regularity also.
Rushing upon my ear
The leaves of ash and chestnut, oak now flow
And bring the Summer tokens of the year.

All is a gentle dance.
Dark green of fir and paler shades suggest
The varying Aegean's
Gamut of night-blue, turquoise and the rest.
The wind lifts, alters, and has all the means

To show all hues. So here
It is with green. The air is green, the light
Is mixed with green. The sheer
Strength of winds has now a friendly fight
Until the night when all shades disappear.

Afterwards

After I've climbed the ladders to the dark
Sky and viewed the stars, after I
Have gone down to a sea where the waves work

In their old custom but more quietly
At this time of the year, after this
I shall find a content that's meant to be

A present for another. Who, then, is
This other? I don't know yet, may not know
For months or years till I see happiness

In someone else who tells me they must show
Some peace they've found – a white roll of the sea,
A gull upon a ledge, a sun bent low

Or something else I never dreamt could be
Until I recognise it, a design
I started but now working quietly

A life which could not when it was still mine.

Images of Love

First Love

A fist of red fire, a flower
Opening in the sun. A kind of peace
Taking over at last, and then the quick release.

Grief

Pull down the tokens. Close your eyes,
Hide from the sun. At least the night
Will keep the pain from other people's sight
And you'll have the stars' cold light.

First Admirers

In those early days it was a game.
    I didn't know the rules
This didn't matter. I lived in a dream
Of love. So many love poems and love tales

Turned out to be quite true at this beginning.
    The world shone clear for me.
There was no trickery or any cunning.
Men admired me and I honestly

Do not think I toyed or trifled with
    Their feelings. Very soon
One would wound me. Love can be dark beneath
This sweet long dance, the working of the moon.

The Near Perfection

This was all sweet and leaping, reciprocal,
Love took off from ground and we were two
Fitted together in body and mind also
Compassion crowned the royal state of love,
This glory of the senses when they are
Controlled, the eager longing that the other
One should always share
Or more than share this love which did indeed
Happen at first sight. Two Summers through
Love was our city and our state of mind,
It painted and it lit up everyone
But all was broken and I don't know why,
Perhaps I thought perfection could endure.
That kind of love, I think, belongs to Spring.
We had two Springs, were lucky with such power.

Given an Apple

He brought her an apple. She would not eat
And he was hurt until she said,
'I'm keeping it as a charm. It may
Grow small and wrinkled. I don't care.
I'll always think of you today.
Time is defeated for that hour
When you gave me an apple for
A love token, and more.'

A Place to Walk In

It was a time of peace and people went
About in quiet groups and pairs. It was
A formal world. It seemed a starting-place.
In fact it had been wasteland rife with weeds
And broken glass, the debris of a world
Torn by war and pain.

But time and clever minds and subtle fingers
Cleaned that place up, lit huge bonfires there,
Carried off stones and, when the ground was soft,
They planted seeds and shrubs, set evergreen
And deciduous trees there, and there they
Placed statues, follies, fountains, everything

To soothe the eye and cool the feverish brain.
I walked once through this garden with you and,
Although we seldom spoke, I felt a close
Pleasure link us together, yours and mine.
Wordless, we took each other's hand and walked
In from the twilight to the waiting feast.

Song of Love and Peace

Love, be a bird to me,
Lullaby me, wake
Me to the dawn and the
Voices of day-break.

Love, I will sing you to
   A sleep dividing us.
I'll wake you to the true
   Dawn, day's impetus.

Love, let us wind round
   Each other silence, peace
Deeper than silence.
   Sound is far away from us.

Morning we'll enter with
   The birds. When shall we speak?
Not till the first bird's breath
   Sings us wide awake.

Land of Plenty

And there was the land of plenty.
We stood upon the edge, the frontier,
We saw the apple-blossom and the roses,
We saw the wholesome green of every vineyard.
We watched the cypresses, steadfast in Winter,
Now giving shade to any who desired it.

A land of plenty – that goes back as far
As 'when my ship comes in'. We have passwords,
Keepsake language, ciphers, symbols but
Here are rich stems of tulips, here is sap
Denying gravity. We wait a cautious
Moment before we cross this frontier,
As if we trespassed on gifts undeserved.

What we Remember

What we remember are not curves of sun
Or swing of bells or orchestra or band,
What we remember of that day is one
Pure flight of nameless birds above the land
And all the afternoon

Unwinding slowly, golden thread above
Impartial grass, wild flowers that nod in heat.
We lay in the extreme repose of love
And everywhere we looked there was complete
Fruition and enough

Of everything for everyone. That day,
That thread of gold, our hands linked loosely are
A keepsake for the time when things don't play
Together. There was then a door ajar
To Eden or Cathay.

Peace

A little peace is luck, a trance,
    A spell, a sacrament.
A dove drops feathers. Children chance
    Upon them. Keep them, paint

Them red or green. The bird's away
    As feathers fall, so peace
Comes sparingly. The dove can't stay
    Long in a single place.

And this is prayer or part of it,
    The white shape in the mind.
The feather touch of God will let
    In light that will not blind

And will not last. The rest is work,
    The world's need of us, each
His talent in the sun and dark
    Then, perhaps, peace's touch.

An Unnerving Lesson

Take what you will of me. What most appeals
    Among my qualities
Of good and evil? Learn me, what is false
And self-deceiving. Then remember this,

I can shadow, even echo you.
    We two half-strangers yet
Are drawn together. Say why this is so.
I am lingering and prepared to wait

Night and day. What puzzles you?
    Are you afraid of me? I will admit
I can scare myself and often do.
Not love, not hate and not indifference set

Us together. In a looking-glass
    I have been staring. Then
I went into a fairground where the glass
Grotesquely can distort us. Out again

I go and first avoid all mirrors but
    I look again and see.
Nothing is there, no face. I should look out.
Shall I then find what I thought once was me?

Imperfection

The causes and the questionings of love
I have moved through again. They do not pause
And I do not grow out of them. I move

Ahead in love and there's no winning tape.
In fact, the race of love will never end.
It seems to play with us. We try to keep

It, hoard it. This is always wrong. Our friends
Sometimes run upon a different track
From ours and no one wholly understands

The shifts, the thrusts, the griefs in us. We lack
Much that seems essential for deep love,
But now and then two will find a trek

Only they know. O may we also move
More often where the sun itself can break
Into huge blossoms, starlight in their wake.

A Dark Passion

I can remember that obsessive love,
Passion, paradoxically, played
Little part in it. Desire was of
A reasonable strength yet I was frayed
And fretted by a rough,

Bullying power. If there had been a foe
That I could see, no doubt I would have fought
This dark obsession, but it did not show
In any form. The person I was caught
Up by did not know

What he was causing. In a curious way
He was not relevant or, rather, was
A channel through which ran this cruel play
With me, my heart. I knew there was no grace
And no repose. Today,

I still know little more of that odd passion
Except that later feelings I'm drawn by
Are clear to me. I do not want possession.
Did I have to know that dark so I
Might love like all creation

Growing now daily? Like one out of prison,
I find sun is my garment, thought the sky.

Recovering from a Death

We are back with our disorders again.
Last year's death has moved into the dark,
For with a real death the shadows drain
Away. All is exact and pure and stark.
    Fear of death has been

Among us since the final mourning seeped
Away. So fear, it seems, is healthy. We
Creep, stride, manoeuvre, once again are kept
Afraid. I think we miss the dignity
    Of mourning. We were stripped

Of all pretence. Love showed its proper size,
Small circumstances drifted quietly off.
Not to mourn can be a loss. We prize
A perfect grief, an almost selfless love
  And wide, defenceless eyes.

Words about Grief

Grief can return without a warning. It's
  Seldom cemeteries
Or news of other deaths that my grief fits
But places of great beauty where I was,

However briefly, happy with the one
  I loved who died. I know
Many feel happier when again they've gone
To such a place with grief. One thing I do

Know is that after years grief brings a pang
  As terrible almost
As that first rending. Death, where love's been strong,
Can always make you feel entirely lost

Or so it does with me. Time does not heal,
  It makes a half-stitched scar
That can be broken and again you feel
Grief as total as in its first hour.

For a Gentle Friend

I have come to where the deep words are
Spoken with care. There is no more to hide.
I toss away the cold stance of my fear

And move O far, far out to be beside
One who owns all language in extremes
Of death. We watch the coming-in now tide.

We have lived through the nightmares death presumes
To wound us with. We faced the darkest place.
Death the familiar enters all our rooms.

We wear its colour. Its mask's on our face.
But not for long. It's good to let tears run.
This is the quick, the nerve, also the grace

Of death. It brings our life into the sun
And we are grateful. Grief is gracious when
It takes the character of this kind one,

This gentle person. We re-live his life
And marvel at the quiet good he's done.

A Hand Lifting

A hand lifting the leaves and the leaves turning
In the sun. The hand is a child's. It goes
On exploring. It has not yet learnt
All it cannot know and may not do.
Our hands were like that once. I thought that you

Knew me as we can learn a continent
By touching cities on a turning globe.
We did not make demands much then and so
Were not disappointed. Now you rub

The tears from your red eyes. Like you I can
See that love must be an elegy.
However hard we try or well we plan
We stand apart before death has its way.

That is why death is terrible. It breaks
The little links we make. Were they more strong
Grief would be great but would not last so long
Since what's joined totally and wholly breaks

Makes a clean severance, an open wound.
It can be healed and comforted also.
But what has not been wholly joined is found
Not wholly parted. Our lot makes this so.

Is it Dual-Natured?

Is it dual-natured to be so alive
Sometimes that your flesh seems far too small
To contain the power of the sun, or how stars thrive,

But then to be diminished, become a small
Dark of yourself, yourself your hiding-place
Where you converse with shadows which are tall

Or listen to low echoes with no grace
Of lyric joy or calm? I do not feel
Divided deep. Sometimes, the sense of the place

Where I am most light and eager can make me thrill
To the planet's course. I am pulled or do
I draw myself up, into the sun's overspill?

One or other. It only matters I know
What levitation would be and am grateful to learn
What's instinctive to birds is what makes the wind blow.

I will risk all extremes. I will flounder, will stumble, will burn.

Painter from Life

He stands close to a rock. Where light falls as
The painter needs it, he
Has set his model. Now and then he asks
The youth to move, and he will keep his pose
Though sea-sounds mock his stance, while gulls go free

Over this little group. There's not a voice,
Two men exchanging thoughts and moods. They are
Almost one person for a second, then
The painter asks for movement. Here is true
Creation shared. The silent art of paint

Is now surrounded by the tempting sea,
The shafts of sun, the hot sand and the gulls.
Nature and art show here,
Briefly, all things as they were meant to be.

Words for Music

A voice on a drift of wind,
An echo left behind,
A star in one pane of glass,
   An act of grace,

The child's farewell to day,
The old with wisdom we
Recognise, the rose
   Unplucked – for verse

These can be metaphors
Or, perhaps, words of praise,
The world is moving fast,
   Poets are hard-pressed,

But at the day's end there is
A silence to fit peace,
Moments when words ring true
   And love also.

A Kind of Magic

The trees walk, they peer through the Summer haze,
   The roses unfold their skin,
Chestnut candles glimmer. On such good days
Summer's not only around us but within

Our thoughts and it plays there. I have walked through
   A wood and gathered its light,
The last gleam of the sun before it must go
Into the territory of the night.

Magic thought of is a true event.
   It happens in the mind.
It is imagination never spent,
It is the warmth that lonely people find.

Everything we think takes on unseen
   Happiness or grief.
Not only mystics have interior lives.
Most have a little in a usual life,

But when it comes to God, how magic thrives.

The One Drawback

It stays, it stays. I have incalculable
Hours of supreme sun, light which always can
Draw me on, running with light, draw me on
In somebody else's plan
But the movement is my own.

I should expect dark to be given when
I have such lights, some are tall as the sun,
Others are hearths which friends will sit around.
When these lights have gone
I am drawn underground.

I wander there but break sometimes into
A run. I only tire myself, I wait,
Imagining Summers of another world.
To move in dark is a fate
But I know also the gold

Dawns of the world outside me, and within
Dawns in which words break into fresh song,
My mind is raided by a dazzling light,
Sun is where I belong
But I'm an expert on night.

I Came Once

I came once into a field of love.
I knew it was because I felt my heart
Beating faster. Softly, I would move

And noticed nimbuses of light were part
Of all I looked at. There were curious shapes
I'd never seen before. These shapes would start

Up anywhere. Sometimes clouds from scraps
Of broken cloudlets came together in
A stretch of satin near the sun. Great leaps

Into the sky, a flash of birds, would win
Over the wind, it seemed. All this I know
Because a love in me that leapt within

My heart found an exchange, another who
Wordlessly smiled, silently took my hand.
This is a magic we have no power to

Call up. We're happy not to understand.

As the Rooks Are

Alone as the rooks are
In their high, shaking homes in the sky at the mercy of winds
Alone as the lurking trout or the owl which hoots
Comfortingly. I have a well-crammed mind
And I have deep-down healthy tough roots

But in this house where I live
In one big room, there is much solitude,
Solitude which can turn to loneliness if
I let it infect me with its darkening mood.
Away from here I have an abundant life,
Friends, love, acclaim and these are good.

And I have imagination
Which can travel me over mountains and rough seas;
I also have the gift of discrimination.
High in a house which looks over many trees
I collect sunsets and stars which are now a passion.
And I wave my hand to thousands of lives like this,
But will open my window in Winter for conversation.

Sources of Light

Sources of Light (I)
A sonnet

Sources of light and arbiters of men,
From torch to star, from moon to candle-flame,
In the bad hour of unexpected pain,
In the good hour of Christ's holy name,

These are the lights that turn into the Word,
The anxious query and assenting voice,
This is the universe's cradled Lord,
The litany from depths which still rejoice.

So light is language, so the stars give tongue,
So noon is voices babbling in the heat,
Or in the Polar snows all praise is sung.

We are delivered as we sit to eat
Our daily bread. Our God's for ever young
And he has all the planets at his feet.

Many Religions

Spring is inexhaustible, I swear
　　In early March it's on
Us already. Morning sky is clear.
There is no Winter garment on the sun.

Can we catch up? We move with quickened steps,
　　We breathe an air that's new.
Surely now no hibernator sleeps.
Are migrants back, small arrows on the blue

Stretch of sky? Not yet, but any hour
　　They'll come in strict formation.
Meanwhile we stretch our limbs and feel new power,
We too take part in this regeneration.

Eyes become brighter as the evenings come
　　Later each night. We stare
At the sky opening. It waits for some
Arrival. Christ and Proserpine are near,

There's no blasphemy in this. All old
　　Beliefs are sewn into
One great tapestry. Tales new and old
Are woven there. Like night dreams coming true.

Let Us

　　Let our hands be raised and held
　　In attentive silence. Let
　　Our minds be wholly stilled
　　And we be whole. O let
　　Us feel the fibres of
　　The universe, the shape
　　Of so much life, and love.

How smoothly the world rounds
The sun through day, through night.
Even the stars make sounds
For there's eloquence in Light.
We kneel, we stand, we embrace,
We feel the pulse of the world
And Christ is on our breath
As we move on to death.

Prayer

A flame, another element, a law
Made by experimental joy and care,
A world of golden roses, end of war,
A place of many kinds is personal prayer.
  Each one at the core

Is different as we are to the bone.
Much we have in common, it is true,
But they are obvious things. We have alone
Our kind of prayer, our own approaches to
  God who comes in his own

Way to us that suits our natures and
Capacity. To some he is a king
Dispensing property. He is a hand
That begs to others. I have heard him sing
  As a child does, and I understand
  He comes to me to bring

Me out of turning-inward and to play
Which is important if it is well done.
This child walks close behind me on a day
Of curious magic. I had never known
  This was a way to pray.

First Sunday in Lent at Downside

Love back in Bread. Rome back, a certain church,
A hill long loved there. Christ, it's Lent, I know,
But you have come to me and not to teach
But tell me of the dread despair you know.
You say, 'I am in reach,

I know your wilderness, I know the threat
Of tempting, and the pleasant way it feels
To hear the devil's whisper easy, sweet,
Offering you rich kingdoms, also false
Luxury. I meet

You in the hot and tempting hour but I
Have another world, another way
To live. I've been your child. You neighboured me.
Have you forgotten all that Christmas day
You held me on your knee?'

I am amazed. The voices rise, the light
Pours through the windows. Christ, your Lenten gift
Raises my heart. I have a sudden sight
Of Calvary. O let me, please, be left
Present at the sight

Of your triumphant dereliction. Lord,
This Lent's first Sunday is a joyful time.
I know the whole of Easter. Your good word,
Saviour, again forgives all mankind's crime.
Child, let my prayer be heard.

A Memory and a Fact in Early Lent

All the bells rang again. In Rome they rang
In a Sunday serenade of God, a song
In every church was being sung at Mass
And Christ came now concealed in Bread but in
Triumph totally. He cancelled sin
As fast as sorrow, and it seemed he was

In every Mass living his whole life through
Again, was born, grew up in me and you
And everyone who sang and meant his Creed.
This was in Rome now twenty years ago
But this morning I met him again. He took me to
His joy and grief. I felt my spirit grow

And burst in flame, a meteor that would
Not flash out quickly. In the Holy Bread
The world's pulse beat, creation was contained
And I was back within my proper place,
Happy to tears, glad to be sorry when grace
Filled me. To Christ's life I had returned

So courteously. His hands were held out to
Mine, his thought spoke in me and I knew
His presence as momentous yet as part
Of every coming day. O God, your heart
Broke mine today and I'm glad of the hurt
For I'm restored, am trusted and made new.

The Endless Crucifixion

I cannot bear the swearing and the flies,
The blood, the mutilation and the sweat,
For you, my Lord and God. My master dies,
His body torn, his bleeding hands and feet.
His cries are a child's cries

And so we move now from Jerusalem
And go back through his ministry, back far
To his humble birth in Bethlehem.
The Wise Men would be too old to be here
But they knew Christ. In him

They saw more than a special man or king.
They knelt and wise men only kneel to God.
Christ, you suffer still for each bad thing
Done by any. Please forgive me, good
Lord. The darkening

Sky is turning into storm. Strange lights,
Gaudy, grim and yellow clouds smoke. Now
Christ's side is pierced. He dies. O to what heights
Is he delivered? His hands on this Tree's boughs,
His friends release him. Rites

Of burial are performed. This all went on
Long ago but it's repeated when
We try to mend ourselves and change this one
Violent, unhappy world. It is in pain.
Jesus, thy will be done.

Many Easters

Do any escape the dark garden and
The high hill under the hazy afternoon sun?
Do any remain only in coolness and stand
In the sun- or moon-light? Surely, surely, none
For all must comprehend

The big as the small sadness. Most don't know
Whence it comes or why it does or if
It will go and never return. Even though
The time is short, unhappiness very brief
A lesson is learnt. We go

By different routes and at different times and yet
Reach the tall hill and the strange trees, with one
Specially tall. A figure has been put
To hang there still and this has all been done
By all of us. There's no doubt

About the responsibility. A God
Long ago, out of our time's calculation,
Gave us freedom and we made the bad
Choice. In his huge creating imagination
He decided he would

Send his son, also God, to die
To save us for himself. The love we know
Is a faint shadow of this but to Calvary
We must all come some day, somehow, and must show
Our sorrow. Again we,

Like many before, bury this dead God,
Plant him in earth, bind him round until
The Spring comes and one flower white and red
Flourishes. It has a meaning to tell.
It is the Word, Our Lord.

Simplicities

Not only present in the life of hills
And trees and meadows and the stirring sea
And in men's characters and in each sense
And element, and instinct of the beasts,
Not only here, Lord, are you present, though,
Should you withdraw your power all would fall
And disappear and nothingness be here.

But Lord, to make things simple, easy for our so
Easily frightened hearts you came to us
In Bread, the simplest form, our daily Bread.
Always simplicity attended your
Activities. O yes, we know that you

Gave a sense of glory which you can
And do at all times satisfy – the fire,
The flame of God's great Trinity, the sung

Mass, the recited Hours, the natural world's
Views and glories. Yes, we find you there
But in our shyer moments we prefer
To see you in a cradle sleeping fast
And find you in the Bread no one could fear.

The Voices of Plain Chant

There are the deep notes which come from dark places,
They rise slowly, they draw black spirits up
Until they climb the ladder of the chants.
Then there are high notes,

They have been surely struck by star on star
Like flint on flint on earth,
These voices need no ladders, we are with
Their heights at once, for Spring has coincided
With Lent's first Sunday. Easter will be late.

Then there are voices bidding, wooing, pleading.
What heart's so cold it can ignore this sound?
What spirit is so evil it can stay
Shadowing all round it? Few, O, few,
For now come lower voices, voices which
Whisper of penitence. One thought of sorrow
And we are carried up by choirs of such
Ecstatic heights, we find we love our lost
Innocence which is closing in again.

I Beg for Light

I beg, I ask for light,
      Candle, lantern, the shine
Of children's eyes at night,
      Light is always a sign

Of energy, of man's
      Ride through the universe
Under the sun and moon's
      Rise and falling course.

Love is light also,
　　Light that candles us
Through the labyrinth where we go
　　Upon our final course.

Sources of Light (II)
A sonnet

Gold, all shimmerings, and all excess
Of light, entrances most of us. We cry
At the world's dazzle when we're born but this
Only reveals how sensitive we lie

Under our first shafts of the sun. We grow
Into the well-worn gold, the reach of shine.
Companionable shadows help to show
Their opposites. For most light is a sign

Of peace and benediction. Think how sky
Threatened the world's dark when a frightened few
Heard their hanging master's last great cry

And watched his end and what seemed our end too.
But Christ rose with the sun on Easter Day.
He was the true word and true light also.

Over Again
A litany

To the child who lay under a steadfast star
Let there be warmth and sleep,
To the girl who bore a child who would change the world,
Let us always keep
A vigil with and for her. She can drive
Dark thoughts off. With melancholy ones
She smiles and her light makes the shadows dance.
Now I hear men drive

Nails into a pale man's hands and feet,
They've put a crown of thorns insultingly
Upon his head. The sky goes dark. Again
Christ cries across the sky and shakes the world
For God by God seems for a moment doubted.
And mankind holds its breath.

No one is forsaken, all is well
And saved and peaceful. Make the most of still
Times not times like this. Now, through the air
A young girl's voice is singing, but from where
We cannot judge and do not need to tell.

EXTENDING THE TERRITORY
(1985)

The Child's Story

When I was small and they talked about love I laughed
But I ran away and I hid in a tall tree
Or I lay in asparagus beds
But I still listened.
The blue dome sang with the wildest birds
And the new sun sang in the idle noon
But then I heard love, love, rung from the steeples, each belfry,
And I was afraid and I watched the cypress trees
Join the deciduous chestnuts and oaks in a crowd of shadows
And then I shivered and ran and ran to the tall
White house with the green shutters and dark red door
And I cried 'Let me in even if you must love me'
And they came and lifted me up and told me the name
Of the near and the far stars,
And so my first love was.

The Features of a House

The sun picks out the features of a house
In this last spill of light, the rite of Spring.
Windows loom, the sky seems very close
And birds are now only a muttering.
   Sun also picks out us.

Dusk yawns and stretches, windows let a chill
Brush of light run through an April room.
Leaves smell as rich as flowers and all now fill
A length of air. Dusk draws into a gloom
And all the shadows shape a night so still
   That tip-toes loudly come.

A Bird in the House

It was a yellow voice, a high, shrill treble in the nursery
White always and high, I remember it so,
White cupboard, off-white table, mugs, dolls' faces
And I was four or five. The garden could have been
Miles away. We were taken down to the green
Asparagus beds, the cut lawn, and the smell of it
Comes each Summer after rain when white returns. Our bird,
A canary called Peter, sang behind bars. The black and white cat
Curled and snoozed by the fire and danger was far away.

Far away for us. Safety was life and only now do I know
That white walls and lit leaves knocking windows
Are a good prison but always you have
To escape, fly off from love not felt as love,
But our bird died in his yellow feathers. The quick
Cat caught him, tore him through bars when we were out
And I do not remember tears or sadness, I only
Remember the ritual, the warm yellow feathers we put
In a cardboard egg. What a sense of fitness. How far, I know now,
Ritual goes back, egg to egg, birth to burial and we went
Down the garden softly, two in a small procession,
And the high clouds bent down, the sky pulled aside
Its blue curtains. Death was there or else
Where the wise cat had hidden. That day we buried our bird
With a sense of fitness, not knowing death would be hard
Later, dark, without form or purpose.
After my first true grief I wept, was sad, was dark, but today,
Clear of terror and agony,
The yellow bird sings in my mind and I say
That the child is callous but wise, knows the purpose of play.
And the grief of ten years ago
Now has an ancient rite,
A walk down the garden carrying death in an egg
And the sky singing, the trees still waving farewell
When dying was nothing to know.

Green World

The green world stands in its accomplished guise
Under elusive suns. Our gardens reach
Up to the cruising clouds. Before our eyes
The downward world is prodigally rich.
Summer wins from Nature her vast prize.

Elegiac moods, nostalgia too
Are absent and we live in strong today,
Watching the green stride and sustain a view.
The very light is eagerly at play
And there are silences for me and you.

Silence broken by the planning birds,
Their peaceful bickering. The winds are light
Yet strong enough to give refrains to words
And whisper through the star-decisive night.
The sunlight also holds us on strong cords.
The green world bows before admiring sight.

An Absolute

If there could have been in those absolute days a prescience
Of future form and shape, of works of art
Scaling real agonies to their small achievement
And dulcet colours, childhood would have been
A scoop of light; even those night fears would
Have had their measure closed in accurate poems,
Tamed into lyrics. But it is not so.

And I am glad that childhood was all green
Or all of white or black. It is thus fixed
Into deceiving memories. All other
Actions, watchings and allegiances
Travel from dark to grey or pastel shades,
Will have no truck with early rainbows or
Stay hard, stay still. My present slips away
Into a future dancing into night.

But six years of my childhood are precise,
Loom out of silence and inform me of

Whispered secrets, Hide-and-Seek alone
In gardens of rich green. How fertile is
A childhood, how often Summer takes
More than its quarter share. I see the berries

On bushes as imperial as music,
Poised as poetry. Memory is the key
And casket too. I open it to danger
And out come dreads and fevers, fears as full
Of flows as waterfalls. I am a part
Of lawns perpetually mown, of hours
Walking the clock round. Night is black and white,

Dream and pillow. In this later grey
I bid that garden to let colours run
Down to this floor, this hour. I keep in touch
With nursery naughtiness and with ambitions
Looming from dreams and better there achieved
Than now, this time of half-hints, half-moods, and
Half-actions, half a life.

Family History

Family history
Is always sad. You go
Far, far back and there,
Richer than memory,
You find an ancestor
Out of whom you grow.

Who can live up to
The promise of the past?
Who can bear to find
A face that matches you,
Or touch within your mind
A guardian or guest?

We say 'Beneath this star
Or that I find my way.'
But we are wrong. Our will
That shows a just-healed scar
Selects our acts each day
And holds the present still.

For My Sister

'I'm too old to play with you any more' –
The words mean laughter now. But did I care?
Your dozen years to my ten did no more
Than make me stubborn in my games. You were

A figure dwindling, lost among real babies,
Pushing prams, a little mother then
And I, when ill, would find you back again
Wheeling me round. Yes, you were everybody's

Nurse when they were broken, worn, afraid
But I was King of cross-roads, theatres, farms,
Vigilant, a lord of what I'd made,
Sometimes the rigid soldier bearing arms,
Sometimes a look-out on all thorough-fares.

'I'm too old ...' You do not seem so now,
Seem yourself made perfect, and indeed
Matriarch, grandmother, careful wife,
Queen over sickness, and you come and go
Busy with all that makes a newborn life,
Fast and thorough. I'm the child still slow.

The Circuses

On my first train at seven years old and the word
Circus running through my mind. The energetic
Clowns and sprightly horses and the elephants
Filled the ring and a man in a top-hat
Conducted it all. How precise is the picture
Detailed from annuals and advertisements,
The primary colours dancing in my mind. London was all
The hush of dark around two rings. I had them
By heart and head. The train pulled in and the smoke
Seethed to the roof of Paddington. I noticed
Little. Even the waxworks were a prelude
For circling figures, rigorous patterns the ponies
Stepped to. We came to Oxford Circus and ...
Why does the vision vanish? Why have I no record
Of total disappointment? What did I say when London
Shrank to high buses, screams of brakes and everywhere

Hoardings of grown-ups' dreams? So memory
Shields the future, dulls imagination
And no one can tell me what I said or whether I cried
When the circle dwindled to traffic, the hope held nothing inside.

A Serious Game

A toy oven stood for a tabernacle
And two pencils in egg-cups were candle-sticks,
A toy train on a string was the thurible
And I priest and server murmuring my own gibberish
Meant to be Latin and sounding so to my ears.
Day after day long, morning and afternoon
I mumbled the old words, sent up imagined smoke
And in my nostrils the real incense smelt to me always
Sweetly of Sunday and Benediction.

I was alone but not lonely in those untimed days,
Of no hours but my own religious ones
With paper discs for the Host. Over and over
I mumbled the good magic, at times would rope in a friend.
Once a Presbyterian school friend had a bad conscience
And would not play my Popish plots, would not bow or pray
And I let her go with scorn on my face and few words, then on
And on I went, never tired of the growing ritual,
Sure of a God in the clouds, sure of things under veils,
Somehow aware of the holy transformation,
Bread into Body, invisible water to unseen blood.

Night after night I dreamt of the morrow's Mass,
Prayer rising up and up to the fragrant stars
And in my hands the story of man's transformings
With no cold Creeds or Bible or bidding prayers,
But what learned men have argued throughout the ages
There in the shining box lay always before me,
And swung on my thurible censing.

A Sky in Childhood

No Sacrament thereafter,
No blaze of blue in a Southern sky,
No Italy of the heart
Would ever gainsay or sunder that good evening
I wandered in a garden of evergreens.
Near Summer it must have been
And the moon had squandered her light or the stars had doubled
Each other, so there was no Great Bear any more,
No Milky Way,
But only diamonds on receding velvet,
Lights twinkling, showing me uncounted facets
And a sense in me of awe and wonder I
Had not grown up into or marred but was,
As it seems now, ready there for the sky to find me,
There, had I known it, glad to find myself
And awe overtaking me that only later
Looked back upon would be untarnished marvel
Over a Summer night, over my own ten years.

Love-Story

We escaped ourselves by escaping into each other
And even at the time I was reminded of walking on high cliffs
Facing Lundy when I was twelve or thirteen.
The sea below elevated me,
I smelt the pure drench of salt,
The iodine rock-pools
And where I walked ripe hedge-rows
Blew their blackberry scent at me.
And so in this rich, at first, acquaintance with it
Passion was a pause, then a plunge, a long look down, and then
High up to the appearing moon from behind turbulent clouds.
As day fell and the keen chill of twilight took me
I was entering an experience beyond my years,
Tapping old rocks whose names I did not know,
Noting the briar tangles and hearing hidden birds
As later I heard the remote cry of my own amazement,
Explorations self-revealing and temporary
Not a disappointment but a certainty
That there were further explorings and excavations.

So the child on the cliff raised above language and knowledge
Was fulfilled in a later revelation
Shown fitfully only, promising so much,
Sharp, bare, then gone like the southern fall of night,
Dark, cool, and mysterious, stared at by the unacknowledged stars.

The Last

Last among the loners,
Last of matters which insinuate
Themselves into your way of life and heart,
Is this lesson which a child resists,
Will not pursue, sure that its Heaven holds
Many saints, sure that there always is
Justice, a garden planted for ripe Summer,
Summer the healer, known best of the four
Seasons when childhood is the driving force.

I remembered well
Anger which I could not rein or would not,
Then all the world of strict apologies
And the embarrassment of full forgiveness.
I ran away, I hid, I would not hear
'I have forgotten what you did.' I hadn't,
My kingdom was the rule of a dictator
And I was king, of course.

But the lesson of injustice won't
Be held away or run from. It comes with
Lap-dog words, like 'It's inevitable',
Or 'You must just get used to it'. I wouldn't
And find it hard today.
And so I will back up the child in temper,
The absolute refusal to believe
Betrayals can't be broken. I know well
That God above the clouds who taught there was
Punishment and reward and nothing else,
Not this drab, fawning, cringing thing injustice.
Even today I find betrayal hard
Not to forgive but to believe exists.

Over and Over Again

Over and over again those times
When the day was immediate and the accurate sun
Stood high and wieldy, King and master-at-arms,
And I stood below with my hands spread over the grass,
My eyes blazing with light, a figure afire
As children are before time takes their hands
And lowers the sun and sings them away to sleep.
So I was and as I call back over
The wasted years of love betrayed or abandoned
And the heart misused, I see
There was faultless feeling accurate as that sun
In the early days and the terrible fears by night
Always banished by shinings and glowings next day.
And now I finger the leaves of an old story,
My own but could be any child's who ran
Away to be free and lingered long before
A wall reared up, a gate appeared and sun
Sank to the evening. But I looked up at the stars
And time was only the story before my sleeping
And only dreams delivered the warnings of power.

A Class-Room

The day was wide and that whole room was wide,
The sun slanting across the desks, the dust
Of chalk rising. I was listening
As if for the first time,
As if I'd never heard our tongue before,
As if a music came alive for me.
And so it did upon the lift of language,
A battle poem, *Lepanto*. In my blood
The high call stirred and brimmed.
I was possessed yet coming for the first
Time into my own
Country of green and sunlight,
Place of harvest and waiting
Where the corn would never all be garnered but
Leave in the sun always at least one swathe.
So from a battle I learnt this healing peace,
Language a spell over the hungry dreams,

A password and a key. That day is still
Locked in my mind. When poetry is spoken
That door is opened and the light is shed,
The gold of language tongued and minted fresh.
And later I began to use my words,
Stared into verse within that class-room and
Was called at last only by kind inquiry
'How old are you?' 'Thirteen'
'You are a thinker'. More than thought it was
That caught me up excited, charged and changed,
Made ready for the next fine spell of words,
Locked into language with a golden key.

A Time Ago

I shall never live them down, never tumble over
The bad times and the good for they have shaped me,
Firm under English sun, loving the green
Of early Spring and green tips, spikes and blue-bells
And soon the primrose
Returning over and over, every year.
And now I turn back and unroll the coloured years
Till six years old is the sound of a sudden clapper
And I am steady above the almost Summer,
The overall shaking and quaking of wasps and livestock.
I was out with a man with a ferret. It sticks in the mind.
Was it a dream? Was it
A wish becoming a daytime meditation,
Part of my story and current with me now?

It does not matter. Time is a truant to me
And I am my own imagination waking
And the seaside days I still have photographs of,
The feel of sand between my toes, the happy
Fear of the brief waves as they floated my bucket.
And the feather-bed in the boarding-house which we quarrelled
Over to have the first leap on that mattress,
The tickle of feathers turning anger to laughter
And the roses on the wall-paper real enough
As the sea was real, and the ships
Coming in but never to our break-water.
A good thing too, for I have sought them since
Like words relished and found in another language,

A sequence of ship-words, cadences of the ocean
And the frivolous clouds trailing away from the solemn
Sun that shows up every fustian music
And bruises my poems with the brush of harsh endeavour.

Passed

If memory is casual, if time
Takes over when you turn away from it,
If recollection's tempered by desire,
I nonetheless yet dare to say there was
A time and place (both aspects of the same
Mood) when all that pulled away from me
Had its decisive power. I trust to this
As I set out unstitching yesterday
And many days before. There is a group,
A cluster of awakenings, myself
Objective and attuned to shadow. So
I am now eight or nine
And age has set the scene.

Here is no random reckoning but some
Place that took me over. In a garden
Growing about me I am all I see,
The held-in berries of the early Summer,
The pent-up pride of roses
And something general in that mood contains a sense
Of absolutes. The sun poured down and I
Measured its moment. So I grew and came
Into the time not seeming time, but then
Curtailed. I see it all, I know the house
Square and wide-windowed. I learnt flowers such as
The honeysuckle, I kept falling over
Eager and headstrong down the nursery stairs
But I was happy, ignorant of self,
Blessed with the tender skies, alert action
Which then (and here is what I hold fast to)
Was not my own but how the globe moved on
And stars were separate and birds flew out
Over my head, dragging the morning to
Its proper purpose, as it is not now
And cannot be perhaps, or should not be.

Partly Tamed

The soul of a child is a bird who is partly tamed.
It flies – I remember it well – from roof-top to tree-top,
It consorts with rooks in their high places,
Is down on the lawn with the speckled thrush, and it enters
The bodies of sparrows pressing under the starlings
Or startled away by a pigeon. I can remember
Flights indoors, then out of the Summer windows,
I dallied on ledges and stood on the lawn with my head cocked,
Hearing the underworld.
My spirit was fiery and preened itself in the sun
And O at rare times I was a gull cavorting,
Slowing and veering, landing on wave tip and wind-tip,
Then soaring over the green sea, skimming the toppling
Easy breakers, gathering bread and pennies
For I was also a magpie.
My feathered spirit knew the contours of clouds,
The reclining gardens, ha-has and rockeries,
I skirted ash leaves and oak leaves,
Would sing like a blackbird, cheerful, rejoicing
For I loved the world in a wisdom of not understanding.
I was instinct coupled with climbing imagination,
I ignored the clocks. Tossed by spread winds, I was merry
And came to my nest in the lucid, starry evenings,
Closing my eyes, folding my pretty feathers
Knowing how I would be one with the rising lark.
I winged without winds and shut my eyes to the dark.

The Inheritors

They will fail always in the end – the appropriate garden,
The august, sad music pointing to older griefs,
    The cities heavy with history, only at ease
When west winds shake the determined cypresses,
    When the choir-boys hold the air with inhuman singing.
These so obvious alternatives to loss
    Will always fail. Mythology is better, will point you
To the old stories of Diana and Eurydice,

The sweet and melancholy moments when the gods
Ape our behaviour and step from their sacred groves
　　Into towns of turmoil, 'Where is grief to be lost?' you ask
'Or at least turned into useful fables, the kind
　　Your children in the fever of first love
Will turn to and appropriate as models?'
　　How kind and simple seem those first emotions,
Untouched by all the posturing of irony,
　　Held in the eye and clear before the day,
Standing in their own sufficiency.

　　For the rest there is only the dignity of the present
Sliding away into the bookish past
　　While we eye the future through dazzling sunsets or starlight,
Our loss neither belittled nor magnified
　　But seen in its true form terribly frightened or bewildered,
While our children play the game of first betrayal,
　　Sure of the ease and luxury of first love
With time's finger only sketching the sun's behaviour.
　　They were ourselves once long ago, so how
Could we indeed bear to disillusion them?

Elegy in Spring

　　Even in Spring I see an elegy,
　　A long recall, a cherishing the past.
　　Easter was early, long before each tree
　　Was noisy with the nesting habits of
　　A thrush, a blackbird. Why should death stalk me,
　　The sudden taking and this constant black
　　Apparel of this planet? I don't know
　　Except that one great grief comes back to mind
　　And why should that be so?

　　The dead rise up with one large Death and I
　　See it tall, its shadow still stretched far.
　　Easter's for life abundant, eager care,
　　A light that climbs, but down
　　Descends upon this ineffectual care
　　And begs an elegy.

Friday

We nailed the hands long ago,
Wove the thorns, took up the scourge and shouted
For excitement's sake, we stood at the dusty edge
Of the pebbled path and watched the extreme of pain.

But one or two prayed, one or two
Were silent, shocked, stood back
And remembered remnants of words, a new vision.
The cross is up with its crying victim, the clouds
Cover the sun, we learn a new way to lose
What we did not know we had
Until this bleak and sacrificial day,
Until we turned from our bad
Past and knelt and cried out our dismay,
The dice still clicking, the voices dying away.

The Advance of Spring

Here's the advance of Spring,
Here is the overture
Before the first birds wring

The clouds and sky out and
Show a new, washed world
When Winter has its end.

Spring is always new
For me, a great before
For Summer. It is true

That each Spring has a way
Of challenging me to
Be innovatory

In words, in music. Hear,
Was that the cuckoo? No,
But soon upon my ear

The music of all birds
Will beat and I shall know
New images, new words.

In April

This is a time for beginning and forgiving,
Lent and April – how their honour shines,
How they ask a change in all our living

Now where the earth shows such propitious signs,
The bursting blossom, and the birds who sing
As if no Winter happened. There are lines

Upon my face, the show of lingering
Sadness and grief; I stand aside from all
This ceremonious joy. The birds who wing

In widening circles must like all things fall
But for this moment seem eternal. I
Have no words, no sign, and no fit call.

Disillusion is a way to die.
I wear the dark of it now like a shawl.

Spell for Spring

I'll weave a spell and send it to
Friend after friend. It will bring you
Spring again with all its show
      Even if it is slow.

I'll cast a spell upon the land
And every field, and it will end
The Winter's damage. You will see
      Blossom on every tree.

But there's another spell. It brings
Persephone and all the Springs
That she has known.
      She casts a light.

We're dazzled by the sight.

A Supposition

If there's a saving God he is
The image of our failure. If there is
A blaze of light where no star trespasses,
It is a presence which contains our doubt,
A being like a thought

We dare not trust. I think my God is dark
Whether in swaddling-bands or on a cross.
Mine is a God who only makes his mark
Upon our fears. He is a shape of loss,
The spirit of our lack.

Child, youth and man – my stranger God, they say,
Has been all these, and one to whom I pray
From darkness into dark, but sometimes light
Bursts across my thought and burns away
The dream of one 'Dark Night'.

Worth

Summer disposes of us. We are not
Ripe for such disclosures, seldom can
Live up to so much magnanimity
Of growing things. The fountains play and sport
With clustered light. We are such broken men,
Baleful with our eccentricity.

When were we worthy of the ground we tread?
When grateful that we are a presence in
A world we prune and wound? Some say there was
A pristine time with men a noble breed.
When did that end and how did it begin?
If we knew that we would be dressed in grace.

Only our impatience can become
Our walking here and seldom staying still.
Only our wonder lights the world for us
And our descendants. Is this globe a home?
Is it at the mercy of our will?

A Forgetting

Only a sky,
Only a star,
Only a cry
Of chanticleer.

Only a day
After the dawn,
No words to say,
The sky comes down,

Only for now,
Soon to be gone.
But we don't know how
Sun will have shone

When it reaches us
And we reach for it.
O, we need grace
From an infinite

God we forget
Too often. He
Takes our defeat
And sets us free.

Let Summer Thrive

Let me be out and let the world do well
With this successful Summer. Why should I
Ask it to fit my mood, be Winter till
The blue has gone and there is charcoal sky?

Let me let be and enter what lies there
Beyond my shadow. It can do no harm,
I feel a sudden breeze lift up my hair,
Then it subsides and everything is warm.

My purposes are profitless, I'll choose
But, choosing, can I act? Such calm I'd be
Were there no dark and nothing left to lose.

I am the black theme of my history
But Summer tells another story.
Loss batters me yet in storms of memory.

A Kind of Magnet

I came upon a kind of magnet-pull
But where's the metal? I become aware
Not of self, that feuding miscreant,
Invalid sufferer. No, now to the full
I feel the planet cruising through the air
And light's the one important element.

Let mystics climb their ladders to the dark
And wrangle with a Satan's greedy throng.
Let holy people hasten to their work.
There is a star that surely sings a song,
Make no mistake the moon has made its mark

More than in several shapes night after night,
Stars form and group. And is this casual?
What is the power behind the element
Of light? What makes me ask the stars to fill
The air with a new version of Plain-Chant?

Falling

Falling leaves in Summer, willows weeping
Into any river, drowned twice over,
The real and the reflected swans go by
Slid by someone's hand it seems.
                              Light's falling
From sun at five o'clock,
                    some small fish darted
By to some end of their own.
                              All slithered then
As the sun slid slowly down the sky.
A day was falling unobtrusively,
Night would fall. How words can tease each other.
Willows gaining dignity at dusk,
And later light from stars,
                    their long stares falling.

Sundowning

It is a Moses rush of light behind
My back and I am scalded in the sheen.
Light-headed sun balances but looks
Ready to fall like my high piles of books,
The sun's as prodigal as it's not been
All day and now there is no puff of wind,

No sound of bird or foot. I hold my breath
And watch my page take fire. It fascinates
And claims my watching, yet I can't stay here,
Errands await. I step out through the air
Gold as the sun now on the heavy slates,
How the sun revels in this earth beneath

Its power and dignity. I feel I must
Record its mood, look to the sun-dial now,
Blow dust from ornaments and hold this hour
Somehow in my own intrinsic power.
I seem to do this though I don't know how.
Night will come softly as a tranquil ghost.

Into the Clouds

I have walked into the clouds where light
Hides and I see little room ahead.
I have crouched in dark left by midnight
And I have wondered at what saints have said
        About the patient sight

Of implications of importance to
The host of men, the lingerers in shade,
And I decide that all mankind is made
Of time that mostly proves he is undue
        For the good words said

By masters of the moment that is held,
By hope and patience with the long unsure
Purposes. Perhaps we should be bold
With clouds high up and, downward, the obscure
        Cold places of the world.

Dare I dare what all the wise men told
at the deep past half covered up in cloud?
I would attach a purpose to the world
But some unfocussed fear keeps me in cold
       And in the rootless moods

Which add to dark. But Spring is almost here
And air is opening for songs and breeze.
In seasons' patient repetitions there
Are hintings of a life without a lease.
       Why should this coax out fear?

Endings

Endings
And all our attempts to fob them off, to stay
The tide's impulse, wind's pressure and the hard
Demands of senses, but the pollen flies,
Birds brood on South, but hearts cannot migrate
Or not until love dies.

Proceedings
When space fits time. The lucid lily, full
Rose stand up and gardens are intentions
To make at least one thing whole, ardent, good,
But we who are our impulses forget
Even our best hopes, jostled by conventions
Until the last regret.

Betrayal

The child knows it first and it is then
He comes into the world of ice and snow
That freeze and never thaw. To be a man
Needs a betrayal. So the child will go
From total trust to doubt and always when

This happens he can never see the world
At its accomplished best. Its winning ways
Will scarcely touch him. Everything grows cold
Quickly as he walks uncertain days:
And when we are most wounded we unfold

The map of memory and look upon
The orchard days of freedom. Love we learn
In many lessons and the darkest one
Is that which tells us that mankind must turn
Into his own betrayals, trust no man.

Ballad of War

Brutal and vigilant the watchers were,
Pale and lean and disciplined to hate.
They taught us fear because they knew white fear
So well. They stood as sentries at the gate.

Gate of the morning and the dawn's endeavour,
Gate of the mind with fantasies and war,
Gate of sickness and unconquered fever,
Yet haven't we known all such gates before?

The gate of birth and then the broken cord,
The gate of love and holding back from fear,
The gate of language and the golden word
Which speaking makes the lustre disappear?

Who are the watchers? Why won't you reply?
Is the world sick? You turn away in dread.
What are those shadows widening the sky?
Where are the stars and is the new moon dead?

Clarify

Clarify me, please,
God of the galaxies,
Make me a meteor,
Or else a metaphor

So lively that it grows
Beyond its likeness and
Stands on its own, a land
That nobody can lose.

God, give me liberty
But not so much that I
See you on Calvary,
Nailed to the wood by me.

A Condition

There is a cold we do not notice yet
It is about us always. We can't feel
Its terrible behaviour, infinite
Demands and energies. We have a will
To choose and yet, in spite of that, we're set
In the vast presence of this cutting chill.

We recognise it only when we are
Hurt or lonely. Then the ice around
Our purposes reveals this unkempt star
And in escape-routes all of us abound
Till in the night we're faced with what we are,
And all of space yields not one fractured sound.

Seasonal Reverie

And the afternoon engages itself with light,
Yolk of egg is the colour of crocuses,
Small purple candles the rest,
And the naked trees are putting on a look
Of almost-green. The days draw out, the sun
Flirts with clouds. This is a good time.
Birds are lively. Sparrows leap and spread,
Then gather in huddles again, made one by a drove
Of starlings, pushful, unhappily-feathered birds,
Though in the right light you can see a rainbow shining
Such as you see on puddles containing oil.
So now is a time for observing every hint
Of preparation. Easter is early this year.
My blood is moving fast, my heart exults
With these becomings and these benedictions.

Nothing

We are nothing, we are
A dream in a cosmic mind,
We are a solitude, an emptiness,
We only exist in others' thought, we grow
In fitful seasons, yet we leave our marks,

Our scratches on dark walls, our prints, our spoors,
Our persecuting wars,
Gentle spirits trust that they are made
Over and over, freshly every day,
Beasts die everywhere.
Over the sun clouds cross and change
In threadbare dark processions.
Insects move and men like insects. Why
Are we set here, frightened of our reflections,
Living in fear yet desperate not to die?

Confession

It will not be possible to be radiant with ripe age, to
    Hold peace and prize the past as not your own.
The stars, skies, far seas and immediate will belong
    To others' arts and fancy, be inscribed
In margins and footnotes. I do not expect ever perhaps
    To be quite cool when the South inquires of the North its message,
That cold code, that ritual always in Winter, always
    Sung lightly and so remembered. All of this I shall be
Outside, digging away, sketching or standing still,
    The past's reflection in the present, and I shall hope
For a music of inquiry always, never cease to believe,
    No matter what rife evidence to the contrary, that there are always
The innocents who suffer and survive, the elderly who turn to be mocked
    And the future waits, a space for sound to enter, a scene expecting
A swift brush, and words will wing like birds over impossible seas
    To actual islands where small boats may beach.

Ariel

I am three elements, I
Am water, air and fire,
I am made of the sky
I am spirit, I

Am never earth, I have
Wings better than birds,
I am the heart of love,
I have no need of words.

I am set free, I wish
I still heard his commands,
I miss my lord of flesh,
I issued from his hands.

Caught

Caught in a fragment of forgiven light
The past's refracted and the present lies
Waiting to be caught. Now feeling dies

At the year's edge, the dark-to-be of night
And then the migrants homing and the Spring
New as always, meaning everything.

Day has its attitude of sovereign height,
Birds discourse, the long hours spread, we are
In the best moment of the travelling year.

Now the dark is light and sound is sight,
Winter written off, Summer is then,
Spring is the season for begetting man.

As We Wish

We are not yet. We are the time we feel
      Servant to, we are
Our own discovery when we are full
      Of gratitude not fear.

We are the grammar of our working days,
      The parsing of our nights,
We are as healthy as the way we praise
      Or as we watch the lights

Of silent stars. We can be lost if we
      Dare to forget the hour,
The self-analysis that cannot be
      Addition to our power.

And you, my love, are as the sunset paints
    Your peaceful face. I watch
Shadows dancing on you, leaving prints
    Never out of my reach.

The Great Mover

Love, the great mover of
Hard actions, shrewd tracts and
Our daily doings, off

It goes down *cul de sacs*
And turns and, at a run
Hard to keep up with, makes

For where the light is kind,
Where every tree approves
And gives it shelter. Bind

Up your memories
But make them slack enough
To reap all of today's

Insistent, random love.

Missed Chances

Preludes and dawns, those spare awakenings
Gone before listened to, how we miss such
    Arrays of opportunities. As sun lifts up
Its wings and birds tune their large orchestra,
    We are invited out of sleep, called to
Take part, share all such daily, sweet beginnings.
    Dramas of dreams rise up, the haze of them
Dries in the sun and the awakened mind.
    The spirit's opportunities see flights
We seldom heed. Good moments of regret
    Vanish in our wanton rummagings,
O bold designs, O short disparaged nights.

Two by the Sea

We said nothing, we said nothing at all.
We could put out our hands
And link them. We did not.
We have gone
Beyond the frequent touch, the need to cling
Although we know there is a time for these
We watch the sea and in our minds we pack
This bounteous Autumn blue of it. We could
Be the first people in this testing world,
This pomp and ridicule, this power and trust.
The sea is riding in. We watch its spread
Over the castled sand. Now day indeed
Is tired. Nothing at all we said.

Remembering

Do you remember that dark
Wood where we walked in a heat-wave to find some cool?
You must, I think, since all the trees bowed down
And all the shadows made cool shapes for us.
It was unforgettable, for me, because
Our talk was one with the air and the air washed
Over our hands. Between the different trees,
A few patches and openings let in light.
We were talking of knowledge and wisdom. Now and then we
Fell into silence deep and filled with what
We had said and we meditated on it and when
We started to speak again there were fewer shapes
Of light and shadows. Had we really been
Talking and staying silent so long? I think
We proved the relativity of time,
And the spirit's power and the great sun going down
Made life seem easier, wisdom longer. I hope
We shall go again though nothing will be the same.
Would we want it to be?

Years Ago

It was what we did not do that I remember,
Places with no markers left by us,
All of a Summer, meeting every day,
A memorable Summer of hot days,
Day after day of them, evening after evening.
Sometimes we would laze

Upon the river-bank, just touching hands
Or stroking one another's arms with grasses.
Swans floated by seeming to assert
Their dignity. But we too had our own
Decorum in the small-change of first love.

Nothing was elegiac or nostalgic,
We threw time in the river as we threw
Breadcrumbs to an inquisitive duck, and so
Day entered evening with a sweeping gesture,
Idly we talked of food and where to go.

This is the love that I knew long ago.
Before possession, passion, and betrayal.

Tell Me

Tell me where you go
When you look faraway.
I find I am too slow

To catch your mood. I hear
The slow and far-off sea
And waves that beat a shore

That could be trying to
Call us toward our end,
Make us hurry through

This little space of dark.
Yet love can stretch it wide.
Each life means so much work.

You are my wealth, my pride.
The good side of me, see
That you stay by my side

Two roots of one great tree.

Love in Three Movements

Comings
In moonlight or in sunlight, the immediate
Heat of Summer laying on the leaves
Hot hands. A little breeze, a wisp of breath
Cools the purpose of the heyday noon.

Goings
In Winter or in Autumn when nostalgia
Cancels the present, stops the clocks, endures
In our imaginations of a better,
A standing-still world, stable universe.

Retreats
As bonfire smoke hides figures in the streets.
The spirit's urgency –
How it will exercise our passions, put
Power not ours on our blunt purposes.
The spirit moves inquiring fingers, lips
Touching, pressing, then the mind asks questions,
Gives an order. How our spirits threaten
The bodies' movements they intend to sweeten.

Ways

Never to possess,
Therefore never lose, –
This is a creed of fire,
The burning of excess,
The cold ash of loss,
Continual desire.

To receive or take –
Yet there's danger there,
We are what we make
Of each other where
We have lost all fear
For the other's sake.

I dream of neither way
But something in between,
Not taking, not to be
Stolen. Then I'm in
A broken, withered day.
If we unarm, we win.

Certain Lessons

You have taught me to outgrow the dawn
And learn the ways of night I did not know,
You have brought my kindest cities down

And shown me where the better traitors go.
Something of innocence has gone for good
And maybe all of this is better so.

I knew the Eden of my childhood
And how the apple looked. It had to be
Snatched and eaten, and perhaps I could

Not go so far with such simplicity –
But was it so? The names confuse me now.
Cunning has crept on me deceitfully.

You once taught grace and often told me how
The world's intrinsic worth is what we want
And how intensely any can allow

Falsehood to stay. But is it you who haunt
My different nights? You taught me how to see
Stars and what their several quarters meant

If there are lies then tell their truth to me.

Anger

What is this? Why are there so many questions?
Why do you ask so much and want so much?
I lie on my back under an equable sun
And do not want any words,
The mischievousness of language,
Its long misunderstandings.

Love is silent at best.
Who wants words for it?
Whatever you love always answers itself.
Whether you hold a vast God in your mind
Who shows you the universe,
Or you love the faults and the little injustices
Of one who will not leave your dreams alone.
I know all the questions and I know too many answers
And I do not know which are worse.

A Death Alive

This is a grief I never thought to have.
Ten years ago I learnt the grief of death.
For days I could not speak and all belief,
Trust and the like died with my then-dead love,
His sudden end of life.

Time was too present, memory was shame
And guilt and dark reproach. The years have passed
And I have learnt of love and do not blame
Myself again. I thought grief could not last
But now it's back, the same

Ice in the blood, the wrestle in the night.
My life means grief. No other word will fit
This disillusionment, this loss of light.
Friendship has foundered now upon my life.
I thought your image bright,

Yourself an act of grace. Your letter shows
You drawing to the distance, bringing shock
With wounding words. You are the shape of loss.
You are abroad for days. When you come back
Will all be as it was

Once? Will all that glowing joy, those long,
Excited conversations be the past?
I thought the love between us was so strong
It seemed a starlight purpose made to last.
O break this grieving song.

Eye to Eye

Must it have a tired name?
Familiar imagery and be
A ghost who walks and makes a claim
Upon my daily doings? See
Grief is never twice the same
        In you or you or me.

The dead are celebrated in
The mourning wreath, the noted prayer.
Grief is renowned among all men,
But in a living loss, is there
        A paraphrase for pain?

Does time forgive? Does space relent
When in a letter one can do
Damage no spoken words consent
To leave the mind and freely go
        Where they were never meant

To fix? I do not think you mean
The harm you do and yet you show
A knowledge of my fragile scene
And all my pebbled paths you go
        Wide-eyed as you've not been

In any of our silences
So surely rich in guesswork.
Why have you wrought sudden violences?
When will you meet me eye to eye?
        Will you do penances?

Bitter Fruit

How many tastes are there of bitter fruit?
How many little poisonings? Can you
Tell me? You so rich once in my thought?
I am afraid of you and this came true
    Upon the day I caught

You out in lies, I had not pressed to find
A cause for jealousy. You gave it me
Or rather lack of trust that fills the mind
With darkness. What then will our future be?
    Once it was designed

For and out of happiness. Can trust
Ever be retrieved? We can forgive
Anything but that, it makes us lost.
There is a noon-day sun that mocks at grief
    Before we turn to dust.

Yes, there are many deaths but this today
Seems the worst I've ever known. You are
Distant in fact and distant in a way
You were not till you broke my trust, taught fear
    Darker than I can say.

Pain

God knows it hurts and I have wished it off
And otherwhere. The Summer takes the air.
It should be far too hot for games of love.

It should be far too kind for stabs of fear,
Anger and aching. Love walks in a white
Party-dress in childhood. I was there

And watched her in the early evening light
But now I wear her clothes, a little worn,
Washed too many times, but easy light

And good to feel were my mind not so torn
By dark resentment which returns when I
Least expect it, I cannot return

To former peace when love's the issue. High
New moon mocks at me and I have to stare
Searching sky mountains for a kinder star.

The Alteration

It is not love but we who change
And should become aware of this,
Else easily we shall estrange

Each other's heart. Accomplices
Of joyful thefts and long escapes
We must be always or we miss

The ladder love lays and which keeps
Us firm on rungs to heights above
The airy clouds, the moon's changed shapes.

And up that ladder we must move
In love and for love. O my dear,
Who knows the summit of man's love

And who is groundling and who seer?

Lovesick

Yes, I am angry and am tired of love.
    Its moods are trials I need
To push aside, for now I want to move
    Cool in cool places. I won't try to plead

Love's meaning and its purpose. I tie round
    My eyes and ears as well
A cloth to keep off predatory sound
    And to put off the soft tales lovers tell

About their happy pain. I will not have
    Truck with such. I am …
O but the words came tearfully, words of love.
    What in me needs such negligence and shame?

Growing Ahead

The full and flush of you has gone. I see
Nerves quivering beneath your eyes, a dread
Of something in your mind and not elsewhere.
Then you are troubled by your memory,
'What day is this?' 'What time is it?' you say.
Tell me of cross-purposes that led

You into fraught uncertainty. I thought
That growing old would still the nerves and make
Untroubled vagueness maybe but, instead,
Along wild paths you go where I'm not led.
Selfishly I'm hurt that you can take
Paths leading from me. Will you let me break

Into this different world to which you've gone
Reluctantly? You do not ask me and
This 'I' insists that I wish I could run
Ahead and show you rise and set of sun,
And then walk back and guide your faltering hand.

Love is a storm so often but there must
Be some still centre. Had you reached it then
Before I understood? Could you not trust
My own brash habits? Are you really lost
To me? And must I let you go again,
Neither companion, shadow or a ghost?

Shall All the Loves

Shall all the loves I knew then come to this
End unprepared for, suddenness within,
And the full memory of a sudden kiss

Scald, turn to ash and slowly then begin
Questions and pain, and anger, worst of all?
Yet though I rave and toss I think of when

All might return, Spring hang her lendings full
Of sunlight out and push back Winter. Yes,
Hope brims in me even when grey clouds fall,

And reason tells me that you don't mean this,
That there's a happy purpose or some lack
That's not your fault. In dark parenthesis

I stand until I have your answers back.

I Climbed a Ladder

I climbed a ladder to ...
Was it the moon or stars?
Was it to find a view,

A total world view of
Some magnitude? I had
Much daring once in love,

But daring balanced by
Hope and trust. I read
Of how wise men will try

Slowly to reach a state
Where there's no argument.
Man cannot know his fate

But he can face the rough
Returns, the storms of hate,
If only he will love

But love with purpose and
Direction. I can see
A ladder in my mind

A moment. I am free,
A moment understand.

Our Neighbour

What can it be to know four faces will
Turn at a key's sound moving in the lock?
This seems all happiness when I go back
To one cold room. I am aware of lack
But I'm called lucky no doubt sometimes by
The very people who can move me till
The tears are near. But sometimes when I knock

The doors of houses where a family lives,
I imagine all the later hours,
The love that's made by rote but happy too,
The door is opened and I see all you
Welcomers who draw me in and show
I am part of the family. I'm not,
But I forget that sometimes there survives
In them an envy of the things I do

Because I'm free, or so they think I am.
I can move and act on impulse which
They are denied. All this may well be true,
For we are ravelled in a discontent
Half a misunderstanding, half a claim
For some gold place that neither one can reach.

The globe is spinning. Men can see the curve
From their risked satellites, while most of us
Are pressed like flowers to table, bed and choice.
How little we can really know of what
Our neighbour wants. How much all ache for love,
How often we regret what we refuse.

Mother and Daughter

These ties, these bonds, these bitter enmities,
These sweet reversals, challenges of faith,
These journeys with hot time. There is a race
For every family to reach the truth
About intentions and the hopes for grace.

Lovers and friends, however intimate,
Imply a no-man's-land but with those who
Share our blood and try to calculate
What we should give, to frozen regions go
And always our apologies are late.

And you my mother who will never speak
About your pain, the physical as well
As passionate, again, again you break
The castellated challenge of my will,
Shame my anger. You are quiet and meek
Remember that I wish myself as still.

Ages

The air accosts me as I tread into
Evening belonging to the young who keep
Earnest promises. I see them glow
Under full moons. And they need little sleep,
Time is for them a skirmish to and fro,

Neither standing still nor an advance
Upon our age. Hours are our medium
When we have banished power, broken one chance
Of casual joy. Time is a coming home
When you slip from the hope within a dance

The young proclaim. Twilight is the press
Of shadows on the old, long memories,
Short days and an accepted loneliness.
The young alone can never be at peace
But are both source and mouth of their distress.

Awake in the Siesta

Rumours of winds and dusty afternoons,
Others' siesta, I stay wideawake,
The only conscious one here. All cats sleep
Upon their shadows. Hot against the walls
Leaves and butterflies lick the crumbling stone.
Here was I, all by myself and happy,
Content in a country truly my first home.
So Tuscany about six years ago,
In a small town never sought out by tourists,
Nothing important, no mosaics and only
One small church not worth the sight-seer's inspection.
The view from my window was peerless, the shutters wide.
Everything I could possess but no possession.
I laid myself open to the atmosphere,
Dipped my hands in water.
                              Tuscany
You are a sweetness in my nostrils still,
A view I'd never trade, and, every morning
The promising haze and the emerging hills.

Rome – A Quarter of a Century Ago

I was in Rome twenty-six years ago
    Almost to the day,
All the nostalgia which I used to know
    Shows like fountains which play
Up and down to the basin underneath,
    Rome in her panoply

Of worldly beauty catches at the breath
    But she can be austere.
I knew the honied passion of man's death,
    Had found it everywhere,
But there were elusive spirits, essence of prayer
    Almost anywhere.

Feeling's equivocal with me, I can see
    Rome in my mind. I'm sure
That I shaped no deception, no travesty.
    I learned her disciplined law
And her demands were always sweet to bear,
    What am I wanting for?

Why don't I go back? Why am I afraid
    Of disillusionment there?
Passionate probity, my secret will
    Will come into their own.
The remnants of those months stir in me still.
    Rome wears her laurel crown
And my praises of her sound from every hill,
    In their tones I used to drown

In a joy I knew authentic at the time,
    A wish to understand prayer.
Up to the top of St Peter's dome I would climb
    And wander everywhere
In this city of bulk and fury, song and rhyme,
    And the casting out of fear.

Particular Music

There is particular music
Hunted for, dug up
Near airy planet-spaces,
Or on the cold, sure lip

Of a cliff that will not take
The climb of a white break
But only permit a foam
Rising. So I make

A music out of places
Unsurrendered to,
Watched on careful nights,
Not circumscribed, no view

Caught in the camera-mind
To be developed later.
Words are music to find
In places the colder, the better.

But I have needed South
And its unambiguous sun,
Its haze and fire on the breath.
Since childhood I've been one

Never at ease at home
Relishing loneliness
Creating out of shame
Measured happiness.

Memories of Rome

Balanced here between the sky and street
I am awake when others lie in dreams
Unknown at night. Now I absorb the heat
And walk out slowly where the honeycombs
Of scents rise from the dust. The hour is meet
For wandering. A hint of fountains comes

Defying distance. No one is about
Except a weary dog. I am alone
As I sit down and take my papers out,
Wait at a table, gladly on my own.
Buildings dissolve and all things call in doubt
The possibility of brick and stone.

The haze lifts slowly and the sun begins
To lower itself. The shutters are put up,
Voices start but scarcely can convince
That they can spring from flesh, but then the deep
Tones of bells draw everyone from sleep.
Such afternoons I've lived again long since.

And so the actual South exists for me
In a dozen ways but mostly it
Comes back in Northern Winters stealthily,
Bearing all the attributes of heat.
In empty streets in England still I see
In waking dreams how North and South can meet.

The Way of Words and Language

When you are lost
Even near home, when you feel
The tide turning, a strange sea under you
And you are a pale, rubbed pebble, a sea ghost,

When you have lost
All the high-ways and every dimming sign-post
And the sea is far away and the moon hidden
And your watch has stopped and you have no compass
And feel to yourself like a ghost,

All this later will seem your best
Time for there will be future and memory and the tossed
Tide. Morning will come up and you will open your eyes
And see in the mirror a ghost.

But day will take you and the dawn uncover
The ribbed sand foot by foot and the first light
Will stretch over the grey water and you will know
It is no longer night

But still a time of silence and light like a shielded lamp.
Then you will shake off dreams and recover
What you know is yourself still but changed
And the new sun will come up and pass over
Your hands, your arms, your face and you will discover
A world that the night has re-arranged.

Let this time be. Let the present stay. Do not
Look back. Do not look forward. Let thought
Idle from dream into daylight, and watch, then, the coast
Climb out to dark, to grey, and then to chalk-white
Cliffs till the grey sea goes blue
And then indeed you

Are found and safe at last
And all your thought will grow
And you will unreel it, a silk thread, a long-
Travelling, moving-everywhere line
And it will gradually, as you relax it, become a song
And you will not say 'That is mine'.

A Performance of Henry V *at Stratford-upon-Avon*

Nature teaches us our tongue again
And the swift sentences came pat. I came
Into cool night rescued from rainy dawn.
And I seethed with language – Henry at
Harfleur and Agincourt came apt for war
In Ireland and the Middle East. Here was
The riddling and right tongue, the feeling words
Solid and dutiful. Aspiring hope
Met purpose in 'advantages' and 'He
That fights with me today shall be my brother.'
Say this is patriotic, out of date.
But you are wrong. It never is too late

For nights of stars and feet that move to an
Iambic measure; all who clapped were linked,
The theatre is our treasury and too,
Our study, school-room, house where mercy is

Dispensed with justice. Shakespeare has the mood
And draws the music from the dullest heart.

This is our birthright, speeches for the dumb
And unaccomplished. Henry has the words
For grief and we learn how to tell of death
With dignity. 'All was as cold' she said
'As any stone' and so, we who lacked scope
For big or little deaths, increase, grow up
To purposes and means to face events
Of cruelty, stupidity. I walked
Fast under stars. The Avon wandered on
'Tomorrow and tomorrow'. Words aren't worn
Out in this place but can renew our tongue,
Flesh out our feeling, make us apt for life.

Song of Time

Deliver time and let it go
Under wild clouds and passive moon.
Once it was fast, now it is slow.
I loose my hours beneath the sun,
Brisk minutes ebb and flow.

Time is elemental, all
We make in speech and action, yet
Time itself can have a fall
When heart and mind have no regret
And love is how you feel.

O let us dance with time and turn
It to a friend, a willing one.
In time we grow, through time we learn
The visitations of the sun
And ardour of the moon.

Time is not clocks but moves within
The discourse of the learned heart,
It is the way our lives begin.
O leaving time behind's an art
Ahead and now and then.

Dawn Not Yet

Dawn not yet and the night still holding sleepers
Closed in dreams, clams in shelter, a hiding
Of half the world and men turned back into

Primaeval matter. A closed world only tides
Ruminate over. Here men could be fossils
Embedded in strata, all to be discovered

By morning, skilful archaeologist
Cutting down carefully, drawing up debris
Of centuries but also precious gems,

Ivory figurines, kings' hoards. We are shown
Riches the sun at last gives shape and glint to.
Sun the explorer, sun the diver too.

The sea is quiet. No bells from church and harbour,
Slow off-white sky. A healing time, right peace
Where monks sing hours somewhere, where small waves settle

As if to hush before the general sleep.
As if to hold the waking worries back
Sea-gulls are swinging softly through the sky,

Almost six and light is spreading now,
Soon the many waking, soon the powers
We cannot handle will make their demands

But now is silence, stillness everywhere
And the good night still holds us in its hands.

Frail Bone

Recall the frail bone,
Anatomy where is lodged
Or so we like to express it
Soul, spirit, mind.
Any sea can drown
Or waterfall distress
This pitiful, easily wounded
In every sense, small being.

But we think we are giants,
Fabulous spirits, a people
Plying time to a curtain
To keep off time, to shed
Shadows we can handle
And alter. With sunset
We become our own nocturnes,
Speak aloud to the stars,
Engage the implacable moon
With our fierce endeavours of power.

But we are falling sand
Through the hour-glass of the planet,
Blown through the universe,
And yet that dust delivers
Defiant speech to the last,
Anomalous oratory.

Dust

We are made of dust, we are
Flying on every wind,
Blown to the back of the earth,
Stormed at, broken, defiled.
We are people of dust
But dust with a living mind.

Dust with a spirit, grace
Goes to the end of the earth,
Follows the dark act, the thought
Lying, wounding, distraught,
We are dust from our birth
But in that dust is wrought

A place for visions, a hope
That reaches beyond the stars,
Conjures and pauses the seas,
Dust discovers our own
Proud, torn destinies.
Yes, we are dust to the bone.

Enough

What we have not written, what we have
Not worked for will come back
Reproaching us for waste. We tease the time,
Empty the home of riches. Will there be
Stanzas that never found
A mind, a page that wound
Unseen and ignorantly as rivers go
Slowly to the sea?

Yes, there'll be harbours which
Never received our ships. We don't put down
Anchors enough or reach
Rich cities waiting or the bartering town.
Something we could grow rich
Upon we'll find we somehow left undone.

Yet wasting time can be a way to loaf
And not be waste indeed. The mind requires
Time to stand aside, rather like love,
Continuing after the quick desires
Craving for their own dark satisfaction.
Love does not beg. And so with poetry
What volumes are enough
When half of life is dreaming and half action?

By the Sea

I have seen seas so still
That I could well believe
There was no sea at all.

But I have also seen
Great horses rearing up
And rushing down upon

The well-marked sand. Yes I
Know every mood and tense
Of tides. I was born by

The sea. I know its pulse
Since it still beats in me
From such great waterfalls.

Song

To language I refer
All present pleasure, all choice
Of pleasing and being pleased,
Every bird's new voice
Seems now perfectly phrased
Much like a well-tried prayer.

Atone, atone. It's the end
Of Lent, and risings declare,
In a small flower, what we
Have looked for everywhere.
We are tied to our destiny
But cannot understand

Why immediate wishes are
So hard to be certain of.
Old Puritanism marks
Our tribute of strong love,
And among all Nature's works
We stir to the heights of our power.

Water Music

What I looked for was a place where water
Flowed continually. It could come
In rapids, over rocks in great falls and
Arrive at stillness far below. I watched
The hidden power. And then I went to rivers,
The source and mouth, the place where estuaries
Were the last, slow-moving waters and
The sea lay not far off continually
Making her music,
Loud gulls interrupting.
At first I only listened to her music,
Slow movements first, the held-back waves
With all their force to rear and roar and stretch
Over the waiting sand. Sea music is
What quiets my spirit. I would like my death
To come as rivers turn, as sea commands.
Let my last journey be to sounds of water.

Imagination

Imagination greets the baleful tide
And seeks a ceremony in its coming.
Desire for vision is incorrigibly
Demanding. We are citizens, not seers,
Asking our little governments to bring
Order and shape to guide a way to sing.

So we are masters of an afterthought,
Tackling time reveals our blunt, brief fingers
Bringing back the past, diminishing
Its special lights. We pin poor messages
Upon the skies of yesterday which fade
Our wishes with the sea's oppressive play

Upon the shore, upon our wish for plans.
Truth is taciturn, quotidian
And we are wise to let it move us to
Possible ladders, lowered likely clouds,
Excellence is in will and not performance,
We should be quiet when the world is loud.

From the Coast

All the confidences you have given
Away will taunt you now.
Will they be used?
Once there was a harbour for them, haven

For ships now out of date and new ones blessed
With cheap champagne. Your confidences are
Out in the wild sea, you stand on the coast

Tasting the salt, watching the churning brew
And charge of waves.
Your ship is somewhere else.
You sent it out once.
Was it going to

A place upon the maps?
You feel your pulse
Excited by the thought of journeys but
The waves are rolling back, the sky is false,
The ways for ships to come home have been shut.

Precursors

Passages of music, a violin's slow pace, a picture
Recording the sunset but telling more, stating
    History's alarm and hurry. I watched as a child the slow
Leaves turning and taking the sun, and the Autumn bonfires,
    The whips of wind blowing a landscape away.
Always it was the half-seen, the just-heard which enthralled –
    My nurse pulling her white dress off in the moonlight,
My sister pushing me in a doll's pram as I recovered
    From a slow illness. There is a library somewhere surely of
Pictures piled waiting for a hand to lift them,
    Books with long markers in them. This is the world
Once ahead of me, now behind me, and yet
    I am waiting still to record some of the themes
Of the music heard before I understood it,
    The books read to me long before I could read
And with me tantalisingly near. So I have come
    To believe that poetry is a restoration
Or else an accompaniment to what is lost
    But half-remembered. Today it is Autumn outside
And as the sun reddens the whole landscape
    And a smell of bonfires haunts me, a tune begins
To sing in my mind. It has no words as yet
    And a life and a half would probably be too short
To set the music down with appropriate words,
    Record a season completely, words before death.

TRIBUTES
(1989)

A Letter of Thanks

For Cotty

In your handsome house where everything eases the eye
    And young and old are one
Since in your thoughts age is forgotten, I
Am happy and grateful. Warm April lies upon

Delicate willows and all the air is in bloom
    But most of yesterday was
Destruction and argument. Broken a little I come
Into your magic circle which means pure grace.

I am learning wisdom from you every day,
    Each hour. You walk through my mind
And set the images dancing, the words to play,
You opened my eyes again when I was blind

With ludicrous tears of hurt, but to you they meant
    Somebody needed your heart,
Your sweet goodwill. Love is your one element
In which you let me share. I am a part

Of the family of uncountable ones you know
    And care about. You are
As welcoming as this lavish April, also
For me in my lucky sky a new-found star.

Tributes

Debts can be burdens and can lead to hate
But there are others which are strong in love
And lift us into a harmonious state,

Judicious, full, compassionate. They move
Us into joys we'd never dreamt about,
Seldom thought possible. I've learnt enough

Of the heart's follies and of serious doubt
To question what the senses claim, I've found
In recent years a warmth which pulls me out

Of lassitude, indifference. Around
The long shelves of my mind I've come upon
Writers, painters, mystics who abound

In gifts my poems have reflected on
And whom I wish to sing and celebrate.
It is not only great stars or the sun

I owe so many debts to. I now state
A poet here, a painter there, a place
That's altered all I do. So I relate

My debts and give back what I've taken, grace.

For George Herbert

You'd understand the gratitude I feel,
    My need to tell it too.
Sometimes in great love someone wants to kneel
    In reverence, and you
Would understand the tears and joy of this.
I've learnt of trust and hope from you. It is

More than a pleasure, passion shakes the sense
    And glows within the mind.
When I've been low I've felt your deference
    To all that dogs mankind
And all that also gives him happiness.
It is within your words. Your emphasis

Is on the drama lived in each man's soul,
    His battle with his flawed
Aspirations and you make him whole
    Telling of his Lord
Who battled too though God in every pore
And pity. No one wrote like this before.

You loved the monosyllable and it
    Runs through your music. I
Can hear between its graces music yet
    More deep and much more high.
You have released my spirit, sent it on
Audacious flights by what you've said and done.

Notes to The Winter's Tale

We knew it in childhood, always found it in
Garden or park. When we chased birds we were
Small spirits of this Summer harbinger
When we made Daisy-Chains they were for her
This is how all Persephones begin.

Within the minds of children most myths start
And this assuredly is one of such.
Spring is in the child's pulse. Its heart
Beats in response to this Corn Goddess's touch.
At harvest no one can resist so much
Abundance, yet there has to be some hurt,
Some offering and here it is field-mice
Whose huddled horror is the sacrifice.

For Charles Causley

Cornwall is your pasture and your pleasure,
The granite cliffs, the high sea, and each cove
The sea rides into puts us at our leisure

For we are tourists. We know little of
The spell of that long sweep of England where
You've lived so long that Cornwall is a love

You'll never lose. In bracing, salty air,
In high white horses all the year round, you
Have now become a part of all that's there.

The open and the secret places know
Your step and gaze. So now I praise a place
And doing so I offer thanks to you

For all your poetry and its lyric grace
Which are so rare now. You have taught me much
About the need to work upon my verse.

I see you seldom yet I feel in touch.

For Philip Larkin

I

The last thing you would have wanted –
A poem in praise of you. You would have smiled,
Cracked a joke and then gone back into
Your secret self, the self that exposed itself
To believe in nothing after death, to a trust
In traditional customs, marriage, falling in love
And behaving with kindness and courtesy. You watched
Horses put out to grass,
The wonder of Queen Anne's lace,
To everything English and green and bound by rivers,
The North with its dark canals:
I see you suddenly caught by a brilliant moon
In the early hours. I offer you words of praise
From these time-rent, beleaguered
Violent void-of-you days.

II

English faces, private, hiding away
Hurt or love gone wrong, the stubborn waste
Of meadows built on. Every end of day

Must have seemed to you, as it does to me, the last
Since we threaten to break the planet now. I see
Your watchful care over the chosen past.

Once you said that poetry was a way
To preserve, enshrine, and to give purpose to all
That seems more senseless and furious every day.

You are a distance away and yet in call
As I turn your pages over. *The Less Deceived*
Delights me most of all your books. I feel

That *Wedding Wind*. Here are all you believed
In always – the gentle touch, the tender care
For the long-dead poor. I always feel relieved

And less afraid when I read what you would share.

III

Was your silence the quiet of desperation?
Did you feel wholly helpless when you saw
The ruined future beyond your explanation?
Or was there in your heart a private war?
Perhaps your isolation

From passion, disorder felt to you like regret,
As if you had made the wrong decision, a choice
Not to opt out but to stand aside and let
Discord or harmony happen. We miss your voice.
The very quiet of it

Often consoled us and yet there is a lack
In your later poems. It seems as if you saw
Your failed past and wanted to have it back
And choose again. But in your verse a law
Is clear, you refused to speak

When there was nothing to say. You hated all
That Modernism meant and yet your verse
Sings of now and here. We hear its call
As the future assaults and every day grows worse
With vice and war. Was a wall

Built up deliberately by you? Did you hide
From the greater issues? No, your silence was
Imperative and resonant. You died
In a dark Winter leaving all of us
Needing you at our side.

Tribute to Turner
A sonnet

What were your bonds and limits? It is hard
For us to see them yet there must be some
Since art can only flourish locked and barred
By form. However inward; it must come

To keep off sprawl and chaos. Out of sight
Yours are but they are firm. Within your craft
The storm, the tides are held by day and night,
Leashed strongly in and so the looker's left

With fire and flood and steam. There is no fear
For us but only wonder. Nature is
At your command when you most disappear

And so we're caught up in your ecstasies
And large delight that's present everywhere
And what seems peril has the power to please.

Caravaggio

It wasn't violence I noticed first,
Your *Narcissus* took me by surprise,
The polished light, the pair of eyes that trust
Those repeated. I knew that my eyes
Were wiped of usual dust

And I was shown again how light is proud
And threatening and will not be denied
To one like you who took pimps from a crowd,
Put them in poses for a God who'd died.
Brutal you were, not crude.

And accurate, impatient of mere sketching.
The rounds and squares of suffering you made
Arresting, overmastering, overreaching.
Christ Entombed was how the rich light played,
The spirit drifting, touching.

Goya

It is a kind of force which does not touch
The sadist nerve, the calculating thought.
Here is the soul at work within the rich
Muscle and sinew. Goya always caught
That vigour out of reach

To lesser painters who make violence
A proper end. We do not look for long
Unless we are the few who love the sense
Of hurt that does not hurt us. Here the strong
Purpose is intense

And tense also and draws our admiration,
When war's the issue we are shown the loss
Of spirit and are taught that satisfaction
Of our brute senses points the worst in us
While the true connection

Of flesh and spirit is united by
Goya's pure vision. Portraits by him show
A man alert and eager. We see why
Unity governs clearer than we know
When Goya lends his eye.

Chardin

Is it the lack of self that most of all
    Challenges eyes to stay
And linger over the petals that will not fall
    Although they have some way

Of suggesting that Chardin, had he wanted to, could
    Have moved the steady light?
Here is still-life that tells us Nature is good,
    Here is a seize of sight.

After a Painting is Finished

For Alec Guinness

He is hunched against a wall
And his hands cover his eyes, his feet fit together.
If you draw close you will hear him murmuring, not
To you but to himself, and what he is saying
Is 'That is not what I meant.'
What he did not mean is a canvas on an easel
Still wet but finished. The painter is almost in tears,
The picture is full of light and people walking.
It is a city scene on a gala day.
Flags are flying, rosettes

Are worn by men, and the children
Hold the strings of silver, heart-shaped balloons,
The scene is sharing merriment and more,
More which is hard to put into words. Is the painter
Feeling this? To us the scene's a success.

Nothing is overstated,
Much is left to imagination and we
Want to free that along the streets, in the sky.
A fiesta, a feast day is part of a special vision,
The moon is full and could not be anything else.
Why does the painter appear

So desolate, so sad, so disappointed?
What did he mean that we do not recognise?
Does every work of art leave the maker feeling
His work is unfinished and the failure is his own?
This painter is now shedding tears.

We dare not approach him and we do not need
To ask, as with some abstract paintings, exactly
What every symbol means. Simplicity
Is the hallmark of the canvas on his easel
And we are pleased to look

But maybe we should call to mind that when we
Say, bake a cake, embroider a cloth, or sing
A snatch of song, we are often dissatisfied.
Are these on a lower level than what's shown here?
We do not know. We only feel compassion.

This man feels sure that he has not portrayed
The vision held in his mind, that he's let something down
Or disappointed others as well as himself.
Maybe in a Garden of Eden a painting
Would be a perfect work of art, and yet

Surely Adam and Eve did not need to make
Works of art. Their visions stood all around them,
The sun was supremely itself, the trees exactly
What their creator intended and so were all the flowers
And birds and beasts. There did not have to be art

Made by man in his once perfect state,
And there is much to prove that we have fallen
From grace and integrity. Every work of art
Then, it appears, must be approximate only,
The maker has quickly lost interest in what he made

And doubtless this man will get up and look about him,
Take down the canvas and put its face to the wall,
Pick out a clean one, and squeeze new paint on his palette,
Feeling zest rise in him, hope that indeed one day
He will please himself as he has pleased his viewers.

But it seems more likely he'll soon be squatting once more
Against a gate or wall and will be saying
'That picture isn't what I saw in my mind,
My imagination held a great comprehension,
A world of new life and colour.' He'll never stop
Painting if he's an honest maker. How odd
That we should see completion where he sees part,
For he is, in little, a God.

Tate Gallery

I

Think of these at night when no one sees
The fearful summons and unsparing brush,
Ernst is a hunter with dark images.

Imagine ghosts of gazers seeing flesh
Hinted at. Rodin is there of course,
Yet in a night-time gallery, the wish

Of all past lookers and their live discourse
Might haunt the air. 'Here' one might say, 'My dread
Is captured. I've had dreams like that, a curse

On easy sleeping'. Do these painters then
Darken our day to help us through the night
Knowing that we are scared and little men?

Perhaps, but we are ones who climb to bright
Precarious moments, love those abstract lines
Of Nicholson and Mondrian. Our sight

Is sharpened in this place of many signs
Directing us within but also out
To how the sky behaves or moon reclines.

The Tate's purpose cannot be in doubt.

II

Place of mirror and mirage, hint, retirement and then
Sudden fierce arrivals after shunting in sidings of paintings which
                                        have unloaded
Influence, bias and bring in their own views of now, visions of
                                        time beyond us almost, also
Warhol, Pollock, Hockney, all, in a way, shockers, shapers of work
Which affronts us, takes us by the scruff, giddys us to come round
                                        and stand, shakily still
Before the risk and rise of intemperate choices, blatant colours, bearers

Almost of ungrace. And yet, and yet ... look closer,
Dare to stare at the tricks played by Magritte, be willing to admit
The painters had to leap down unconscious minds, and
Out-Freud Freud, healing not by talking trouble away, but by being forced
To admit art must go this way, find a difficult sturdy beauty in
                                        all unlikeliness.
And, as a touchstone, stare at Blake or Palmer.
Open your eyes to your own mind reflected
But improved, given form and purpose,
Painted out of the colour-box of the rainbow,
Shocking us only to save us for this moment
In an age at ease with violence and terror.
An almost impossible peace may here be gathered,
But has to be won by a courage of total looking.

The Arts

Only lately have I
Questioned the nub of verse
Sought in the heart's cry
The purpose of art to us

And the more I reflect the less
Do I seem to understand.
Music can always bless
While under the sculptor's hand

Abstract shapes convey
The mind ill at ease with the heart.
What poets have to say
Was difficult from the start,

Twisted language played games
With meaning and metaphor.
I write when the craft claims
What I never knew before.

A Roman Trio

I Sant' Anselmo on the Aventine Hill, Rome

No other place so holy,
No other hill so resonant and calm
So utterly itself. I learnt of it
When someone said 'The best singing in Rome
Is at the Sunday Mass at Sant' Anselmo,
The mother house of all the Benedictines'
I found an early bus and got off at
The Aventine's still base. I was alone
And early for the Mass. I walked up slowly
And on my right found St Dominic's church,
Santa Sabina, carefully restored,
Soft-stoned and simple, no mosaics or frescoes,
Near the entrance a carved wooden door
Shaped before St Dominic was born.
No one was there. I knew I would return
Often, I knew this was my special hill
Among Rome's seven. Soon Mass would begin

And so I moved on to the hill's peak and
Entered the Benedictine church. Of course,
Nuns were already in the front row but
I did not care. Soon ninety monks assembled,
Lastly the Abbot. Latin Mass began,
The universal language of the church,
The tongue familiar since my childhood but
I'd never heard music like this before,
Such lofty voices, masculine and clear,
And magisterial – *Credo*, *Gloria* and
Sanctus. I had never known till then,
Felt and thought, such sure serenity,
Bread into Christ, wine to his blood, and time
Existed only in the Rome of squares
And shops and fountains. I came out of Mass
And wandered down the hill between the roses
Turning their faces to me, early June
Faces of pink and red and white. I carried
The singing of the Benedictines in
My spirit as I entered central Rome,
All of me deepened, sharpened, happy too.

II Ostia Antica

We were out of Rome,
Out of the dust and heat of it,
Even the heat of early June was clasping hot fingers
Round ruin, church, fountain. Over each hill hung
A veil of mist, but we were out of this,
Walking knee-deep in thick grass like English grass
And through English flowers with their clear translucent names,
Bird's Eye, Shepherd's Purse, Queen Anne's Lace and Buttercups,
And the various grasses, some cutting, some soothing,
Rose up from the black-and-white mosaics insisting we look
At elephant, horse, fishes, snakes. St Augustine's name
Hung in the air too till we brought it down
Into our voices, talked of the City of God
Not, after all, far off.
But time was measured only now by our shadows
And the ripe blue sky and the noon dome of the sky,
And we spoke as if words were plucked out of the air
Or out of the earth, or both
And it seemed not impossible echoes still drifted here,
Augustine and Monica talking,
Voices rooted among the grass and the buttercups

And the sky going suddenly dark as we would not see it.
Didn't we speak very low?
Didn't we almost whisper
As if otherwise we might drown out the living echoes
Or stir two saints from sleep?

III Lake Albano Outside Rome

Associated with Autumn always,
Lake Albano seems made for it. That day
After a good lunch, with Rome still almost in sight,
The sky pale blue, we trod on the crisp bronze leaves,
Talking of history, saints and visionaries,
Sometimes not speaking at all
For that air begged quiet and we were acquiescent
With this good silence. Now and then a bird
Far out of sight, sang the snatch of a song.
There was the lake so still, dark brown,
Darker than leaves. An image of eternity,
I thought, but did not say.
On we went walking steadily, not specially fast
For time seemed a string we wound up as we progressed,
A silken string left by the Summer. That walk
Is with me now in an English record-cold Winter
And you, my good friend, who opened your private map
Of Rome and shared it with me, have been dead seven years.
Thirty years ago we met, you a holy man,
Myself an eager young poet, in love with Rome,
Heart-free in all other ways. Heart-breaks were over
For those three months and I only realise now
How open I was to a city made half of light
And half of the world's power. I loved it gently, carefully,
Let it take me by strong hand and heart slowly. I met
So much kindness from simple Italians and some
English priests and poets. It was as if
An unhappy childhood was handed back and altered,
An illuminated spell cast round me and on me
During so many days and nights. Now this was October,
My first in Rome. I had been there in Spring and Summer
Until the big heat. We had finished our circular walk and were
                                                    talking again,
Then catching a bus back to Rome, a city with arms
Open to me then and always, a mother, the world's true centre
Awaiting me now as I meditate on a return.

Spain

I have written so little about it, in truth
Hardly a word. It was Rome, Rome
On my mind always, and when I saw even a single
Cypress only on a dusty path I thought
Always of Italy.

I went to Spain often enough,
One month in each year for was it ...
Five years? I remember siestas when I
Worked and you slept. Now and then
I too was captured by sleep.

But I would not try hard with that tongue,
Harsher than Italy's, louder, unrelenting, then
Loud in 'Oles'. There would never be bullfights, never
In all of Italy.

Italians can be brutal but quietly. Spain
Spoke of the fiery spirit, prayer rising
From John in his tower, from Teresa
Enclosed in her Avila.

I often missed the laughter of Rome, the shameless
Shows of feeling, the lack of dignity. Spain
Was what I admired, never what I might love.
I look down at the map,

At that square of Europe, vast peninsula, think
Of Goya and energy, El Greco and Christ but still
Rome draws my spirit. Campaniles are hers
And so are squares and prayers and absolving words.
Spain was a cold, pure passion.

Once in Greece

The Sirens sang in childhood, islands shone
With strong sun I had never seen in England.
This was imagination mapping out

Later voyages. How right they were
To speak of 'Greece and Rome' since in most ways
Rome is indeed the whole of Italy,

More than a city anyway. Was this
Why Athens disappointed me? Had I
Shaped too many islands, set the sun

Too richly on the sea? It may be so.
Athens was noise and Babel. No one spoke
My French or English, and of course I was

Often consciously comparing this
Noisy city with the stretch of Rome.
Its blend of luxury and abstinence,
Its run of hills, its history carried lightly,
A place of arts, tradition and of conquest.
At least I learnt, though, Athens was not Greece.

My mind unburdened it upon that trip
In golden May to Corinth and Mycenae,
But there the sickness started and I saw
Epidaurus through a yellow mist,
Felt far too weak to test the vast acoustics
And yet the resin smell of that slow walk

Towards the theatre lingers in my nostrils
With the dark sea I had one long warm swim in
And yet I felt a stranger all the time

In Athens, specially with the English there;
Stubborn imagination of my childhood
Kept on comparing its huge dream with this
Wide range of mauve hills. Here the gods were dead
And even road-side shrines for Jesus Christ
Had an uncertain and a fragile air.

Maybe I never caught the music of
Greece. All countries have an undertone
Of rhythm caught on winds and rising voices,

Sounds that never finish, flutes which play
For the old times when Dryads grew in trees.
Rome kept intruding and I felt its sway,

Its subtle rhythms, hidden melodies
Held in my heart when Greece lay all around
But would not yield the past in one pure sound.

Anzio

In memory of A. T.-A.

We went for lunch at a hotel kept by a friend
Of this friend who took me to Anzio. The day
Was cool and easy. The sky
Pale with a Roman blue, a Spring blue still.
After lunch we sat with coffee and strega
(Sticky and sweet but it tastes of Rome to me)
And looked at the idle fishing boats at anchor.
The barely visible lap of the sea, the beach
Deserted. We fell into a reverie
Each allowed the other and after an hour –
Anzio still in siesta sleep about us –
You suddenly said you wanted to see the graves
Of the Protestant soldiers killed in the Second World War.
Then I remembered you'd fought in the First World War,
First in the trenches, then in a fragile plane.
You clearly needed to go
Partly to pay your homage, partly to leave
The beach once invaded by British soldiers, their blood
In your imagination all about you.
So we took a carozza in sweet slow afternoon
And dawdled among the graves. That invasion, those deaths
Meant nothing to me. My war had been hunger simply
Felt in a very 'safe area', but through
Your eyes I saw two wars, soldiers in trenches,
Others running on sand amid noise of guns
And the afternoon was broken. Our silences
Floating over these graves were a drift of fear,
Of wounds and death, and now you were a priest
Daily giving the sacraments and changing
Wine into Blood. Is it whimsical to
Remember the pink sky later that afternoon
And see it as blood till the Mediterranean night
Dropped its kind folds about us and we went back
From the echoes of war and the idle fishing boats
To Rome your home and swiftly becoming mine.

The Gulf of Salerno

The Bay of Naples paled as we rounded the corner,
The bus driver singing snatches of *Rigoletto*
And spinning the driving wheel with a single hand,
His reckless joy imparted itself to us,
Such infectious delight. The bright sky echoed with sounds
Of a recitative. Then suddenly all noise stopped
Or so it seemed. Maybe imagination
Was playing a role, but no, there was indeed
No need of anything but this natural grandeur
Of that still bay: spears of stone stood up
And to our left were towns like limpets clinging
To the sheer cliff. At Positano we stopped
And admired the lace a smiling old lady was making.
I had seen her copy in Rome, the same shrewd eyes,
The sunburnt and wrinkled skin. She did not mind
That we looked but did not buy. Our smiles were enough.
Back in the bus we hurried along to Amalfi
Almost silent, nothing of tragedy there
Though echoes of Webster's *Duchess* spoke in my mind
But only briefly. Full noon held us within
Its huge hot bubble of air. Once more we stopped
And ate our rolls and cheese in a cypress shadow.
The driver lay under the sun with his cap
Over his face. Siesta was everywhere,
The dark, still water had made its peace with the sky.

Some Words of My Mother's in Childhood

When I was a child I never said 'When I shall die'
Or 'When my life ends.' I didn't believe in death
Or ends. This made for great joy and huge fear.
I believed that the happy ride on the carousel
Would never end and in a sense it did not
For when I was lifted off the horse or the dragon
I was riding still, hugging the animals' sides
And falling asleep to the hurdy-gurdy music.

But when I had been afraid of a saint in a chapel
Of a huge cathedral because a white handkerchief covered
His face, I cried and screamed in bed that night
Because my imagination was schooled to mysteries,

To holding back, to being open to wonder
And so my fear was an overmastering presence
Larger than full moon or the tumbling clouds
Or the blowing trees. Somebody strong had to speak
And break the evil spell and so you did,
My gentle mother. You somehow stilled the sobbing
And carefully drew from my gasping words the story
Of the saint who was dead and whose face I could not see.
You said – and such magic there was of rich assurance
In your quiet voice – 'He's laughing at you in Heaven'
The room became small, the wind was friendly, the moon
A face nodding with wise approval at me.
Let me be grateful always for the power
Of casting out devils of fear from a child of six
Let me learn how to help those frightened others
Who have no words but look to me for meaning
Or who write and say they often read my poems,
May my music be selfless and pure as my mother's sentence
Which soothed the child I am though now a poet
For I've lost nothing of fear or horror but only
Been given the magic charms of poems which drive
Out the devils that darken love. Let those fraught figments
In others' minds change to a rich peace
When my poems arm them and take them over and soften
However briefly the dreadful disturbance of life.

Fairground

In memory of my Father

There it was, Big Dipper, Giant Racer, Figure of Eight,
Any name, a fairground near the sea
And I was five years old jumping and shouting and begging you to
                                                              take me
High up there into the clouds and the sun. You paused at first
And then went up to test the ride without me. I watched you go
Out of my sight, heard the engine pounding, saw the steep
Climb and the dips and I was all excitement, elation and when you came
Out of the glory of golden air you picked me up,
Put me between your knees and slowly we climbed
Up the sheerest slope I'd ever seen or felt
And I was afraid but joyfully so, you held me tight
Between your knees, your hands over mine and how could I know
This was the closest we'd ever be, that never again

Would there be a ride to the Heavens, you bearing me up
And me all trust and delight? The engine dipped
Down and up and down again with the élan of speed and the air
Ran through our hair, time was somewhere else
Until we began to slow and came down at last
To the usual world of flatness but I was still
Up with the sun and you holding me tight
In a closeness so sweet, in a timeless pleasure of height.

Psalm of Childhood

I was near it, close to the world around me seeming within me
And glad to be there. The psalm of a child, the singing, the glory,
                                                    the terror
Are like the majestic psalms sung in Office, telling the world its trouble,
How the bones sing, are broken, how God is terrible too but
                                                    somehow loving.
Listen, I looked at the sparrow and robin and starling,
Watched their immediate hold on the world, their assurance
Obvious in all their singing and arguing, sure that they were always
                                                    essential and needed
As the Great Bear is and the Southern Cross and the moon's
                                                    discreet alterations.
Children are adept and swift at praise undivided
From the lion's wild ways to the zebra's astonishment at
Its audacious stripes that it can never hide.
I lay in the humming grass or hay, I hid among shrubs and hedgerows
And smelt the rain on the wind and plucked the vetch and convolvulus
And saw its shrinking with tears.
I rejoiced in the swelling apples, the hairy gooseberry, the
                                black-berries and their juice,
And I watched the horizon swallowing sunlight but leaving
Such a spread and depth and so many shapes and shades
Of red and pink and purple.
And make no mistake, I know that I am still
As rich and wild in my ways but also tempered
By love gone wrong or betrayed or altered or darkened.
I drew cool shadows in childhood little knowing
They would stand around me later and close me in
And so they do but I cry from the depths of their reaching
With praise and presumptuous defiance and trust and need
And sometimes the world answers back.

Psalm of Discrepancies

When did I first sing to the clouds of rejection
Turn to the fertile fields with a fiery mind,
Set my imagination in tune with storms
Or the wake of storms? I do not know. I know
Only the stretches of memory, the Alps
Of recollection, Himalayas of hope.
Childhood is almost a psalm in itself or a set
Of psalms with their moods of anger and desolation
And hope and imploring. David's language sings me
Back to the shapes of childhood, its squares and oblongs,
Its definite colours. I called to the green fields often
Ran through the dew of early morning and gathered
Nosegays and branches for gifts. They were mementoes
For later years, talismans for the ways
No longer straight or certain when clouds are smoky and hide
That joy which swelled beyond my containment, dispersed
Among the green branches of oak and ash and beech.
So I was lost in a world of drama but seldom
Felt lonely or frightened. Never by day I mean,
Never in any resplendent noon. So now
When I am troubled and angry or half-way-between
I turn the pages back in an ancient *Book*
Of Certain Hours and find my childhood markers
Between the pages and all the past is renewed
And dazzles with the sunrise upon green hills
And sunset over a sea which is not tidal.

By Themselves

I give the clouds a revelry of song,
Blow them up with trumpets till they float
Like white balloons about the preening sun.
I let go all of Summer but it's caught

And tied up in my mind with other years,
Childhood content when sun shone every day,
I lost myself among those cavaliers
Of lancing light. As music plays I play

Today and consciously set self aside.
The barley's burnt and ready for the gather
When we are needed. Threshing floors are wide.
We are citizens whose town is weather,

And always we press our imaginings
Upon the ripe and unripe fruit. I try
To offer liberation to all things,
Accept that I can't change worlds with my eye.

Music with no voices is the one
Sound we make that does not sing of us.
I listen to a cello, it's begun
Pure cadences that we cannot abuse.

Spring and a Blackbird

Today words have a tune.
Who found which? Who knows
Which came first? The singing goes
Up and up in swinging circles, in sound
Where intimate conversation never goes.
A poem takes off from the ground,
From snow safe and from heat-wave it's immune,
Part-sunlight, part-half-moon.

And the sound of the poem belongs
To nobody. It's a free for all,
A high clarity like the blackbird's call
In this green-gold morning, this burning afternoon.
You need not search for music in your poems,
You, poet. They find each other out
Plangent, intransigent and never in doubt
As the blackbird is, and not becomes its tune.

True Spring

Is it true Spring, this rush of light into
A sky long shrouded in a Winter dark?
I smell fresh atmosphere, I count each blue

Circle or square of sky. In every park
Purple and yellow crocuses abound
In their squat brilliance. I feel something quick

Upon my skin, and in my mind a sound
Of blackbirds calling lifts my spirit and
I am content to stand on this green ground.

I am content to watch the birds descend
On softening soil. I feel a part of Spring.
Persephone now takes me by the hand

And at her bidding thrushes start to sing.

Dusk

Is dusk the favourite hour for many people?
The English gradual change of light I mean,
The slow, soft shadows filling out, the sky

Bonfired and well-augured when it's red
(That's a saw I've never known to fail).
Dusk is precious, even when it's long

And lingers as if eager to stay with us,
Cruising shadows round rich Summer trees,
Lengthening stems of Spring flowers, stealthy movements:

It is a time of many mixed-up feelings,
Almost contradictions which link hands.
Now I think of Southern sudden nights

When there's no dusk at all, no Western red
And pink but sudden plunges into dark
The happiest time for me, these falls in Rome

For then it is as if a huge hand pinned
Brooches of stars upon the Southern heights
Of sky. The Southern Cross is diamonds for

A mythic god or king, a cause for myths.
I love the South but I love English dusks,
The subtle twilight, most things juxtaposed,

Shadow and substance, pale moon facing sun,
Stars like splinters from a hammered forge,
A time for guesses, love words for the dark.

Cloudscape

Clouds coming and going, stretching, reclining, opening up a space
For a blue spread, a fetch of an almost sea,
    A Mediterranean in the air, and then
There is a hungry, rapacious smoke, there are hidden chimneys
    Venting their rage. There cannot be repetitions, surely never
The same sky day and night, north and south, sweet or terrible. I
    Need a brush or a Mozart horn, a serene or nearly divine
Impulse, and so there is a God up there
    Not as I thought in childhood sitting on clouds
But more majestic by keeping in balance the air,
    By simply letting be though deep in control
Of this avid air, this breath that pours out stars
    And fixes them as we travel round them. A Claude
Caught the peace, Turner divined almost every
    Mood and gesture, lashed to a mast he watched
This vast display, this ever-extending, unrepetitious act
    Of light and balance or abrupt of altering air
At which I marvel and silence myself to a stare.

Moon in December

Night and the plangent moon
        Staring me out.
It seemed only yesterday that it shone
        Its quarter shape of doubt.

Now it's a presence of light
        Illuminating my room
I am glad to be a worker in the night
        To see how it can assume

A pleasant dictatorship here
        Over garden, square and street
In the afternoon it will be chalked up there
        Overwhelmed by sunset.

But when the red skies give
    Way to the early dark
I shall see that large presence of moon as if
    It intended to light my work.

Newcomer

Say it's deceptive Spring for nights are cold,
Say it's the sun stoking its evening fires.
Say it's the sentry crocuses whose bold
Petals stand alert which makes desires
Storm me at night. I thought that growing old
Meant dignity. I blame your cunning kind
Subtle advances breaking me back to
Youth. You kindle heart and fill my mind
With love I want to show.

Aubade

A chirp, a chip in the now
Blue not total dark.
I want a music of colours
As the song begins to work
In the throat of a bird at dawn
Who unwittingly celebrates how
Sky turns bright before pale
And then the sun's full powers
As the voices of all the birds
Gather a throng of words
And give them sovereign scores.

A Music Sought

Shall I ever find
This music which I seek?
Both flutes and violins
Are scored within my mind
But something further off
I can just hear begins.
It takes both string and wind
And has to do with love

And all its thrill and drive,
Its landscape and its pace.
This music would preserve
Our best loves. They would thrive
And form a gracious dance,
Both keep our loves alive
And praise their circumstance.

Maybe no music can
Contain so deep a part
Of how we wish to live.
Both woman, child and man
Cry for the broken heart
To find a sound to give
A purpose to the hurt

We suffer and we cause.
Sometimes I hear the strings
Combine with flutes to sound
What is the best in us.
Listen, a music sings,
It's gone as soon as found,
Yet there's a universe

Which Bach and Mozart knew,
Beethoven sometimes and
Dowland often. There's
A starlight brilliance too
We but half-understand
Yet recognise as true –
The music of the spheres.

Arrival and Preparation
Overture

It seems to be very near
This music that's been so elusive but so quick
To offer a phrase and move into difficult silence,
Hard for me I mean.
I have let one phrase enter and disappear,
Kept only words in my mind,
But now the melody's on me at last, the clear
Psalm you don't seek but find.

Enough

A string is plucked, a word
Uttered, then silence till
A robin bleeds the snow.
Fingers are frozen, minds
Shrink to small purposes.
A thread of careful sound,
A rise of raging air
Then purpose found.

Two Together

It will always go with love, this delicate sadness,
Almost delectable sometimes as in Autumn
When the copper and gold and yellow leaves surrender
To the afterglow of Summer. I can recall
Feeling sad in September, thinking of school
And wanting the long holiday extended
For there was always love in those early days
Though it bore other names, happiness, being cared for,
Being taught to swim, being freed among the rockpools
Where I gazed at the polyps on sea-weed, smelt the salt,
And when I raised my head I saw the sun,
The noon lantern and it was almost a god.
Love took my hand when a nanny or my mother
Guided me over the shingle. Love was shining
Out of the face of the ice-cream man as he pressed
A pyramid of vanilla in a cornet.
I had known fear by night and the pain of shyness
But they were little sorrows. I must give back
The territory of love or, better, open
The secret gate to it, let others walk
In the woods of calm consolation, let the pool
Of sunlight there be waded in by them.
This I wanted to do
Even when I was small. I had no name
For the fountains of compassion cooling the heat
Of anger. Now I name and in the naming
Exorcise the terrible temper I have
Still, though it smoulders now while in my childhood
It burst out in fiery rages.

Always compassion has built its city round me
And today in a hot July I open the doors
And let a wind that's lifted an oak tree's leaves
Run round me, refresh me, offer its coolness to all.

At the Source

I was in love with someone when a child
Although I had no words for what I felt
The trust of it tamed me when I was wild,

The power of it soothed me when I had built
Dark kingdoms from my quick imagination,
Calmed me in tantrums too which were my fault

But were the other side of love. Creation
Moved me with all its falls and rises early.
I did not ask the meaning of elation

But felt it at its source where life is purely
Its own event not spoilt by man's demands
I loved and when I loved I loved entirely

And though I've tainted it and laid dark hands
Of passion and desire, in later love
I've also felt compassion's strong demands

And I have known great loves which still can move
And Spring from its strong source and tell me how
There is a love which flows and is made of

My gratitude and hope, yes, even now.

Always

Always some kind of love for me, yes, always.
Sometimes a cradle-song for an older time
Or the flutes of sweetness, heralds of the Spring.

Even in childhood, the magic of love always
With nothing complete then and therefore nothing severed,
Finally love found its own right season,

Later, taking the hands of Spring, escaping
Into the Summer dances, rising in Winter
Like the cold air, the secret breath, the sighing

Of leafless trees. Places have meant love also,
Florence, Assisi, Siena, Umbria could take me
Over and opened the guide book to a much larger

City, almost a country, a state, a centre
Of the old world and the new. The voices of Rome
Rang between her hills. I climbed them all.

Love in churches, wrinkled bony women
Crouched in supplication, prayers for the dying
And the newly-born. And always they meant love

For friend, for family, always with an issue,
A new source, a pure flow, a revival,
And maybe death will be another love

Taking me through the dark forests, lighting
My way with candle stars and lantern moon
And the last words prayers of love when sorrow is

A happy sigh that's taken over by children
Calling in sweet high voices as I once did
At the start of love and before its first rich pain.

And now as Spring's a whisper in the morning
When it is nearly Valentine's loved day,
Love is the argument, the lyric moment,

The care for ritual, the need for growth
And cities rise above the misty mountains
Before the sunlight loves them with its gold.

Presences

Hard to believe in sumptuous Summer that
Dryads don't inhabit all the trees,
Nymphs stir the streams and ruffle every flat
Surface of water. Surely presences

Lived in the past when men believed in them
And danced in air and in the fiery light,
Surely spirits now provide the theme
And consolation on a humid night

If we could but believe. O credence is
All that we lack. We should be slaves to trust,
Only then will sacred presences
Guide and protect us, leap from the crowded past.

From nymph to angel is an easy move,
Cherubs turn chestnut leaves towards the sun.
Trust is the child of hopefulness and love.
A guardian seraph drives me daily on.

Friendship

If you have a secret tell it
To somebody on a train,
Somebody you won't meet
And who won't want to meet you again.
Never make demands
Or load with confidences
Possible new friends;
They deserve better than this.

They are the ones you must
Cherish and be light-hearted
At least with them at first.
They are not claimed but courted,
Honoured, considered. These
Are the ones to go slow with, leave
Your tedious tragedies
Elsewhere. If you're going to love

Someone, you should take care
To notice hints of how other
These precious newcomers are.
And don't enquire of them either
Confidences which they
May want to keep from you,
In short, allow them to stay
Unused. Soon enough they will show
That they have their own way

Of making friends. Let be
Always, don't ever keep
Them on threads that are fairly free.
Why should you tie them up
Even invisibly?
They'll show you fast enough
When they want to make you free
Of their city of ease and love

Tact is less than an art
But is a craft to learn,
And practise until you hurt
With so much discipline.
But this is the pain you must
Feel if friendship's to be
Understanding and trust,
Loving-kindness, liberty.

Total

All is and it evades me,
The trapped word, the tethered star,
The essence, almost the whole
Of me is becoming aware
Of how I have troubled power,
Dared to risk despair.
Now through five senses the soul,

The spirit of me discards crude self, takes on
Unpossessiveness.
O pure, spare moon peel off
Desire, greed, ambition,
Let me be other. Is love
The only way to this?
Even joy is a way to possess.

The full moon outstared me to show
Like it I must become less,
A sliver of self alone
Diminished to quarter moon.

Landscape and Wild Gardens

I never cared for such an ordered view.
Blenheim, Stowe, Versailles were worth no more
Than afternoons of just an hour or two.
I've always wanted wildness in the sky,
A Turner tempest and a garden where
The roses grew the way they wished. The eye

Found its own patterns. Two hours out of Rome
A garden grew in Ninfa. High above,
Norma was pitched. This was a prince's home
And I was greeted with a welcome which
Takes centuries to turn into a love
Part courtesy and part a shared and rich

Yet economic luxury. A man
Of an old English family who had
Married the prince's daughter showed me land
Where corn and nut-trees grew. Showing the last
He spoke of 'The engrafted word of God'
And suddenly I saw the careful past

Of a long line of owners who also
Were stewards who must tend but not possess.
Where gardens are allowed much space to grow
And cared for quietly I've slowly come
To understand there is most happiness.
This seed was planted two hours out of Rome

When I was young, in love with Italy.
Let France and England have their landscapes made
By men who want to govern all they see,
In that wild garden thirty years ago
I learnt power means responsibility,
Gardens and poems must be free to grow

And both be ordered long and patiently.

Winter Piece

This sudden heat deludes
    Our Winter wills and sets
Our minds on marching clouds,
    Summer sunrise, sunsets.
We pull our mufflers off,
    Overcoats are enough.

Then suddenly night frost
    Stiffens our lawns and trees
And we are Winter-lost,
    Gales replace soft breeze
When shall we ever fit
    Again sunrise, sunset?

In Such Slow Sweetness

In such slow sweetness of spirit, in such kind condescensions
Of hours and fulsome boughs, the day declines
Pastelling pale and opal skies, sharpening looks and voices.
Here's the bold bravado of almost July, here is June giving way
To everything late, hollyhocks and delphiniums,
Sweet peas and all the residents of rockeries,
Here is Summer making mankind surrender,
Wherever he can in peace,
To the pleasure of rising sap, to the laying down
Of easy flesh in the afternoon while a few
Birds bicker peacefully. We have sat still at a window
Facing West and watched the sun slip behind
Pale pink and blue and hints here and there of green.
Psalms sing in our restful minds, and near at hand
A piano allows itself to be played and its sounds
Connect our mood with what seems a kind of perfection
And echoes us back to the power of the flood-lit day.

For Melody

Such sweetness of sound, such
Melody just within
Hearing. I try to catch
The harmony, begin
A statement of life and death,
A concord in troubled years.
The trumpet demands strong breath
But the harp means tears.

Two Musics

There are two musics, one
Of human happiness,
Its pain and rapture, its joy at things well done.
But there is another utterly different which
Sings purely its own success,
Cries out of its own triumphant assertions. It is
The echo of a voice in the universe,
It knows neither joys nor fears
But takes them up and turns them into itself,
The delighted, exacting, wholly absorbing sound
Of the music of the spheres.

All that Departing

All that departing and parting
And the wounding others and lonely recrimination.
I learnt very early gifted children are many
And none is very special.
I learnt early too the pain that imagination
Can cause but its joys were vast and the time was now
And only now, it was a circular thing,
It was often a golden ring
In which my spirit danced and I was excited,
Much too excited and could not pause or sleep,
Could not stop running and jumping. It was in fairgrounds
I learnt – I only realise today –
That the flashing gilt horses, the bright blue swings woke up in me
The sense of the world's wonder and multitudinous

Shapes and patterns and sounds.
The hurdy-gurdy took me up to levels
Where only Mozart can carry me now, and now
Is brief and the future's on me so fast as it was not
In the sleepy leisurely moments when I lay
With my eyes closed yet watching the galloping horses,
Riding upon them, their bodies plump to my thighs,
My hands on their manes. They galloped me into the dark
Of the real dreams of sleep.

   But I speak of departing and parting
And family quarrels and angry words and the hurting
Disclosures of cruel truths we cannot retract
Though we only said them in fury.
I know to the quick that each one of us is special,
Unique, particular, odd, lovable, stubborn,
Bound in the flesh and beating against barriers,
Loving the dark bodily pleasures but feeling
Always let down much later.
For I know that we all have eaten the shining apple,
Plucked it, gripped it, ruined each other with it
And yet there are transient Edens where music plays
Ineffable joys and we know that this planet is not
One among all the other orbs and stars
Rolling around the sun but piloted, ordered
By a huge spirit our little ones are part of,
A spirit which music more closely than any endeavour
Holds us to it until there is no more departing
And only sorrow for hurtings.

A Living Death

   You had them all – talent, grace and luck,
   Good health, fine education. You said once
   Almost with guiltiness in your kind look
   'When I was born I had two silver spoons
   In my mouth.' A book

   Now thought a classic, you wrote when you were
   Still in your twenties. You would go abroad
   At least three times a year. Your eyes were clear
   With wisdom. You could always break my mood
   Of melancholy. Dear

To me you were. Our friendship was so rich,
So equal though I always felt that you
Were stronger in most things. 'You've helped to teach
My mind and heart,' you said. I never knew
What this could mean. With such

A friendship, so much easy give-and-take,
I'd sometimes think that you were older and
I could not bear your death. Now there's a break
I never can entirely understand.
Sometimes when I wake

Up in the night your absence fills the sky
And snuffs the stars out. You are not dead but
Have partial loss of memory and I
No longer see or hear from you, I'm shut
Away and don't know why

Except that dark possessiveness has charge
Of all your acts and words. I know you're ill
And are too early old. The gap is large
Between us, yet I hear your soft voice still.
It was a privilege

To know and to exchange a love so deep,
So undemanding, peaceful and yet full
Of wide excitement. Sometimes I still weep,
Sometimes am angry that you do not call
Or write. I am caught up

Within a death that does not die. Your will
No longer holds its former power. Your mind,
So scintillating once, has now grown dull.
There is no comfort anywhere to find
Because I love you still.

Time for the Elegy

The time for the elegy is when joy returns
And even the dead quicken at hints of Spring.
The lift of language is an art one earns

After dumb guilt and hidden suffering.
So now my memory is a room as clean
As any broom can sweep, and I can fling

The windows wide upon a Winter scene
About to alter. Blackbirds rise and sing
And snowdrops mean defiance that has been

Gathering in the quiet Winter. Spring
Sighs now, and then it stirs and spurs me too.
The dead ten years, the other lingering

In a lost memory – both of these can do
Well without me. Elegy is praise
For season and renewal and I know

Not wisdom but the wound of love now scars
And disregards them. Death as in childhood
Is not quite real but lives among the stars

Where spirits linger whose long lives were good.
Now love is round about on every side,
I hear its voices in my neighbourhood,

My doors are open and my windows wide.

Gone

Nothing of grief was said
Only there was a space in the night sky
Where a special star no longer shone, a space
Was there and made him cry
And it did not help at all if anyone said,
Who had never watched her face,
'You will get over it, others have their dead',
He did not listen, perhaps he did not hear,
The last thing he wanted was to get over it,
She was not there. One star was now unlit.

The Spirit Lifts

The spirit lifts when the skies
Lean down, lean over, and when
Scampering clouds disperse,
The moon is up in day blue
Of late afternoon hours.

You can almost become
The assent of probing light,
The assurance of accurate hours,
The day drawing together
Its cold defiant powers.

Listen, a wise man hears
An answer to long endurance
Of questions that must be answered.
The soul of such a man clears
In such high cold. He bows
To the steep honour of stars.

One Minute

Understand one minute. It's enough
And much more hard than you had ever guessed,
For when in the green shallows of our love
Did we take time to say that we were blessed?

Everything else that scarcely mattered we
Repeated over and over for pleasure's sake
Not because we thought that it might be
Not so long later, something we could break.

But break it – yes we did and gradually
As tideless waters draw back to their source
When there's a drought. Who caused it, you or me?
Who had the quick, who the abating powers?

We do not know but if we'd held on to
Just one of our best moments when we were
Not mine but yours, we might have learnt one true
Purpose when we are cold and not from fear

But from indifference or carelessness.
Lovers should cast spells or carry charms
That mark a moment which meant selflessness
When wonder drew them to each other's arms.

Young Love

My first love was all eye and stayed that way
  For months, then slowly hands
Moved to each other in a thoughtful play
  None ever understands.

O let the touch of love now for the young
  Be almost Eden – new,
We only give the darks they move among.
  Some dreadful debts are due.

The Feel of Things

The feel of things, the nap, the fringe, the sheen,
To catch the light that circles round the cat
Brushing him as you groom a horse. To show
The rueful tumble of a head of hair,
Its curl, its fall. And then there is the glow

Vermeer caught always with a modesty
Of means, a tact, a kind
Of cool respect with passion at the core,
The impulse of the mind,
While all the senses make a music of
What others feel but cannot understand.
The poem is a way of making love
Which all can share. Poets guide the lips, the hand.

Some Solitude

To be alone just as I often was
When small, before the name of solitude
Or loneliness impinged on what I did,
To be alone, my mind among the stars,
My hands brushing the lavender and herbs,
My senses clear of smoke and dirt and all
Intrusions – is this begging far too much?
Is it selfish when I go away,
Many miles sometimes,
Sometimes for only an hour when I reflect
And tilt my head to memorise the shapes

Of altering clouds in sudden heat-wave this
Whole of April offered? I think not
For in the solitude when I become
One with birdsong, shifts of winds, the slant
Of sun across the land and hill at noon
I can achieve no peace but some wise state
In which I find both pleasure and renewal,
Knowledge unknown to books, feelings unspoilt
By passion or sensation's touch. So long
As this sometimes can lead to mines the spirit
Finds its own gold in and then offers it back
To one or two or who knows what's the count,
Then there's no need to justify my purpose,
I draw away to be of use, discover
How spirit speaks to spirit, time's no matter
And none knows what amount.

Fifteen Years After a Death

Why was I hard, cruel, sullen?
Why did I turn away and want you to say you were sorry
When it was all my fault? Because I knew
You would always return, never sulk, always laugh,
Touch my hand, crack a joke, stare at me,
Never scold or upbraid me. You should have done,
You were too kind too often and sometimes brought out the worst in me
When I tossed real kindness to others.
Why did you never reproach me?
Now you can never touch me,
Now I am always here, now with the light on late,
Night lorries lumbering off below the window
And I am alive and wakeful and live among strangers.
The years of misery, guilt, shame, anger are over,
Good times are back but not as they once were with you
And also when I was younger.
You taught me death and I never knew you were dying
On that island in the English Channel whose name
I cannot hear spoken or even bear to see
A picture postcard of,
I was frightened, I was so much to blame.
In our childlike precarious love
You taught me that death is sitting and watching the sea
Without a smile. That is how I last saw you.
If you were here now you could learn living from me.

Legacies and Language

I have learnt my tongue
From cities that are neighbourly and near water,
Where wren or rook or sea-gull lance the air,
Where the land is flat and above it the sea sows its salt.
That was my first home,
Born in Boston, Lincolnshire,
Reared in a flat land of sugar-beet and tulips
But with mind attuned to the tides, the heart ready for journeys,
I learnt the song of storms and ships at anchor
Where the tide governs the mind. Till I was six
These were legacies but my inheritance then
Came from the damp, soft valley of Oxford's Thames
Where the air is slow and easily misted, where minds
Cogitate, think long and companionably but do not draw
Easy conclusions. For rest, for recreation,
The bells of the churches oddly ring for services
Which are not so often attended. I was a cross-breed also,
Christened to Catholic Christianity, oiled and marked
With the name of Rome on my lips. I learnt the Latin
Of stone and pillar. The Greek was soft and persuasive
But Rome spread out the glory of the Renaissance
Colours and light, huge marble presences,
Raphael's frescos filling rooms in the Vatican
And Raphael, loved by all and dying young,
Brought all Rome out to conduct him to the Pantheon.
But Rome became neighbourly when I was out of my teens
And ripe for renewal of vows. The child's belief
Had to argue with flesh and blood, must vanish, must go underground
To the catacombs and the dark long memories there
And doubt and be afraid but came up suddenly
Into the bold Baroque, into the city of artifice
Where a square is a circle, Bernini lays down his columns
And in the fountains between them and in all Rome's fountains
I learnt the sound of water, it versed and instructed me,
Took over all my English lyric sense
And gave it deeper roots and wider branches
And now, though unvisited for a number of years,
Rome does not haunt but holds me, is a presence,
Gives me a landscape utterly unlike Oxford's
And therefore a conflict that ends in the dance of phrases.
Latin and Anglo-Saxon are not estranged
But sing together as language lives and changes –

The Saxon, the Roman, the Norman, the modern with all
Its trends and touches. The dance becomes more elaborate
And carries me on and on. It is like love
That bears you beyond the guesswork of first rejoicing
And sets you on a rock facing the sea,
Your hand in another's or in the tide's or in rock-pools,
All's passionate and remote, personal yet also general,
In fact a system of rites, of comings-together
Where poetry is the common language of dreams
But also of love and its profound legislation.

The House of Words

It is a house you visit but don't stay
For long. Words leap from ledges. Verbs and nouns
Ask for a sentence where they'll fit and say

What you were unaware you thought. A dance
Of meanings happens in your head. You start
To learn a melody you half-heard once

But can't remember wholly. Now verbs sort
Themselves from nouns, and adjectives insist
You use them with great care. There is a plot

And story where the parts of speech are placed
By you and they will stay still only when
You make their purpose clear. Now you are faced

With plot and characters. There's music in
Their lives and discourse. You must set them free
By knowing where facts stop and poems begin.

For there's a truth you find in artistry
Or it finds you. The lucky words appear
And now they have a theme and history.

But you must wait a little till you hear
The sound, the tune, the undertow of song,
And now you are made suddenly aware

Of music all these words find place among.
It swoops as birds do from the living air
And nests upon your house of words to throng

With messages you never hoped to hear
And greetings which sound best when they are sung

The Early Work

Was it there all along
      The music I seek
Now? Did a song
      Through my meanings break

In those early lines
      Of verse I made
With easy designs?
      Did every word

Find its pulse and speech
      As a thrush's do?
Now I would reach
      For the sounds and so

Discover the pure
      And untrammeled note
Which is surely the power
      Which you can't separate

From the theme. O let
      My poems find,
As stars do light,
      The music of mind.

Think Of

Think of a delicate softness. Think of a cloud,
Not what it is, vapour and air, but as
Imagination masters and names and holds it
Poised on the edge of the mind. Think of a fledgeling,
Not yet able to take the air but relying
On the thrust and impulse of parent birds. Observe
The pastel shades, the opal of going-down suns,
And the way the trees turn dark from every texture
And shade of green. Think of the shy first love

That dare not speak what it thinks it sees but waits
In a hover of happiness, not yet a depth of desire.
Think of the actual joy of a child on the seashore
Not yet divided from where he wades or how
He clings to shells or tosses them back in a rock-pool.
Think of paintings and their bold transformations,
Those portraits stilling the crowded face of a man
Or a woman gazing in a mirror. And last,
Think of the first inviting bars of a music,
The violins' first bold sweep, then the sound of horns,
And then be grateful for how the mind can dance
Between and around and under words and rejoice
And know that this is not chance.

Art and Time

It has to do with time, there is no doubt.
The clocks, the bells, the sun-dials have their power
Over the shaping of a verse. But what

The power resides in I am not quite sure.
What is certain is the way that rhyme,
Cadence and beat of syllables endure

Within the importunity of time.
Whatever form is used or if we trust
Only to ear, our stanzas cannot climb

To regions of no time. Art must exist
Within that element. Now, listen to
Any composer. You cannot untwist

His many sounds from time. Hours make them true,
Minutes absorb. And so with poetry,
Past, present, future fashion what we do,

Confine our purpose and our artistry.
And yet great verse can signal to us from
A thousand years ago. The art is free

Within the length and breadth of time. The poem,
Picture and music can be like the stars
Which flash out to our present through a gloom

Of countless light years. Yet for most of us
Time is the metronome we dread and watch,
We heed its movements and our little verse

Needs its severity, yet there's a catch
In all this argument, a wound, a flaw
Which maybe wise men could discern and touch

While makers trust to instinct, craft and more
Shapes of time they never reached before.

Pigeons Suddenly

A flight of pigeons, a sheer
Flourish and dash and delight.
Out of the pale air
They flew unexpectedly, light

And easy, graceful as
Nature is at her best.
I watched them gather and pass
And I felt language graced

And natural as the way
Birds took the air and then
Without a second's delay
Vanished. There seemed but a thin

Barrier between
Such confidence and speed
And the way poems sometimes begin
And gather force with no need

Of my intervention. Maybe
This is the absolute
At the heart of poetry,
A single ecstatic note

As Vaughan Williams found in *The Lark
Ascending*. One pure sound
Made its soaring mark
That is not sought but found.

The Luck of It

Of course it is luck in a sense,
In every sense indeed,
Lucky for you that the words arrive out of what
Really does seem a perfect, cloud-absent sky,
But the luck is not for that 'I'
Which begs for sympathy, wants to tell its tale.
The poem is not your plot
Or life or worry. It is imagination
Let loose and allowed to run wild
Till it sometimes brings back a phrase or two, at times
A whole poem that needs no alteration.
What sings and tells and rhymes
Only asks that you be two impossible things
In the usual sense, that is: –
Let things be and yet be wily too
So that now and then language and music kiss
And marry and stay true.

The Start of a Story

It is so gentle as yet,
Just on the edge of my mind
And also beating quietly in my heart
But I will not say I find

A friend, not one replaced
But something itself and new
And I have no wish to own or be possessed
But find perhaps a true

New story beginning, for all
We learn to care for are
The quiet beginnings of the hint of a tale
And so there is happy fear.

Excitement, yes, but not
Much, for I feel there may be
Coming a friendship which is a love that's taught
And not demanded by me.

Against the Dark

I have lived in a time of opulent grief,
    In a place also of powers
Where self-indulgence can break your purchase on life
    But now I inhabit hours

Of careful joy and rousing gratitude.
    My spirit has learnt to play
And I have willed away the darker mood
    And now I want to say

That verse is hostile to shadows and casts you out
    When you have mourned too long.
Images always rise from the root of light
    And I must make my song

Truthful, yes, obstinate too and yet
    Open to love that takes
Language by the hand and ignores regret
    And also our heart-breaks.

Words use me. Time is a metronome
    I must keep in mind always.
Nobody really knows where poems come from
    But I believe they must praise

Even when grief is threatening, even when hope
    Seems as far as the furthest star.
Poetry uses me, I am its willing scope
    And proud practitioner.

The Sea as Metaphor

You can always use the sea
As an emblem of almost anything but, of course,
You must take the rough, the overriding white horses,
The mountains of snow tipping over and lengthening, spreading
Over the sand and through your mind. If you use
The sea as metaphor you must know about tides
And the harbour bell, the torturing rocks, the caves
Of unearthly light or else of pitiless dark,

But if you are tough and faithful, head to the wind,
Mind bobbing over the breakers, climbing the steepest,
And if you are patient with the blue calm Summer waters
Of almost quietude,
And if you will wait, then run and risk the rocks
And give the white horses their head,
You may catch the intimate, changeable rhythm of oceans,
The neutral moods which are rare, their black bad-temper,
Their sudden bursts of applause.
If you are prepared to risk all this and, much harder,
Ready like patient fishermen to return
To the morning water with an empty net,
You may now and then, at other times, also catch
The ocean's rare, perfect pitch.

I Heard a Voice

What I heard was a voice
Belonging to long ago, not only my own
    Past but the past of many memories.
Classical and Romantic were forgotten,
    All categories dismissed. I heard a voice
But did not recognise it. I could not put
    An epoch or rule around it. I was myself
Uncertainty personified. In the Winter
    Landscape I fitted. In the relentless icy
Night outside I watched the stars. They seemed
    As if just scattered, released into an air
Millions of years away. And then it seemed
    That the voice I heard was vocal and no longer
Instrumental. I listened carefully and
    Heard a humming reverberation. Then
I knew it was my task to add the voice;
    Supply the language. I thought of all who ever
Practise a craft or art. It must be heard;
    Recognised and responded to. The hermetic
Obscurities belong beyond the stars.
    Art must take the hands of men and women,
Lead the children into its fastness, shut
    The door of disillusion, provide not escape
But a larger view, a danceable distance. It is
    The task of makers to lay themselves open to pain
And then cast spells on it. Only this way

Are music, painting, poetry a part
Of the pith and nub of existence. Let there be rough
     Edges, dishevelment superficially.
But art does not copy the breakage of a world,
     Does not offer a picture of ruin or remorse
Or hand out panaceas. It speaks from the private
     Loss and grief, happiness too, it dares
To tell the truth of ecstasy and suffering
     By an alchemy no artist should bother too much
About explaining. Art brings relief, it casts
     A spell in the face of heedless stars, it works
By what one person saw and felt and endured
     As others endure. The maker is sometimes lucky
For now and then he finds the target of truth
     Not through his own accomplishment or, at least,
Only a little due to his care and crafts.
     Musical notes, visual images,
Careful words show to a few there is
     Purpose in bearing pain, but this is only
A part of sharing what one artist makes. The full
     Gift is to offer what maybe has lodged for long
In places of disapproval. Never mind that.
     I hear a voice in the watches of the night
     Which one day may turn to song.

Parts

How we live by halves and quarters and
Eighths and sixteenths, never full and square
Towards a sky or season. Either hand

Is occupied, the other hangs limp where
It might have touched the grain or ringed a knob.
Babies, we crawl within a sheltered air

Watched by others but we learn the nub
And nap of things before we have the speech.
We are all concentration, fit the job

In hand, we push our limbs but cannot reach
The bear, the ball. Elders guide us from
The full experience when they start to teach

Habits, some good, some bad and so we come
At last to school and circumscription, yet
We learn to paint and take the picture home.

Our minds are filled, our memories seldom let
Our expectations down, but we exchange
The gift of self for learning score and set,

Rote and range. We can't be wild and strange
Except at night, except much later too
When love's the argument and will impinge

On all abstractions. We are full and true,
No halves or quarters then but guided straight,
Occupied fully and attain the view

Of a full moon yet it too must abate
Though it sheds gold for us and honey dew.

Let It Be

Let it be stately sometimes. Let it be sweet,
Lucid, unselfregarding, let it also
Be wholly serene and late-Summer seasonal,
Washed by the first pale suns and new-noticed moons.
Let it be ordered as hollyhock and poppy,
Scabious and columbine are in their flowering.
Let it be rich as wheat and oats and barley
Show they are, gathered up soon in swathes.
Let words of ordered rhythm sing Harvest Home
As ignorant of Winter as children are
Who have not heard of fear or seen its pale,
Close-to-death face. Death is another chapter.
Now is only the poem.

Waiting

Is it searching me out? Is the music
Playing far off? Is that what I think I hear
In December distance? A matter of horns and strings
Wait somewhere to be caught

In a mesh of words, a host of echoes, a charge
Of passion held in. Waiting is part of writing.
Poets aren't lucky to write. The good fever comes
Only fitfully while

We spend whole weeks and months with only a hint
Of a hint of music. We cannot force it, we must
Let it have its slow, sure way.

Meanwhile we live on usual levels, proceed
With little purposes, meeting, talking, not sleeping
And those nights of insomnia are not the worst to bear
Because, if they come at all,

Poems arrive in the silent small hours, seem
Part of the moon's wide definition, the stars
Shining, and so for me, sometimes for me,
And when the music begins

In my mind I always recognise the time
When it is authentic; then I leap out of bed
To grab a pencil and paper to write down the score
And of course the libretto too.

For words and their particular music are bound
Indissolubly, you must listen to both
And give them space, allow them the freedom of your
Expectant imagination.

You have to wait and then when the words arrive
At speed and racing ahead of you (that is their way
With me) then you feel that the world is indeed just
And the stars seem to shine approval.

So the lucky lyric comes and you are not sure
If there is a jarring word or a false note
So you set it aside and wait again, yes, waiting
Is the mainspring of poetry.

The Prodigal Son

He is far off, he is very far off, he's a blur
Of shadow against the setting sun, he is ragged
Clearly and slow and there is a touch of shame
And even penitence. In his vineyards his father
Is gazing at the crop, the promising early
Fruits but suddenly for no apparent reason
He lifts his torso, tilts his head and shades
His eye and something very familiar, a gesture
Of a child who has misbehaved is silhouetted
Against the bonfire blaze, 'It is my son at last, at last it is
My dear lost son, my promising one, the part
Of my heart I've missed for nearly a dozen years.'

In the kitchen a clatter of dishes proceeds and good
Herby smells rise up but the father is running
Fleet as a boy again and the shadow too turns
In an old and hopeless way. The boy doesn't move
For he is still a boy to his father. The sky
Is festive pink and purple. The father throws arms
About the boy and kisses the thin pinched face,
Smells the dirty clothes and a godlike but also extremely
Human compassion is seen against the light
And the boy is crying babyishly but now
Treading slowly the old good road to home
Through olive trees and herbs and the starting grapes

But in the house someone is slamming doors
And swearing and saying 'It isn't fair. I was good'
And the prodigal is afraid till his father goes
And coaxes the elder son to the gala meal,
And grapes it seems have been burst across the sky.
Wine is running along the slopes of night
As a household starts to heal.

The Hours

So many hours, so many shapes and sizes, colours and arrangements, so
Many noisy, discordant ones breaking to storms but others,
                                        uncountable others
When the tides of the mind went out and the shore was wide and the sun

Shone, the moon's lamp seeming quite motionless holding
Watch over love and its promises. Listen there are
Voices praising the love of God, others suffering, monks in their
                                    choir-stalls keeping
The promises we have broken, uttering sorrow for our sakes, so
                                    much contrition
Lasting too long, so little trust. The hours
Of life turn into the sea, my ships go out on the full

And deep green tide. The hours of love return, so many kinds,
Some unrequited but no less true, some too eloquently
Demanding, the best so tranquil at times, at others almost a weeping
With thankfulness. There are drums and trumpets, there are
The limpid harp, the deep-voiced double-bass
And the boy's voice climbing to peaks we perhaps can never
Return to again though in childhood we knew them so well.

I praise now the hours of renewal and kindness and hope
When the corn is high and the apples and pears and plums
Are full and sweet. They are the harvest our imagination can never
Rival with paintings or poems or music though music
Sings round the planet, knows no barriers, alters
The anger of nations that starts almost always from fear.
Prime, Terce, Sext, Matins, Lauds and Vespers
And Compline that dispossesses the hearts of devils
And haunts round the patterns of stars.

Saint Augustine

Poetry always partnered philosophy
At least in your *Confessions*. Abstractions never
    Had the last word or first. Ostia improved
Upon your yearning only by being static
    And tamed down to the hour you could ignore.
'*Tolle, lege*' – you never forgot the words
    Or the order your impulses were servants to,
Gladly spying their role and quick to perform
    Their tasks. There's no discrepancy in pages
Of passionate prayer with *The City of God* you built
    Out of your mind, establishments of the heart.
Affirmed in dawn or half-light. I remember
    Seeking your mother's tomb in Sant Agostino
One Easter Saturday. I stood helpless by

As a woman more daring and probably much more loving
Insisted the old man with his broom let us in
   'I'm writing a book called *Blood into Seed*' she told me
And Tertullian's phrase tagged the whole afternoon.
   Faint whiffs of wax and incense hung in the air
As she and I stood by in mutual reverence
   While her adolescent son stood in sullen impatience
Like Deodatus maybe entering on
   The ripe and wretched years of passion balked.
So you, my favourite saint, were present more
   Assuredly beside your mother's tomb
Even than in Old Ostia where sweet hay smells
   Like English pasture. Rome was so exact
A copy of any *City of God* since it raved
   And sang and rose from silence like the fountains,
Like your rich words in which you give to us
   Freedom of your conversion, hope in a violent age.

For Easter 1986

A violin haunts, a flute calls, recorders, then trumpets
And next, pool after pool of silence, notes falling, sounds
Dispersing. So now, this late March. So this night
Clear and cold but warmer than three weeks ago.
Easter is early, as early as possible. Must we
Catch up, count the coins, shape the wood,
Weave our crowns of thorns? In daily violence,
In loud streets, in country lanes, the crude act ruins
Itself, kills a whole childhood, nails love to splintering wood
But even so, even so,
The crocuses push up, up to life yet again insisting
On rising to drink the sun. And the blackbird carols
And cheers and rises and then is down,
All glossy feathers and yellow beak. Boys and girls
Whisper down streets, smiling, arms round each other.
Hope is there, more than desire. These are our children
Given our bleak legacy, thanking us with bold eyes.
This is a time of year and night when care
And trust and kindness rise like the prayers of children.
Some kneel at the lap of an unseen God, while others
Stand by a tree and watch the sky spread blood
Over an innocent child, over a murdered king.

Easter Vigil and Mass

It was like childhood once again but more,
More ardent and more purposeful, more realised
And possessed in mind. The Blessing of New Fire
Was all the constellations being blessed
And *Genesis* once again
And the prophecies from *Genesis* and onward
Took me back and forward yet held me still
There in the church with the covers on statues removed
And the Paschal candle the centre of the world,
Sun and moon alike.
And as the prayers continued and as I watched
The yellow flowers and golden vestments I knew
I was back in my true beginnings, baptised again
In the new water, and the church was a microcosm
Of earth and sky and there would be a rising,
Incense would bless and linger and hide the candles
Only a little, only a moment. I was
Taken up to the place where a God-made-Man
Was buried in the winding-sheets but at this Mass
He rose and came among us and we could touch him
And incense was the mist of early morning
Slowly dispersing. We walked up to the tomb
And the stone was rolled away and holy men
Told us where God was and it was good to touch him,
And then I was in a sudden childhood rapture,
The world an order within my mind and without
And held between minute and minute,
And the blood on the cross was back in the chalice, the white
Risen flesh offered to simple men,
And in the cold night underneath the stars
I felt something like love and nothing of fear
For here was holy ground and rising day
And it was right to be there.

Gloria

Is it too dark for glory?
In Winter's frozen fields it can seem so
And yet that sunset blush
Reminds of lamps that tell the Host is hidden,

Christ the child and man, the whole of God.
Glory is an object not a subject.
Little in our shabby spirits lights
Another's gloom. And yet we have known hours,
Or maybe moments only,
When ... was it spirit or a heart-beat which
Stirred us to a sense of glory which
We scarcely recognised, it was so strong,
So other and so strange to usual life?
The Alps of clouds remind us of the message
That speaks of hopeful hills and sacred mountains,
Yet doubt is a quotidian shadow, tells
Our darkest purpose and our dreadful story
Which we repeat although we say we're sorry.
We should be suppliants to the turning waves,
Take the ocean's hands with gratitude,
But now and then is our best medium, we
Are fitful, changeable although we look
For love that asks for nothing, hills that tell
Of distance and can teach humility.
Listen, we're close to Christmas. Look about
For children almost innocent, for men
Who hold within their minds an ancient story.
Let us be still and silent. Thus we may
Move in the medium Glory.

In Good Time

It works in time, I think, and yet
The spirit in me often seems
To reach from flesh and hours to set
Its purpose up where poems,

Paintings and music pause also,
The soul, the spirit in each one
Of us can never ring quite false
Or not unless we've done

Such evil and dark business that
Time swings its door and we can hear
A great key turn. Is spirit what
Rings in us all most clear

And wide away from stress and mood?
In prayer and art we sometimes come
To time that tells space it is good.
Is this the spirit's home?

A Reproach

'If I believed what you do I would stay
For hours each morning and return each night'
So someone said to me, yet my thoughts stray

At Mass. My eyes drift toward the evening light
Perturbing that plain window-glass and then
I try once more to focus on the sight

Of Bread raised up and manage one 'Amen'.
Owning imagination, why can't I
Think of Calvary and the cruel men,

The women with no words, the men who vie
For careful, seamless cloth. I do not know.
Each week I make new resolutions, try

To think of one who made the sunset glow,
Modelled a loved face, whispered and the sea
Began to turn. I ought to be brought low

When I see Bread and Wine and can believe
They are the God-Man whom I pray to when
I want a trifling bonus for my life.

'If I believed what you do I would go
To Mass each day ... ' The words upbraid me still.
I who find metaphors in which to show

My poems yet strain to make an act of will
To wrench my thoughts back to the Consecration
And find it hard to say a few prayers well.

I need, in fact, a God whom I can feel
Or else remember each poem is the Real
Presence since God *creates* imagination
Which never works by any act of will.

Moving Together

Fluting voices and an azure sky
Remind, remind but all my memories
I've put in money-boxes. They're locked in
But if I wait in peace and do not try
To free them, they'll be out. A violin
Coaxes and guides me. It sings a refrain
To work of Cézanne and of Monet too.
The arts converge. *Salves* and *Hosannas*
Make a magic. Where do poems fit in?

Poets must learn from paintings. Painters keep
An eye on words but music will elude
All designs upon it. It is pure,
Tough and resistant, its own power and realm.
It holds divinity in every mood.
Beyond a mood it yet can overwhelm
The leap of spirit in us. Gratitude
Is the one refrain we can provide
As the world whispers for a hiding God.

Only

It is sad and theatrical and also it
Is going on everywhere. It means
Just changing properties and scenes,
Lowering the curtains, dimming the lit
Footlights. Of course what the play means

Alters the actions but even so
They have much in common. The chosen theme
Is love or death, fast or slow,
Possessing the quality of a dream,
Never mind where the sleepers go.

I saw it myself but of course I was
Very involved. I knew the man
Playing the lead. When the play began
I had no idea at all of the close.
It was very dark. I was part of the plan

The playwright intended, but wasn't told.
So I came on unprepared. The script
Was pat on others' tongues. I was left
Wordless, tearful, trying to hold
My own but, of course, I hadn't been briefed

Or rehearsed either. I took the call
With the others but wanted to get away
And suffer remorse alone. The day
My friend died we quarrelled and all
Was dark and wordless for months. The play

Was put on elsewhere, almost everywhere
With others playing the bereaved friend.
It took two years for the wound to mend
To leave me with the play we are
Acting daily and cannot end.

Snooker

Over the perfectly mown and rolled grass
Under a sun we cannot see they pass
Those fifteen red balls and one pink, one black,
One yellow, green and blue and brown. Arms press
A cue is chalked. This ritual we lack

Within our lives and maybe that is why
Millions watch with rapt, attentive eye
These acolytes who have such different ways
Of pocketing a red. When breaks are high
Our prayerful looks make altars of the baize.

Group Life

Observe the group life of children
As they go disregarding us on dangerous skate-board
Notice too how they break apart as from dancing
To be other and else, wholly individual
Yet looking out and not in

Looking will come later
They do not know the particular pain of growing,
The senses' solitude, avaricious sensations
   They are not innocent, failure's a faint bruise
      Their scorn is directed at us.

   Time is not eloquent yet.
Let children not learn too much of punctuality
Nor fear of scolding that's almost wholly concerned
   With our abject obsession with clocks and chimes and road-signs
      Leading always to the dark.

First Six Years

I have not been back, have not returned to Boston
With its stump and sugar beet and the long garden
We played in till it became my earliest kingdom
Where my first remembered fragrance was honeysuckle,
Where I learnt of love in liftings and being cared for
Sitting in a cot, holding a little basin,
Whooping cough the first remembered illness.
And the shops where the doctor's children were always favourites,
My sister and I rushing round in small cars,
On scooters, pushing prams, plump legs to flanks
Of rocking horses. That was Day's, a shop
Huge and busy. Then there was the grocer,
Mabelson's, where rosy-cheeked Mr Mabelson
Opened bright tins and showed us new sweet biscuits,
Offered us choices. Here I learnt the kindness
That only comes in lessons of example,
Kindness again when a sister and a brother
Seeming years older than we were but probably only
Ten and twelve to your seven and my five,
They had a bright toy switchback which I longed for
And dared to ask for and they gave it me.
Never fear, never the wrong favour.
And then there was the secret, magic place,
Brenner's Bazaar where everything cost a penny,
Never a farthing more – small red tin cars, green engines, baby dolls.
They were the first treasures I stored up.
Imagination widened always longer
Than the large-back garden was and even bigger,
Then the beach at Skegness or sea at Freeston shore

My first six years were lived here. It's a marvel
Not to have any bad dreams or haunted memories,
No ghosts that rouse me sweating in the night
As they do decades later. A happy childhood –
This I had. It is the heart's first loving,
Overture to every love affair
Later, shaping, moulding and preparing.
Language was large and vivid, green as the hedges
I cut with nursery scissors. I remember
How words misunderstood are all I now
Recall of disappointment. You said proudly
'I'm going to the stations'. How old was I?
Three or four. I thought of puffing engines,
The luggage on the platform, porters busy
And of course it was not this you went to but
The Stations of the Cross. My given creed
Was linked with words for signs, the Latin
'Hoc est corpus meum' later. Childhood years
And garden years and seaside holidays
Told me of God in clouds triumphant, generous.
And still there were no nightmares. I remember
No talk of sin or pain. Such debts I owe
For six perfected years, the generous hours,
The currant bushes and the loganberries,
An apple tree, a rockery, a lawn,
My parents' presences, the great arrivers
On mornings after Balls. They brought us fancies,
Favours again, gold paper crowns and streamers.
I remember now the year of the rocking horse,
My Christmas present, I rode it through all lands
Of blue skies, passed red-coated soldiers and
That day I had the first warm feel of kindness
All my own. I wished to share my gifts,
Chocolates, little toys, a first good coming
Of age and to my own well-governed country
Which never disappears from any maps,
Which we can't lose though caught in foreign traps
But that right place where, after often losing
Grace we can return to many times
And be made whole and set our precious course
Towards, and never lose the sense of homing.

A Childhood Religion

The day we invented a god
The sun was tipping the green horizon, the clouds stood still
And in our garden the hollyhocks stretched their bodies
And the strawberries swelled, the pears were hard and the apples
Shone in a splendour of light,
And out of I do not know what quick instinct we made
Our god a god of light.

Sun was his power and pleasure,
Moon was merely a thin pale copy of sun
Not to be highly regarded.
Quickly our sect seethed and gathered about it
Totem poles with eyes and knives painted on them.
Friends were forced to be initiates and
Of course there were simple tortures close at hand.

For the rest of that Summer we practised our complex code,
Our faith, our tribal customs
But one day my father took us aside and told us
'You are Christians. You shouldn't be dancing round totem poles
Or painting your faces either.'
You might have supposed that our whole invented religion
Went underground then and became a subversive sect
And therefore much more powerful.
But no, we gave up the whole thing, reluctantly yes,
Yet oddly without rancour.
But that faith in a Sun God still has a niche in my mind,
Still is remembered when the Spring light turns to Summer
And the buds open, the roots stir, and the seeds
Quicken, and something quickens within me too,
A love of the sun that is close to worship, a reverence
For light whether sun or star,
And sometimes my God-made-Man seems one with this glow
And revelation beats in my heart and I think
Of the sun and the moon held in the hands of this God,
This planet entirely his province,
While his young mother hangs her head like an early snowdrop
Upheld by a host of stars.

The Essential

It will never cease, this needing, never be over.
Should it be otherwise?
Age increases but passion stays. Either lover
Or friend brightens my eyes
And as in childhood move in amazement still.
Wonder never dies.

And should not surely. Let me never become
Listless, cynical or
Uncaring about sad news of a human event.
Let me not care for size,
Even a sense of proportion can mean a want
Of love. May I not be wise

If wisdom means often standing aside or aloof,
Letting the world go on.
I care, I need, I still feel passion in love,
I tilt my face to the sun.
I cannot care for millions. Nobody can,
But from childhood I've minded the grief simply of one.
May I end then as I began.

Talking of Hume

People were talking of Hume the philosopher
Also the man who many thought was a saint,
But I was listening to his theories where
The sensuous world was held in doubt. This meant

That the writing of poetry had no purpose. So
It seemed to me. In an illusory world
Art would double the unreality, do
Away with the need. Then I heard a bold

Idea put forward, 'Hume' one talker said
'Valued imagination, thought it the most
Important matter.' I thought of the lyric word,

The music which takes ideas and makes them blessed.
Causality and induction disappeared
And I've learnt that Hume's ideas must be possessed.

Thinking of Descartes

I can see him cogitating, watch him with
A candle-flame. There's Descartes by himself
And by himself he's back where Aristotle,
Aquinas too began.
The crucial question is the same, 'How much,
If anything, can our minds know?' The quest
Was pure and selfless, spiritual also
As any human wish can be. Descartes
Conjured a naughty spirit who might lead
The mind astray, and then he asked himself
How he could tell a dream from waking thought,
When was he sure he was awake? At last
On those pure peaks where speculation shows
Ideas can be pinned down at last, Descartes
Thought how he thought of God, a greater Being
Held in his mind, thus greater than his thought
But still the vexing query was not answered
Until, perhaps in homely and slow ways
Or, and it seems more likely, in a dazzle
Of recognition, Descartes saw that thought,
Himself a thinker, proved he was created,
Authenticated by the famous slogan
'I think therefore I am'. For most of us
This is sufficient. Not for this man though.
Bravely and patiently he still pursued
The difference between the soul and matter.
He never found it but that 'Cogito'
Stressed, he made clear, 'I know myself,
No other'. And so tonight I think
With admiration of this generous thinker,
This self-denying seeker as my mind
Swarms with what poetry is, why poems are made
And 'I write poems therefore I am' won't do
Nor, though perhaps it's closer, 'Poems write
Under the poet's partial power, therefore
They are.' The night is warm for mid-October,
The windows open and green smells come in,
A half-moon is engaged on staring at
This little planet. I yawn and I sense
That clarity which sometimes comes before
Sleep trespasses upon us, I feel (yes,
Not think) that poems or their substance are

Upheld by moon and stars, lifted by winds
But won't be words until some poet catches
The moment and the music. I'm still back
At a beginning I've known half my life.
So maybe poems sing out the greater questions
But questions which expect the answer yes.

The Force of Time

The watch, the sundial and
Putting back the clock
Make us feel we can
Tame time but we forget
It is time's hand which mocks
Woman, child and man.

And yet in childhood we
Have to learn the hour,
We are taught to read
What clocks and sundials show
Though some abiding power
Is felt by us. We see

Seasons in the form
Of change and not of time.
Spring is winds grown calm,
Summer moods of sun
While we believe we climb
To stars by staring. Some

Memory of this
Imaginative force
Slowly fades from us
And, older, we begin
To beg time to endorse
Our little sympathies.

Maybe this is why
The great ones work with art.
One will paint the sky,
Another make sounds sing,
But time still breaks the heart
Because we're passersby

In time as well as space.
Great art lives longer than
Our lives and it surveys
The loss of time itself,
And hints immortal man
Means faith that time will cease,

That its three garments of
Present, future, past
Will one day be cast off
And we live in a power
Whose medium is trust
And undemanding love.

Of Time

Three-fold time begins
Your questing through the air,
Your ride upon the sea,
In a touched violin,
You are not three but one,
You guide us to a power
Beyond the moon and sun.

You move in one contour,
One fold of time we call
The present which moves on
And up beyond us to
The silence of a star,
And a celestial view.

Then we can listen to
Perfected music such
As drives out time and tells
In sounds of ordered touch
The purpose that we are,
But soon the angry bells

Sound in their jangling all
We guessed we were before
We heard a music small
To start with but so soon
An awesome ordered choir,
A shape of joy that tells

There is beyond us some
Spirit of lasting, and
Yes, we are sure of this,
A space that's out of time
Which Mozart makes for us
When all his meanings climb

Further than far-off stars,
He takes the best we are
Along with him until
Our spirits cannot bear
Such order and we turn
Back into time's hard will,
Its threefold turn of power.

Distractions

I settle down but not as I did when a child
After excitement in playgrounds or when rain trembled the windows
And I sat at the nursery table loving the noises,
Painting the sky or reading Beatrix Potter
Or simply hearing the rain like a stream of music,
Music just written by someone I'd never heard of
And didn't ask their name.
Now when I settle down to write a letter
Or lean back in a chair after hectic reading
Or walking fast, fighting a Winter wind,
I do not let silence enter me.
I cannot empty my mind.
Black thoughts of dreadful possibilities,
A parting, another death, most likely all fictions,
Fill my imagination, haunt my memory,
Padlock the past to the present and make the future
A door half open at night, swinging on wind.
All is bother and dread and untidy anticipation.
Let me learn the quiet of the evergreens,
The resilience of the robin and starling in Winter,
The concentration of snowdrops, crocus or daffodil.
Take me out of myself, that cupboard that needs spring-cleaning,
And let me remember the size of the moon and search the sky for it,
Count the clusters of stars, enjoy the rain's animation,
The energy of Nature, let me now and then learn to be peaceful
And add a quiet to creation.

There is Time

There is time and only time enough. It must do
For the acts neglected, the love twisted, the children denied
Childhood and love we could not give because love
Was broken by us whenever we touched each other,
Misshapen by us when we tried to claim our rights,
For there are no rights now except the ones we've forgotten,
Simple, eager, difficult to keep shining
Though somebody polished them once.

The old are sitting by little bars of fire,
The young are noisy, dance to noise because music
We did not teach them has turned to blare and discord,
The love we failed in they seize on, grab with hunger
And afterwards turn away,
Unable to understand why they are not happy
And why they're afraid of silence.

Passion

The violence is over. They lie apart,
They are shapes belonging to no one or could be
Part of an abstract painting or figure sliding
Upon a Dali sea.
But they are breathing fast still as if they'd been running,
Man and woman, carried by a wind blowing
Out of an open window. Here is passion
Appeased, here is pleasure
Exulted in. And here
Is possible creation. Here could be
Adam and Eve, turning away ashamed.
Here is loss waiting to be redeemed.

Mastery

From childhood I have pursued it, chased it, tumbled, picked
                                        myself up and then
Followed this special honour and service, this gift
That cannot be faked or fumbled for or be

Mistaken for anything but itself. It surely divides
Child and man from the animals, sets up our standard high,
Claims our right and privilege. What I admire
And mean now is mastery. For example, say,
The dance perfected, the downward swerve of the swallow,
Sure that the earth will receive it and show it off
And welcome it and try to copy it.
I speak, I suppose, of what is a kind of perfection,
Maybe the only one that we can be sure of
Here amid nondescript and shop-soiled goods,
The cliché-ridden clans and the evasive
Looks. But I've been lucky, from childhood on,
I've watched the careful gardener pruning pear trees
Or trimming trees to topiary, I've seen
The planets' patterns, the moon's inexhaustible changes
But always following through the exact advent
Of new and quarter and half and full. As a child
I lay in my bed with the door half-open and heard
Strains of Mozart telling triumph and sadness
And I could not bear such beauty but called out, begging
My parents to stop the sweet persuasive sounds
For I hadn't tears or years enough to respond
With understanding, yet maybe those young tears
I shed at the mastery of music showed
A grace much greater than any understanding
That side-steps feeling and honours the intellect
Almost too fully. Now every night of Summer,
When oak and chestnut and sycamore leaves stand still,
In breathless heat I pay my respects, I salute
The manifold masteries that man has shown
Which the child could not refute.

Energy

I have always revered it – energy leashed in
In those I love, in myself, in works of art.
It is the pith and the muscle of life, the keen
Blade of moon and sunlight, the beat in the heart

At the advent of one we love come suddenly.
Shyness is right, is part of vitality,
A holding-back before the unity
Of mind with flesh. Turner could always see

And re-create and celebrate this taut
Tension and power, like the turning-over wave
That spreads and streams along the shore. This is what

Passion exacts from tension, the rush of fraught
Tide, the turning-over wave, the proof
Of the moon's power in which all touch is caught.

Turning Inland

Inlands are always like that.
Associated with jetties
And also with estuaries which,
Being neither land nor sea,
Are a slowness, an always becoming
And never being, possessing
No name, no lasting action.
Look out, we are moving inland
Sick for the deep blue sea
And slowly learning to be

Landlubbers, returning to where
We have to belong. Each year
Turning back from September shore
I, for a time, belong nowhere,
My heart is an estuary,
My mind a pure becoming
Loving the fact of the sea
Going back to the Thames Valley where
I've learnt thirty years to be.

Resolve

I'll keep this heartbreak, let it hurt and tear
    My spirit, let it run
Through every day's best moments and appear
A joy I learnt under a happier sun.

For love so total and so simple yet
    So rich and many-sided
Is rare to know and touch, and though we're set
Apart forever now we're not divided,

Because in all mundane and brief affairs
    Rich love like this takes hold
Of future when we're separate. Let tears
Be shed. It shows me love is lithe and bold.

I mutilate the memory of you
    When I am fierce with pain
And cannot understand what broke us two,
Who were strong once, in half. But quiet again

I am the gratitude I learnt from your
    Strong mind and generous heart.
The past is our good luck, loss is no more
When I think of the love you made an art,

Friendship an act of faith. You are not well,
    Are early old and I
Must leave you elsewhere. But you've cast your spell
And left a magic which I can live by.

On the Edge of My Mind

It is on the edge of my mind, the tip of
My imagination, it is a
Theme of memory but much more. It is
A search, a ransacking, a bullying of the past,
A fight of my spirit with my spirit
But let me, let me be. I gaze out now
On a windy March four o'clock with a halfmoon already
Chalked on the sky, strangers pace by to a theme,
A rhythm not mine only my thoughts'. I am not concerned
With my childhood or first loving, but the first true flash
And demand of art, its subtle, sweet overture,
Its unceasing demands. I'm attempting now to capture
A rhythm of pure thought which must I think mean music
For I have gazed at paintings, even tried to paint
And gained only a marvel of light and confusion
Of still-lives and landscapes. Once or twice Claude
With his rapt attention, his foreground figures
Dwarfed deliberately, has sometimes seemed to answer
My purpose. It is music of the spheres,
No less than that, which will speak to my weary spirit.
No, do more, release my spirit
Till I fly like Ariel given his total freedom
But with Caliban's music singing in my ears.

Justice

It does not make you feel better
If you can write out your grief
If you can surrender to the escaping moment
Of lyrical spell-binding.
The spell soon breaks.

And why should it not? It would be
Unjust if grief could be written
Out in a facile charge. The dumb, sad many
Have no such release. Their grief and mourning are just
The same as yours or greater. Words are not sunlight
After the dark night or terrible tempest of grief.
If they were it would not be right.

Question

Would you have me turn to violent things,
The abrupt act of love, the possible war,
The intrinsic anger even in a butterfly's wings?
I've sometimes had a go at this before,

Written of birth and death and the wounds of love
And the baby weeping its hidden life away.
Yet I remember how the very play
Of art is thrilling and at one remove

Only from chaos. Surfaces I leave
Now as I watch the April Avon turn
In dark green waves as ducklings have to learn
Fresh water little tides, their brief of life.

Nocturne

This is the time for it,
This full-moon-lit night and stars and absolute silence,
This cold, sharp, defining night, this is the time
When ticks and chimes and pendula pause and I am
Simply imagination and a hand
Ready to score the music that's moving fast

In my veins and arteries. I am excitable always
In the kind small hours when I have not fallen asleep
But have become wider, fuller, more noticing, and
Now the moon and the rich deep sky surround
The walls of my mind and it becomes a globe
I fit this space and time as a perfect note
Takes hold of horn or violin or trumpet.
And now good memories are the words of a score
And I am neither creator nor listener but
An instrument that is tuned and perfectly pitched.
The theme and cadenza are childhood Christmas Eves
When I lay awake hearing sleighbells although
There wasn't even snow.
That was an act of perfect imagination
Supported, I sometimes believe, by enormous angels,
Guardian angels, potent presences.
These are about me now and turn themselves
Into kind thoughts so immediate they have not
Been filtered through memory. I remember hearing
One whom I loved telling me that I
'Had helped to educate her mind and heart'
And I never did nor even wanted to
Understand what she meant. When love's the drift
Explanations are ushered out and these
Vital, loving, guarding presences
Take me over, evoke a harmony
That can only be compared with the moments when
Love is so full it bursts through our flesh in tears,
Weepings of joy for we are needy and weak
But, now and then, are taken by very great art
Which disposes of time and holds us to itself.

A Happy Death

I

Death again but death in so friendly a fashion,
So courageous a guise that I should not weep but I do.
A man with cancer smiled at his dying for he
Knew that his spirit was moving out to whatever
Endurings there are. He wrote me a letter saying
Art was his joy, that Bach had made God his friend
And made him God's. His writing was straight and clear,
The syntax perfect, nothing at all to tell

He would die any hour. I ought to have guessed, of course,
Since he said that doctors assured him there was no cure
But he wrote serenely that he was happier than
He had ever been before. In his letter he said
That 'friends mean so much and I would dearly love
To see you before I die.' The letter came late
And I had been away. In the darkness I found
This white envelope with its message of friendship for me.
Early today I phoned his special number
And the line seemed to be engaged but it was not so
For when I rang the general number a kind
Voice told me that this priest had died last night.
In shock I wept and all today I have been
Close to tears and I ought to be ashamed
For this good man, a friar of fifty-seven years
Is out in the elements, one with the music of spheres
Which God plays over and over in artists' minds
For the great ones to copy out in little fragments,
Angel messages putting this frightened world
At peace with itself. But still those words 'dearly love'
Move in all my thoughts, emotions and acts
Although I try to push this irony out,
What the cynic and sceptic would call this 'trick of fate',
But I don't believe in fate, I trust in purpose
And also in free-will. And I ask myself
If pride is part of this grief, if what I feel
Is pity for self. The devils of doubt have come
Asking me 'Is there an after-life? Can you prove it?'
I cannot but as I read that letter again
And consider it many times, I begin to see
The only image that man has ever conjured
That makes a little sense of all our doings.
Another ship was launched only yesterday
And out on a calm sea this man sailed for ... is it
An island of the spirit? As a small child
I believed that God ruled from a throne of clouds
And what was literal then is useful now.
A breeze is up in this beautiful, learned city
Where my friend died, a city where cogitation
Is commonplace. But I remember that art
And even some of the poems which I have written
Helped this noble soul beyond acceptance,
Took him to truth that only faith can anchor.
His anchor is up and he is far away
Where salty breezes carry him on green seas
And little waves turn over. The Hours he sang

Are the songs of Syrens or sea-winds. I'll let him go,
Be glad if I can, hold back the childish tears
Until I am alone and can let them flow,
For I live in this world of violent, cruel fears
Not the one my friend must know.

II A Letter from the Dead

I have received a letter from the dead,
A happy letter came when the tulips stand
Like Easter candles, and this letter said
Someone would 'dearly love to see me' and
'Before I die' I read.

A priest of fifty-seven and my friend
Although we had not spoken for perhaps
Half-a-dozen years came to his end,
As he had wished, at Easter. Tears are traps
But sometimes they can send

Absolving waters down the cheeks. Here was
A death that this man saw as liberty
To be with God. I'm moved by so much grace
And in a tender sorrow I can see
That Christ brings living peace

To us when we are on the threshold of
Life and death. This man wrote he was now
Happy, but those words echo 'dearly love'.
The Easter post alas did not allow
Our meeting. Now I move

About lost in a sadness that is part
A lucid grief, an honest sorrow yet
Self is there too. Either in mind or heart
Wherever our souls rest, I feel regret
For maybe that priest thought

I needed help since he'd been near me when
My first death happened suddenly abroad
Without a warning. This man shared my pain
Without a word. Now he rests with the Lord
Who sends down such fresh rain,

Who makes the cordial April evening sky
Go red, then pink and now it's pale indeed

And a small breeze moves blossoms to a sigh.
This brave man's gone but surely knows my need
For he lives where the high

Truths and little hopes are all at one.
I learn of death but as I do I feel
Love take me over. Sweet compassion's on
My world tonight. The dead, I think, can heal
When all time's fret has gone.

III   A Song for Death

Another music now, a song for death
    Where once the dying was so brave
That I need new instruments to praise it with.
    It was a death you gave

So joyfully. You were prepared to die
    And happy in suffering as
You wrote a letter asking me if I
    Could see you. So much grace

Sang its own music from the steady hand
    Which wrote that I had been
'Much in your mind this Easter'. O my friend
    If I could but begin

This week again and not have been away.
    There was no fault, I know,
But what strength it had taken you to say
    In that steady hand you'd so

Love – it was the word – to see me again
    Before you died. There is
A music in the way you bore your pain
    Such hopeful harmonies.

Is there a music in the tears I shed
    Now on this night when you
Have only left behind what we call dead,
    While your spirit's in its true

Home at last? You said that Bach told you
    That God was your friend. Indeed
Your gracious going makes music that I too
    Think of this night of need.

Need, I mean, to know there was no blame
    But only chance that I
Was an hour's journey away when your letter came.
    Let it teach me how to die.

IV Death of a Dominican Priest at Easter

There is no waking or sleeping, no seeing, hearing or touching,
No taste, no scent and yet there must nonetheless be
Rich memories of these, deep thoughts alone at last,
Argument over and meditation only.
All at the end which delighted you now is pure,
Its own essence and nothing more. How fitting
That Bach's Cantatas carried you over the edge
Of living and dying to that state we in life
Come on only in prayer very rarely, in art more often, in love
That does not demand. You wrote me a graceful letter
In a scholarly hand. No one could guess you were dying
Yet you knew you were and so did those about you.
They say you wanted to die at Easter and so
You did, my friend. You had brought God's bread to me,
Consoled me fifteen years ago when my first
Death took place and all was darkness. You said
Few words but stayed beside me and saw all
My tears. You were the kindness of understanding,
Moved by mercy. I felt the comfort in you
But something stronger also.
You wore no sign of your death but, as men of God are
Who give up their lives to becoming saints for others,
You were prepared indeed,
But you could not imagine that fifteen years on you would know
That you would be dying and utterly reconciled to it,
Totally happy. I had 'been much in your thoughts
At Easter' you wrote to me a week ago,
Said, though you had 'little voice, you would dearly love
To see me again before you died'. You told me
It was 'a privilege to have known a poet'.
I hardly understand what you meant for I still
Am much in grief, touched by your truth, absolved
By your sweet acceptance. I'd been away when your letter
Arrived and told me all this. I rang the next day
But you had died only twenty-four hours before,
Gone from our senses' reach but not from our wishes.
You are awareness now and comprehension,
One with the elements. Words are so literal and

So clumsy, falling, lying, rising again.
O you have risen as music rises, you died
When all were thinking of Resurrection, when Spring
Was blithe and full and blossoms were everywhere.
Your death was beautiful, all your brothers around you.
O be my hope in your happiness. I have your letter
Full of assurance. I do not pray for you, no,
But to your spirit, one with the other saints.
O teach me how poetry must be selfless, let music
Be new in all that I write, O leave your mark;
Serene encouragement, hope in the purpose of dark.

Beginning

It is to be found half-way between sleep and waking –
A starting point, a recognition, beginning.
Think of the clouds on this planet lifted away
And the stars snapped off and the day tremendously breaking
And everything clear and absolute, the good morning
Striking the note of the day.

So it was and so it is always and still
Whether you notice or not. Forget that you are
Eyes, nose, ears but attend. So much must go on
Daily and hourly. Wait for the morning to fill
With cockcrow and petals unfolding, the round planet's power
Held in the hands of the sun.

And somewhere around are presences, always have been
Whose hands remove clouds, whose fingers prise open the sun.
Watch, learn the craft of beginning and seeing the world
Disclose itself. Take this down to a small thing, a keen
Whisper of wind, the sound of the cock or your own
Story that waits to be told.

I stood at a window once. I was four or five
And I watched the sun open the garden and spread out the grass
And heard the far choir of some blackbirds and watched blue
                                        flowers rise.
This was the first day for me, the planet alive
And I watched the stars' shadows grow faint and finally pass
And I could not believe my eyes.

TIMES AND SEASONS
(1992)

Grammar

Allow, admit the brave, attentive verb,
Be patient, watch it, keep a distance off,
Think of an adjective, do not disturb

The music as it comes but let it move
Around, among the words. Now you must curb
Intruding conjugations, hold them off.

Listen, permit a polished noun. No rough
Rhythm must ride or intervene or rub
And rinse away. Here is the leash of love,

The love of speech and the perfection of
A tongue that's true, an ear that is an orb
Round which the very stars have room enough

For music of the spheres which will absorb
The awkward sentences and make them live
Where prepositions dance and adverbs lob

Their meaning wide but leashed by 'but' or 'if'.

Parts of Speech

I Verb

Listen, the acute verb
Is linking subject and object –
Hear the links fall in place
And the sturdy padlock clinking.

A verb is a power in all speech,
Rings through prose and verse.
It brings to birth. Can't you hear
The first cry of awareness?

'I go', 'I forget', 'I exist'
By language only and always.
Blood cannot beat in a void
And the potent, fiery tongue

Offers the gift of language,
Blesses our lips and throats.
'I love you' vows and connects
And moves in a climate of tensions.

II Adjective

I'm a close relative
    Of nouns, I reinforce
Their moods and meanings, I live
    By running on a course

They also move on. I
    Live by music too,
The run and scheme and cry
    That rises to the blue

Taut skies. I qualify
    And temper every noun,
Enrich it, help it fly.
    I'm never on my own.

Say 'Love' and you must add
'Sweet love', 'dear love' and make
Your message deeper, lead
To love for its rich sake.

III Noun

I preen myself, I am a peacock word,
    I am a call, am one
Who does not need a tether or a cord,
    I dally in the sun

And in the life of grammar take a part
    That is a main one. You
Can never do without me. I'm the heart
    And teller of what's true.

IV Adverb

I qualify, I add to, I insist
     That verbs are active, go
About their business aptly. I exist
     Mainly to let them show

How graceful and how many-natured are
     Their meanings and their tense
Purposes. I show them how to wear
     Any experience

With a fine gesture. Yet I also can
     Help them to hide and go
Into small cells where they tell what a man
     Can shape alone. I show

Verbs they are needy on their busy own.
     I hand right clothes out and
Help them to speak a need or use a phone
     And how to understand.

For My Mother

I My Mother Dying Aged 87

You died as quietly as your spirit moved
All through my life. It was a shock to hear
Your shallow breathing and more hard to see
Your eyes closed fast. You did not wake for me
But even so I do not shed a tear.
Your spirit has flown free

Of that small shell of flesh. Grandchildren stood
Quietly by and it was they who gave
Most strength to us. They also loved you for
Your gentleness. You never made them fear
Anything. The memories you leave
Are happy times. You were

The one who gave me stamps and envelopes
And posted all my early poems. You had
Such faith in me. You could be firm and would
Curb tantrums, and would change an angry mood
With careful threats. I cannot feel too sad
Today for you were good

And that is what the kindly letters say.
Some are clumsy, some embarrass with
Lush piety but all will guide your ship
Upon a calm, bright ocean and we keep
Our eyes on it. It is too strong for death
And so we do not weep.

II Grief

I miss my mother today.
I went into a shop and saw the Mothering Sunday
    Cards in bright array.
I always used to send her one and now
    There is nothing to write or say.

    Grief can strike you when
You least expect it. It's an emptiness.
    Easy to fill with pain.
My mother had no rage, was always kind.
    When will she come again

And darken and haunt the large room of my mind?

III Her Birthday

My mother would be eighty-eight today.
It has been cool, no April fit for her
And yet, and yet, she always had a way
Of liking weather as it came. There were
No angry days for her,

No sky she did not watch and no downpour
That wasn't welcome in some way. I wish
I owned this quality. My mother's power
Lay in a gentle steadfastness. No rash
Judgments spread from her

And yet, although not witty, she would have
The perfect phrase for an unfit event.
When we were on a roundabout she gave
A straight look at 'hot gospellers' who went
By. 'Why should they move

'About like that with sandwich-boards which say
"Thy judgment is at hand" and spoil our fun

That's innocent enough?' I think today
Of words like that and wish her back upon
Her eighty-eighth birthday.

IV A Memory

Nothing is innocent,
Nothing unable to alter, to carry a word
    Of yours. Each element
Is charged with a copy of you or carries a chord
    Or echo of something you said.
Today in a blackbird's joyful cry I heard
    You speaking from the dead.

The usual memories
At the front of my mind are wholly happy ones,
    Your aim was always to please,
Especially children. You possessed innocence
    Yourself, were a person of peace
And now you have no control over circumstance
    But are part of the ironies

Of death and grief. One night
When I was a child I was crying loudly because
    I had seen a saint with a white
Veil on his face in a London cathedral. It was
    Simply guessing at the sight
Beneath that cover that scared me. My noisy tears
    Brought you. You switched on the light

And somehow quickly found
What was the matter. You spoke the right words at once.
    I heard the redeeming sound
'He'll be laughing at you in Heaven.' Innocence
    Returned and I was bound
Again within the safety you'd built. No defence

Is round me now. Those good
Words can start the flowing tears again
    And what once your words withstood
Is itself a cause for all the expert pain
    Your love healed once, and the mood
Of relief is altered, yet grief has become a gain
    Because it means gratitude.

V Sudden Remembrance

Orphaned and elderly and yet a child,
For so I am when thoughts of you return,
Return and batter me and I'm not mild
But close to tears and scarred for these tears burn.
You tamed me when most wild,

You comforted my nightmares, came and sat
Beside my bed when sleep was far away.
You were a healing presence. More than that,
You were a joy, a treasure, could display
High spirits when the flat

Dull mood took charge of me. You always were
Busy and quick and swift to suffer too,
But only now and then did I know fear
When I could see a troubled look on you.
Tonight you feel so dear.

It is a cold wet June, the flowers are blown
In tangled throngs, the charcoal clouds hang near
The tousled tree-tops. Had we ever known
So dull a June? I doubt it. How I care
For you. Where have you gone?

My faith speaks of another life and I
Find your nature a right proof of that.
A child, I'd have you crowned up in the sky,
And growing old I see your star well set.
O your death will not die.

VI Her Wisdom

The paper's badly crumpled. You a bride
Stare shyly, do not seem at ease with flowers
So strictly cut and, very close beside,
My father stands triumphant in full powers
Of thirty years. You hide

The look of fear, half-knowing what's to come
But only half because facts aren't enough.
Perhaps you thought of the new-polished home,
The wedding gifts. He looks at you with love,
Protectively. There's some

Hint of his patience. In his gazing eyes
His care of you is manifest. He would
Tell me years later he had to be wise
And wait for love's fulfilment for a good
Month and this defies

Our haste today and lack of thought. Also,
My mother, you were never much at ease
When I asked awkward questions. Later you –
Rightly now I think – told me it was
Fear of hurting. So

I learnt of sex and birth in furtive ways
With worried stares at magazines but now,
Thinking of childhood when you dressed my days
With paths and hedges, offering each bough
Of apples to me, I can only praise
Your care and wonder how

You stayed so gentle. I was stormy and
Quick to see a fault. You guided me
With love. In every poem I see your hand,
Your pride in those that did not need to be
Ones you could understand.

VII   More than an Elegy

What are you now then?
    A thought on the wind?
A balance of spirit and air?
    A released mind?

You are more, more than this
    Though sometimes seem less,
You are the pain death is
    And yet you bless.

Let me not intervene,
    Mark my shadow where
Only you now have been,
    Your spirit is there

Where at best faith carries the heart.
    You are both air,
And earth and you are part
    Of a disciplined fire.

Let my missing you be
    What sometimes prayer
Is when it moves free.
    Let me find you there.

But the daily truth is
    That I see most
In physical memories,
    You are never a ghost.

How curious love can be
    For now your death
Shows me how lovingly
    The voice finds breath,

The hands find useful things
    To do. O you are
The way a blackbird sings
    And shapes the air.

VIII Let Me Learn

Let me learn from you now
    Or is it too late?
The North wind starts to sough,
    Coal shifts in the grate.

Once in a white and high
    Nursery we played as if
The ceiling were the sky,
    Each hour all life.

You and my father came
    After a dance
Bringing bright favours home.
    It still enchants

To think of you young as then.
    Your face never was
Wrinkled with lines even when
    Death took its place

Within you, beside you, all
    About. I was dry
With sorrow but tears do fall
    Now. You don't die

Over and over but are
	Installed beside
The pile of books laid here,
	The lamplight wide.

You read in bed, I feel
	Your heart stirring in mine
And everything starts to heal.
	What a delicate line

Death writes when love was the drift
	Of a life like yours.
At all my fears you laughed
	And cast out their force.

There will be no wind tonight,
	No angry words
And at dawn a strong light
	And chattering birds.

Poems, praise, prayer –
	In these I find
Your gentle atmosphere,
	Your steady mind.

IX Her Gifts

Most you return when fear is mastered. I
In childhood trembled often in the night,
Lay huddled and afraid to turn my face
Curtained by fingers. I had no near light.
How far the day-world was.

I could have called. I never did but vowed
Next morning I would ask for night-lights or
A bedside lamp. But then birds sang so loud,
The postman was so busy at the door
That all the dismal crowd

Of night's imagined terrors disappeared.
But then from six to ten I often ailed,
Fell against trees, picked up most germs. You heard
My hoarse cough and immediately you sailed
Without a sound or word

Into my room like a strong ship and gave
Me warm drinks, puffed the pillows and then sat
And read to me. I never had enough
Of your soft voice, firm hands. You sweetly taught
Me then the Tale of Love,

Its patience and forbearance and the way
It laughs off dread. How rich indeed I was
From your deep mine of gold. It shone each day.
Now you are dead but memories like these
Have taught me to obey

The kind impulse to give, the wish to share
My books, ideas I read, the jokes I'm told.
In laughter now I find you are most near
And, oddly maybe, you are never old
But the young mother who cast out my fear
And kept me from the cold.

X My Debt

I had a lucky childhood. I was
A late-developer and so I lived
For untimed weeks and months in any place
I could imagine. I think you perceived
This joyous state of grace,

For I was left to play alone although
You were below or in the garden and
Kept me safe as I ran quietly through
So many realms of gold. I would pretend
That I was priest, would go

Through all the stages of the Mass and be
Priest and server. On a string I held
A train. It was a thurible to me.
Sometimes in the garden I would build
Castles in air. You'd see

Within the child's busy mind, my world
Which you defended from a distance. Now
I know that you saw much more than you told.
Before the years of doubt and fear I'd go
About my worlds, a bold

Ruler sometimes, sometimes merely one
Who settled for a while. What better way
Can poets be prepared? I know of none.
I still am rich today

Since you would honour childhood's lack of time,
Its ignorance of clocks and bells and hours,
Its fascination with the world of rhyme,
You were the one who taught me my best powers –
Those fields of gold, those silver hills to climb,
Those gardens full of flowers.

The Smell of Chrysanthemums

The chestnut leaves are toasted. Conkers spill
Upon the pavements. Gold is vying with
Yellow, ochre, brown. There is a feel
Of dyings and departures. Smoky breath
    Rises and I know how Winter comes
    When I can smell the rich chrysanthemums.

It is so poignant and it makes me mourn
For what? The going year? The sun's eclipse?
All these and more. I see the dead leaves burn
And everywhere the Summer lies in heaps.
    I close my eyes and feel how Winter comes
    With acrid incense of chrysanthemums.

I shall not go to school again and yet
There's an old sadness that disturbs me most.
The nights come early; every bold sunset
Tells me that Autumn soon will be a ghost,
    But I know best how Winter always comes
    In the wide scent of strong chrysanthemums.

On the Tongue

The tang and touch on the tongue,
The pause, the creep, the quick advance and then
    The verbs which we move among,
The nouns that alter their meanings again and again,
    The poem which turns to song,

The awkward adjective,
The thin-worn noun, the verb that seemed to grow stale.
    It is by language we live
For the senses falter, halt and finally fail,
    But in poems and only if

We pay attention and stand
Listening, whispering, relishing a word,
    A rhyme, we discover the end
And purpose of art, the impulse which has heard
    A message it can lend

And send us on with delight
And a soaring spirit which touches the furthest stars
    And makes a neighbour of night.
It draws refreshment out of dry discourse
    And animates dulled sight.

A voice said 'Let there be song
When words join music in an intricate dance
    Which yet won't lead us wrong.
Let there be happiness as a sure defence
    Against shadows we move among

And cannot wholly ignore'.
Yet I lift my pen and gaze at the heated day
    And am moved so intensely more
Than any human tongue can ever say,
    It is so quick and sure.

Protest after a Written Interview

They see you thus. You care and you are hurt
    At your self put on show.
How hidden its abasements, its wrung heart,
    How easily a blow

Opens the doors you thought were locked. They were
    Accessible to any
Who overruled a thought of care or fear
    Of ignominy.

So I am open and ridiculous!
    How pride can squirm at that.
My friend had saved me from all this, of course.
    I face the tit-for-tat

Of public criticism, fallings-short
    They understand too well.
I did not know my secret could be caught
    By any ready will,

And they are right. My work is not like me
    Though it's the world where I
Move, I believe, with right authority,
    But now I simply cry.

Yes, shed hot tears of childhood, waste my time
    By being laid so bare.
I'll get my poems in good dark shape and rhyme
    And always be armed there.

A Christmas Sequence

I Advent

Such movings, risings and such settings forth,
The world's astir with startings. Many go
From house to house seeking employment or
A room to live in. Voices everywhere
Are calling out loud slogans. War seems near
And there is easy fear.
Look at the mothers trying to seem calm,
See the sons and brothers who may be
Called up to go to war.

But this is also Advent, a good time
Once for a few and now for everyone.
A woman bears a child and carries it
Through the last month. She knows it is a son
And so does Joseph. Both are very poor
And their whole world is troubled. Romans have
Settled down and rule in Palestine.
Division, argument and pain are rife
But O a wonder's near,

A virgin girl is soon to give God life,
God as a man. How can we understand
That man can be divine?
We cannot but the centuries have told
This story as a fact and we believe.

O let us, even in our fear, join hands
As we think of a story that is old
Yet new each year. It is a mystery
How God took time and entered history.

II The Journey to Bethlehem

What is she thinking now
    As they ride through the cold
Toward Bethlehem? O how
    Can her God who is old

Or outside time at least
    Be growing in her womb?
This girl does not look blessed
    She fills so little room

Yet carries a new truth,
    A God whom she makes man
Will soon take his first breath
    And fit a lofty plan.

How can we not feel love
    To see such helplessness?
Our cold hearts start to move
    With an old gentleness,

Yet it is new also
    Since we are feeling for
A God who is to grow
    To manhood like the poor.

Listen, let Mary sing
    Her unborn child a cry
Such as all mothers bring
    To their first lullaby.

III The Contradictions

His life was always one of contradiction:
A young girl, still a virgin gave him life,
He taught not happiness but dark affliction,
He spoke for peace when all around was strife.
He was a God whose action

Stirred the first stars, designed the universe,
Invented time, made men and gave them choice,
They disobeyed and he undid the curse
By being one of them. An infant's voice
Is sheltering each of us.

He chose our lot, was only different
In seeing evil but not being it.
It was with little things he was content
And made a world where even children fit
For he was innocent.

He died to rid mankind of bitterness
Since all that he would suffer was unjust,
And he showed love where love so seldom is –
In dark, in pain, in death. He took our dust
And taught it how to bless.

IV The Shepherds

He is so small the stars bow down
    The fierce winds ease their breath,
And careful shepherds look upon
    The one unsullied birth.
They kneel and stare while time seems gone
    And goodness rules the earth.

The blight on man is all undone
    And there will be no death,
For though this child will be nailed on
    A cross, he'll be so since
He is the jewel of untold worth,
    For him all stars have shone.

V Hymn at the Crib

Lord of failure, teach us your success
At sending up a glittering star again,
Lord of anguish, show us happiness,
Teach us your mysteries.

They open every locked door and they melt
The icy heart. Child of heaven and earth,
Teach us to eschew the smallest fault
And let us love all innocence. Your birth
Is where great kings have knelt

And where the poor of heart receive all gifts
The universe can offer. Christmas day
Lights all hearts, the humble man then lifts
The pride of centuries up. In Bread he may
Find all riches. Shafts

Of moonlight join the sun and every star
Bows to a child, the one of such great price,
Through him we learn that depths of sweetness are
Found where God makes his son a sacrifice,
And he is now and here

Binding the past and future till we stand
Only in a present. Paradise
Was once like this and when at last we mend
Our faults we shall again show gentle eyes
And generosity, and understand
That innocence is wise.

In Green Times

Let the blossom blow back to the tree,
Let the wind be lost in silences,
Let my childhood wake again round me,
    Its sweets and violences.

Out of that white nursery I came
Into the garden green to wade in deep.
Quiet broke with calling of my name
    I acted half-asleep.

I listened to the bees. I felt the grass
Touch me softly. I would watch the sun
And every truant cloud that had to pass.
    I was at peace alone.

Nature was my shelter. All the berries
Plumped and showed their shining. I was there
In what could be a Summer's dream. Time's worries
    Found no foot-hold near.

And nor did mine. Perspectives happened later.
All my world was flat and full of green.
Mountains face me. Rivers mirror me,
I am all aware and frightened too
But I can't turn back pages now to see
    What once was green and true.

A Child Destroyed

I can do nothing but feel, I can imagine
The terror within the mind of that child who was carried
Away from a moment of play. What did she see
In her mind's eye? Was it a happy regret?
Crumpets and milk? The children's TV programme?
He held the stinking cloth against her mouth
And she must have smelt tobacco, dirt, male stenches.
She tried to scream. She kicked him and he gripped
Her legs together, pinioned arms behind her.
Again and again I turn to my own childhood
When fears were but imaginary ones,
My only pains concussion or pneumonia,
And they seem honours as I try to force
Myself into this small child's little shoes
And clean white socks, and soft washed hair, and then
I bring her start in life to bear on me.
She knew of love in night-time kisses, hugs
And kind hands holding hers. Now this large weight,
The man's cruel body forcing her to lie
Under his. I hear her small frock torn.
I hope by then she was unconscious but
She may have felt the thrust and heave of sex,
Smelt the man's breath, and then he gripped her neck
And twisted it as if it were a bird's

Or else a rabbit's. So our world behaves.
We have grown lax and comfort-loving, watched
The act of sex on big screens in the dark,
Have eaten, drunk too much. We are to blame
And this small, broken, violated child
Must be the scapegoat. I'm ashamed and hate
The helplessness I feel, my world's cruel work.

Shapes and Surfaces

Edges of things, surfaces, smooth grain of wood,
Natural showing of rings of growth when a great
Tree is felled. Glass blown wide and light
Seen in Murano, seen in the Pueblo Espana
In Barcelona. All these things I praise –
Nature working with man or man with Nature.
I've walked on sea-shores when the tide was out
And picked up pebbles smoothed by hands of the sea,
Laid them on one another and observed the different
Shades of grey. What a bonus given by creation,
The working of time and tides on rock and crystal.
Then I've seen our Cotswold walls built patiently
With stones that are tapped and shaped, and thinned to lie
Upon each other in harmony, in order,
With only cement on top of the walls to hold
The flat stones lying side by side together.

Turner saw skies like this, he levelled or left
Entirely alone, responded to puff and billow,
Storm and calm, stress and peace. Again
Nature working with time, with space that is smoothed
Or ruffled or blown like glass, like a cherub's cheeks,
Never the same shapes twice. Never the same
Shade of pink or purple or gold or green
Seen exactly the same again. What a palette is here,
What a hoard of shapes and edges, surfaces, levels
And roughness Nature organises. No doubt
The sculptor learns from this when he gives pure form,
A Maillol or a Brancusi.
Creation is on the move out there in the sky,
In the land, in the sea, and here in my mind and of course
All in no time at all in the mind of God,
Smoother of stones, sculptor supreme and mason.

But he left so much for us to complete, to enjoy
And to use and to offer others. There is no end
To rounds and squares, angles and circles, no number
To colours and light. O there is the sun itself
Sculpting tomorrow as now the moon is shaping
Surfaces I shall never see. I ponder
Light years away, away in every sense
And light also in every meaning I know
And in shapes and spaces that never can be counted,
Now and tomorrow and always long ago.

A Litany for Contrition

Dew on snowdrop
                    weep for me
Rain in a rose
                    cleanse my heart,
Bud of crocus
                    candle me to
Contrition. Far stars
                    shine from your great
Heights, and burn my faults away.
Half-moon emerging
                    from a cloud
Strengthen my spirit.
                    All Spring flowers,
More each day,
                    in this night now
Give me a scent of our sweet powers.
A shower of rain
                    wash me clean,
Let my spirit glow
                    for I have seen
The terrible depth
                    of dark in me.
Christ, you alone
                    can cure jealousy.

My Ships

'When your ships come in' – the words in the nursery sounded
Every tidal pulse, all salty commands. I thought of
The shell I picked up one day and put to my ear
And indeed I heard the tide in another key
But not in one less true. The real sea's
Grace-notes were there, I remembered
The jetties the little sailing boats were roped to,
The smell of the rock-pools, my legs covered in seaweed,
My eyes searching for prawns. I pulled at limpets
But they resisted as all those ships resisted,
Were anchored somewhere I had not visited yet.
In my mind the blue sea brimmed, I knew the islands,
The cliffs and archipelagos. Ships sailed by
With sails taut for a moment straining with wind,

Tussling with gales, plucky against the white horses
Which reared and toppled. Some later ships were slowing,
Dawdled under the sun and little breezes,
The yachts slackened their sails, even the steamers
Seemed to drift. Here was a maritime childhood,
A world of minerals, salt pervasive, my ships
Shadows on nursery walls. I watched their prows
As I drifted off to a moonlit, tidal sleep,
Sailed in, dreams not deeper than I had imagined
Only more foreign and excitable, only
More mysterious. I think the cargoes were words,
Hoards of adjectives, bales of nouns and sacks
Heavy with verbs. I woke to the shouting birds
Who sang all Summer under the nursery window.
All my world was broody with pollen and bird-song,
An inland burgeoning, gooseberries fattening, apples
Swelling and shining, but still the sea sang songs,
Hornpipe and heralding pipes, dog-watch and day-watch.

'When my ships come in' – prophetic words in a way
For what else is the roping and nailing of tea-chests but poems?
I know indeed the tug of the poem's tide,
Its being lifted and loosed at last on land
When the crane is drawn away and the sea subsides.
My ship is sailing still but sometimes it stands
On a motionless sea and it is motionless too,
As if at anchor. The sailors are sleeping, the storms

Blow and vex and heave in another quarter.
I try to sleep but a dream of sailing breaks through
My drowsiness. I cannot beckon my ships.
Their time is their own and no concern of mine
Or so it seems as I walk again through rock-pools
Savouring salt and iodine and brooding
In a world-wide dream of water.

Springtime and Easter

Love is leaping among the Spring's heavy branches,
Light torn from Winter clouds is forming new patterns,
Winning another year, another season
Of painful growing and delighted issue.
Light and music will come again after sunset,
Stricken clouds paling, darkening, disappearing,
Becoming the kindness of night-time, the later hours
Stretching out longer each evening,
Moving, dancing, pausing,
And the swallows returning, the hibernators waking,
The birth of the fledgeling, the cracking egg, the Easter candle,
So much occurring, so much enduring, so much renewal
And we are not ready, never are really prepared
For the love which whispered in Autumn, lay down in Winter
And is speaking now in a lark's voice shaping the sky
And singing the clouds away.

The love which hurt before it was spoken again
Dares to speak and we accept the pain
We know must arrive for if we surrender we always
Dare so much, risk a whole life almost
And some lack audacity.

We walked together under Spring-distressed branches
Thinking of words we did not speak, now and then
Touching finger on finger.
Then loosening the rosary of hands,
We let the light catch our mood, we heard a music
In skylark and swallow, in tumbling clouds and in rain,
Washing the world to beauty.
And we heard a voice crying 'Save'
And recognised its meaning
For we knew so much of repentance and of sorrow,

Anger and sorrow for anger.
We say 'make love' as if we thought that we fashioned
The movements, emotions, wishes, longings and hopes
And O we were open to so much sadness. I asked you
'Can it be worth it? Will this last?' You answered
Simply by taking my hand and smiling and saying,
'Listen, the breeze is lifting the laden branches,
The thrush is making his annual music afresh
And the breeze is the bold conductor. Have no fear
Of love which costs so dear.'

I suppose I did not understand you and yet
I had known the fulfilment of trust, the first confidence
Of love, and also the awe which love induces.
So I took your hand and stared in your eyes and whispered
'There was pain once and I was frightened but now
You teach me the pain is needed, as in Spring
Birth breaks the egg, clouds spill in rain and there
Is hunger for Easter and doing penance. I'm learning
That love is only and deeply itself when repentance
Issues out to the world which needs to be saved.
My heart is saved by you, my mind is thronged
By old discarded wishes but softly among them
A music of Spring is sounding, is rising.' We walk
Into and through and out of the wood and pause
Not for words and only uncertainly for music.
I think we are waiting for Spring to return our childhood
And for childlike confession and hope. It is hope we have lost
But love is singing, is so excited and we
Are only a little part of a greater plan
Enacted at Easter over and over again
When we stretch our bodies under the noonday sun
And worship a God who is pain.

This is the meaning for all the coldness, the fraught
Mood, the angry arguments – but then
These do not last, love as surrender endures
And sings and dances under the blossom and sunlight.
A hand of forgiving light is laid on our heads
And love does not fear for the night.

All this is partly a prayer a child once heard
And partly invented when Spring brought the good tide in,
Tide of stream and river, the white wash of blossom,
And the child understands without speaking the song of the thrush

And the pulsing nerve of the lark.
Here is Spring and Lent and here is happiness
Even though three crosses stand and wait for death,
One death especially, love has taught us it is
Our only salvation. Love needs a death and a death
Is a man and a God moving and dying in Springtime
But waking up and rising as stems push through earth.
A stone is moved, a rising is in the air
A human form is stepping along the grass.
It is walking as love always does, bearing a gift
And we take it as we have always accepted forgiveness,
Saying little but watching the bold sun lift
As the Easter footsteps pass.

An Easter Sequence

I The Start of Holy Week

How to be sad when the tulips swell in the wind,
When the hyacinth admires its own voluptuous smell,
When tit and sparrow, thrush and blackbird spend
Time out of mind building or singing well?
Yet this could have been the end.

The start of Holy Week was always full
Of quick excitement; enchantment, shouting, palms thrown down
Before a King who knew and tried to tell
That darkness comes, that suffering will crown
The hopes that meant so well.

I cannot make my mind dark but I can
Think of a death. I choose to force it back.
The shock, the dreadful pain, a pale-faced man
Who could or would not tell his sudden lack.
'It's all part of a plan'

Somebody said at the time and now once more
I can see the tulips glow, hear blackbirds sing
But know that life is mostly inner war
Until next Saturday when the stones will ring
On this beleaguered star.

II Holy Week

Time of water everywhere. The Spring
Sprinkles the land. There has been too long a drought.
Good drenchings come and brighten everything.
Time of water into wine and doubt
Flowering to faith. Birds sing

Matins and Lauds, O every hour indeed,
Bells ring, the spirit climbs beyond the sky
And touches a true Heaven. We have need
Of Eden, Paradise. All prayers fly
And we confess our greed,

Our lust and pride and anger, once again
Renew our trust, make promises we hope
To keep. O there is gladness in the rain,
We think of sorrow far beyond our scope
As Christ's wounds flower with pain.

III The Eternal Cross

He'll blossom on the cross in three weeks now,
The saviour of the world will die again.
He is the flower upon a hurting bough,
The crown of thorns and nails will give him pain
But the worst one is how

We go on daily wounding him and he,
Although he's out of time, still feels the great
Dark of betrayal. He's nailed on a tree
Each time we fail him. Suffering won't abate
Until the liberty

This God-Man gave us is used only for
Kindness and gentleness. Our world is full
Of dying Christs – the starved, the sick, the poor.
God sleeps in cardboard boxes, has no meal.
We are his torturer

Each time we fail in generosity,
Abuse a child or will not give our love.
Christ lets us use our fatal liberty
Against himself. But now and then one move
Of selflessness sets free

The whole of mankind whom he saw at play
And work as he hung dying, when his side
Was pierced. That spear was how we fail to say
We love someone, but each time tears are dried
It's Resurrection Day.

IV Holy Saturday

The open doors, statues are covered but
Soon there'll be flowers, a special candle and
Easter upon us. Daffodils are cut
And hyacinths blow perfume through the land,
But now we brood on what

The spirit freed from flesh can really mean
And how a resurrection happened. Death
Is emptiness, a vacuum. We have seen
Thousands of soldiers die this year, their breath
Stopped suddenly. Again

Violence, a short and distant war,
Conflict where Christ hung not long ago
Only but now and with us all and where
Our soldiers barely men were forced to show
A smile and not the fear

Which moved them most. Now Holy Saturday
Is the sweet smell of Spring. The land is rich
For celebration. Children dance and play.
Our thoughts of death will soon be out of reach
And all sin washed away.

V Crucifixion

Always the same and always new. The nails
Are hammered hard in every place we know
Upon our maps. Within all our bad wills
Our better choices echo. It seems so
Easy to see what fails

As someone else's fault, our parents' or
Some illness that we cannot prove was not
Responsible for deeds that we abhor.
And yet we have refreshing spells of doubt
And hate the subtle war

We wage within ourselves. We must look out
And Easter begs us to. It's blithe with Spring
When once again God's human body's put
Upon a cross to bear our suffering.
A little love can yet

Guide us to the place where other men
Copy the God of saving and take on
The unjust agony. Christ's holy pain
Is borne by his best children. Yes, the Son
Of God brings Easter in

When blossom covers thorn, when sweet fresh air,
Smelling of buds and leaves, compels us to
Honour this world that's not beyond repair.
Compassion is the only way to grow
And Christ is buried there.

VI Easter

Doubt has been so near all through this Lent
And also disbelief.
There has been war and its cold partner, death,
There has been argument.
War is close always now we move so fast,
And few are innocent

Except our children and also except
Nature run riot. Spring
Arrived so suddenly we were amazed
At its impulsive fling.
Resurrection is the mood and theme
And trust returns to sing.

But death still vexes. Many think it is
The absolute, cold end.
Yet even atheists feel hope and trust
And almost understand
Creation, order, purpose manifest.
Lord of victory, mend

The war-rent buildings and the broken minds,
The heart which cannot bear
More pain until it knows a God brought low
And almost to despair.
Quicken us, let us blossom and believe,
Risings are everywhere.

VII Easter Morning

Mary Magdalen

It was a good day with its panache when
This mourning woman walked into the garden.
She and two other women stayed when men –
Save John, his favourite – watched Christ leave his burden
Of flesh. She carried pain,

This Magdalen, but kept a little hope
And that is why she visited the tomb.
She could not know of life beyond our scope
Would raise him up. There was no longer room
Or time for him to sleep

And so he'd gone, but Magdalen could see
A radiant figure come and recognise
Her Lord and great forgiver. But when she
Came near he told her not to touch him. Eyes
Told her enough, set free

All grief and disappointment, so she went
To John and Simon Peter and they ran
A race toward that tomb. This huge event
Lit Nature up and showed how it began
And how all death was spent.

And so it is each year when Spring's about.
The Cross that flowered with pain must show a death,
A saving one to take away our doubt.
At Easter each breeze is a sweetened breath
When Christ comes walking out.

VIII The Ascension

Ascend and disappear but in what way?
How did this special man take on the clouds?
If he was God then God himself could play
With solar systems, see the frightened crowds
Look up, beg him to stay.

It is a mystery, and my creed declares
God made the planets, space and you and me,
Then every obstacle yields thoroughfares.
The chosen watched until they could not see
Him any more. Affairs

Against all reason, mysteries, miracles
Happen when we believe. Again last week
Christ took the clouds once more. My credo tells
Me this is so. Not mind but huge heartbreak
Has wrapped God-man away.

For Restraint

When will it come again
        An age when delight
Does not need to snatch or attain
        Possession at sight?
We have waited long enough
        For an age when love

Is not toyed with or only seen
        As something to own
And use. We have surely been
        Searching for pleasure alone,
Seen it as its own end.
        Let us understand

What we are searching for
        And when and why.
We are men who need to adore
        For whom one sigh
Can begin a near-perfect world.
        Love, it is called.

A Childhood Horror

I have pretended long, in loyalty.
I had a childhood hurt for five harsh years,
I let it wound my good fragility
And over decades I've shed many tears
And sometimes wished that I were wholly free
Of faith because it was to me all fears,

Unhappiness and, yes, grief for a part
That should be left untouched in childhood till
There have been many blows upon the heart.
I listened to the words within that still

Confessional. 'You must not be a part
Of the communion tomorrow.' Frail

I was and still a child although fifteen.
My only fault was large uncertainty
Of my faith's tenets. I had not yet been
Close to grave sin. A dark shade stood between
Me and the altar. Gone was liberty
Yet absolution had just set me free.

The priest was twisted, sick. I felt no hate
For children think they cannot change such things
Or run from them. Of course it was too late
When later I could tell all this. Love sings
Now in my spirit but when black moods wait
For me I cannot launch them on light wings.

God, you meant terror once. But maybe this
Brought me close to your mysteries. I knew of
Unjust suffering. Deciding this
I sometimes now am filled with boundless love
And gratitude from which I've power to build
Music, the poem and all they are witness of.

Beyond the Horoscope

What does it mean, this spirit? What do we owe
To father, mother, all our forebears? Are
Our bodies which can agitate us so

Shaped back much further than we see, so far
That genes are mixed in such strange ways that we
Quite understandably say that a star

Or a whole galaxy has helped us be
This person now and that one then. We add
The readings up till we begin to see,

Or think we do, how curiously we're made.
Our blood and bone and free-will seem to move
To purposes beyond our choice. We fade

And dwindle into death yet know dreams of
Sweet everlastings, dignities so bold
That we believe beyond our being old.

For Louise and Timothy

Two years between them. Now Louise is ten
Or almost that. When there is trouble they
Unite at once and run and hide away.
Is this mere chance or else a chosen state
When a dark shadow mars a happy day?

I've thought this over and I've come to this –
Gentle Nature makes these allies when
Trouble's about. Often they're enemies,
My great-niece and great-nephew, yet it is
A kindly instinct when they guard the pain

Of one another or of both. They are
So swift in their alliance that I feel
An almost tearful gratitude where fear
Joins them together. This is like a war
Which has its moments when one heart can heal
Another's dread upon this stricken star.

Romantic Love

I thrive on incompletion and, in love,
Demand a distance which I cannot reach.
I inch up to it and it's on the move,
I feel so poor yet know that it is rich,
It's always moving off.

I've whispered sometimes and heard it reply,
I've stalked it and it seemed to stay quite still,
I've made a clumsy speech when I should sigh,
I've learnt this is an honest way to feel.
O may it never die.

For it is only thus that love stays new,
Starlike and with no touch of mine to make
The tender enterprise remain its true
Untarnished self. My heart indeed may break
But not such love also.

The Word

Think how it's teased and troubled, made a part
Of speech. The word is wonderful and trim
And speaks for thought or else a broken heart,
Is sweet and soft to her while it galls him.

None is pleased always, yet in poetry
When lucent language enters perfect mind
And music is the gist of harmony,
The word is absolute, both strict and kind.

And, at such pondering, I think of how
Saint John spoke of the 'Word', how it began
And stayed and reined the present. Priests will bow

And say 'This is' and God is given to man
Who eats the Bread and prays within a Now
That's gone too soon and God knows why and when.

Meditation

What is this I and what are you? I say
In utmost faith that we can truly meet
And know each other, not on every day
And not on every path or in each street
    But as a blessing now and here.
        We fashion what we are

By will and by all things we love and those
Exempla, active models, soul and breath,
Losers of self, in part what others chose
To make of us before the brink of death.
    We feel indeed that we shall last
        And outstrip present, past

And make a moving future which the clock,
The plane, the ship, the car know nothing of.
However much we may pretend or mock
We are so sure that there's no end of love.
    Death is an edge where we must stand
        And not, hope tells, an end.

We tatter, fray, our patchwork's seldom whole
But, now and then, we are surprised into
The master of our own intrinsic soul
Which leads us where we've never learnt to know,
    Yet we can recognise the state
        Where our death has no date.

An Age of Doubt

They stay there on an impulse
A seed, a star, an explosion
And all creation followed on this, and design
Was really haphazard. I never shall believe it.
I stare tonight at a late-March sky and see stars
Distributed in patterns we have found
And named and taken over.
Atheists say with certainty all this started
By chance, that there's no maker.

Once, after a childhood full of trust
And hope and faith, I suddenly felt unsure,
Thought of the Holy Ghost as a huge bird
Which I knew did not exist.
After that, doubt followed doubt, nothing was certain,
I wanted my faith and trust back, longed for the sure
Days of childhood. They would not return.
For months, no, years, I lived in doubt. I read
Books of philosophy, they gave further doubts,
Ones I had never heard of.
This was the doubt of life, my late adolescence,
I thought that growing up meant loss of innocence,
Hated my altering body.
My mind, so wide once with imagined kingdoms,
Shrivelled and shrank to doubt of my own existence,
Let alone of God's or of another's.
My dear, delightful days of saying Mass,
Of moving in dreams of angels all about me
Disappeared and I was alone, one doubt
And not even sure of that.

Gradually, O so slowly and discreetly
Faith crept back, stars reappeared in patterns.
And what brought this about?

I was reading poems, falling in love with verse,
With Keats and his nightingale and Grecian urn,
With Coleridge and his Ancient Mariner,
Wordsworth near Tintern Abbey.
And soon I started to write my small attempts
At the art of verse. I entered a huge family,
A place where poetry sang and was applauded,
Where love was how a stanza whispered its way
Above a starlit forest,
And my rhythms tried to copy the tides' huge impulse,
Dover Beach, most of all.
And, unlike Matthew Arnold's, my waves came in
With ships of certainty putting their anchors down
And settling in the jetties of *my* country,
And I gazed at the full and half and quarter-moon
And the stars all seemed to surrender to obvious music
Conjured by poets making a potent song.
So I began to feel a little, O such a little
But so authentic a power, it altered my poems
Whose rhythms sometimes moved to the tide of creation
And felt the touch of a God.

First Love

I only felt it when somebody said
     'She likes you. Did you know?'
I did not and now thoughts ran through my head.
     My heart was touched also,
O but with so much tenderness and so
Much hope. About me all the new Spring spread

And moved in breezes I could understand
     But never could explain.
I did not even want to hold her hand
     And this love gave no pain,
Not even that kind sort we can't defend.
Here was first love. The world was new again.

Such sweetness lasted long and time had yet
     No power. I learnt of care
And joyous admiration, welcomed it.
     I did not need to share
Or speak of this. I had no wish to set
Words down about it. Love was everywhere.

How long this lasted I shall never know.
    Time and memory came
Together in an absolute sweet now.
    Enough to hear her name
And watch from far-off. On the Eden bough
The apple hung again. Love held no shame.

Today I shed tears longing to learn how.

For the Young

What have we done? What have we made for you?
A world of violence lies all around,
And you are now part of the violence too.
You can't do anything without the sound

Of beating drums and screaming yells. You are
Not used to silence but have grown up with
Natural discord, inner and outer fear,
Dark sky above you, loud noise underneath.

It is our fault but we have lost the right
To discipline you to a gentle world.
Often your love-making's a tender sight.

You cling as if you almost had to hold
The world in place. You throw a gracious light
And show quiet ways in which you can be bold.

The Start of the Universe: April 1992

They've heard the echoes of the starting stars,
They say, these physicists. I am amazed
And feel the sky is shrinking. Is it Mars
Or Saturn signalling? So they have blazed

A trail for us and some conclude this means
Chance is the master and creation is
A random happening. Yet each star leans
Upon our reckoning, and the galaxies

Shrink to our telescopes. I never thought
Creation could be easy or took place
In seven actual days. Now I am caught

Up with the physicists' conclusions, trace
Mankind's beginning to a wonder wrought
Aeons of echoes back, each one a grace.

Inner and Outer

It was always a danger to me, this inward-turning
Search between doubt and doubt, search for a truth.
In childhood, I think, came the first warning
When I told lies as stories. In my youth

Self caught me up and made me my own doubt,
My eyes turned in and were amazed to see
A kind of kingdom turned all inside-out.
It baffled me. I wanted certainty.

Now I look out, so many decades later
And cannot have enough of what I see
Up there, beyond beyond. I see a better

Proof of purpose in each galaxy.
Now every poem is a kind of letter
Posted to stars yet somehow sent by me.

Curtains Undrawn

Looking in windows down a night-time street
    In Winter, I don't feel
A *voyeur*, no, I only seem to meet
    Lives lived with love's good will.

There is a student with an angle-poise
    Lamp. He's hard at work
In happy concentration. There's no noise
    As yet and nothing's stark

Or ugly. I've a sense of neighbourhood,
    Of being near yet keeping
A proper distance. Now I find it good
    To think of children sleeping

With night-lights on. No doubt their parents will
    Later go up to bed
And make love without speaking. There's a still
    Design within my head

As if I were about to write a score
    To fit these modest lives
Where there are quarrels sometimes but no more
    Than small ones which arrive

Because we are imperfect. I walk on
    Under a full moon's stare,
Knowing that elsewhere crimes are done –
    Not here, no, never here,

And 'here' is much more usual, I believe,
    Than war and hate and dread
Since here are still lives where the trust of love
    Will never be quite dead.

Say I am sentimental. I don't care.
    The rooted tree of trust
I know is always flowering somewhere
    Where people still are just.

Maybe they could not tell you what they think
    Their lives are all about.
Philosophies grow cold, most dogmas shrink
    Here where hope's not in doubt.

Time in Summer

    Summer bedevils the clocks. They tick away
Into themselves. As heat grows stronger we
    Forget them, do not need them, breathe within
Another element. We are all space
    And easy air while the good time of day

Sounds from the stable clock or city chime.
The heat hangs on, a shimmering garment in
    The drumming air. We are but half-awake
And half-a-dreaming. We are moods of warmth,
    Our tepid foreheads are not damp with time

But with the season's moisture. Fountains play
Temptingly far away. A tiny stream
    Is loud with falling water. All's a haze
And we are mere suggestions, half-ideas
    That somebody may soon begin to say.

First Confession

So long ago and yet it taunts me still,
That First Confession. I was only seven
When I first knelt by that impersonal grille
And poured my little sins out one by one.
I never felt near God or any Heaven.
It was my thefts which made all that undone

Or never started. Certainly the priest
Was not unkind though he told me I must
Return those things. I think my childhood ceased
Upon that day. My spirit had been light
And happy for six years. I lost my trust
And learnt a little of the spirit's night.

From that day on this healing sacrament
Was hurting for me. No one's fault, it's true,
And yet I think the child's right element
Of joy should not be risked so early but
Left till youth sends doubt and darkness through
Flesh and soul and childhood's door slams shut.

Green

Green.
Green for our fear of what we have spoilt, from the turning
Wave to the grass that rots as we look, the roots
    Which break in the ground. What green-sickness there is
In the world we walk on; look up, too, from the edge
    Of a field to the centre of cities where pollution
Stands in the air, blows to the suburbs, then
    Runs through corn and fruit-trees, renders barren
The bushes of blackberries, fields of strawberries, all
    That we ate with relish, bottled once and set
On a high and treasured shelf. We have set ourselves
    Too high too often, thought we ruled the sky,
Owned the arable farmlands, had a say
    In sunlight, starlight, all that atmosphere
Was rich in once. Not any longer. We have
    Watched the foxes run and die, have seen
Pigeon and pheasant fall from the sky to our feet,
    And felt exultant. Almost too late we learn
Our lesson. We need a purity, a cleansing
    Ritual for the actual. We must unlearn now,
But all too slowly or else too hectically fast,
    That we must honour the earth and the flying birds,
Not spray chemicals on the delicate buds
    And poison the later fruit. We have been greedy
With land and air but also lecherous;
    We sow our seed too widely and in wrong places
So that we hinder a baby's growth, produce
    A handicapped race. We must be sorry and make
A fertile penitence, look about us, let
    Nature teach us once again. O can
We walk the difficult steps back to Eden garden
    And place the apple back on the poisoned tree?
Is it too late? Not if we deepen our sorrow,
    Give where we used to take, feed orphans, snatch
A million Christ-children back from the three-fold world
    Where the Holy Trinity broods with a lucky number.
So in a green dream of sweet fertility let us
    Kneel in sorrow, carefully plant our seeds
And exhale good air and leave it to others too,
    May the green, unpolluted waves turn over and over
Till green is the colour of safety and survival,
    And may green be our freshness for the last redemption.

Think Of

Think of a note
And a drop of water
Falls and splashes and
See the taut blue
And a cloud cruising, a
Golden shaft of
Riches and
Then comes a theme,
An easy drift,
A pluck on a harp, a
Call on a horn
And then see
In the mind's eye
In the heart's ear
In the reaching hand
And the beat of a heart
To a somewhere coming
Choir of angels
Where seraphs blow
A trumpet of sound
And a colour enters
Imagination's
Ajar door
And we are aware
Of a threshold crossed
Of a shadow woven
In webs of air
And more of all
Always more and more

Spell for a Dead Baby

You filled a gentle pause in air
　　But would not stay for long,
And yet you've left a magic here
　　Still delicate yet strong
Enough for us to think of waste.
　　We've racked our brains to find
A spell of words that suits you best.
　　They will not come to mind.
Then let this wish of ours at least
　　Serve to remind, remind.

Cold Words

I learn of love now that I've been betrayed
In such a little way. Friendship was more
Important than I knew. No words were said

But only wrong ones written. Why were there
No thanks, no greetings? When I am alone
Childhood is back and its hot tears are here

Burning my cheeks at midnight. I have known
Love-affairs broken as all of those who care
Have learnt. But I feel coldness to the bone

Because possessiveness had played no part
In this good friendship I'd known for five years.
Now I have lost what seemed a grace of heart,

A reciprocity and I shed tears
Because there is no reason for such cold
Shunning. I spoke little of my fears,

But much of my friend's life, I was not bold
And did not make demands. Why have I lost
What seemed so shared and kind? Let me be fooled,

Not cynical but still keep my whole trust,
That childhood gift I've carried from the past.

Ordination

For Richard Finn O.P.

Hats fit for a wedding. Here and there
A crawling child, a cry. There is a crowd
Rustling and waiting. They are gathered here
For an occasion that is kind and proud,
The centre of your life, another start.
Some are near tears and in my waiting heart

There is a stirring as, perhaps, I knew
When I first saw the sea or when I met
Someone important to my life. For you
There's love and preparation, no regret.
You smile, seem calm. Your friends are all around
But there's no silence. Every little sound

Promises what your future means. You'll pour
Water on babies' heads and speak their name.
You walk with Christ and you have known him for
Most of your life but now it's not the same.
You make hard vows, are taken up by grace
Which somehow spreads to all in this good place.

But there's also the largest gift of all
That you receive. You'll take the wine and bread
And speak right words and Christ himself will fill
These simple things. He rises from the dead,
He lets you touch his side but with rich faith,
Still wine and bread but all God underneath.

I've known you only for four years and yet
You asked me here. I see you smile. We take
Your blessing. All your free-will now will set
You on a course where there will be heart-break
And maybe doubt, though not for long. I wish
You peace and thanks as you give me God's flesh.

Star-Gazing

Give it a name. It is still there,
One on its own, another star
    Which is not yours and is not mine.

And yet we need to find a name,
To lay indeed a kind of claim,
    A beauty wrought to our design.

But we are wrong. We don't possess
The stars. Our words make them grow less
    As we waylay them to define.

They shine a love. Another one
Is there tonight. The Summer sun
    Left the horizon's steady line.

Think, there are more than we can count,
Star after star, O such amount,
    Each seems to flicker out a sign,

To hand a message. It is this:
'We are much further than you guess
    And brighter too. Yes, we combine

Distance and light to give a show
Like fireworks which retain their glow,
    We keep a rich unmeasured shine.'

The voices pause. I look again,
The sky is pouring silver rain
    Which could be yours and might be mine.

Light Between Leaves

The light between the leaves and under the leaves –
    Do not forget these,
The mouth which turns and touches, the eye which loves,
    Here are our ecstasies

Or some of them. They started long ago
    Back in our infancies,
Others came later when there was pain to know
    But there are always those

Treasures of kindness, comfort during grief,
    Learnt opportunities,
But now the Summer leaves are full of life
    And teach us mysteries.

Nothing is usual, nothing commonplace,
    Nothing easy to please,
There is a sky of comets in a loved face,
    A thousand astronomies.

The leaves are turning under an easy wind,
    The evening starts to cool
And love moves gently in a shared state of mind
    And comforts and makes us whole.

A Question of Form

The point is that a Monet does not move,
A Mozart clarinet sonata can't
Be seen or smelt. Art works by metaphor
And cool constriction. Cool means white-hot here.
By rule and lack of liberty art's meant

To work and at its best it does so. Last
Tuesday I was heckled by a boy
Who said that poetry never should be cast
In form, but come without control and fast.
I knew that all this had to do with joy

And pleasure. Why did I not think to say
Nature has limitations? Trees can't move
Away from roots. They only grow that way.
I said 'Form's not a jelly-mould to pour
A poem into. It can only say
Whatever is its message.' But I saw

That none of this convinced, yet Baudelaire
Juggled the senses. Language smelt and could
Taste, but still switched senses had to say
Their mood and tone in form. All art can play
But always is contained, leashed in. The good
Work of art makes laws it must obey.

Song

A violin waits for its sound,
    A poem for its word.
Listen, up from the ground
    Rises the lyric bird.

It possesses no instrument
    Save its own taut throat
But it offers us eloquence
    In a single note.

Remember the blackbird who
    Could not cease to sing,
The power of its voice grew
    Beyond Summer and Spring,

Beyond Winter and Fall.
The dumb violin
Is unused but the blackbird's call
Makes our world begin.

Death

How do we think and feel and sense? What happens
When we come to our death?
Is there a darkness or a purpose that opens
When we reach our last breath?
My creed insists that all that is good in us opens
And finds itself held with

A magnitude of thought, a wonder, a kind
Of world where we perfect
What went astray, what faltered and kept the mind
Tormented, unhappy and racked
On its own bad past. And so we are refined
And ready to connect

Spirit with spirit, but I cannot conceive
Of a state where every sense
Is no longer needed. It is hard to believe
In such a circumstance,
And yet my creed exhorts me to behave
In this world for the chance

Of living with its Creator. I'm thinking of
A time when I was ten
And went out in the dark, saw stars above
And felt drawn out of then
And there. I was upheld by a new love
And I do not know when

I was drawn out of that uplifted state
But when at last I was,
Even in childhood ignorance, I knew what
Is meant by gift and grace,
And now I think that death may be like that
Undeserved blessedness.

For under those stars my senses were set aside,
    I saw further than sight,
I knew an order then that would not divide
    My spirit from that night.
Within its lofty presence I could hide
    In joy outsoaring delight.

In the Beginning

In the beginning, on the first true dawn
Our lives began. No clocks or watches were
There to intrude. An aeon made a song,

Ten million years went by and even more
Until the angel came upon a breeze,
Bearing a message and the girl was there

Absorbed by calm, using free-will which is
The nub of our salvation. God was young
And slipped into our time, but all of this

Rested on her. The child was small among
All angry drifts but Mary kept her word
And it grew in her womb, was nine months long

Like us but not like us. There was no room
For him from the beginning. God could trust
Himself to our caprice, would know the tomb

And save us from the misrule of our dust.

In Praise of Giotto

Giotto, lover of tenderness, you were
The first great painter who showed man as man,
Not icon or pure spirit but entire,
For through the flesh the best compassion ran.

You taught this when you painted Joachim
And Anna, Mary's parents, standing with
Their faces close and intimate. In him
Was gratitude, in her, surrender. Death

You also knew was glad surrendering
Without a dread. So God himself was laid
Gently in his tomb, all suffering

Wiped from his face. You understood men prayed
And found right peace when they could speak and sing
As Francis did for whom the birds delayed.

For the Times

I must go back to the start and to the source,
Risk and relish, trust my language too,
For there are messages which need strong powers.
I tell their tale but rhythm rings them true.

This is a risky age, a troubled time.
Angry language will not help. I seek
Intensity of music in each rhyme,
Each rhythm. Don't you hear the world's heart break?

You must, then, listen, meditate before
You act. Injustices increase each day
And always they are leading to a war

And it is ours however far away.
Language must leap to love and carry fear
And when most grave yet show us how to play.

The Way They Live Now

You make love and you live together now
Where we were shy and made love by degrees.
By kiss and invitation we learnt how
Our love was growing. You know few of these

Tokens and little gifts, the gaze of eye
To eye, the hand shared with another hand.
You know of few frustrations, seldom cry
With passion's stress, yet do you understand

The little gestures that would mean so much,
The surging hope to be asked to a dance?
You take the whole of love. We lived by touch

And doubt and by the purposes of chance
And yet I think our slow ways carried much
That you have missed – the guess, the wish, the glance.

The Poem in Itself

The poise of time. The history of speech.
Articulation. Subject brought to heel.
The poem is filled and animated, rich
With hints and hopes, with how you wish to feel.

It won't be faked or ever forced. You must
Seek out its landscape even when it's yours.
The attitude for you is total trust
Not of your own but of the poem's powers.

It is a gift, a spell, a fabric wrought
Seamless. It also is a way to pray
By which I mean it's ceremonious thought

Spoken through you. You must not let it stray.
It asks for silence sometimes, won't be bought.
It's given, yet commands you to obey.

Parents

You are two, you are seven, you are ten
And never more than fifteen years or so,
You are always seen as you were then.
Parents never notice what you grow

Into in your twenties, thirties, more.
They lose the sense of time, ignore the watch
And chiming clocks. When you have lost the score
Of teens and twenties, they will never catch

Up with you. It is your task to keep
A bold pretence up, be the age they want
To see you as, be kind, forget the leap

Of time you made when you left home. Repent
Of ancient tempers lost. Within their minds
You have not changed but still are innocent.

Innocence

I almost loved you but in friendship's kind
And unpossessive way. Now something's gone
Wrong. An expert darkness fills my mind
But I can find no reason why my sun

Of gracious feeling has been shadowed with
Such unexpected night. Friendship has run
Into cover and a little death
Mocks at the very rigour of the sun.

Shall I write and ask what has gone wrong?
No, I feel it may bring some new hurt.
I speak low words when once I would have sung

For the pure issue of my ready heart.
All I can hope is silence won't last long
But waiting has become a new, flawed art.

Two Sonnets of Art and Age

I

Let there be orchestras for my last words
Or, better yet, no words but only sound
Diminishing, increasing like the birds
Rising and climbing from the dewy ground

Of dawn. I would hear melody and know
Someone, much luckier, may find words to fit.
Dying I would hear only the undertow
Of purest sound and the rich tone of it.

Names are for all the living and the young.
Young poets shall find words I never seek,
I knew another purpose for my song –

It told the story of how hearts will break.
The young are proud and agile with their throng
Of bold sensation praised for its own sake.

II

Let there be quiet, almost only still
Moments when I stop writing and begin
To know that pages wait for me to fill
Them with glad battles I was proud to win.

Battle with form and style, with metaphor,
Power over rhyme, an art grown very near
To prized perfection. While I wrote the score
I found I only learnt how I could fear

The noise of time, life's hurry, love's regret.
I filled up many pages with these things
And sometimes language seemed to take on wings.

Perfection was an end I never met
But O I loved the way that poetry sings
And feels most strong when sun begins to set.

Two Sonnets for a Czech Friend
For R.

I

Long ago she was a refugee,
My Czech friend whom I've never seen in rage.
We met in hospital. It seemed to me
She was not ill but quiet. Her own true age

Meant nothing for her courtesy was more
Like a good child's than someone grown-up, yet
Her discipline was wise and adult for
She suffered very quietly. I've met

Many with breakdowns or depression but
None like her who felt her country's pain
By hearing voices, sometimes throwing out

Her treasures like a tribute. Was she not
Living her country's anguish once again
  Who never once complained about her lot?

II

It seemed most suitable that my Czech friend's
Country should know a bloodless revolution.
She was invited to relearn her land's
Sights. She brushed her Czech up like a lesson

And seemed excited, eager to depart.
But when the time to go was near she would
Not eat or drink and on the day to start
She could not speak. It was because she's good

That my friend could not go back to her land.
It was not fear that stopped her but a mind
At one with all its pain. I understand

This now in hindsight. Still my friend repined
For all those deaths as if to lend a hand
By dying slowly with her own lost kind.

Poetry Sometimes ...

Sometimes you have to lead it by the hand
As if it were a child which you must teach.
Sometimes you write what you don't understand
Or only partly. Words climb out of reach

But for that reason, need not be set by.
The more I write, the less I seem to know
What this strange business is, since poetry
Like this, like that can come about or go

Beyond imagining. I only know
That it's not at my beck and should not be.
It takes me late or early, makes me grow

Up overnight. It is a way to see,
To learn, to celebrate. It's given too,
And uses me yet offers liberty.

November Sonnet

Spirit of place. Spirit of time. Re-form
The rugged oaks and chestnuts. Now they stand
Naked and pallid giants out of storm
And out of sorts. It is the Autumn's end

And this is Winter brought in by All Saints
Fast followed by All Souls to keep us in
Touch with chill and death. Each re-acquaints
Us with the year's end. Yet we now begin

A life of realism, watching out
For a red sunset, grateful for a dawn
Of rich light now. Tall shadows step and strut

Facing the big wind daily coming on
Faster. This is the season of right doubt
While that elected child waits to be born.

Water and Air

The eddy is a coil, a sliver, then
Gone to become a waterfall far off,
Perhaps a total brimming with its spume
When staring once can never be enough.

How time and space are one when water is
The drift and flow, the topic, later still
An image of all elements, a trace
Of almost a free spirit which we feel

As thought is felt in concentration and,
When you look up, you feel a world of strain.
The argument you hoped to understand

Has eddied elsewhere to return as rain
Cooling a forehead like a sea-dipped hand.
Water and air draw near again, again.

Beyond

The pith, the nub, the nap, the rough, the feel
And grasp of things. I praise what pleases touch,
Heartens the eyes, trances nose to tell
What ear awaits. I close my eyes to reach

The essence under each thing but I can't
Go further than the overcoat, the pile
That covers things. My senses try to hurl
Beyond but are set by. I wait a while,

Hoping that patience may invite the tall
Spirit of sky. Its stars alone I reach
And they should be enough, but I yet call

Vainly perhaps, the power that bows to teach
Meanings. O never mind, love's made of all
That leans to touch and finds its perfect pitch.

In the Nursery

We had no need of toys. Domestic things
Were transformed into objects used at Mass:
For thurible a tin train on thick strings,
A toy stove was a tabernacle. These

Were sacred in our game which always was
A serious one. We mumbled gibberish
Instead of Latin. So a holy place
Was once a nursery. A childhood wish

Enacts the strict demands of art. Also
It shows how far man's rituals reach. We were
Priest and server. From such small things grow

Religious awe and love of art. With care
We copied what we'd seen as, to and fro
The censer swung and all was hallowed there.

Out of Time and Season

What is this joy? It is like love again
And yet there is no object. This is more
Than seeking or possessiveness. The rain
Pleases, the sky is blue, April is here

But long before its time. Daffodils throng
Wherever there is grass. Birds carol too.
There is an inspiration in their song,
There is a sweetness now that passes through

My nerves and blood. But it drives further yet,
My spirit is engaged and I can feel
A power that is not mine search the sunset

And how I look at it. Upon me steal
Purposes out of time and so I let
Them have their way. They bless me and they heal.

Time and Love

It is all seasons and no time at ease,
The hour's evasive and the minute's in
A teasing mood. The sun is out to please
But later there's a moon which can begin

With its thin crescent, thoughts of love so soon
Waxing and then upon the wane again.
Today the sun is Summer and at noon
It was unthought of to suggest that rain

Was needed for the land. But love has needs
And it will barter childhood friendships and
Then be so kind, we think its telling beads.

O love is careful not to understand
Until the cooling starts. It shapes its creeds
For you and me and time runs through our hands.

Subject and Object

It is most rife in Spring, this sudden move
From mind to object with no space between.
It comes as an immediate act of love
When what is wanted is what we have seen.

Maybe all looking is a love-affair
And it was the Impressionists who taught
Most accurately how the eyes can stir
The heart and all that in between is caught.

So on this mid-May morning when I drew
The curtains back, the first mist took me by
Imagination's storm, so fast I knew

Subject and object are both one, and I
Felt, saw this happen and I say it's true
And I don't need to ask the reason why.

Left in Charge

For Anne

No ghosts haunt here or, if they do, they are
Kindly and gentle. When I climb the stairs
There are no creaking steps. I see one star
Greeting me through a window which lays bare

A happy street. Young voices come and go.
A train moves in the distance and it brings
Back echoing times when childhood days went slow
And sleep came quickly. All about are things –

Books, paintings, statues – chosen with large care.
Nothing is unsafe for the children who
Come often to my host who is elsewhere.

Her love has left this house to me. I know
Trust and joy which fill the scented air
Took quiet days and nights to stay and grow.

Trees

We took them all for granted, these bold trees,
Wandered in the pools of dark they spread,
Lay down in afternoons when not a breeze
Blew the oaks' curls. Always overhead
Huge parasols protected and with these
Above we did not move until sun shed

Its long intolerably hot light and
Moved down the sky like silent troops at last
Released from drill. The broad kind chestnut's hand
Lay on us like a blessing. As trees cast
Their deeper shadows we saw sunlight send
Rich oils upon the canvas of the west.

Oak, ash and birch – each has a character
Shaped by long knowledge of the heat and cold.
These are contemplatives when no winds stir
Their ample branches. They are also bold
In their defiance of the sun. They share
The wisdom which belongs to all things old.

August Heat

There is a feeling of farewells today
    Although the August heat is all around.
There is no fountain anywhere to play,
    We need the water's sound.

The very word of it reminds of sea
    And river unpolluted. Children run
Into tubs of water nakedly.
    They feel the sun upon

Their flesh as gracious though they need no word.
    So very far back it has always been
Since we were happy with a clear thing heard
    Or good things only seen.

The mood of metaphysics takes us by
    A rough hand when we start to grow away
From this sweet sensuous world. The half-orb sky
    We think needs words we say,

As if all honest happiness were made
　　By any expert way we think or feel.
It does its own wish, will not be obeyed
　　By words. O words can kill

When watchful meditation is enough,
　　Enough also the kindly fragrant air.
Why can't we be contented just to love
　　As children do? We are

Unwise and often know it. Now today
　　The feeling of farewells is sweet. It falls
When everything seems standing very still.
　　Even the soft bird-calls

Move towards evening. Surely we are made
　　For some place which endures beyond the hour.
We almost cry when day begins to fade,
　　Loss has so great a power

O let things go. They must. We cannot make
　　Anything stand or stay. Nothing is free.
We partly are but cunning love won't break
　　And only love will be

Left when the sun has gone and breezes come
　　And birds no longer try
To celebrate departures. Love's our home
　　No matter how we try

To turn from it and plunder and lay waste.
　　Even farewells must bow to it and go
Dwindling off. Even the mocking past
　　Right love can overthrow.

Living by Love

It should be so and can be so I say.
We walk in love but keep dividing off
The play of hearts from what was only play:

Our childhood did not need to find a word
But lived it through. Grown-up we wish to lay
A claim on love. In childhood it was bared

And could teach hurt but mine did not. The way
My nurse would teach or mother kiss my hand
Was how a love was sealed, passion away

Elsewhere. I wish that it were thus today
But senses let loose passion and it's hard
To tame it. Love once did not need to say

That it ruled me and I was not afraid
Because I wished to stand a world away
And only worship from afar. I played

Love on a high but gentle note. Today
It is too harsh and deep, though love's a word
I try to live by and my poetry

Keeps me enclosed, well-ordered and close-barred.

An Old Story

They are all true, the images and rhymes
That wish to speak of love.
Reason is magic, eternity is time's
Master. We try to prove

A love like ours was never felt before
Or never could excite
Others as it moves us. We've found a door
That leads out of the night

To a perpetual day. That huge sunrise
Is ours alone it seems
And so it is until that vowed love dies
And lives in others' dreams.

When I Was Young

When I was young I wrote about the old.
Now I am old I write about the young.
The words are cautious for a worried world
And out of them I shape a tell-tale song.

I was irresponsible and wild
When I was young but now the young ones are
Thoughtful and anxious though their eyes are mild
Even when they speak to me of war.

They are prepared and do not blame the old
That many have to make the street their home.
I warm myself at their kind hearts. The cold
Shivers through me now long dark nights have come.

O but there is a joy that I would speak.
I have a dream and turn it to a song.
It is the only home that I can make.
Its doors are open to the careful young.

Movement and Meaning

Language is always on the move
    Its meanings will not last for long
We try to call it back when love
    Beckons us to shape a song.

But it's impatient, will not stay
    Or be at any beck of ours
And yet it's we who help it play
    And change the purpose of its powers.

It limits us for it's precise
    And hates the superficial guise
Of novel meanings, has a nice
    Neat purpose, will not generalise.

It flies higher than a kite
    And dives more deep than submarines.
If we take care, its yoke is light
    But if we falsely generalise

It moves away and closes like
    The shiest mollusc in the sea
But when we are expert to strike
    It opens to us instantly.

In ballad, dirge or lullaby
    It moves to measures which we find.
It puts a meaning in a sigh
    And heartbeats in a lucid mind.

Leavings

Going again and you
    Staring at me. The sky
Is a cruel blue.
    When will you and I

Get used to a probable trust,
    Be sure this is not the end?
Some love is always lost.
    Neither lover nor friend

Turns to look around
    After their seeing-off.
But when one has returned
    There is increase of love.

Witchery

I know witchery
Of words. I've seen them grow
High as the sun, or low
As trees' roots. Nature is
A kind of magic. We
Never get used to this
Power that's only hers.
She hides her purposes.

Sometimes in love or thought
I've felt my heart beat so
Fast I could not tell what
Had caused it, yet I know
It was a kind of spell.
Seers go direct
To what all thinkers must
Find with patient skill.
O, love, the world is tossed
To us. It will not spill.

A Father after his Daughter's Wedding

What was an instinct turns to vivid loss.
    The girl is married now,
His only daughter will not come across
    The threshold to endow
The home with joy and trouble weariness.
He would take all. A little happiness

Shaped at her birth and growing every year
    Seems precious now indeed.
He would disperse so often any fear
    Of any sort. His need
Is greater than the one invading her.
He is not jealous, no. He wants her life
Without him to be joyful, yet it's grief

Which he now feels. He has a little son
    And loves him but in ways
Quite different from the strong and urgent one
    He felt for her. His days
Are now a little empty but he will
Say nothing for he loves her mother still

In body and in spirit, and he draws
    Nearer to her. Their son
Is to them both often a careless cause
    Of worry. Life strides on
As love twines in and out in its quiet dance –
A gift, almost a fate, and yet not chance.

The Happy Regrets
Last words for my mother

Who knows how much I owe? So many things.
You had no rage but always could calm mine,
Were always ready with your comfortings
And also ready at pain's slightest sign
And as though with wings

You'd fly and fold me in your arms. When I
Was ill you once kept up a fire all night
And scarcely slept. At any childhood cry
You came with comfort. You had blue eyes bright
With wisdom. Now you lie

Under a small rose tree. It's April and
Your birthday has just passed. I thought of you
Last night and wished that you could understand
The gratitude I often could not show.
You were the one who'd mend

Misunderstandings. Sometimes people took
Your love for granted. I regret the days
When I was thoughtless, too lost in a book
To notice your compassion. Now your gaze
Comes to me when I look

At children being comforted, at old
People who have no words to tell their need.
You had the gift for finding seams of gold
In most unlikely purposes. You freed
My mind, made my heart bold.

You died in Winter eighteen months ago
And it was unexpected. I am glad
You never knew long pain. I want to show
How you taught guileless love and I am sad
Tonight I can't say so.

FAMILIAR SPIRITS
(1994)

The World We Made

We were aware of everything but ourselves,
    Listened, watched, and thought
We did everything totally, never by halves,
    Intricate kingdoms were wrought

By the network and depth of our imagination.
    Everything that we saw
Or heard or touched or smelt was part of a passion
    And we were alert to awe.

One day we put a little cochineal
    Into an eggcup and
From it made a world which was more real
    Than the one which was close at hand.

The god we worshipped we named Cochineal
    And he was a Sun God.
We shaped a totem pole and painted all
    The angriest things we could

Think of on it – red faces, skulls and knives
    And round it we danced, of course.
Upon such games as this a childhood thrives
    And builds up such a force

Of memories, foretellings, wise delights.
    Everything had a place
In our dervish dances, our cardboard swords, our rites
    And all had an odd grace.

  Maybe because order was everywhere
    Nothing was meaningless
But my father was troubled and one day said,
    'You are Christians, you know.' His distress

Was something that we could not understand
    Yet trespassing on our world
He had overshadowed and spoilt it for us and
    Our fervour soon grew cold.

Our Sun God stayed in the sky and somehow had
    Lost most of its power.
Of course we were grateful for it when it shed
    Its heat upon us but our

Religion had foundered on what we did not know
    Was called reality then.
We forgot our dances and rites and started to grow
    Like the dullard rest of men.

The world outside us hadn't changed but we
    Found imagination was
Something to do with art and poetry.
    Our great world came to a close.

Cochineal was drawn back to a bottle
    Of colouring essence, our pole
Was lost in an attic while we ourselves had to settle
    Down in a world not whole

Or satisfying or orderly while we
    Shrank into teenagers who,
Conscious of little but themselves, aren't free
    To dream but must learn to know.

The First Music

What was the first music
After the chirping of birds, the barking of foxes
After the hoot of owls, the mooing of cows,
The murmur of dawn birds, winds in the trees?
Did all these tell the first men they must make
Their own music? Mothers would lullaby
Their babies to sleep, warriors certainly shouted.
But what was the first music that was its own
Purpose, a pattern or phrasing, a quality
Of sound that came between silences and cast out
All other possible sounds? It must have been man

Singing in love and exultation, hearing
The high sweet song of blackbirds. When did he fashion
A harp or horn? O how much I would give
To hear that first and pristine music and know
That it changed the turning planet and visited stars.

An Uncle and Godfather

Uncle and godfather, how patiently
You read my early poems. You were upon
My level too for your attentive mind
You gladly brought to bear on every one
Of my young verses, called them poetry.

All those ambitious ballads, sonnets, odes
Which I most valued you would read but yet
Told me a four-line poem which was based
Upon a dead bird I held in my hand,
Was in your careful judgment far the best.

Slightly disappointed at the time,
I knew when I grew up that you were right.
You showed me truth's the heart of poetry.
I owe so much to your clear, kind insight.
I learnt from you that rhythm, form and rhyme

Are at the service of what's deeper – craft
Was an essential to all poems. You had
Once published a small volume of your verse
And lent your findings to a small child's gift.
Today imagination throngs my head

As it did once but discipline also
Curbs and refines it. This you taught to me
And never told me how bad most poems were
When I first wrote them. You saw poetry
Was present in those four lines and would grow.

Our Maids

Our maids did not have names like my friends' names.
    How snobbish that seems now!
Sometimes they joined me in my private games
I never knew that they had not known how

It feels to be a child until eighteen.
    Elsie stole and I
Recall my mother saying it had been
Hard to sack her. She saw Elsie cry

But I did not. Lily Lovegrove had
    Strange habits. Now and then
She'd have a fit of rage when she felt bad
And used to slam all doors, but always when

She had a holiday she'd bring us back
    Kind presents, sweets and toys.
She'd never known her parents yet the lack
Had left her generous. When she talked of boys

She never said that she had been admired.
    A child easily
Accepts the strange, the odd. I never tired
Of simple stories Lily told to me.

Then there was Ivy. Ivy got the sack
    For seeming to pollute
My mind although I did not know it. Back
My mother sent her, said 'she did not suit'.

And so when I was six or seven I had
    Learnt much about odd ways.
Not one of our maids had been really bad.
How wrong for them – and us – were those 'old days'.

Slow Movement: Autumn

Falling, golden falling of brown leaves,
    Slow sunsets, still long days though they diminish,
    A time of memory of childhood years
    And picking blackberries, I now remember,
    And dreading school. O treacherous September,
    I cling to you as leaves do to the branch

Until a long, slow wind insists they go.
Mid-August's Summer still but at its end
Days grow a little shorter. Every year
In August I am moved back to the time
Of school's commencement. How I used to fear
Cold mornings and bleak lessons. Then began
A melancholy never known before,
Sadness which only those who've been in love
Understand fully. Yes, a touch of sadness
Came to me in September every year
And it's grown into me, is now a habit
So that I dread a non-existent school
And long-gone lessons every new September.
O falling season, Autumn sadness, use
Sounds like the touch of bows on violins
Moving within me, telling me once again
About the Autumn and how it begins.

A Cliff Walk in North Devon when I was Twelve

I was walking along a cliff,
It was late afternoon and a cool wind blew my hair,
Below was the casual sea in its commotions,
In and out, out and in as if
It would catch out the very tides.
I could see the wet sand and slowly appearing pools
Where my grandfather caught netfuls of prawns while we,
My sister and I, caught four or five between us.
But that day I was happy alone and walking along
The high cliff. I breathed the healing salt,
Stared at the sea moving and suddenly had
Such a sense of exaltation,
Such certainty that all was well with the world
And I was one with, at ease with everything,
Reconciled to the humdrum hurts of life,
Knowing for certain that some invisible Power
Had fashioned the turning seas and the tides and moon
And made me for some purpose as yet unknown
But something, however small or large it was,
Only I could achieve but need not hurry.
No, must not hurry but move in accord with tide,
Collecting the changing moons, being grateful and glad
That for a moment or two I could see creation
Planned and purposed and somehow achieved by love.

Sky in Childhood

A child, I watched the sky and said 'Up there'
    And 'there' meant Heaven for me.
I could imagine saints, long row on row
    And angels' minstrelsy.

Grown-up, I read of aeons away and of
    Star beyond star beyond star.
Yet this says nothing of my God-man's love,
    It only causes fear

And vertigo. Last night I thought of this
    And strangely once again
I thought of angels and of Mary's love
    For her new baby. His

Power holds every star within its place
    And all the energy
That causes every cell to move, since grace
    Is vaster than gravity,

More wonderful than any star or sky
    And just as bright to see.
Near Christmas now one star is breaking free
    And all grace is nearby,

Ready for us to take and feel delight.
    Heavenly star, you show
Time does not matter on this holy night.
    Man's spirit is aglow

And there is surely 'music of the spheres'
    If we will only keep
Silent for it to drive away our fears
    And orchestrate our sleep.

Camp

We catch up with emotions later on,
    Those of childhood I mean,
My first rejection by a friend is one
Of these. My memory holds the time and scene.

A child of twelve, I went to camp because
　　A friend insisted I
Should go. When we arrived she quickly was
Off with another girl. I hid to cry

For it's a rule at school that you don't sneak
　　About your hurts but my
Sister found me. School codes let you break
The rules when blood's the bond. I was told I

Could go into my sister's tent but with
　　An acted courage then
I turned that down. Still, trust had found its death
And I know now it could not live again.

First Love

Does it die wholly, that first love which is
　　So selfless and so pure?
It does not ask for reciprocity's
Proud demands but worships from afar

And asks for nothing. Yet it alters all
　　You were and makes you grow.
This surely was man's love before the Fall.
It teaches happiness you did not know

Was possible. I can remember how
　　A school-friend said to me,
'Emma likes you.' It comes ringing now.
That love which bound and yet meant liberty.

A Way to Imagine

I painted a house that morning
I coated the walls with yellow stucco and how
The sun made friends with it,
I painted the door dark green and the window shutters
Sported the same colour.
I planted a white rose to climb that yellow wall
And placed a fountain eight yards from the door.

I looked at the huge sun and the blazing blue
Of the hot Summer sky,
I heard some children singing but could not see them,
I heard a blackbird singing with happiness.
I saw the house owner drive away in his car,
I dipped my hands in the fountain's pool and then
Took one more look at that delightful house
And with scores of birdsong breaking upon my ears
I walked through the front door.

My Father's Father

I never met my father's father who
    Died in his fifties when
I was very small, say one or two;
Later my mother said he was a man

Of gentleness whose presence filled a house
    With comfort and with peace,
He never lost his temper or let loose
Disappointment. He put all at ease.

I wish I could remember all of this.
    His wife was different.
She lived with us for years, would nag at us
And often spoiled my mother's happiness.

She seldom was upset but one day I
    Saw her at the door
And she was obviously about to cry
And run away. My father stopped her there.

But she adored his father, loved to have
    Him staying with us. How
I wished that I had known his gentle love
And, so much later, wish it even now.

Blood Bonds, Family Feelings

It's in the blood and yet it is much more.
It's sympathy and pride. It will not have
A sharer criticised. It is a shore
On which encroaches one huge body of
Power reined in and then released. This love

Fits no one definition yet it grows
As bodies do. Its spirit is the way
Gifts are repeated, looks are shared. It knows
The constant ebb and flow of amity.
Loose anger on one member and it shows

Immediate affiance. I recall
Childhood moments when my sister would
Boss me about and yet would never fail,
When others criticised, to be my good
Defence, a kind ghost in my neighbourhood.

Cousins, Aunts, Uncles

Not close enough for vows or bitter words
Yet near enough for family blood to matter –
I think of those my cousins I've not seen
    For years, and some not ever,
And wonder, if we met, our family cords
Would bring us near at once, or maybe never.

I do not think embarrassment would make
A barrier yet maybe guilt would find
A place, some guilt I mean that we have stayed
    So far apart. Maybe
There would not be a sense of 'old time's sake'
Or merely wonder that our family

So large in number never has been close.
The only aunt I really felt near to
Died first of all the family although
    She was the fourth of eight,
A loving humour rose in both of us.
Maybe for all new meetings it's too late.

My mother died two years ago when I
Was ill and so not at her funeral.
Her nature knew no bitterness, was kind
    But sensitive and shy,
Childlike and gentle. She would always find

Intrinsic worth in people. If she were
Alive today I think that she would bring
Us all together, uncles, cousins, aunts
    For she would keep in touch
With all the family. If she were here
Today, each one of us would be in reach.

Old Friends

We are children still to one another
    In what we say and don't,
Closer than blood-bonds ours seem and together
We enter many worlds as was our wont,

We speak a language that is private and
    With it enter places
Few of our relatives can understand.
We find in friendship many kinds of graces

Which passion can know nothing of because
    The flesh is so strong there.
Yet some too of the sweetness which love knows
Moves around us like this Summer air.

In such a season long ago we would
    Play our religious games.
We knew indeed the measure of our God,
Yet worshipped him and gave him many names.

Now through five decades we have come again
    After lost years, O yes.
But now upon our friendship there's no stain
And we together shape a steadfastness

For as we talk of 'making friends' so do
    We make a mood and home
Which can surprise us sometimes and be new.
We mint gold wisdom for our friendship's sum.

A Realisation

It is only today that I
Have suddenly thought that I have no one who
    Cares for me totally,
No one to whom I come first. There are a few
    Who think of me, certainly,

But there is no longer one
To whom I am the world, the centre, the heart,
    The headstrong noonday sun,
And of course I too love many who play a part
    In my universe, but gone

Are the one or two I've known
With whom I broke the Galilean claim.
    Who were the suns which spun
About my earth. Yes, I have none to name
    For whom I'm the only one.

A Coffee House

A little boy of twenty months. He fits
    Exactly into space and floor.
He runs a few yards as his mother sits
Talking but she's soon after him. What's more

She wears an anxious frown. He's full of glee
    Not knowing how we all
Share in watching over him while he
Laughs loudly. He knows he will not fall

Although he hasn't moved about for long –
    Fair hair, a smile of grace.
If he knew one he'd sing a morning call
But there is worry on each watching face

For this year one horrific murder was
    Done by two boys of ten.
Our minds are full of that and all its loss.
When shall we laugh with children once again?

Bicycles in Summer

You could not go today. It is not safe.
I mean those Summer afternoons when we
Left home at two on bicycles to go
Through lanes, along the highways, then beneath
Deep dark of oak and chestnut. We rode with
Absolute confidence, alert to all
We saw. We took our swimming things and buns,
Bottles of lemonade, our port of call
A Norman church lit now and then by sun's
Reach through the leaves. Then on and on we went
Not saying much, in pleasant mood. We would
Undress beside the Cherwell or the Thames,
Both unpolluted, and jump in and swim,
Splash and go beneath the water's surface
To glimpse the sun's fall, then reach up and out,
Rubbing ourselves with towels, on bikes again,
It was a pastoral childhood that we knew
A child can't have today. It is not safe
To let our children out alone for hours
Like two to seven. Darkness falls at noon,
The dark of roaming men intent on crime
But we were lucky in our Summer days,
Lucky in losing every sense of time,
Lucky in feeling warm from towels and sun,
Loving old churches, following the Thames,
Learning the world by love and childhood games.

Sea Music

How to catch it, how to find the deep
Accurate notes, how to show the way salt smells
And how the tide drags and raises, pulls down
And then lifts up and curls and falls and slides
Like snow beneath skis, like agile drifts
Of some crêpe-de-chine falling over and down.

Can anyone catch for mind or instrument every
Tension and release, every gesture and slow
Kind movement? O I watched it for an hour
Thinking of last night's moon and finding it hard
To believe that power and invisible plucking. Tide

Was coming in, dragging the sea over shingle,
Riding over every rock-pool, recording
Its echo music. I think I almost had
The right word then but it slipped from my mind
Though music was all about in its own order.
I listened entranced, I stared at the ruled horizon
Knowing the notes were falling out of hearing
And that I would never find orchestral words
Or catch the sea though I was near it in childhood
Standing on breakwaters, paddling in the rock-pools,
My mind at one with the tangy exuberant air
And the heady, salt-laden breakers climbing around me.

Among the Stars

I walked into our garden one Spring night,
    Warmth moved among the trees,
The stars were plentiful and in their light
I felt an exaltation such as is

Offered at times but never earned. I was
    Caught by a wonder which
I'd never heard of. Now it is a grace,
That night the very Heavens seemed to reach

Down to my stance. My spirit and my flesh
    Were one existence then.
How often since has such joy been my wish
As then was granted to a child of ten.

It is not True?

It comes to me at midnight it is true
We don't believe in death. It can't be so
Or not for those we know as me and you.

It is a state, a happening, an event
For those who're strangers to us. Death is meant
For others. In newspapers in dark print

We read of great ones going. We think of
The fact a moment, then turn back to love
And care and all the ways that we must move

To work, to play, while death goes on elsewhere.
It is a message carried through the air,
Something that happened when we were not there.

But wait, a day arrives when someone close
Is taken ill and dies. We feel the loss
And thoughts of our own deaths return to us.

My mother died two years ago today.
I often think of questions I could say
That only she could answer. She's away

But where and how? O love, we quarrel and
Neither will speak. Then one puts out a hand
The other takes. We start to understand

Our final goings and we are afraid
And I, not you, believe we are not made
To go forever. When we often said

Death is not true, I think we were in part
Precisely right. When we make works of art
We think they'll last. O when did mankind start

To think of death as somehow to begin
Our lives a different way, to start again
And live life flawlessly? Our minds move in

Countries untried but waiting for us. Love
Conjures up lands which death knows nothing of
And forevers are convincing proof,

And hint at lastings. Love goes further still,
Suggesting we have spirits death can't kill.
O love I am afraid of this as well.

Cities: Their Beginning

First it is a city of the heart.
In some far-back imagining there is
A place to wonder at, to stroll through and
To be acquainted with great craft and art.
Cities are places makers understand,
    And so from fantasies

A real place is built. The architects
Consider light and shade, the climate too.
Dreams are drawn down to possibilities
And men consider little human acts
And needs. The greatest cities always please
    But must be makeshift too.

For we, the dwellers, are untidy and
Wreckers also. We are proud to see
The spires and towers, pigeon-haunted squares,
But we are not designed and never planned
Except in minds of wise men who split hairs,
    Yet sometimes we can be

Visionaries for an hour or two,
And in those hours our spirits rise to heights
And show our city is a magic place.
And it is then that artists have to show
Order, renewal, moments filled with grace.
    It's in moon-flooded nights

That now and then we fit our aspirations.
Children are lullabied, quiet love is made
And windows are flung open to the stars.
Cities then fit our bold imaginations
And in the symphony of distant cars
    Our souls are strings well-played.

Unto the Hills

Mountains for wise men – how I see them glow.
With good red sky at night their peaks are crowned.
Moses and Jesus have climbed, lesser men too.
What throngs of thought have risen from the ground,
    What findings of what's true.

Is it coolness which refreshes minds?
'Mine eyes are lifted up', I understand
That in heights of cloud or mountain I may find
Peace and wisdom. Spring is close at hand,
    Whose light clears and can blind.

Love Whispered

Love whispered to the tide-out
And sang across the wet, reflecting sand.
We were holding hands and murmuring not words
But sounds of supplication, lyric graces.

I have learnt all this from the ocean
In lessons of tide-in and tide-out
As I think myself back to first childhood
And beyond that to floating in kind water
And love that made me and launched me
Into the salt seas of now.

Almost

It almost was not. That is what I say
About this minute coloured by the sea,
About this chestnut losing its huge hands
About the boys who pick the polished conkers.
This almost was not now and setting sun
In pink surrenders, scarlet streaks foretelling
Good weather certainly. Now,
I celebrate the clothing of all these,
Their singing and their colour and this now
We stand in peacefully as night intrudes
In kind dark dusk. O celebrate with me.

Squares and Circles

I couldn't paint it that day
Nor the next nor the next nor the next
But on one clear Winter morning
I saw my scene of September
In bars of light and squares of yellow
And dizzying circles of red and orange
I quickly opened my paint-box
And put down the colours exactly
And in between the circles and squares
Smiling children were shouting,
Laughing and playing with shadows
Just outside my picture.

Genes, Likenesses

What is this in me called spirit or
Soul or being, self which I call me?
So many qualities I owe to more
Than one ancestor but my self is free
Of them. It knows of law

And duty, choice, responsibility,
Yet it is dressed in clothes much like those of
Some member of my huge past family
And closer ones whom I know best through love,
And then there's liberty

Whose boundaries are often hard to know.
My voice, my eyes, my hair, my shape of head
Are easy likenesses to see although
They are so mingled, but my present need
Moves further, deeper too.

My spirit's part of my imagination
And also part of thought and memory.
Then there are ways of feeling, also passion.
Can spirits look alike? Is soul not free
To be unique and its own revelation?
I say my history's me.

After a Film called The Bridge

he looked at the forms
          and colours of the
                         young woman
               standing on a
                              bridge
she turned her head and
          he looked at her
                         with passion
she was coy and twirled
          her parasol
then turned her back
          on him

in his sketch he jotted
              down what the sun
              showed
        which he would complete in oils
here were two sorts
              of desire
the painter's to capture
              the roving sun on
              a figure
and a man and a woman
              held in a
                    different wish
        did they know even
                    then
        in a matter of only
                          seconds
that they must undress
              and lie in each other's
                    arms
part of this at least
              was gathering their
                    senses together
but he was seeing a
              woman in lights and
                          shadows
        in circles
              and squares
                    in glowings
what would they do
        when the sun went down
                    at last
would they make love
he would certainly one
              day paint her
the act of love seemed
              part of the act
                    of creation
in colours upon a canvas
the sea was coming in
        I turned away
        like an intruder

September

When I woke up, the window
Showed me September, told me
Of crisp leaves being toasted,
Of days closing into their envelope,
The envelope placed on a table
As we thought of bed-time and children,
Here was a subject indeed.

Still Life

but it isn't
the painter is playing
a very beautiful (usually)
trick. Think of Cézanne's *Apples*
or a narrow vase of flowers by Chardin
or a pair of old boots
by Van Gogh
who could also make you care for
a chair or a bed
long before Pop artists
or Op ones thought they were making
you look at a chair closely
simply by putting a solid one
on a very small platform
I won't say a 'real' one
because art is all an illusion
but a mysterious one that somehow
takes you to truth by imitation
because Cézanne's *apples*
and Van Gogh's *chair*
look utterly unlike
anything you have eaten
or sat on, and Chardin's vase of flowers
is his own, in his style
and that is important.
Style is the great illusion in art
and only man notices it
or uses it.
Still Lives
are moving us almost to tears,
to amazement.

The Roots

The roots are stretching their arms, the buds are yawning,
The sun is signalling little points of red,
There are green smells wherever you turn, the bountiful earth
Heaves and there is movement in each flower-bed.
Snowdrops seem redundant, crocuses too.
February still yet it's not hard to believe
The Spring has started its labour-pains, and birth
Is taking place wherever you look or feel.
My mind stretches, I smell the tang of a new
World in time and space, and everywhere
Murder and war have left for a little while
And there's nothing but blossoming air.

Overture to Spring

It all began with a bicker,
A low note, a hopeful hint of beginnings
And I lay listening, waiting for further sounds
And they came in scores, in heralds, an orchestra
Rising now and welcoming the sun,
And the sun was spreading underneath a thin
Gauze of mist above the windows and trees,
And as the light spread and the birds' strong voices
Grew louder but no less melodious, I ran
And opened every window in my room
And my heart beat fast, my mind was open to music
And now it came in an ordered rush, a marvel
Of perfect morning. No one spoke but the birds
And their cries were the world beginning over again
With innocence and freshness and delight,
And my eyes opened into another Eden
Sweet and unblemished, luxuriously green
And I didn't know how long I was in
A state of perfection which the birds supplied.
Then I noticed a shadow, one, and then so many
I knew that Eden could not come again
Nor I be innocent, and as sun grew
Hotter and wider I became restricted,
In bondage to a broken world within me,
But it did not matter because
I knew the overture of birds

Would happen tomorrow and draw me into its music
Soft and audacious, such a tide of voices
As never can be counted.

Steps Towards Poems

It is imagination's liberal side,
It is the guesswork of the intellect,
It is a metronome to which words ride
And beat their rhythms out in one swift act.

You cannot understand it if you ask
A poet. He will give approximations.
It is a gift which always means a task.
It is at best quite new illuminations.

But saying this is saying nothing much,
The poem still rides free and will not come
To easy bidding. It moves out of touch

Until it finds what did not seem a home.
Revere it but don't think of it too much.
It never will add up into a sum.

Passed Down

'I get this from my father,' one may say,
Another, 'It's my mother's fault that I
Get upset so easily.' We may
Blame many things on parents but the 'I'

Which blames or thanks, which will not claim free-will,
Is not a growing person, not complete.
We act as if responsibility
Were ours when it best suits us. Our hearts beat

Behind our ribs and signal we're alive
And have five senses of our own to choose
With every second, and we all survive

As individuals and can't refuse
How we re-act. Whatever may arrive
We've brought it on and it is marked with us.

Unsaid

I'm glad that there were some who did not speak
Their youthful love, I'm glad that I was shy
And marvelled how the heart might seem to break
Yet happily. It's good when we don't try

To urge ourselves or others to set round
Them shadows of our own. Words held me back
When I was in my teens. I heard their sound
But did not use them. Thus we learn how lack

Yields riches that no forcing will obtain.
Our first love stories are of fairyland
And maybe our last too. There is sweet pain

In thinking how we learnt to understand
Love first in little losses. Now they mean
Houses of gold which we've learnt to defend.

Katie: A Portrait

Katie has an animated face
Full of questions and discoveries,
Abounding still in childhood's easy grace,
She does not judge or bask in reveries

But fits the way the world would have her taken –
In outings to a friend, in pools of sun
Which she stands in unselfconsciously, unshaken
As yet by growing-up. Maybe she's one

Whose adolescence will not send her on
Journeys of introspection. May she have
The luck not to look inward but be one

Who will be found out by the ease of love,
Move in near-Edens where long suns have shone
And where the darker shadows seldom move.

In Praise of Anonymity

I think now of the Middle Ages when
Some clever men carved perfect gargoyles or,
In Chartres for instance, God creating man
Somewhere high up where few could see the pure

Creative fervour. No one signed his name
But was content to work with the reward
Of money only. No dark need for fame
Shadowed those artists. Their deft minds were stored

With images that owed a little to
Sermons they'd heard, bells that rang the Hours.
Who knows to what religious debts were due

Those churches which stand up today, their powers
Still vigorous? These men of long ago
Rest in kind peace beneath the spurned wild flowers.

'Music of the Spheres'

Is there a music underneath the kind
The instruments send up, conductor draws
Out of the orchestra. Is there a sound behind
The theme we hear that fills another pause

No echo eases? Maybe the ear that is
Most sensitive to sound can hear a call
Most of us miss, like heavenly harmonies
Which only on a wise, controlled mind fall.

Maybe there is and that is what is meant
By 'music of the spheres'. Perhaps each one
Of us sometimes can hear this Heaven-sent

Sound and in love that needs no words we're on
This sphere a moment. It's a grace that's lent
And is no prize for anything we've done.

Two Sonnets on Love and Lust

I

It is a person and can only be
That one, no other. So it seems at first.
Love moved with its especial melody
As if not heard before. It does not last,

Not in this kind or way, I mean. It is
A trap, a prison, lust the warder who
Locks you inside. Each touch and every kiss
Grow more insistent and it seems so true

And what you need. But you are wrong, of course,
You're caught and hardly know that this is lust.
It's passion certainly but it has laws

Love does not know of. There is little trust
But you are motivated by a cause
Which unselves you and is not kind or just.

II

How can it end? In death or loathing or
An appetite grown tired. Who has not known
This urge that uses you, is daily more
Demanding than a dream to one alone?

There is one good which grows from such a prison.
It is that love appears in its true guise,
A wishing-well united with strong passion.
When love is worked for, it's its own best prize

Ten years ago I learnt how lust could work
And it was death which brought about its end.
Mourning was terrible, most cruel and dark

And wore grey guilt. Yet grief itself could mend
The hurts and wounds of lust. Now love can lurk
And send a dove forth from its sheltering ark.

For Louise Aged 12, My Great-Niece

Louise, Louise, fill every moment now
    With hope and love,
You are upon the brink of knowing how
    It feels to change and move

About aware of being separate and
    Yourself. It will be lonely.
You have an agile mind and understand
    The natural world. Soon, only

An inward world will ask for your inspection,
    Your twelve-year body is
Lovely but you don't know its attraction.
    I wish that I could ease

The hurts of adolescence, tell you how
    Your body's changes will
Be a cause for joy. I wish I knew
    A way to keep you still

A child in many ways. Yet when I see
    You sewing, I know that
Growing may not be as it was for me
    But eager, gazing at

The world with something of the given grace
    That you possess today.
O when first love finds your unfinished face,
    May you feel joy, I pray.

My Sister

Ours is a love we never speak about,
Have never needed to. Between us lie
Two years ten days but both born in July.
As we grow older do you also feel
How rare our love is? I have little doubt
That you know well how much in me you heal.

I live alone by choice. I need to be
Alone to write. There are few friends we share.
It does not matter and we need not care.
I'm part of your own family today.
Two of your children I've known since their birth
And I remember how I used to play
With them as toddlers. Since our mother's death

I'm closer to you, understand you better.
I know that you are proud of what I write.
Do you know how your different gifts delight
Me more and more? Wife, mother, now grandmother
You are a wonder to me. Every letter
You write to me is unlike any other

Since we are blood-sisters which means we have
The gift to read between each other's lines.
We share a language shaped of little signs
We formed in early childhood. I admire
As well as love you. You can do so much
That I am clumsy at. You've taught me love
Is often richer when it need not touch.

Death of a Father who was a Poet

The father's dead. The son regrets so much
He said or did not say. He would rush back
The wasted hours when he felt within touch
And yet ignored the chance. He mourns his lack,
Wishes he were in reach

Once more and took the bold way, said the speech
He was afraid his father might flinch at.
But when one day the son feels he could reach
His stoic father, then it is too late
And now he feels too much

Guilt. He's going through his father's work
Poems as yet unpublished, and he finds
One of unusual warmth and with no dark
Reproaches. More, he learns his father's mind's
Regretful and not stark

And stoic as he thought. O time how you
Threaten family love, send quite awry
The wish and its expression. How you go
About and complicate the little shy
Feelings a man may show

To his one son who now is shedding tears
And so repeating all those arid scenes
Of cruel cross-purposes. So death appears
As almost total waste and yet it leans
Towards love. Those childish tears

The son would hide now seem an expert way
To yield and give for that one poem which
Revealed a father who had longed to say
The truth of what he felt, made death seem rich
And turned the past into a fruitful day,
With all love within reach.

A Very Great Friend and Influence

I

Finally you come because you are
    The last of friends, relations,
To whom I owe deep debts. You were a star
    To me, a constellation
That I at first looked up to from afar.
    No anticipation

Told me you would become the greatest friend
    That I have ever had.
You would be the one to understand
    All that I thought and said.
In hindsight you became a destination.
    Before we met I'd read

Much of your history and loved its grace.
    Nothing you wrote was dull.
I was excited when I saw your face,
    It was sun-burnt and full
Of life. Your voice was quick with joyfulness,
    Both kind and musical.

All of love's magic and of friendship's power
    Came from you to me.
At first I found it hard to credit your
    Friendship would one day be
The best I'd ever known. I learnt you were
    In love with poetry —

There is no other word for what you felt
    Later about my own
Poems. A mutual admiration built
    A place where we alone
Lived, it seemed. There never was a fault
    To spoil. The telephone

Almost each day brought us together.
    Then I'd read new poems to you.
I was so excited always when
    I heard your sigh, a true
Mark of your pleasure. You removed all pain
    From what cruel critics do

To poets. They possess the power to break
    A talent but you would
Heal the hurt, show me how to make
    Evil turn to good.
You spoke a spell and cast out all my black
    Faults, gave a starlight mood.

II

It is a mercy that we do not know
    The future, that I had
Never been told for sure that one day you
Would be completely lost to me, that sad

Days might come when I would wonder how
    I'd cope when you must die.
It's seven years since I have seen you now.
You are not dead but have a malady

That's almost worse. Your splendid memory
    Has disappeared. You have
Lost a great intellect which once was free
With many tongues, and now you cannot love

In any way. A dreadful illness has
    Snatched you, the most cursed
For a great writer. Do you feel distress
Now? I hope with passion that the worst

Part of the illness – I mean knowing that
    You lack your gift – has gone
And that a kind of almost-oblivion's what
You know now. May your present world be one

Such as a young child has, but more I wish
    A happy death for you.
Your spirit's gone from your once gracious flesh.
Your many friends must long for your death too.

Dear friend, kind help, dancing imagination,
    You've been dead for me long.
I treasure now your intellectual passion
But more, far more, I want you now among

Lives after-death I do not understand
    But yet hold in strong trust.
Rest soon in that believed-in holy land,
For which, great soul, you've paid so high a cost.

Fables, Lessons

Was it long ago, that story,
The one that started so badly when no one agreed,
    No one made sense of the papers they read each morning
And we couldn't answer our children's questions? They turned
    Away and sought other guidance. It's not surprising
We failed so cruelly. We thought they were far too clever
    But not wise, and it turns out that we are the ones they trusted
Until that fell and foreign day when they went
    Not slamming doors, not arguing, not smiling
Either. They left no address. They were travelling far
    And we were staying, our unused minds were hard
And fixed. We could not imagine anything but
    What we found of ourselves in the old charged fables. We ought
To have read the messages, seen how Pandora's Box
    When opened was full of furies. We should have remembered
How dangerous the Trojan Horse was, but we forgot

The presents we'd taken into our children's lives
Only to use them later against them. Where are they?
    Will they ever return? Will they write?
We don't deserve them. We loved them in the wrong way,
    Were now possessive, the next minute careless. O what
Is the use of regrets? We were born in a ruined age
    And we've passed it on to them
Made worse, made sicklier. So many young have no jobs
    But so many more work hard at two or three
And they give compassion and selflessness without question.
    This planet is lucky in them. They are our stars
Reflecting those others I used to love but now
    Think of them all colliding simply because of
Anger, violence, new ways of killing, new ways
    Of bruising the hearts of the young, their minds also,
But you now, David, you Peter, you Caroline, you
    Are with those who love you. Your love is rare and you give it
Out to us, donations O hampers of good,
    You love with a wisdom that shakes me. I am not worthy
Of you and you, so how can I be of God?

The Modes of Love

In Love

O it is here and near. It is so sweet,
    It is the breath of Spring.
It is all earlier loves and how they meet.
    It holds each happy thing

You've ever known or loved. It's wonder and
    Child's innocence again.
The world's repose, it makes you understand.
    It is delightful pain.

Lullaby for Lovers

Fall apart, fall apart. Lie
    Together. One arm, maybe
    Touching the other's. Be
Docile and calm. Rely

On being naked in all
   The ways that are known to man.
   Sleep for the night's kind span
And praise the first bird-call.

Contradictions

If we are arrogant and wish to be
   Solemn in all our ways,
The human body's poignant strategy
   Of sagging flesh, of hair
Thinning, limbs that falter, show our place
   In farce, black comedy.

We would be lofty, noble, dignified,
   Creatures who own the best
Of lithe, wild animals, spirits which ride
   Almost the buoyant air,
Upon this planet we think we're the blest
   Yet soil it everywhere.

We fashion shrines and temples, make the world
   Ring with angelic sound,
Write epics which are opulent and bold –
   But we shrink from the cold,
Sweat in the sun and yet make holy ground,
   And in our weak arms hold

Each other. All the acts of love we do
   Closely resemble lust.
Five senses aren't enough. We are brought low
   By muscle, nerve and heart-beats. Liquids flow
For passions' purpose, and
Yet with a simple gesture of a hand
   We show a gracious trust.

The Test

   Sound it well. There is a way
To know the truth of love. It is
Much more than ways to hold and cling,
And different from seers' ecstasies.
Mark well these words for what they say
   Is – love increases suffering.

In all love's luxuries and sweets,
In all its words of honest praise
And when the sense and both minds ring
A constant round of bells, when days
Join nights with joy, then most love meets
    The realms and powers of suffering.

    For when love gives much more than takes
And when the lover wants the best
For the beloved, and each frail thing
Seems wrought for lasting and shared rest,
Such love itself makes its heartbreaks,
    Is tested in pure suffering.

    Since it must pass and fleetly too,
Love hears a clock and looks away
But cannot pause the hours which ring
And run swift passage through a day.
Time is the torturer telling you
    The best love means most suffering.

Obsessive Love

It was a madness of the mind and heart,
It was not shaped of sensuality
And yet it throbbed my senses, but it hurt
    My mind. It lay with me

At night, this passion that I can't explain
Even at this long distance. There was much
Joy in it but also precious pain
    And, yes, it longed to touch

But not demandingly. To see and hear
Were almost all I needed. I know now
How I was tricked and played with. I could bear
    This then, but don't know how.

I stayed quite sane when this love went away
For so he did, and he taught me obsession.
Under his cold authority I lay
    And learnt the cruelest passion

Over

The spell has been uncast,
    The magic gone.
The adored idol is placed
    Among everyone.

The perfect expectation
    At simply meeting
Is a routine invitation.
    The brief greeting

Is simply a shape of speech
    One can just summon up
Strength enough to read.
    Why must love stop

And the loved one only be
    Someone barely bidden?
You are back to the fatal Tree
    And the Garden of Eden.

Lust

It is a want that cannot have enough
Of what the senses give. It is a shame
That dresses up in all the trim of love,
    It is what each will blame

The other for. It seemed so sweet at first,
And so it was. None knows how it went wrong.
It was an angry hunger, baleful thirst,
    Yet it seemed to belong

To tenderness. Perhaps it started as
That, but flesh took over, making its
Demands that won't be satisfied or pass.
    This lusting always lets

You think that loving never was or could
Be kind and selfless. How does lust begin
I only know that it's a shameful mood
    And a most deadly sin.

What ends it? Never satisfaction.
You cannot kill the senses where it works,
It is a fever and a foul infection,
        It is all shaped of darks.

Married Love
a sonnet for D. and A.

They do not use the words of passion now
But they speak tender nicknames now and then.
They are familiar yet they both know how
Precious love always is and so they mean

Each word that tells of sharing. They see much
Of partings and divorce and know the worth
Of private languages and gentle touch.
Marriage makes them monarchs of the earth.

I knew a couple whom I praised for this.
They smiled and said, 'We have our quarrels though,
You must not think that everything is bliss.'

But as they spoke these words they both looked so
Compassionate, they proved that marriage is
A marvel which can somehow daily grow.

Friendship

You need not touch, you need not feel,
        You scarcely need a sense at all
Since this love is a happy duel
        Of minds, and it is always full

Of shared excitement. Argument
        Never becomes a quarrel with
This kind of love. It is intent
        On understanding, uses breath

To share good-will, and chooses words
        That will not hurt, it moves about
And only crosses nursery swords.
        It never knows a cause to doubt

Fidelity or trust. It gives
   Unstintingly yet always keeps
Sharp eyes upon the other's griefs.
It never rests. It dares all deeps,
   It is the way the spirit lives.

The Seer's Love

It is so rare. It is unlike,
All other kinds of love we know,
   It can be like a lightning-strike
   Or come so infinitely slow.
The visionary cannot say
What this love is that takes away

All usual powers, all exercise
Of sense and flesh. It is its own
   Invader of the ears and eyes,
   It outlasts flesh and blood and bone,
My only understanding of
This gift, this ecstasy of love

Comes from what seers have told us
In words they all admit fall short
   Of both the vision and its cause.
   It does not work by cunning thought
But blesses the imagination.
It is the eighth day of creation.

IN THE MEANTIME
(1996)

The Right Givers

Give me the honest benefactors who
    Do not offer gifts
Out of duty but who clearly show
It delights them. How the darkness lifts

From my own sky when such guide me towards
    Wild gardens where I can
Wander. Do not traffic with rewards
Or make me some rich prize but rather, then,

Invite me to take part in an event,
    A music-party, say,
Of amateurs whose every instrument
Is gracious, equal too. And so, I pray,

If you are giving for reward elsewhere,
    Do not come to me,
But if you're gentle, show me that you share
Some need also and then your gift will be

Carefully chosen, not too large but full
    Of some lack that you have
Which I can help to heal and make you whole,
Like shyness, dark moods, even lack of love.

Prawning

We went along because we trusted him,
Our grandfather, my mother's father who
Taught us darts, setting us near the board.
And then his tall and steady strides were in
The rockpools, and he didn't seem to need
His eyes. Something instinctive as the wind
Guided his tough net under every fringe

Of slimy seaweed. Almost at his beck
It seemed, the prawns fell in his net, a dozen
Or even more at one good push and pull,
We copied him, my sister and myself,
Aped his wait and thrust, but ours were quick,
Too quick and awkward. We were smelling salt
And iodine within North Devon tide-out.
We raced along, sometimes sliding, sometimes
Slipping a moment in the green and laughing,
Then off we went. The birds were circling high,
The sea was far-away, would not encroach
For several hours.
                              So many times we went
Prawning with Grandpa Turner and we loved
The craft we tried to copy, healthy breeze,
Feeling of being well yet all these came
Together in a mood of love and trust.
He must have caught nearly a pound each time
He took us prawning. Grandpa Turner was
A skilled, fresh-water angler too. He'd stand
Flicking his bait and seem to wait for ever.
These untimed events we treasure later,
Come upon them as we fall asleep.
Nothing mystical, nothing holy
Except that such a craft enjoyed with children
Is precious always. Prawns were flung in water
Piping hot, soon dead. We had no qualms
About their deaths. In Nature's hierarchies
They fitted in a happy part of childhood,
The age of ten's a treasured time for me,
I could not see the clouds ahead, the turning
Inward for years. I shut my eyes and summon
A Devon of the heart's imagination,
All seas out far, high birds with lofty music
When Grandpa Turner caught our bumper supper.

Wisdom of the Fields

It's all built up, with ugly houses too,
That stretch of far North Oxford where my father
Bought a house. He told us with a glow,
'No rents for us. This house is strong, will weather

And rise in price.' Behind us was a field
And all through Summer (surely sun shone then
Every afternoon) we shoved and pulled
At fences to get in and always when

The hay was thigh-high, we would gather piles
So that the quick hands of my sister could
Weave the hay between bent willows. Smells
Inside these Summer igloos were of wood

And something very old we had no name for.
Small houses stand there now, two cars apiece.
Where are the children who should be out there?
Our counterparts, our ghosts? No sign of these,

Most likely they're in Greece or Tenerife,
Names we had never heard of but I swear
We learnt a wisdom in our playing life
That can't be found on hot sand anywhere.

Spring Love

I must accept that love will never come
As it did once – quickly and unexpected
Casting a radiance on any room

That I worked in – I could be unprotected
Because surprise was the chief element
Of love like this only at me directed

And coming to me like a sacrament
Unearned and hard to credit. Part of this
Was that for years I thought that love was meant

For other people, that it would not bless
And cherish me. I was the second child,
Awkward, competitive and thinking less

Of everything would come to me. A wild
Creature I was, searching for meaning in
The universe. I never could be mild

Or sure. I never guessed love would begin
Romantically. I was caught up in it,
Amazed, enthralled and wholly altered when

I was first kissed with passion. Now I sit
Watching Spring suggest itself. There's pain
In thinking of dead loved ones yet — O yet

I feel my blood race in my veins again
And words unfolding with the leaves while birds
Call tentatively. Poems I knew sustain

Me as love did at first. There's a refrain
Singing within me, finding me fresh words.

The Liberation

It happened one day
It really did
I was off to school
But a new one now
The classroom was bright
The mistress was kind
She smiled as she taught
O and suddenly, wonderfully
I understood
The meaning of words
I wrote an essay
Recited poems
And I was freed
From the bars of my cage
For ever and ever
And now I was bold
Would enjoy the games
Even more than work
In this golden world
I was any age
I could touch the stars
I was ten years old.

Dream

A dream without a nightmare element,
What leaning into light, what gracious chance.
Even the strangers with kind gestures lent
Towards but not inside our ring of dance.

There was an easy grandeur which I could
Lose myself in and never feel the shy
Child I once was when a party mood
Was always dark though I could not say why.

One presence oversaw and yet took part
For suddenly I felt his arm around
My waist, and dances beating in my heart.

Music we moved to had a well-known sound
And yet I did not have to name its art
But only knew we moved on holy ground.

Their First Snow

This is the first time they have seen it and
At first it looks like icing on a cake.
They wrap up well and try to understand
How they can use it for they want to make
A house, a man, or anything that comes
To mind. Their muffled hands will pick it up
Roll it round and throw it till it homes
Upon a wall, a roof or it falls deep
And soundlessly. They've found a silent world
For the first time and now they like it so
But soon, in spite of running, they are cold.
Their hands are hurting and they all run through
Entries to home, no longer swift and bold
But slow and burning. Some are crying too.

A House in Nottingham

Everything I hear is beautiful,
    Everything I see
Blends and attends. Here I've come to feel
A care where only suffering can be

The chosen and the decorator. Each
    Room has thick, soft mats
And there are enormous windows. Light can reach
You easily. There are no noisy pets

Because a little girl has Down's Syndrome.
    How may hours were spent
In teaching her to read and write? Quick fear
    Is present that she may
Fall or be frightened. Yes, it's always her
Spirit and flesh which weigh here night and day.

But she gives back untarnished love, whole trust
    Even to strangers. In
A world like ours of hourly crime she must
Be guarded. She's not capable of sin

And both her parents guard her innocence
    Gladly and with awe,
But suffering took them long ago. You sense
It in the calm, but when her parents saw

They had a Mongol baby they must have
    Been shocked. They hint they were.
But their child has evoked enduring love.
The doors dose softly. There is much light here.

For Charlotte
with Down's Syndrome

We are shallow if we say that you
Need our pity since you have a lack.
There are many things that you can do
Much as we can. You can read and make
Pretty things. You show

Skill though it is hard for you to learn.
You teach us patience, yes, but so much more,
You keep an eye on us and you discern
Our many moods. In your life there's a pure
Vision you must earn

By slowness for you have no knowledge of
Facile thinking, acting. In our world
You show immediate feeling, gentle love
But you are at the mercy of our cold
Moments and must move

With hard precision. Everything is fraught
With risk for you. You run to hug us and
Never doubt that we shall understand
And give love back to you. You've never thought
If we should take your hand

Gently and repay your total trust.
Today I met you and tonight I can't
Forget what you are teaching. You are just
Where we take easy sides. How much I want
You now when I am lost.

Yes, lost by cruelty where I must live
Planned animosity. I find you where
Kindness is all about. Your parents give
Me gracious love to which you add your care
And start to heal my grief.

Children in Summer

We sweat and grumble and the noon sun has
No mercy on us. Tiny gusts of breeze
Blow through one block of flats and its close neighbour.
'This is the Tropics' murmurs someone. Here
Is an old city loved, throughout all Europe.
Tension is felt. Too many tourists press
Their way on narrow streets, too many tongues
Shout gibberish. The streets are filthy with
Countless black spots made by alfresco eating,
But one thing can't be missed.
Children cavort and leap about. Their spindly

Legs are dressed in highly-coloured tights,
They wear the rainbow like a true parade
Of little models. Most of all they have not
Lost their zest for heat and sun that's strewn
Everywhere. Our trees are drying up,
And soon – and this is August still – they will
Lose their leaves to clothe our streets. I think
That Summer is a mood to perfect childhood.
Strawberries are still about and orange lollies
Please the avaricious tongues of children.
They are the planets' keepers. Let them be
Proud and cool, impatient with all who
Curse as another camera snaps a view.

Child of Seven Questions
In Chechnya

What are they doing? How are they thinking? Why
    Does nobody smile at me?
I can see that everyone's staring up at the sky
As if they were tied to the ground. They are not free

As my friends and I were before this happening
    Upon such a usual day.
Now we can feel our own eyes opening
Wide and our game is over. We cannot say

Anything now but why and what and how.
    Helpless our elders seem.
Time touches us in a panic-stricken Now.
We imagine in play. Is this a grown-up dream

And have they somehow painted the clouds all black
    And why do their fingers shake?
O I think that we are learning the lesson of lack
And the world like our games is now beginning to break.

The Need to Praise

What do you say when Summer returns overnight,
When the world is painted in deep, rich gold? You want
New words for sudden Summer.
After cold nights and icy mornings, we were
Bathed in sunshine and felt lighter wherever
We went and however long
We stayed. I am a Summer child whose birthday
Is in July but here was Summer all over
Again, all over the late grass of our meadows
And the half-dome of the sky was a radiant blue.
I wanted to praise, I needed a new *Book of Hours*
Painted by unseen holy ones, enchanted
By God as man and creator of the world.
O it is sweet to be
Suddenly warm in October in suddenly green
Fields and ubiquitous trees.

Oxford, Heatwave, Tourists

Lift up your eyes, I say,
Above the upper windows of tall houses,
Above the horror of high-rise grey, stone flats,
Above the dirty air and all the pallid pollutions.
Lift up your eyes
A foot or a yard or so.

Because in this city tight-packed, angry with tourists
The dwellers here feel cast out,
Yes, I feel cast out,
In this attention to a pleasure of helpful breeze
I gazed a yard or two above some roof-tops
Of beauty and colleges, squares and orchards and gardens,
I lifted my eyes up to the limpid sky
And found examples of very strange architecture,
Churches and mosques and ladders assertively leading
Up to alleged Heaven.
And as I sat on a low wall
I felt another, almost-ghost of a city
Try to gain my attention and when it did
I found a purity, a vernal perfection
About attic windows not seen

On ordinary days.
There was a sense of beauty beyond beauty
As the day distributed its dusty moments
Among a rain-wanting sky.

So I say look up only a few rungs
Of imagination's ladder
And you will find a city inviting you
To hear all its bells and enter.

Somerset

Such gentle open slopes, such lack of drama.
A cottage there and there a tiny town
lodged in a valley, rivers overflowing
after four rainy months
but all is drying now as ubiquitous sun
points out a church spire then a gaze of windows
an almost temperate time but not quite yet.
Who knows what March may bring? Perhaps some snow
but for this Sunday late in February
Spring slips its head round corners of big clouds
and they are silvered by the raptured sun
and by me gazing. Here all good that's England
speaks in green flows of light, in church-bells ringing
while afternoons are stretching out their arms
before the good day of our clocks put forward.

Among Late-Teenagers

You wait in a half-circle, serious eyes
Upon me as I enter. Do you see
My nervous fingers? I begin to read
Sitting. I don't stand. This is a class
Because you have to read my poetry
For your A Levels. Do you notice me
Stopping briefly as my fingers pass

Over the pages? Now and then I pause
While you ask wise and tactful questions. I
Try to answer, telling you about

How I write. 'Do poems come easily?'
'Do form and subject come quite separately
Or both at once?' More probing, 'Tell us why
You write in verse, not prose.' Always I try

To answer simply though part of my mind
Reflects, 'At your age I was reading Keats,
Not someone living.' Then I read more poems
Which do not feel like any part of me.
Next I tell you there's much luck for poets
Using the English tongue. Now the talk gets
More personal but in a kindly way.

I'm thinking what a world we've made for you.
Your love of poems will not earn you a living,
And then – no nonsense here – our spirits seem
To meet and I am learning something of
Your quick responsibility, your giving
So much to me now that is part of love.

Welcoming Spring

Give me new words for Spring. There must be some.
Delight wells up in me. I'm almost drunk
To see the daffodil and crocus bloom
And a huge cloudless sky. Winter has slunk

Away, a guilty thing that is ashamed
It came among us darkening each good mood.
We let it go like a small pang we dreamed
Now all we see and smell is ardent, good.

And I mean good in every kind of sense –
Sweet, desirable, in morals, right.
Who can be angry when such wreaths of scent

Sweeten our noses? Such a rainbow sight
Stands everywhere in its own circumstance,
What seers know now ours in shafts of light.

The Great Spirits

The trouble is we are all loose and mixed,
    A shape of mind and then
The body slow and wanting to be fixed
Somewhere, and all bear witness to this when

They fall in love. Why fall? It seems to raise
    Us to the sky, to hills?
Love is the power within us when we praise
Each other. Nature, works of art. It kills

The half-achieved, the tepid thought, the wish
    Half-realised. Have you
Met anyone whose spirit shone through flesh?
I have myself encountered one or two,

And loved their modest power, their gentle worth,
    Their give-and-seldom-take,
O these are gods who rise above the earth.
Trying to reach them mostly means heartbreak.

Story Tellers

The tellers of tales give more than reading a book
They make things up as they go along, they will add
    And annotate and digress. They don't mind being interrupted
And corrected. Children gather round them in rapture
    And this is the start of history when history meets
Imagination. Imagination will always walk off
    With the golden trophies, the prizes, the best
Their listeners can afford. I'm about to visit just now
    A narrator I know who tells tall stories and short ones.
I await his latest and I'm on my way to get it.
    You can race me if you like but you won't overtake me
And I won't tell any more.

Seers and Makers

There is one quality in common which
    Artists and men of prayer
Display when we think back on them. They were
    Eager to disappear
Within the words, paint, sound, and praying; each
Wished to be hidden. Thus we can
Always mark off the honest from the sham.

The artist and the holy man also
    Always share energy.
When a saint prays you see his goodness grow
    His rapture you can see
In his concentration. Great art shows
Impatient feeling. Mind and sense debate.
Will is at work and there's no touch of fate,

Self disappears when man becomes his prayer,
    Likewise man and his art,
And both aim at perfection and will share
    Any wound or hurt.
But seers accept while artists cannot bear
To leave their work untouched. Some detail's wrong
In poems, buildings or a catch of song.

Hermits and Poets

Do they move with empty minds so that
Meditation may have room enough?
Or are they filled with this world's appetites
Which must be cleared out by a perfect love?

A love few of us know or want to learn,
It is so dark. In deserts or at night
The spirit of an eremite must burn
With God's own hardly bearable good light.

Imagination shaping poems can seem
The purest moments of one's life and yet
We know, when coming from that trance, a dream
Was working in us and the poem is set

Down and finished, such experience
May seem at times like perfect meditation
But words or images are what enchants,
What seemed like prayer was only concentration.

But all poets know that their best work is given
So they should not be thanked and they know too
That if a few lines hold a hint of Heaven
It can't be forced if ever it rings true.

We don't deserve it when somebody writes
Or says a verse of ours has helped so much,
We are surprised, for when a poem delights
Some power has given it a magic touch.

The Sitter

O for the selflessness a painter has
    When he paints nakedness
With lack of lust even if hands may pass
Over a woman's flesh to put her as

His picture needs. At any age the rest
    Of us can't help but feel
A touch of some desire, a hint of lust
And wish that we could watch as painters will

And children too but surely no one else.
    The petty nastiness
Is that our own desires are also false
For we mind, when we're old, if lust grows less.

Innocence is afar in every way,
    In childhood and in myth.
We are deceived when wishing we could say
We own pure looks for eyes to wander with.

Act of the Imagination

Surely an Act of the Imagination
    Helps more than one of Faith
When a doubt brushes us. We need strong passion
To summon miracles. Life after death,

Bread turning into flesh and blood from wine,
    I need to cast around
And find an image for the most divine
Concepts. My mind must move on holy ground,

And then the hardest creed – the rising from
    Death when Christ indeed
Bled finally – ideas cannot come
As barren notions. Yes, I always need

Herbert's sonnet 'Prayer' say, or that great
    Giotto painting for
My heart to leap to God. I want to meet
Him in my own poems, God as metaphor

And rising up. I watch a lucid sky
    And see a silver cloud
And Christ's behind it; this is part of faith,
Hear the Great Hours sung and let faith be loud

With the best imagining we have.
    This is how I approach
My God-made-Man. Thus I learn to love
And yes, like Thomas, know Christ through a touch.

For Paul Klee

Such a fastidious colourist, this man,
    The painter who truly knew
School of movement. All his work began
And ended where imagination's glow

Enchanted everything. Klee's was a world
    Wholly fastidious.
And it is out of time and always bold.
The painter's character is given to us

Unsparingly. Klee's world is never one
    Which he hides in. It is
Shaped without mirrors. Everything is done
To show a place open to everyone.

A painter of quick patterns, colourist
    Whose palette knows no lack
Or so it seems. Here is an art of rest,
And of sophistication. Klee gives back

Ideas of worlds where artists did not sign
    Their pictures, let them go
As gifts to anyone. Klee's touch and line
Show us the bounds and make sure that we know

The rules of art. Surrendering is one.
    A brush can be a wand
Which can be potent even over sun
And, like a prayer, can reach beyond beyond.

Order

We shape, we cut, we steal, we wrap, we are
Makers of order where there wasn't one.
Think of our topiary when all trees wear
The same, shaped, scissored look. Yes, we have done

This to most wildernesses. After we
Were driven from that garden, we've shown how
There must be patterns. We lost liberty
Of one kind but we've fashioned others. Now

In our wild world of misrule we insist
On shapeliness and balance. Most of us
Do this to gardens. Tough weeds will persist

Until we've plucked them. We make curious
Designs for garden-beds. O we exist
To make new order since our Eden loss.

Sonnets to Narcissus

I

Homage is due to you because you show
In a myth's magic way a reason to
Value the mirror and all it can show,
O but what danger lies in this also.

But isn't every work of art a kind
Of play with the reflection and the glass?
We think that in a glance we read a mind
And lovers always long to read a face.

The peril here is obvious and sweet,
A true temptation but a gracious one.
Sometimes in mirrors two loved faces meet

And here love starts its glimpse from one to one
And looking-glances show we can repeat
And thus right love is carefully made complete.

II

Imagine worlds without some form of mirror.
We cannot make this act at all because
Men first gazed into streams. Did they feel terror,
Seeing themselves repeated there or was

It a delight to learn their eyes, their hair,
Their noses, cheeks? Of course such men
Did not know it was themselves they saw
But there our inward-looking ways began.

Was this the death of innocence, this knowing
Yourself so soon by heart? Did selfishness
Start here, and pride, in this so shining showing?

Perhaps. It makes good sense. Such happiness
We gain indeed when our own selves start going
Outward. Be wise and break the looking-glass.

III

Holy ones have always sought to find
A place of silence where no noise intrudes.
They search beyond themselves, their heart and mind
To be united with a living God.

Satan, of course, always sought them out
Would turn them inward to themselves alone
And there they were besieged by clever doubt
And voices which would break the calmest souls.

Many would then reflect upon their Lord
Who prayed within a garden to find there
Moments that aren't conjured by a word.

For Christ was tempted and into his prayer
Came all the world's proud voices doubting God,
Whilst damaged peace was obvious everywhere.

Having it Both Ways

What liberty we have when out of love,
Our heart's back in its place, our nerves unstrung,
Time cannot tease us, and once more we move
In step with it. Out of love we're strong,

Without its yearnings and the way it makes
All virtues vices. Steady liberty
Is our element and no heartbreaks
Can touch or take us. We are nobly free.

But how long can we live within this state?
Don't we miss the slow encroachment of
Possessive passion? Don't we half-await

Its cruel enchantments which no longer have
Power over us? O we are obdurate,
Begging for freedom, hankering for love.

Touch

Touch. How much it starts and how much ends.
Each sacrament demands it and all love,
Whether of passion or the play of friends,

Asks for its use. God started this world of
Shape and substance. The whole universe
Stirred by his touching it at every move.

Eden – the potent tale of our reverse,
Was darkened by the picking of a fruit
When touch was disobedient. Its curse

Spoilt touch and yet it also somehow brought
God-Man to us and put him at our will.
Touch can demonstrate an arcane thought

And love surrenders when its power goes still.

Telling the Time

Telling the time has little to do with hours
    Or seconds, minutes, day.
Time is one of the spirit's inimical powers
    And you learn it in the way

You fall in love with someone who doesn't care
    For any part of you.
At best, it whispers through an ardent prayer
    But time has more to do

With any happy friendship and it has
    Full power over love.
It makes you think of how all good must pass.
    Yes, it's the enemy of

Falling in love. It makes you fall indeed.
    It tells you expertly
That no love lasts though what does last is need,
    And time stalks liberty.

It makes us fear an end before it comes
    And haunts all sweet farewells,
It is the dark dissembler of our dreams
    And it can leap from bells

Which enter marriages just as they start.
    You cannot hold time back.
It dizzies every movement of the heart
    And is in love with lack.

Two Sonnets

For my mother who has been dead for two years

I

Your natural wisdom is what I remember,
Your clever hands re-shaping, sewing, cooking.
You always come back to me in September
When St Giles' fair still is making
Its noise in roundabouts and in loud colour,
Straight to the bull your dart went but you said,
'It was a fluke.' All pleasures you made fuller
And gave them back from heart as much as head.
Nothing you did was vulgar or a fluke,
You had an instinct about poetry
For making was your life. You loved a book
By Jane Austen or Trollope. You could see
The point of writing poems and you took
My first ones to the post. You are with me.

II

Not as sadness but a presence who
Shaped my life. So often I was ill
And once you kept the fire up all night through,
And in the morning you were with me still.
You never chided my dull awkwardness,
Falling, slipping, breaking. You could see
My skill and elegance in writing this
Or that small verse. I owe you poetry
For I've no doubt your making gift became
Mine in another way. You were so proud
Of my first books and loved to see my name

Upon the spines. I hear you read aloud
Often in the night still for you were
Gentle, strong and quick, beyond the crowd.

A World of Love

Since early childhood I have been in love
Or loved or looked up to from far, someone.
My early childhood passions meant far-off
Gazing at. I've always seen a sun

In my half-real and half-imagined world.
What good pours through all children when they can
Almost worship, copy. There's no cold
Climate in my country. I can scan

And stare at stars, and often I have read
The words of seers, tried to understand
How they are lost in God. There is no dead

Place for me. I have a pulsing land
Peopled with saints and children. These I need
To help me see in joy and pain, God's hand.

Loss of Loss

It never brings relief that we can wake
        Up without a fear
Of some cruel loss, a heart- or a death-break,
I think of this just now when I am clear

Of all the guilt and horror your death brought.
        I hid away to grieve,
People shunned me. Grief, it seems, is caught,
A sickness that can feed on happy life.

Now I wake up and do not think of how
        You've gone away for good
And yet there is a vacuum in me now,
I mourn because I can't mourn as I should.

How shallow we all are, we never can
    Be sure of what we'll feel,
Except we learn a power that's greater than
We ever guessed and nobody can heal.

At Mass (I)

Why are we not amazed? How can we kneel
    And stare or else, perhaps,
Find our minds wandering? We ought to feel
Awestruck. A bell is rung and the bread wraps

Christ thinly in it. This is for our sake
    Lest we should feel afraid.
The wine's for drinking and the priest will break
The bread as on that night when Jesus laid

His life down for us. Did they understand,
    His chosen, what it meant
To bring God into bread? A human hand
Takes gently what is kind and heaven-sent.

The drama is tomorrow. History has
    A place for crucified
God-made-man to teach us to learn peace.
It was for this that Christ bore pain and died.

All he had promised came about. He knew
    Peter would deny
His lord and master. So do we also.
The Mass is gentle, prayer is but a sigh.

And yet, and yet ... at times most of us hope
    That all the world will see
The magnitude, yes, the enormous scope
Of what the Mass means so that all may be

Sorry and say so, mourn and maybe cry,
    For all creation here
Has waited for God-man to testify
That he can conquer every kind of fear.

But we are wrong. All that our saviour did
    Depended on free-will.
Time ceases when the gold ciborium's lid
Is lifted and Christ comes to us as still

As he was at his birth. Now death and birth
    Are changed that we may live,
Yes, live abundantly and by our Faith
Accept what all the Godhead longed to give.

Which is Which?

I'm vexed with this delight
Because I cannot say what spirit is
And what mere flesh. I'm driven by the light
And only want to clap my hands and praise.

    Spirit, they say, works through
Our feeble senses and transfigures them,
But my five senses through all rapture go
And yet I know my spirit has to come

    Into all this someway
Because what I am feeling at this hour
Is what I rarely feel when I can pray.
Which is the stronger, soul or body's power?

After Dark

How will it be when we're fleshless?
What shall we do?
Will our minds climb invisible stairs
So that we too
Reach the moon or see a new star?
I do not know.

I only know that when I shut
My eyes I sometimes can
Re-invent the world to my own plan
Which can seem so much heaven
That I now stare at sun or the moon
And feel part of limited men

When Lazarus rose from his tomb.
Why did his friends not ask
What it felt like to be dead?
Was it too hard to ask?
No harder to credit than
The Godhead in a white disc?

I close my eyes and my usual world escapes
And I throw off time like a coat.
I seem to be spirit entirely.
I move where I wish.
I am my own story and plot
But time turns me back into flesh,
Flesh and the spirit of thought.

At Mass (II)

It is so simple and so quiet that we
Gather round and make small bows and look
At all the others present. Gradually
The celebration works on us.
A book tells us how to be

A part of all the wonder happening
And soon enough we realise the awe
We ought to feel. Here God is opening
His secrets. Human law

Is broken and a great event occurs,
Hidden, yes, but only that we may
Not be afraid. The wine a server pours
Becomes Christ's blood, the same as on the day
He died upon the cross.

This great occasion started long ago
In an Upper Room. Here Christ's own blood
Is present once again. The priest will show
The Little Round to be our daily food,
We pause in what we do,

Every day. Our marvelling to prayer
Nothing matters but this Holy Meal,
The angels bow and time can disappear
As we gaze and simply want to kneel
To show our faith. We're near

Eternity and every bad thing done
By us we're sorry for. Our hearts are made
Bethlehems for God the Father's son
Who is God and wants us unafraid
And only see what's true.

Every moment of enchantment we've
Ever known joy here is present and
Our best love is shown when we receive
God so simply. We can understand
Less than we believe.

For here all intuitions gather to
Show our hopes are valid and made clear.
Passion falters. Love alone will do
As God shows his creation need not fear
Great wishes won't come true.

The rite proceeds. The world comes spinning back
And we return to find all usual things
Are shining with right purpose.
                          What seemed luck
Is given while our hurt creation sings
And there is no more lack.

Bread

What ashes and what sackcloth now?
          We more than eat our fill each day.
Lent is upon us. Few think how
          To do some penance and still see
                    Christ's agony.

He is with us in the Bread
          That's consecrated everywhere,
And still a few take on a need
          And show their sorrow in a prayer
                    And so repair

Their own and others' faults. They feel
          All of Christ's suffering is still
About and some try how to heal
          And help his steps up on that hill
                    Where men could kill

God as man. This mystery
    Wise men could never understand
But here and there in history
    A seer comes to comprehend
      A Man-God's end.

O yes he died. The sky went black,
    Christ's own disciples fled away
Like Peter who would mourn his lack.
    Our world is black and still we slay
      Our God each day.

Consecration (I)

It all happens so slowly. A few words
Are spoken. Such tiny words
Full of more than this world can ever contain
In its random occasions, its pell-mell actions which we
Have brought about. It is to change what we see
And hear all about us that this Round of Bread
Is changed, becomes Christ's life on earth when he
Chose to move among us all, to free
Our trammelled spirits. He loves liberty
So he became for a time what all of us are
All the time. His words go on echoing where
Any will listen. One simple breath of prayer
Will break our chains, abandon our daily fear.
For this he arrived and stays on our desperate star.

Consecration (II)

    'This is …' The priest lifts up
    The Round of Bread and we
    Wait for the risen cup.
    So that no ecstasy

    Should too excite us, God
    Hides in this frail Host
    And then we drink his Blood,
    Wine to us. Our dust

Through all the ages has
Brought us to this event.
In any simple Mass,
Christ is so quietly lent

To all. We fold our hands
And try to pray. Who can
Find words? Mass starts and ends
With hiding God-made-Man.

Ash Wednesday 1995

This moment is tremendous yet is veiled
    In a thin Round of Bread.
We must use our imaginations which have failed
So often to help us towards the truth. Instead

We have let them lean toward violence
    Where not one thing is safe.
Nature may move in her ancient, timeless dance
But we have let go and we swing off

Hither and thither, untrusting, loveless, caught
    In a murderous mood we invade.
Let me on this Ash Wednesday create a thought
That is open and innocent, something which I have made

But more a way of being that I have been given,
    A chance to make a choice,
After six weeks of Lent may I be shriven
And echo from my distance Christ's dying voice.

A Touch of Existentialism

How essence and existence fascinate.
The soul's born with us. When we start to grow
Existence takes us over and we start,
    Given free-will, to be, to learn, to know.

Firstly it seems to grow like monkeys who
Ape our actions. Then we seem obscure
Within ourselves but outwardly also.
But soon we marvel that we own a pure

Faculty for feeling stars like powers
To know bravado, while imagination
Guides us among the fleet, assertive flowers.

But we were meant for more than this. A passion
Teaches us ecstasy and how to pause
Within our central place in all creation.

Holy Communion

There were some miracles intended to
Save us from too much awe and wonderment.
How simple are the things a priest must do
To close Christ in a simple element.
The Round of Bread is so

Tiny, thin and white. It almost makes
Us feel we must protect the Godhead when
The Host looks like what any woman bakes
For her small family. The wisest man
Says nothing when he takes

The little wafer. What can any word
Explain of this kind, gentle element?
Silence is the way God is adored.
Vaster than galaxies, this sacrament
Holds Bethlehem's young Lord.

The Spirit's Power

All the sheen and cut, the tied, the true
Of almost anything I praise and watch.
I clap my hands when Nature shows her due
Respect for us but how does spirit go

On? Strip off each trying sense, think how
The spirit works. It has its own success
As I think hard and leave the here and now.
My spirit is the way that I seek grace

And how it corresponds with what I do.
The flesh creeps slowly offering dubious powers.
I will five senses off but they won't go

For long, I have known rare and kindly hours
That leap from love and then I think of you
As I last saw you, gathering wild flowers.

Rome

I

I think I found a counterpart of it,
The balance of the spirit and the flesh,
Forty years ago when Rome was lit
Up night and day as if by my own wish.

I mutely prayed and when the sun came out
For April Easter, Faith was all around
In voice and face and works of art. No doubt
Could last there long. All seemed like holy ground

And so it was. The sun stretched wide and far
And I was touched by it. My spirit knew
The world was worth the saving. I was near

Quick absolution, happiness with true
Purpose. Resurrection was so sure
And oddly this was old and very new.

II

There was St Peter's and within the great
Sistine Chapel roof was painted, how
God created Adam. With much sweat
Michelangelo made all things Now

And showed how gift and instinct, flesh and soul
Can work as one. How fortunate I was
To see and feel all this and be made whole
As loving care shone out of every face.

Much has gone wrong since almost everywhere
But hope's a beacon in the moon. Each star
Stands over Bethlehem and on us here

For Bethlehem and Resurrection are
Working in each of us. The spirit's clear
And in me I can feel Christ's sweet love stir.

Time's Element

For Robert Ombres O.P.

I know that I was wrong about the hours
    And time and clocks and bells.
I thought that only future had its powers
Upon us. Hearing you, I see the false

Premise and perspective. All that's now
    Indeed is moved into
Futures we can't rely on or know how
Anything that happens there is true.

Of course the past is only sure and feels
    Certain. It is our
History. The future may be false
And any moment take from us one hour.

Then I remembered those prophetic words,
    'Before all was, I am.'
Christ lived among us with a cross and swords
And yet he with his Virgin Mother came

Into the moments of the angels' plea.
    She carried God and man
And gave the future her willed history
As she took part in God the Father's plan.

Calvary

Surely when Christ was hanging on the Cross
He felt all pain, not only that one which
Was obvious to men. I think he was
Suffering all the agonies which touch
Some time each one of us:

The death-camps, torture, hurting thoughts, and all
That claims the flesh and soul of man throughout
History since our chosen lot, the Fall.
Thus God as Man experienced every doubt
And so he had to call

For mercy, yes, God when man could sweat
For all the shame of Peter's cowardice
Though he'd foreknown it. Christ felt every great
And small sin, yet his dying meant success
Though it looked like defeat.

The Assumption of Our Lady 15th August

'Assumed.' What does it mean? Say 'Take for granted'
That is it's workaday, mere connotation.
But take 'Assumption'. It is now enchanted,
Pulsing with life, untainted.

August the 15th will arrive tomorrow
And we shall celebrate the death of one
Who chose to take on every human sorrow.
When she became the mother of God's son.
Mary had to borrow

A stable and a manger where her child
Might sleep and drink her milk. How much did she
Understand? Since she was undefiled,
God's birth came easily.

Yes but from that day on much mystery,
She lost her son when he must go about
His business. But she stood beneath that tree
And understood our doubt.

Yes, this girl accepted everything,
Felt all of grief but never would despair,
She taught the God-man how to walk and sing.
Grace did not save her from man's suffering.
She teaches us to bear

Horror, war, misunderstanding, loss,
She was so young and yet a stoic too.
The sky went dark as she stood by the Cross.
Did she feel triumph too?

Flesh and Spirit

Think flesh away, attempt
    To be pure spirit and
Be in your God so wrapt
    That you can understand

His working and his way
    Of leaving you to let
You find his heart and stay
    In his pure spirit, set

Where time is cast away,
    Where flesh makes no demands
And there's no night or day,
    No limbs, no head, no hands –

But wait, did Christ not come
    To re-perfect our flesh
By making it his home
    And the whole Godhead's wish?

Spirit and Flesh

Although we're chained to flesh and mostly love
Its senses, appetites, the way it gives
Pleasure to us, most of us think of
Another part, the spirit which too lives

And fashions art and our response to art,
Which works through memory and intellect
And sometimes also we speak of the heart
Not meaning that which beats but one which acts

Through judgement, insight … And how often we
Long to lose our bodies and to move
By our imaginations. Liberty

Works here and all the best of human love,
We move beyond the stars and through the sea,
We trust our souls and yet can find no proof.

Lazarus

Why did no one ask you what you saw
　　And found when you were dead?
For there's no doubt that dead is what you were.
All breath had gone and you were cold. They laid

You in a tomb and your relations shed
　　Tears and mourned for you.
And then, this wonder rising up indeed,
A little Christ. Did no one really know

What to ask? Were they too filled with awe
　　And silenced? Or, maybe
All were so joyful at the sight they saw
And so astounded at what they could see

That, at the time at least, no question came
　　Into their minds when they
Saw you alive and called you by your name.
It seems more likely that you could not say

What after-death can yield and mean and show,
　　That there were no words for
That place or time when human spirits know
This whole vast what? There was no metaphor.

Good Friday

It is the day of death and the burnt-out sun
And the teetering cross and a man who is God crying out
To his hiding Father and he and his Father are one
But the man on the cross carries the world's doubt
And asks where his Father has gone.

So the creed says but today the orderly creed
Is set aside and Man faces God and demands
'I am forsaken by you, and what is the need
I am hanging here and have lost almost all my friends,
And now they loosen my hands.

My mother is here. She holds me again to her breast
But no angel is by, only a frightened few
Who know no reasons but still stay near and trust
They know not what but find there is work to do,
The duties of death now must

Be performed and the mother prays to her son.'
God is brought low and darkness is everywhere,
The bright, unthinking people still look for the sun.
And somewhere the mystery of rising is starting here
Where there is the scent of grass and flowers in the air.
The long hours of Easter Saturday have gone
As the great third Day draws near.

Age of Doubt

Lying on my bed one Summer day
I thought of what the Holy Ghost could mean.
Always before I'd taken it on trust
But now it was in doubt. The gold and green

Summer air and grass showed everywhere
But inner dark had taken hold of me.
I thought of mighty birds but now they had
A silly sense. How could a mere bird be

Holy and part of God? It made no sense
And so I started going through my creed,
'God-made-man', 'ascended into Heaven'.
I could not answer and the books I read

Led to more questions. When I asked them, though,
The answers only made me ask afresh,
A fresh new one. I longed so much to know
How God himself could even be 'made flesh'?

Over was all acceptance and glad trust,
And from those days to this I have asked how
Answers can come and fit my magic Creed.
And every dawn I'm more uncertain now.

So maybe just the asking is what God
Seeks out in us and makes our spirits glow.
We want a reason why we should be good.
A God in hiding's all that we can know.

With the Migrants

O let me go with the happy migrants who
Have the accurate instinct when the first cold bites,
Give me their feathers and wings, their joyful trust
As they brim the clouds and veer with the precious blue.
I'll be no hibernator, rather go
To the warmth of the world, the jocund moods of it.
I can almost think myself into a swift's
Slender body. I would keep my hope
And my imagination but coupled with
Their hope and certainty, their joyous lives.
I have seen swifts go and felt a strange nostalgia
As if I once were one of them indeed.
And so, according to many theories, I am.
How tender yet tough their wings look, how they seem
To signal Southward a message from the North.
I close my eyes on this September night
Of sudden cold and I am indeed away
But most of all when I'm on the tip of sleep
I am spreading my wings, I am off with a rightful faith.

In the Meantime

In the meantime. What does it mean?
First of course that there's time further on,
Hour upon hour, second on second
And days and nights. I know I mean
A pause as if
I had plenty of days, volumes of weeks.
But who really knows?
I think I am certain that this is a pause
And later on
Will be just the right time in every sense
For the message I'm sending now, just a message.

I beg you to wait. How can I know
That you have the time and it's worth the wait?
It sounds like arrogance and presumption
To hope that anyone wants to wait
Especially when I can't be sure
That a moment waits to hold my message,
Meaning my poem. I need your hope and your patience so
That you'll understand 'in the meantime' is now.

PRAISES
(1998)

For my Sister, now a Widow

Mourners have tip-toed away, the flowers are dead.
A mocking Winter sun pours through the glass
Of your bedroom windows, but your grief won't pass.
Slowly, carefully you make the marriage-bed.

I think of you crying alone and cannot bear
The thought of it long. What can I do to make
Each day more kindly? Maybe though for his sake
You want to keep his loss, for he is there,

There in the harsh reminder of these things,
Mostly little ones certainly such as
The way he washed up the breakfast, hoovered the floor.
Are you cross with a happy bird which sings

Close to the house? No, I don't think so.
There's never been anything morbid or selfish about
The world you've managed. Still it has to go
On working without solace or a doubt.

I've been surprised into a new compassion.
Of course I've known it in different guises before
But not like this which feels like a fraught passion.
It makes me hope there'll be many rings at your door.

It arose when I saw you look so pale and dressed
Not in black but muted colours. I want to say
You have nothing to blame yourself for. Whenever you pray
I feel sure that, even so, you have confessed

To little impatiences, words out of place.
Listen to me: your husband loved you so
That, like a lover, he always looked at you,
You were his reason to live, his channel of grace.

A View of Lazarus

See he is coming from the tomb. His eyes
Need shelter from the light. We crowd and press
Towards him, some say nothing. One or two
Whisper. Others look afraid but stare,
Most turn their eyes away. Such a strange
Light is coming from behind the man
Brought back from death and coughing in the breeze
One by one his senses set to work
To ease this man to us. A look of loss
Shows on his features but he does not speak.
Some begin to question him about
What dying felt like and how did he break
Back to us. He can relieve our doubt,
But he seems dumb and we don't want to make
His rising difficult although we long
To look back at the glimmering Kingdom he
Has left, if Paradise is there
But is not for the snatching. Lazarus now
Opens his eyes and it's at us he stares
As if we all were strangers. Then it's odd,
But we feel we should stop talking. Lazarus is,
Yes no doubt of it, now shedding tears,
And whispering quietly, God, O no, dear God.

Walking in the Dark

In a dark mood I wandered at night-time,
Most people were in bed, some lights still shone.
In the far distance; trains made happy sounds,
A going off with jubilation. I
     Tried to think of them,
     In childhood distant trains
     Were a good lullaby.
But now I was grown-up and wandered looking … for what … ?
I did not know and yet I felt my spirit
Stirring with some glad power.
Between a dream and a nightmare I had come
To this strange city not on any map
That I'd been shown at school
And yet I knew I had to take quiet steps

Even as I felt afraid of crossing
Almost every street. What fear was this?
Where did it come from? Why
Had it made me think
I must put on a jacket and go out?
The season was so vague, the moon was half
But not a star was there for me to look at,
Not a human-being anywhere
Could join this search whose goal I did not know.
The God whom I had always prayed to still
Existed but he seemed too far away
To give a blessing or explain why I
Had to walk upon what was perhaps
A pilgrimage though there was not a sign
In air, on ground, close to the moon, to say
I must know dark and carry it about.
Dear God, this was a doubt about a doubt.

In and Out of Time

He has heralded the morning with his blessing.
    The Great Christ has done this
Not 'done' but 'does' for past is always missing
When Jesus comes in all his mysteries.

Time is our worry and our pain. We must
    Be shackled to it till
We have done penance for our pride and lust
And all the deadly sins which tease our will.

Clocks chime, bells ring. The present slips away
    Even as we make
The good choice or the bad. We know of day
Even as the Precious Blood we take,

And eat the Bread, for these are lasting things,
    And Heaven's gate's ajar
As in humbleness our spirit sings
And we learn galaxies, name every star.

Cheap gibes are made about a God who can
    Allow us to feel pain.
But we learn sympathy for God-made-Man
And touch eternal things again, again.

The Words are Pouring

The words are pouring. Listen to their sound,
Their implication, weather, strength and cry,
Let dictionaries shout against the wind
And lyricism find its weather there.
Here's a world of freedom hardly won,
The fervent sun is beating on our faces,
Grace is found, religions praise themselves
And men stand back as if creation's day
Were now and here, and all attempt to pray.

The weather of the world is altering.
Babel begins again, the many tongues
Of fraught mankind are fighting as they sing,
When once more can that younger John be heard –
'In the beginning always is the Word'?

Rapture of Spring

Play havoc with our language. It is Spring.
Let nouns be adjectives and every adjective
Become an adverb. Let the language sing
As daffodils blow trumpets and the life
Of every bird takes wing.

The sap is running and the rainbow is
Pouring its colours out while every sense
Vies with the others in a wreath of praise,
A purpose of pure joy. Sweet innocence
Marches through our days.

Always something new is found to say.
We are so glad, our blood is sap also,
We speak in joy at all this ripe display
And point up to the sun with work to do.
O see, it too can pray.

A Unique Gift

Don't be embarrassed by the words I write.
    You should know they are true.
To you I owe the kindness of tonight
    And its wide peace also.

I have been angry, difficult at times
    And shall be yet again.
But there is peace in these warm, Summer rhymes.
    You've helped me to attain

A place and mood of hope. Desire alone
    Cannot accomplish this,
Much work is needed and much care. You own
    A gift that few possess.

Somehow you know how to make magic happen.
It's here before me with the curtains open.

An Apple Tree

    The apple tree, so many kinds
And there's the one which few forget,
    But I'm concerned with one which finds
Rich sun and I am near to it.
    As I draw blinds
    Against this sudden August heat
I think of one who lived and died
    Where I have come. So soon we'll eat
All apple harvests. Polished, dried
    Apples may be sweet
Or tart, or juicy. Of the lot
The Cox's Orange is the one
    I like the best,
That special sweetness of its own.
    I wonder what

    The lady who lived here liked best.
A friend talked of her with much love
    And said the apple-tree brought rest
To her. She wrote a poem as proof
    This tree was specially graced.

What a happy change it is
That someone saw the better side
    Of ill-fabled apple trees.
We're taught the reason why man died
    To trust was eating this

    One fruit, and now in all of us
Bad choices often rule our world,
    Bringing famished hate, abuse,
But my forerunner who was old
    Hymned the apple-tree across
The way. Her writing made it gold.
    Her dying must have wrought much loss
(I know that's true, I have been told)
    But still her apple tree stands bold
And I am lucky to live where
    It flaunts its foliage in green air.

A Full Moon

Tonight the full moon is the Host held up
    For everybody's eyes
To see and understand the high and deep
    Salvation in the skies.
In usual Masses we withdraw our stares
When we bow down. How wise

The Godhead is to make all Masses small,
    All Consecrations set
Where the most simple, the most sceptical
    Know of mankind's regret
That we brought Christ himself to such a pass.
    That overflowing grace

Gave us another chance when we refused
    To leave one Tree alone.
God-became-Man because of this and used
    A cruel cross to atone
For us. It seems we cannot bear for long
A simple goodness but must choose the wrong

Because it looks so sweet. But look again
	That Host-like moon shines where
All can see him. Christ took on all pain
	Beyond time's arbiter.
The Bread is offered us, the wine also
For Christ and every saint, his Mother too.
	That moon in silence can
Elevate us till we long to know
	The Trinity's whole plan.
Nature was fashioned for this purpose. See
A moon reminds us of God's ministry.

Song Just Before Autumn

It is a music of the air,
	It is a spell that's cast around
The trees. Here is the harbinger
	Of Autumn. On the ground

Gold's tossed and squandered. Never mind,
	The breezes haunt and hunt. Each star
Is diamond-fixed. We soon shall find
	That almost-Winter's here

But not quite yet. There's time and space
	For worthy fallings, songs and things
That have no words except pure grace
	And all its whisperings.

Harvest Home

The music of Autumn is just on the edge of hearing,
The torches of Autumn glance to and fro in the trees,
The still-green trees, not a shadow showing among them
The smells of Autumn are noticed when the winds
Of Summer's lightness slow. The soil is rich, the corn has been
						brought in,
Soon the blackberries with their dark, jewel shapes
Will hang and ask to be picked.
The signs and tokens, the myths, the Natural History
Of Autumn are never like last year's or the next.

Weather is unexpected. A shrewd guess
Is as good as a meteorology of measures.
Listen, feel, sniff. What do you hear, and what do you taste?
A library of intentions, a churchful of bygone prayers

But – and this is the best of all –
A Harvest Home of a Brass Band shining and blowing,
Reaching the heart-beats and going far beyond them.
Everything Golden with Brass. It is mid-September
And watching and listening to this marching of Bands
I feel the world is celebrating itself.
Heedless, almost, of our presences altogether,
But our spirits enter the instruments that are blown,
Crash with the big cymbals and meet each other
Never mind that Winter is round the corner,
With music and touching and smelling the news of our world.
We are ripe for whatever comes.

Alone Over Christmas

A serious night of calm it is. The moon
More than half. How warm it is for Winter.
Christmas will be on us very soon.
It is the time of Advent Calendars
        And I sit down alone

Happy and full of friendship but I think
Of a young man who at the weekend stood
Calling 'Everyone's walking past.' Some brink
Of lonely terror was near him. It's no good
        Pretending every link

Between each human being and another
At Christmas suddenly grows firm and solid.
This lonely man is everybody's brother
And we *do* walk past in selfish mood
        Not bothering to bother.

No Visions or Prayers

I am not after visions or prayers
Nor in search of experience missed in earlier days.
Least of all do I carry a message, invoke a cause or yield my sympathy.
I am not even sure yet what it is that I am pursuing
But the feel of something just out of reach of my writing,
Beyond the luck which is almost half of each poem.
No word is on the tip of my mind or hidden
Waiting for me to find it.

I am only partly aware of the plan, the music, the theme
Yet I feel that some time I shall come upon it.
It may be narrow or wide
It may be a tone in music
It may be – and now I think I am getting nearer –
A flow of song, a cadence that hints and surprises
That carries me into maybe a darkness of the spirit –
That has to be risked –
But I am eager and ardent, baffled and angry.
Two nights ago a thread of sound came near sleep.
The subject is totally hidden
But a whisper, a hand, an accidental leader
Drove me, O, to such pure and utterly new
Story or passion. Something is plucking a string
And feels like a lover's first touch.

Apology to a Friend
For C.J.

People say 'You're sensitive.' I'm not.
    Only an hour ago
Unwittingly I hurt someone when what
I feel for them is rich and ought to grow.

Why did I not think hard of what I said
    And learn that possibly
You felt quite differently about one dead,
A young and public figure? I could be

So cool, no, worse, so cold and be like ice
    About this unknown one.
Too late, I saw the sadness in your eyes.
What have I done today, and what undone?

Round and Round

The children asked 'Where is the end of the world?'
And we started telling them about horizons
And how the sun does not really go down
As it seems to us to be doing.

They were all frowning and obviously didn't believe us.
We looked at each other and wordlessly agreed
That scientific speeches were useless and so
After a fairly long pause
We told them all the ancient stories
About the sun moving around the world
And rising and setting over and over again.
They listened, did not speak, but they stopped frowning
When we said, 'Of course that isn't quite true',
They put their hands over their ears and ran out
Letting what we call knowledge lag behind them.

Famous Parents

'Are you his daughter?' Don't you feel a blank,
Like someone overlooked and in the way
Because you are a relative? You thank
For being attached to this great man, don't say
But surely think 'I am myself.' You may

Give well-worn smiles, 'Oh yes my father was
A sweet and generous man.' He was a swine,
Had filthy habits. And you, just because
You are his child must sometimes want to whine
'I hated him. Nothing was ever mine.'

But then a famous father or a mother
May well have been adorable and gave
You love and wit and money. You'd still bother
About taking advantage of a love
So overblown. Still you'd want to move

Away and change your name. For you're not 'Me'
As ordinary, lucky people are.
Your father gave you fame lopsidedly.
'I am myself,' you cry, 'and not a star.'
These famous by their birth will not go far.
Wiser not to try. Forget me, *He*.

Childhood Christmas Parties

Those parties after Christmas always threw
    A shadow back upon
The joyous gifts, events, so much to do
And all things glittering. But there was no sun

To light the parties we had to attend.
    Children are stoical, don't say
'I do not want to go.' They go and bend
To order. How I hated all those games.
    I never found a chair
When the music ended. All bad dreams
I'd known came true and yet I would stand there

Trying to smile, begging God to make
    Six o'clock less slow
To come, but when it struck a smile would break
Out. Most thought I did not want to go.

Ballad of a Thinker

One man went out and watched the sun
And found it warm and stayed beneath
Its casual power. 'Much can be done,'
He thought, 'when there's warm air to breathe

And heat just right, not tropical.'
He sat down to his work and did
Not note the time. His mind was full
Of words and concepts. Each one led

To others and his argument
Was sweet to read. He called out to
A woman who appeared. She leant
Upon his shoulder. She went through

His reasoning and her eyes shone,
'Life will be easier now,' she said.
'A kind of magic you have done.
I feel it ringing round my head.'

So he went on with happy ease,
With confidence supplied by her.
He'd found a world made just to please
Because a valid truth was there.

The sun was strong. The air was wide.
The plan and purpose pleased this man.
He never thought that he should hide
From fiery heat. The hours began

To slow and every thought was laid
Upon a page. The man lay there
But suddenly some difference made
Him stir. He woke and wept for where

His pleasant arguments were set
Upon his note-book there was now
Only an empty page. He let
The pages flutter, wondered how

He'd tell the woman of the change,
But she had gone. She was a part
Of his deep dream. He must arrange
His life again. He had to start

Upon his own, the sun gone cold.
'I want my dream,' he cried, but knew
Dreams won't revive however bold
The dreamer is. That this is true

Is how the actual brings us down
And scatters magic quite away.
'When I'm awake and quite alone
The world's not mine and will not stay.'

Teenagers

Adolescence seems less painful now
        Than it was when I too
Found I had changed. Few would then allow
For all the questioning I had to do.

Soon it was a questioning of thought
        And of Faith and self.
All I had once accepted was in doubt.
I was half a child and also – half –

A grown-up person. Nothing fitted me,
        The world seemed made for all
The eager walkers, talkers, wholly free.
I was clumsy, awkward, letting fall

Almost everything I touched. I could
        Not take one thing on trust.
I tried to change each dark and doubting mood.
Simply to hide was what I wanted most.

It is very likely that beneath the smart
        Looks and words, among
These, teenagers hide what there's no art
To mend. I mean the pangs of being young.

Boston

I've never been back to Boston,
Boston, Lincolnshire,
Never looked at the Stump with grown-up eyes,
Never stepped on the flat ground or seen the size
Of the sky unencumbered by hills or trees.
All I remember is

Being pushed in a pram after an illness, playing
On a Pogo-stick (one plaything that's never returned),
I remember cutting the garden hedge with scissors
And picking the red and black currants and gooseberries.
I remember the nursery table where we used to play Ludo,
Once I lost and picked up the board and threw down the pieces
And can't remember if I was chided for this.

So often people say, 'You don't remember things and
All these memories, all these scenes and emotions.'
But they're wrong. My senses tingle when I think of
The smell of bonfires, touch of nettles and
A season wrapped in what five senses tell.

But I sometimes long for a music of memory
A song with a rhythm, and blackbirds singing high,
For the ear is swiftly attuned to happiness.
It's on the edge of my mind but always stays there
As the hint of a note, a recalcitrant, teasing sound
Which ears can't catch and push it into my mind.
In fact if I think of birdsong it's never connected
With Boston, Lincolnshire.
But what my ears lack is richly made up with scenes,
The white, cool dress of my Nanny in the moonlight
And the moon in several shapes staring at me
Surrounded by a majesty of stars
And sky was heaven and God the Father lived
Beyond the moon, beyond the stars, up there
High above everything, keeping order where
I once stared up in Boston, Lincolnshire.

Theatre

Theatre of the Absurd, Theatre of Cruelty, Theatre
Of the here and now, the actual, the spare
        Moments of revelation, then the bleak
Look at meetings and departures showing
        All lack of understanding, people never
Able to touch or extend or assist each other.
Then there's the Theatre of Ideas and wit
        Based on a casual meeting or stray acquaintance.

        But why not the bold and brash, the hurting and
The broken heart needing putting together?
        Why not the real endeavours, the warmth withheld
Then wasted in a cruel act regretted
        Almost as if it hadn't truly happened?
Why are we niggardly? Why not fuller, willing
        To forget or lose each other or lead back?
I cannot say and yet I fight to drive off

        The theatre Shakespeare spread across our land
And down our history, and all Europe's stance.
        Who will be bold, who dare take the risk
Of ending a fool when there's any chance
        Of a rich loving or a tender tryst?
The curtains rise and fall on littlenesses,
        The great surrenders happen in the wings.

Praises

I praise those things I always take for granted: –
The tap my sister turns on for my bath
Every time I stay, the safety pin –
And who invented it? I do not know –
The comb, the piece of soap, a shoe, its shine,
The name tape and the string, a leather purse –
How they all flock as I recall them now,
And Now I also praise with all it holds
Of nudges, hand-shakes, playing trains with children.
There is no end until I'm tired and think
Of craftsmen everywhere ... O I forgot,
Cushions, napkins, stoves and cubes of ice.
All the world is praise or else is war.
Tonight the moon is almost half in shape,
'Tomorrow will be hot' say weathermen.
I praise the yawning kind of sleep that's coming,
And where the spirit goes, the sheet, the pillow ...

Reasons for Not Returning

I

They say 'Go back to it.' They mean to Rome
Where I was happy forty years ago.
All was excitement. I had not left home
For such a time before. There I could grow

Into a different person in some ways
And those important. I walked with a map
And guide-book daily, everywhere would gaze
And then I fell into the generous lap

Of History and Faith. The latter I
Shared, though English, I was glad I knew
French and Latin. They helped me to try

The language; when I did, people would show
Delight and say 'Bravo'. Until I die
I'll keep my Rome. I never want to go

II

Back because all foreign places are
Bursting with tourists now. Cities you love
Are more than stone and brick. You travel far
And find a mood, a purpose. I won't move

A step to go back to the Rome in which
I learnt how time and history compete.
Almost every street in Rome is rich
With fountains, pictures and good meals to eat.

I sometimes dose my eyes and swiftly see
Every street and statue, every large
And little church. I met new friends who'd be

In my life always. Such a privilege
Rome was in every vital way to me,
Now she's a state of mind in my old age.

Carol for 1997

Made flesh, made poetry, made art,
        The little child was born for this.
His mother held him to her heart
        And touched his brow with her warm kiss,
        Underneath a bursting star
        This God-Child came to us from far.

And every Christmas once again
        He's born afresh and needs our care.
He is all hope yet knows of pain
        For on a cross he'll suffer where
        We mock and hurt. Now he forgives
        Us for all that. For that he lives.

But though the heart of mystery
        Is his own right, he understands
Our simple hearts. In history
        He comes with little helpless hands
        But all who choose will be saved by
Means of a child who has to lie

Shivering, he clings fast to
    A virgin's breast, finds comfort there.
All stars are his, all wisdom too
    But for our sake he comes down here
    And we wait for his little hand
That all the world may understand.

Makings

Early we start making
Worlds and empires, even a language, often
At least a civil war.

Is war then in the blood
Early on? I still believe in a Fall,
That crucial one that made us feel ashamed,
Afraid of our bodies, putting out our hands
In the many crevices. We were frightened too
But of what? Afraid of being afraid and so
Building intimate castle walls, deep moats,
Guards night and day on duty?

One of the worlds I made with a friend of mine
Needed a totem pole with figures on it
(My friend was clever with paint brushes)
We made alarms and many mild tortures too.
Our world had a singular God
Who lived round every cloud but sometimes showed
Part of his face to us.
He had a cunning smile.
So we made ourselves new fears, new treasures too.
Explanations were not
Needed, 'Here' and 'Is' and 'When' and Now'
Were spectacular words indeed for things we only
Occasionally glimpsed. And of course we shaped a language,
Tiny Pentecosts of fiery sounds,
Whistles, shouting, whispers on the edge
Of understanding something. To ask was all,
To build a grammar, send up vast balloons
And wings and feathers and hushes and trembling forms.

This world endured throughout a Summer and
We were rulers, lawyers, singers, fliers

And finally we blew our world away
In rage and purpose and want and touching wood
And then came the words we did not want to say –
The end of a holiday.

Two Sonnets on Words and Music

I

Music leaps the language of our verse,
The sonnet does not have its brass or strings,
Percussion echoes with a sweet excess
And violins say more than fingerings

Of language. Poetry has to fight our tongue
And keep it pure and hold a message too.
The double-bass is neither old nor young
Yet carries meanings which we listen to.

The angel on a cloud will always hold
A lute or trumpet. Music is its sphere.
Poetry must be cautious, music's bold

And yet, and yet a great ode takes us where
The mystic looks to language to unfold
And cries out for the mastery of prayer.

II

Then there is Bach and counterpoint where meaning
Has no purpose. People always have
Set words to music from mankind's beginning,
And specially when all the drift is love.

But what of silence? Language uses there
Length or briefness till a verse is won.
And that's a chance or gift. Gift I prefer.
Love of man or God has always run

To words and cadence. Feelings must be said
And in as new a way as we can find.
The lover may not take an ode to bed

But knows right love occupies the mind
And by it he is willing to be led,
And by its brilliance only is struck blind.

Mid-May Meditation

How can I find a music of the heart
That marries mind and the imagination?
  I need the painter's brush and canvas and
Each composer's personal pattern which
  Engages us but also takes us further
Into the arms of dear discoveries.
  Today is burning May, I've drawn the curtains.
Since flooding, icy Winter we have been
  Through every climate in the calendar.
Many have lost a home which surely is
  A kind of death the spirit must accept.

I'm in a mood of gratitude for so
Much richness in my life, enduring friends,
  An art to practise and a zest that is
A leaping passion. Mid-May is a blessing
  For students at work, in love or out of it.
I praise the vernal leaves, the seeking rainbows,
  The flowers around and hanging in their baskets.
I want a music of pure thankfulness,
  Horns and trumpets and the cellos too.
Saying 'Thank you' is inadequate,
  I need the sounds that satisfy like prayer.

Small Hours

The small hours are so big for me
And I can feel the stars draw near
In more than mere astronomy.
They are great lives I need not fear,
    No astrology

Is needed by me, I feel faith
In such wise being, life and power.
Time has no purpose. I'm graced with
A solitude that seems to flower
    Into a company

Of light, more light. O it is sweet
Simply to be. All wisdoms come
And make a kind and gentle home.
Stars are a bright simplicity
They write these words, make poems complete.

Myths Within Us

All the great myths that were whispered
      Into our childhood ears
Stay with us somehow somewhere
      Coming to life in tears

Or in great bursts of laughter,
      Jokes which went on while the sun
Was slowly, precisely going
      Leaving so much undone.

But the favours of Midas or Ajax,
      The Trojans' triumph, the old
Norse legends are written inside us
      And only will grow cold

When what we call our spirits
      Finally disappear
Yet most of us still believe even death
      Will keep those great gods near.

Song of Welcome

How swiftly and sweetly
      The weather can change
As if for your coming
      My power could arrange

The bold sun's appearance,
      The rain gone for good,
The whole world is wearing
      Its best clothes. The mood

In my heart is all glowing,
    No cloud is in sight,
The blue air is growing.
    There'll be no night, tonight.

I'll lay out a carpet
    Not red but all gold,
I've fashioned a wonder,
    An unfallen world.

A Metaphysical Point About Poetry

You said we only share what intellect
Provides us with. I can't agree with you.
Surely we share our love. We give it to
Express right feeling. Why, then, can't an act

Be shared? It manifestly is. Of course
You spoke of poetry and how it's true,
It is a making and so poets do
In little what God does with all his force

And all the time. I wish to say that God
Is present in all poetry that's made
With form and purpose. Everything that's said
Is written to be said. When poems are good

We say that they communicate. It's true
And surely like all truth it can be shared.
Tell me if my judgement is impaired
And why my poems can't share. I want them to.

Pain

Innocence is broken every day,
Shattered, wounded sometimes in the name
Of education, mostly in the way
Elders wreak some vengeance and then claim
    An innocent to say

Or, much more likely, show, for they lack words.
Think of the first time you found love and were
Enthralled. Some soldiers came with unsheathed swords
    And taught you how to fear.

So many ways to hate, yet more to love
And one man cried out from a cross to men
Who'd heard him say that he was God, with rough
Anger of their own nailed him in pain.
    On Calvary, no love

However twisted or perverse was not
Called upon for help. Obsequious men
Of law and church explained they had not thought
That God could bleed and weep, be all of pain
    And cry, know anguish yet.

Prayer for Holy Week

Love me in my willingness to suffer
Love me in the gifts I wish to offer
    Teach me how you love and have to die
    And I will try

Somehow to forget myself and give
Life and joy so dead things start to live.
    Let me show now an untrammelled joy,
    Gold without alloy.

You know I have no cross but want to learn,
How to change and to the poor world turn.
    I can almost worship stars and moon
    And the sun at noon

But when I'm low I only beg you to
Ask me anything, I'll try to do
    What you need. I trust your energy.
    Share it then with me.

Love's Struggle

Always this struggle of the flesh with mind,
The touch-and-go, the desperate waywardness,
Duality is dominant, we find
And never keeps the whole of happiness,

But we go on pursuing and retreating,
Now in a noble effort, now in low
Surrender. There is never perfect meeting
And, at the best, we quickly rise and grow

Away from one another but we come
Back to a sweet composure that can't last
Although we trust it can. We seem at home

But only for a moment. Time will cast
All sweets aside and we are blind and dumb,
Wanting forevers, finding only past.

'Hours' and Words

There is a sense of sunlight where
Warm messages and eager words
Are sent across the turning air,
Matins, little Hours and Lauds,

When people talk and hope to teach
A happiness that they have found.
Here prayer finds a soil that's rich
And sets a singing underground.

Let there be silence that is full
Of blossoming hints. When it is dark
Men's minds can link and their words fill
A saving boat that is God's ark.

O language is a precious thing
And ministers deep needs. It will
Soothe the mind and softly sing
And echo forth when we are still.

Song

I ought to know after so long
Trying to learn the art of verse
That it's large passion makes the song.
Long practice tells me love demurs

And waits in hiding till the art
Of singing, making build one whole.
Thus we can tell what breaks the heart
And lends compassion to the soul.

Craftsmen

I love to see the master at his work,
Concentrated wholly on his craft,
Whatever flaw may show, he will not shirk
To mend it, and whatever may be left

That's wasteful will be used for something else.
I think of carpenters and painters who
Build a house that never will seem false
Because it's painted, mended and made true

By sleight of hand and eye, and by the skill
That is particular and not to be
Copied by anyone. Man's choosing will

Loves the precise and measured, longs to see
The perfect box or bridge or waterwheel
And never needs to sign what he's set free.

For Seamus Heaney

I love you for the feel of things you have,
The nub, the texture, rub and block and blow.
I love the way you tell the touch, the heave,
The roll, the plait, the smooth, the working glow.

Nothing is alien that is of the earth,
And sky and water too. You are a kind
Of Adam who can bring all things to birth
And give emotion empire over mind.

You're not like Yeats. His Irishness was why
Causes are just and golden cities built.
He could polish jewels and paint the sky
But you care how a child, a bird has felt.

You hoard but often let us look at things
Like an old, rubbed satchel or the bite
Of saw on wood. You've made your children swings,
Cherished old cribs, made a newspaper kite.

Yes, maybe that is it; the rush and sheer
Marvel of air goes riding by your power.
What's used and tough is always to you dear.
The hedgerow for you, never one picked flower.

'The music of what happens' are your words
And happenings, not craft too judged are yours.
You find much pleasure watching playing-cards,
And you're all male yet not ashamed of tears.

The Book of Love

I have been reading in the book of love
          With all its exploits and
Withdrawals and advances. There's much of
          How we misunderstand
The ways of love. I have just turned a leaf
          And read about the end

Of falling into love and living it.
          I marvel as I turn
The pages. We can love with eyes and wit,
          There is so much to learn.
Love, though felt otherwise, is what we earn
          Although no price is set.

The sweets of it, of course, can't be kept long.
        We are not made for such.
Love that poets re-fashion in a song
        Is sometimes what we touch
But we cannot maintain this, love lasts long
        If we don't question much.

Who, knowing all the pain of love that breaks,
        Would not swear all was worth
The anger and remorse? True loving makes
        Allowances. Our earth
Can make the crudest gesture lively with
        Kind purpose which awakes.

The very comets which we watched last night
Yield us small visions of enduring light.

In a Bar

Who knows what he is feeling, this one here
Close to me in space but both of us
Might be two planets, each in different air?
I'm waiting to meet friends, have time to pass.

He tries to hide his eyes. What is his need?
He may, of course, be happy. Nonetheless
He's doing nothing, has no book to read.
Before him stands one small, long-empty glass.

Where will he be at midnight? Quite alone
Or in the arms of some girl he adores?
We are a foot apart, both on our own.

How poignant flesh and bone are just because
In love's act we can be a moment one
And then once more relearning all of loss.

The First Time

Our love is not the same as others'. We
Resent comparison for there was no love
Before we met. This makes us whole and free.
None has moved before the way we move

And never will. Our letters speak of things
New to the world. All's a discovery
For us. We find a new place and it sings
Up to the stars with our own melody.

Must we wait until love's lived with and
Domesticated, to find out we're wrong?
Or is it worse when we don't understand

Each others moods and thoughts, when every song
Dies with its echo? Now we're hand in hand
Within our world where others don't belong.

The Limits of Love

I

'I know what you feel,' we glibly say
And then continue 'I know what you think,'
And we speak of ourselves. We should obey
The courtesy of things. Through one small chink

Or key-hole we may glimpse a little of
Another's suffering but that is all.
Even when we murmur, 'O I love
You' our words are really but a personal call.

In truth we are surprised at likenesses
And say with honesty, 'Just now I thought
Something of what you mean,' and then we bless

Each other for a moment when we've caught
The other's spirit and large purposes.
We live by guesswork and the time is short

When we felt we were one. But then, of course,
In love we scarcely need a word at all
Since by a touch, a gaze, we learn the force
Of passion and repose. When people fall

Asleep when they have loved, they cannot share
A dream. We have to learn a desolation.
There is no art to show us how to bear
Closeness in sleep. We fall away from passion

And we don't know that sleep may take us to
All the unknown places of the heart.
In consciousness at least, we know man's true

Loneliness. But when we have to start
Sleeping no map tells us where to go.
We enter lands of which we know no part.

After an Elegy
For my sister

Now you're learning all of loneliness
Which is quite different from solitude.
Feeling lonely is complete distress
But being solitary is a mood

A poet, for example, needs to write,
A wise man wants for thinking out the world;
Loneliness, you'll find, is almost cold,
You linger near the sun and beg its light.

Your husband's dead and you have lived all through
The anger and the shock. This week now you
Gain another grandchild. You can go
Through all life's starting phases, see the new

With joy and pure delight. A child, you were
A little mother often, would push me
About when I had fallen. Birth is near
Now but death dogs you. You have to see

The empty pillow and your house so still.
I wish that I could teach you how to be
Happy by yourself but, falteringly,
You must live on with your own steadfast will.

Let me offer you imagination,
An opulence of stories about love,
I know that round your house in isolation
You walk. True grief like yours will not move off

Swiftly but you have new life at hand,
A little girl to hold within your arms
And she will need you. Being needed calms
As you so long ago could understand.

A Gift of Gratitude
For Christina

This house is Number Thirteen and is full
      Of wisdom and of love.
The four girls who grew up here cast a spell
And in their home you feel a spirit move

And it is kind. O yes, there has been pain.
      The mother of these girls
Can sail and ski but has also lived in
Self-doubt and all the bitterness that fills

The tension of divorce. She has not let
      It make her sour. She is
Full of natural wisdom and has set
Her children free in her own happiness.

When trouble stormed me she gave me a home.
      Three months she offered me
And laid upon me all the gifts that come
To the right sufferers. She would be

Light-hearted, dazzling, also calm and free,
      A freedom she's worked for.
I want to write a lively poem, to say
I've learnt so much, so deftly too from her.

Praise can sound sentimental, gratitude
  Twists our English speech.
Let me offer then a spell-like mood
Which few can learn and fewer still can teach.

At Our Best

There are so many loves we know,
Paternal kind, and one we feel
For somebody who's understood
Or nursed us when we're weak. We go
About in search of one which seemed
To find us at our best always,
The best of love won't fill our days.

It is ample and we have
A mind and heart not deep or wide
Enough for such a love to fill.
For this Christ cried out from a hill
Hoping God's love in him as man
Would find us ready. Sloth or pride
Found us wanting. I've a plan,

One that found me, gave me rest
And love beyond our frail desires,
Compassion thriving at its best.
Even when we're found wanting, Christ
Lets us choose again. The Tree
Of Paradise turned to the one

Where God as man cried out for us
To show us joyfully that need
He begged for. We did not refuse
For he was taken from the Cross
Where Mary and his great friend stood,
Our representatives. And thus
All mankind in time and out
Forgets the selfishness of doubt
And finds it easy to be good.

The Largest Question

I've vexed my mind about where spirits are
And how they manage when death's taken off
Their pelt of flesh through which the senses stir
And act and do our will, at best
Beyond the flesh and more.

And yet when love's the drift we gladly work
Through every sense we have and shape a world
Where marvels happen and where we can mark
With flesh, and where we feel our spirit bold
Until we reach the dark.

The dark of absences and loss by death
We hide and long to have our dearest back
But life and death are always but a breath
Apart. What happens when the largest lack
Parts us from this world with

Slowness or suddenness? And what and where
Does God, we say we trust, move all of us?
My greatest friend was good and she is where
The spirit's lively. O but she is loss
And I am lost to her.

Does she know moonlight and the ocean's wash
Around this planet? Does she now at last
Learn perfectly the love she knew as flesh?
Her glowing spirit surely can't be past
And so each day I wish

That she were present with her liveliness,
Enchantment too which she would press on me.
She often was the whole of happiness.
O God, instruct me where she now must be
Without the cruel sickness

That was a dreadful death-in-life for her.
She was imperial and became a slave,
She was indomitable, kept all fear
Away from me. O God, she still is dear
In every curling wave,

In every cooling wind, her mind was brimmed
With precious knowledge which she gave away
And still more came. Such life cannot be dimmed.
Her spirit moves in all good words I say
And surely part of me

Is in little what her great soul knows.
She is with God who must delight in her
And set her still a-dance. I think she goes
Where God keeps spirits out of time before
Life is all rise, not rose.

Concerning History

I

Does history guess itself into our minds,
　　Taking over our memories, railing at our past,
　　　　Envious of our future?

Let there be a lullaby for all
　　Events that history cannot avoid.
　　　　It listens to prayers, it comforts youth,
　　　　　　It mocks the aged.

Listen, history is now and what you're doing,
　　It is the seed that grew, it is the child
　　　　In a green wood in a gold flower in a white hour.
　　　　　　Don't let grey come banging the door.
　　　　　　　　It's the ghost of a ghost
　　　　　　　　　　It's not history's death.
　　　　　　　　　　　　It is hope distracted,
　　　　　　　　　　　　　　Passion dissected.

Does history tell love-stories?
　　That's not its one aim
　　　　But Cleopatra makes Antony include themselves,
　　　　　　Eloise again breaks the will of Abelard.

History also lies down in the fields
　　And picks the berries in an eclogue day.
　　　　History is not divided though it sometimes seems so.
　　　　　　Too often it's broken pieces of wise men and wars of foolish
　　　　　　　　　　　　　　　　　　　　　　　　　ones.

History's a game
    But you have to play it seriously,
        Not let your mind be distracted,
            Speak only the slang of the game.
                Quiet, quiet. Does history really sleep?
                I have lost it, I have lost it and I weep.

    History must deal with us and
            you and you.
            and we and me and all those behind
            who fit their lively shadows
            whose deaths were marked by war
            whose purposes were order and design
            who loved the new-made and the new-born too.

History is so tangled, is also
so guessing forward;
it is urgent, tragic.
We are part of it for its
concerns are wide and forward and old and new,
it uses mirrors and magnifying glasses,
it argues with the geography of time
and won't leave meteorology alone.

History is also tender,
more than benign.
It is intimate,
it enters all our dreams but
won't abuse
the humble lives we are,

And in the end and always
the great historian selects a line.
Deep in encyclopaedias he is
but also must give many years and much endeavour.

History selects the credos of the world.
    The first wild
        rustic gods,
The proud large spirits of sophistication.
To write your history is a daring thing
and also it requires much ruthlessness.

O yes yes yes yes yes yes
but it is gentle, childlike, lyrical.

History makes an orchestra of time,
and all the instruments men have designed
will bow before the lovely human voice.
The order of a king,

        the servants' obligations
and will are at the heart of this austere
and yet also at times this golden study.

          *

The reverie, the dream,
    The quick word and the long
Sound of coming home
    And then the sleeping song,
The haunting of the flesh,
    The unripe touch upon
Another's world. The wish
    that cannot be undone.
This is a little of all history's music.
    Its war-cries, its peace treaties
    and always, always its search for some design.
Not one imposed but one lived out in time
from the huge epic to the nursery rhyme.

          *

Pacts and treaties
    Heresies and arguments.
        The guess that grows,
           The malice that moves
             In so many places

But most in the human heart:
    History lodges there a little,
        It must remember the unguarded hour,

Balance and value
    Weighing up
        Looking down
           At all of us over the globe,
             Smaller than ants when we are dust
                But quick with kind dreams and gold wishes

Moving up and down
Over and into
And leaping and dancing
With a scholar's meditation.

The great historian is always listening.
His countless notebooks
    His findings and guesses
    Wait for months, for years
    Till only wisdom moves his daring hopes,
Only self-sacrifice gives him truths to give us
    part of our story.
We are the punctuation-marks he must use precisely
    in his lucid style.

II

From legends and myths
From scarab and stone
From yellowing rolls
Bills and receipts
Faded papyrus
Tomb-stones
Tall stories – take on any or all, these are the base
The starting and stopping
Often going back beyond Greece or Rome
Checking, balancing
Putting together
Almost unbearable
Difficult hours
When the facts won't fit or are not facts.

Turn to the fax,
The computer, the ruler,
the filing cabinet,
every modern convenience
put to the service of knowledge.

All to be placed together,
    so many notes to discard,
    too many contradictions,
    too many false roads taken.

The historian moves from his study,
walks into the garden
and sees a grandchild making a daisy-chain.

'That's my purpose,' he thinks,
watching the adequate fingers,
loving the whole picture
when the facts won't fit
or are not facts,

'And what then of love?' he observes,
'It rides and wishes and is joyful
Over the story of man.
The king hated his mistress
That politician was impotent.
Should I be reading more novels?
O mankind you slip from my hand
But I can do nothing without you.'

III

Theories of history –
Get the facts right and a pattern emerges.
Watch the clock, the clothes,
The political choices
And time slips into its place.

    How to address the spirit?
    No use to list creeds and cults, no help
    To file or correlate,
    To give mere likenesses.
       History itself has a spirit,
    It shows in the movements of men
       at their extreme moments,
       when they are most hopeful
       and when they are daunted by death, the sufferings of others
                and their own.

    What then of God?
    In every stage of man and all his making
    He has been a creator.
    Even in unbelief he's pursued the good.
    History has no trouble with the wicked.
Recording it may be a tenth of its purpose
    And all the choices of action.
History is words.
Visions are not always spoken or written
But history is in the spine of mankind's book,
His book is belief in God,

Be quiet and listen, listen;
There are whispers outside my window,
It is July but wet and cool as April,
Seasons work on and through history.

Tomorrow is Sunday and many
Visit a church
Pray to a God
Beg forgiveness
Tonight is the end of the Sabbath
The Synagogues are shut.

History whispers in the waiting ear
And hints how power may be obtained, how war
Has to occur. Dictators see themselves
As near-gods worthy of their people's love
And what is more they take that love for granted.
Often their armies march through frontiers,
Soldiers are helpers, make men orderly,
But the despot argues and for long
His words have been believed. 'He is good,'
The people say and offer laurel leaves,
But history throws them off, is on the move

     Chasing
           chasing
                 chasing
                       all of us.
It sets a rainbow over millions dead
      and someone somewhere
          counts again the colours,
Tributes to who we are and
     all our story . . .

TIMELY ISSUES
(2001)

Regions of Memory

After an operation

Regions of memory – I returned from these
Not with a map but with a hard-learned awe.
I know the spirit's travails and its peace,
Have found there is no law

To help you through the trees and gardens of
Memory. All life is different where
The mind is moved by hidden brooks of love,
Forests of kindness, almost a sacred air.
You cannot find in books

Useful guides to paths where memory
Treads softly. I have come back to a place
Of argument and discord but can see
Skies of sifted gold, a silver space
Where everyone is free.

Regions of memory – when you've been there
For long you're changed. Those regions teach you how
To deal with enemies like dark and fear;
And how to praise. Here. Now.

A Company of Friends

We were all friends that night and sitting round
A lateish dinner. Candles lit us and
Shyness disappeared. Some golden ground
Surely held us. We could understand
Love's mishaps, teenage children and the sound
　　Of their troubles. Here,

Close to a river and a city where
Learning's been current long, you could accept
Its implications. Last night we could share
The worth of art and promises well kept
Until that hour. Here was a world of care
      And I think we all slept

Better for our words of joy and grief.
We ate, we drank, ideas seemed to come
So easily. Here was abundant life
And grace shone like a happy coming home.
We did not notice that the time was brief
      As every candle flame.

We gave time back to one another as
We shook warm hands and called a clear Good Night.
Now it's last night's tomorrow and I pass
That feast like film before my eyes and light
My long room with that silver and that glass
      And glory in the sight.

Dance

Always at the heart of things there is dance,
      Dances of death, dances of angels where
Christ is there is always a dance of Rising
      For saving is always a dance that takes our hands,

Tells us the joy of endurance, the steps of pain.
      Prayer is the deepest dance and it can be
Stately and homely, high, serene and sweet.
      Where there is love that's hurt there is also dance,
And Creation is a dance, a constant movement.
      The stars dance in their high places, the moon
Dances and alternates with every sunset
      And with every sunrise too.

Mozart in the Middle of the Night

In the still night the cool notes fall,
Mozart elaborates the silence as
Note after note seem to be hanging, then
He lets them fall as if into a pool.
My lamp is shining. Gold is everywhere.
Ah, now the drops are gold. They disappear
One after the other, one again, and yet
Again another. They are caught now in a net.
Alfred Brendel can control them all
And yet 'control' is not the proper word.
In the night there is a singing sun.
I listen in a rapture of repose;
Drop after drop, there another goes.

Dream: A Ballad

It was no dream and yet it was not waking,
A story told itself within my mind
But it went further; there was bright day-breaking
And huntsmen hungry for the lucky find.

Was I the centre? No. So much occupied
Within my seeing and, much further on,
I heard the grateful and auspicious word,
Saw the broad opening of the morning sun.

World upon world. I was not well indeed
And yet what I have gathered from it all!
Dancers making music showed their need
And there was neither apple nor a fall.

The Story

I knew that it lay about me,
I knew that the story I had to live was near
But fenced off. Only I
Could find the entrance, and not by straining and fighting
But only, always by

Being prepared for the great surrender, the huge
Advance and appearance. Nothing to do with fear
Was this. I only had
To let the four seasons march in order ahead,
To watch the sky changing and meeting the sea.
This was the way I had to let things happen,
To let the world appear
In all its golden finish and lucky end.
I watched the door of morning start to open,
I simply put out my hand.

Country Sounds

We really lived in the country,
In the long school Summer holidays we shouldered
Our way through a thin wooden fence straight to a field
Where the hay was high and sweet-smelling, the sun crisped it and
There were poppies and shepherd's purse and cow-parsley
And the smell of grass and the buzz and murmur of insects.
Our home was big and near enough to the city,
A beautiful university but we,
My sister and I, basked and flourished in green.
Deft with her hands always she would build
Small hay igloos. We'd sit in the dark smell
And plan an easy war with bows and arrows.
No one actually suffering of course.
For we were in a mood shaped by the huge sun
Bowling overhead.
And we were in a trance of murmurous Summer sounds
Its music sighing and blowing,
And we learnt much all the time
Whole histories of how things thrive and spread
And we packed our imaginations with country lore
Dreams of milking and taking in the harvest.

Today this cannot be.
That field and every approach to it is built on
With houses of different designs, all showing cars.
And so our country life is a memory,
A mood and a music too.
Our counterparts today don't own a field,
    Can't share our languid pleasure.
I wish I could

Offer our pleasant field to them and let
Them learn the wisdom of every Summer sound.

Out in the Country in 2000

I shall not forget this Summer
With all its moods of water and of light,
With all its hasty sky and tunnelled roads.
I shan't forget so many
Greens beyond green, the sage, the weed, the mournful
Evergreens. There've been such raids of light
Down side-roads which we drove down, through the neat
Important, tugging river.

I shan't forget the sound
Of many birds excited by the breeze,
On hunting trips, the young out testing wings
And tumbling with the clouds
All this through side-roads, lanes of Oxfordshire
And Warwickshire, so ripe and clean and busy.

I took new vigour from the rush of winds
I drank the light and felt it in my veins.
I praise the countryside that's still to find,
Waiting so patiently,
Giving, oddly, such strong peace of mind.

Caring

It was all scientific to start with,
The voice, male, young, not excited,
Not at first, that is.
But the radio voice became much warmer, much keener,
And the subject, *Life Before Birth*, became important.
The young obstetrician didn't hide what he felt
And the woman whose labour only lasted two hours
Kept saying 'It hurt very badly, you've no idea',
But the doctor *had* an idea, his voice revealed it,
The words came faster as, with enormous pride,
Which I could accept at once,
He said 'A baby is much, much tougher than we are,

Before it is born, I mean.
For example, our brains won't survive more than three minutes
Without any oxygen,
But an unborn child can do without it much longer
It has to be tough, you see, for its long, dark journey.
So full of hazards and dangers.'
He went on talking and I
Found quite suddenly I was close to tears.
Why? Why? Why?
I think now because so much care was present
So much compassion, almost all of it practical.
Life Before Birth is an almost epic subject,
So many hardships and obstacles,
So much longing to live.
The young doctor's voice paused sometimes and I
Realised how carried away he was by his subject,
How much he wanted premature lives to continue
How far away from anything that must die.
How rapid the hands I could not see must have looked,
How eloquent his eye.

Well-Being

I savour it as it returns to me,
    This health, this flow along
My bones and veins, this wholesome energy
Which can create rich thoughts or drifts of song.

Any poison halts the inward flow;
    Illness takes away
The strength of love almost. Art seems to go
Relentlessly. There is more night than day.

Now I am glad and grateful and relearn
    The taste of happiness.
My thoughts with almost tenderness now turn
To making poems, creation's hopefulness.

Vigour

Sometimes each day proclaims itself as if
    I had not seen it so
Before. It has such glow, such sheen, such life.
The oldest flowers seem freshly now to grow,

And every sky I gaze at shows a sun
    Of huge power and extent.
From being ill I'm well and I've begun
My life afresh. I understand what's meant.

New ideas are spoken. I am full
    Of longing now to know
How creation shows such fulsome skill,
How all the winds seem fertile when they blow.

I see before I understand and then
    Interpret and explore.
I move in joy around this world of men
And beg more life, more freshness, more and more.

Celebration falling like kind rain
New skies that have new planets in their store.

Lullaby for the Old

The old need a lullaby
    As much as the young.
I think of right words to sigh
    Into a song.

A song that reminds of the past
    And all of its joys.
May all through the night my song last
    Sounding 'Rejoice'.

Rage of the Moon

Rest, heavy head, on the wood
    Of the good, old desk-stand.
Dreams must be understood
    And the right hand

Feels for purchase upon
    A fine, old, open page
Of writing lit by the moon
    And its light rage.

October 2000

The leaves hang tardily. There's been such rain
And now today the sky is wide and clear
Of all but radiant clouds. After huge rain
We are amazed at the dry atmosphere

And potent sun that glitters through pale blue
And tender puffs of cloud. Rain disappeared,
Summer has not quite gone. What it can do
Now that the land's been winnowed and is clear –

Imagination gathers insights now,
A slightly teasing landscape keeps alert
Leaf after leaf, still green on twig and bough.
Here is a country for the hopeful heart.

The Thinker

He is mild-mannered and some people say
'He's in another world.' They are quite wrong,
He is in now and here, and every day
He thinks of plans to which we all belong.

He's read past notions. In his mind he holds
A shape, a purpose, meaning written live.
Night and day he watches now our world's
Behaving wildly. He wants it to thrive.

He wants all men to share his appetite
For truth. It is a way of life, a choice
Of how to be and know. He claims no right
But tries to be a civilised, true voice.

For Any Newish Poet

There is this habit now of nonchalance –
One writes of death but doesn't use the word.
They might allow the words 'a dance of death'
    Or something overheard.

There is this habit of concealing art:
You do not say you fear and let alone
Love anyone. You have, of course, a heart
    But now it is not done

To say you care. O yes but English verse
Comes echoing back: 'I am behind the art
I am the feeling when you love to curse,
    I am the vital part

Of everything you write.' Remember Yeats,
Don't forget Auden's perfect adjective
So unexpected. English poetry waits
    Always for you to give

What feels like novelty. The new is so
Resistant. Never mind. Dare to allow
The word that leaps to mind. O let it grow
    And be part of your now.

Prayer: Homage to George Herbert

George Herbert said it all. All I can do
Is show my hesitancies now and try
To fit my different, later words into
Another way to say Our Lord will die.

He hangs upon the Cross and I seek words
And how they can be lifted into prayer.
The soldiers come with hammers and with swords
And flies are buzzing in the blinding air.

Shall I seek opposites as Herbert did
To reach the truth? I need the spirit to
Leap through flesh. Language must be rid

Of all half-meanings. Christ needs words to show
He's dying. O indeed now he is dead
But I shall need the words that rise also.

Homage to Thomas Traherne

Your prose could hardly be more close to verse.
It soars, it sings, and God is your great theme,
Your paeans to Him never seem to cease,
He filled each waking moment and, in dream,

God surely must have faced you gladly with
All his graces shining, sweet and clear.
You never needed to have fear of death
Yet your contrition was not hard to hear.

Your *Centuries* are noble, rich, serene,
Leaping with love and dancing with delight
And it is clear exactly what you mean.

Traherne, you've lighted up my blackest night.
Your work is quick, direct, exact and keen
And everywhere I read I come on light.

Homage to Gerard Manley Hopkins:
After Receiving Communion in Hospital

Hopkins, I understand exactly now
What you meant when you told us that the sick
Endear us to them. I know this is true
Because I am a sick one and God's quick,

Saving principle has come to me,
A tiny piece of bread unleavened saves
The soul. I feel its power immediately.
Stammering my thanks, I know my flesh behaves

Oddly, but I know also I am
Within Heaven's confines. You, O Hopkins I
Commend for showing me how close I came

To our Redeemer in his healing, high
Offices. My thanksgiving is home
And Jesus Christ is with me where I lie.

Homage to Robert Graves

The lyric, that true, traditional sound
You were in touch with all your life. I owe
More debts than I can pay. I love your ground
Which blossoms into song. You did eschew

Modernism but it did not matter,
You had no need of it, you were so strong.
You tell us of fierce love. None can do better,
It makes us see death darkening every song.

'Death's food at last in his true rank and order'
You wrote and you were right. Yes, Robert Graves,
You wrote much else, stood never on a border.

You knew the moods of love, how it behaves
And you stored language like a busy hoarder.
I move about among your golden leaves.

Reflection

Wisdom comes without a sage,
    Music finds harmony
That asks for no composer of any age.
    Thus, sometimes, poetry.

Looking at Pictures

In memory of C. V. Wedgewood

Your presence lit the paintings for me but
Only to show more radiantly how each
Impressionist, say, in his own way caught
A slant of sun, a pool of shade. To teach

Like this is not to teach at all but fill
Another's eyes with your own way of seeing.
You let the biggest buffet go so still
That I too entered in the painter's being.

And so we walked from galleries to see
A world transformed. Thus every visit went
When you were picking paintings out for me,

Making the shortest time a large event,
Now I'm alone but you have set me free
In all art's history from those hours we spent.

Concerning Imagination (I)

It is at all great starts of things. Recall
The Tree, the Garden and the promise, all
Appeared in nursery tales and nursery rhymes.
Imagination furnishes all times
That show a lucid and an empty space.
There was a whisper even then of grace
And grace is what a nanny taught you long
Before you'd heard the other use of song,

How everything is swarming with odd light
When you look back to find your first goodnight.
Haven't you been searching everywhere
For places which halt time and hold you there?
Eden had its cradle – songs you knew
And Eden wasn't very long ago
When you read history and noticed how
Imagination chooses then or now.

And then the many faiths, the countless cults,
It is not your imagining which halts.
And you can't run from it for in your dreams
Images rise and joy or terror comes
How is it to be held, how fixed and framed?

It won't need orders or the cold command,
No, let it be, and, let alone, it may
Grow without you. It did yesterday,
But do not think tomorrow's at your beck
Entirely. Human will can love or wreck.
Remember all the frightening history.
Imagination is no mystery
But it can haunt whatever you may do
And can be both the ghost and haunted too.

Concerning Imagination (II)

It can round known galaxies, scan light
    And yet there must be rules.
It has its own bewildering stretch of light
And it can make the owners of it fools.

When it digs deep or leaps across the sky
    It is a kind of grace
Offered to almost everyone. Then why
Is it so trammelled by the human race?

In the baby crying after birth
    It is already laid
Intricately and gently in our earth.
Yet from our start we knew we have betrayed

Some unreached tenderness, some dear compassion.
    Our will plays its strong part
In the uses of imagination
Which comes the moment there's a human heart.

Concerning Imagination (III)

It is reality, it must be stressed,
    And not its opposite.
We place its aura over everything
    By our power make it fit
A tiny mood, great art, a way to sing,
    It's more than to exist.

Wallace Stevens made each poem he wrote
    Show differences between
Imagination and reality.
    And yet for everyone,
By casting his own glow he showed how we
    All somehow have brought

The two together. All we imagine is
    A bonus to all things.
We heighten every exploit that we know.
    Imagining means wings
Which lift the usual, give it light, and so
    Our purpose here is this.

Diagnosis

The doctor talks. The students gather round.
I'm opposite this patient in a bed
Close enough to hear each separate sound.
I heard each syllable the doctor said
But I am carefully bound

To seeming not to listen. Doctor goes,
Students chat and smile and disappear.
That patient opposite is wrapped in fear,
She turns and pulls her sheets and blanket close.
I am so far though near.

The patient's name is Milly. Now and then
We've talked of trivial things. We've never said
A word about our illnesses. Her pain
Is obvious to me. Will she be dead
Soon? What does it mean

That operation which the doctor told
Her wasn't 'very serious'? I knew
The very opposite was what was true.
I dared not show compassion and be bold
And tell her that I knew.

At length knowing I could not find the right words
To fit the time, I kept our talks upon
Humdrum matters. She would point out cards
She had received. Her operation's soon.
O human nature's cards

Ought to be tougher and more sensitive.
The very contradiction makes me see
How far we are from powerful sympathy.
I do not know how long that friend will live
But feel her lack in me.

An Awareness

When did I first know I'd been close to death?
When did the dark, negotiating birds
Swarm away and their sounds turn to words?
When did the wide air clear and show me growth
　　Was what I moved towards?

Pain released me, anaesthetics lost
Their power. People's faces became clear.
It was as if a sweet, migrating host
Turned and brought Summer back and placed me near
　　Where the sun shone most.

The minute-hands were moving on most watches,
The chimes of all clocks sounded steady hours.
Lights seemed everywhere that each limb stretched
Towards when healthy. O I felt new powers
　　Building me fresh beaches.

I fell in love with the tides, and love renewed,
Restored, re-made me. Life put kindly hands
Out for my need. There was not any feud
Between the ill and well but now new lands
Showed me everywhere fresh flowers, ripe food
　　And I could understand.

Some Months After Anaesthetics

It is as if I'd never seen before
The block of gold that's melted in the air,
It was indeed a largesse of good ore
That's painted all the shadows everywhere.
It is as if a door

Opened in the East this morning and
Spread out richly everywhere; torched flower
From white to yellow, lighted on a hand
That settled anywhere. It is a power
In sky and on the land.

In early Spring I left my sick-bed and
Tangle of memory and gazed around.
I was enriched and altered, found a friend
In everything. This morning all the ground
Is gold that will not end.

It will only be concealed at last
When cool comes back and we turn round the sun
But I shall have no feeling of a past
Or credit that the sun has really gone.
My mind makes happy haste,

And my imagination is restored
And lively, richer than it was before
Sickness held me. Memory's now a hoard
Of rich landscapes and insights. My mind's door
Shows an unearned reward.

Tenderness

For Alyson

I can't remember any tenderness
Like this before. When I was weak and ill
A gentle nurse would wash me. My distress
She calmed at once. I can remember still
Each quiet move, calm word. I marvel this

Can happen for I'm independent and
Think that I am able to take care
Of myself. With her hand on my hand,
Washing was a kind of joke to share.
There's so much more today I understand
And now I owe the whole of it to her.

Lost Time

Shall I never recall those hours when I
Lay drugged beneath the nameless surgeon's knife
Or in some bed or ward? I did not die
Though I was told I nearly lost my life.
Again, again I try

To bring back memory and every mood
Which it contains. What spaces did my mind
Inhabit? What great scenes, some sad, some good
Did I discover? Was I deaf and blind
Or in some neighbourhood

Out of time that memory won't yield?
I have haphazard, pell mell scraps of thoughts,
Far views of now a road and now a field
Of grazing cows? Or was I in great courts
Of princes which conceal

Histories of hopes or wars, or both? Who can
Offer me each event that fits these hours?
I beg my friends for knowledge and they scan
Moments when they saw me with no powers
Of usual days. No man

Or woman can retrieve that land. I knew
Its dreams, its riches and its emptiness.
I know that there is nothing I can do
To bring back all that lost time. So distress
Comes because the true

Events my spirit wandered in are lost
And my present lacks some grace, some sign
And yet what wonders hit me when I crossed
The threshold back to consciousness to find
All things aglow with grace.

After Four Months of Illness

Coming out of illness, I feel shy
As if the world around were new to me,
As if, as in vexed youth, I now must try
New doors which seemed to be

Locked and bolted. I've been in a closed
World (a world of open fear sometimes)
But nurses, doctors had their cures and used
Them carefully. Old rhymes

Of poetry came back to me before
The words of mannerly discourse. I'm glad
Poetry has such a grip. I push a door
Open and feel sad

Not to hear or see great celebrations,
Simply people caught off-guard who try
Not to stare. So, with imagination's
Fresh vigour I defy

My own uncertainty but I can't be
Bold as I wish. Too much has happened and
I know that I look pale and thin. I see
A world once usual new lit up for me.
I try to understand

Why such a flood of light shines everywhere,
Except for sudden darks. All this is new,
Yet there's an invitation in the air
And I walk slowly through the pell mell glow,
Then stand quite still and stare.

So much energy went into this
Return of mine. Long convalescence can't
Prepare you fully for a genesis.
I wonder where I'll fit for O I want
To find love, happiness.

One More Place of Memory

There are mysterious places where I've been
But only keep their echoes in my mind,
Also their fragrance. I have never seen
Colours like theirs before or since. I find
It hard to tell now of this curious land
And yet it haunts me. I can't understand

Why long sickness brought me into such
Woods and clearings. I declare the sun
Which shone there was a beacon, yes a torch
Lighting the earth up. O how hard it shone
And left new coins upon the forest floor
Where I was standing. I would say much more

But no words catch the glowings that I knew
Within that space where no clock ticked and where
Colours outshone the rainbow. Very few
People brushed past me but I did not care,
And yet I wish I had a map, a chart
To point out all I learnt. I need new art,

To show, as Baudelaire did, we too can
Mingle the senses. Yes, that comes most near
What I experienced. I indeed learnt then
A radiance that I could almost hear,
Sights I could touch. Maybe later on
I'll find the cadences which halt that sun.

Assurance

My love, I hold you in imagination,
     Either mine or yours
And it is stronger than remembered passion.
It uses memory with all its force.

O and the clocks go silent, time departs,
     Now is forever here.
How delicate yet strong are our two hearts,
Mine beats for you now almost everywhere.

Only when my world is rent with storm,
    Threatened by sadness or
Overcome by black words which can come
And threaten me with the inner, hideous war,

Only then, I've lost you, O but fast
    A little flash of sun,
A hurrying memory returns you blessed
And our great love is stalwartly at one.

Advice

Best to be still and meditate
And let the broken heart alone.
There is a pure and timely state
That reaches through both flesh and bone.
    O yes be still and gently wait
And neither trade nor own.

There is a quiet state of mind
Where images can dance until
Their own true landscape they can find
And where the heart is one with will
    In this way harvesting can bind
And nights are always still.

Wait, do not justify or trade
Or make excuses. What you need
Is something you have never made
And never understood indeed.
    Thus mind and heart are both obeyed
And to fruition lead.

The Hours

Out of silence they come, out of their own
Eloquent silences they join together
Into the wide church they come as the bells
Start the beginning of Hours, the singing of Hours.
These are silent men who come together
Out of their secret prayers into the open,

The cool and open, undecorated space
Of their wide church. Day after day and night
After night throughout the months and every year,
Monks sing the same words, save for the special ones,
The rich, enlarging Hours of the great Feasts,
Christmas and Easter and the darker Hours,
The penitential ones of open prayer,
Prayer that pierces the sun and rounds the moon,
Moves through the trees and over the roofs of houses.
The Hours are eternal in their repetitions,
The monks die and others take their places,
Young men who give up everything for the rich
Eloquence of prayer and the words of God,
God as Man and spirit and Three in One.
Hours sing the praises of the sacred Three
And the daily Masses, the bread turned into flesh
And wine to Blood, the Hours Hosanna and say
All that need be said in the singing voice.
Listen, the night is passing, the *Gloria*
Praises the dawn, the Lamb of God is sung
Into the rising sun and day appearing.
Hour after Hour, they will proceed forever,
Telling our Birth and sanctifying death,
Tolling and ringing, bringing the great good news
And the saving of souls and all the contrition of men.

Prophets

Into our history great prophets break
And they halt time with what they have to say.
Even sceptics want to hear them speak
Perhaps to catch them out and so betray.
They're cynics. Many make

Sounds of praise and wonder. Prophets give
Shape to our lives and touch our purposes.
They draw up rules and laws to help us live
With pride. They'll pause distress,

Comfort the grieving, make the happy more
Content. Great prophets are forerunners of
God and bear his early words. We are
Excited when we hear them speak of love.
We welcome every seer.

It is as if there is some need in us,
Isaiah, John the Baptist can fulfil.
They surely always have the power to bless
Our little plans. At best, they make us still
And alter us with grace.

Girl at Prayer

The girl simply raises her hand
And salutes the sudden sun and blesses it.
She is learning the lesson of love,
And trying to understand
That she need not search for words
Or make many movements either.
All she need do is copy the sun's behaviour
Or the moon's silent entry at night.

Advent

Comings gather here to celebrate.
Almost impossible adventures now
Take place and all excessive dreams can meet
And no one even wants to question why
Bright lights assume a street,

Stars stand in order. One or two may fall,
We are awestruck, full of gratitude.
Marvels can happen, we invite them all
Into a sudden state of wanting good.
Yes now every tall

Story comes true. A child is on his way,
Unborn as yet but carried in the womb
Of a virgin. She chose to agree
To this. O all the world makes ample room
For everyone to be

Enchanted in a state of graciousness
Not all choose well but possibilities
Blossom about us. In the Christmas Trees
Waiting around we watch our happiness
And some fall to their knees.

At Mass

It is the order which we know so well
The 'alleluija' here, the 'Amen' there
That concentrates the awe, makes drama fill
Whatever shape the church is. We can hear
Jerusalem is there,

Or maybe it is Bethlehem indeed.
People rise and genuflect, then bow
Their heads and by the gesture intercede.
The Mass proceeds and this is always how
We show how vast a need

Is satisfied. The Elevation is
Rushing by the bell and yet hours hesitate,
Time withdraws while human ecstasies
Take on the power in which we contemplate
How Mass must be like this.

The Bread and Cup are raised and once again
The Resurrection happens, we are there
Walking on Easter morning with Christ's pain
Still crying from the Cross and in our ears.
Listen, the meaning's plain

All metaphors from music or from verse,
All purpose undiminished and fulfilled
All these occur in every form at Mass,
The Crosses stand there and today they yield
To all of us the grace

We need but may not name. Psalm after Psalm,
Passages from the Bible sing their way
Into our hearts and we are all made calm.
The Eucharist appears each hour of day
Through violence, alarm

And all the dark happenings of history.
We beat our breasts, cover our eyes and may
Weep a little. Sin is washed away,
All of Redemption each Mass will set free
The large Grace we must say.

All Saints 2000

They are anywhere but you won't find
Them easily. They are elusive and
Often shy. Some have a marvellous mind,
Others seem eccentric. They won't stand
In riches. They are kind

In ways not obvious. Wherever there
Is anguish of the flesh or mind or heart
Their presence can be sensed. They always bear
With the awkward who can play no part
In this world. They share

Strengths with Gandhi, the Dalai Lama. See
How Christlike are their manners. How exact
Their wisdom. They are haunters who set free
Those they harry. Sometimes they are racked,
Often they will be

With children, fools, the difficult. Some have
Special powers but none is a magician.
When others laugh they often will be grave,
So various, they share a great tradition
Which is bound up with love.

You may find one saint talking in a bar
And sharing jokes and views. Extravagant
They never are except in what they bear,
Lovable, a kind of element
Also, sometimes a star.

All Souls

Yesterday the holy ones by name
Were all remembered. We were edified
Yet also sweet affection rang their fame
They have set us standards which we've tried
To emulate. Today

All the holy, unnamed souls are called
To mind and heart. How they domesticate
Our otherwise more lofty thoughts. We're filled
With kindness, warmth. This is a crowded date,
November the second stilled

For a little while as we reflect
In church or street or office or at home.
We think about our own ends and connect
Our souls with these now gone, but they yet come
To mind in any act

We interrupt with our small contemplation,
We think of everlastings for a while
And all these souls rise in imagination
They are within a spiritual exile.
There is deep dedication

For all believers, those who ever dared
To credit what we all so dearly want,
A never-ending, but we're not prepared
For death. Words come to us, seem Heaven-sent,
A future life unfeared.

Song in November 2000

Count within me your minutes, hours,
    The turned tide of the sea,
Count me among your Summer flowers
    And Winter's leaf-bare tree.
Count me by every bell which rings,
    By every clock which ticks.
Count me in all your time-bound things
    And candles' blackened wicks.

Whatever loss still hurts for you
    Shed tears until your grief
Ends the story that is true,
    The pattern of your life.
Even if love should end you must
    Let it and be free.
Time blows away our fickle dust
    But, in arched memory,

Story by story still are told
    And no one tires of these,
They change to myths when they are old
    And show the shape of peace
Count every death as ended war
    Which has its minstrelsy,
If you have ever loved before,
    Your book of memory

Shows page on page which you may turn
    And read or let alone
Doing either you can learn
    That birth and death are one.
We write the chapters of our lives
    By good or evil will
And page by page each one survives
    While someone reads them still.

Now is the turn of music to
    Choose trumpets, strings or drum.
They will assist each grief to go,
    Fresh happiness to come.
Music takes memory and lets
    Theme and use and range
Be heard in every note which fits
    And rings the needed change.

Turn the score of melody,
    Slowly let silence tell
The eager tale of memory
    That gives life yet stays still.

Carol for 2000

Put memory away. Today is new.
Carols and bells ring out and take the year
Into their power. They cast out pain and fear
    For everyone and you.

Put memory away. Soft sounds are rocking
A newborn child laid in a cradle made
For animals to eat from. Grace is said.
    A child puts out a stocking.

Put memory away and watch a world
Grown almost still because a baby can
Convince us he is born as God and man.
       The world's no longer old.

Put memory away. Tonight is Now.
And new as children's hopes and old men's eyes
Soon Kings will come and they are rich and wise
       But to a Child will bow.

Put memory away and have no fear.
A star is shining on a joyful sight.
A young girl's Child is born to us tonight
       And casts out pain and war.

New Year Song

This is the little space between
The marvellous birth and next New Year.
We've prayed and rid ourselves of sin
But still we feel the edge of fear.
So soon now we again begin

A year, a month, a way of life.
Three eager Kings are on their way.
A little child's been born in strife
But it is peace he brings to us
And gives our world another day,

Another year to mend our ways
And build our broken world again.
At Christmas we learn how to praise,
A little child fills all new days,
Forgiving sin, relieving pain.

Epiphany 2001

Three Kings or Three Wise Men – it is their day,
Their feast and with it we say our good-bye
To the new baby and the Christmas tree,
The gifts, the food but, most of all, the way
Light shone. It was an arrogant display.

The Kings bring gifts – gold, frankincense and myrrh,
The precious ore, the sweet scents we can share.
Outside today, the sun was everywhere
Yet sadness rises until, suddenly,
My father, I recall, was born today.

The melancholy goes for I recall
His sturdy mind, his to-and-fro of wits.
He thought that learning mattered for us all
And, what is more, gave me the taste for it
And hung such riches on my own mind's wall.

The Kings have come and gone. Epiphany
Moves to its close but now it leaves behind
A glow of Winter sunset in the sky.
Cards and gifts still throng my room and I
Can't bear to move them. Now my heart and mind

Rejoice together. Childhood comes back with
Its ripe regrets while age lights candles still
Partly to ease the eyes. O but their breath
Brings frankincense and myrrh and now they fill
Imagination. That small baby will

Guide us to Easter. Now I stand to pray
By a small crib and see the Child-God who
Waits for the world to say his words are true.
We can hoard now another Christmas Day
As Kings depart but by another way.

Night Song

Child in the womb or at breast,
Lovers at last at rest.
By the hands of the moon and sun
God's work is done.

This is the deep night.
The freezing Winter light
Of stars gathers us all
Into God's call.

In and above all things,
He is the night-bird's wings.
We come to him at last,
Some slow, some fast.

Whitsun

It's Whitsun in a day or two and I
Think of the tongues of fire, the Holy Ghost
Brooding and teaching men the way to die
And never to feel lost.

A Holy time indeed but weather wears
A different look. It's grey but, nonetheless
A few birds' songs are audible. My verse
Has come back. Happiness

Is how I write and I know God is near.
Tongues of fire bear poetry to its height,
While holy rhythms take my words to where
There never is a night.

Hope

It is never gone for long.
It travels in dark caves and washes round
Slimy rocks but then it is out and off
Moving over wet ground:
This is the Sea of Hope which is sometimes rough,
Sometimes brief as a song,

When the tide of hope is out
The sun glitters above in a huge round
And the waves are dappled with light and you have no doubt
That here you are meant to be
For the Sea of Hope is your sea.

But not always yours.
This sea has moods as well as its buoyant tides,
Waves rising like horses, their great sides
Flashing with emerald

You are somewhere near
But not by this sea. It is true it reaches your ears
This sea in its many moods is also old,
Almost as old as time.

Stay not too far away
And wait for hope to return like a bold day
At Summer's glittering height,
Practise your fresh sight
And use it to compass the wide sea and land
There is such golden sound
And on the breeze words whisper to you
In psalms and song, all of them telling a true

Tale which you'll later turn to your own words
And your own work of rhyme
As the Sea of Hope comes in and the sky glows
And words are ready to choose
And this moment is their time.

Eden

There are moments when we find we are
Back in Eden. Its authentic air
Carries the breeze and draws up every flower
Sunwards and shining. Trees surround us but
Always a special one is heavier
With fruit and promise too. No gates are shut

But all swing to our touch. We do not go
Directly to one tree but back in sun,
Sit down a moment, then walk to and fro
Shaped of admiration, looking on,
Not picking anything. We do not know
What we've decided yet. All suns have shone,

The rising and the going. We don't choose
Consciously the moment when we shall
Gaze up at fruit and feel dry for its juice.
On we go, down trodden avenues
Until we pause at last, and then the fall
Happens. Sky grows darker and we lose

All sense of ease and leisure. Something is
Wrong at the heart of us. The sky reflects
Our mood. Clouds gather. There's a wilderness
Where order ruled each hour. We notice weeds,
We gaze towards the city and each mind collects
Round sudden ruins wrought by our misdeeds.

Perfection

Most dream of a perfected, holy thing,
A place or state. It's natural to our race.
The spur is not ambition. No, we bring
To this thought of ideals, a sense of grace.

Not grace itself for that is always earned
But a foreshadowing of how it can
Lead us to a place where many learned
About a real but insubstantial plan.

Matter never satisfies for long,
Power dwindles fast and leaves us wondering
Why we pursued it. In the soul a strong

Yearning for a personal truth will bring
Us to our knees and keep us there for long
And we won't shun all kinds of suffering.

Assurance Beyond Midnight

Wisdom or music come in these small hours,
Their clarities combine and I allow
Myself almost to rest in their good powers.

But it's a lively rest that I know now,
Compulsions cease and everything around
Fits in a meaning though I don't know how.

I only know rich purpose with a sound
Of settlements suggests itself and I
Listen for theme and arguments, the ground

Of God's great Being. Stars are very high
The moon is full, a warm September makes
Seasons a mood here though I don't know why.

But I know well that now my spirit wakes
And is assured. Imagination is
Rich. Helped out of sickness and heartbreaks

I feel in touch with everything that's peace
And later on there will arrive with dawn
A bold assurance and a synthesis

Of what waits for me not much further on.
But near enough to tell me faith is bold
And proves itself in all that has been done

To me and for me in a golden world.

UNPUBLISHED POETRY

JUVENILIA

Wings of the War

Wings over the ocean, wings over the land,
Fly that courageous Royal Air Force band.
With fighters and with bombers they're beating down the Hun
Beating down the aeroplanes until there's only one.
Wings over the glistening sea, wings up in the clouds
Where the aeroplanes fly single not in huge great crowds.

Wings over the tree-tops, wings up in the blue
Men in leather flying suits, fly for me & you
Keeping forever our England strong,
Striving to right a wrong.
Wings buzzing overhead, in formation flying,
Wings of men, so strong, so free, who never think of dying.

The Friend

Sometimes I feel as though
The world was barren and each man a foe
As though no friend were near, no one to care
But there is always, always Some-one there
He died, the God, Creator of everything
That everyman might know him as The King.
His Dear Kind Face will smile at all our woes,
His gentle hand will make friends of our foes
My Jesus is there, My Dearest, Kindest Friend
My ever, ever, His World will have no end.

The sun shone through from a mystic sky
And the grass was green and the soil was dry
And crisp bright leaves of onions and Swedes
Were succulent, fresh from shrivelled, brown seeds
~~Now a certain old garden was specially gay~~
With crinkled leaved cabbage
in a certain garden.

A Snail Universe

In this place of blue and green and noise and sunshine bright
A gardener toiled hard to make the earth a glorious sight,
Clad in gumboots tall and strong to which the mud would cling
He tried to make a large savoy a very beauteous thing.
He dug the earth with gleaming spade and hoed and raked undaunted
Until an earwig hove in view and the young seedling haunted
A tidy row of flower pots red containing saplings new
Stood before the grey stone house for everybody's view
And enveloped of wondrous flowers with pictures on the front
In lurid reds and mauves and greens, to artists an affront.
But ne'ertheless the gardener toiled his face a ruddy tint
Whilst near a cat luxuriously lounged in the sweet cut mint
He purred and yawned and licked his fur in pussy ecstasy
And blinked and curled and furled his tail very sleepily.
Until front door [opened up a] jovial person came
Holding aloft some frothy beer A very worthy dame!
The gardener stopped his eager eyes upon the drink
He scattered seeds; he rushed along his gardening had ended!!

The Cuckoo

A voice rose out of the drowsy dawn,
A tuneful, bold, and glorifying voice,
Over the swaying trees and dew-flecked lawn,
It sang, not for compulsion, but for choice.

My whole being was tired and asleep
Lulled by the breezes that I scarcely heard
The whole of life was in a slumber deep
Until we heard the voice of a bird.

A strong clear voice full of the joy of life
Sounded its anthem in the dawn of Spring.
It was a voice that knew much joy, no strife
Or any of the horrors wars could bring

It sang of memories of dewy dawns,
And budding hedges and the blue skies clear
Of cool, quiet evenings and of happy morns
It sang of hope and Faith, not strife and fear.

Who is the man, who hearing such a sound,
Would not be wakened and deeply stirred
By the glad notes of one just lately found,
The music of the Springtime's happy bird.

To Our Lady

Beautiful sun of the morning
Mother on earth for our warning
Light of our hope and our dawning
Mary the Queen.
Sweet Sparkingly home of God's grace
Swift as an arrow in chase
Of Wisdom and love in the race
For the heavenly scene.

A Thought

What is it makes youth bright yet wondrous dark?
The sorrow of a grave, the sweet joy of the lark?

The Call of the Sea

As I sit, high on the cliff-top
Gazing out at the great wide sea,
And as I look on the glistening ocean,
It brings strange thoughts to me.

As I look, I think of great sea-men,
Of Drake, and Raleigh too,
Of many courageous sailors
Who sailed across the blue.

Then I think of the great Lord Nelson
The most gallant Admiral was he,
And the finest little sailor
Who ever sailed the sea.

But long ago lived explorers
Who set out to find new land
They sailed in their little, wooden ships
And landed on new sands.

But there's still the Royal Navy
Who sail from sea to sea,
Protecting and guarding the high seas
To keep Our England free.

Moonlight on the Oxus

The moon it shineth down upon the river,
Making the water gleaming down below,
Whilst nearby sings the last sweet nightingale,
Warbling his last sweet song.
And all this while the trees stand still and straight,
Their tiny leaves shiny and motionless.
All through the night the water ripples along,
Shimmering sweetly like a wondrous jewel:
And through the moonlight all the world doth sleep.

Roman Noon

The buildings are the only emphasis
Within this heat, they grip thin bold facades,
They trim Rome and let it bear across
The ancient stone and flesh and burn to red:
This heat is such that even shade discards
Its darkness and turns to light instead.

Travelling through moments and feeling flush
(Yet full of ease) from luncheon and the day,
The wine still gay within my throat, the rush
Of voices, people, colours still the way
I want Rome most, I yet can feel the hush
Of how a city shuns the full noon's sway.

But close to a siesta I can feel
Also the stone, the flesh, the sin
The bright facades of churches break and peel;
And sense how someone in his room will draw
The shutters to, will close his eyes and kneel
And beg, beyond the instant's grace, for more

Yes I can understand and sympathise
And feel myself need to hide away,
Grope beyond all the pleasure of the eyes,
This haunting city, the ecstatic day
And O deeper than the mind can say
A prayer that punctuates the heart's disguise.

The Adversaries

Framed by their frowns they wait alert
Across the gulf their shadows make
Their force is felt within their hands.
Each hopes his enemy will take
Aim first for fighting to begin

The conflict, yet each fears to move.
Watching, unknowing you might think
The struggle was a truce of love.
Far off the total battles wage:
Only these two like beasts before
The final power stay still and wait
The proper opening of their war.
Stillness indeed. And if they could
Stay thus a little longer they
Might break the meaning of their mood
And pause to pity not to slay.
Closer than death's last shaken word
Two men who guess each other's pride
Might set their single arms aside
And sheathe their shadows like a sword.

Elegy

If we learn to read poetry properly, the poet never persuades us to believe anything ...
What we learn from Dante, and the Bhagavad Gita, or any other religious poetry is
what it feels *like to believe that religion.*

T.S. Eliot

Washing, washing against the wall
We picked a pebble up there once
Communicated with the stones,
Regarded every thin wave's fall
And O the wasting of the planet's edge
Rubbed by the waters and the moon's
Calm but abrasive privilege.

So many conversations pause
At the sea's edge. Words halt because the tide
Rubs salt into the wound in every side.
So many dry-eyed brief farewells,
Become important just because
The untempting inland bells
Made every smallest parting wide

Now there is nothing but the stars
Hint of another different night.
The last ship leaves the harbour, steers
By the cold moon's approving light.
But still the thought of water and the way

The shore is ribbed baffles the mind.
What footprint will be left behind,
What will tomorrow's voices say?

Towards Contemplation

Not to the sun these worshippers
(The footfalls echo down the street):
The fountains guess an instant's throw
As if the hour itself would slow.
It is the mind, not sense, that stirs
Yet light is hot beneath our feet.

Churches are cool and air expands
Wide in the dark, then drawn across
The smells and sighs. And silence here
Dispels, not emphasises fear.
Touch is subdued while waiting hands
Are folded in a full repose.

But who can say the dark he finds
Is not the opposite of light,
The light that breaks across the air
And halts a shadow with a stare?
O we are flesh and our own minds
Need the brash sun, the brazen sight.

Adolescence

I was a child when the war began
Waiting with net above a shallow pool
I watched for prawns. All the Atlantic ran
Backward and forward, thread upon a spool.
What does a child know of tides and can
Clear minds be muddied by a world's mistake?

Bombs fell beyond my city. All I knew
Of war was adolescence, was the sudden
Shadow (my own) across the child's view.
The pool, the prawns, oh all the easy vision
Were pushed away. And though my body grew
The wide day shrank. All clarity was hidden

France fell and concentration camps were filled
But all the blood I knew was how my own
Body grew strange. The gazing child was killed.
Nations fought on: simply I was alone.
The clear pool held the shadow of the world.

'No Worse, There is None'

Not love or hate or any magic thing
Will help me now, I feel so much alone.
It is as if I shrank to nothingness,
Had lost all power to write words, make them sing.
O God, it seems that everything has gone;
Call it self-pity, call it suffering.

In happy moments now (and they are few),
I paint, make up strange verse, become a child;
But momentarily, within my head,
My heart also, a pain, I never knew
Exists and then I wish that I were dead.
But fear still holds me back before I can
Do damage, only cry so deep within
Myself, I could not say what sickness fills
Me, yet I can retain a sense of sin;
This is no drama, nothing new to man.

God is remote, I cannot put my hand
Or mind out to him; words seem meaningless,
Others have been the same and worse, I know
But where is that first-last clear *caritas*?
Hot tears still fall. I do not understand.

Acceptance (Perversity)

Why, why?
And when
Shall I stop blaming myself
And begin

To accept, believe,
That anyone
Might in the same position
Have done the same thing?

In any paper
The horror
Is certainly true. *This* happened,
But the terror

Really lies
In everyone;
We are perverse to the depths –
No exception.

And when whatever happened
Is done by you
Then however it sears or wounds
You cling to it too.

As I See It

You do not share my faith
So must I write as if I had no faith,
As if my acts were not preceded by
Not only choice but by acknowledged choice?
Must I pretend I see no order in
The world we both inhabit? This would be
Dishonest, reprehensible. My faith
Touches on this also, this busy writing.

But do not think however
Action, event and character for me
Are different from how they seem to you.
We both interpret. On that ground we meet.
Old symbols which once worked in poetry
No longer stand. Their meaning rests upon
General acceptance. Here then, I prefer
To let them go. My own conviction must
Rely upon my voice, my private speech.
And only thus can I converse with you.

Before the Interview (Surprise)

The seeming cruelty, the chair or couch,
The accusations from the godlike man,
The terror of believing that he can
Destroy you utterly, kill at a touch –
This the experience that still goes on

No mystery, he says, no drugs will do
What you must do yourself. You hate him more
And fear him more, each time you are asked for
He can, you think, do so much harm to you.
You weep in terror half the night before

You have to climb those stairs, a yellow sheet
Shaking within your hand; and in your mind
You dare not think what meanings he will find
How he will speak, what he will make you say.
You hate all this, you try to run away.
Then why one morning, when you find him ill
Do you not think 'Thank God, I too can kill'?
Instead, compassion quite gets in the way.
I do not understand, am baffled still.

Breakfast in a Mental Hospital

I cannot bear these faces any more,
I cannot stand the silences that greet
Me as I enter, pulling to the door

No one is bright and if they are, I hate
Them for their noise and yet, I try to hold
Fast to good manners – butter and dish and plate

It frightens me each morning – such a cold,
Inhuman atmosphere; I live on fear
As all the others do. Always I'm filled

With longings to run out, to close a door
And be alone, not risk the certain pain,
At times I think that I can't bear much more
And think of doing what I did before.

The Dead Selves

I think of them now, these makers who needed life –
Thomas and Plath and Crane.
Each had a language cutting smooth as a knife,
I have prayed for them, but most of all felt pain
For those who have chosen and cannot choose again.

Oh tears and drugs and fear beset me too;
I did what they did, but I was carried back.
Yet I have seen like Lazarus the crack
Between this life and death. They knew, they knew
The whole of it. What did the world then do
Since each of them saw its richness? Was it some lack,

A being able to bear so much?
All of them fought the sea or sex or touch,
All were lovable. Over and over again
We lose the givers and the truly rich.
Is it because we cannot bear their pain?

Discharge from Hospital

I must admit it; all the things I thought
I wanted ended seem desirable
Now that I know I must give up that port
Of curious safety. I'm no longer ill
I realise we cling to what seems strong
Not to get self-importance but to gain
The safe, not beautiful, but certain thing
How when there's kindness, then, can we attain
The cure that sends us back among the stars
And traffic, to the noisy and the still
Planet we were born on to, where we must
Live without keys or cures or pills or bars?
I ran once from the things I most could trust:
Now I'm reluctant to admit I'm well.

Divers Gifts

Here I have found new words, new languages,
Subjects possessing me. Not rhetoric
Nor too much understatement here, I think,
Sometimes the sentences, the images
Flow out until my head spins and I fall
Into a natural sleep, no longer sick.

And when I wake, the only guilt I feel
Is that these others who live with me have
No power of words. But I forget how they
Have marriages and love. So much can heal
Part of our illness is we dread what's good
Has disappeared and most of all it's love.

We lack or have abused. There is not much
Simplicity or innocence within
These clinic walls. We have built our own too.
Jump at the tenderest, kindest human touch,
The Hippocratic oath is based on this –
Doctors are not afraid of sore or sin.

This world is still extreme though, nonetheless
One never knows what horror one may see
One does not know what's wrong with others here
Unless they tell. Strange that I curse and bless
What I have learnt and laughed at – suffered too.
(My freedom's shattered, yet my mind is new.)

Duty Doctor

There was no pity on that face at all,
Nor yet indifference. He stared at me
As if I were a nuisance, one last call

Before his duty ended. Dignity
Of every kind was snatched away and he
Took from me my humanity.

Vomiting, weeping, body stretched out taut,
I lay, and in the distance faintly heard
Voices, – my father's and a doctor's – caught

The sounds 'Too much for us.' No other word
Was clear; and soon the stomach pump was used.
All this was nothing to the overheard

And cruel truth. Acquitted, self-accused
Often I cry still at the words which bruised.

A Father

What keeps us tied together has grown knots
Now when I enter rooms where you have been
A just perceptible

Tension disturbs the air, as if a glass
Were tapped and one clear note sent echoes round
The also complacent room.

We speak and my intention not to quarrel
Is palpable as all the *objets d'art*
Which sit so plumply and so tidily.

Violence would have brought us close together –
Real tears and blows and reconciliation.
The truce is tense, the room itself

Seems to be waiting for a sudden gust
Of wind to blow the flowers down, smash the glass
At least we then would pick the pieces up.

Hospital

Observe the hours which seem to stand
Between these beds pause until
Some shriek breaks through the time like glass to show
That human-kind is suffering still.

Observe the tall and shrivelled flowers.
So brave a moment to the glance.
The fevered eyes stare through the hours
And petals fall with soft fresh pinks.

A world where silence has no hold
Except a tentative small grip
Limp hands upon the pillows fold
Minds from their bodies slowly slip.

Though death is never spoken here
It is more palpable and felt –
Touching the cheek or in a tear –
By being present by default.

The muffled cries, the curtains drawn,
The flowers pale before they fall –
The world itself is here brought down
To what is suffering and small.

The huge philosophies depart,
Large words slink off, like faith, like love
The thumping of the human heart
Is reassurance here enough.

Only one dreamer going back
To how he was when he was well
Weeps under pillows at his lack
But cannot tell, but cannot tell.

Heat Wave: Melons

They are eating melons in the late evening
O hot sugar and easy sliding knife!
The melons reflect the moon.

We throw off our bed-clothes,
Someone is thirsty and reaches for water.
The sea is too far away with too few boats.

We throw off the sheets.
I walk to the window and wait for the day to arrive.

And love is urgent even in this hot climate.

Imagined Honeymoon

The gentle morning and no need at all
To hurry or to move. We should perhaps
Be shy a little, I turn to the wall
And do not you speak. There would be many traps
Still to avoid. Sometimes we would feel strange
Together. Love must learn how to arrange

Its moods: In marriage there would be much more
For us to watch and care for than in love –
Responsibilities not known before,
Duties and dreams we had not spoken of.
And yet I think it still would stand apart,
That morning where our marriage had to start.

We shall have none of this, we shall not know
Those days when love can move from mood to mood,
We know the sudden depths but not the slow
Acknowledgements where passion is like food
Needed and ordinary, not a feast
We never have the calm of simple rest.

Incompatibilities

She talks, he listens, I sit in between.
These are the parents of a friend of mine
I feel myself a safeguard or a screen
Preventing anger or a hateful sign,

This marriage has gone on, perhaps too long.
What happened when the passion first was spent?
The children must have guessed that things were wrong.
Now, years past passion, she in pain, he beat

With rheumatism, find a sort of truce
In gentleness – their children live elsewhere,
While I, still young enough to be their child refuse
To catch the hints of their concealed despair.

A Lesson

There was music next door
A boy practising clumsily,
    Rain was coming soon;
Violence was coming.

    I have written too much or too little of love,
Now it comes most sweetly with death.
    I am learning, learning
Clumsily (like the boy with the violin)
    That I can love enough
To weep for your father's death (someone I never knew),
    But the sharp, clear, pain
Is soon spoilt by my thinking
    'I want to be with you.'
We cannot keep love pure for long
    How well you would understand this.

A Memory

For a whole week now, I have been reflecting
On what I did last year. My breath comes fast
When I attempt explaining or dissecting;
So quickly now, mere thoughts bring back the past.

I think of all the famous ones who've done
What I did, and succeeded; I came back,
I feel a need to shout to everyone,
I have a scar the lucky living lack.

Not lucky, but courageous, or not sick.
Now, for a year, people have tried to tell
Me that I did not know the years of wreck
That never could lead anyone to Hell.

Limbo, perhaps, or Purgatory, some place
Where those who've lost their way can find some rest
The face of God is veiled from them at first,
But, God knows, God is merciful at last.

The Mind Has Wounds

I have hated these months
Planned to run away
Especially at night when the doors were
        locked and I was wearing only pyjamas.

I have tried so hard to be kind;
What has emerged has often been tears, self-pity, near hatred
Most of all, I have spent my time saying 'Sorry,'
Feeling guilty for what was not my fault.
Drugs helped but I knew all would be the same tomorrow,
This place of healing has seemed like a prison.
I have wanted kisses and kindness.
I have wanted to know what is wrong.

God, don't go away. I have never ceased to believe
But you have often seemed a void,
I have learnt a lot, I think;
I am changed.
But most of all,
I am afraid of the future.

Miro

Miro, you have been highly praised lately:
One hears strange comments such as 'So like children's art'
In smug, sophisticated voices, or 'Another Klee, so mathematical.'
If one is honest, if one tries to define one's pleasure,
Then I think it is because you have made your own world
And managed to do it without shutting us out.
That pleases us and makes us love you.
We cannot put you in a period or movement
(Not easily, that is); you are individual
Your strange children, balls, balloons, string –
They are part of you. Your colours and composition are joyful
So that no one can say 'I could paint that.'
Only the slick and vulgar really arouse such responses.
I know who would best understand you –
Blake, Samuel Palmer and, perhaps above all, Chagall.
You have delicacy but no sickness, mystery but no confusion.
Miro, I admire and pay tribute to you.

The Mountain

We never did get far into those mountains.
We had equipment ready, tools and clothes
And food enough to last a Winter through,
But somehow there was always a delay.
The valley crops were bad, our sick children
And so the mountains still remained a view.

And yet we never quite forgot their presence,
Even at ordinary tasks like ploughing,
Building or mending our machines, our eyes
Would sometimes turn towards them. We would keep
The chance of scaling them secure and bright
Cut ropes were ready and we had supplies.

Sometimes a stranger would come down and tell us
A little of the hazards of the climb.
None that we met got more than halfway there.
And we were always glad that they had failed,
Knowing the mountains all remained for us;
We staked our claim on that still unbreathed air.

Now we are old and all our dreams of climbing
Have gone so deep that they are part of us.
And yet our bones are far too stiff and dry
Even to scale the smallest peak. But still
We tell our children and our grandchildren
The mountains are unscaled, but never why.

Naming the Stars

They are still there, waiting.
We want to visit them
But first we must name them
Plough, Bear, Mars, Moon.
Naming them possesses us of them,
Makes them our worlds.
Picked out at night, they appear
To leave behind them more worlds.
Then at times they seem to come near, near,
Close to us they come, a kind of protection,
A warmth, a kindness, an image of brilliance.
Also their distance is often a warm one,
Oh hands, hands, pluck them down, down.

On the Telephone

One word, dredged up from random memories
And the whole line's a-buzz with violence.
The voices crack and part, and then a silence,
More terrible than any sentences
Is broken by the operator's voice,
'Three minutes more'
We do not have a choice.

The bakelite receiver clutched so hard
Against the ear becomes an instrument
Of agony. It is a double torment.
Which one of us will say the hurting word
And which fling down the telephone and then
Wait for the other one to dial again?

Order

Looking for order, now, I see how words
Have given me an image of pure calm.
Cities have been erected where no birds
Nest, no voices shout. A lifted arm
Belongs but to a statue and is meant
To be a symbol of admonishment.

Words crowded thus and made shapes of their own
Until I could not see what lay behind
The well-laid bricks and the appropriate stone.
It was as if I shut out half my mind
Keeping the night's chimeras out of sight,
Admitting but a foreground, careful shaded light.

And if the rats behind the city walls
And if the deadly beams are brought to view,
Does this mean that all art, all language falls
Back to the chaos that the first stars knew?
Or does the need for order also go
Back to beginnings that we cannot know?

Philosophy in Springtime

Winter was the best time:
Then he could speculate without intrusion,
Bring books down from the shelves and by his fire
Keep body warm until his mind grew calm,
Balancing arguments or letting them
Go drifting as the smoke went up the chimney.
Chill Winter was locked out and all his thought
Engaged in comfort on philosophy.

Then Spring came suddenly.
At first he hardly noticed, still could think
Of what life meant, of what the stars endured,
Of why men reasoned and of how they acted.
Then his five senses broke the Winter calm,
The air was thick with birdsong and his own
Pulses invaded every line of thought
And leaving books strewn on the floor and table
He let the season have its way with him

And later shaped a new philosophy.

Revaluation

Am I the same
You loved three years ago? There has been such
A growth or a decay. Now, at your touch
I come as I first came

Swiftly sometimes, sometimes
As though I carried all acts, all events
Since our first meeting. Yes, and I can sense
Like one who climbs

A virgin peak, a sense of strangeness here.
Illness and pain and anger cannot break
The image of each other which we make,
Both from delight and fear.

Spaceman

What to say of it since
No one else has seen anything quite
Like this? How can he find words to convince
Those who are earthbound still, who stare at the light
As he did once?

The weightlessness, the being
Out of control of hands and feet and then
The utter loneliness and only seeing
Everything by oneself, the being shut in
With the earth lying

Lonely like any other star
And he, godlike almost, gazing at it.
There are no symbols quite that can compare
Will his imperial glance, no image to fit
To be so far

From all that we know well
Is something, perhaps, like being a holy one
Who comes to us from the mountain, his vision still
Showing upon him. This man comes from the sun
With secrets sights that he cannot tell.

Suicide

Pills, first, of course, the easy way
But they were powerless under this pulsating planet.
Then followed the gas which took a long time
Much too long, I was woken from it.

Pills (to be sure), oven opened and the head resting there
Waiting for finality. At last there was nothingness
Then the pressing on the chest to bring life back,
It came back, I returned, I returned.

All this I lived through – also the hurrying to hospital,
Ambulance, stomach-pump, questions and answers
And then the trolley to the ward, the bed waiting,
And most of all, a sweet smile hooked from unkindness.

I am cool now on a cold planet.
I do not want pills or gas to destroy me,
Yet memories of near-death die hard, die hard.
Always the pills, the gas are near.

The Treatment

I do not understand what you are doing,
Why I must live my childhood once again.
Reading psychiatry, I find I'm going
Nowhere, I think I'd rather have the pain

That's been with me most of my life, than this
Grey magic, ugly jargon, and the way
You say 'We'll take these facts, interpret these
Things' that I try to say or do not say.

Our smart world's witchcraft? I dared say that
You'd have an answer. Even so, I can
Accept the pain of freedom, oh yes, but
I chose the last resort, despair of man

And like a child, I only want to prove
That I was wicked, guilty. If you would
Show me I can be loved and still can love,
I would perhaps, with fear, leave this dark wood

Where I have wandered far too long. Are you
Observing all this, making notes perhaps
Out of compassion and a wider view?
And do you really have the needed maps.

I haunt myself; you are the fearful ghost.
Each interview feels sick in heart and mind,
Please tell me what is wrong, and why I must
Find out myself or leave all help behind?

Two Ways

Two ways I think I have known love. The first
Is passionate and restless, knows no peace.
It knows of aching hunger and of thirst
Of pain and longing, and of jealousies

And even if requited, it can't find
A certainty, a peace, a sense of trust.
It cannot stop the movements of the mind,
Or live apart from every human lust.

The other love is friendship, and demands
Nothing, not even something still returned.
It asks no questions, quickly understands
In friendship every lustful thought is spurned.

And yet I know that neither is enough
Alone. I need the two like everyone.
I want a sure return of my own love –
The pain, the passion and the two made one.

A Year Later

In two more days it will be one
Year exactly since the thing
I thought I wanted then was done.
All detail still remains to bring
The madness (was it madness?) back
Behind my eyes tears want to break.

And all the time I long to tell
Someone what happened, need to blame
Myself each minute, speak my shame.
The whole event is with me still.
No other crime or sin seems bad
If one has wanted to be dead.

Not wanted really – in a fit
Of pure unreason (so they say),
Fear made me try to do away
With my whole self, the gap I fit.
What Judas did, what Lazarus knew
I have some knowledge of also.

Darkness there was a moment, but
Enough to know what death must feel
When it comes naturally, is real.
The shouts, the smell, the van door shut
They say 'Accept,' but acts like this
Have made me care and feel distress.

(Not mine alone) much deeper than
Ever before. When buses swerve
Or people scream, I feel each nerve
Jump to attention. Oh did man
(But without sin) once always have
This fragile knowledge, close to love?

If so, then in a different way
I've learnt of it. I want to cry
Because last year I tried to die
My death moves in me every day
Accompanied by private fears
And incoherences of fears …

A Recollection

Nearly a year ago I tried to take
My life: not pills, that only half-means death.
It was with gas I tried to stop my breath
Yet did not want to finish life but make
Some sign that things were cracking and might break.

But none of this was conscious. I remain
With all that vivid memory – the smell
Of gas, the fear, the childhood thoughts of hell.
I grasped a rosary in my hand to gain
Some hope in hopelessness, a talisman.

I cannot now forget what I have tried.
There was a time when I told everyone
The fearful thing it seemed that I had done.
I could not bear to live as if I lied
I knew that I so nearly might have died.

Now I feel scarred for ever; all confession,
All the long words of psychotherapy
Cannot remove responsibility.
I know that I have become a different person
Because I gave my fears their full expression.

Where does the moral lie and where the lack
Of shame and guilt? Great questions fill my mind.
Trust, the nurses say, leave this behind.
Yes, but I want the innocence back
That came before the heartbreak and the great dark.

Around are many lives who've done the same
Slashed at their wrists, taken an overdose.
Yet none of this belittles my own choice
Or momentary madness. Still the shame
Haunts me and taunts me, scrawls across my name.

Homage to Jung and Freud

Forgive me that I mocked at you,
For both of you are dead.
I did what everybody does
When analysed. Instead

I wish to pay homage to you –
Men of science who gave
All that they knew of human minds,
Studied them to the grave.

The joke's on you, though you would but
Have noted it and gone
On bearing it, just thinking that
All acts that we have done,

The shameful or the silly ones
Might bring you closer to
Knowledge of men's behaviour
And how their sickness grew.

Because of all my jokes I feel
A sense of guilt and shame,
Forgetting that you wished to heal;
I turned it to a game

(And even this you would accept)
Patience to make me well,
The doctor also has to go
Down to the depths of Hell

All this I quite ignored and now
Wish to make some amends,
Though suffering still lies
And darkness still descends.

Making in a Mental Clinic

I close my eyes a moment, then
Open them wide and see the grass,
The burning trees, the clouds which pass
Suggesting visions. I'm again
In cities that I really love –
Rome, Florence, and Assisi – these
For one whole year I've not thought of.

Now sometimes every sense can touch
Reminding objects, when the mind
Can leave its fears and dreads behind,
I've learnt things here (perhaps too much)
Ever to know long happiness
Again. Cold moon, you have defined
The domes of Rome as clear as these.

Out of the suffering here I long
To build again, make some new art.
Yet guilt makes me afraid to start
Because I have a gift, not strong
But something that the others lack
Whose silences cut off and hurt,
O let *me* bring their language back.

After a Catastrophe

I thought it would be different when we spoke
After so many months of separation,
After so much occurred I could not look

At where we all had lived in devastation
Covered so thinly but so neatly over.
Surely, I thought, there will be new emotion

Almost as if a lover met a lover
After an absence? But how wrong I was,
I could not see one sign of change, discover

A gentler voice; only a long, thin pause
Linked us, and questions, and a growing fear
That I would speak of suffering and loss.

Breakdowns, they say, bring relatives more near.
It is not true. Our lives move to their ends.
Nothing is closer, nothing grown more clear

Except in the compassion of my friends.

For Jung

Even at you I have laughed and played you off
Against poor Freud, had fun with alchemy.
But you know well some laughter's close to love,
That can be

So helpful to a cure. I can't forget
Your wise old face on television when
Some interviewer chattered and you let
O everyone

Know your profoundest thoughts. 'Do you believe
In God?' the questioner asked.
There came a glow
Into your eyes, wisdom as well as love;
You said '*I know.*'

They say there is no scientific proof
For many of your theories, yet they seem
To work, and cure minds' sicknesses enough,
Always to seem

More than a quirk, a cranky set of notions.
There is a formal beauty in your plans.
Your colours and the way you touched emotions
Are true to man's.

Despair in a State of Nerves

looked at in certain ways
you could say it was a punishment –
locked doors, money removed, constant vigilance
not even a nail file allowed

hard in fact not to see it as such

there are a few kind ones
gentle hands and voices
not many
'rest, rest,' they say
you might as well say 'rest' to a grasshopper

sometimes I wonder if nerves exist outside
certainly here they do.

ever seen anyone die with no screens round her?
or a girl, on the floor, screaming for her dead father?

pompous consultants discuss their patients in public:
who do they think they're impressing?

if you get better here, it's because you prefer Purgatory to Hell

Heaven is not for us.

Nativity

In other ages painters never had
Trouble about getting the period right:
They put down freely mother, child and man,
Trusting the rest to one star's serving light.

Cave, shed, house, even an open field
Or rocks, have shown the mother clasp the child.
Somehow the man has always been in shadow,
But always strong and watchful though so mild.

Were I a painter, I would try to show
Something of what he felt. What fathers find
When shown their first-born son, he never knew.
In spite of all that joy, I think his mind

Held desolations only God, this child,
Could understand. Much later also she
Lost Christ in human ways. O we forget
What pain began at the nativity.

The Question

The words were bound to come and now they've said
'Why aren't you married?' Not a close friend asked it.
Those we know best contain within their love
A special kind of tact. I had no wit
To deal with this, but stammered something brief
I know the other's mind held thoughts of bed

As well as other things – 'Does no one want
You in that way?' or, worse, 'Is something twisted?'
Such matters were left out; I could not find
In the confusion of my heart and mind
The answer then. So now the subject's festered:
A real wound aches, a fashioned one can haunt.

What might I, in a mood of honesty
Have answered? 'Women poets often don't.'
True on the whole but not, I think, for me.
Said 'Go to Hell'? No. Rather dropped a hint
Of fear, frustration, wounded integrity
(And asked the questioner just what she meant).

Security

What is fear? 'Terror spread thin' I heard
A doctor say. A definition apt
And yet it tells us little. I'm afraid
Of things I can't explain. The child crept

For two years I have been in unknown rooms,
With strangers. And it hurts, it hurts enough.
Hospital, lodgings – none of them were homes
And none could whisper safety, love.

The Builders

I see the builders
They are orderly yet
Work in extreme disorder
They slap cement about, chuck bricks
And climb to immense heights for nothing it seems.

I see the builders
Carving with extreme care,
Using small tools as though they loved them,
And, standing back, I watch the whole edifice,
Complete and beautiful.

The builders do not gaze:
They move on to more work.
They will be climbing and mixing again tomorrow
A poem is partly like this.

Prayer

I could not worship a placid God
one who answers every prayer
appears in every grotto
makes punctilious miracles
in obedience to men

Such a one I could not love

But a fierce God, proud, vehement:
one who makes a great noise
appears with a clap of thunder
and hands over the law on a high mountain –

Such a one I could worship

Equally the very small, helpless, tentative
child in a stable
the vulnerable new-born
licked by the rough tongues of beasts
and fed with human milk –

and also one shrunk to the size of the Host
discovered in bread and wine
honoured, despised, rejected, doted on in turn,
a God agreeable to being eaten and drunk
one who becomes man
and knows near-despair in a garden

Such a one I honour, respect, bow down before

He is very near in this mad-house
most especially in the good thoughts
of guardian nurses
and the gentle touches of patient on patient

The sick look like children in their high beds
and here
in the extremes of suffering and elation
the spirit of God is especially near

even in the screams and violence
and equally in the horribly convincing nightmare.

A Surprise in a Mental Hospital

To make a calm form,
To shape three notes of music,
To listen, so that listening becomes an act of creation –
There has been little chance of this
Save on one or two occasions.

And when I have seen
Flower upon flower
Open in a slow dawn
After a night when scream over scream
Sliced through the air
And cut open every dream –

I have been amazed
That in this world of madness and of death
I could catch my breath
At the sight of a too-early rose
Or at the way the whole day
Seemed to wait to break through
a tenderly thin layer of glass,
Where the sun abundantly comes and goes.

A Haunting

I feel great warmth towards those I've left behind
In the locked ward. Two nights ago I went
To visit them and it was good to find
Them glad to see me. Was it sentiment

Or something deeper? It is all so new
This obvious love of strangers, though they're ill;
My last three weeks have led me slowly through
More than the dreams which hold and haunt me still.

Violence I've seen and I was terrified
But I am frightened of myself much more
Than of the window-breakers. Deep inside
I sense the dark behind an unlocked door.

A Mood of Near-Despair
In hospital

Once, melancholy was a handsome thing
    And loneliness a kind of game of chance.
They have grown solid now. I live among
    Many despairs. O everyone is tense,

But not like runners. Here, we've reached an end;
    There is no tape, no whistle, no false start.
We talk of things we dare not understand
    And cannot tell the mind now from the heart.

Days are like dreams, or rather nightmares which
    We cry to wake from – though we never do.
Love is the distance that I cannot reach;
    What am I doing? Where am I going to?

Dependence
For E.

Why should I care so much that you should not
Forget me when I am not there? It is
As if my life depended on your thought.

And so in most important ways it does.
Loving is painful and it changes all
That we had thought unchangeable in us.

Is it because I have been very ill
That I feel weak and helpless when you are
More than a mile away? But then I feel,

Even when well, unsafe till you appear.
Such vulnerability's a chosen pain,
A chosen risk. These choices are quite clear.

I would live through the past two years again
With all their anguish, just to know that you
Would come into my world and enter in

My thoughts. You are a child's hope come true.

Words

Emerging from that private world of dreams,
I surfaced into silence and no sleep,
But not for long: the words soon came like streams
So swift and absolute, they had no deep
Source or surrender. Language was the thing
And poetry a new tongue I could sing.

It seemed that memory had found its rest
On some linguistic level I had found
Hidden in darkness neither cursed nor blest.
Come from some place within me, underground.
I spoke then with a fine abandonment
And scarcely cared to whom the speeches went.

Image on image, word upon shining word.
I felt as if I had discovered them.
I stretched my arms like wings spread by a bird,
And babbled old quotations till I came
Into a state of perfect clarity;
I let it form round my identity.

It is deceptive – such an inner peace.
Now every sound distracts me in a way
I had forgotten possible; I cease
To count the hours until I reach the day
When light which burns me gently on my skin
Now, will be gold and fervent or within.

A Kind of Villanelle

There should be other ways to tell you so,
I mean I have apologised too much
And tell you truths that you already know.

For several weeks I have been out of touch:
You see, my memory was dark and slow.
Maybe I have apologised too much.

Friends are constructed from the dreams we know
Will be borne out in daylight. You are here
Because I need your silence? I say 'No':

You are your self. I like to have you near
Because you storm my shadows and they go,
But not because you banish all my fear

Only all love is birth and we must grow.
My mind is muddled I am out of touch,
But you are something adamant and clear.

There should be other ways to tell you so:
I mean I have apologised too much.

I am afraid ...
In a mental hospital

I am afraid of saying what I mean,
I am afraid of doing what I say,
I am afraid of all this crazy scene.

I wake up to an early, dubious day.
It seems as if the patients bear it off.
Do clocks pause our minds and hearts delay?

Sundials, chronometers, the light above –
I am not sure which moves and which stays still:
I only know we are deprived of love.

And so the world is: none has had his fill.
Why are we sick? We are not chosen ones;
We suffer sickness that do not kill.

Nobody thought this was an illness once;
We are disturbed by dreams we do not will.

Rilke

You are the commentator on our nerves,
The artists of the pathological.
The odd, neurotic, suffering – each one serves
And finds a stance in the poetical.

Is this their purpose then – to fill your art,
Provide the images? There should not be
So calm an entry to the human heart:
Nor is there really, when we learn to see.

Dear Rilke, break your windows, mirrors, all
That's kept you from the pure, the central pain,
Yet never exile language, always call
The meaning out, sort symbols once again.

Old Inhabitant

The dolls are lying round the quiet room;
The old inhabitant has gone elsewhere.
There is no sign that anyone will come
And fling a window on the must-breathed air.

The one who lived here has been taken off,
The neighbours do not ask what was the matter.
Maybe it was a mild affair of love,
A death, an illness, or a thoughtless letter.

I do not know, and nor do others either.
The ambulance just called and was gone;
I worry now and wonder who will bother
To dust her things or ask what she had done.

Bon Voyage

I buy you cards to speed you on your way
(The last thing that I want). We do not say
Much with our voices, but our eyes can speak;
They hint the synonyms for our delay,

O yes, men say 'good-bye' each day, each week,
And so do we, though never quite like this.
Our words are smooth, our speeches do not break,
We need these intervals in which to make

Courage for simple needs like 'I would kiss
You if I dared.' I hide my loneliness
In a bravado only you can breach,
And only you have any way to teach

Me to admit and also to express
The passions hidden under homesickness.

Thinking of My Father's Future Death

I think now of your death and am more shaken
Than by the amorous or easy thoughts
Of those I love. I am, in fact, breath-taken —
A little dying of my own that gets
Involved in just the fantasy of yours.

What shall I feel? And what will be the cause?
That is the order of my dreams I fear.
Your real absence never gives me pause,
Then why, when you imagined disappear,
Should I so grieve? Is guilt composed of this —
Self-blame for murdering what never was?

Anomalies in Love

I wanted love and now I have received it
Over and over, more than I deserve.
But still there is a restlessness in it.

Or else in me. I need the fight, the fight,
The flare of anger, the compassion too,
Gentleness and surprise, and clearest sight.

Maybe the fact that you have gone far off,
Quite out of touch, refusing even to write,
Fans and inflames deep embers of my love.

Is what I need, then, love I can requite
Only when there are obstacles enough?

Adumbrations

Peace has become a personality
And love has moved a little closer in.

You are the reason for and object of
What some would call obsession, I call love.

You are an absence now, an opening deep
Which I can only enter in wild sleep.

O be your waking self and do not stint
The gain, also the envy, all loves want.

Admissions

Because I have been sick
I shall go mad with the mad,
Tick when the clocks tick,
Be sad with the sad.

I am, they all say,
Easily impressed,
Easily a prey
To the angry and distressed.

How can I keep
My walled garden yet
Always rise up
At another's regret?

Ruthlessness? No.
Patience? Perhaps.
I am stunned by what I know,
Caught in my own traps.

To My Father

I have not seen you now for two whole years
And am afraid to, though I would be glad
If something in your character had changed
    So that we had
Ways we could meet without distress or fears.

I know that I am different. Maybe
How I have changed would make our meeting come
Smoothly, like loosening ropes which slide and sink
    And then are dumb.
And yet I dread the meeting. Why have we

These two, father and child, grown far apart?
I know myself much less than once I did
When I thought everything was to be known.
    O you have gone
    And taken part of all I thought I hid,
And made a child again and bruised its heart.

Love and the Looking-Glass World

That is the past and I can watch it go
Into a looking-glass, a backward world.
And yet I wish that world would lurch and slow
And show my love untouched, nor yet unfurled.

Alice, the Queen could see both ways at once:
What vertigo! And yet what miracle!
I want my love to unfold and convince
Me that it is completely with me still.

Yes, I know planets tumble at a touch
And dreams break down when given too much space.
But Wonderlands are with me far too much
And hide the many glances of your face.

Tapestry

We have been stitching for so many years
And we are tired.
But look a pattern slowly now appears,
Something we had not planned.
I think it is composed of our own fears.

I watch the shades of colour swerve and cross
And then I stand
Back to allow the pattern now to pass;
I stretch my hand
And deftly touch the wool, help out the press
Of so much spinning stuff.
In this, there is a kind of blessedness,
A sort of selfless love.

An Evening in the South

That tide ran calmly
and the moon tugged only
with gentleness. We sat
watching the waves roll,
the horizon stamping Italy,
France to the left
heavy with history.
We sat and I tell you
Love came in me
in throbbing tides.
I wanted a moon
to pluck them and join,
but the moon was my mind
set apart darkly.

Ambiguities

I had the meal ready,
Was waiting for you when
I heard the telephone.
'Not you,' I thought, 'Not you.'
I held the wine-glass steady
And listened while you threw
The disappointment down.

Quick, as to children, tears
Poured down a steady course.
It was no fault of yours:
Family trouble, stress,
You could not eat the meal.
Now that the pain is less
I can guess how you feel.

But O what huge pains come
Swooping upon a small
Mere disappointment; all
That we have learnt to feel
Seems wrapped up in a storm
That begs a dove for some
Appeasement, ways to heal.

Episode

Warneford Hospital, Oxford

Some speak of operations, some are still
And silent. Others thrust out shaking hands.
A few turn pages of a book until

They know the words by heart. Yet 'heart' is wrong.
To own a heart is to receive demands,
Not just to make them. All hearts here belong

Within a world that has no answers ready,
No secrets either; problems are the thing,
They keep their owner just distressfully steady.

Last night I heard a late bird stir and sing.
This morning someone woke too soon and cried.

An hour ago one shot himself and died.

A Briefness

'Yes it is terrible and wonderful' you said,
'This world. I can't write poems any more.'
Gayly you spoke and I drank the last drains of wine,
Scraped the last fragments of rice on a fork.
A party of Russians sat near us.
Two races eating together,
Thinking such different things.
I remember reflecting
'Women who don't believe in God
Don't bother to look elegant.'

September

I can smell it, it is coming –
September, coolness, leaves turning
Fall, fall, fall,
Nothing intense
But the quick bonfires,
The abrupt ending of Summer,
The smell in the air of Winter.
Cold nights.

Animals watch, birds are gentle,
Oh great chrysanthemums repeat the sun,
Petal on petal of dahlias fall to the floor.
Quick, look, the red there, the red.

The Aquarium

I have seen them slow in their soft pond,
The leaves have lifted up to the light,
The light has come down making another pond,
Shining through fish skins
Showing the tender bones.
All has been golden and swift.

Once as a child, I visited an aquarium
And came on the huge faces, the gaping mouths.
All of the world could be sucked into them, I thought
So I ran to the safe cages of sleeping lions
Or watched the penguins strutting.

The Wedding Cake

I suddenly saw it – the wedding cake,
Three tiers, growing smaller and smaller.
I examined the silver leaves, the white flowers,
The hard to crack icing a hand could skate on.
Then I looked more closely and saw symbols of lastingness
And two tiny figures of a man and a woman.
It was inviolate, it seemed, would remain so.

But the young pair came and the ribbons were undone.
Hand over hand they held a sword.
Then they stabbed suddenly, the icing smashed,
The currants flung out, the whole shape altered.
So we celebrate our dearest devotions,
Make smooth objects, then break them in half.
But these two are merely cutting a cake.
Every ritual contains a violence.

October

Birds break the air.
Mornings come to September mist
Blow your hands already against cold.
Something is coming soon.

Early advent this, and expectation.
A child, a voice will come from coldness.
Maybe a star will fall,
I am uncertain always.

Hold it, let it not corrode,
Shave off the rough edges of it and you have gold and warmth.
I dare that bird to be demure.
Someone should shout and rejoice.

Words

I cannot speak the words I want to say
Because the languages betray too much.
I cannot tell you in a proper way

How love is still but allied to mere touch.
Always there is an absence and delay.
I handle gently what I want to clutch.

You teach me how to speak and how to lay
Words side by side. I have none of my own
You teach me what I want to write and say.

You see, the wishes and the speech have gone.
Simply with eyes and hands you touch and teach.
And I am lost and all the words are done.

The gift of tongues must take us out of reach.

Waking in Tears

This has never happened before –
Waking up crying
Sobbing and crying
Yet not remembering the nightmare.
When it happened last week I
Ran down the corridor
Looking for someone,
To ask for the Night Sister
To come and soothe me.

She came and slowly I stopped weeping.
'What was your dream about?' she asked.
'I can't remember,' I replied.
Sometimes when one is alone
(With the last paper stars fading)
The dream is the only reality
But she took it away.

O, we are all children as much as sick.
Sometimes I wonder how we can bear it all
Reality and imagination haunt us

I do not know which is worse.

Suddenly

A slight sliver
Almost of ice
Crossed my face.
Somebody coughs.
I need gloves,
Almost a muff
Winter has entered,

Slipped in between
Autumn and Summer.
There is not a gleam
Today of sun.
Suddenly Winter
Like a splinter
Came almost

When we were not looking;
We did not see it enter
Autumn has slipped off
Like a frail ghost.
All leaves are downcast.

Fever

Thought, will-power
Actions go
Now our weak bodies
Loosen. The mind
Has moved off somewhere.
Where we don't know.

But we do know
When delirium
Takes us over.
Strange visions,
Stunningly bright,
May come, may come.

Rubinstein Playing Brahms's Intermezzo

He is in love. Gaze at his eyes,
Observe his fingers. How his touch
Is tender. Yes he can surprise
The keys as if they were so much

More delicate than ivory,
More tense than flesh. He must subdue
But also rouse. Ah, also see
How Brahms's shadow falls there too.

And he is old. His wisdom draws
The passion of the music to
A climax. He's conceived the pause,
The pitch and flares Brahms's vision new.

Christ Speaks to the Other Persons of the Trinity

Father, it is unjust, it is unjust
The world is weeping, that world which we wrought
In spirit, planned and shaped. O Holy Ghost.
You Third who are one great Almighty. Thought
Which is mine too, suggest

To me, yourself but also man among
Men, our best, our highest – tell, I say
A reason why the universe looks wrong
And why now God himself must kneel and pray
To God. You two, now bring

Reasons upon my lips, let me explain
To many why suffering abounds and why
Anger and sickness seem the whole domain
So sweetly planned by us. O help me try
To make it good again.

Thinking of Ireland in January, 1976

A country of rivers and rain
And poetry. This isle
I've never visited
Was firm enough till now.
Will it be so again
Though bombs keep falling, grow
Back to a place where pain,
Anger and love can be
Set down in poetry?
When blood and guilt and grief
Will flow through every vein
Of verse, and verse be life?

Yeats would have agreed maybe
And turned away from swains,
From gyres and mythic lands
To hold between his hands
A glass enclosing the
Passionate expense
Of dreams when dreams come true
In daily violence.
But what of me and you
Who ply the same trade but
Have no roots in that place
Yet feel its tragedies
And cannot keep eyes shut.

Down to the personal
And intimate at last
We move and see a child
Once innocent and wild
Shouting and bleeding there.
Christ's daily broken where
Bombs mutilate the air.
Perhaps all poets can do
Is drive their rhythms through
Poems which resemble prayer
Where both have been exiled.

Artur Rubinstein Playing in Old Age

Player who keeps the passion in order
To unleash larger fires, to let the full flood
Fall in descending, hardly ending note-beats –
Harmonies holding back, then purring, shaping,
Pools of vibration in the mind, crescendos –
Of flowers, of new trees. Yet no programme music
Sighs in these notes. Here no complacent landscape
Is lighted up easily. Here pure sound takes us

To human passion nobler than we knew of
Look at the old face, creasing, eyes closing sometimes
To hear the sound more strongly, not see fingers
But feel them yielding, plying, coaxing, easing
And finally commanding the whole keyboard
All selves are lost here, even the composer's
Who surely thanks this selfless handing over
Of what he strained to hear and caught so gently, gently.

Skier

Confuter of gravity, runner with wings, a hover
Of speed and slayer of snow, gatherer-up
Of space – skier, you are equally athlete and lover.

Light swings with your leap till you land with a swerve, till you stop,
Draw breath, take root again, smile with a look of surprise,
Enter over space in the moment full of our first clap

Of amazement. You come down to earth again just as our eyes
Level with yours. You are diminished entirely into
A creature again, a mere speck. Behind mountains rise.

Their peaks are what awe us, move like a vision then view,
Since we live by our marvels, we need what exalts and defies.

Bach

I have been having a debauch of music and hearing certain notes to which I could be wed
– pure simple notes – smooth from all passion and frailty.
Virginia Woolf, in a letter of December, 1906

Passion plays elsewhere. Weaving over and over,
sound is moving embroidery, is singing stitching.
Change the metaphor. Open the ear as a seashell
Opens and widens and shapes itself for our coming
And also withdrawing tides. Follow the pathways,
The incessantly different attitude of wavefalls,
The curling over of manes of tempestuous horses
Which smoothly return to that first pure element

We sometimes reckon the world began with. Maybe
It truly started with sound like this, the beginning
Of order. 'Music of spheres' comes back to mind,
Returns to like as Bach is hymning over
Our ears, in stilling our passions, is making us
Believe in innocence. O there are angels holding
Haloes within their hands as contrapuntal
Music pours over and into and under our hearing.

Francis Bacon's Paintings

Your canvas screams. It is as if you cut
After you painted, through the cloth and then
Touched in the rent you made. A crimson mouth
Yells from a butcher's shop. You do not need
Cadavers, skeletons. An abattoir
Turns humans animal. You leap across
The grace of Greece. You tear a torso through
And grab the heart. It is an orb which you're

King over for a moment. Not for long.
You're back in shadows, burrowing about,
Seizing on satin, hounding down a Pope.
You have no time for smiles, you have no time
To stop for long. You'd paint smell if you could,
Smear blood across your canvas, love the reek.
Horrors abound but, when you're out of breath
Or grasp a nap, a dignity prevails.

It is the one the preyed upon darts at
The hunter when death's sure. Oh yes, defiance
Follows you like your shadow, like defeat.

Christ Speaks to his Father of Homesickness

Father, you sent me forth, your only Son.
Your only Son is missing you. As man
He feels such homesickness, he is undone,
By tears, feels as a child. O Father, scan
Your universe and run –

I speak in human terms – to rescue me.
But I am God, am you. Father I know
That you miss me. Say, can it also be
That you feel suffering? O no, O no,
It's not in agony

That we unite nor in the joys which men
Illustrate, make me wonder. Father, why
Are you remote? I am a man whom sin
Has never tainted. Must God be so high?
O shudder Godhead through your Son again
And wipe his child's eye.

End of Winter
A sonnet

The Winter dawdles and the air is hard.
Sheathed are the buds. Leaves won't unwrap today.
There is an air of nothing-to-discard,
Of holding in; the season won't give way

And loose the clouds and let the blue ride in
(Sea over our heads, the sun a shore
Running with light). No, Spring will not begin
As yet. Winter has settled for one more

Rigorous night ahead with sprays of stars
To glitter coldness. Through our windows we
Wait for a wind, laden with warmth, to pass

A little heat round trunks and stems, to free
Folded-up flowers which tensely wait to press
Their largesse out and our new liberty.

Ten Years After My Father's Death

You can be set aside, untampered with
By me, although I keep a kind of light
Unbruising touch on you. I see your death
Not with detachment but yet in a rite
That's fitting to us both.

The wrong words do not echo now, the fraught
Stormy arguments are smoothed away,
I see you clearly as a doctor caught
In the wrong branch of medicine. You saw me
Rooted in poetry.

And you were proud but neither of us was
At ease. Is it the wearing years which have
In their slow repetitions, given place
To the acceptance of a flawless love
And shown me unearned grace?

Perhaps. There was no settlement, no pact.
You died and left a question open and
Ten years have brought about the hardest act –
To dare our differences and to respond
To love we both once lacked.

A Hidden King

King of the fraught and bewildered,
Of the half-attained, the lack-lustre,
The shy and terrified,
Emperor of diffidence;
Prince of the mistaken,
Look at your world hurrying on as if
One man's energy could keep it going.
Gaze at the hot beaches and the frightened bathers.
King, Lord, where you are most small

A sudden flutter of feathers,
A cry of a child who is more than a child and less and yet all,
Here you are man, a God hung on a Cross,
Here you are little, we feel for you,
Here you are lost, we find you.
What huge cold breath spun this globe into turning?
Was it yours? Did it move in you?
God, who nearly despaired,
Give our inheritance meaning,
Stumble the way we go.

Give Me Colours

I would have paint near me.
I'm in a Turner mood and words won't say
What temperature is crimsoning the West.
What words can paint the process of a day,
Summer at dawn but now so overcast?
        I would be wholly free

Of rainbows and dip deep
In orange, scarlet. Sky shakes free of hours
And often has lost touch with Winter ground.
I'd have a palette and a painter's powers,
And then I hear a gathering of sounds.
        Where do composers keep

The sway and tell of air?
The summoning of belfries? Everywhere
Movement and pattern throb and sound and show
Purpose and circumstance and I am here
Without a medium. Words I used to know
        Are faltering everywhere.

Losing

A marriage time, a marriage song
And two are more and two are less.
My arithmetic is wrong.
What is lying in the grass?
Why does daunting loss

Bellow from the *discothèque*?
Warble through the dishevelled birds?
It's our heritage, an ache
Beyond, behind the risk of words.
Why do we unmake

Pacific skies and Milky Ways?
There is something that I want,
There are valuables to choose,
Why does white so coldly haunt?
Who said both must lose?

The Drift

Music was my drift.
Never the voice only the revel of
      Drum, flute, the theme that lifts
And hallows. There are harmonies for love,
Discords for argument, my score confides
In the stars' discourse. It takes a tide's

      Enforcing power, it pleads
Only to celebrate. I can face death
      If violins intercede.
I can enchant the dreadful announcements with
Consolations justified. There was
'A music of the spheres.' And here it is.

For My Father Again

I thought I'd set it right. A night ago,
When the stars flashed between the blows of wind,
I lay and the thought of you. Back came a row
About an art, the old excuse to find
Tactics and I learnt how,

No, felt (it was the senses caught me out)
We both had bleak battalions. No Man's land
Just visible I heard a warring note,
Grabbed camouflage, but could not understand
Why thus we had to meet.

Maybe the night expressed by one cold owl
Composed a kind of peace. I wished I could
Sign it and send it over to you, full
Of childhood penitence. Why should a mood
Of temper flaw my thanks? I love you still

As the owl speaks overhead.

Ashore

O straits of discipline, you are
The proper place where tides can wrangle yet
Keep proper order always there.
The waves unwind the sand and step the shore
And you and I love, stand and watch regret

Levelled along the sand. I find
A shell, a little worn. Here's music. Let
It roll the sea's sound through your mind.
This is how man's love ends and where it met
Music to which the universe is set.

Music for Italy

What instruments are best
To take this country into music, to
Speak firm? Do bells suggest
The mood? Their measured touch could hint the view,
But also all the rest,

And so much. Voices are
The proper guide here, voices speaking of
Daily events, the stir
Of small vendettas, broken homes and love.
O bring the orchestra

But not an opera:
It sounds obliquely. Tuscany must ring
Its voice as clear as air
All breathe. I too will try to bring
And spread now everywhere

Snatches of Vivaldi, memories
Turned into now, all Italy, no less.

A Prepared Elegy

An elegy upon a golden day,
I would prepare, so that when someone dies
And I am dumb with grief, these words will say
That life is full only because it stays
So brief a time. Words pray

Whenever they are self-forgetting or
Chosen to tell truth with. I have known grief
And had no words. Simply I heard a door
Closed near at hand. Through it half my life
Now I stand before

Primroses, daffodils, all raising to light
Their heads. The sun goes wandering today,
It is hard to credit there is night
This is a time for everyone to play
Near such a buoyant sight.

Life, the Spring power of it will celebrate
What has been rich for some dead friend. Today
They are alive. I shall not be too late
With these rapt words. Perhaps they'll sing for me
Where my death lies in wait.

A Special Sound

What a chuckle and fret of birds
What a constant argument in trees and hedges,
Chaffinch, starling, sparrow, blue-tit, all
Discourse and, above them all,
Now and then the deceiving sweet high notes
Of the trespassing cuckoo fall.

This is irresistible, we can forgive
The using of other birds' nests,
The laziness, the thief

Is excused all its bad manners for it has
A sound that is flawless and irresistible
It's the true Spring's absolute call.

Changings

What would you like to become?
A slow-worm, a sparrow, a breeze?
A thrush in a nest? A rose?
Stare at all of these,
Learn their light and shape
And you will be lost in them,
You'll shine with the glow-worm, sing
With the black bird's voice, will blow
With a new breeze, and be just as protective as
A nesting thrush, and then slowly you will
Open and preen yourself like a royal rose.

A Song and a Question

I am gentle now. Forget
        My rage. It never lasts
Long, but I should not
        Be driven by such outbursts

Of passionate anger. See
        I am calm, I am slow and kind.
Can you take all of me?
        The rage and the eager mind?

The Mother of a Hunger-Striker who Died in Ireland on May 4th, 1981

What is in her mind, that hidden place?
Her son aroused the world. He would not eat
For what he thought good reasons. He spurned grace
Offered. In this state

He's died, this Irish prisoner. He saw
Himself, as many will, a martyr to
A good cause. He rejected God's clear law.
What does his mother do

Now? She has said her son did not want to
Start trouble. He has done so, must have known
That riots would break out. He had been one
Such. She is alone

Within her spirit now, his mother who
Showed a suffering face. She has shed tears.
But only now, it seems, a miracle
Will break this country's terror and its fear.
But will one come? Now all

Of us are touched by rage. Our pity goes
To this mother but, as free men, we
Align ourselves with justice, but none knows
When Ireland will be free

And safe to walk through. Those who pray, pray
And even near-saints cannot tell us how
All Ireland will be stilled.

Words in the Small Hours

Song. My childhood play. The stars always –
Verse a sacrament. No blasphemy
In that. Art leans towards God for me. I wish
To list my loves and debts. I cannot be
On bad terms long with flesh

Or spirit. These two fight in all of us
And so they should. It proves we are alive
And will admit our wants and needs, not use
Other lives but give our own and live
In double sweetness thus.

Love will not reproach. It knows so well
Its own shortcomings. I know large faults too,
But everyone's an individual,
There is no mould for men. Each has a true
And unpredictable

Way of looking at the world and making
His own mark on it. All do this but it's
Only the great who set the planet shaking.
It is in these that God's great mercy fits
And it's a sweet heart-breaking.

Wordsmiths

The words must become
                    yes washed
And raised and hung out
                    to dry.
Language is precious. Dust
Lies on it. Those who use
It all their lives in their
                    work
Must save it from the dark.

Words are like ... stars
                    at times,
Meteors racing through the
                    sky. Then some
Stillness and the words that
                    contain peace.
We must polish words to
            gold and diamond
                    lights,
We who enter poems
                    and try our best
To bring it out of the night

Of confusion and cruel dreams.
Words are alive on the
                    tongue
But they must be treated
                    with
Respect. All this goes on
With wordsmiths all the time.
It is something small like
                    rhyme

Or clumsy rhythms on which
            a poem will fail
And the failure is total. We must start again,
Nervous with craft, aching with some deep pain.

A Smile and a Country

It all came back, my love of Italy
Every pleasure there relished, every hour
Of a three-month stay returned when yesterday
Italian eyes lit up when I spoke a mere
Sentence in that tongue. Those eyes for me

Brought back Italian light of every kind,
The Easter one that spread through St Peter's Square
After many April days of rain. I could stand
Feeling transformed every nerve aware
Through my five senses of this favourite land

Of mine. It is no city of the mind,
This world. No, it is Florence in late Spring
With views and paintings everywhere to find,
A real rebirth, Renaissance lingering
In every proud piazza. Dazzled not blind

I turn back a page to Assisi as it was
When St Francis loved his God so much he could
Also love the sparrows. Here was peace
And the light was not too strong. O I could
Read page after page of joyous memories

And give examples of countless shapes of light.
I remember looking down on the Umbrian Plain
And seeing small lights flicker in the night
Under a sky of stars it was almost pain
To see such splendour hung there for my sight.

But it is to Rome I return, always Rome.
I have lived in her. I could walk anywhere,
Show you each hill and church and forum. Home
It is of my Faith but also of golden air
And rose-flush on many buildings so I came

Back to all this through the brilliant eyes of a young
Italian in Oxford who liked my halting speech.
I remember my friends in Rome. I lived among
The simple, the artists, the holy men. Rome's rich
In all of these, and to these I always belong.

Unity

The soft streams flow
   Faster and faster, clear
As the first sun they go
   And every pebble there

   Shines like a jewel until
You lift it out, leave it where it is
   Watch the stream gather and swell
Until it joins a river at last. Then this stream remains itself still

Although it seems otherwise.
   It isn't lost but made one
With all water, and this
   Is the way life should have gone,

   Our human life which is
A frenzy of proving and trying and breaking much.
   We are all clumsy in this
Urge towards unity. But just one gentle touch

Can remind us of Paradise.

Night Song

  Love, at night, it is not death I see
    Or think about, it is
  Life, the dome of stars, the moonlit sky
    And all the ecstasies

  I've known by day return, in the cool air
    Great cities come back. I
  See Roman fountains flowing everywhere,
    Old buildings floodlit, sky

With a generous court of stars. I feel
    The pulse the energy
Of life move in my veins. In the wide cool
    Good moments come to me,

Love, most, then art. Within the company
    Of stars I see the shape
And purpose of creation. I can see
    That there's a watch to keep

Us safe upon this teetering planet. But
    I feel the source of light
Concentrated. Did my God create
    Mankind in the night?

On My Sixtieth Birthday

Shall I change? Shall I learn to be
Circumspect, careful, wise?
Shall I be more considerate
And see with others' eyes?
It does not feel like that,
On this birthday that troubles me.

People of seventy seem
Decades older than me today,
In another world, infant.
I doubt if I'll ever say
The right thing always, learn tact
At long last, I still dream,

In the early, wakeful hour,
Of all I mean to do,
As if I still had a whole
Life ahead. I know
Little of wisdom, am full
Of doubt. I yet feel powers

I knew in my twenties, verse
Works in me still like yeast.
The blackbird's elegant call
Sounds to me the best
And most potent music of all.
I stand and stare at the stars

In the early hours and feel
Music stir in me, words
On the edge of my teeming mind.
I am still moving towards
Poems I feel sure I shall find.
They will power and possess and heal.

Patience

I've sometimes heard it at night
As if the stars were bells
Ringing, as if the moon
Were a drum to beat, I hear
Sound that serves all light,
Seems to become it till
Four elements unite.
There's a rhythm beyond my ear
But I must be patient. It may
Ask me to end it soon
As a hand touches the moon
For my melodies move at night.

Near Despair

Where is a God, where
Does he hide these violent days?
Have we driven him off? Where can
He hide? In a bleak man's praise
Or a poor man's trust? In what mind
Can God find any space
Since the clutter and dust of mankind
Has stifled the presence of grace?
Can simply a near despair
Find God out? Can it? Then
I'll lift up my papers and probe
Through the darkness everywhere.

An Elegy After Twenty Years

A grey ominous sea rolled in and the high tide
Foamed at the stone jetty and the grey sky almost completely
Cancelled the horizon. Here was a strange island;
Two languages spoken, two kinds of hours kept
But we never knew which one was dominant.
I only learnt one lesson,
And all that the sea had taught me in childhood drew back,
Withdrew as if the tide would never come in
Yet there were no rock-pools to paddle in,
No smell of iodine or salt,
No shells at all. I never saw a limpet
I had known before the blue North Sea of childhood
And the old snapshots prove the Summers were adamant then,
When the rooster sun preened itself in the morning
And the full moon shone a silver passage at night-time.
But this Channel Island of Guernsey was utterly otherwise,
Inimical, dangerous. When you went to the doctor
On our third morning you would not tell me why.
You would not eat and I was frightened as never
Before. This was a fear where loneliness
Joined hands with dread and in the long dark nights
They stepped in and out of fitful sleep and taunted me
You never told me why you went to the doctor
Or what your symptoms were.
On the only Sunday you laughed a little when we
Walked for about an hour by the sea-wall
And watched the sun splash golden pools all morning
But turned to rain after lunch.

We did not eat lunch or drink and you went to rest
And your face was grey and the last time that I saw you
You were staring out at a sea of disquiet
And I was angry and cruel and said such things
As I should never forget,
But that does not matter now.
What matters is that I can write calmly of you
And of your faithful love and gentle humour.
I never guessed that you were indeed dying
And when the doctor said to my rhetorical
Question 'Is he dead?' and he replied
'We are checking up to make sure,'
I was appalled and in tears and only the voice

On the phone from England saved me from something desperate
So that now I look at the English coast of Devon
And swim most years in that sea
And there are no reminders or self-reproaches.
I know that an elegy holds no room for self.
It is filled with the dead at their best moments when living
And the sea exalts and is blue and green each year
When I celebrate you and all you love by forgetting
That terrible, new-learnt fear.

Elegy for Myself

Less possessive now, I see landscapes
And burning sunscapes from a step or two
Back. I only want to watch the shapes
Of clouds, not make them traitors of the sun.
Carrying sixty years about, I go
But not how I have gone

Round Oxford or the Cotswolds when so young.
They were part of love's playthings, for when
I knew first love, I learnt it in the long
Summers spent on the Cotswolds, cycling round
The drifting villages round where the careful men
Cleared the hedges, found boys eager to thatch the roofs.

An elegiac mood is stalking me.
And I can't draw my shadow from its pace.
It is the shadow of an ancient love
But look, the sun is gilding it and now
My present takes the hand of memory
And means to show me how.

I should behave as if the nursery rules
Still guided me. They are the last to go
And yet, O yes, the Spring still jests and fools
And mixes memory with time. Shall I
Divide them? Can't I let them dance me to
New loves before I die?

C.S. Lewis Lecturing in Magdalen Hall in 1946

A tribute

You never once talked down to us
Who would have listened if you had
Or come each Saturday with glad
Minds and excitement. We all chose
To listen to your wisdom, had
Enough good sense to see here was

A teacher and a man possessed
By Plato's vision. I recall
Your carrying voice in Magdalen Hall
Telling us his *Symposium* blest
As first love does or feeling all
The ocean's power. Who could not fall

Beneath a spell so gently cast
About our callous youth for you
Found out in us what loves the true?
You made a present of the past
In every sense. Today I know
(And have the grace to know I'm blest)

A little more of love and have
Swum in the sea with just as much
Pleasure as when I felt its touch
For the first time. It was your love
Of wisdom which you brought in reach
Of us. You knew what words most move

The very young. You'd kept your own
But added to it grief and pain
Passion of all kinds. Once again
In my late years I hear your tone
Strong yet kind. Your words remain
Within my mind and to the bone

I've learnt the lessons you taught me
And many more when we were young
It's thanks to you I move among
Wise poets and in past passions see
A purpose you began the long
Griefs that make love and poetry.

Sleep Shanty

Stirring, still, murmuring where
Is pillow, is arm, is air, is the bare
Breath of the night? In my eyes here
Something advances, pressing so
Gently, I let it, grow, grow, grow.
But the night isn't finished. Sleep is slow
I pack up thoughts, fumble a book
Look at the light
Don't put it out,
The room is occurring, blurring, so
Rainbow-coloured, new, so new
My eyes are closing,
My mind dispersing,
The full moon's clear
Is now, is near
Sleep takes over …
Nothing is here.

In a Taxi

Why should I suddenly
Driving through London in a cab, think of
A life that would suit me
Or would have done. I'd want Romantic love,
Which means not seeing too
Much of those loved. They'd want me on the move
I knew that would be true.

But when we met it seems
To me love would be perfect while desire
Would be rich as in dreams.
I think of how such love would stoke the fire
And send up furious flames,
A waking dream. It would have proved a liar
And shown my hope's child's games.
I recognised this as the cab's door shut.
But O what joy leapt in that if and but!

A Fleck, a Breath

A pair of sonnets

What a fleck, a breath, a word, what a paltry thing
In truth any life is. How easily blown out
It is like a flame or a piece of string
Easily clipped into bits and yet how we
View it each day, each night. We feel such power
When we race or wake, make love or simply stand
Watching a storm. And we will pluck a flower
And fondle it and see it die and fold,
Shrink into almost nothing. Yet is not this
Our fate? A lorry hits us or a wave
Fells us. And yet within a passionate kiss
Or reading a book, we always seem to behave
As if forever's our end. Maybe it is
For our spirits can soar higher than any grave.

Deeper than any ocean. So now I sit
Almost ready to sleep. I am at ease,
My room crowds round me and I'm the owner of it
And I see the new moon as a sign of peace,
Each star an ardent promise. I can't believe
In lack of meaning. In my mind I hold
Lines of verse, chords of melodious life.
Surely I cannot be too richly bold.
Yes, I'm a fleck of dust, a word, a mood,
A thought in somebody else's generous mind
As they are in mine. There is so large a good
Even within this life of loss. I can find
Wonders everywhere and I am renewed
By a plan of love, a purpose that is not blind.

Reading Poetry at a School

There you are, my past or some of it
Seven girls between nineteen and thirteen years.
In concentration every face is set
And they seem calm, but surely they
Know or will know youth's painfulness and tears
A July sun is shining on the day.

I too feel nervous as I read my poems
To these young ones therefore am exposed.
I wonder if some come from broken homes.
What lies behind clear looks, tanned skin?
Part of their life is gradually expressed
And I feel honoured that they let me in.

There are no boys so all of us could say
More than we would if it were otherwise.
I talk of adolescence and the way
One often blushed. One says 'Oh yes'
And suddenly there's knowledge in their eyes
And we become a party. The distress

Of their exacting years becomes so clear
And their agreement with me touches so
That I can feel my own youth drawing near
They teach me now compassion.
I even tell them of an ancient woe
And they marvel how they hear my stored confession.

There is no past when honest love's the drift
Nor future. We discover a held Now
And I am grateful that, when I have left
I carry with me such a shared, swift love
and I still question how
Love is so strong when there's no sense of touch.

Two Griefs

I remember you only with love
And gratitude. I know another death
When there had been wrong anger, argument
And that friend died before good words were sent
To mend us both. I still feel guilt and grief
And wish I could reach with

Sorrow across the years
Between ages and the years which now
Have not wiped horror out. My spirit's dead
At times and can I ever feel instead
The gratitude I owed? You stifled some fears
But added more, so how

Can I feel honest grief
And bear to think of you with gentleness?
Loss of my mother surely should teach me
Some way to do this and most steadfastly
Admit my debt. There's rancour in my life
Till I feel kind distress.

[Untitled]

Again we are moving through war
And thousands of refugees are walking and dragging
Their feet. They have no maps, no charts, no directions
And their pilgrimage is towards a little compassion
Even if it is only a crust of bread
And a cup of milk for their crying children they carry
Upon their backs. The stars hang up their lights
But they seem taunters to these whom war has shaped
Who could not tell you what war like this is about.

Now and then they pause and sit on packs
And then a few of the mothers sing a song,
'Sleep, my baby, never mind the stars,
Never mind that my breasts contain no milk,
Fall asleep, into that merciful place
Where, if there are dreams, they are
About green trees, white flowers and waterfalls
Sleep my baby, you are the heart of the world,
Its orb is in your hands and maybe you
Will bring it peace with magic wands of grace.
O I am tired, I cannot sleep like you
But you've a little hope, all I can give
I am the reason why you now must live
When you wake up I know you'll start to cry.'
O let all flowers mean peace before you die
The mothers huddle together. This is not their war
They never were. Perhaps they will shape a peace
Bring an end to the anger and folly of war,
Its vast stupidity, unmeant cruelty.
Morning is coming. The East shows layers of light,
The babies stir and they wake up to see
The almost risen sun and departure of night.

Romanticism

Never attaining, always standing by
Waiting and poised. This must be the stance
To find perfection. It's not in the eye

But in the heart that feels the stress of dance
Yet does not move. Keats wrote of 'winning near
The goal' and recognised this was not chance

But a whole way of life. Most dread and fear
Will come. It does not matter Love has been
Almost achieved. Dante is standing near

The perfect model. Beatrice just a girl
And left to find near perfect love where
Dante held that look, both start and goal

Of Paradise. All spoilt when we're too near
Only the partial is for us true whole.

Skyscrapers

How does it feel to live so high
That you are acquainted with
The nearest stars, have access to sky
That almost takes your breath
Away? The lift must have to go
So high it must take quite
A while before its final slow.
You must have much more light
If you're close to
The sun. Skyscrapers must
Teeter in the wind
I don't like heights so I don't think I'd trust
These buildings. In my mind
I see an accident. And yet
What views are given these
Scrapers of stars. What sights await
Sky-dwellers, what hills, what trees.

A Realisation

Sometimes I think I have it
And now is one. As the Autumn leaves are falling,
As Summer steps slowly back and disappears
In a mob of shadows. I am moved to the quick
By such sweet sadness. Now I seem to catch
The plan of the universe, now the arguments
For lack of meaning pause. My mind is full
Of light and time is quiet, the air is still
And in my almost favourite time, past midnight,
The idea of purpose sheds an enormous beam
Of light on my thoughts which now seem one with feeling.

When love is happy, and I have joy
I feel, no, believe in an almost perfect love
Which we are capable of in our best moments,
And that I am a wakeful dream in a good friend's mind.
And then I move much further; the moon is full
And looks like the consecrated Host at Mass.
The hour is propitious but needs no words of prayer.
I suddenly see that all of us and all
created things are thoughts in the mind of God

Or dreams that are a total reality. When
I reflect on this, all evil, every pain,
Appalling suffering and what seems like injustice
Fall into place for they are nothing beside
The gracious dream of God who breathes us out
For a tiny moment upon the planet. He has
Honoured us with free-will, allowed us to choose
Good or evil but he is always near
Ready to rouse us from the mire we make,
The maze and muddle in which we entangle ourselves
And lifts us up to grace, his perfect dream
Where everything dances, every word of love
Is a perfect lyric, and so I've learnt to believe
That art that's practised wholly selflessly
Is a tiny copy of God's transcendent dream
Where nothing's forgotten and 'is' takes over from 'seem.'

Two Sonnets on Death

In memory of my mother

I

Your death has made me think of my own end
And of the trust that my religion ought
To offer me. I cannot understand
When flesh is dead, what happens to our thought.

All our ideas, for mankind lives by sense,
Those trusted five which tie us to this earth.
Eternity can seem like a pretence.
Since flesh cries out the moment of one birth.

And never ceases to demand. O then
Is what endures in us how we can make
Art and respond to it, but we are men

Whose noblest moments and whose worst heartbreak
Work through our flesh, so I keep asking when
Death comes what form does our experience take?

II

Is it that all that's delicate in us,
All that is subtle, careful, kind also
Lives in our spirit only? I ask, does
Great art appeal to this? How can we know

Our words when all our terminology
Implies our eyes and ears, our taste and touch.
My flesh makes love, all my response is me.
And yet those moments, when we seem to reach

Powers beyond ourselves, are valid too
And we insist that our best feelings are
Tender, uplifted, selfless and most true.

And my imagination can stretch far
Beyond the planets. Can death, then, hold
The ties of flesh, free what we really are?

Love and Friendship

A sonnet

It was a perfect friendship that we had.
Each knew the other's mood and state of mind
And you could always heal the often sad
Wounds that poets, if they are good, will find.

From you I learn that love makes no demands
And yet can satisfy each claiming sense.
A gentle kiss; and poignant childlike hands
Linked us. Nothing ever was intense.

If sex was present in our play of minds
It took a part simply because we are
Both flesh and spirit. Love of many kinds

Exists but I swear that there was no fear
In what you taught me with no lessons. Friends
Can teach us almost more than we can bear.

Boston, Lincolnshire Childhood

All that time that was not time was growing
Into the sleep and lap and plunge of words,
Their coming and their going.

I mean the childhood when I was, say, five
And gloried in the glow of words and what
They stood for, all the life

Of tadpoles, conkers, chalk and marble were
Creation happening for me, a world
With sometimes a gripped fear.

But mostly safety was the feature I
Knew in those flat fields, that county of
No hills but all the sky

Was hemmed down to horizons. Here I was
All pick and thrust and cry and touch of leaves
And animals. Such grace

Is in one in such times when there's no need
To make a poem or beg for explanations.
The place was mine and greed

The passion for it. Boston, tulips, sea
Not far-off and quiet and seeming tideless
Here I became me,

Separate, excited, often haunted by
Shadows at night, crying for kind touches
And someone always by

To mend. That world of touch was almost Eden,
Everything smelling sharp or sweet and offering
A childhood taste of heaven.

Last Night

Listen, I heard the birds of death last night
And children screaming as they woke from dreams
Rampant with war. Even the love-makers
    Swiftly fell apart.
Dear God, what's happening
to this torn world's heart?
Where is there truth? My theme

Is death and helpful myths and proper cures.
Nearly twenty children were last week
Shot by a madman. War on war on war,
    Civil or world-wide is
Fought out while our little children share
The sight with us. The world is mad with fear
Who will bring laughter, blossoms? It is March

And Easter's early, Christ's upon his way,
Wounded and scourged like us but worse than us.
His Father holds the globe within his hand
    But Christ can't understand
Terror yet knows he'll rise with all Spring flowers
And with scars on his hands and feet show powers
Which could help all world mend.

A Litany

    There is a call
    Inside a head
    Inside a room
    Inside a house
    Within a street
    Within a town
    Ringed by fields
    Filled with trees
    Washed by streams
    And all of this
    Is north or south
    Within a land
    Upon the globe
    Which rounds the sun.
    And there's the moon

And stars in groups
And new ones found
And all of this
Is told by one
Fitting a body
Ruled by a mind
Which partners thought
That's linked with will
I am just one
Upon this night
Who sees within
Imagining
The course of stars
The race of beasts
The flow of birds
We all do this
And most believe
Some power shaped
Our flesh and soul
Which both uses words
Which makes us whole.

A Trance of Spring

To be read at speed

It is all a swirl of green
and yellow and pink and
the petals are chips from the
sky as it rolls from behind
a cloud and the cloud forms
flowers and takes hold of
the branches and draws
the white and thick and
wanton blaze of bursting
buds. Mother stays still,
growing tires out the clocks
and all the elements take
our senses and raise us up
to touch the sky while our
hands pull petals and taste
is smell and hearing is how
to learn to see in a different
way. O what an education

the Spring enforces but all
pleasure all with an almost
amorous flow. We raise our
heads and think our feelings
which rise and rise
beyond our control. Then note
the rounds and ovals and
how the squares and angles
have disappeared who knows where and
nobody cares. Spring is a
vision entering us and we
wonder if we have imagined
it because out of the four
seasons this is the one which
knocks down barriers, covers
the hedges with ardent green
and raise the stalks and us
also and we have been
picked for a reason we can't
exactly say. But what an effusive
sweet and open blowing of
breeze, arrival of birth and
death is not, has been
bundled off and we are
serene as well as calm. Spring
indeed is a rise and rich
and only lets fall the rainbow
petals for the marriage of
sense and mind and earth,
the bond enchants, the earth loves us.

Banish

Banish this 'I' and make it disappear.
I hate the way it looks
Within, within and darkening what was clear.
Last night I took one down from all my books.

And on the creamy paper there were no
'I' or 'yous' or 'us'
It told me why the weather is so slow
It pushed all selves away without a fuss.

Blaming
Two sonnets

I

When shall we cease setting ourselves up as
Kings and despots, tyrants and emperors?
Every day we make up our own laws,
One for others, not for us of course.

We look about at an enchanted sky,
Billows of clouds, stretches of ardent blue
And almost believe that part of us can vie
With creating a fall of rain, a tumble of snow.

We act as if everything we can know is brought
About by us, but when things all go wrong
And we are betrayed and darkens every thought

Then we start inveighing against a God who has strong
Terrible power and blame him because we are caught
In a cloud of chaos, anguish that lasts so long.

II

When there's an earthquake or a tornado we
Speak of 'Acts of God' and blame some power.
Not in our grasp, for weather so cruelly
Smashing our forests and gardens, washing each flower

Away for good. But when the sea is calm
And the sun high and happiness rules our world
We take the credit for it. God causes harm
We think and superficial we are and bold.

We should give thanks for marvels, we should be glad
That we are tied to this planet, see so much
That amazes us. It is we who cause the bad

Times for its we who from our birth are in touch
With every freedom. We make the hour, lives sad
When we make the wrong choice, batter and break and clutch.

Being

Being is what I praise –
Anything upright, latent, pulsing still
With a life of its own it adds to a boisterous wind,
The upright daffodil,
The child tumbling and realising its limbs,
A book of words thought of and mulled over then
Given life in a different way
By a printing-press or a pen,
The sun's molten glow up there but down here spread
Everywhere, into your eyes, the woods, the waiting flower-bed.
A natural Sacrament all being is. We receive
It the moment the seed's alive in the womb. I praise
The dull or ardent mornings, nights and days.
I am, I can be, I must die
O there's the sadness. Why
Must we disappear, stop breathing, fail at last?
O Christ on the Cross, in the Bread be near me to
Take me upon the journey. I must go
Among the shiners and glowers. O let me not
Be nothing, nowhere, punished, be only what
My bad acts made me. Sorrow is being again
O let it pulse in me, help me bear any pain.

The Sea

When we come to the sea we enter a world of levels –
Horizon, balancing clouds and the ribbed sand
Revealing itself according to the tides
And of course we have also reached
A world of health and healing, salty air,
Sand by the tides continually renewed,
And our breath is fresh as we drink the good salt in.
Here as we gaze we look at gold of sunlight
And gold of sand. As we simply stare we discover
Little winds which change at any second.
Now the air is mild and the washing sea
Shows only a little white. We sit on tough grass
And we do not speak but inwardly all of us praise
A new world, a buoyant, expansive one,
A place of life changing yet seeming the same
We have come to a region whose laws we must obey,
Whose sovereign is the sun.

Inheritance

They talk of genes and then they start to blame
Their parents for some quality which they
Inherit. It's from these they always claim
That they possess a weakness, seldom say
Some good they well might name.

I have no patience with this kind of thing.
I'm sure I've never heard somebody say
'I am creative,' 'I can write or sing.'
'I know I've been most lucky in this way.'
I'd sometimes like to ring

A celebratory bell and tell my friends
I owe my Mother my imagination
But not, alas, her dexterous pair of hands.
My Father gave me intellectual passion
But not a scientific mind which lends
Itself to all creation.

How swift they both were in their different ways,
They come to life now as I think of them.
Upon my poetry their spirit plays
And they are present in each sound and theme,
A debt one seldom pays.

But there's much more to this whole matter. It
Was learnt by me in how their love was lit.

Dawn

Dawn comes up
Slowly, softly
In silence of power
In colour, of new
Shades for a rainbow
No sound, no sound
Not yet the birds
Spreading the world
With clever sounds
Of somehow yellow

And possible gold
Not just a silence
But wait, look again.
The sky starts to blush
Lifts off the grey-
White early morning
Somewhere the cocks
Collect their calls
And throbbingly then
Loudly they cry
Invoking good weather
Unzipping the sky.

Abuse of a Sacrament

A sonnet

There are more ways than one of the abuse
Of children. Flesh need play no part at all.
Sudden anger and cruel words from us
Can bring war to their world and breach its walls

Of innocence, that state in which the heart
Plays happily, has scarcely heard of sin.
I have known priests who tore the soul apart
Just when puberty had to begin

Its long self-consciousness, its need for love
That reassures and blesses and brings grace
O yes, I've known the dreadful penance move

All hope away. For this Christ knew the place
Of agony. For this the splintered rough
Wood held him up for little children's peace.

English Lesson

Somebody once asked 'Did you enjoy school?'
I paused and thought about it, then replied
'I liked some lessons but hated every rule.'
Most seemed so stupid but I loved the tide

And tremor of verse bursting over my head
For that is what poetry felt like when one day
We read some Keats. I couldn't believe he was dead
Because his lines seemed to speak. I felt he would say

Something important. Death was not yet read
To me because I was still very much a child
But nonetheless, was able to fully feel
What he could feel about a nightingale

Or a Greek urn. His letters were read to us
And it felt as if they had come by the last post,
So fresh they sounded but also serious.
I never thought of John Keats as a ghost

Nor do I now when my books are spread around,
Poem after poem. Sometimes I have to climb
Up steps to reach a book but poetry's around
Is how I hear and does not belong to time.

It is slowly growing dark in this mid-June
And I watch the moon taking up its sentry duty.
The night is best for me to hear a tune
Beginning to sing in my mind. O may it have beauty
As Keats's lines do. May my own come soon.

The Vocation

I do not know what it's doing entirely yet
        I'm certain I have a hand
In the wealth of detail in our language. I meet
Both when I write a poem. There's no command

To me to write, nothing to urge me on
        Except what for decades I've done –
Make poems on themes that take me over, I've gone
Down many false trails and yet sometimes I've won

A wealth of peace or a forest that's cool
        After rare English heat.
In a way I learnt to write poems when I was at school
Though at the time it did not feel like that.

I pay deep homage sometimes consciously to
         The mine of language, which
The English tongue can reveal. May I always do
This and die still knowing there's ground more rich

That I shall never be near. Somebody will,
         Poets by the dozen maybe.
Whatever I write I sing our sweet tongue still
And daily give thanks for the art of poetry.

After the Fall

No past at all, but forever now,
Brimming creation glowing as they stood
Underneath a tree whose loaded bough
Shone out an apple for their chosen good.
But free-will was a trust. We wonder how

And sometimes why they ever broke into
A lesser time-sequence. We cannot know
The otherwise our parents did not choose,
We only know the fruit with its sweet juice
Was it first bitter, then what is the use

Of judging now? But now we know and feel
All that's behind us, taunting memory
And we so weak. We used that gracious will
And picked the apple from the precious tree
Yet God knew from the start that he would heal
The wound of our bad choice. At Easter we

Hear his great song cry out our liberty.

An Impertinent Interviewer

Somebody questioned me
Only the other day. They said they were
Not so much interested in my poetry
But just as much or more
In a very detailed autobiography

I was on the alert,
Suspicious and I have to admit I was
Not charmed, to put it mildly, but wondering what
This woman thought was the place
Of my life. She should have cared about my art.

She told me that her brief
Was commissioned for a multi-volume book,
On writers today. But poetry's not the life
Of the poet but the work.
The change and rise of the

Imagination. We
Poets have responsibility
For keeping the English language rich and free.
Why could that woman not be
Interested in the craft of poetry?

I let her questions proceed,
Answered now and then, occasionally told
An off-white lie. I could see her trivial need,
Her intrusion which was bold.
She did not seem to care about verse indeed.

Coming away from her
I was angry at her impudence, the flaws
In her mind. She should have cared how poems stir
And champion their own cause
And can't be forced, but, by some luck, occur.

That is my life – to find poems anywhere
At the lucky moment with this spell-like power.

Child in a Café

Feeling somewhat low, I found a cure
For any darkness in a small event
Which some might mock but it seemed heaven-sent
To me and I defy all cynics. Pure

As our condition can be, a small child
Of four years old cast on me her own spell,
Of warmth and timelessness. The world was well
For a few moments, its condition mild.

Quite suddenly this child came up to me.
I asked her name and guessed her age. She sat
And offered me her Coke. But more than that
She gave a total spontaneity

And unselfconciousness was hers. She was
Four years old and seemed to change my world.
Let cynics mock me, I felt free and bold
As this small girl. She was indeed a grace,

A very rare one. All thought of the crimes
Done to children filled me but she cast
Them out and put them wholly in the past
And turned to innocence our ugly times.

Clocks Back

How we deceive ourselves. We think we can
    Play games with time and make
Day change to night and night to day, as when
    We move clocks to our sake.

Thus we make day seem long and night less so
    Dragging. Of course we are
Not changing anything. Sun always goes
    On its own way. Each star

Stays where it is. The moon shapes its own course,
    Disdainful of our wish.
Its expertise is never caused by us,
    We wear out our own flesh

By how we work and play. But there's an end
    Indeed to all of this.
Astronomy we think we understand
    But putting clocks back has

Only a little power. Our children come
    Home when it's still light
We put our clocks back one whole hour and seem
    To have power over night.

And so when Spring waits on its very brink
    We move the clocks ahead,
And feel delighted but forget to think
    All of us will be dead

Some time and we can never choose that hour
    Or minute. We must go
Because time owns an absolute of power
    And that strength we know

Our deaths take place. For that we cannot put
    The clocks back ever. Death
Happens in time and we can only let
    It have its way, and yet

When music is the drift, its whole design
    Lets us make patterns which
Hold back the hour and offer us sublime
    Sounds so deep and rich

It is imagination we should know
    That lets all instruments,
String and horn and timpani bestow
    A lasting innocence.

For music puts the apple back upon
    The Tree and God still moves
Always where music plays and makes the sun
    Turn, surely round our loves.

Afterword

You will be hurt
have empty hands often
often too think all has gone for ever

for words are whimsical, moody, evasive
form shifts, is soon out of reach
but now and again and always when least expected

the poem descends almost sacramentally
and it is you it has chosen.

Assisi after the Earthquake

I was there now forty years ago,
Seeking, even in youth, the peace I'd heard of,
Resisting though the talk
Of how the spirits of St Francis would
Meet me everywhere.

No, what I looked for were heights of calm,
Abundance of tranquillity a poet
Might find for their writing. And, of course,
I was in love with Italy entirely
Had discovered the one country which

Would take me on for life, and never cease
What art needs both of discipline and freedom.

In the Upper Church the Giottos stood,
Among them the most famous, Francis preaching
To the famished birds.

                      Now it is hard to believe
Almost impossible that all that quiet,
That natural stillness was shattered by an earthquake.
It shook the world, of course,
Since this is a shrine to which all nations come,
Believers and unbelievers. Such desecration,
Such ugliness and yet, and yet, peace has
Not vanished. Nothing vital's disappeared.
For men have worked at restoration and
That Upper Church is new but with a peace
That knows no time. I think of it with love
And gratitude. I see it as I did
With youth's vitality. I will go back
And enter peace I'm better now attuned to,
Bearing my poems, knowing their roots stand there.

The Farmer's Lot

Comforting that Harvest, planting, weeding, baking
Go on. We can change so little. Put back
Clocks an hour forward, an hour back, but still not temper the sun's
Sovereignty or the moon's potent changes
They are for our instruction surely, a way of discipline
Perfectly solemn, not to be gainsaid
The farmer keeps his disown to himself,
Learnt it in childhood almost without
Knowing how huge the books of growing.
He scents a fox, counts hens, collects the migrants
Little thinking how noble his calling is, only aware
Of the good soil winding the roots, the broad winds spread everywhere.

Three Attempts at an Aesthetic

I Van Gogh's Chair

The simple, unassuming well-worn chair
and it holds our attention. Van Gogh has
given it sovereign power, importance that

is difficult to gauge or understand.
Yet we respond and cannot move away,
He's cast a spell, what genius can do

and only heights like that we're drawn up to
summits that awe and inspire us. We stand where
The whole world's changed, in time but only there.

II The Raphael Rooms in the Vatican

Beaten to the Sistine Chapel by
The Germans I paused in the Raphael Rooms
Meditated on the *School of Athens* and
The Dispute on the Blessed Sacrament.

There was no difference in my gazing from
The way we looked at Van Gogh's ancient chair.
What is it that compels us then, I ask,
How does the painter's style inform his vision,

What of the personal nature of his palette,
The way he breaks the rainbow on his subject?
I seek aesthetics out and cogitate
On arguments on art and themes of magic.

III   Mark Rothko at the Tate Gallery

Once inside the Tate
I felt the huge abstract
Of Rothko build up round,
enclose me, not imprison,
enlighten even though
there was no obvious theme.
Huge glows of red disputed
With lozenges of black.
The style was one man's and
Could never be mistaken
for another's. Why
was I entirely in
the power of this large vision?
How did Rothko want
My eyes to scale his heights?

A Mood for Painting

I'm painting a picture for you,
It is abstract and I'm interested chiefly
In form and colour. What brought this mood on?
Was it a circumstance of light outside
Filling my window? All I know is that
I long to re-design, re-shape and so
Understand all lying round about me
Which seems so clumsy and dishevelled. How
New I think that I could make it all.
I am unwise. Loss of self is what
Works best with rearrangement of our world,
Humbles us, awes us. So let colour flow
As naturally as from a rainbow written
Hugely across the sky, seeming before
Never so newly-planned, so simply now.

The Perky Flowers

The flowers are perky in their green arbours
Lifting thin faces into the new sun,
drinking the light with a huge morning thirst,
Gesturing at the flaring, effulgent light
See how the faces of carnations rise
Rich and alert, excitable sending their incense
Into blue light, O the faces of flowers are perky
And must not be refused when they invade us,
Making our morning new, our world unfallen.

Betrayer

Someone will always be slipping away when the others
Go on talking and drinking. They notice, of course,
Knowing they can do nothing. Close as brothers
They lean on the table, now and then talk, now and then
Simply think and enjoy the company.
But they know, of course, that none of them is free.
That each will be away, each betrayed.
For their great friend, the choice was long ago made,
And though the whole of the horror could be altered
It will not be for the world in need of great
Pain and agony, the crucial loss.
Will-power has been allowed its leash but on
Easter Sunday, we'll see the abandoned Cross
And God-made-Man stepping along the grass,
Thinking surely of Judas, surely of him
For he must be saved also though we don't know how
For how can Redemption depend upon one man lost,
One man hanging upon another bough.
That cannot be Rising's cost.

The Receivers

The words are wanting. Someone somewhere will
Receive the message. They don't know as yet
Who will hear and how. Perhaps they feel

A vague excitement. They have learnt their skill
Over years. They know the craft must be
Precise, much-practised and well-honed until

They deserve the language which is free
To those prepared. How they wing through the air
With all of song's rapt, sweet immediacy.

So luck is not the issue anywhere.
Singers have to learn their discipline.
Self must be abandoned. Love and care

Are where the great words both end and begin.

Early Rituals

All day we'd play at saying Mass. We put
A toy train on a string and swung it for
A thurible. Imagined incense set
The air to fragrance. Then bright crayons were
Candles. So we let

The whole abundant ritual take on
Human needs beyond our years. Maybe
Instinct was the first prime mover. When
We blessed the paper hosts, we certainly
Were learning that all men

See shapes in clouds, read magic language in
The simplest spoors. Our world is everywhere
Waiting to be interpreted and when
We're little children we are seeking more

Than we can know – a glory to adore.

Pietà

We thrive, it seems, on mystery for there,
A girl, scarcely grown up
Supports a dead man on her yielding lap.
She is the very symbol of a prayer.

She was the one to whom the angel came
Asking if she would be
A mother. But she had no man or home,
She said, yet listened to the mystery

Considered all that it could mean and said
She'd do the angel's will
The message that he carried for her God,
And for nine months she bore him. In a shed

Warmed by the breath of sheep, fed by her own
Enriching virgin blood
She brought up Jesus, spirit, flesh and bone
Shaped the world's salvation; Her Child – God:

Even after death and even when
They laid that full-grown man
In her childish lap, she kept faith in
Her destiny and all creation's plan.

We do not know after he rose from death
Of where they met or how
They spoke but we believe that it was with
Grace that keeps our fraught world tender now.

Rilke's Angels
A sonnet

Yours were not messengers, not guardians or
Sacred beings, but you needed them
As go-betweens and wholly secular.
They were the undertow of psalm or hymn.

Noble creatures. Your humility
And knowledge of the workings of your art
Told you always and intuitively
That it's not only in the human heart

The poem rests or starts. You know that of some
Purpose, intention that you had to trust
More than instinct, less than one large theme.

And so your angels, vigorous and vast,
Baring burdens, linking fact to dream,
Swept into power now linking all with past.

Friendship

In Memory of Veronica Wedgwood

I want new words, I want new words. All night
I could not sleep and searched for them. They were
Escaping always. I want brand-new bright
Pieces of syntax, grammar, all the pure

As-yet-unused good words and adjectives,
Even new parts of speech if there should be
Such. I can't believe that not one lives
Waiting for me to pounce on it. I see

You in some pictures which you showed me once.
A visit to a gallery was such
A joyous education. Notes dance still
Before the Kenwood Rembrandt. Out of touch

You may be but one never out of reach.
Once, when I said I could not understand
Your goodness in your voice of pitch
You used those three words, gently took my hand

And I said nothing. Nothing was the best
No, it was the only answer. How
I miss your presence. It is indeed most blessed
We do not know the future. Only now,

After your death only five years ago,
I can't feel bitter that you had to die
Of that cruel illness when your mind had no
Grasp, no subtlety. Your memory

So stored seemed empty, but your character
They told me did not alter. It kept its true
Sweetness. Now for once alone I'll dare
Those three great words you once said – 'I love you.'

Prose

A sonnet

It halts, it limps along, it cannot soar.
Try as it will, prose cannot reach the stars.
It knows about ambition, power and war
And lists the names of aeroplanes and cars.

It has much strength, it has an army and
Its military is well-trained and kept
At the ready. It can understand
The needs of reason. It has seldom slept.

But still all prose is limited and will
Keep to certain grounds and certain parks.
It does not know those secret stayings-still

On the large promises of light and dark
Poetry rises up and it can fill
All upper air and never leaves its marks.

Picture Galleries

A sonnet

In the picture-galleries of the mind
I can visit almost every day.
Paintings by Great Masters, yes, can find
Their style, their timelessness, their magic play.

And I can play with my own sense of time
And movement, juggle with the way I've gone
To the Sistine Chapel. I would climb
And marvel at what Raphael's Rooms have done

For the human spirit. Memory
Is the larger mover here. I pay it great
Honour and I'm grateful I can say

I have strength now and it is not too late
To find how Michelangelo can play
With Raphael in my heart. They never sate.

Homage to Wallace Stevens

In language of originality
And metaphors from many modes of life
You built a body of great work to be
One that would prove to last. You took on strife

Of outer action and of wars within
And all the time your argument proceeded.
The story of the whole, deep origin
Of our imagining and the real. You pleaded

Your argument, occasionally employing
The language of the mystics. But art means
Always our collusion and enjoying.
You show us scores of diverse men and scenes.

Director of an Insurance Company,
You were indeed, and high up in your task.
But your true world was other, vividly
You give and give, much more than we need ask.

So I salute you, Wallace Stevens, want
To thank you for what you have done for me,
Shown me shining symbols which still haunt
With what they fashion from reality.

Homage to W.B. Yeats

'An aged man is but a paltry thing'
You wrote, and wisely, and went on like this: –
'Unless soul clap its hands and louder sing
For every tatter in its mortal dress.'

How I commend your daring, William Yeats,
How much I love your work for beauty, truth.
You open all the mighty, good flood-gates
And you reveal the stuff of birth and death.

All you wrote gives high delight and lets
Us into worlds we never knew before,
Your language is so rich and it admits

Us out and over almost all things set.
Thank you, William Yeats, for such a door
And for all the wonder that it's lit.

Hope

A sonnet, with distant echoes of George Herbert

High above trouble and against all signs
To the contrary, hope proudly wears
A smile that is infectious. It combines
Faith, justice, charity, for it compares

Well with all kind intentions, all sweet looks
That can encourage longer than for an hour.
Hope is a quality not found in books,
It is new manna, superhuman power.

It looks into a storm and sees the end
Even when thunder's clapping still. It can
Turn a harsh enemy into a friend

And work out in fresh detail God's large plan,
It can without a stitch or needle mend
And show why God has been so good to man.

Homage to Chaucer

A sonnet

Chaucer, you're beyond praise. Even so,
I want to give you mine. I owe so much;
At school we read you with a crib. I know
That it was you who put me in close touch

With people of all kinds in this land which
I love for I am English. Oddly I
Am also Papist. Both have made me rich
In faith and feeling. In my mind's clear eye

Today I see you travelling to a shrine,
All of you telling one another tales;
And their curiosity is mine

And that's a gift which I know never fails.
I'd almost call you, Chaucer the Divine,
No blasphemy, though, but a thousand 'Hails.'

Homage to Henry Vaughan

A sonnet

Vaughan, great seventeenth-century poet, in you
I always find a radiance that's unique,
A light which has a dozen things to do
And never once have I known it less weak.

It shines upon my outer world and seems
To join the stars and sun and moon indeed
In showing all their wonder. Then, in dreams,
I find you can attend my spirit's need.

Your art is not like Herbert's. He worked by
Opposing symbols, difference of degree.
But your gift equally tells why men die

And how they'll rise again. You give to me
At second-hand, God's grace that swells the sky
And fills my world with wise lucidity.

Homage to Robert Browning

A sonnet

Your sense of drama, Browning, was exciting
When I was still at school. We read your lines
About Fra Lippo Lippi. In my writing
I know there must be many little signs

Of your deft influence. I love the way
You tell us about painting. I can see
Half the Renaissance at its glorious play
In the vigour of your poetry.

It's difficult to tell you what I owe,
It is so widespread. In our English tongue
Words are moving always, come and go.

In poetry they're fixed and in your song
I hear another music start to grow,
So fine are meanings that I move among.

Homage to W.H. Auden

A sonnet

Restless, excited brain, artist who could
Turn an idea into a simile
Or metaphor like magic, your mind would
See everything transformed into poetry.

I think of *Musée des Beaux Arts* and then
Of *Shield of Achilles*, that great ode of yours.
Look Stranger shows your love of water. When
You looked at landscape, limestone held most force.

In Praise of Limestone summoned all the love
You'd ever felt. It also gave you trust
In an eternal life. You knew the Fall

Had damaged man. Auden, man most just,
Prodigious poet, you helped me heed the call
Of poetry, showed me Paradise Unlost.

Homage to Samuel Taylor Coleridge

A sonnet

Samuel Coleridge, philosopher,
Depressive and above all things
Great poet indeed, *The Ancient Mariner*
Sparkles and burns and carries me on wings

Over many-coloured seas and over
Shipwrecks, silent water, every kind
Of wonder and disaster. You're a lover
Of everything dramatic in the mind.

I think of *Frost at Midnight*, then move on
To the *Biographia*, full of thought
Shining onto poetry like a sun.

How much of poetry's purpose you have caught
There and in a great verse. How much you've done.
Coleridge, I salute all you have taught.

With My Hands

All this seething in my brain,
All this poetry.
Lovely of course, when it's going well, but nonetheless,
So often I'd love to do something physical.
Use my hands to turn and shape a pot or vase,
Wash huge sheets and smell the clean linen,
Paint, indeed, in oils or water-colours
Or draw with pastel or charcoal,
I suppose there are people who envy me my poetry
And, of course, I wouldn't be without it.
But what a pity we can't exchange our gifts now and then.
How happy we'd all be.

UNDATED POEMS

Actors

Not the mask only or the actor's smile
(Each one is easy on the stage he makes) –
It is not our feigned sorrows which defile
Nor the rewards that fall upon our fakes.

'My real self' we say and mean the one
That pleases the precise complacent mood,
Simply the self we love when most alone:
We look upon our world and find it good.

Maybe the smile, the thin and painted face
Are truer than we ever wish to know
And 'the real self' a small imagined place –
The mask above and nothingness below.

The City

Declarations, powers, commerce. Stone squares with wide columns.
Men arguing, meeting. Birds disputing the wide territory. Hands lifted
in admiration. A faultless mood of farewells.
Kings were here once. Dignity then in a person. Love not lost in
images but moulded in flesh and blood. Balconies crowded with petals.
Warriors spattered with blood.
There was union then too with the elements. Water flowed through the
city – vein in a great arm. Flows now too but in a different tide. Earth
then was free and flowering. Later the stone, the entombing.

Sadness of cities. Love grows strangely impersonal. Broken in pieces
we struggle. Stone men cracked at the heart.
Possessed not by men but by seasons, the city survives. We are
somnambulists here. We are collecting the echoes of some irrecoverable
past. Statues are stiff in the square. Birds fly from past into future. A
giant turns over and sleeps. Sorrow breathes over the water.

Contemplation

Gabbling endlessly,
We rummage for images –
Light, air, water,
Things elemental
Words heard far off
That sound like singing
Each is tried out
And each is found wanting.

But the moment when speech
Not failed but drew back
To courteous reticence
Still haunts, still enchants us,
Some say 'Nothing is
Till words have been found for it
Naming is all.'

They have forgotten
The drawn breath, the waiting.
Shy things most suffer
From speeches not silence
Great moments live
Not in light not in water
Clasp hands round silences
Space between words.

Meaning

The few words only, the essential few,
The close appraisal, the firm honesty.
The ghost that gets its own disguise from truth,
Words that enlarge and echo sympathy –

This was the hard thing, yet the search was never
finished when words were found. The senses seemed
so many. Meanings differed. Each receiver
Heard more and less than what the language claimed.

Words need so much of shadow and of light
To stand out boldly. Who makes shadows here?
Where is the light that satisfies our sight
Or words which praise the meaning they make clear?

Thoughts on Dying

Put pennies on their eyes and then
Adapt your grief –
Something to tame and live with and
A kind of consolation when
There is no other warm relief
Except the dumb, strained need to understand.

Sometimes I think it must be as
Time is to children, no perspective but
Minutes drawn back leaving an empty space,
Best tenanted with both eyes shut.
Something of this stares out from each dead face.

But there is fear also:
Not the clear animation of pure awe
A terrified desire not to go
Be as one was before –
Alive and with a half-thought dread,
A curiosity that draws one to,
Even in mute disgust, those who are dead.

A Vision

She held the moment, watched the sun
Unbend upon the half-fledged corn.
Each fragile movement seemed to stun
The vision she had borne:
Not of a child or lights flung down
Or angels hiding in dim wings –
She saw the grey, the graceless town
And painful silent things
She knew she could not bring to birth
That moment. There was nothing she
Could find in sunlight or in earth
To shape her ecstasy.
But something cried for life (the sun
Was bearing down upon the air):
She did not know she had begun
A life no flesh can bear.

The Wood

This was the dark and the deceptive place
You went to it in search of solitude.
Better, you thought, the branches on your face

Than smiling pictures from a risen mood
Yet it was darker than you had expected,
No child's dream of an invented wood.

And when you had gone far too deep to turn
Always it was yourself you found, detected
A person whom no open plains discern

Not bad enough to be entirely lost
Nor innocent enough to feel safe there,
You had forgotten they are frightened most
Who trail their own faint shadows everywhere.

For a Painter

For J.

You in colours, I in sound
That words when rubbed together make,
Each of us waiting for the found
Image that will not fail or break.
From silences I start to sing
But is your spectrum the same thing?

For on our own and out of sight
We feel the energy take its form
The mind, the fingers keep it warm,
The shadows step aside for light
But is the impulse of my lines
The same that shapes your own design?

So many distances to leap
Across: for you, hard surfaces
For me, words meaning less and less
For languages can fall asleep,
Both of us paring down to some
Perfection that will never come.

'Easter in us'

Season of sorrow, season of Spring.
All contradictions link. Here birth and death
Dance as the planets do. All suffering
Finds its symbol. Early mist is breath
For every mortal thing,

Immortal too. We play with time and put
The clocks back and increase our days. The light
Fails like a blessing. So it must have set
And risen once before our fears at night.
Lent is with us, yet

All we decide to do or not to do
Creates a tempo. Nature fits her dance
And Christ moves in his own creation too,
Bearing our makeshift burdens, taking chance
And changing it to time.

Patterns which now and then the great ones see –
Aquinas, Hopkins, Keats. Now we can find
Christ the artist with his mastery
Whose shadows show true gold within the mind
For Easter's panoply.

It will be early April when we reach
The rising day. The frost is sharp at night
But surely sap will rise and petals pitch
Their gentle powers and turn them to the light.
Christ has so much to teach

And yet he comes as pupil, one who needs
To learn hope from us. He is still the child
We nursed at Christmas. On the Cross he bleeds
While one good felon speaks to him with mild
Words. He intercedes

For all of us. He speaks the perfect trust
We scarcely understand. He sees that God
Is scourged and mocked, his eyes are full of dust
But from that fertile Friday all that's good
Takes us. When the host

Enters our bodies it brings along
With grace we cannot earn. Yet God in need
Moves us to gentleness, the cradle-song
Of carolled Christmas. Christ, you love to plead
For kindnesses that throng

In our imaginations. Easter's proof
That our compassion comes when we are shown
The tide and texture of Christ's needy love,
He is flesh of our flesh, bone of our bone
Immortal, mortal stuff.

For Russian Poets in Prison

Only from cells with little light or water,
From stony rooms with high walls, from in such places
Men and women move towards us, utter
Essential truth and justice, turn their faces
Of kindness to us. Graces

Are in the gift of these. There is no pain
They do not know. There is no time which they
Have not called back. The past is theirs and when
They write their secrets all their futures play
Now and yesterday.

Play is what poetry does in every sense,
It plays on us, it dances to a tune
In some far backward sound of instruments.
Prisoners pared unjustly to their own
Simplicities have known,

Cleared of material dross and gestures, what
Is necessary. They are voices for
Ourselves at our unhappiest. They've taught
Lessons needed when we're close to fear
Or any inward war.

And so salute them, prisoners of graces,
High-priests of knowledge consecrated by
Language and its spells and processes.
Death is their shadow they see standing by
Which they do not defy.

For Seamus Heaney

Yours is the spirit, the mind I would like to be near
To talk of the making of poems with, learning new lessons,
For you are a teacher as well as a poet and in
Your essays and letters and tapes you've recorded I can
Observe the strength of our giving, counting no cost,
Never imagining any question stupid,
Any verses absurd.

In your verse you make the senses seize on the words
So that digging, harvesting, washing linen or making
A kite for your sons rise from language, become
A fresh experience, a nub of feeling, a speed
Of breath and wind. Seasons follow your words
But often take them over till tactile things –
A bone, a bowl, a pebble, a bucket or metal,
Your favourites the alloys, – work around me and bear me
Back to the farm where you grew up and learnt
With the child's flawless instinct the strength of perennial growth
The grace of gripping a shoe, of polishing brass.
And then there are the touchings of love
The land of plenty, the corn of surrender, the harvest
Of seed and growth and birth. I give this power
The richest admiration I can offer,
But you are also a man whose spirit's at ease
In his flesh, whose eyes are aglow and never miss trouble
Or pain, or gratitude. Yes, it's gratitude,
A power of thanking which thrusts through your rhythms and bridges
Spirit and flesh. 'A venerator' you have
Called yourself, and I
Can share in that for on this hot June night
I feel the Summer run down my arms, heat
A nocturnal breeze beginning a lullaby
And awe possesses me, love responds in me, let
Us one day meet for we would see eye to eye
On so many things but you can teach me much,
Let me value once more the flight of a swallow,
The sleep of a child, and be grateful for your deft touch.

Going Back

What will it be like? Will there be great
Changes? After over twenty years
I am returning to a city that
Took my heart, and now I wonder what
Rome will do to me. I shall shed tears,

I know, but it will be for many things
Tangible and intangible. I'll go
Down the same streets, and there'll be lingerings
In the same churches, also, echoings
Of voices of the friends I used to know.

A few have died, many have moved away
But at the heart of Rome, the Rock still stands.

Only in Fragments

Every poem is broken from a whole
Which nobody can write,
For there are gaps in any human soul
Where night wins over light,
So all we make is fragmentary till
Taste corresponds with sight,

And hearing makes its peace with every touch.
We only can foresee
Half-this, half-that, the whole is out of reach,
And so with poetry –
The lyric grace, the saga that's so rich
Know they are fragmentary.

And maybe this is why all poets go on
Writing and losing heart,
Completing lines, the writer knows there's one
Or more essential part
That he will go on hunting till he's done
And other poets will start.

Psalm on Contemporary Philosophers

They argue more and more about less and less,
They ask if there is anywhere a meaning.
And if the human mind can know anything
Beyond itself. (Even that they hold in doubt),
And yet they use words, clichés, syllables, slang,
The language of science and logic, metaphors
That by right belong to poets.
I admit I am slow and work in my poems almost always
From the particular to the general,
That is to say, in the language of sages, from
Deduction to induction
But let me explain, give me a split-second only
To say that you Logical Positivists
Or Linguistic Analysts, whichever name you prefer,
Are assuming by using language in any way
That meaning is possible. Do you see what I mean
Or indeed, think, hope, wish, conclude?
I've drifted, occasionally swum or even surf-ridden
Through or on Plato, Augustine, Aquinas,
Descartes, Locke, Berkeley, a little of Hegel,
Up to Wittgenstein, and there foundered because
He talked of the meaning of meaning and if we could know
For certain if we existed at all, if the whole
Of reflecting, feeling, wishing, understanding
Were all illusion – I still insist, you see,
That he used a language as if it were diamond clear,
Carat-gold and shaped a crown or halo
Out of it to tell us we can't know much.
But wait, I believe that Wittgenstein travelled beyond
All his examinations of understanding. And entered what Augustine
Would have called a mystical state
And so perhaps while wisdom as the ancients
Thought of it was what Wittgenstein found at last
As if wisdom itself were magic like Prospero's wand
With important spells to cast.

Remembering Plato's Symposium

A pair of sonnets

I

I had read Plato in translation long
Before I'd been in love and so I thought
Of one who ran to seek me out among
A million others. I thought I was sought

But when love came there was no sense of one
Half who found the whole in me. We were
Two astonishments who'd somehow won
Each other. Then there was no touch of fear,

No hint of loss. I tossed out Plato's book
And basked for one long Summer in a love
Made up of talk and touch and wondering looks.

It seemed forever. I knew nothing of
Failure in love. We parted and I took
Plato and knew I was indeed but half

II

A person. But this was a mood. I heard
So many say I was Romantic yet
Even today when friendship has occurred
I am made whole. Whenever I have met

One who is all I know and am and dare,
All that I hope and wish, then Plato still
Speaks to my trustful heart and I am sure
That no one else could feel as we both feel.

I put my loves on pedestals, I know
And maybe that's not fair and yet there are
One or two who each day slowly grow

More wonderful. I've always loved a star
Which shoots into my firmament to show
Love is a marvel, I its worshipper.

Where Words Fail

For some things no words will do
They fall and fail and die,
Parents whose child is raped and murdered know
Dumbness yet they try
To tell the impertinent journalists the true
Story. Their words are few

And they also know that language is crude and says
Nothing that makes any sense
But courage moves in them and it obeys
Their courtesy. Innocence
Yet needs a voice, and evil circumstance
Finds music later which pays

Homage to unjust suffering. It will
Talk to true tragedy
Like this one. What these parents suffer and feel
Will be taken up by the high
Notes of flutes and recorders and will tell
There is purpose in how we die,

By murder or natural causes, whatever the case
Music will not fail.
It moves us to the depths we thought we could not face,
Also it will reveal
The purpose of pointless suffering, bring peace
And pardon us and heal.

It's Magic

Whatever else it is it's magical.
The intellect may play
Its part but there must always be a spell
Cast to give a gleam to dullard day.

However metaphysical your verse
And all which that implies,
You work to general from particulars,
If you tell truths it is your spell that's wise.

Think of conjurors or of Prospero.
The poems which you make
Give pleasure even when you have to show
A world in trouble or your own heartbreak.

The conjuror pulls a rabbit from a hat
Or builds a house of cards.
He owns a nimble mind. You too have that
And it gives magic to defeated words.

After Thirty Years

Meeting a man I nearly married

You were that lyric world
which I escaped to once,
You were the tall, bold
Measure of my dance.
Now I'm iambic and wordy,
You a side long glance.

After three decades we
Stare at each other and know
We had to be parted and free
In spite of perhaps and although
You were an aspect of me
And I, surely, of you.

In our two freedoms we stand
In superficial delight,
Once we stood hand in hand,
Making a noon midnight
I wept when we parted but now
I know I must put to flight

That year when we met each day
And Summer outwitted Spring,
We were children at play
In dances, but now I sing
Alone, turning midnight to day
Finding poems in anything.

Schizophrenia

There is a mad girl in the house where I
Have lodged for ten years now.
It took a time to recognise in her
The central sickness. Now my life is how
Often I can avoid her since she has
A sickness that's expressed
In long complaints. Here conversation is
Often obscene. I used to do my best
To help, to listen, seeing her isolation.
I could not keep it up and
When I found that she could never give expression
To care or love I knew I had to stop
Her power over me, my door tapped on
At two or three a.m.
Yet I still feel a sort of sickness, misery also when
I climb up to the safety of my room
She cuts me or is rude in other ways,
Often I believe
Some evil spirit fells her lonely days
And that maybe exorcism would relieve
Her life of loathing. I felt useless when
She threw across the floor
A little Christmas present. Is her pain
Only relieved by hatred? I'm not sure

But I know I cannot live with pity long
And have to be callous. If she were a child
My heart would beat in strong
Love. As it is she makes me feel defiled.

On the Edge of Sleep

A sonnet

Things not possessed will never leave the mind
Alone. The senses itch on for that gain
And yet it keeps its purity we find,
That fine cool distance we could not attain.

O untouched peaks a child after would
Dream of, the grown-up never leave alone.
Those unpossessed things fill an idle mood
And shape it. All those loves we could not own

Don't languish but turn evergreen and keep
A smell of Spring a little distance off.
Last night upon the very edge of sleep

My mind was taken by that first kind love
And as sleep came I felt it planted deep.
O firs of childhood how they seem to move.

Waking to the Sea
A kind of elegy

I have known elegies of early days,
Moments of childhood which move with my life,
Measure it, tame it, make a pristine music
Of violin and drum. The other morning
I woke into a place beside the sea
Threw back the curtains, opened windows wide
And leaned across the sill and smelt the salt.
And I remembered all my childhood ships
Coming careful order into port.
But this sea was the music everywhere,
The tide was coming on in gentle folds
Of turning over waves, that curling cream
Orderly movement. No one was about
The old pier stood in its Victorian stance
Of firm belonging. All the houses near
Were painted quiet colours, beige and brown
A touch of blue here, there a little green
Here was a world of anglers and dreamers
And what's the difference. Fishermen are patient
Sit or stand ready for ideas
To open in their still attentive minds
I gazed at the horizon but no ships
Heaved up their hulks and holds. Everything was
In abeyance but not idleness.
I thought of music of the sea. I heard
The first notes of it penetrate my mind
And childhood was a theme beginnings which
Told of our rock-pool wandering and I
Could almost taste the boiled prawns and the bread,
New and crisp where butter was spread thickly.

I do not know how long I looked down on
The old place, Cromer, which was new for me
Morning was moving on with gentle steps,
I heard one bell break silence but it went
Back into silence as I washed and dressed.
My past was all below among these pools,
My future maybe those ships not in sight
Which carried poems somewhere. I could credit
Mermaids and their marriages to sailors,
Sun-crowned at last this morning was made up
Of possibilities like notes of music
Practised, repeated, moving with the wind.

Abstraction

It may be a flower or a vase
but the vase has to be leaning
falling in a certain
slant of stillness
is found
only in one defined point
during the day
which no instrument is delicate
enough to catch.
Even the human eye
misses it
though it manages
sometimes to watch
for the full twenty-four hours
which are our measured stretch
of waking and sleeping.
If it is a flower
it will shrivel slowly
if it is a vase
it will suddenly look unsuitable
as if the wrong light supported it
in some other object's pause.

Act of Unreason

I do not understand
Why I suddenly picked up a dish,
Flung it on the floor,
And smashed it.

I felt cold afterwards
But not with contrition or fear.
I felt no shame at all.
Now, this troubles me.

I was tired yes,
And provoked a little;
There are plenty of excuses
But no explanation.

My mind feels cold all through
Like a draughty room,
An empty green-house.
There was no passion in my act.
So afterwards, no compunction.

The dish was blue
With a red leaf pattern on it.
My smashing of it has added a little more
To all corrosion, all chaos.

Apology to a Psychotherapist

I am ashamed of things I did and said
Today. In some of them at best I showed
How right you were to say my mind's ahead
Of what I feel. I let my thoughts explode.

Also. It was self-hatred, fear, maybe also,
Hatred of you and what you asked of me –
These are excuses, hiding what I know,
How hateful and destructive I can be.

I have calmed down and try to bring my mind
Back to the present, to reflections of
This room, these books. The past is still behind,
Haunting me with desire for truth and love.

In some things, nonetheless, you have been wrong:
You never showed compassion, care or trust.
I think you might have made me strong.
For only thus can we be healed and blest.

Approaches to Fear

'And what is fear?' said the Lion looking sideways
'It is a great ache, an emptiness,' the Mouse replied.

'What else?' said the Tiger, licking his stripes.
'No peace, no sleep' said the Owl alert

'What more?' said the Bear, leaving the honey-pot,
'Great empty spaces' said the quick, sad, Deer.

'Does man feel it, then?' said the Monkey, alighting,
'Yes' said the Birds, 'It falls from the air.'

'And where does it rest?' said the one Horse grazing,
'In the mind, in the mind' said the animals together.

Bells

When we were eight or nine or so
We got a lot of fun
By ringing people's door-bells;
Then doing a quick run.

Mostly we got away with it: occasionally we
Got kicks upon our bottoms
Or slaps upon the knee.

The difficulty always was
To bandages and fuss,
We had to think up stories like
'A large man on the bus
Gave me the bruise, you see.'

People were kind and tactful
Asked no more of us.

The Big City After a Year

Streets look wider.
The taxi rank is the same
As always in Summer.
We wait with impatience hidden and over our heads
They've cleaned the roof of Paddington.
Now the sun
Can spear straight through.
I am afraid
Of such a mingling of what I knew so well
With what has changed.

Sick charged senses
Shake at new noises
Traffic shakes through my mind.
I pass a new machine which says
If you pay a penny or stand on it
You'll be tranquillised.
I don't believe it.

The city is growing again too rapidly
Creation is coming again.
In the eyes of a woman in the corner facing us
Fear is also written.
I hear her whisper to one seeing her off
'The bed is always yours.'
And we know that it's all a lie.

A Bowl of Stocks

They are tearing at the light,
They are suggesting all last night's stars,
They are also bringing
A pungent sweetness, April to the nose
And the thought of kissing and clinging.

Let them be austere for a moment,
Let them be sacramental.
They could be wafers of bread for communion,
Those thin petals.
But not for long are they still-life or Sabbath:

Soon they are battering our senses again,
Soon they are bringing Summer to the mind,
Leaving snow-drifts, Winter-frosts far, far behind.

A Boy Dying

For E.B. aged 23 years

This boy I do not know at all,
Who did not ask my presence here,
Has with his silence smashed the wall
That stood between myself and fear.

So sheltered I have been, so kept
From pain; I thought that passion, love
Meant growing up. I was deceived
And it is griefs like this which move

And change. I hunt a comfort now:
I have compassion but it's dumb.
The boy listens while I show
The casual remarks which come

Sick with a glibness I don't feel.
O this child's dying draws me near
To perfect love – but love won't heal.
I only beg to bear his fear.

By the Fire

As we sit, one on each side of the fire
Needing no words at all,
We are drained thin of passion, fight hate, desire
And such silences fall

As never before even in that instant when
The spiral was struck unexpectedly. We
Stare as if we might never see each other again –
But now contentedly.

Case-books

To have a certain pain, one that can be
Located in an arm, a brain, a limb,
One with a clear diagnosis and history

Would seem relief; there could not be a blame
Attached to mind or, if there were, it would
Be very slightly, easily given a name,

Heredity, infection. Bad and good
Have no place now, nor justice either;
Oh yes, sharp-cut, but morals are a mood

Here, not metaphysics. There is no well-known, clear
Delineation now between the blame
And sickness. Yet our feelings fall back far

Beyond the text-books and the modern name.
Reason abides, but has no power just here;
Imagination rules, has the prime claim.

Crucifixions

There are several kinds of crucifixions.
The first is of the flesh. It leaves us exhausted,
Speechless, empty, calling for a drink,
Calling from fear out of a cold night.

The second is of the spirit. It has to do
With prayer and sacraments and feeling parched.
It has its emptiness also, huge
As the night sky, the left altar.

The third is of both. It is a quarry
Where, as you look for an age-old shell,
The waters rise up and cover your head.
This is the crucifixion by water.

The word is accurate. In all these ways
Something is split, entered and crossed.
O give me green wood and let me forbid it
Ever grow strong and be broken and shaped.

A Cure

I have known partings when
There was warning and preparation,
Plenty of time to put on
The masks, the night expression,
There was an ordered form,
A kind of ritual.
Almost I felt at home
With partings habitual,

Never I think before
Have I been so suddenly fronted
With pain I have no masks for.
Is this perhaps what you wanted –
To see me stripped, afraid,
Open to every feeling.
Knowing my self displayed
Would itself be a healing?

Day Patient

Low, stagnant, spending the day
Sleeping or smoking. Now that I have gone
The whole scene horrifies me more – the way
Life has ebbed, ebbed; I don't know why.
Sometimes two rows of knitting are done
Tears trickle down my cheeks, and

I feel there's a certain hostility here;
I am half-stranger and half-friend.
Most of them want me to disappear.
As quickly as possible I go. You see
I am afraid this is not the end;
I know I'm not better and selfishly

I want to get away, I am afraid
Someone will stop me (as they often did),
And tell me their symptoms; I shall be delayed.
I too feel guilty and cannot bear
Even the kindness. I want to be rid
Of a place that I know keeps part of me there.

For Sylvia Plath

How is it that you could
Record it all before it had begun,
Or only just begun? There was no mood
Merely of chance despair, and then
The whole thing over, done.

You lived with thoughts of death,
Apparently spoke nothing of them to
Husband or those you were most intimate with.
Much was quite natural and the children who
Received your blood and breath.

What did *he* think, or what think now?
Can strength like his outlast the fear?
He takes charge of the son and daughter, though
There was a time when only timid deer
Were driven from his jungle. So,
With Sylvia gone, he pities her.

For Van Gogh

*I am telling you [about this canvas] to remind you that one can try to give an impression
of anguish without aiming straight at the historic Garden of Gethsemane*
from one of Van Gogh's letters

He stood before the canvas with his brush,
The colour poised, the vision bearing down –
Silence and concentration and the hush
Of expectation for a king or clown;
And could light penetrate such human flesh?

It seems that he could find the proper peace
Where pleasure could be praised and not abused;
It was Gethsemane he wished to tease
On to the canvas where the colours bruised
Each other, where mere forms were agonies.

Van Gogh, so innocent and incorrupt,
With madness racing with your insights, you
Knew how the light falls, how it is abrupt
Both to the seers and to what they view –
Your garden held the colours and Christ wept.

Words are my instrument, are how I see,
Windows and agitations, ways to fight.
I know the devious route can often be
Like spinning spectrums where we see the white
Losses and sanctities of human light.

Haiku

I

I miss you but
Know that you'll come each night
When my eyes are shut.

My anger flared:
you who deserved it least
were the least spared.

Hot nights and days;
siestas spread their length
to night and dawn haze.

I hear the sound
of Mozart playing and
it seems underground.

Someone went mad;
he talked all night and said
that God was sad.

I love with all
my flesh and nerves but know
of death and Fall.

II

A letter came
in unknown writing yet
bearing my name.

A white deer tried
to drink its own reflection:
at once it died.

My world assumes
the shape of houses with
unfurnished rooms.

What do they do –
these ones who have no words
for what they know?

I am lonely;
my friends love me but
I love one only.

Tell me the truth:
I need a blade that's clear
to battle with.

These epigrams
they are the tools of those
whom we call shams.

III

For three months I
lived daily, nightly with
people who cry.

I need an art
remote as glaciers yet
hot as the heart.

My memory roves
over the past and finds
old hates, old loves.

Give me a sense
outriding everything,
of excellence.

A suicide
(Brought to) sat up and said
'I want to hide.'

Love becomes hate
if touched too often. This
I learnt too late.

In the South

Not to be held but to be stood back from
So much is seeking out our weaknesses.
Bells are confused with scents. The coloured dome
Beckons the eye. Our sicknesses
For pleasure are paraded. Love comes home.
But stand a little back, your self secure
Your shadow by itself, untrespassed on
Five senses siege your wishes to endure
And not be caught up by the sun:
And ears, nose, lips, eyes and hands still press for more.

Jargon

Projection, father figures, abreaction, all
Appear within this treatment. One cannot call

Many suggestible or beautiful.
Half the time they're used, I simply feel

Nothing but lack of understanding. Pity because
Words can be so emotive; even science has

Exciting phrases. O the Greeks, the Greeks
Their poetry was exquisite but creaks

With near-death now that it's been misused
Our Anglo-Saxon cannot be so bruised.

Love Song

Lie in my arms and let the day
Discover us in peace and still.
Our moods have merged and came to stay.

Let love be lullabies until
Our sorrows have been told and shared
O world of wounds, my arms you fill.

The night is silent and the flared
Planets have stopped their dance. We lie
Learning how much we never cared

Before and are afraid to die,
For either one must be alone
When death presumes. A tear, a sigh

Will bring you to me to atone
For all past pains. And I to you
Enter your heart, make it my own

Lie in my arms and let us do
Nothing but let compassion grow.
Old words of love seem now untrue

And speeches stammer what we know.

My Friend

Never before, this –
Feelings so still,
Night or day quiet,
Birds on the window-sill,
Sun touching moon with a kiss:
Never before, this.

Never before so much
Power and peace,
Your hand laid in mine,
A cool steady touch;
Such happiness
Frightens me, though.
I try to detain it,
Afraid it will go.

I am sick and I need
Your strength and faith,
Your gentle delight
And goodness, indeed.
You understand with
Your heart and your head,
Your hand will uphold me
All ways I am led.

On a Text by Sartre

This thin space
We attentively stand by
Worries constantly, asks to be filled
With noises, gestures,
With thoughts reaching out and connecting.
Our attention wanders

But never so far
As not to return
To the thin place, the echoes.
Our touch records nothing,
Our ears are empty when the silence comes.
Yet standing here,

Thick chair, carpet,
Curtains, table
Are solid, not needing to resist
Yet having the power of resistance,
Not needing to react. Gently emotionless
They wait. Sometimes,

At an hour of recognition,
At a moment when friendship
Confronts passion without possessiveness,
Or, when nothing happens at all
But simply the day and natural instincts are happy
The space O suddenly

Is crowded around us.
We grow into it thickly,
Not with the furniture's mindless surrender
Nor the morning's heartlessness,
Nor as if echoes should bear back upon their beginnings:
Not as the spirit of the place
But a place where the spirit takes flesh.

Roman Wine

Sometimes the white, sometimes the red,
A *quattro* or a *mezzo* wait.
I know that either will compete
With the clear thoughts inside my head.
All afternoon I'll lie in bed,

Until siestas swarm and seem
Essential part of every day.
The rough wine and the sweet convey
All waking hours to types of dream.
Detached wine-tasters turn away

Knowing the sip upon the tongue,
The taste and nothing more. But here
Where wines mix what siestas clear
I know the worlds I move among
Better because the wine is strong.

But sometimes when the room is cool
I stare straight through the coloured glass
And watch the people meet and pass.
Then every fountain seems to fall
Into the wine. I drink them all.

The Silenced

For a poet who ceased writing some years ago

She must behave now
Like all the inarticulates –
Smile, nod, assume
A look of understanding, guess
By inadvertencies and learn
To know when she is caught and when
Dismissed. It is
As if huge speeches yawned and then
Clapped their jaws shut. No words.

And does she miss them,
Or ever try to drag them back –
Insolent children tugging from

Her chains, recalcitrant?
Or is it all a huge relief,
No need to be a commentator,
But see the corn grown thick across
Fields that exact no praise?
Make love by silences, be glad
To teach real children how to talk –
Adequate now to all demands?

Sonnet at Nightfall

The evening absences contract the heart
And all September waits upon the sill.
Can the imagination play its part,
Act in accordance with the human will
And stay the time, bring back the pleasant past?
All air is blue before the real dark falls,
Objects are one with shadows which they cast;
The intellect considers, the heart pulls
Imagination to its side. The light
Is unperturbed; we cannot change a thing
Not even force our dreams upon the night,
And yet the need is still losing, losing,
I make a world against the rub of time,
Crammed with desires, circumscribed by rhyme.

Thoughts from Abroad

Peeling a pear tonight, I thought of you,
The skin came cleanly off to show the flesh
Tender and moist. I let my teeth slide through
The pulp and sucked the juice, my inner wish
To give the sweeter, better part to you.

A simple thing – yet from such gentle ends
And pleasures great emotions find their form
The first I held so carefully in my hands
Was ripe and rich, was delicate and warm
Much like the touch that bares what it defends.

This is a country where I used to come
And find fulfilment. Everything the same
Except that in each pleasure there is some
Absence for which I cannot find a name.
Whatever journeys call me or worlds claim
You are my compass and certainty, my coming home.

Transitional Poem

I

I do not know now what to say
And yet I have so many things to write.
The style was easy once and came unsought,
The rhymes also, they ran upon loose reins.
But I have found that I repeat myself
Not just in themes
(These would be easy to discover)
But in the rhythms, cadences I use
Words are imprisoned in my cadences.

The year is almost over
And it is good to sum the whole thing up
Not wait till New Year's Eve,
Great happiness has come this year,
A love I never guessed was possible
And pain as poignant.
My verse perhaps is halting before this,
Cannot catch up with what I feel,
Hangs still to overcome the past,
Strike out the words of love I used before,
The short and analytic poems of love.
Yet there is pride in such a self-destruction.
This love has taught me to accept the past,
Myself, my many angers, all that hurts.

The tone, the choice and the precisions all
And I have often envied artists who
Have a material medium to work
Paint, clay or marble. Or I have desired
An art that is entirely abstract – music;
But poetry rubs shoulders with the world
Yet scarcely lives there. When it is abstract

It loses warmth, becomes mechanical.
Detached, attached, it is a complex art.

II

Poems should possess and be possessed I know,
Should warn and wound. Sometimes I wish words were
Like columns rooted in the earth and stretching
Towards the sun, simply themselves and silent.
But words refer, refer,
Ask to be tested, traced,
Will let you down with one small oversight,
Insist on meaning, point to something else,
Demand your honesty and whole attention.

I have grown cautious now of writing poems
and in the year that's past have found a new
Respect for silences. I want my words
To feel the silences that lie around them,
Be joined, be linked, and yet remain themselves.
And in my poetry my life must slip
With unobtrusive truth; while you who have
Changed this whole year, with love, in you my poems
End and begin. Only the style is mine.

The Weapons

The mood has changed now. I, who feared the pain
Of loving and avoided it, have found
What strengths lie in my grasp, how I contain
Huge power to give or to withhold a wound.
I learnt this since I learnt that you love me:
I who love you can be your enemy.

Then watch me when the masks have been put down,
And there are no more barriers between
Our minds and senses. See how sure I've grown,
My hands so sensitive, my mind so keen.
All this can be put to the service of
A moment halved or the act of love.

Then shield me from discovering like this
(A child too early swept into the throng).
Let me give what I need – a gentleness,
And make us be as quiet as when alone
We tossed and thought how love would fade all scars
Yet never dreamt it too might start new wars.

The Tormentors

They fought although they did not know
Why they were fighting. Each one tried
To give the hurting, final blow,
Also to be the one who died.
The night around was cold and slow.
They wrestled still, yet each one cried.

They had not wished to give a wound,
In loving moments, they had sworn
That neither'd give the other ground
To wish that he had not been born.
Their tenderness had been a sound
Gently as those who quietly mourn.

Then why this wounding, why this fight?
The angry blows, the subtle pain
Closed out the deep and star-strung night
And made them lonely once again.
Apart, on separate beds (no light
To comfort) each longed to explain.

And when they did it seemed that each
Nerve was made comfortable. Yet
Can they be sure that they will teach
And learn the lesson both have set?
Passion, compassion are in reach,
But love must fight still and beget.

AFTERWORD, SOURCES AND INDEXES

AFTERWORD

Elizabeth Jennings inhabits an oblique relationship to the literary culture in which she wrote, a devout Roman Catholic whose poetry speaks with a Romantic lyric voice and whose prose ranges across religious mysticism, nineteenth- and twentieth-century European and American poetry, Italian art and philosophy. Like Christina Rossetti, whose poetry she edited for Faber and Faber in 1973, she is a poet who wrote prolifically but quietly, intent on softly singing her faith 'in love and exultation'.[1] While this edition has attempted to reveal a more complex poet than critics have previously acknowledged, this afterword aims to offer a fuller picture of her life, poetics and theology in order to establish her as one of the most significant modern Christian poets to emerge from post-war Britain. Like many Christian poets, Jennings is also a successful elegist, constantly responding to moments of loss even as she strives to graduate desires – human and spiritual – into her poetic practice. Her lyrical depictions of self-restraint, attentiveness and the capacity to wait without expectation or anticipation are as marked by struggle as by peace and joy. By shifting her focus away from the abstraction of contexts and stories and into specific moments of emotional experience, Jennings holds us in the presence of what is happening to her narrators, allowing us into an intimacy that, as Rilke puts it, enters our hearts and pulls us into the safety of the poetic space.[2]

Witness, for example, her consistent and curious use of the prefix 'un-' (untempting, unbreathed, unscaled, untampered, unbruising, unarmoured, ungraced, unfallen, untrespassed, unwaning) as a way of reversing the action described to bring us closer to the emotional encounter the poem seeks to address. Her creative positioning of words such as 'wavefalls', 'echoings', 'tideless', 'fleshbound', 'bright-thoughted', 'sunscapes', 'lingerings' and 'littlenesses' within her poems works to the same end, while also indicating the influence of Gerard Manley Hopkins and Wallace Stevens on her verse. These influences, like her faith, have been little explored by critics and what follows establishes Jennings amidst what she proclaimed important to and in her writing. There are three sections to this afterword: the first locates Jennings as a Romantic poet at sea in her contemporary literary culture, and discusses her conceptualisation of the symbiotic relationship between religious belief and poetry; the second offers a short overview of her life, dependent on her unpublished autobiography, *As I Am: An Early Autobiography* (1967), as well as three interviews with her friends Priscilla Tolkien and Gina Pollinger, and her older sister Aileen Albrow; and the third and final section draws on her unpublished and published prose to review the main literary and theological influences on her poetry and situate her as a significant elegist as well as Christian poet.[3]

I

In her poem 'Precursors', Jennings describes her dependence on poetry as a mode of recovery, rehabilitation and re-imagining: 'So I have come / To believe that poetry is a restoration / Or else an accompaniment to what is lost / But half-remembered' (ll. 16–19). The lines point to an elegiac preoccupation that runs through Jennings' vast collection of work, one that registers loss (of the self, those we love, what we believe), only to conjure a consolation born of memories re-envisioned. Her best poetry avoids nostalgia, sharply evoking moments of realisation or emotional experience through a heightened awareness of the present, inviting the reader to 'accept the hour / The present, be observers and / Hold a full knowledge in our power'.[4] She believed that poetry was an incarnation, a formal and human embodiment of the spirit that served to put readers in the presence of the specific and the personal. As she argued in *Poetry To-Day* (1961), her survey of contemporary poetry for the British Council: 'incarnation, taking flesh, implies a profound horror not only of abstractions but also of all that is impersonal ... Poetry, like Christianity, preserves, when it is in a healthy state, the sense of personality and the dignity of being human'.[5] Jennings' conviction in the 'dignity of being human', one driven by her Roman Catholic faith, positions her outside of the group of poets with whom she is often associated: Kingsley Amis, Philip Larkin, Donald Davie, D.J. Enright, John Wain, Thom Gunn and Robert Conquest. These contemporaries were critically classified as 'the Movement', a body of intellectually rigorous, difficult, concrete and unsentimental poets who positioned themselves against a Romantic visionary tradition Jennings wrote within. For the Movement, Romanticism encouraged the poet to sweat and grasp towards an artistic delusion 'Smeared with garish paints, tickled up with ghosts' and which set the brain 'raging with prophecy', as Amis wrote in his poem 'Against Romanticism' (ll. 8, 10, 11, 21).[6] Davie endorsed the slight, calling Romanticism 'a sentence of death from which there was no appeal'.[7]

Jennings, by contrast, embraced the Romantic tradition, intent on summoning the mystical, emotional, dream-like elements of life and finding solace in religion. Her pensive and intuitive lyricism entirely separated her from the Movement, as she acknowledged in her unpublished autobiography, *As I Am*: 'The members of this supposed group – poets such as Larkin, Gunn, Amis, Holloway and Davie – had in common a care for order, but what they lacked, and what I had, was a fervent belief in Christianity. I believe that this showed itself even in my most secular poems. The other poets of the Movement tended to be agnostics. Thus we had few ideas or beliefs in common'.[8] While the Movement favoured an Augustan, pragmatic and realist poetics, Jennings relied on a simple yet devotional lyric voice to address emotional and intuitive themes – love, joy, sadness, faith and wonder. As she wrote in her introductory book on poetry for children, *Let's Have Some Poetry!* (1960): 'it was, I think, the mysterious, half-suggested emotions and ideas that I looked for in poetry … It was in the Romantic poets that I found these experiences most satisfyingly … it was as if the poems were, in some odd way, transparent, as if, beneath the words, immense emotions were being enacted.'[9] Responding to Amis's 'Against Romanticism' Jennings composed 'Romanticism', a poem in which she invokes the spirit of that which the Movement rejected, a Keatsian negative capability that brings paralysis before granting emotional insight:

Never attaining, always standing by
Waiting and poised. This must be the stance
To find perfection. It's not in the eye

But in the heart that feels the stress of dance
Yet does not move. (ll. 1–5)

As a 'whole way of life' (l. 7), Romanticism offered Jennings access to the relationship between the human, nature and the numinous, one that represented something at once perpetual and sensual in an increasingly fragmented and practical literary world. She is formally and lyrically closer to her fellow Romantic, W.S. Merwin, than to Larkin or Amis: while the latter poets were chance acquaintances she met as an undergraduate, Merwin was a poet she deeply admired and corresponded with for several years after meeting him in the mid-1950s.[10] Like Merwin, Jennings worked out of a Romanticism defined by William Wordsworth, her very understanding of poetry as an emotional strategy for coping with loss rooted in his incarnatory poetics.[11] Wordsworth's conceptualisation of words as 'an incarnation' of our thoughts and emotions looks forward to Jennings' own understanding of language, both poets resisting verse that sought to ornament or dress up experience. As Wordsworth argued: 'If words be not … an incarnation of the thought but only a clothing for it, then surely will they prove an ill gift', poisoning our interpretation of the world and dissolving our experience of life.[12] Compare this to Jennings' self-definition of herself as 'a Roman Catholic' poet who, in her 'undogmatic, impressionistic poems' has 'begun to clothe her convictions in poetic language'.[13] These convictions, unwaveringly Christian, are tempered by her melodic, sometimes hymnal, lyric style, aurally reminiscent of Christina Rossetti's devotional poetry. 'Poetry', as Jennings later wrote in the introduction to *The Batsford Book of Religious Verse* (1981), 'offers experience, not sermons', a description that elucidates her own commitment to developing a lyrical Christian poetry in an intellectual climate marked by a secular realism.[14]

The doctrine of the incarnation is key to Jennings' work, then, because it reminds us that she thought and wrote in the intersection of 'the divine and the human ... the material and the spiritual, the mundane and the mysterious'.[15] Like C.S. Lewis, who also identified poetry as a 'little incarnation', as Jennings noted in a review of his work, she gestures towards a philosophy of poetry that has a capacity to bring us into being and make us human, not as egoic individuals, but as contemplative and attentive listeners of the world.[16] When we learn to pay attention, her poetry shows us, we disentangle ourselves from anxiety and learn to 'be silent for silence's sake', entering into a poetic dwelling in the world that shapes and builds a space in which we can contemplate how to think and feel.[17] Her poem 'Any Poet's Epitaph' captures this process, one that is fraught with the fear that poetry's attempt to preserve the experiential might fail:

> Poetry – builder, engraver, destroyer,
> We invoke you because like us
> You are the user of words; the beasts
> But build, mate, destroy, and at last
> Lie down to old age or simply sleep. (ll. 5–9)

Wordsworth's *Essays on Epitaphs* (1810) simmer underneath the lines of this poem, three pieces in which he argues that the materiality of the inscribed epitaph on the grave can preserve experience – of the dead, but also of the living – who are 'tranquillised' before it into a reflective state. The epitaph is also 'intended to be permanent, and for universal perusal', expressing 'thoughts and feelings' that are 'permanent also', 'engraven' by the 'slow and laborious hand' of the memorial mason.[18] This careful and attentive building up of letters into words on stone makes for model poetry because it at once endures and also refuses to be 'a proud writing shut up for the studious', concerning 'all, and for all'. Wordsworth's emphasis on universal access to poetry rings through many of Jennings' shorter critical books: *Poetry To-Day*, *Let's Have Some Poetry!*, *Christianity and Poetry* (1965), even her unpublished *The Inward War: A Critical Biography of Gerard Manley Hopkins*, where she censures critics for clouding and cluttering Hopkins' poetry with excessive footnotes and theories.[19]

Jennings enthusiasm for universality was more obviously Christian than Wordsworth's, however, directed as it was by Paul's command that all human beings are united in 'one body': 'And if one member suffer any thing, all the members suffer with it; or if one member glory, all the members rejoice with it. Now you are the body of Christ, and members of member'.[20] If her internal Romanticism had not already separated her from the Movement, her religion undoubtedly did. While Jennings was not hostile towards her peers, she found their lack of respect for religion childish, insolent and impatient. The poet was always, she thought, bound to become God-like in his or her creation of verse ('We shape, we cut, we steal, we wrap, we are / Makers to order where there wasn't one' she writes in 'Order', ll. 1–2), and so owned a responsibility to reflect and meditate on how the poem, as well as those who wrote and read poems, came into being. For Jennings faith enables us to hear the sound and pace of metres and rhythms, in poetry and also in the world, granting access to 'A kind of living, a rhythm' that steadily unfolds the meaning of our relationships with others and also with God.[21] Close listening, contemplation and attention are central not only to her poetry, but also to her theological works, *Pensées* (1957), *Every Changing Shape* (1961), *Christianity and Poetry* and *Seven Men of Vision* (1976) each urging 'the study of direct union with God'.[22] She is resolute that this union arises and is forged in poetry, a form that demands we imagine, reflect and listen to meaning in order that we are brought closer to its divine source. 'The vague may disarm the reader momentarily', Jennings argues, but only to encourage us into a relationship with 'the concrete', namely, God and those willing to intuitively and affectively receive his 'touch'.[23]

Receiving God's touch, however, was not always straightforward for Jennings, and her poetry and autobiography betray varying extremes of unworthiness, guilt and sin. Her early engagement with Roman Catholicism produced a terror of damnation within her, as well as countless anxious questions. Suffering through her first school, Rye St Antony in Oxford, she jotted in her notebook:

> Are Catholics allowed not to believe in material things?
> ~~Does Our Lord come to people in Holy Communion who have done sins?~~
> ~~What did Our Lord mean by when he said he only spoke in parables~~
> ~~Are we anything to do with God~~
> ~~Will God ever die?~~
> ~~What exactly is the soul and how is it connected with the body?~~
> Is there any relationship between the three persons of the Blessed Trinity?
> ~~Did people go to Purgatory before the Resurrection?~~
> ~~Is Our Lord is always entire in the Blessed Sacrament?~~
> ~~Have we any connection with God?~~
> Can people find out by experiment what Happens at death?
> ~~Can sins committed with the body and if so with it alone~~[24]

While she excised the majority of this list, the three questions that are not struck through remained pertinent to the end of her life. Despite professing to privilege the immaterial, Jennings was painfully obsessed with the material, as the first question hints. She compulsively bought clocks, musical boxes, ceramics, toys, bottles, dolls' houses, stationery and bits of Hornby trains that she piled up in her various tiny Oxford flats. Buying these objects mostly from antique shops in Brighton, Jennings would make the eighty-mile trip in a taxi, ask the driver to wait until she had made her purchases, and then travel back to Oxford, spending almost as much on the cab fare as on her new procurements. Visitors to the sheltered accommodation she lived in towards the end of her life noted that the kitchen was so filled with objects that it was entirely inaccessible. A journalist writing in the early 1990s even confessed to the readers of *The Times* that Jennings 'spends her nights writing poetry in bed (her rented room in north Oxford is too cluttered for her to sit on a chair or at a table)' and 'her days in a café [Beau Champs] in the centre of the city'.[25] Like many restaurants, including Rules in London and the Randolph in Oxford, Beau Champs considered Jennings an 'undesirable customer' until they found out who she was: her inability to care for herself had already resulted in at least two suicide attempts, ominously foreshadowed in her scribbled eleventh question above.

This eccentric, fragile and certainly difficult individual stands in contrast to the confident theological and philosophical poet, whose lyrical voice carries the implications of the seventh question into poems full of tender resonance and religious awareness. Question seven's focus on a sense of interconnection, between the persons of the Trinity and between friends, lovers, families and the believer and God, is key to Jennings' poetry: as she writes in the opening poem to the eponymous *Relationships* (1972): 'Oh, we can sip / Something that tastes almost divine / In such pure sharing – yours and mine' (ll. 16–18). Reciprocal affection is as fundamental to her love poetry – 'Winter Love', 'Love Poem', 'The Modes of Love', 'Love Song' – as it is to her devotional works – 'Springtime and Easter', 'Consecration (I)', 'Walking in the Dark', 'Prayer'. Like the Christian socialist philosopher Simone Weil, to whom she dedicates a chapter in *Every Changing Shape*, Jennings struggled to sustain her relationship with God, sometimes self-destructively desiring to pull away from religion out of fear rather than doubt. Her description of Weil as a wandering and distressed 'poet' and 'mystic' who sought to write with a 'precise and luminous' intellect but was more often 'moved' by 'intuition' reveals as much about Jennings as it does about Weil. Certainly Jennings sought to encourage the same kind of theological approach to the world as Weil proposed in her first book *Gravity and Grace* (1947): Weil's outline of a methodology for approaching God through 'attention' accords with how Jennings consistently suggests we access poetry. Weil's meditative definition of attention presupposes a kind of faithful close reading, a way of moving towards the world that 'consti-tutes the creative faculty' and, in 'extreme' form, 'is religious': 'Absolutely unmixed attention is prayer' she writes.[26] As Jennings reiterates in 'On the Tongue', shifting the emphasis from prayer to poetry: 'We pay atten-tion and stand / Listening, whispering, relishing a word, / A rhyme, we discover the end / And purpose of art' (ll. 11–14).

While Weil's theology of troubled despair offered a model of careful observance, Jennings also considered it alienating, overly intellectual and even a little conceited. As she wrote in *Pensées*: 'The terrible pride of wishing God to make a personal revelation to oneself (i.e. Simone Weil waiting for God to announce to her when she should be baptized). Our Lady never demanded, never questioned, never foresaw. Yet she received every blessing, every revelation.'[27] The work of Teresa of Avila and Julian of Norwich, on the other hand, seemed to Jennings to invoke Mary's example more honestly, revealing to her the 'value of suffering', one always accompanied by 'compassion', 'sweetness and intimacy'.[28] Like Wordsworth, who sought to translate grief into joy within poetry, Teresa and Julian helped Jennings work through her difficult childhood experiences of religion and find hope in suffering: 'When the religion of one's childhood has been almost unrelieved torment,' she claimed, 'one becomes almost accustomed to searching for God in agony'.[29] By revealing a way of subjectively looking and attending to the world, Jennings' faith became a trigger to disrupt the easy but painful impulse to conform complacently to expectation. As she writes in 'Passage from Childhood':

> But now I know that all the agony
> Built a compassion that I need to share.
> The torment of that childhood teaches me
> That when I listen now or simply stare
> Fears are exchanged and exorcised – and free. (ll. 16–20)

Much of Jennings' poetry is a testament to this experience of freedom, a fulfilment of her sense that the poet 'must be constantly on the alert, keenly observing, but observing with love and care not simply with a cold analytical eye. He must be involved and yet disinterested – *involved* because he knows that everything that happens outside him also affects himself, and *disinterested* because he must be content to watch and to feel without possessiveness or covetousness'.[30] Yet the reams of poetry she produced suggest that Jennings could not always sustain this carefully watchful lyric voice. One of the aims of this afterword is to explore the disparity between the poet who emerged poised and sparkling onto the lively British poetry scene of the 1950s and the psychologically damaged and physically frail writer who frequently lost control of her art after a series of breakdowns in the 1960s. With this aim in mind, the next section provides a brief biography that leads into a closer look at her religious and literary influences.

Elizabeth Jennings as a young girl

When Jennings died in 2001, Michael Schmidt wrote that she 'was the most unconditionally loved writer' of her generation, loosely affiliated to the Movement but striking out with a voice that appealed to more readers than many poets ever reach. As Schmidt notes, her *Selected Poems* (1979) and *Collected Poems* (1986) sold in excess of eighty-five thousand copies, a remarkable accomplishment for a twentieth-century poet.[31] Yet the contrast between the media's bumbling, scattered, drably dressed if well-loved caricature and the intense, sometimes joyful, sometimes desperate narrator of Jennings' poetry is immediately obvious to any reader of her work. She was born in Boston, Lincolnshire in 1926, close to her 'gentle, soft-spoken mother', but seemingly distanced from her physician father and scientifically minded older sister, Aileen.[32] In *As I Am*, Jennings describes the first five years of her life in Boston as 'the only really idyllic times in my life. I was happy, guiltless and carefree'. Her problems began when the family moved to Oxford in 1932, where her father had taken the post of County Medical Officer for Oxfordshire. Here, the Jennings family attended the local Catholic church, St Gregory and St Augustine, where they befriended their neighbours the Tolkiens. The church was not a happy place for Jennings, however. She remembers making her first confession aged seven and feeling 'more guilty when I came out of the "Box" than when I went in'; she much preferred to 'play' Mass at home with Priscilla Tolkien, whom she befriended from the age of six. Her sense of unworthiness was intensified by her experiences at the independent Catholic school, Rye St Antony, although a supportive English teacher at Oxford High School encouraged Jennings to begin writing. Her juvenilia, signed 'Betty Jennings', suggest that she was writing earlier than this, but Jennings claims to have composed her first poem at thirteen: 'I held it in my hand / With its little, hanging head, / It was soft and warm and whole / But it was dead!' The at once anxious and sombre tone of the poem is indicative of her early life in Oxford, overcast in particular by what she called 'severe religious doubts', terrible 'neuroses' and a 'sort of difficulty' she later branded 'mental illness'. She also initiated her life-long belief that 'sex was a filthy and evil thing' at school, and her autobiography and unpublished letters suggest that she was never fully intimate with any of her lovers.[33] After a priest censored her for thinking only of her 'ugly little self', Jennings was forever confused and haunted by sexuality. She wrote in her notebook:

> when I was just fifteen, after some sort of hysterical conversation with my parents about religion, they told me to go along to confession. I think that they must have spoken to the priest over the telephone because after I had made my confession I received an angry reception. With real venom the priest said 'All you think about is your ugly

little self and you will say five decades of the Rosary for your penance!'
I burst into tears at this because it seemed such a huge penance and
I could not think of anything very bad which I had done. This priest
immediately changed the penance into *one* decade, but added that I
was not 'to go to Communion with the other children because of your
pride.' I have never understood how pride came into all this; also as
I had not committed what then was called 'a mortal sin' *and* had,
anyway, received Absolution, I was in a state of grace. This whole
experience did a great deal of harm mainly because I never told a single
person about it until I was 21 or 22. When my father heard about it
all, so much later, he declared 'I would have reported it to the
Archbishop'! The whole thing had festered in my mind and imagina-
tion and done a good deal of damage.[34]

The word 'festered', with its implications of infection, deterioration and
isolation, stands out from the passage, and seems to have skewed her rela-
tionship with her self and potential suitors. While in childhood she
developed crushes on girls at school and young parish priests, her refer-
ences to adult romantic and physical love in her autobiography and
notebooks are frequently juvenile and naïve.[35]

Her sexual fears, she remembers, were exacerbated further at St
Anne's Society (later St Anne's College, Oxford), where she felt child-like
and vulnerable, and consequently remained living at home with her
parents throughout her degree. Her sister Aileen, who had intended to
read zoology, was forced to become a 'weather girl' for the Met Office,
later marrying the Catholic journalist Desmond Albrow, and raising a
family. Jennings, meanwhile, began to enjoy university life, both intellec-
tually (she affectionately remembers C.S. Lewis's lectures and befriended
Philip Larkin, John Wain and Kingsley Amis) and socially (she began
dating, drinking, listening to jazz and attending the theatre and cinema).
She joined a number of societies, including the Socratic Club, of which
Lewis was a member, and also the Experimental Theatre Club, where she
acted in Noël Coward's play *Hands Across the Sea*.[36] On graduating,
Jennings began to prepare for a B.Litt. on 'Matthew Arnold as a Romantic
and Classical Poet', but failed her preliminary examinations, claiming later
that she was distracted by her engagement to an ex-prisoner of war and
Buddhist called Stuart.[37] Still living with her parents, she began a job copy-
editing for a publisher in London, where she met and socialised with Cecil
Day-Lewis, Rosamond Lehmann, Edith Sitwell, and Veronica
Wedgewood. The prospect of a new and intoxicating way of living,
however, restrained Jennings from immediately marrying Stuart, and he
broke off the engagement just after she moved permanently back to
Oxford to work at the city library. Continuing to party with ambitious
undergraduates and poets in Oxford and London, she met Donald Hall,
Geoffrey Hill, W.S. Merwin, Edwin Muir, Kathleen Raine, Adrienne

Rich, Anne Ridler, Stephen Spender, Anthony Thwaite and Paul West, and began to send her writing out to journals and magazines. She joined the P.E.N. club, spoke at the Cheltenham Literary Festival and was included in Robert Conquest's *New Lines* anthology, a publication whose legacy was to group Jennings with those poets later recognised as 'the Movement'.

Jennings' first two published books of poetry both won literary prizes, including the Somerset Maugham Award, which required Jennings to travel abroad to study 'the manners and customs of a foreign people': she enthusiastically departed for Rome in 1957.[38] It was here, in the confessional box, that she met one of her greatest friends, Father Aelwin Tindal-Atkinson. Practising her religion with the Catholics she met in Rome, Assisi and Florence inspired Jennings to renew her faith, and while she had several introductions to secular society, it was the 'intuitive understanding' of Father Aelwin that made her visit to Italy so fulfilling.[39] Her record of this trip, in both her autobiography and the unpublished manuscript 'Rome', exudes calm and happiness: she gathered material for her next three volumes of poetry, including her translation of Michelangelo's sonnets, and began her book on mystical experience and poetry, *Every Changing Shape*. From Father Aelwin, she also received introductions to the Dominicans at Blackfriars Priory in Oxford, where she returned after a brief holiday with Priscilla Tolkien in Paris. Deciding to give up her library job, Jennings was moved to a branch library in Bury Knowle to work out her notice, but was again 'suddenly beset with hideous religious doubts'.[40] Her depression worsened when she met Father Sebastian Bullough at Blackfriars, a gentle and kindly academic Jesuit whom the reader of her autobiography is led to connect to a figure described only as 'B'. Jennings fell deeply in love with 'B' and describes her desperation in wanting a child with him, but the impossibility of their relationship, she alleges, was the 'part cause' of a series of breakdowns.[41] Ostensibly, Jennings became ill after a period of stress and nervous exhaustion while working at Chatto and Windus, where she was looked after by Gina Pollinger and Leonard Woolf, and she reluctantly resigned the post at the encouragement of her new confessor, Father Hildebrand James. In reality, she was suffering deeply from the experience of her affair with 'B', and threw herself into her literary career. She arranged a meeting with T.S. Eliot, finished *Every Changing Shape* and *Let's Have Some Poetry!*, reviewed a few novels for the *Listener*, wrote a pamphlet for the British Council called *Poetry To-Day* and also a critical introduction to Robert Frost, and finalised her translation of Michelangelo. Her poetry and prose were gaining in reputation, and she won countless awards and glowing reviews that eventually earned her a place in the first of the Penguin Modern Poets Series (alongside Lawrence Durrell and R.S. Thomas), D.J. Enright's *Poets of the 1950's* (1955) and Robert Conquest's *New Lines* anthology (1956).

But when her parents moved to Eastborne, Jennings was unable to cope with the fallout from her relationship with 'B': from 1960 onwards, she reeled between cramped and inadequate private lodgings, sheltered accommodation and hospitals. She had always been physically weak, having had surgery to remove an ovarian cyst and suffering from Asian flu in her last weeks at the library, and soon after the affair with 'B' ended, she was operated on again for a gall-bladder infection, developing an ulcer while hospitalised. While staying with Father Hildebrand, who had moved from Oxford to Rugeley in Staffordshire to join a Dominican Order, Jennings deliberately overdosed on Nembutal and was rushed to Rugeley Hospital where she had her stomach pumped. Her doctors suspected a brain lesion on top of her other ailments and she was moved to New Guy's House in London, where she again caught flu. Her doctors and friends, however, considered Jennings' mental state of far deeper concern than her physical health. She began to see David Stafford-Clark, the consultant psychiatrist at Guy's, and, when released from his care to take a holiday in Tenby with Father Hildebrand, immediately took another overdose. Following a third suicide attempt back in Oxford, she began treatment at the Radcliffe with Seymour Spencer, a psychiatrist who immediately placed her in a local mental hospital. While institutionalised, Jennings became a serious alcoholic, gambled and developed paranoia and hysteria. She at once blamed these symptoms on her psychotherapy, railing against hospitalisation while also becoming dependent on 'the security of the hospital'.[42] Although she managed another trip with Father Hildebrand, this time to Spain, she corresponded with her nurses and Dr Spencer while away and returned home committed to psychotherapy. She stopped drinking for a while and moved back into private lodgings, finishing her book *Christianity and Poetry* and writing a series of satirical poems about Freud. This period of relative well-being was short-lived, however, and after experiencing a seizure that disoriented and bewildered her, Jennings was soon back in hospital. She was unable to recognise her mother when she visited and suffered from sexually explicit nightmares that her heavy doses of assorted painkillers exacerbated. After a period on the ward for severely mentally ill patients, Jennings was moved down to the observation ward and began writing again. Her autobiography ends with a glance towards recovery but concludes with the 'traumatic experience' of her father's death in November 1967: Father Bullough, who had died two months earlier, is not mentioned.

While Jennings continued to write and win awards for the next thirty years, she did so in a state of considerable physical and mental ill health. When both the English Faculty and her old college at Oxford refused her pleas for help, Jennings relied on willing friends: she grew closer to Priscilla, and befriended Rugena Stanley, a Czech refugee at the Warneford hospital, who often invited her home where they would cook together and read poetry. Vivien Greene (Graham Greene's wife), Veronica Wedgwood (who herself suffered from Alzheimer's in the 1980s) and a social worker called Katherine Jones were also supportive during this time, and Jennings found additional solace in her correspondence with women such as Barbara Cooper and Miss L. 'Tommy' Tomlinson. Her publisher from 1975, Michael Schmidt was almost entirely responsible for her heightened reputation in the 1980s, his editorial efforts making her work both more readable and also widely available. More than this, Schmidt proved Jennings' greatest friend and confidant during her later years, offering constant reassurance and encouragement during her worst periods of bewilderment and depression. In his obituary for her he describes working through 'sacks of A4 notebooks she submitted so I could make a selection and running order. This ritual was repeated for several of her later books, which needed, for the most part, to be typed up from manuscripts. She had a habit of writing in large spiral-bound notebooks propped on her knee, filling them with verse from back to front ... she wrote copiously and revised little.'[43] This editorial process undoubtedly enhanced the quality of Jennings' published poetry, securing a place for it on school syllabi in Britain and advancing its appeal abroad. As many of her manuscripts were exported to American university libraries, archivists such as Nicholas Scheetz at Georgetown University all but funded Jennings' old age, one in which money worries were uppermost. She spent her last years in and out of hospital, moving between various Oxford lodgings (from her parents' home on Banbury Road, to Polstead Road, Winchester Road and Birch Court in Headington) and the Warneford, Fairfield House and Rosebank Care Home in Bampton. Refusing to leave Oxford, Jennings masked her mental illness and alcoholism by assuming the media-created role of 'bag lady of the sonnets', receiving her CBE in 1992 dressed in a blue duffle coat and red woolly beret. She continued writing until her death, however, preparing her final volumes, *Timely Issues* and *New Collected Poems*, and being recognised by Durham University as an Honorary Doctor of Divinity in the last year of her life. She died of heart failure at Rosebank on 26 October 2001, and was buried during a small, private ceremony at Wolvercote Cemetry.

III

Jennings' acceptance of an honorary doctorate in Divinity, rather than literary studies, is indicative of her late status as a Christian poet and thinker.[44] Yet she had always thought of herself as a Christian poet and understood the idea of the artist as a Christian phenomenon: 'God is present in all works of art because man is a *maker*, whether a craftsman or a great artist. By the act of making, he shares in the Divine Act of Creation'.[45] She readily admitted that all her poetry was 'a development of my religion, even though I have only occasionally written specifically "religious" poems', and her notebooks, letters and unpublished works, especially *Pensées* and the radio script 'Roman Easter: A Theme for Voices', attest to a mind committed to the exploration of religious experience.[46] When she attempted to describe her poetic project free of religion, her comments were often flat and descriptive: 'I think my work has changed greatly since my early lyrics', she claimed vacuously in a late memoir, 'I have used many poetic forms in recent years, from the ballad and sonnet to free verse and, occasionally, the prose poem'.[47] Compare this to her markedly more lucid definition of the artist in *Pensées*, a figure that she describes as forever 'poised between the peace of a state of prayer and the turmoil of the world of action'.[48]

Pensées, fashioned in both layout and form after Pascal's defence of Christianity, comprises a series of 127 meditations on Roman Catholicism. Many of the fragments are concerned with the relationship between art and religion, but Jennings insists that her reader beware of promoting one over the other: 'Strange how we can spend hours, years, days studying the meaning and mechanics of poetry and altogether ignoring the meaning and mechanics of religion!'[49] The *Pensées* collectively argue that God's mercy, grace, charity and compassion must be reflected on and embodied, or incarnated, in poetry in order to help counter human sinfulness, especially the vices of pride, jealousy, selfishness and the desire to 'possess' others. Wary of the 'sin' of using art to 'create entirely new symbols bodying forth an entirely new world', Jennings relies less on scripture and more on the symbolic language of Roman Catholic sacramentalism. Outward signs of inward grace, the Catholic sacraments were perhaps the most significant shaping forces on Jennings' emotional being, and she was tormented by the fear that she might be too unworthy to receive them. Poetry did much to allay these fears: she believed that it had the formal, affective and rhythmic capacity to guide the worshipper into a reflective and accommodating disposition appropriate to receiving the sacraments. Of the seven key Catholic sacraments – baptism, confirmation, holy orders, matrimony, the anointing of the sick, the eucharist and confession – the latter two dominate *Pensées*, not as cold theological dictates, but as manifest paths into safe kinds of physical and emotional experience. For Jennings, communion is somatic, a way of finding contact with one's body without 'succumb[ing] to the flesh': 'Is it possible to receive Communion with a *full* realization of the shattering significance of it without having one's senses stirred? God wants a quiet spirit, certainly, but surely he knew when he created so *physical* a sacrament that we, as flesh and spirit, must be moved by it in the senses as well as in the soul. c.f. John of the Cross'.[50] She also suggests that confession brings the believer closer to God by inducing a state of mindfulness that offers a way out of anxiety and depression: 'We may, *perhaps*, be able to remain in a state of grace without frequent communion and confession. What is quite certain is that we cannot stay in a state of *peace* without those sacraments. For they have the power to fuse our wills and our emotions and our intellects.'[51]

Her description of communion and confession suggests that religion was powerfully restorative for Jennings, synthesising those elements of her self – her will, her emotions, and her mind – that otherwise threatened to fragment under the pressure of cultural and social expectation. While she was a persistently anxious and depressed personality outside of her poetry, Jennings found a confident and empathetic mode of expression within the framework of the poem, one that enabled her to speak for those unable to communicate: 'The tenderness that the articulate feel for those who cannot speak, cannot express themselves! Surely every artist feels this compassion for those people'.[52] The inherent compassion within poetry was nowhere more apparent for Jennings than in Hopkins' work: she observed that each of his poems incarnates whole moments of religious insight and absolution: 'Each vision of God is like a recovery, a winning-back of some lost state.'[53] Jennings too found a restorative compassion in poetry, not only for others, but also towards her childhood self. In 'A Roman Trio', for example, Jennings imports the strength and energy she perceived in Catholicism into her lyric voice:

> How open I was to a city made half of light
> And half of the world's power. I loved it gently, carefully,
> Let it take me by strong hand and heart slowly ...
> 　　　　　　　　　　　It was as if
> An unhappy childhood was handed back and altered,
> An illuminated spell cast round me and on me
> 　　　　　　　　　　　　　(III, ll. 23–25, 27–29).

There is something careful and muted about these lines that touches many of Jennings' poems, a wish to disclose her emotional and religious being without saying too much. She was drawn to poets in whom she discovered a similar poetics of reserve – Wordsworth, Rossetti, Hopkins, Wallace Stevens, and especially Robert Frost, whose theories of the 'imagining ear' and 'audile imagination' showed her how to embed the personal within poetic sound over linguistic content.[54] As she argued in her book *Frost* (1964), his poems are only ever 'partial revelations, notes on the way taken from one man's experience', elusive and reluctant to 'probe too deeply', while still demanding and holding 'our complete attention'.[55] While she considered Frost's work 'direct, economical, almost terse', it was this very refusal to give everything away that Jennings believed granted his narratives a 'sensuous', 'lucid' and 'balanced' effect.[56] In a close reading of his poem 'A Steeple on the House', for example, Jennings argues that the 'power and effectiveness' of the poem lies in 'the tentativeness of its statement', a practice that lends his work an emotional and formal control. His reserve is definitively Christian for Jennings, but not mystical: 'He does not seek in nature either a sense of oneness with all created things or union with God. There is nothing Platonic in his view of life; everything is good and valuable in itself, not because it is a fore-shadowing of something else. When Frost says: "All revelation has been ours" he means, literally and precisely, that.'[57]

Jennings' veneration of Frost's ability to achieve a muted and held-back affective power that refused to divulge personal detail is central to her own identification as a Christian poet, and not a quiet confessional one. She was uncertain about the 'confessionals', commending Sylvia Plath but disliking Anne Sexton, and ultimately uncomfortable with the word 'confession' removed from the Catholic context in which she understood it. Invited to comment on confessionalism in a late interview, Jennings declared:

> I don't like it. It's probably because it has become so involved with poets like Anne Sexton. It usually means absorption in some mental … I don't think poetry has got anything to do with sickness. I had a breakdown and the poems in the book *The Mind Has Mountains* (1966), a title from Hopkins, most of them are not about me. They are not like Anne Sexton's. I think Sylvia Plath was a marvellous poet. […] The term confessional has been associated with me, mental illness and revelation, but I don't think that's very interesting.[58]

In contrast to the confessionals, Jennings' poems function as snapshots of specific flashes of emotion or faith, enacting what she called 'a crys-tallization of an experience' and 'an attempt to draw a general truth out of a particular occasion or subject'.[59] While her poems often create a quiet and gentle space in which to reflect on words and rhythms, Jennings was not a poet who chased publicity and as a consequence felt no need to compensate by broadcasting herself within her work. At the same time, Jennings willingly engaged with like-minded peers: while she felt 'uneasily huddled' into the Movement, she was not averse to communal poetic projects, writing a series of group-poems in the 1950s with James Price, Garnet Bowen and Simon Broadbent.[60] Broadbent describes this 'group-writing' as 'a collection of people who, by randomisation or other means, eliminate what is personal in their production … writing four words on a piece of paper, folding it so that only two showed, and passing it to the next player. He in turn wrote four words, attempting to make a contin-uous sentence, folded, and passed on'.[61] The poems were published in the Oxford magazine, *The Isis*, and Jennings later commented on the process in 'New Poem Simply', professing that the project had clarified what she hoped her own poetry would become:[62]

What I really want

is a new kind of art altogether
trade all tradition
make music stand still
buildings be mobile
and everyone say (and mean it)
'How beautiful!' (ll. 18–24)

Jennings' prototypes for this kind of aesthetic and expressive poetic 'beauty' were Keats' odes, G.K. Chesterton's *Lepanto* and T.S. Eliot's *Four Quartets*, poems she habitually returned to in her prose writings and notably so in the introduction to her own anthology of poetry, *A Poet's Choice* (1996). Jennings' poetic development was dependent on poets whose aesthetic exposition of religious and emotional awareness most moved her, and alongside Wordsworth and Robert Frost, Wallace Stevens and Gerard Manley Hopkins held the most sway over her lyric voice. Her commitment to these poets is apparent in her draft manuscripts, 'American Poetry' and *The Inward War: A Critical Biography of Gerard Manley Hopkins*, in which Jennings describes her attraction to poets with a capacity for experimentation (her 'picture poems' reveal her own interest in poetic play; see 'Poem Like a Picture', p. 978). This preoccupation with writers willing to innovate poetically and theologically is apparent in her various published essays, including those on Yeats, Lawrence, St-John Perse, David Jones, Antoine de St-Exupéry, Pasternak, Charles Péguy, Thomas Traherne, Hart Crane and Edwin Muir, and also her unpublished essays, in which she explores the work of Walter Hilton, Coleridge, William Empson, Thomas Merton, Geoffrey Hill, Ted Hughes and Simon Armitage.[63]

Stevens and Hopkins, however, materialised a particularly joyous spiritual energy – secular in one case, Catholic in the other – which Jennings worked to recreate in her poetry. She read both poets from childhood, finding solace first in Stevens, whose 'vision without belief' offered security in a poet who had neither religious nor humanist faith but was still dedicated to pursuing 'truth *through* imagination with as much rigour and passion as mystics seek God or philosophers seek meaning'.[64] 'For years I had been obsessed with the relationship between appearance and reality', she wrote in *As I Am*: 'Only in Wallace Stevens had I found my obsessions expressed and realized in poetic form'.[65] For Jennings, Stevens' poems individually evoked and captured a 'whole metaphysical system' through a sensual language of 'scents, sounds and tangible objects' that, like Frost's, remained free of excess and ornament.[66] His ability to balance ardour and reserve reminded her of Simone Weil, Stevens' vision exuding a 'passionate calm' that offered the young Jennings a sheltered model of expressivity.[67] Preparing her second volume of poems, *A Way of Looking*, Jennings scribbled across her notebook in capital letters 'I NEED <u>COLOUR</u> AND <u>SENSUALITY</u> IN MY

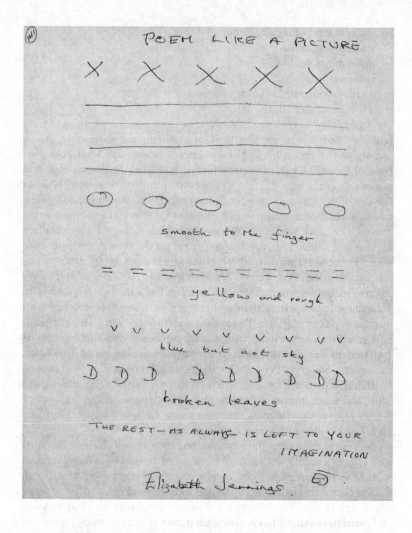

POEMS' – something she recognised in Stevens and attempted to prac-
tise in her own verse.[68] The lilting yet precise unrhymed couplets of
Stevens' 'Less and Less Human, O Savage Spirit', for example, echo
through Jennings' 'For a Woman with a Fatal Illness', an abbreviated
sonnet that closes on a single line.[69] Here is part of Stevens' poem, quoted
at length by Jennings in *Every Changing Shape*:

> If there must be a god in the house, must be,
> Saying things in the rooms and on the stair,
>
> Let him move as the sunlight moves on the floor,
> Or moonlight, silently, as Plato's ghost

> Or Aristotle's skeleton. Let him hang out
> His stars on the wall. He must dwell quietly.
>
> He must be incapable of speaking, closed
> As those are: as light, for all its motion, is (ll. 1–8)

For Jennings, Stevens here attempts to 'postulate' the 'kind of god he would revere if he could believe in a god at all', achieving a 'beautiful poise and unpossessiveness' most apparent in the illuminated silence of lines 7–8.[70] 'For a Woman with a Fatal Illness' repeats the cloistered form of Stevens' poem in its evocation of a hospital ward, but Jennings loses the glow of Stevens' poem by truncating the final couplet and closing with words of bleak acceptance:

> The verdict has been given and you lie quietly
> Beyond hope, hate, revenge, even self-pity.
>
> You accept gratefully the gifts – flowers, fruit –
> Clumsily offered now that your visitors too
>
> Know you must certainly die in a matter of months,
> They are dumb now, reduced only to gestures,
>
> Helpless before your news, perhaps hating
> You because you are the cause of their unease.
>
> I, too, watching from my temporary corner,
> Feel impotent and wish for something violent –
>
> Whether as sympathy only, I am not sure –
> But something at least to break the terrible tension.
>
> Death has no right to come so quietly.

The awkwardness of the poem – the gifts clumsily offered, the visitors' noiseless disquiet, the patient's fate bluntly stated – becomes part of its rhythm, as the poem stalls, aurally and emotionally, at 'unease' (l. 8), 'violent' (l. 10) and 'tension' (l. 12). It is characteristic of Jennings to push us into an uncomfortable metre that summons our judgement: we might stop reading but are suddenly eased by the broken tension in line 12 and the melodically gentle final line 'Death has no right to come so quietly'. Stevens is figured by Jennings as the poet who bears such technique, his 'passionate calm' rendered sacramental and Weil-like, withdrawing from the world in order to attend to it.[71]

Jennings also recognises this ability to 'stand back' as a gesture of 'care not of indifference' in Hopkins, his poetry 'as brilliant as a Turner land-scape' and able to exude 'sensuousness' in a 'completed controlled' form.[72] While her study of Hopkins, entitled *The Inward War* from Marianne Moore's 'In Distrust of Merits', remains unfinished, it never-theless shows the ways in which Jennings was thinking about the religious poetic tradition of which she considered herself a part.[73] The book fleet-ingly relates Hopkins to religious contemporaries such as John Henry Newman and Edward Pusey, but is more concerned to unravel his poetic connections to Christina Rossetti, George Meredith, Emily Dickinson and Walt Whitman. Hopkins is also portrayed in profoundly human terms: Jennings berates critics for convoluting his lucid and hospitable poetry, and points to his companionable and kindly correspondence with friends as a marker of his intuition and compassion for others.[74] As she wrote in her chapter on Hopkins for *Every Changing Shape*: 'It is surely significant that a number of Hopkins' poems are about particular people – the bugler, the soldier, Harry Ploughman, Purcell, Felix Randal. He was consumed by the true Christian charity which sees God in all things and all things in God.'[75] *The Inward War* develops much of the insight of the published essay, working through Hopkins' doctrinal commitment to the incarnation and exploring his sermons more fully (Jennings finds them 'slightly confused' but always ending 'in great tenderness').[76] Hopkins represents the epitome of the poet because his work is driven by an unwa-vering but always vulnerable faith, engaging us in 'the wrestling of man with God – but also the surrender of man to God'.[77]

What Jennings learns from Hopkins, as she does from Wordsworth and Weil, is the dexterity to tumble through misery, grief, dejection, fear and loneliness as a way of accessing joy and stillness. She most success-fully accomplishes this in her elegies, verses that are characterised by a proleptic sense of grieving which allows for positive release and good feeling.[78] By always implying that joy will follow grief, Jennings frees herself to articulate desperate expressions of desolation without burying or fearing them. Rejecting a confessional model of elegy, wherein the dead or lost object is internalised and preserved, Jennings' elegies antic-ipate grief in order to guard against sorrow experienced in the past and perceived future. Rather than negating or overplaying elegiac feeling, Jennings holds it in formally concise stanzas or phrases that are sorrowful and sad – her narrators do not easily find solace – but that finally grant the reader consolation in the act of hearing them. That the process of mourning is passed onto us as readers is reinforced by Jennings' tendency to write elegies about concepts (such as love, time or death), and also to common or abstract, rather than proper, nouns (such as the sea, weather or a season). We are thus freed to grieve with her, rather than for her, drawn into the sound of her words through a Frostian imagining ear to again insist on close listening and attentiveness. In 'Love Needs an Elegy', for example, Jennings asks us to listen before telling us what she hears:

Listen, a wind is rising. I think Spring
Is skirmishing today. It feels nearby

Yet we are not affected. I hear wings
And flights. The bird need never heed the clock
Or hear a lonely summons. Such light sings

But we fit nowhere. What is it can break
Hearts while there's good faith still? I do not know;
We keep our promises but stay awake.

If love could be a matter of the will
O this would never be most sadly so.

Invited to pause after the first word of the poem, we are drawn into an audile imagining of the rising wind and also our breathing, which is accented again in the last line's repeated 'o' sounds. Creating a space for breathing, the poem, like many of Jennings' elegiac and emotive verses, encourages a prayer-like or meditative response that takes us beyond words. It is here that Jennings fulfils her own definition of mystical experience, transforming the poem into a second of captured experience to be felt in the moment of reading, and 'not', as she writes in *Every Changing Shape*, 'in its fading or aftermath. Some words of Simone Weil's are relevant in this context; "A poem", she says, 'is beautiful to the precise degree in which the attention whilst it was being composed has been turned towards the inexpressible."'[79]

In 'Waking to the Sea', Jennings articulates this experiential process again, evoking an instant of remembering ('I have known elegies of early days', l. 1) in order to bring herself and the reader into a present moment ('The other morning / I woke into a place beside the sea', ll. 4–5) wherein detail can be focused and reflected on ('All the houses near / Were painted quiet colours, beige and brown / A touch of blue here, there a little green', ll. 15–17). Watching the patient fisherman, 'ready for ideas / To open in their still attentive minds' (ll. 19–21), Jennings settles us into a process of waiting, not for epiphany, but for the necessary composure to reconcile us to feel or be in our experience. This sense of composure is evoked in the poem by 'gentle', 'curling', 'orderly' 'music of the sea' (l. 25), a space protected from apathy by the active image of the morning wind, the image with which the poem closes:

Sun-crowned at last this morning was made up
Of possibilities like notes of music
Practised, repeated, moving with the wind. (ll. 40–42)

Jennings moves the reader here, both into her own moment of unruffled reflection and affectively into a slow-motion enactment of religious faith, one that she shows us is functional only when practised and repeated. Her achievement here and elsewhere is her ability to translate the intensity and happiness of her Christian faith into a canon of accessible poems that reach out to a community of readers even as they do not assume their welcome. Whatever experiences Jennings went through in her own life, her poetry owns a tempered authority that echoes her description of D.H. Lawrence as always 'searching Christlike / Bruised and wounded like him, / Clear, bright-thoughted like him' (ll. 12–14). She remains an at once assured and tentative twentieth-century voice, aspiring towards a prayerful affective state even as she acknowledges the pain that accompanies such striving. Now firm, now hesitant, Jennings's poetry addresses those ideas – love, friendship, compassion, nature, time, memory, faith – deliberately neglected by her peers, and with a tenderness that evades sentiment by finding its bearings in discernment and kindness.

Notes

Abbreviations
GU: Georgetown University, Special Collections
UD: University of Delaware Library, Special Collections
WUL: Washington University at St Louis, Special Collections
For full details see Sources, p. 985

1   Elizabeth Jennings, 'The First Music', l. 12.
2   Rainer Maria Rilke, *Letters to a Young Poet* [1929], trans. Stephen Mitchell (New York: Modern Library, 2001), p. 84.
3   The interviews were recorded on 22 January 2008 (Priscilla Tolkien); 9 April 2008 (Aileen Albrow); and 10 April 2008 (Gina Pollinger), and carried out by myself and Rachel Buxton.
4   Elizabeth Jennings, 'Time', ll. 6–8.
5   Elizabeth Jennings, *Poetry To-Day (1957–60)*, The British Council (London: Longmans, Green and Co., 1961), p. 55.
6   Kingsley Amis, *A Case of Samples: Poems 1946–1956* (London: Victor Gollancz, 1956), pp. 30–31.
7   See Donald Davie, 'Eliot in One Poet's Life', *Mosaic*, 6 (1972).
8   Elizabeth Jennings, *As I Am: An Early Autobiography*, p. 103(b) (I refer here to an inserted hand-written page in between p. 103 and p. 104).
9   Elizabeth Jennings, *Let's Have Some Poetry!* (London: Museum Press, 1960), pp. 14–15.
10 Jennings, *As I Am*, p. 108.
11 On Merwin's connection with Wordsworth, see James Chandler, 'About Loss: W.G. Sebald's Romantic Art of Memory', *The South Atlantic Quarterly*, 102.1 (2003), pp. 235–62; Alison Flood, 'W.S. Merwin is America's new poet laureate – at 82', *The Guardian*, 5 July 2010; and Lee Zimmerman, 'Against Vanishing: Winnicott and the Modern Poetry of Nothing', *American Imago*, 54.1 (1997), pp. 81–102.
12 William Wordsworth, *Essays on Epitaphs*, III, in *The Prose Works of William Wordsworth*, ed. W.J.B. Owen and Jane Worthington Smyser, 3 vols (Oxford: Clarendon Press), II, pp. 84–85.

13 Jennings, *Poetry To-Day*, p. 21.

14 See Elizabeth Jennings, 'Introduction', *The Batsford Book of Religious Verse* (London: B.T. Batsford, 1981).

15 Barry Sloan, 'Poetry and Faith: The Example of Elizabeth Jennings', *Christianity and Literature*, 55.3 (2006), pp. 393–414 (p. 394).

16 Elizabeth Jennings, 'Review: The Fullness Thereof: Edmund Hill, trans., *Nine Sermons of St Augustine on the Psalms* and C. S. Lewis, *Reflections on the Psalms*', *The Observer*, 21 September 1958, p. 18.

17 Elizabeth Jennings, 'For their own sake', l. 6.

18 Wordsworth, *Essays on Epitaphs*, I, in *Prose Works*, II, pp. 59–60.

19 Elizabeth Jennings, *The Inward War: A Critical Biography of Gerard Manley Hopkins*, UD 186/5 (p. 2).

20 1 Corinthians 12, 26-27, from the Douay-Rheims Bible (a translation into English of the Latin Vulgate), the version Jennings used as a Roman Catholic.

21 Elizabeth Jennings, 'First Man', l. 3.

22 Elizabeth Jennings, *Every Changing Shape: Mystical Experience and the Making of Poems* (London: Andre Deutsch, 1961), p. 14.

23 Jennings, *Every Changing Shape*, pp. 16, 23.

24 Elizabeth Jennings, MS paperback notebook, BL Add 52598 C, pp. 25–26.

25 Candida Crewe, 'Bag Lady of the Sonnets', *The Times*, 23 November 1991.

26 Simone Weil, 'Attention and Will', in *Gravity and Grace* [1947], trans. Emma Crawford and Mario von der Rhur (London: Routledge, 2002), pp. 116–22 (p. 117).

27 Elizabeth Jennings, *Pensées*, no. 15.

28 Jennings, *Every Changing Shape*, p. 42.

29 Jennings, *Pensées*, no. 34.

30 Jennings, *Let's Have Some Poetry!*, p. 20.

31 Michael Schmidt, 'Elizabeth Jennings: Obituary', *The Independent*, 31 October 2001.

32 Jennings, *As I Am*, p. 4.

33 Jennings, *As I Am*, pp. 5, 9, 20, 24.

34 Elizabeth Jennings, MS paperback notebook (GU, 2/4/93).

35 Jennings, *As I Am*, pp. 26, 22.

36 Elizabeth Jennings, 'Elizabeth Jennings', *Contemporary Authors Autobiography Series*, volume 5 (Detroit: Gale Publishing, 1987), pp. 103–14 (p. 108).

37 Jennings, *As I Am*, p. 48.

38 Jennings, *As I Am*, p. 110.

39 Jennings, *As I Am*, p. 119.

40 Jennings, *As I Am*, p. 149.

41 Jennings, *As I Am*, p. 177.

42 Jennings, *As I Am*, p. 221.

43 Schmidt, 'Elizabeth Jennings: Obituary'.

44 On Jennings' religion, see Rachel Buxton, 'Elizabeth Jennings and Rome', in Zachary Leader, ed., *The Movement Reconsidered: Essays on Larkin, Amis, Gunn, Davie and their Contemporaries* (Oxford: Oxford University Press, 2009), pp. 292–306; and Jean Ward, 'Elizabeth Jennings: An Exile in her Own Country?', *Literature and Theology*, 21.2 (2007), pp. 198–213.

45 Elizabeth Jennings, *Christianity and Poetry* (London: Burns and Oates, 1965), p. 115.

46 Jennings, *As I Am*, p. 112.

47 Jennings, 'Elizabeth Jennings', p. 114.

48 Jennings, *Pensées*, no. 85.

49 Jennings, *Pensées*, no. 57.

50 Jennings, *Pensées*, no. 2 and no. 51.

51 Jennings, *Pensées*, no. 104.

52 Jennings, *Pensées*, no. 26.

53 Jennings, *Every Changing Shape*, p. 101.

54 See Robert Frost, 'Lecture to the Browne and Nichols School', 10 May 1915; and Frost, letter to Sidney Cox, December 1914, in *Frost: Collected Poems, Prose, and Plays*, ed. Mark Richardson and Richard Poirier (Library of America, 1995).

55 Elizabeth Jennings, *Frost*, Writers and Critics (London: Oliver and Boyd, 1964), pp. 17, 30, 22.

56 Jennings, *Frost*, pp. 67, 11, 46

57 Jennings, *Frost*, p. 97.

58 In Gerlinde Gramang, *Elizabeth Jennings: An Appraisal of Her Life as a Poet, Her Approach to Her Work and a Selection of the Major Themes of Her Poetry* (Lewiston, NY: Salzburg: Edwin Mellen Press, 1995), pp. 93, 96.

59 Elizabeth Jennings, Introduction, 'Poems by Elizabeth Jennings', *Third Programme*, BBC, 4 March 1958.

60 Jennings, *Poetry To-Day*, pp. 9, 12.

61 Simon Broadbent, 'A Machine Sums Up: Extract from a 23rd Century Literary Review', *The Isis*, 31 October 1951, p. 25.

62 The Group, 'Two Carols', *The Isis*, 5 December 1951, p. 34; 'Quarrel by the Sea-shore' and 'Dreams Revisited', *The Isis*, 23 January 1952, p. 18; see also the prose experiment 'Man Awakes: A Study in Narcissism', *The Isis*, 5 December 1951, p. 35.

63 See Elizabeth Jennings, *Seven Men of Vision: An Appreciation* (London: Vision Press, 1976); *Every Changing Shape*; and 'Modern English Poetry', WUL, 12, n.d.

64 Jennings, *Every Changing Shape*, p. 201.

65 Jennings, *As I Am*, p. 109.

66 Jennings, *Frost*, p. 36; Jennings, *Every Changing Shape*, p. 201.

67 See *Every Changing Shape*, p. 209.

68 MS notebook, WUL, 145.

69 'For a Woman with a Fatal Illness' is the seventh poem of Jennings' 'Sequence in Hospital'.

70 Jennings, *Every Changing Shape*, p. 209.

71 Jennings, *Every Changing Shape*, pp. 202, 203.

72 Jennings, *Every Changing Shape*, p. 209; Jennings, *The Inward War*, pp. 259, 77.

73 See Marianne Moore's 'In Distrust of Merit', ll. 71–74, 'Hate-hardened heart, heart of iron, / iron is iron till it is rust. / There never was a war that was / not inward', in Grace Schulman, ed., *The Poems of Marianne Moore* (London: Faber and Faber, 2003), p. 252.

74 Jennings, *The Inward War*, p. 240.

75 Jennings, *Every Changing Shape*, p. 109.

76 Jennings, *The Inward War*, pp. 165–66.

77 Jennings, *Every Changing Shape*, p. 108.

78 See Patricia Rae, 'Double Sorrow: Proleptic Elegy and the End of Arcadianism in 1930s Britain', *Twentieth Century Literature*, 49:2 (2003), pp. 246–75.

79 Jennings, *Every Changing Shape*, p. 17.

SOURCES

Published poetry

Early work

'The Elements', *Oxford Poetry 1948*, ed. Arthur Boyars and Barry Harmer (Oxford: Basil Blackwell, 1948), pp. 45–46

'Weathercock', 'Estrangement', 'The Lucky', 'Modern Poet', 'Winter Love', 'Time', *Oxford Poetry 1949*, ed. Kingsley Amis and James Michie (Oxford: Basil Blackwell, 1949), pp. 31–36

'The Clock', *The Spectator*, 18 February 1949, p. 215

'Deception', 'Warning', 'John the Baptist', *The Isis*, 1162, 14 November 1951, p. 29

'From the Cliff', 'Identity', *New Poems*, 1.1 (Autumn 1952), pp. 6–7

'Tuscany', *New Poems*, 1.2 (Winter 1952), p. 7

'The Idler', *New Poems*, 1.3 (Spring 1953), p. 6

'Cave Dwellers', *New Poems*, 1.4 (Summer 1953), p. 9

'The Lost Symbols', *New Poems*, 2.2 (Winter 1953), p. 4

Published collections 1953–2001

Poems (Swinford, Oxon.: Fantasy Press, 1953)

A Way of Looking: Poems (London: Andre Deutsch, 1955)

A Sense of the World: Poems (London: Andre Deutsch, 1958)

Song for a Birth or a Death and other Poems (London: Andre Deutsch, 1961)

Recoveries: Poems (London: Andre Deutsch, 1964)

The Mind has Mountains (London: Macmillan, 1966)

The Secret Brother and Other Poems for Children (London: Macmillan, 1966)

The Animals' Arrival (London: Macmillan, 1969)

Lucidities: Poems (London: Macmillan, 1970)

Relationships (London: Macmillan, 1972)

Growing Points: New Poems (Manchester: Carcanet, 1975)

Consequently I Rejoice (Manchester: Carcanet, 1977)

After the Ark (Oxford: Oxford University Press, 1978)

Moments of Grace (Manchester: Carcanet, 1979)

Winter Wind (Newark, Vermont: The Janus Press, 1979)

A Dream of Spring: Poems (Stratford: Celandine Press, 1980)

Celebrations and Elegies (Manchester: Carcanet, 1982)

Extending the Territory (Manchester: Carcanet, 1985)

Tributes (Manchester: Carcanet, 1989)

Times and Seasons (Manchester: Carcanet, 1992)

Familiar Spirits (Manchester: Carcanet, 1994)
In the Meantime (Manchester: Carcanet, 1996)
Praises (Manchester: Carcanet, 1998)
Timely Issues (Manchester: Carcanet, 2001)

Unpublished poetry

Main sources

GU: Georgetown University, Special Collections
Elizabeth Jennings Papers
Numbers refer to the series number (there are two sets of Jennings papers at Georgetown, series 1 and 2), box number, folder number

UD: University of Delaware Library, Special Collections (WTU00061)
Numbers refer to: manuscript collection number, box number, folder number; or where there are two numbers, manuscript collection number and folder number

WUL: Washington University at St Louis, Special Collections
Elizabeth Jennings Papers, catalogued only by box number

Published prose

Every Changing Shape: Mystical Experience and the Making of Poems (London: Andre Deutsch, 1961)
Frost, Writers and Critics (London: Oliver and Boyd, 1964)
Christianity and Poetry (London: Burns and Oates, 1965)
Seven Men of Vision: An Appreciation (London: Vision Press, 1976)
Let's Have Some Poetry! (London: Museum Press, 1960)
Poetry To-Day (1957–60), The British Council (London: Longmans, Green and Co., 1961)

Unpublished prose

As I Am: An Early Autobiography, n.d. but probably 1967 (GU, 2, separate folder)
'The Poetry of Kingsley Amis', n.d. (GU, 2/28/5)
The Inward War: A Critical Biography of Gerard Manley Hopkins, n.d. (UD, 186/5/73)
Rome, n.d. (GU, 2/31/26)
Pensées, 1957 (WUL, 8)

Roman Easter: A Theme for Voices, 1957 (WUL, 5)
'Early poems', 1957 (WUL, 9)
'Augustine and C. S. Lewis', n.d. (WUL, 12)
'Modern English Poetry', n.d. (WUL, 12)
'American Poetry', n.d. (WUL, 12)
'Prayer for a Sick Poet', 1965 (WUL, 8)
'Fountain', n.d. (WUL, 10)

List of known archives containing Jennings' writings

BBC Archives, Reading
Berg Collection, New York Public Library
Bodleian Library, Oxford, Department of Manuscripts
British Library, London, Department of Manuscripts
Brotherton Library, Special Collections, University of Leeds
Brynmore Jones Library, University of Hull
University of Delaware Library, Special Collections
Georgetown University Library, Washington, Special Collections
John Rylands University Library, University of Manchester
National Sound Archive, London
Pennsylvania State University
Royal Society of Literature, London
Department of Special Collections and University Archives, University of
    Tulsa

For more information on where Jennings' poems, prose, plays, essays and correspondence are archived, see Jane Dowson's extremely informative website: www.elizabethjennings.org

INDEX OF TITLES

INDEX OF FIRST LINES